# THE FIFTH FIELD

## The Story of the 96 American Soldiers Sentenced to Death and Executed in Europe and North Africa in World War II

Colonel French L. MacLean
UNITED STATES ARMY, (RET.)

With a Foreword and Legal Analysis by Attorney T.G. Bolen

Schiffer Publishing Ltd

4880 Lower Valley Road • Atglen, PA 19310

Designed by Justin Watkinson
Type set in Mom'sTypewriter/Typestar/Minion Pro

ISBN: 978-0-7643-4577-7
Printed in China

Published by Schiffer Publishing, Ltd.
4880 Lower Valley Road
Atglen, PA 19310
Phone: (610) 593-1777; Fax: (610) 593-2002
E-mail: Info@schifferbooks.com

For our complete selection of fine books on this and related
subjects, please visit our website at www.schifferbooks.com.
You may also write for a free catalog.

This book may be purchased from the publisher. Please try
your bookstore first.

We are always looking for people to write books on new
and related subjects. If you have an idea for a book, please
contact us at proposals@schifferbooks.com

Schiffer Publishing's titles are available at special discounts
for bulk purchases for sales promotions or premiums.
Special editions, including personalized covers, corporate
imprints, and excerpts can be created in large quantities for
special needs. For more information, contact the publisher.

*For oak and elm have pleasant leaves*
*That in the spring-time shoot:*
*But grim to see is the gallows-tree,*
*With its adder-bitten root,*
*And, green or dry, a man must die*
*Before it bears its fruit!*

*The loftiest place is that seat of grace*
*For which all worldlings try:*
*But who would stand in hempen band*
*Upon a scaffold high,*
*And through a murderer's collar take*
*His last look at the sky?*

*It is sweet to dance to violins*
*When Love and Life are fair:*
*To dance to flutes, to dance to lutes*
*Is delicate and rare:*
*But it is not sweet with nimble feet*
*To dance upon the air!*

*So with curious eyes and sick surmise*
*We watched him day by day,*
*And wondered if each one of us*
*Would end the self-same way,*
*For none can tell to what red Hell*
*His sightless soul may stray.*

*At last, the dead man walked no more*
*Amongst the Trial Men,*
*And I knew that he was standing up*
*In the black dock's dreadful pen,*
*And that never would I see his face*
*In God's sweet world again.*

*Like two doomed ships that pass in storm,*
*We had crossed each other's way:*
*But we made no sign, we said no word,*
*We had no word to say;*
*For we did not meet in the holy night,*
*But in the shameful day.*

Excerpt from the *Ballad of Reading Gaol,*
— Oscar Wilde

# Contents

# Prologue

*"What is history but a fable agreed upon?"*
— Napoleon Bonaparte

Sixty-five miles northeast of Paris is a macabre secret. The secret is buried in the ground; but it is not a treasure chest of sparkling diamonds, gold or silver. It is not hidden in a deep, dark French forest; nearby bright, white marble crosses can be seen from high in the air. While off the beaten path of most tourist destinations, it is not isolated behind a towering mountain range. Travelling to the location does not require a rugged expedition with Sherpas and pack mules to uncharted destinations; quality hotels – providing excellent dining fare – are available in Château-Thierry, Soissons and Reims, all within a half-hour drive. Visitors are not required to slash their way through dense jungles; it is easily accessed by automobile from Paris via toll auto-route A-4 to the Château-Thierry exit, turning left onto highway D1, continuing north about six miles to D310, turning right and heading east for another six miles to Fère-en-Tardenois. One can also take a train to Château-Thierry and then hop a taxi to the cemetery.

Fère-en-Tardenois is a village of 3,364 souls in the Aisne department of Picardy in northern France. A mile and a quarter northeast of the commune is the nine-hundred year-old Château of Fère-en-Tardenois. Today the château is a luxury hotel, where guests may play a round of golf, swim in the hotel pool or play tennis. After exercise, the pampered visitors may choose their dinner wine from a selection of 20,000 bottles. If the guests are fortunate, they even may be able to tour the fabled wine cellars; the rows of bottles have a fine coating of dust on each flask – testament to a lifetime of uninterrupted pampering and peace.

However, located one and one-half miles away from this serene life is a remembrance of interrupted youth and violent death. The Oise-Aisne American Cemetery and Memorial, bordering the hamlet of Seringes-et-Nesles, contains the remains of 6,012 American war dead – most of whom lost their lives while fighting in this area during the First World War. Some 597 additional markers are labeled "unknown." The gleaming white crosses, aligned in long rows and surrounded by lush, well-manicured grass, lie on a gentle downward slope. Each cross proudly displays a soldier's name, his unit, the state from which he entered the service and the date of the soldier's death. It is simple, but moving. Leafy trees and beds of gorgeous roses flank the burial area, divided into four fields – A, B, C and D – by wide walking paths. At the intersection of the four plots are a circular plaza and a flagpole. Flying proudly on the staff is the American flag. This is hallowed ground and lies on the very spot that the Forty-Second Infantry Division, the legendary "Rainbow Division," fought and bled by the bucketful – losing 2,058 men killed in action and 12,625 wounded in action.

The memorial, built of rose-colored sandstone with white trim, is shaped as a curving colonnade and flanked at both ends by a chapel and a map room. The ten double columns bear the division numbers of the American Army units that fought in the general area: the First, Second, Third, Fourth, Twenty-Sixth, Twenty-Eighth, Thirty-Second, Forty-Second, Seventy-Seventh and Ninety-Third Infantry Divisions – a veritable "Who's Who" of American military sacrifice and glory of the era. On the monument is an inscription:

THESE ENDURED ALL AND GAVE ALL THAT HONOR AND JUSTICE MIGHT PREVAIL AND THAT THE WORLD MIGHT ENJOY FREEDOM AND INHERIT PEACE

Within the chapel is an altar of chiseled black granite. Visitors may silently look upon its "Walls of the Missing" and see 241 names – engraved in stone, the letters painted gold – of American soldiers, who initially were believed missing in action. Over the years, master stonemasons have added rosettes to mark the names of those whose remains have since been recovered and identified, but many remain unknown. The map room's multi-colored walls portray the American military operations in this region during the final year of the First World War. The service buried most of the soldiers initially in temporary cemeteries during the war. After the conflict, the Army asked the next of kin if they wished their loved ones sent for permanent burial back home, or interred at the closest overseas cemetery. For these 6,012 soldiers the choice was the Oise-Aisne American Cemetery.

For thirty years, the peaceful country cemetery remained undisturbed. Then, after the next world war – World War II – the U.S. Army faced a dilemma. During this second global conflict, in the North African/Mediterranean and European Theaters of Operation, on gallows and firing-squad-posts, from the hot dusty sands of Algeria to the grim, granite fortresses of wintertime Belgium, United States Army General Courts-Martial convicted and ordered the execution of 96 American soldiers for desertion, murder and rape between 1943 and 1945. These were not crimes against enemy soldiers or against civilians supporting the enemy. These 96 GIs murdered twenty-six fellow American military personnel, murdered thirty-five British, French, Italian, Polish and Algerian civilians, and raped thirty-six civilian women of various nationalities.[1]

Moreover, these executions were not pseudo shot-in-the-back-while-trying-to-escape killings. General Dwight D. Eisenhower or another theater commander personally approved every single proceeding. The Army did not trumpet the crimes or the soldiers that committed them, although some accounts made it into newspapers. There were no last-minute opportunities to avoid the noose by volunteering for a suicidal mission à la the fictional account of condemned American soldiers in the motion picture *The Dirty Dozen* – although that was contemplated.

What did the American military gain from putting to death almost one-hundred soldiers? Aside from seeking justice for the victims, an argument is these stern punishments helped maintain the order and discipline required by the U.S. Army to defeat the vaunted German *Wehrmacht* – while generally maintaining decent relations with the civilian populations in the vast areas of operation of North Africa, the Mediterranean, the British Isles and Northwest Europe.

Now, after "Victory in Europe Day," those wartime civil-military relations took a different turn. Now, there were 96 bodies of executed American soldiers in various temporary military cemeteries throughout Europe, where if nothing was done, they would lie in perpetuity. That simply would not do; military leadership wanted to ensure no stigma, "actual, imagined or implied," be attached to the heroic soldiers from the First World War, now in the vicinity of the temporary resting places of the "dishonored dead."

Before that was the question of where to bury the "honored dead," quickly mounting in numbers in this Second World War. Beginning in 1942, the Adjutant General of the War Department, Major General James A. Ulio, requested assistance from the American Battle Monuments Commission (ABMC).[2] The ABMC recommended that the American military section of the Brookwood Cemetery in Brookwood, Surrey, England be used

for the burial of U.S. military personnel who died in England, but this ruling did not address executed soldiers, as none of the honored dead at Brookwood met their death in this manner.[3] In 1943, the situation changed, and a "Plot X" at Brookwood – located in forestland near a compost heap and some tool sheds to the north of the main military cemetery – became the home of temporary graves of executed soldiers. By the end of the war, eighteen American soldiers in England were buried at this plot at Brookwood.

After the war, the ABMC determined that all American dead in England would be buried at the American Military Cemetery at Cambridge. This would include those executed troopers; re-interment of these eighteen graves occurred in 1948. However, shovel and spade could not undo popular emotion. Pressure mounted from the British government concerning the eighteen, as most of the perpetrators had murdered or raped English civilians. Many British citizens still harbored bad feelings toward the offenders, as did civilians in France, Belgium, Italy and Germany, where dozens of other crimes occurred.

Therefore, the Quartermaster General of the Army, Major General Thomas B. Larkin, began to search for a single suitable site in which the remains of all 96 men could be interred. General Larkin knew all about the situation. In 1945, he had published orders setting the place and date of execution for six of the condemned men. It would be a "dishonored plot" and secure from the public eye, not due to any perceived judicial discrepancies, but as so to not publicize the Army's "rotten apples." As Studs Terkel would later pen, it had been a "Good War;" this chapter was not to be a part of Glenn Miller's *Sentimental Journey*.

The 96 executed men did not represent "the service, achievements and sacrifice" of the 416,800 American military dead in World War II. It would be a tough slog to find such a place. Then, George C. Marshall, former Chief of Staff of the Army, resigned as Secretary of State in January 1949, but could not completely detach himself from the national scene and became the Chairman of the ABMC. General Marshall was well aware of the judicial proceedings during the war and the sticky situation General Larkin was attempting to handle. It was just as well that General of the Armies John J. Pershing was dead, as he may have been unenthusiastic about putting these 96 criminals anywhere near his beloved troops from the Great War – for the ABMC commissioners had chosen a plot of land adjacent to – but technically outside of – the First World War American cemetery of Oise-Aisne.

Designed to be secret in existence and inaccessible to the general public, it is called "Plot E" by the ABMC; others often refer to it as "The Fifth Field." With General Marshall at the helm, re-interments from England to Plot E began in May 1949 and finished that July, as did those from France, Italy and North Africa. While the cemetery proper is open daily to the public, access to Plot E is extremely challenging. Located behind the superintendent's quarters, it is separated from the main cemetery by a high, stone wall, concealed from view by thick laurel bushes and pine trees, and is closed to visitors. Twelve French groundskeepers do all the work in both the cemetery proper and in Plot E – they keep their mouths shut about what they see. The challenge to enter is not the perimeter walls – static defenses have been breached since Troy. The ponderous, federal-level bureaucracy defeats intrusion. Only the ABMC headquarters may grant permission to visit. In the past, it has been seldom dispensed. In part because of the secrecy, stories swirled around the subject of U.S. military executions during the war. Even historian Stephen E. Ambrose became carried away and wrote that forty-nine American soldiers died by firing squads. Wilder claims included that of a British executioner:

"'We hanged twenty-two Yanks in one morning,' he told us. 'They'd got people all over the place who had been sentenced to death in this country and in Europe. They brought them all to Shepton Mallet in Somerset, where they had a big military prison and they brought us [several hangmen] in. We did the lot in one morning.'"

Other mysteries have been harder to unravel – murmurs of late night courts-martial, command influence, a British executioner travelling to Normandy to hang a GI there and an anonymous American hangman driving a truck with a portable scaffold atop its trailer across Europe, carrying out dozens of executions. Hushed tales involved botched hangings and firing squads and a "death train" that moved the remains of the 96 to their obscure final resting place. The whispers did not stop; questions still exist concerning what remains are still in that obscure cemetery and if one of the 96 men actually escaped execution and surfaced in California in 1949. All these rumors and questions have made excavating the truth extremely difficult.

American tax revenues finance our military cemeteries in Europe. In France, a separate treaty gives the United States control of the land in perpetuity for honoring our war dead, although the ground belongs to France. Now, seven decades after the war, the ABMC extended an invitation for the author to visit Plot E. Someone has to cut through the swirling fog. It is time to know. In January 1944, an attorney – for the family of one of the 96 – wrote an urgent letter to the Office of the Adjutant General. In it, he stated, "This boy has written his father that he has been in some serious trouble in Africa and that someday they would find out about it."

That someday is today.

While the crosses at the Oise-Aisne American Cemetery are bright white and stand tall, in the "Fifth Field," the 96 grave markers are dull white, flat, marble stones sunken below ground level and inscribed with only numbers instead of names. In silence, these stones scream that something happened – that they are the keystones to a mystery that ends here, but begins somewhere else. French locals out for a stroll would call them *clefs de voûte*, were they allowed inside the Fifth Field, which they are not. With just numbers, it is difficult to identify where each condemned lies, who they were, what they had done, how they were tried and how they went to their deaths during that tumultuous period, without knowing the keystone to this complex historical secret. The cemetery has no original "official" master list of the burials, and relatively nothing of the crimes, courts-martial or executions leading up to the interments.[4]

This book is that *clef de voûte*, that *keystone*, for the entire mystery of the 96.

# Acknowledgements

The following wonderful people are the modern-day heroes of this book.

**Office of the Clerk of Court, U.S. Army Judiciary, Ballston, VA.** This office started it all. Brigadier General David Carey, Colonel Malcolm H. Squires, Jr. and Mary Chapman helped me extensively. Without their support, this book would never have been written.

**National Archives and Records Administration, St. Louis, MO.** Thomas "Tom" Hayes and his cohorts Dean Gall, Susan Nash, Eric Kilgore, Karen Schwarm, Donna Noelken, Theresa Fitzgerald and Chris Secrest, are some of the best archivists in the world.

**American Battle Monuments Commission (ABMC), Washington, DC.** Michael G. Conley, Director of Public Affairs, kindly granted permission to visit the cemetery. In Europe, Brigadier General Steve Hawkins, Jeffrey Aarnio, David Atkinson, Geoffrey Fournier, James Woolsey and Nathalie Le Barbier assisted me greatly. She is the most knowledgeable person in the world on Fifth Field burials. Because of their hard work, the cemetery will likely be much more transparent in the future.

**National Archives and Records Administration, College Park, MD.** The archivists here have been instrumental in researching every book I have ever written. Dr. Timothy K. Nenninger played a key role in locating the mysterious Army hangman.

**Judge Advocate General's Legal Center and School, Charlottesville, VA.** The Judge Advocate General Regimental Historian and Archivist, Colonel Fred Borch III (U.S. Army Retired) served as the principal advisor for the chapter on the Army legal system.

**U.S. Military Police School, Fort Leonard Wood, Mo.** Kathy West, James Rogers, Staff Sergeant Andrew W. Peppers and Bob Gunnarsson (Ret.)

**Paul Fraser Collectables, Bristol, England.** Director Adrian Roose, allowed me to see selected scans of the execution ledger belonging to English hangman Albert Pierrepoint.

**French Citizens.** Michel and Aurelien Jacquesson of Beaunay; Monsieur Louis Massard of Plumaudan; Anita Queruel, Guy Lebrec and the grandson of Madame Berthe Robert, Mesnil-Clinchamps; Monsieur Etienne Viard, Mayor, Canisy; Monsieur Georges René, Mayor, Étienville; and Monsieur Daniel Bellamy, Mayor, Le Pernelle.

**Unique Individuals.** Herman J. Obermayer, of McLean, Virginia, provided a wealth of information on John C. Woods. Dr. Stephen Weiss spent several months at the Loire DTC in 1945 and provided significant information on this facility. "Hammer" Smith, a historian in Kentucky, located a grave of one of the 96. Thomas Ward, former supply sergeant at the Loire DTC, described activities there. Chandler Williams worked wonders in photo development.

**My Lawyer.** Once again, T.G. Bolen stepped to the plate. He read the files, commented on cases and showed me the differences between the legal world and world of an Army line officer.

**My Heart and Soul.** For this project, my wife went "above and beyond the call of duty." When we arrived in France to visit the crime scenes, Olga took charge, saying, "Find each mayor's office; they will know what happened; I'll do the talking."

# Dedication

*"He was a good boy before this awful war began."*

This book is dedicated to every United States Army Military Policeman (MP), disciplinary training center guard and commandant, General-Court-Martial member, Trial Judge Advocate, Defense Counsel, appointing authority, reviewing board member, confirming authority, Chaplain, medical officer and graves registration officer listed in this work. It is also dedicated to every unnamed "buck" sergeant and junior enlisted man associated with the following 96 death penalty cases.[1]

Yours was a thankless task; upholding the administration of what you and the Army believed was a modern, fair judicial proceeding, while maintaining the standards of good military discipline and order, all in the middle of a war for national existence. In the years ahead, others may vilify and condemn you – those who have never walked in your boots, from a vantage point of seventy years into the future, a future that no man or woman can ever see in the middle of the tumultuous events in which they are participating. Those critics will never know the mental anguish you endured performing your duties; for some, your nightmares lasted forever.

In fact, you already have been castigated. Your critics began in 1953 and have continued to this day. First, were the historians examining the Eddie Slovik case; they opined that the defendant was "singled out" by the Army for punishment for desertion. You know better than that; you know how many chances he had to soldier at the front. Later books emerged saying that you were racists. One publisher, in presenting two cases where in one, a white officer was acquitted and in the other, a black enlisted man was executed, boldly asserted that because of race, Army Courts-Martial represented one of the ugliest chapters in the history of Jim Crow. You know better than that because you were part of both trials; you read the transcripts and witness statements; you saw the demeanor of one defendant on the stand. You know which defendant pleaded self-defense and which defendant admitted doing the shooting without provocation. You know that the overriding factor in the outcomes of these two trials was that the Army proved in one case that the defendant murdered the victim and in the other case, you ruled that the defendant acted in self-defense and thus acquitted him.

Along with the historians, came the sociologists, commenting on U.S. military justice in World War II, and they did not only had an axe to grind toward the Army, they had a whole hardware store of tools to sharpen. They started their arguments with broad conclusions that the Army was associated with oppressive government, was unpopular and an organization of which people had always been suspicious. Some then continued their arguments with unproven generalized assertions about officers and soldiers that included that you no longer had the capacity of individual thought, because the Army had drummed it out of you. Once that leap had been made, it was time for the sociologists to comment on the Army's judicial system: they concluded that at trials command influence trumped due process. One expert opined on death penalty cases in Europe by saying, "Certainly some of those convicted must have been guilty."

Some? Then the experts insinuated that if they could not prove improper judicial conduct that was only because the Army covered up all the examples of it.

Even you "Sky Pilots" – the Chaplains – have not escaped condemnation. One sociologist inferred (through supposed sixteenth century evidence) that bishops sent their "most questionable clerics" for service as Chaplains in the military – and damning you with faint praise by concluding that you were the "cleanest" of the "dirty workers" at military executions – apparently he never heard of the U.S. Army Transport *Dorchester* in the frigid water off Greenland in February 1943, where four Chaplains gave their life jackets to others and then locked arms and went down with the ship.

Sociologists may correctly demonstrate that treatment of black American soldiers in World War II was different than treatment of white soldiers, was often unfair in terms of respect (or lack of it) – and in many, many instances was downright despicable. However, it is a leap of faith to conclude – without hard evidence – that individual jurors and trial officials convicted and sentenced defendants based on their race. Since this is the first work to detail all the cases based on the official records, we can conclude that this level of investigation has not been previously done.[2]

You individual jurors, Trial Judge Advocates and Defense Counsels of yesteryear already know that. You did your best and belong in the "Greatest Generation" every bit as much as the rifleman, fighter pilot and submariner. It ate at your guts and even may have led to several premature deaths; and for the most part, you received no individual decorations for your service in the war. It is time for the story of these cases in the U.S. Army in North Africa and Europe during World War II to emerge from the shadows. Your story can now be a piece of the Army's story, which always will be a part of the American story.

This book is also dedicated to any of the 96 who may have been wrongfully convicted. Historians and lawyers will undoubtedly argue the merits of your cases for years into the future, stating what should or should not have happened at trial and perhaps even attempting to make overall societal judgments of the nation seventy years ago. I do not know which of you, if any, may have been wrongfully convicted, as judging whether a man is guilty or not guilty of a serious crime can never be done fully by simply shuffling through a sheaf of musty old papers. Therefore, if you truly did not commit the crime attributed to you, you have our deepest and sincerest apologies. You may take some solace however, in knowing that because of identified flaws in the judicial system during the war, the military has succeeded in improving the overall fairness of the process.

As we continue to progress, we cannot look into the souls of the 96, but we can look into our own humanity for the inner fortitude to examine the whispers and the shadows. It is for that reason that I wrote this book.

# Introduction

*Begin the Beguine*

It was a time and place much different from today, from the music to the way one thought of one's country, and I was not alive to experience the events first hand. This is not a legal text. Every reader who expects this book to be a treatise on the merits of the famous *Ex parte Richard Quirin* (upholding the use of military commissions for the trial of German agents landed by U-boat as spies in the United States) will be sadly disappointed. What I do bring to the table is thirty-four years of Army service, the first four as a cadet at West Point and the last thirty spent as an Infantry officer. I have served on court-martial panels (juries) and, as a commander, have had the unpleasant duty of bringing court-martial charges against some – but fortunately very few – of the soldiers in my unit.

My personal compass in these judicial matters has been to act in a manner I would want my commander to act if I had been an enlisted man facing these proceedings. My father – the most significant role model in my life – was an enlisted man, a private first class in the 39th Infantry Regiment of the Ninth Infantry Division in World War II. He fought in the Hürtgen Forest and in the "Battle of the Bulge," receiving a pair of Purple Hearts and a Silver Star for "Gallantry in Action." German *Fallschirmjäger* later captured him after he was wounded in the head and he "did time" in a German *Stalag*. Therefore, a second guiding principal, as I administered military justice, was, "What would my father, as an enlisted man, think about my actions?"

I believe that my experience as a colonel serving as the Inspector General (IG) for the United States Army, Europe (USAREUR) from 1999 to 2001 helped me in this endeavor. Inspector Generals do not deal with legal issues, but sift through investigative reports concerning professional conduct, training, maintenance, unit morale, fraud, waste, abuse and other issues the commander wants examined. Legal officers talk in terms of "beyond a reasonable doubt" while IGs speak about "more likely than not," and "preponderance of evidence." My closest associate was the Judge Advocate General (JAG) for USAREUR, Colonel Dave Carey. Many times, we trooped into our four-star commander's office to give him some bad news and our recommendations on how to fix a problem. USAREUR was the name for the organization that during the war was the European Theater of Operations (ETO.) Our commander was General Montgomery C. Meigs, and I sometimes found it interesting that if I had been the IG for the ETO I would have briefed General Dwight Eisenhower on many of the same things. General Meigs' door was always open to us and I suspect that General Eisenhower's would have been also.

I am also a military historian, a job that many Infantry officers gravitate to when they get "long in the tooth." A year before I retired, I asked to go on "Operation Iraqi Freedom" as the historian for the Army's Fifth Corps, finally getting to Baghdad in April 2003 twelve years after fighting in a mechanized infantry battalion of the Third Armored Division in "Desert Storm." Bracketing that 2003 deployment, I taught at the National War College in Washington, DC.

During those post-Nine-Eleven "professorial" years, I came across a collection of historical files at the Washington National Records Center at Suitland, Maryland. I had been working closely with the Clerk of Court, U.S. Army Legal Services Agency in Arlington, Virginia researching a history of military tribunals. One of the marvelous staff of the Clerk of Court's office finally asked me, "Would you like to see the death book?" What I found was an "ancient" green, oversized ledger-book, with hand-written entries concerning capital crimes cases involving Army personnel in World War II. I spent hours poring over the entries; while I had recalled reading about the Eddie Slovik case, I had no idea that there were dozens more cases ending in execution.

In fact, it was more than dozens. The U.S. Army executed 96 soldiers – American soldiers – in the European, Mediterranean and North African Theaters of Operation alone. Many more executions occurred in the United States and in the Pacific. I returned the ledger, at which time I heard the question, "Would you like to see the case files?" I was hooked and the Clerk of Court's office just started keeping the files over there in a semi-permanent status, when they knew I was coming. It was at that point that I suggested to Brigadier General David Carey – who was then with The Judge Advocate General in Washington – that someone should write a book about all this, as it was a key piece of Army history in World War II that had not received the attention it deserved. He agreed, but insinuated that his office already had enough to do with Afghanistan and then Iraq on the docket, so I started to make copies of some of the most crucial documents in each case hoping someday to put it all together.

The U.S. Army did not attempt to limit what I saw; it did not attempt to guide my research – in short the Army made no attempt to influence this project in any way. The only question I ever heard from anyone at the Clerk of Court Office was, "May I use the copier for a moment before you start on the next file?"

The reader will note that this book is not written in the style of many history books. It often uses words and expressions widely understood during that period, but not in use today – a fault that most historians avoid like the plague. However, I wanted to write the book, as a colonel of that Army in Europe would have, had all the facts been known then. Hence, you will find World War II Army slang, disparaging remarks about the enemy and references to period "Big Band" music. The profanity used is not inserted for shock value, but the words used by the actual participants; these dozen or so examples assist us in getting to the frame of mind of the men engaged in life and death events. An example here and there of gallows humor is my decision to lighten what could otherwise have been a completely gloomy account of this history.

This work is not a political or social diatribe against military justice in general. While we may contemplate how we might have done things differently back then, the Army has an excellent history of critically looking at its past and current practices and modifying them. The United States Army of today is not the same as my father's Army. Nor – since I retired on a hot August afternoon on "Last Stand Hill" at the Little Bighorn Battlefield in Montana in 2004 – is it the same as the Army in which I served. Its history, tradition, experience and heritage flow like a river – and this story is now part of that history.

# Foreword

*"No battle plan survives contact with the enemy."*

Reactions to this project have been many and varied. They range from "I didn't know any of that" to "Will you get in trouble writing this?" Because of these questions, I will use this section to describe the book's methodology.

I first determined that there should be several basic elements to report. There was an accused soldier. There was the crime itself – to be described in plain talk devoid of terms such as "with malice aforethought." There was a General Court-Martial (GCM.) There was a guilty verdict and various legal reviews. There was an execution and there was an interment. I wanted to describe all these events to a level of detail to assist future authors to produce more in-depth accounts of any or every case. I knew I did not have the resources to examine every officer, who sat on the court-martial panels, or examine every death penalty case that ended with a life imprisonment verdict, and then compare those cases to these 96 cases. Without a law degree, I could not examine truly legal facets of the trial, so my description of the GCMs is broad-brush.

The first problem was the files themselves; eight were not present. There was nothing sinister in that. In fact, it is amazing that so much paper has survived countless filing and refiling over six decades. Each file present was unique; there seemed to be no master list of required documents to be included. Almost every file had the confirmation of sentence order. Most files had the record of trial or at least parts of the record of trial. Most had reviews of the cases, by either the judicial section of the headquarters that convened the trial, the judicial section of the various theaters of operation or by special boards of review located with the theaters of operation, but that actually were assigned to the JAG in Washington, DC.

Sometimes statements made by the accused or by witnesses were in the file; in one case, the actual murder weapon – a knife – was in a thick envelope in a file, but I did not have the presence of mind to photograph it! Only a few of the files had photographs of the accused. At that time, I had no intent to publish a book on the subject. However, I wanted to collect enough information to become an expert, since obviously no one else was. To amass this information, I started to xerox parts of the files …, xerox …, and xerox. I brought in reams of paper

and deciding that copying everything would be impossible, I concluded I needed to create enough of a file copy for each of the 96 to be able to describe the crime, the trial, the execution and the interment. The interment was easy; there was nothing in the files, as "Plot E," the "Fifth Field" of the Oise-Aisne American Cemetery, did not open until 1949. Another gap in the available knowledge occurred in the case files from the North African/Mediterranean Theater of Operation. There were no reports of execution, unlike the files for the European Theater of Operation. I could only assume the stockade at Aversa, Italy did not generate an execution report, or that those reports did not get to Washington. That assumption later proved incorrect.

In 2008, I began assembling the project in earnest and discovered I had a paucity of data about the background of the executed soldiers. While the case files mentioned race, previous court-martial convictions and date of induction into the Army, I knew next to nothing about the personal side of each man's life; the legal files, for example, had the date and place of birth for less than half. I attempted to find the families of some, but found only two surviving family members. I turned to the National Personnel Records Center (NPRC) [Military Personnel Records] at St. Louis, Missouri. It initially proved very difficult as the bureaucracy there has Byzantine rules of access for almost any file. Still worse, the NPRC classified these particular 96 files as "Vault files." All had written on their covers:

**Reasons for retention in classified file are
<u>EXECUTION</u>**

Access to the "Vault" is very limited; it has heavy security doors and fireproof walls. My Freedom of Information requests were turning up nothing, as since I was no longer an active-duty Army colonel, I now had to follow a variety of, frankly, onerous procedures. More importantly, I was unable to convince the records clerks of the interest this project would surely generate with the public. This remained so, until a new facility opened in St. Louis in May 2011, the National Archives and Records Administration Building, which now houses many of the older files formerly stored in the NPRC facility on Page Avenue.

On July 12, 1973, a terrible fire devastated the NPRC, destroying up to 18,000,000 official military personnel files; the exact number will never be known. The blaze affected almost 80% of the files for those Army personnel who served between November 12, 1912 and January 1, 1960. Thus, my initial inquiries on many of the 96 files revealed fire had destroyed them – end of search. That is the answer provided me for file after file located at the NPRC, even though later information would show that all but three of the 96 personnel files escaped the blaze.

The personnel at the National Archives were more proactive and I finally obtained personnel information on most of the 96 that has made this study a much better product. As some of the personnel files in St. Louis had information for many of the "missing in action" files at the Clerk of Court, I was thus able to make a decent reconstruction of the misplaced cases. I found many of the execution reports from Italy. Finally, I was able to identify the actual hangman involved in many of the executions; in my review of the thousands of pages of judicial files at the Clerk of Court in Virginia, not a single document had ever revealed that mysterious name. In 2011, The Clerk of Court for the Army directed that all judicial files of the 96 be transferred to the National Archives in St. Louis from Washington, DC, making my travel easier.

While this work is primarily a history book, I did need to subject my writing and conclusions to a trained legal eye just to make sure I was in step with the law, and my good friend and long-time lawyer, T.G. Bolen volunteered his services. Mr. Bolen actually tried murder cases and has read almost every page of trial records that I have read; in this work, he has taken several cases that can be instructional tools for military lawyers, analyzing the evidence and testimony.

In a perfect world, I would have found these case files three decades ago and written the book at that time. In 1980, there were participants in these events; with each passing day, there are fewer and fewer eyewitnesses to these significant proceedings. That is why toward the end of the research project I decided to travel to France and visit a substantial number of French villages – where some of the crimes and subsequent executions occurred – to see if I could find, what was still there, to shed light on the events and to locate witnesses from that period of history. In a stroke of luck, at the end of the project, the actual supply sergeant of one of the disciplinary training centers in France and the son of an officer at a disciplinary training center in Italy both contacted me with a wealth of information, after reading my website.

Sometimes it is better to be lucky than good.

# Legal Foreword

When Colonel French MacLean, asked if I would be interested in writing a foreword for his latest book, I welcomed the opportunity to contribute. He informed me that the book would deal with the execution of 96 U.S. soldiers in Europe and North Africa during World War II – each following a General Court-Martial that imposed the death penalty. The book would set forth details on each of these cases, and the reader could decide whether the proceedings produced a just result or not. Colonel MacLean's thought process in asking me to review the cases was that it would be interesting to see what a civilian lawyer thought of the evidence and procedure.

I am a lawyer in general practice, having practiced in Decatur, Illinois since my graduation from the University of Illinois Law School. My only contact with the military came from my enlistment in the Army for two years during the Korean War. Discharged as a corporal, after spending my time in the Army in charge of a battalion personnel office, I can assure you that I had no experience with the serious type of matters found in this book. I was a ten-year-old boy at the time these events in World War II took place, and like everyone, I followed the progress of the war avidly in the newspaper every morning and recall the reports that Private Eddie Slovik faced a firing squad in Europe for desertion. Every publication stated that he was the only U.S. soldier executed for desertion during World War II. The result of that statement was that civilians misread it to assume he was the only soldier court-martialed and executed, rather than the fact that he was the only soldier executed for desertion. As this book shows, 95 other soldiers faced execution, but none of their convictions was only for desertion, their crimes being murder, rape, or a combination of the two. I had thought I was a well-read, thoughtful person, but when Colonel MacLean showed me the cases files, I was shocked.

As a practicing lawyer for half a century, I prosecuted cases and sought the death penalty, and I defended clients accused of capital crimes. However, that was in the small fishpond of central Illinois. Here in Colonel MacLean's study were case file after case file with trial records, witness statements, confessions, crime scene photographs, legal reviews, sentence confirmation orders signed by some of America's greatest military leaders, and chilling reports of execution.

When I started the project, I thought about how to approach the analysis, as I think most persons reading this foreword might assume that civilian lawyers would be critical of military courts-martial in capital cases. Civilian lawyers might feel that the trials would be hurried, with a defendant's rights not being fully guarded and the guilty verdict being preordained, with little chance of a successful appeal. Conversely, there might well be a general feeling that military lawyers would look on the civilian criminal process as dilatory or overly concerned with protecting the defendant and not the victim, and subject to endless appeals, which might cause the case never to be finally adjudicated. There may be a kernel of truth in both of these views, but that certainly does not represent a completely fair reading of their procedure.

Lastly, I considered the fact that I should not easily start through a group of capital cases, reading them as though they were presented in what might be a time and space vacuum. I realized that I had to consider that the personnel involved were not simply disinterested – in the sense that a civilian juror might be. They were men in the middle of combat, where their own personal safety rested in the hands of their fellow soldiers whose conduct might imperil them and their mission. The fact that a criminal defendant was charged with the murder of another service person or the murder or rape of a civilian upon whose goodwill the Army depended would surely be a part of the mental process anyone brought to the criminal procedure. Violent crimes against the civilian population were a serious matter, since the American Army was on foreign soil and hoped to be viewed by the civilians as liberators and not conquerors.

I quickly concluded that it was not fair to view a case, conducted under those circumstances, in the same light as a civilian capital case – conducted by neutral and disinterested parties and jurors. The second factor that influenced my thinking was that I should also consider the period in which these cases occurred. Clearly, the general civilian population of the United States did not view capital punishment in the 1940s in the same light as it is viewed today. Then, capital punishment was a way of life in the U.S. criminal justice system, administered sometimes fairly and sometimes unfairly. The consensus was that certain crimes should cause a defendant to forfeit his life and people trusted the government and the court system to handle those cases fairly. Everyone believed that there was a need for the administration of a criminal justice system in combat areas and no one doubted that the appropriate military authorities did their best to maintain a system of justice under difficult circumstances.

This is because jurisprudence has divided criminal acts into two separate categories. The first is labeled *malum in se* and the second is *malum prohibitum*. Criminal acts belong to one of the two categories as defined by the nature of the act. *Malum in se* crimes are crimes, which constitute an act that is so obviously criminal that it would not be necessary that a specific statute be violated. *Malum prohibitum* crimes are not intrinsically evil by themselves, but are found to be a crime because they violate the laws of the jurisdiction in which they occur.

An example of *malum prohibitum* is a competent driver who is operating an automobile, but who is driving with an expired driver's license. The fact that he is driving the car is not evil in and of itself, but it is a criminal act because the statutes of the jurisdiction provide that it is a crime to drive a vehicle without a valid license. The *malum in se* crime is a crime such as murder and rape, which is criminal in and of itself, without any definition by statute. In all the cases in this book, the only one, which is not a *malum in se* crime, is the Slovik desertion case in which the charge arises by virtue of a violation of Army regulations. Once you consider the definition of *malum in se* criminal acts, it explains all of the murder and rape cases reviewed in this book. These cases constitute a violation of the Articles of War, but that is not the reason for the charge. The reason is that they committed acts, which civilized countries deem by virtue of their very nature to be criminal. The fact that they are charged with a violation of an Article of War is simply a procedural matter in order to get the case before the court.

The attitude toward capital punishment changed substantially to the point where my state of Illinois had capital sentences abolished by the governor on the basis that the criminal justice system produced such sentences on such a unilateral and inconsistent basis, that a civilized society could not allow them to be enforced. His actions brought no huge cry of protest; the population generally accepted that there might not be a fault only in the criminal justice system, but that capital punishment itself might be an inappropriate sentence. Some Supreme Court justices have even ventured in written opinions that capital punishment might in and of itself be

unconstitutional, a legal idea that would have been nearly inconceivable in the 1940s.

**Reversible Error,**
**Aggressive Lawyering and Avoidable Error**
Errors in a death penalty case cannot be "undone" after an execution. When we hear that error was committed during the trial of a case, and ask anyone if an execution should go ahead when there was error in the trial, the almost unanimous answer would be "no." If you explain further that the proof was clear and convincing beyond any doubt and the error consists of the prosecutor calling the defendant by the wrong name several times and then ask if that case should be completely retried, again the almost unanimous answer would be "no." This illustrates the problem that reviewing courts continually contend with as to whether or not the error denied the defendant a fair trial. The reviewing court will look at the record for "reversible error." That phrase tells us that if they find reversible error, they will send the case back to the trial court. The phrase "reversible error" defines the problem and solves nothing; it is in the eye of the beholder. When a court determines that the defendant seemed clearly guilty and the problems that occurred during the trial were not as egregious as to prejudice the defendant's right for a fair trial, the court simply states that the errors did not constitute reversible error. This is a sensible standard and one that acknowledges that any human procedure is still an imperfect product. This situation is well set forth by William G. Otis, a former federal prosecutor and Special Counsel to the White House. Mr. Otis's analysis states:

"The question is not whether you can avoid errors. The only realistic question in an adult mind is which set of errors you are going to accept. You have to be mature and honest about it, and understand there is the risk of executing an innocent person."

That fairly sums up the analysis of error and the risk inherent in the procedures in the courts-martial cases in this volume. To put that into context, in my opinion, in no case in this compilation is the error so significant that you feel the accused is not, in fact, the person who physically committed the act. You will see cases where the question of innocence or guilt is closer than you would wish, but that is a result of the facts of the case, not of trial error.

The reviewing authorities in each case approached it with a standard that asked if the trial was properly conducted with no serious misconduct.

If so, there was an affirming opinion in all these cases. Before you draw any conclusion from that, you should realize that there were tens of thousands of courts-martial during this period and some of them were reversed or the sentence commuted. We have only chosen to examine files where the capital sentence was carried out – and only those in Europe and North Africa. From that view, the reviewing authorities acted properly and concluded that in none of these cases had error in the trial that would require a reversal.

Colonel MacLean – who has studied these files for a decade – believes that he would have voted guilty, with the death penalty, for thirty-seven of these defendants. For another twenty-seven defendants, he believes that he would have voted guilty, but would have voted for the lesser sentence of life imprisonment. In another four cases, he would be prepared to vote not guilty. That does not mean that any innocent men were convicted, sentenced to death and executed. What it does mean is that different tactics by the defense counsels could have produced different results. What those tactics and lines of defense could have been I leave to each lawyer.

Reviewing the case files also sparked in my mind that I now had an opportunity to select examples of what we settled on calling "avoidable error" – procedures and decisions that could be called into question at some future time, not overturn a verdict. They are in the realm of calling into question aspects of the perceived fairness of the particular judicial system. These "avoidable errors" should be further studied by current and future military lawyers with the intent of assisting them to avoid making the same potential mistakes in their own cases. From a legal standpoint, we do not seek to condemn the judicial personnel of the past, but rather to learn from these significant trials.

# PART I

Historical and
Legal Underpinnings

# The Big Picture

*"All of these cases, except for the one for desertion, are the clearest and worst kinds of cases of cold-blooded and premeditated murder and fiendish and atrocious rapes, with few or no mitigating circumstances."*

President Calvin Coolidge once said, "The business of America is business." That is not true for the nation's Army. Sometimes the business of the United States Army is to implement social change – leading the way on racial integration after World War II, enforcing Civil Rights legislation in the 1950s and pioneering the assimilation of women into previously closed aspects of the work force in the 1970s and 1980s. Sometimes the business of the Army is to protect citizens and defuse domestic turmoil, as in many major American cities in the late-1960s. Sometimes the business of the Army is to conduct peacekeeping operations in places like Kosovo in the 1990s. Sometimes the business of the Army is to help communities respond to natural disasters such as immediately after Hurricane Katrina in 2005. In the history of the Army, however, these types of "business" have always been secondary.

The principal business of the United States Army in World War II was, frankly, to kill people, and business was booming. During the conflict, the U.S. Army – including its subordinate Army Air Corps – very likely killed several million people.[1] Most of those dispatched were Germans and Japanese, who – when the pain of these losses became too unbearable – unconditionally surrendered. Some of those killed were Italians, until September 1943, when Italy smartly changed sides in the war; a few were unlucky Vichy French in North Africa in 1942. Over 400,000 American military service members also died during the war – including at least 116,912 Army infantrymen – but the stakes in the conflict were so high that America was prepared to pay that "butcher's bill."[2]

Many American soldiers were involved in this grim business. Some 10,110,103 men were inducted into the military, with 2,670,000 trained for ground combat.[3] From January 1942 to May 1945 in the ETO 4,182,261 American soldiers served "over there."[4] Included in that total were the 96 American soldiers in the North African, Mediterranean and European Theaters of Operation, who were convicted of capital crimes, sentenced to death and executed.

That sounds like a high number today, and it may have sounded like a high number back then – although it was miniscule when one considers that in 1944 alone the U.S. suffered 495,052 casualties. On April 22, 1946, Colonel John P. Dinsmore, the

Special Assistant to the Chief Legislative and Liaison Division in the U.S. Army in Washington, DC, sent a memorandum to the Under-Secretary of War – its title, "Comparison of Executions during World War I and World War II." Dinsmore, basing his findings on the time period December 7, 1941 to February 22, 1946, reported that throughout World War II the U.S. Army had actually executed 142 of its own soldiers – that total included the North African/Mediterranean and European Theaters of Operation, as well as in the Pacific and in the continental United States. Colonel Dinsmore examined the major categories of offenses and reported that seventy-two were for murder, fifty-one were for rape, eighteen were for double crimes of rape and murder and one was for desertion. In comparison, Dinsmore wrote, the U.S. Army had executed thirty-five American soldiers in World War I.

That probably still looked like a high number, so Colonel Dinsmore enlisted the support of the Statistics Division, Office of the Assistant Chief of Staff, G-1 (Personnel), which calculated that American involvement in World War I lasted 2¼ years, during which 4,000,000 soldiers served in the ranks. This equated to "roughly a rate of 4 men executed per year for each 1,000,000 men who served." Using the same methodology, he concluded that World War II "saw 142 executions over a 4¼-year period, among some 11,000,000 men who served, or a rate of about 3 men executed per year for each 1,000,000 men who served." Therefore, the execution <u>rates</u> during World War II and World War I were about the same.[5]

Then Colonel Hubert D. Hoover, the U.S. Army Assistant JAG, got into the act. Hoover assembled a comprehensive report – Dinsmore's memo had been only a page and a half – and sent it to the Secretary of War. Hoover cited 141 executions, not 142, and compared these military executions to death sentences in the civilian system. Based on information from the Census Bureau, the Army calculated that there were approximately 150 executions of civilians per year, out of some 40,000,000 males in the country – excluding those in the military. Using the same methodology in the Dinsmore memo, Colonel Hoover concluded that there were, therefore, 15 executions per year for each 4,000,000 male civilians, or 3.75 per million. *Voila!* This <u>annual rate</u> nestled perfectly between the four soldiers executed per million in World War I and the three soldiers executed per million soldiers in World War II.

Then Colonel Hoover opined why the executions were necessary. He had been the U.S. Army Assistant JAG for the North African Theater of Operations; Hoover, who was no desk jockey, but had had actually seen military justice in the field, wrote:[6]

"All of these cases, except for the one for desertion, are the clearest and worst kinds of cases of cold-blooded and premeditated murder and fiendish and atrocious rapes, with few or no mitigating circumstances. They were the crimes of hardened and proven criminals and in most cases were deliberately planned and premeditated some time in advance."

The numbers may still have looked high. Shortly after Colonel Hoover submitted his lengthy report, Major General Thomas M. Green, the U.S. Army JAG, sent his own memo to the Under-Secretary of War. The wordy title was, "Final disposition of rape and/or murder charges tried by General Courts-Martial, December 1941 to April 1946, and analysis of evidence establishing identity of accused in such cases as resulted in the death of the accused." From the lengthy heading alone, it is obvious the civilian leadership wanted to know much more information. General Green began by discussing evidence offered by the accused at trial. He presented that there were 140 soldiers executed – he did not include the single case of desertion in his analysis. Green stated that in 37% of these cases (52) the accused offered no evidence of any kind at the trial. In another 33% (46) of the cases, the accused admitted the crime but "attempted to excuse it on such grounds as self-defense, drunkenness or accident." He added that in 18% (25) of the cases – all of which were trials for rape – the accused admitted being with the woman but denied that any act of sexual intercourse occurred or claimed that such an act was voluntary in nature. General Green summarized this part of the memo by stating that in thirteen (9%) of the cases, the accused offered a simple denial and uncorroborated alibi, while three (2%) accused offered very weak alibis that were "obviously" rejected by the court.[7]

General Green included a supporting "Analysis Report," which presented that between December 1941 and April 1946, the Army charged 2,799 American soldiers with rape and/or murder. In 55 cases (2%) the chain of command disapproved the charges at higher levels; GCMs in 731 cases (26%) found the accused not guilty; and in 509 cases (18%) the accused was tried, found not guilty of rape and/

or murder, but was found guilty of some lesser offense (which would not have warranted a death penalty.) Therefore, 1,295 (46%) accused avoided a guilty capital conviction. But not all of the accused were so fortunate; GCMs found 1,136 soldiers guilty, but sentenced them to imprisonment and not death – a further 226 initially received the death penalty, but had this sentence commuted – leaving 140 to face the hangman or a firing squad.[8] In his "Identity of Accused" second supporting report, General Green delineated how the identity of the accused was determined before or during the trials of these 140 death cases:

| | |
|---|---|
| admitted by the accused at trial | 47 accused |
| positively identified by 1 or more witnesses at trial and admitted by the accused in pre-trial statement or confession | 22 accused |
| positively identified at trial by three or more witnesses to the crime | 23 accused |
| positively identified at trial by less than three witnesses to the the crime | 7 accused |
| positively identified at trial by less than three witnesses to the crime | 18 accused |
| admitted by accused immediately after the crime and not denied by the accused at trial | 1 accused |
| admitted by accused in a pre-trial statement or confession and connected by strong circumstantial evidence | 17 accused |
| partially identified and/or connected by circumstantial evidence | 5 accused |

Major General Green then included a few sentences on each case that illustrated what happened at the crime scene, but not what transpired in the courtroom, or at the gallows or the firing squads. To be fair to General Green, much of this information was reported on during the war and was accessible to at least the readership of major American newspapers. On January 21, 1945, for example, the following headline appeared in the *Chicago Tribune*, **"U.S. Army Tries 3,185 in 2 Year Stay in Britain."**

In the article, Army officials summarized that in Great Britain alone over two years, the U.S. Army conducted 3,185 General Courts-Martial with 2,858 ending in a conviction. Courts convicted nineteen soldiers of murder; of these seven had been executed. GCMs convicted twenty-four military personnel of rape; three of them had been executed. The article did not present the circumstances of these cases, but the magnitude was clear. With that, the "death book" and case files went into storage, where for the most part they have remained. The Army implemented improvements to the judicial system. Today every defendant in a GCM has a real lawyer defending him or her. Trials are not rushed; time is now measured in months and years – not days and weeks – before proceedings begin. Forensic evidence has come a long way since then; now DNA is revolutionizing the conduct of trials.[9]

However, times were different in World War II, so it may be helpful at this point to review the legal system then in force, before we examine the cases themselves.

# The U.S. Army Judicial System in World War II

*"Innocent, I would prefer trial by a court-martial of the United States Army than by any other tribunal in the world. Guilty, such a court is the last I would choose."*[1]

## Intent and Objectives

The U.S. Army's military judicial system in World War II was a straightforward process designed to fulfill several different objectives. One purpose was to keep as many soldiers as possible in the war effort, not in a jail cell. Therefore, only soldiers who had committed truly serious crimes were incarcerated, as military prisons tied up guard personnel that could be better used in the various theaters of operation.[2] Additionally, many leaders felt that some soldiers would "opt" to commit minor crimes, if they knew they could avoid frontline duty by sitting in a safe, warm jail cell. It was not just a feeling, either. On February 11, 1945, the *Chicago Tribune* reported that more than 45,000 soldiers were under arrest in the Army, using this headline, **"One Out of 185 U.S. Soldiers in Army Custody."**[3]

Another goal was to have a streamlined process of military justice that was devoid of lengthy delays. First, the vast majority of officers who sat on courts-martial were not members of the Judge Advocate branch. Therefore, they had other important functions to perform, such as leading their units in combat and performing unglamorous, but valuable staff-work to keep the Army supplied and moving. The longer these officers were tied up in lengthy court proceedings, the more their other duties suffered. Speedy proceedings also ensured that witnesses would be available. Units were constantly moving; a witness whose unit was near the proceedings today might be gone tomorrow. Casualties also played a role; unfortunately, a key witness might be killed or wounded in a few weeks or months, before he could testify.

A third objective was to maintain good order and discipline. Commanders believed that if a serious crime occurred, only swift and sure punishment could have a deterrent effect. As a result, knowledge of the results of courts-martial and executions was not treated as a closely held state secret. While executions in England occurred at Shepton Mallet Prison, once the Army landed in France, executions frequently occurred in public, often in the same village in which the crime had occurred. The Army brought witnesses to the event from other units, also permitting French officials and selected townspeople to attend. According to the diary of Kay Summersby, secretary for General Dwight Eisenhower, Major General Bedell Smith briefed his theater commander that murder and rape cases were causing complaints by the French and Dutch. Eisenhower (noted as "E") responded: "E suggests there should be a public hanging, particularly in case of rape."[4] To achieve these goals, the Army employed a logical sequence of events before, during and after a trial, and a multi-tiered court-martial system to dispense military justice.

## Types of Courts-Martial

The Army used three levels of courts-martial, based on the severity of the charge. The least severe, a Summary Court-Martial could only impose up to one-month confinement, restriction to a limited area for up to three months and could fine a soldier two-thirds of a month's pay. During the war in the ETO, some 83,456 men received Summary Courts-Martial.[5] A Special Court-Martial could sentence a soldier to six months confinement and fine a soldier two-thirds of a month's pay for a period of up to six months. In the ETO, at least 43,103 accused faced this type of court-martial.[6] A General Court-Martial could impose the death penalty and other punishments. In the ETO from January 1942 to May 1945, the following appeared as defendants in GCMs: 1,005 male officers, eight female officers, one female enlisted and 11,105 male enlisted.[7] All of the trials discussed in this book were General Courts-Martial.[8]

## Joint Offense Courts-Martial

Sometimes more than one soldier was involved in the same offense. In those instances, the commander preferring (bringing) the charges could decide if the defendants would be tried together or have separate trials. According to *A Manual for Courts-Martial, U.S. Army, 1928,* "consideration should be given to the increased labor, time, and expense that may be involved in separate trials."[9] One or more defendants could present a motion to sever the trials; this request would be considered, but it could be denied.[10]

## Capital Crimes

Violations of the following articles of war qualified as capital crimes (in which the death penalty could be adjudged) in both peacetime and wartime: 64, 66, 67 and 92. In wartime, violations of these additional articles of war were considered as capital crimes: 58, 59, 75, 76, 77, 78, 81, 82 and 86.[11]

*Article 58 – Desertion*: the absence, without leave, accompanied by the intention not to return; or to avoid hazardous duty; or to shirk important service. Two soldiers were executed in North Africa and Europe after being convicted of this article of war, but only one – Eddie Slovik – for just desertion. In the ETO, GCMs convicted 1,963 soldiers of desertion and sentenced 139 to death. The average sentence, as approved by the approving authority, was imprisonment for twenty years.[12]

*Article 64 – Assaulting a Superior Officer/ Disobeying a Superior Officer*: striking, drawing a weapon against, of disobeying an order related to military duty. One soldier was executed in the in Europe after being convicted of this article of war, in addition to another article. In the ETO 1,424 accused were tried by General Courts-Martial for this article of war as follows: *Willful Disobedience* – 1,112; *Striking an Officer* – 120; *Drawing a Weapon against an Officer* – 97; and *Offering Violence to an Officer* – 101. In combat, the average sentence was fifteen years; in a non-combat zone, the average sentence was five years.[13]

*Article 92 – Murder/Rape*: unlawful killing with "malice aforethought (either premeditated or unpremeditated); unlawful carnal knowledge of a woman by force and without her consent ("mere verbal protestations and a pretense of resistance are not sufficient to show want [lack] of consent.") Ninety-five soldiers, executed in in North Africa and Europe were convicted of this article of war.

## Procedures before Trial

Once the suspect was under arrest, the commanding officer of his company or battalion would order that he be temporarily confined to the guardhouse or placed under guard if in the field. For capital crimes, the commander of the arrested soldier would appoint an officer – usually a very thorough one – to conduct an impartial investigation to ascertain the facts and "what disposition of the case should be made in the interest of justice and discipline." He informed the accused of the charges of which he was suspected of committing. During this investigation, the accused could cross-examine witnesses against him, inform the investigating officer of witnesses on his own behalf, and give his own statement – after being informed of his rights.

That investigation would then go to the commander. If the commander was considering a GCM, regulations required that he "refer it to his staff judge advocate for consideration and advice."[14] Then an officer – often the first level commander, would prefer charges. A judge advocate would turn these charges (what really happened) into a formal technical charge (the Article of War violated) and specification (what happened in a legal sense) so all the elements of the offense were properly included. An example might be:

> *What really happened*: Private Smith shot and killed Sergeant Jones.
> *Charge*: Violation of the 92nd Article of War.
> *Specification*: In that Private Joe Smith, 1st Engineer Battalion, did at London, England, on 27 May 1942, with malice aforethought, willfully, deliberately, feloniously, unlawfully, and with premeditation kill one, Sergeant Sam Jones, a human being, by shooting him with a rifle.

A defendant could face more than one charge at trial. There could also be more than one specification listed per charge.

## The Appointing/Convening Authority

The appointing authority was the commander who had the authority to appoint and organize a court-martial, and that often exceeded the legal authority of a junior commander. Commanders of regiments, detached battalions and detached companies could appoint Summary Courts-Martial. Brigade and regiment commanders, and detached battalion commanders could appoint a Special Court-Martial. For a GCM, the appointing authority could be the commanding officer of an army, a corps, a division or a separate brigade. The *Manual for Courts-Martial, U.S. Army* specifically stated that no appointing authority should direct a trial by GCM until he had considered the advice of his staff judge advocate. Once the decision was made, the legal system appointed the participants in the trial, as the proceeding could start within a week or two.[15] By war's end, 118 GCM jurisdictions operated in the ETO.[16]

## The Trial Judge Advocate, Defense Counsel and Jury

Any officer could serve on a GCM, with the exception of warrant officers and members of the Army Nurse Corps; there were no enlisted personnel on a GCM. Thus, for an enlisted defendant it was not truly a jury of his peers. If an officer was the accuser in the case, or a witness for the prosecution, or in the case of a rehearing the officer had been a member of the first court, that officer would be ineligible for that particular case. By regulation, a GCM jury must have at least five members. Most GCMs had officers from several different branches (Infantry, Cavalry, Field Artillery, etc.), but this was not a requirement. As required by the *Manual for Courts-Martial, U.S. Army*, the appointing authority for the court,

"shall detail as members thereof those officers of the command who, in his opinion, are best qualified for the duty by reason of age, training, experience, and judicial temperament; and officers having less than two years' service shall not, if it can be avoided without manifest injury to the service, be appointed ..."[17]

For each GCM, the appointing authority selected a Trial Judge Advocate (prosecutor) and a Defense Counsel, and one or more assistant, keeping in mind it was "desirable" to have an equal number of assistants for each side. The assistant Trial Judge Advocate and the assistant Defense Counsel were to be competent to perform any duty required of their primary.[18]

The Trial Judge Advocate was the prosecutor in the name of the United States. He was not required to be a lawyer, although he often was, only that he "be carefully selected." His duties included obtaining a suitable site for the trial; that was sometimes more difficult the closer one got to the frontlines. His most important duty, however, was,[19]

"To prove beyond a reasonable doubt, by relevant evidence, that the offense was committed, that the accused committed it, that he had the requisite criminal intent at the time, and that the accused was in the jurisdiction of the court."

The Trial Judge Advocate was not free to achieve those results at any price. The *Manual for Courts-Martial, U.S. Army* stated,[20]

"While his primary duty is to prosecute, any act (such as the conscious suppression of evidence favorable to the defense) inconsistent with a genuine desire to have the whole truth revealed is prohibited."

Having said that, the manual went on about the Trial Judge Advocate saying,[21]

"Except to the extent that this manual may otherwise require, it is not his duty to assist or advise the defense."

The Defense Counsel was also "carefully selected." The accused had the option of asking for an officer by name, usually someone he knew from his unit, to represent him. The one restriction was that the named officer had to be "reasonably available." In most instances, the appointing authority selected an officer from another unit. In many cases, this officer was <u>not</u> a military lawyer. Some had been lawyers in civilian life, but were not serving as lawyers in the JAG Corps. A defendant could hire a civilian lawyer, but overseas, that was unlikely. The Defense Counsel's main mission was to,[22]

"Guard the interests of the accused by all honorable and legitimate means known to the law."

The manual charged the Defense Counsel with defending the accused to the fullest, even if he had his own opinion that the defendant committed the crime. He was to be provided "ample opportunity" to prepare his defense, but "ample" was never precisely defined – so he had to work quickly. In the interest of getting through the trial, he was encouraged to join in appropriate stipulations of fact concerning unimportant or uncontested matters.[23]

All members of the jury had an equal voice and vote. Each member swore an oath to do his duty. Any improper conduct by a member of the court was a military offense. Each GCM had a "president," the senior in rank of all members present. The president – a voting member of the jury – maintained order, gave necessary directions for the proper conduct of the trial, expedited the trial and all its charges, and spoke for the court where a rule of action was prescribed by law and regulation. In the absence of the court's "Law Member," the president of the court would accomplish those functions.[24] Nevertheless, the president of the court was not a judge, who in theory was neutral.

Each GCM had one member designated as the "Law Member." By regulation, this officer would be an officer of the Judge Advocate General's Department, "except when an officer of that department was not available" according to Article of War 8. That seemed to be the case early in the war, at which time the Appointing Authority selected an officer of another branch who was "specially qualified" to perform the duties, which often meant a field grade officer or officer who had served before on courts-martial. The Law Member – who was also a voting member of the jury – would rule in open court (in front of everyone) on all interlocutory questions – questions that dealt with admissibility of evidence, competency of witnesses, continuances, recesses and propriety of any argument or statement of counsel or Trial Judge Advocate. Concerning admissibility of evidence, the Law Member's ruling was final. On other matters, if challenged by the Trial Judge Advocate or defense, the court would be cleared and the court officers would vote on the issue.[25] In many respects, the Law Member was the most important officer on the entire panel.

The Trial Judge Advocate or the Defense Counsel could challenge officers assigned to the trial. Each side could make one peremptory challenge, which did not require a reason or grounds for why it was being made. That officer challenged would then be excused from further duties. The Law Member could not be peremptorily challenged. Then each side had the opportunity to challenge one or more court members for cause. Among the valid reasons for challenging an officer for cause included:

- that the officer was not competent or not eligible to serve on the court;
- that the officer was also the accuser in the drawing up charges, had been the investigating officer for the case, or would be a witness for the prosecution or defense;
- that the officer had already formed an opinion about the case;
- that he previously participated in the trial of a related case;
- that the officer's presence would involve an "appreciable risk of injury to the substantial rights of the accused."[26]

Challenging an officer with a peremptory challenge was dicey work. Lieutenants were often thought of as "wet behind the ears," and some "barracks lawyers" thought that "butter-bar" lieutenants would fall for any story or excuse, unlike the older field-grade officers. The more experienced officers had an easier time telling when a Trial Judge Advocate was "out of bounds" and the old, senior, colonels, legends like Colonel Harry A. "Paddy" Flint, often did not give a damn what anyone else thought about their rulings, and were thus completely unpredictable.

**Procedures during Trial**

Both sides could present evidence and witnesses during the trial. Previous statements by the accused, made after he was made aware of his rights, could be introduced. In a joint trial, the statement of one accused was not evidence against his co-accused. It was possible for the Trial Judge Advocate to enter into evidence history of past courts-martial of the accused. It was also possible for the accused to have character witnesses speak about him or have their statements admitted into trial.[27] To convict, the jury had to be satisfied, beyond a reasonable doubt, that the accused was guilty of the offense. The manual addressed that concept:[28]

"'reasonable doubt' is intended not fanciful or ingenious doubt or conjecture but substantial, honest, conscientious doubt suggested by the material evidence, or lack of it, in the case. It is an honest, substantial misgiving, generated by insufficiency of proof. It is not a captious doubt, nor a doubt suggested by the ingenuity of counsel or court and unwarranted by the testimony; nor a doubt born of a merciful inclination to permit the defendant to escape conviction; nor a doubt prompted by sympathy for him or those connected with him. The meaning of the rule is that the proof must be such as to include not every hypothesis or possibility of innocence but any fair and rational hypothesis except that of guilt; what is required being not an absolute or mathematical but a moral certainty."

Concerning the charges (Articles of War), possible findings could be guilty; not guilty; not guilty, but guilty of a violation of the Xth Article of War. As to specifications, possible findings could be guilty, not guilty, guilty with exceptions (with or without substitutions) or not guilty of the exceptions. Exceptions usually referred to word changes from the original specification, often name changes. The court could find the defendant not guilty as charged, but guilty of a lesser-included offense. That could be in the case where the court did not find the defendant guilty of desertion, but did find him guilty of being absent without official leave (AWOL).[29]

The first part of the trial addressed whether the accused was guilty or not guilty. If the court decided he was not guilty, the trial was over. If they returned a guilty vote, the trial would briefly adjourn for a short break (often just a few minutes) and then re-assemble to hear matters of extenuation and the accused's prior record. Civilian convictions were not considered at this stage in the process – but later on, the various higher-level judge advocates and commanders did review them. For enlisted men, the jury could consider previous court-martial convictions, but in theory only those convictions in the previous year.[30] To convict for an offense that had a mandatory death sentence, or to sentence a soldier to death where the choice was between death and life imprisonment, 100% of the jury members had to vote for death for it to be imposed. To obtain a sentence of life imprisonment (or to any confinement of more than ten years), 75% of the jury members had to vote in favor of it. All other convictions required two-thirds majority vote. Fractions went in favor of the defendant. For example, for a jury of five officers, convictions requiring a two-thirds majority vote were not met unless four members voted for it. For a jury of seven officers, a conviction required five votes. For most of the war, it was possible for 75% of the jury to vote guilty in that first (conviction) phase and 100% to sentence to death in that second (punishment) phase and the defendant had a valid death sentence. Voting was done by secret ballot; deliberation before the votes encouraged "full and free discussion." In theory, rank had no place in the jury room, per the manual:[31]

"The influence of superiority in rank should not be employed in any manner in an attempt to control the independence of members in the exercise of their judgment."

However, every court-martial member knew that the convening authority would not have ordered a court-martial, unless he thought that the accused had likely committed the crime.

## Duty of the Military Court
Military courts-martial were not designed to produce indecisive results that necessitated a re-trial or engage in jury nullification. They were to examine the facts, determine if the accused committed the crime and determine an appropriate punishment. Like most organizations in the Army, when a court-martial jury did not accomplish that mission, they received feedback after the trial as to what was the proper standard. This was a concept foreign to civilian juries

in our country, and to military juries today, as any type of admonishment of a jury became illegal in the 1950 Uniform Code of Military Justice (*Article 37, Unlawfully Influencing Action of Court.*) That feedback in World War II could come in the form of a letter of admonishment from the approving authority to the President of the Court, directing him to reassemble the court members and read the letter to them. These letters of admonishment often read:[32]

"The action of the court in not finding the accused guilty may indicate on the part of the members of the court a lack of appreciation of their duties and responsibilities in such matters."

Judge Advocates often felt that failure to admonish courts-martial in these cases would give the impression that silence by the approving authority would constitute tacit approval of the court's actions. As a senior Judge Advocate wrote:[33]

"In the review of the Staff Judge Advocate it was recommended that a letter censuring the court for its action be dispatched to the President of the Court to be read to the members. Appropriate admonition will be directed to the court, if such action has not already been taken."

## The Approving Authority
The approving authority was the same commander as the convening authority. Now, he was just wearing a different hat. The approving authority – assisted by his Judge Advocate that would review the entire record of trial – was supposed to ensure that the sentence was within the limits prescribed by the manual. He could not add to the punishment; nor could he commute any part, or all, of the sentence; he could only simply approve or disapprove. After he made his ruling, the approving authority would send all of the trial paperwork up to the confirming authority – the most powerful officer in the World War II judicial chain.[34]

## The Confirming Authority
In non-death sentence cases, the approval authority, after approving the results, could order the sentence to commence, under the provisions of Article of War 50½. For the death penalty, one more officer was involved, the confirming authority. In peacetime, the confirming authority for sentences of death was the President of the United States. In wartime, the confirming authority was "the commanding general of the army in the field or by the commanding

general of the territorial department or division," declared by an Act of Congress on June 4, 1920.[35]

This meant the commanding general of the theater of operations would first issue an order of confirmation, which confirmed the death sentence, but withheld the execution of the order – the designation of the time and place for the execution. Sometime later, the confirming authority would issue a GCM order that gave those specifics. This order was generally ten to forty days before the scheduled date of execution. The confirming authority could lessen the penalty – he could overrule the death penalty – this happened 226 times during the war.[36]

## Reviews

In addition to the Judge Advocate of the approving authority and the Judge Advocate of the confirming authority (the North African/Mediterranean and the European Theaters of Operation), the review process required that a special Board of Review – consisting of not less than three Judge Advocates – review the entire case. This review occurred in the Branch Office of The Judge Advocate General with each theater of operations headquarters; it could be considered similar to an appellate court, as its members did not work for the theater of operations commander, but rather their master was The JAG in Washington, DC. These boards were originally headquartered in Cheltenham, England and later moved to Paris, France. This was a powerful board; in fact, the Confirming Authority could not direct the execution of a death sentence until this review board officially informed him that the record of trial had been found legally sufficient to support that death sentence.[37]

In addition, the theater Judge Advocate had a requirement to mail a copy of the proceedings and review to Washington, DC, where the Army's JAG – normally in the form of the Assistant JAG, a Brigadier General, would also conduct a separate review. In some death penalty cases, Washington would actually offer specific comments, rather than just approve the verdict and sentence. However, these review boards were only quasi-appellate forums; the accused was not present at these review proceedings nor were there any counsels representing the accused before these boards. In fact, the accused did not have the right to have any evidence presented on his behalf at these boards.[38]

## The Death Penalty

Conviction for violating **Article 92 – Murder/Rape** carried a mandatory penalty of either death or life imprisonment. **Article 82 – Being a Spy** carried a mandatory death penalty. The court had the choice of selecting the method of execution – hanging or shooting. The *Manual for Courts-Martial, U.S. Army* considered hanging "more ignominious than shooting" and it was the usual method of execution for spying, murder in connection with mutiny, murder or rape – while shooting was typical for death in a purely military offense. The manual did not mandate selection of either one; each jury had to decide on its own – what the juries in Europe and North Africa in 1943 and for most of 1944 did not know was that the Army had no qualified hangman.

The locations where prisoners faced execution included the Peninsular Base Section Stockade Number 1 at Aversa, Italy; the Loire Disciplinary Training Center (DTC) at Le Mans, France; the stockade at Oran, Algeria; the Seine Disciplinary Training Center at Paris, France; the Delta Disciplinary Training Center at Les Milles, France and Shepton Mallet Prison in Somerset, England. Many other executions occurred in villages and towns in France and Belgium, when the U.S. Army wanted to show the civilian population that justice was being done.[39]

An often-overlooked feature of the death penalty in World War II was the phrase in each sentence of death that read "dishonorable discharge from the service and forfeiture of all pay and allowances." These were administrative functions, the tangible result being that the executed man forfeited all pay and allowances, and the $10,000 GI Life Insurance Policy benefit did not go to his next of kin. As the Insurance Act of 1940 stated, "No insurance shall be payable for death inflicted as lawful punishment for a crime."[40]

In the following section, each of the 96 cases is reviewed. For them it was not a matter of legal tradition, review safeguards, confirming authorities or next of kin benefits. For these 96 soldiers, it was simply a matter of life or death – and all of them lost.

# PART II

## The 96

*"He displayed a contemptuous defiance of authority and a callous disregard for human life. He showed no spark of remorse, but rather the heartless defiance and ghoulish pride of a cold-blooded braggart."*

*"It is requested that a plea for clemency, in the case of Private David Cobb, be considered. It is felt that Private Cobb actually believed that he was fulfilling his duty as a guard by not relinquishing his rifle until he was properly relieved. This is brought out by the fact that he continued walking his post after the fateful accident."*

## 01      Private David Cobb
### 34165248
**Company C, 827th Engineer Battalion (Aviation)**
**Murder**
Hanged on March 12, 1943

When a man is hanged, there is a lot of damage to the body. A World War II Army pathologist would describe that there would occur a rupture of the cervical spinal cord, at cervical vertebrae C1 and C2. Examination of the upper cervical region would reveal a complete dislocation of C1-C2, with complete rupture of intervertebral ligamentous attachments. The separation between the first and second cervical vertebrae would be so great that several fingers of the examining medical officer could easily be admitted in the gap between these vertebrae. The doctor would find hemorrhage – subdural (subtentorial), subarachnoid (occipital), and into muscle and facia planes about the site of dislocation. There would be hyperemia in the lungs, liver, kidneys and pancreas, and abrasions and lacerations in the left submandibular region.

He would conclude that the cause of death was a rupture to the upper cervical spinal cord, due to dislocation of vertebrae C1 and C2. The men who witnessed Private David Cobb's execution – and the eighty-eight other American GIs hanged in Europe and North Africa during the war – would not have understood all that technical medical jargon. They would just say that the condemned man died of a broken neck.

What had an American soldier done to deserve this horrific fate? The simple answer was that while standing guard, Private David Cobb had shot and killed Second Lieutenant Robert J. Cobner, who was serving as the Officer of the Day, on December 27, 1942 at Desborough Camp in Northamptonshire, England. Corporal William Mason, Jr., who was

serving as the Sergeant of the Guard, filled in the details. The "two-striper" said that Private Cobb, one of the guards assigned under him, had walked his post for eight hours, from midnight to 8:00 a.m. on December 27. According to Mason, Cobb was then to have eight hours off, but because there were prisoners to be guarded in the guardhouse, this period was shortened to four hours. Then Mason brought Cobb back to walk guard at 10:00 a.m., just two hours after his last guard tour. At that point, Mason instructed Cobb to walk his guard post until he was relieved.

At about 11:45 a.m., Lieutenant Cobner – of Swissvale, Pennsylvania – and Corporal Mason arrived in a jeep and truck respectively. From that point, Mason and Cobb had different versions – and the unfortunate Lieutenant Cobner was soon to be in no position to corroborate anyone's testimony. Mason said that Private Cobb told the lieutenant he was not going to stand his guard post any longer. Lieutenant Cobner called another guard to arrest Private Cobb. Cobb then leveled his M1 Rifle at the soldier, who stopped. Lieutenant Cobner then told Corporal Mason to arrest Private Cobb; Mason started to approach, but again Cobb told him to halt. Finally, the lieutenant took matters into his own hands and approached the accused, attempting to reach for Private Cobb's weapon. Cobb fired a single round that struck the lieutenant, who toppled forward, face-first. Although the lieutenant was armed with a .45 automatic pistol, Mason said the officer kept the weapon holstered. Private Cobb told a different version. He asserted that after Corporal Mason and Lieutenant Cobner arrived, Cobb asked:

"Sergeant of the Guard is it possible to get a relief so I can go eat dinner and go back on my main post?"

Cobb said that Mason did not answer him, so he repeated his question to Lieutenant Cobner, who allegedly answered:

"It is not any of my business whether you get a relief or not because it's not my fault you have to walk guard – it's the fellows in there (meaning the prisoners.) Do you want to go in there with them?"

At that point, Cobner told Corporal Mason to take Cobb's weapon. Mason hesitated, at which point Lieutenant Cobner said, "Are you afraid of him?" Cobner then approached Private Cobb – who said he started to back away, calling "Halt" half a dozen times. He said he warned the lieutenant he would not give up his weapon as he was on guard, and that the lieutenant then drew his pistol and drew the hammer back, bringing the pistol downwards. It was at that point, according to Private Cobb, that he shot the officer - but added that he was aiming for his hip. The shot struck Cobner halfway up his chest mortally wounding him – the lieutenant probably died within just a few minutes.

MPs arrested Cobb at 12:42 p.m., about one hour after the incident. The following day, Major General John C.H. Lee, the Commander of Services of Supply (SOS), ETO, appointed Lieutenant Colonel John J. Nealon, an Inspector General, to conduct an investigation of the incident. Nealon completed and forwarded his investigation on December 31, recommending that the case go to a GCM. A GCM convened on January 6, 1943 at the Court of Quarter Sessions in the Guildhall in Cambridge, Cambridgeshire, England to try the accused, who pleaded not guilty.[1] The trial started at 10:30 a.m. The defense declined to challenge any members of the jury.

Cobb and Mason stuck by their stories. Private Samuel L. Jacobs, who was serving as a guard during the incident, went on the stand and stated that he did not hear the conversation between Lieutenant Cobner and Private Cobb, only that Cobner approached, at which point Cobb shot the officer. He added that he did hear Lieutenant Cobner tell Corporal Mason to arrest Private Cobb and heard Cobb tell Mason not to come any closer. Most importantly, Jacobs maintained that Lieutenant Cobner kept his pistol holstered. Private Cashie Mason testified, stating that he heard Cobb ask the lieutenant if he could be relieved and he heard the lieutenant say he could not. Mason also testified that he heard Lieutenant Cobner tell Cobb to put his weapon down and act like a soldier or he would put him in the guardhouse. According to Private Mason, Cobb replied that he did not care, as he was on restriction for six months anyway. Mason also

confirmed that the officer's pistol was in the holster and that Lieutenant Cobner approached Private Cobb with empty hands.

Corporal Nathaniel Walker, next on the witness stand, added that during the conversation between Lieutenant Cobner and Private Cobb, the lieutenant said something like "cut it out, you will be relieved." Private Cobb then took the stand. A black soldier, he had been in the Army for just over a year, had eight weeks of basic training and had training in conducting guard duty; additionally, he had been on guard about twelve times before. He said he had first received an M1 Rifle on December 7, 1942, but had not been trained to fire it. He stated he had no advance notification of guard duty prior to midnight, when he began his tour. After the incident, Cobb continued to pull guard until brought back to the barracks. Cobb added that he did not know that Lieutenant Cobner was the Officer of the Day - but did know that he was an officer - and that he had been instructed not to give his weapon to anyone, while he was performing guard. He added on further examination that had he known Lieutenant Cobner was the Officer of the Day, he would have given him his rifle.

Finally, Private Robert L. Brown testified and he was devastating. Concerning the accused's actions immediately following the shooting, Brown said, "He [Cobb] said is there anybody else out there that didn't like what he was doing." The trial lasted six hours and 22 minutes. The jury convicted Private David Cobb of murder, a violation of the 92nd Article of War, and sentenced him to death by hanging.[2] The *New York Times* covered the story on January 7, 1943. The *Philadelphia Inquirer* headlined the story:

"SOLDIER IN BRITAIN TO HANG FOR KILLING; Negro Sentenced By Court-Martial For Shooting Officer"

However, unlike in many other courts-martial, the defense did not rest after the verdict. Captain Richard L. Tracy, Cobb's Defense Counsel, wrote a letter on January 12 requesting clemency to Major General Lee. In the letter, Tracy stated:

"It is requested that a plea for clemency, in the case of Private David Cobb, be considered. It is felt that Private Cobb actually believed that he was fulfilling his duty as a guard by not relinquishing his rifle until he was properly relieved. This is brought out by the fact that he continued walking his post after the fateful accident."

Tracy continued that he felt that the guard duty training of Private Cobb was so deeply ingrained that Cobb acted instinctively without considering the consequences of his actions. His was a lone voice. Major General Lee approved the sentence and forwarded the record of trial for action. Lieutenant General F.M. Andrews, in command of the European Theater of Operations, confirmed the sentence on March 1, directing that the execution take place on March 12, 1943 at Shepton Mallet, Somerset, England, at the Disciplinary Training Center Number 1.

• • •

Shepton Mallet – constructed during the reign of King James I – was Britain's oldest prison, It had been cleared of English personnel and transferred to American control under the provisions of the 1942 Visiting Forces Act, which allowed for American military justice – with respect to American soldiers – to be conducted on British soil. To enable the executions to take place, carpenters constructed a two-story brick structure to one of the prison's wings. It included a new British-style gallows on the first floor of the building, with two cells, within the main building, converted into a condemned cell – where a prisoner was held immediately before his death. The prison and town were located in Somerset, England nine miles northwest of Glastonbury. Glastonbury had long been associated with the uplifting legends concerning Joseph of Arimathea, the Holy Grail, and King Arthur and his Knights of the Round Table. Down the road at Shepton Mallet, however, the goings-on were less inspiring.

• • •

Meanwhile, a JAG Board of Review (JAGs B. Franklin Riter, Charles M. van Benschoten and O.Z. Ide) for the ETO met on January 23, examined the case and found no serious errors in the trial. Brigadier General L.H. Hedrick, the head of the Branch Office of The JAG with the European Theater of Operations, sent a letter to Lieutenant General Andrews summarizing this review. Hedrick stated:

"As stated in my recommendation to the Commanding General, it is my opinion that there were no mitigating circumstances, but to the contrary the offense was aggravated by the conduct of the accused. He displayed a contemptuous defiance of authority and a callous disregard for human life. He showed no spark of remorse, but rather the heartless defiance and ghoulish pride of a cold-blooded braggart."

Later, Brigadier General Hedrick added:

"To do other than to confirm the death sentence in this case, in my opinion would seriously jeopardize discipline. That no race prejudice enters into this case is shown by the fact that the witnesses to the tragedy and upon whose testimony the conviction was based, are all members of the same race as the accused."

David Cobb was born in Dothan, Alabama on November 14, 1921, the son of a reverend. He dropped out of school in the seventh grade to become a newspaper delivery carrier. He was married in 1938. He and his wife had two children, but his wife subsequently left with the children and moved to Philadelphia. Standing 5'10" tall and weighing 151 pounds, he enlisted at Dothan on January 8, 1942. Cobb stated that he went absent without leave in May 1942 for thirty days, while assigned to Fort Dix for basic training. Doctors diagnosed him with gonorrhea shortly afterward. Cobb departed Fort Dix, New Jersey on December 5, 1942, sailed to England, and arrived on December 16.

As Private Cobb waited to die, his family – and the Community Social Club #47 of Philadelphia – wrote letters to President Franklin D. Roosevelt and First Lady Eleanor Roosevelt. The letters requested both to intervene and appoint a committee "of Negroes and Whites" (Lieutenant Cobner had been white) to determine the cause of the shooting. The President did not acquiesce and instead forwarded the letters to the Army. Lieutenant General Andrews wrote the family, stating that the trial had been fair without racial influence.

On March 4, 1943 at 12:45 p.m., Lieutenant Colonel T.W. Gillard, Commandant of DTC Number 1 at Shepton Mallet Prison, read Court-Martial Orders Number 4 to Private Cobb. These orders stated that his execution would occur at Shepton Mallet Prison on March 12. Cobb responded, saying that he was guilty of the shooting, but that he had committed the crime without malice or premeditation. Authorities then placed Cobb in a death cell adjacent to the death chamber in the prison. The day before the execution, the two civilian executioners, Thomas Pierrepoint and his nephew Albert Pierrepoint weighed and measured the condemned man; Albert noted in his execution ledger that Cobb stood 5'10" tall and weighed 158 pounds. From that data, the executioners calculated that a drop of 7'2" would produce an instant death.

At about 9:00 p.m. on March 11, the Chaplain began a four-hour spiritual session with the accused – who was dressed in the prescribed uniform of a private without decorations, medals or service chevrons. At 12:40 a.m. on Friday, March 12, 1943, Lieutenant Colonel Gillard assembled eighteen officials and witnesses in another part of the prison and explained the proceedings to them. He then led the group to the death chamber, where they arrived at 12:48 a.m. At 12:58 a.m., Thomas Pierrepoint and Albert Pierrepoint entered the death cell and strapped Cobb's arms behind his back with a leather strap. The Commandant, accompanied by four guards and the Chaplain, led the prisoner the few steps into the death chamber, which was bright, "spotlessly clean" and painted white. They arrived at 1:00 a.m.

Over the next 3½ minutes, the following happened in rapid succession: the Commandant read the pertinent GCM order in its entirety; he then asked Cobb if he had a statement to make; Cobb replied, "Yes, sir; I just want to ask them to pray for my soul." The Commandant thanked him. Then the Chaplain asked if Cobb and anything to say to him. Cobb replied, "No, sir; no, sir. Just to pray for my soul as I asked before."

Albert Pierrepoint then dropped to his knee and bound the prisoner's ankles – in case Cobb decided at the last moment not to go gentle into that good night. At the same time, Thomas Pierrepoint placed a white hood over Cobb's head and face, and adjusted the rope around his neck; the Chaplain recited a prayer and upon a silent signal from the Commandant, Thomas Pierrepoint actuated the trap doors.

• • •

The use of British executioners was part of the Status of Forces Agreement between the United States and Great Britain, signed in 1942. The American Army had a small problem – it did not have an official hangman in Britain yet. When required, the Americans would pay a British executioner and his assistant for each separate hanging and that the U.S. would abide by technical customs of the British, different from an American hanging. The hood in a British execution was a white bag, dating back to the days of strangulation in public. The hood served to mask the contortion by slow strangulation, which was too horrible for even the ghoulish English public – who had always relished a good public execution. The two, hinged trap doors on a British scaffold measured precisely 8'6" long by 2'6" wide; when they dropped into the vertical position they were locked in place by rubber-backed spring clips, which prevented them from swinging backwards.

The goal in a British hanging was the "fracture dislocation of the two/three cervical vertebrae; spinal cord severed." Thus, there were no knots in a British hanging rope, simply a metal eye at the end. The hangman made a loop by running the free end of the rope through the metal eye and fastened the free end of the rope securely to the top of the gallows. Soft wash-leather covered the noose, with the eyelet adjusted for a snug fit just in front of the left ear – unlike an American hanging where the knots securing the loop stood behind the right ear. According to Albert Pierrepoint, this was a significant difference, because with the pull of the drop on the noose, it gyrated a quarter-circle clockwise, the rope ending under the chin. This violently threw the neck back and broke the spinal column. According to the British executioner, many American hangmen's ropes gyrated from behind the right ear to behind the left, which only propelled the head forward – not killing by spinal severance but by slow strangulation, which could take upward of fifteen minutes. The American system at the time, according to Albert Pierrepoint, also used a standard five-foot drop – drop defined as the distance a body fell until the rope became taut – while the British used a variable drop distance, based on the weight of the condemned and his physical condition (i.e., 6'8" for a man weighing 150 pounds.) Both nationalities pre-stretched the rope the day before the execution to take the "whip" out of it.[3]

• • •

The six-foot drop and British noose did indeed break Cobb's neck, but according to British procedures, the three medical officers (Major Einar L. Andreassen, Captain Ernest A. Weizer and Captain Stanley Altschuler) waited a full hour before examining the body. At 2:08 a.m., they pronounced David Cobb dead. A graves registration unit then took the body to Brookwood Cemetery, where a physician conducted an autopsy.

The *New York Times* waited thirty-nine days to publish the story of execution. By then the Army had buried Private Cobb at Brookwood Cemetery in Surrey, England in Plot X, Grave 1-1. Cobb's family requested that the Army ship his remains home; this occurred and David Cobb now rests in an unmarked grave at the North Highland Street Cemetery in Dothan, Alabama. The Army had already buried Second Lieutenant Robert J. Cobner at the American Military Cemetery near Cambridge, England.[4]

• • •

Albert Pierrepoint later published his memoir about his many executions. In it, he stated that, "At an American execution you could be sure of the best running buffet and unlimited canned beer." This refreshment was presumably set up in the commandant's office away from the death chamber to fortify the many witnesses. Pierrepoint later commented in the memoir on his first execution for American authorities, which would have been David Cobb:

> "On my first execution at Shepton Mallet, long before the drop fell, the officer of the escorting party surrounding the scaffold was flat on the floor in collapse."

There is no mention in the official records of just who may have become unconscious that evening – other than Private David Cobb.

> *"For members voluntarily to vote for a death sentence and then immediately to recommend that someone else commute it smacks of a lack of courage of their convictions."*

> *"It is a rather solemn occasion when you take a man's life legally or in any other manner."*

## 02    Private Harold A. Smith
14045090
Headquarters and Headquarters Company,
First Tank Destroyer Group
**Murder and Escape from Confinement**
Hanged on June 25, 1943

In 1941, Harold A. Smith was a 5'8", 116-pound white soldier, who was once described as a person who walked "with a slouchy appearance," whose ears were "unusually prominent" and who "always seems to be in a sleepy daze." As a child, he suffered from measles, mumps and whooping cough. Smith was born in Troup City, Georgia on January 4, 1923. Prior to his induction, he worked as a waiter in "Charlie's Café" in Columbus, Georgia – making sandwiches at $7 a week. Smith graduated from grammar school, and spent three years in high school, but did not graduate. He liked to ride a motorcycle. He enlisted in the Army on February 4, 1941; he soon after came down with influenza. After basic training, he joined Battery B, 17th Field Artillery Battalion as a gunner. A Special Court-Martial convicted him on July 7, 1941 for loitering as a sentinel on post. On August 3, 1942, Smith transferred to the First Tank Destroyer Group at Indiantown Gap Military Reservation in Pennsylvania, as a cook's helper – even though he noted that at "Charlie's Café" he did no cooking. By this time, he was 5'10" and 145 pounds. However, Smith's Defense Counsel asserted that his true age, at the time when he shot and killed a fellow soldier, was only sixteen and that assertion led to one of the strangest jury actions during the entire war.

The story started on December 31, 1942, when Private Smith and a fellow prisoner, Harry L. English, escaped from the guardhouse at Chisledon Camp in Wilts, England. The pair fled to London and remained there a week before Smith returned to camp on January 9, where Smith appeared at a mess-hall kitchen. Soldiers of a guard detail from Company E, 116th Infantry Regiment befriended him, providing some food and a spare bunk in the barracks. Smith repaid them for their generosity by stealing a .45-caliber pistol from a bunk in the squad area. Outside the barracks, at 4:00 p.m. on January

9, Smith encountered Private Harry M. Jenkins, who was walking guard. Smith drew his new pistol, chambered the first round and fired several bullets into Private Jenkins. Jenkins suffered for 28½ hours – despite an emergency operation; one bullet had injured his spine while another blew a hole in his kidney; the wounds were mortal.

Private Smith fled back to London; English police apprehended him early on January 11, confiscating the murder weapon. After charges were preferred against Smith, an investigating officer examined the evidence on February 7 and the Staff Judge Advocate prepared the charges on February 12. The following day, Colonel Charles O. Thrasher, the Commander of the Southern Base Section, referred the charges for trial.

A GCM convened at Bristol, England on March 12, 1943.[1] The prosecution presented a statement by Private Leroy K. Reed of Company E. Reed said he had spoken with the accused prior to the shooting and later heard three shots (he initially thought it was a truck backfiring) and heard someone shout: "Help! Help!" Reed found the victim, who pointed toward a weapons carrier 135 feet away, saying, "That corporal over there shot me." Reed started toward him and recognized the man as Smith; however, Smith fired twice at Reed, who then ran away. Reed added one key point – Private Jenkins' own pistol was in his holster. Prosecutors introduced Jenkins' statement to Private Reed as a "dying declaration." The prosecution also introduced a statement by Robert Churchill, a well-regarded London gunsmith and ballistics' expert, who stated that he had examined three bullets and declared that that no pistol, other than the weapon found in possession of the accused, could have fired them. However, authorities could not positively identify the bullet taken from the victim's body, nor was there a solid chain of custody established for the bullet's admission as evidence.

Smith elected to remain silent during the trial. However, on January 11, he had signed a confession, later admitted as evidence. In that admission, Smith said he took the pistol, intending to keep it as a souvenir. He stated that he did not intend to shoot anyone; just prior to the incident, Smith explained, he and the victim exchanged words and that the victim, stepping toward him, brought his right hand back toward his holster at which time Smith fired in self-defense. He said his first shot struck the victim in the stomach and that he fired one or two more times into the victim's back as he fell. On March 22, 1943, the GCM found Private Smith guilty of murder, a violation of the 92nd Article of War, and escape from confinement, a violation of the 69th Article of War.[2] By a unanimous vote, the jury sentenced him to death by hanging. Then matters became highly unusual. Within hours of the verdict, nine officers, who sat on the court-martial, signed a plea for clemency, which stated:

"It is urgently requested by the Defense Counsel that the undersigned officers, members of the court, that in view of the extreme youth of the condemned, clemency be considered by the reviewing authority."

Major Riley and Lieutenant Frankfurter of the defense team signed the letter, as did Lieutenant Colonel Peters, Major Kahn, Captain Farrior, Second Lieutenant McCaslin and Second Lieutenant Moberg of the jury. Moreover, Major Meedham, the Trial Judge Advocate and Captain Hayman, the Assistant Trial Judge Advocate, signed the request as well. Major Riley continued his effort to assist his client on April 5, when he obtained a statement from Captain Donald L. DeMuth of DTC Number 1, who wrote that Smith's conduct had been excellent while in confinement.

A Board of Review examined the case on April 23 and submitted their findings upholding the court's decision to the Assistant JAG in charge of the Branch Office of The JAG with the ETO, but noted some discrepancies. On May 20, 1943, Lieutenant General Jacob Devers, the Commanding General of the European Theater of Operations, confirmed the sentence for Private Harold A. Smith. He withheld the execution of the sentence. The same day, Lieutenant Colonel J.M. Pitzer finished the Staff Judge Advocate Review of the case. Pitzer found that there were at least seven "irregularities in the proceedings," but that the trial was legally sufficient and there were no errors "injuriously affecting the substantial rights of the accused." A hearsay document, showing that the murder weapon was stolen, had been admitted. The President of the Court, rather than the Law Member, ruled on some interlocutory questions. The chain of custody of the lethal bullet was broken. The court admitted the report of the attending physician as hearsay, rather than direct testimony. The prosecution impeached its own witnesses without adequate justification. After argument, but before the court closed, the court received a copy of the accused service record; that should have happened in the penalty phase.

Brigadier General L.H. Hedrick forwarded the results of the Board of Review to Lieutenant General Devers on June 11, 1943. General Hedrick took the members of the court to task for their submission of a request for clemency, writing:

"The recommendation for clemency by members of the court is not easily understood. A death sentence requires a unanimous vote, hence each member must have voted for it in this case. However, the death sentence was not mandatory; and the youth of the accused, the ground for the recommendation, was known at the time. For members voluntarily to vote for a death sentence and then immediately to recommend that someone else commute it smacks of a lack of courage of their convictions. Such a recommendation must fail to impress."

So how old was Private Harold Smith? Official records show him a few days over twenty, when he killed Private Jenkins. His Defense Counsel claimed that Smith was born on March 23, 1926, which would make him less than seventeen when he committed the crime. Photos of Smith show he looks very youthful and most of the court, at least in the hours after the verdict, seemed to agree. The Board of Review analyzed his age and said it was correct if Smith entered school at age six, standard for the time. Only if Smith started school at age two years and eight months, "an absurd assumption," would the defense's claim work. When Smith enlisted, both his parents signed an authorization form on February 3, 1941 stating that their son had just turned eighteen when he enlisted.

While we may never know the exact date of Harold A. Smith's birth, we do know the exact date and circumstances of his death. On June 16, 1943, the ETO published General Court-Martial Orders Number 9. By command of Lieutenant General Devers, the Chief of Staff Major General I.H. Edwards instructed that Smith would be executed nine days later.

The day before the execution, Thomas and Albert Pierrepoint weighed and measured the condemned man; Albert noted in his ledger that Harold Smith stood 6' tall and weighed 151½ pounds. The executioners calculated that a drop of 7'5½" would produce an instant death. Prison personnel removed all rank insignia from Smith's uniform. Tonight, he would die as a common criminal, not dressed as an American soldier.

At one minute after midnight, Friday, June 25, 1943, Major James C. Cullens, Commandant of DTC Number 1, at Shepton Mallet Prison, assembled eight officials and ten witnesses, and told them it was his duty to supervise this execution. He instructed the gathering that at the proper time they would follow him to the death chamber, where Lieutenant Colonel Frederick Whitaker would indicate where everyone would stand. Cullens then prepared the group:

"It is a rather solemn occasion when you take a man's life legally or in any other manner. I shall expect that each of you shall conduct yourself with that fact in mind. If there are any questions, I will be glad to answer them if I may. If there are no questions, I shall assume that all of us are familiar with our duties for this evening."

Cullens then recessed the group until 12:32 a.m. when he gathered them and gave some additional administrative instructions ending with, "The witnesses who have been detailed at this execution will keep their eyes on the prisoner at all times until the execution is completed." The personnel moved to the death chamber, arriving at 12:47 a.m. At 1:00 a.m., Private Harold A. Smith, accompanied by the Commandant, Chaplain and two guards, arrived. The Commandant read General Court-Martial Orders Number 9 and then asked Private Smith if he had any statement to make. Smith replied,

"Well, I want to say good-bye to my friends and I wish my fellow members here, the officers here, I wish to hold no grudge against them. I hope that Jesus Christ shall forgive me for my sins and that I shall dwell in the House of the Lord forever. I wish the Lord shall see that He blesses every one of you and my mother and father shall be taken care of and my brother and sister and the people I have lived with on the earth. I hope that the enemies of the nation I was born in shall see their errors and God will take care of them and they shall not perish. I hope the two Chaplains will say a prayer for me."

The Chaplain then asked Private Smith if he had anything to say to him. Smith responded, "Chaplain, sir, I wish you would say a prayer and I also wish that Chaplain Hutchinson will say a prayer too, sir." Thomas Pierrepoint and Albert Pierrepoint then prepared the prisoner for execution. Albert adjusted the prisoner's stance so he stood directly on a chalk "T-mark" under the noose; when so positioned, the arches of the prisoner's feet were directly over the crack formed by the doors joining. Once the positioning was "Bob's your uncle," Albert pinioned Smith's ankles together with a leather strap and buckle.[3] Thomas, facing the prisoner as he always did, then pulled the white hood over Private Smith's head and face and adjusted the noose, ensuring the eyelet was correctly positioned, while the Chaplain said prayers.

On a silent signal from the Commandant, the executioners released the trap door at 1:05 a.m. The senior medical officer, Colonel Robert E. Thomas, examined the body at 1:20 a.m. and pronounced Smith dead. A graves registration officer, Brookwood Cemetery Detachment, signed for the body at 1:22 a.m. The Army originally buried Smith at Brookwood Cemetery in Plot X, Grave 1-2. After the war, his family arranged for the body to be reinterred in Georgia.[4]

*"I won't say I did it, but I won't say I didn't do it; because I was too drunk to remember."*

## 03  Private James E. Kendrick
14026995

Headquarters Battery,
    14th Armored Field Artillery Battalion,
    Second Armored Division
**Rape and Murder**
Hanged on July 17, 1943

The victim was a little girl – nine years old and small for her age – born with clubfeet and barely able to walk. Late on May 28, 1943, the little girl's mother came to a nearby U.S. Army camp accompanied by an MP. She held a picture of the little girl and was crying, asking the accused and others if they knew where her little girl was. Five days later a search party found the child, face down. An American doctor said she had been raped and that her death was caused by asphyxiation because of her nose and mouth forced into the ground by pressure on the back of her neck by her killer. In her right hand was a clump of grass – the result of a grasping hand, clawed "in the agony of death." When the doctor turned her body over, he saw that her facial muscles and tissues were entirely gone – maggots had eaten them.

Private James E. Kendrick, a twenty-one-year-old white soldier, had earlier befriended the family, who lived in Ferme Blanche, Algeria, outside of Mascara. The Americans had landed the previous November, and by early May 1943, they had driven the German Africa Corps out of North Africa. For three weeks, the 14th Armored Field Artillery Battalion had been bivouacked just outside the village. Earlier in the day, Kendrick had driven a truck to the family's home, departing with the victim and her eight-year-old brother at 4:00 p.m. over the objections of the girl's mother. Kendrick, who was seen by numerous witnesses, said he was just taking the children to visit his camp. Shortly after the accused drove away, the little boy returned home, saying the accused had given him twenty *francs* to buy a bottle of wine, but had then left him.

When the girl did not return home, the family went to the Americans and began asking questions. Immediately, authorities suspected Private Kendrick and arrested him that day. Once the body was discovered on June 2, Captain William C. Smith, of the Second Armored Division Provost Marshal, took Kendrick to the scene of the crime and questioned him. The accused voluntarily made a statement, claiming he had been highly intoxicated, so drunk that he "could hardly see the road." He stated that

the truck was going forty to forty-five miles an hour and hit a big bump in the road – which caused the victim to fall out of the truck, with one of the wheels running over her. He stopped, but saw she "was past help" at which time he brought her body to the field in which she was found. Captain Smith pressed Kendrick with more questions, asking about a rape. Kendrick replied, "I won't say I did it, but I won't say I didn't do it; because I was too drunk to remember."

With that tepid denial in their minds, a GCM met at the headquarters of the Second Armored Division on June 12, 1943. Kendrick was charged with rape, sodomy and murder. The court noted that he was twenty-one years old, had been born on March 22, 1922 in Picayune, Mississippi and had served in the Army for two years and seven months, with no previous court-martial convictions.[1] Numerous witnesses placed the accused with his truck the afternoon of the crime, while family members of the victim testified that he drove away with the children. After receiving his rights warning, Private Kendrick took the stand – and changed his story. He admitted that the child had not fallen from the truck, as he had previously stated. He said that he had stopped the truck and with the little girl's consent had sex with her. Then, the girl had gone into a seizure, "shaking and frothing at the mouth." Scared, Kendrick jumped into the truck, left her and went to camp.

The court found him not guilty of sodomy, but guilty of murder and carnal knowledge, both violations of the 92nd Article of War.[2] The only question concerned the punishment. The court asked Captain W.L. Harris, a doctor in the 92nd Armored Field Artillery Battalion, about the accused's intelligence. Dr. Harris replied, "He appears to be about a dull normal."

James Kendrick attended eight years of grade school and one year of high school, before quitting, becoming a truck driver and making $12 a week. Standing 5'7½" tall and weighing 179 pounds, he was granted a waiver to enlist, being thirty-seven pounds overweight; Kendrick had blue eyes, brown hair and a ruddy complexion. He enlisted at Montgomery, Alabama on October 29, 1940 and after training as a motorcycle mechanic, reported to the Second Armored Division at Fort Benning, Georgia. His service record indicates that he was rated as having a poor character and unsatisfactory performance; doctors treated him for influenza, a bruised ankle and a bruised knee in his first year in the Army. Kendrick departed New York for overseas on December 12, 1942 and arrived at Casablanca on December 24, 1942.

The court unanimously sentenced Private James Kendrick to death by hanging. Major General Hugh J. Gaffey, commander of the Second Armored Division, approved the sentence on June 19, 1943 and forwarded the record of trial up the chain of command. Lieutenant General George S. Patton, Jr., the Commanding General of the First Corps, approved the action in one day and sent it to his commander, General Dwight Eisenhower, with the comment, "I approve of the foregoing action and urge that final approval be expedited."

A Board of Review examined the case on June 28 and submitted their findings upholding the court's decision to the Assistant JAG in charge of the Branch Office of The JAG with the North African Theater of Operations (NATO.) Lieutenant Colonel Tom E. Barratt concurred. On June 29, 1943, General Dwight D. Eisenhower, Commanding General of the North African Theater of Operations, confirmed the sentence, but withheld the execution of the sentence. But not for long: General Court-Martial Orders Number 10 of the North African Theater of Operation, published shortly thereafter, set the execution date for July 17, 1943.

The Army hanged Private James E. Kendrick at 6:25 a.m. on Saturday, July 17, 1943, at the stockade near the southern edge of Oran, Algeria – probably under the supervision of Major Matthew C. Stewart, the commandant of the 2615th MP DTC. Doctors pronounced Kendrick dead at 6:41 a.m. and conducted no autopsy. The Army buried Kendrick in Oran, Algeria in the U.S. Military Cemetery in Plot U, Grave 1-1, but reinterred his body in 1949 at the American Military Cemetery at Oise-Aisne in Plot E. He remains there in Row 1, Grave 5.[3]

> *"The act not only violates individual concepts of morality but also reflects upon our national honor, which is a combined national conscience of all of our people without regard to race, color or creed."*

## 04    Private Willie A. Pittman
34400976

Company C,
249th Quartermaster Battalion
**Rape**
Hanged on August 30, 1943

## 05    Private Harvey Lincoln Stroud
33215131

Company C,
249th Quartermaster Battalion
**Rape**
Hanged on August 30, 1943

## 06    Private Armstead White
34401104

Company C,
249th Quartermaster Battalion
**Rape**
Hanged on August 30, 1943

## 07    Private David White
34400884

Company C,
249th Quartermaster Battalion
**Rape**
Hanged on August 30, 1943

The case of Willie A. Pittman, Harvey Stroud, Armstead White and David White was a textbook example of how swiftly military justice during the war could run its course. On July 10, 1943, the Allies invaded German-held Sicily in "Operation Husky." Seven days later, at the village of Marretta on the southern coast of the island – almost before the gunfire had ceased echoing in the island's hills – four American soldiers from Company C, 249th Quartermaster Battalion entered the home of a Sicilian family at 1:30 p.m. and took turns raping a Sicilian woman in front of her husband and infant child. A civilian rode to a command post of the First Infantry Division, and a noncommissioned officer took a detail to the area of the crime and arrested eight "Negro" soldiers. Nearby, he attempted to arrest four more black soldiers, saying, "Four of you boys went to a

house and did some raping." Willie A. Pittman, Harvey Stroud, Armstead White and David White promptly fled, but "Big Red One" soldiers came to their unit and informed their commander what had happened. The NCO then drove one of the two Private Whites to the division command post, where witnesses identified him as one of the attackers.

At about 8:30 p.m. that day, Major Mitchell A. Mabardy, Second Corps Provost Marshal, began duties as the investigating officer. He took sworn statements the next morning – after advising the suspects. All admitted to having sex with the victim; each implicated the other three. Major Mabardy took twelve black soldiers to the scene of the crime, put the dozen men in a lineup and had the victim and her husband identify the four perpetrators. Both witnesses separately identified the same four soldiers – Pittman, Stroud and both Whites. Mabardy recommended that the quartet face a court-martial. Charges were preferred on July 19. On July 20, the commander sent the charges to the Judge Advocate. The Staff Judge Advocate wasted no time and referred the charges for trial, which would begin the next afternoon. The four accused would face separate GCMs. On July 21, 1943 – just for days after the crime – Private David White's trial began at the corps headquarters, at Caltanissetta, Sicily.[1] All members of the jury belonged to the corps staff, whose commander – Lieutenant General Omar Bradley – had convened the court-martial. The Army had sought a joint trial for the four men, but defense counsels insisted on separate trials.

Private David White pleaded not guilty. The prosecution presented the witnesses, along with the statement of the investigating officer. The defense offered no evidence, nor did Private White take the stand. The court found Private David White guilty of carnal knowledge, a violation of the 92nd Article of War.[2] White, who was born on July 12, 1919 in Shamrock, Florida, later lived in Jacksonville. He had been in the Army for ten months, having been inducted on September 5, 1942 at Camp Blanding, Florida. He was married and had been stationed at Camp Atterbury, Indiana. The court sentenced him to death by hanging. His trial began at 1:55 p.m. and ended about 5:30 p.m. – about three hours and thirty minutes in duration.

Private Stroud was next; he also pleaded not guilty. The trial proceeded in the same way as White's, with the exception that Stroud elected to testify. He admitted participating, but said he realized what he was doing and stopped, adding, "I desire the mercy of the court." What was unusual was that the jury was the same – to the man – as the jury in the first trial. The defense did not raise any objections. The proceedings began at 6:15 p.m. and ended at 9:00 p.m., with the same verdict and sentence. Stroud was born in Merrwell, Georgia on March 26, 1921, one of seven children. His parents divorced in 1932 and later Stroud spent sixteen months in the Navy, discharged on July 17, 1941 for astigmatism; he was single and was a general house cleaner. He was inducted on October 31, 1942.

Private Armstead White was the third to be tried. The 26-year-old, inducted on September 5, 1942 at Camp Blanding, Florida, pleaded not guilty and elected not to take the stand. The court, with the same jury, opened at 9:30 p.m. It was finished at 10:30 p.m. – sixty minutes. Again, the verdict was guilty and the punishment was death.

The court proceeded to the case of Private Willie A. Pittman without taking a break. Born in Campbellton, Florida on August 26, 1918, he was Protestant and married. Pittman stood 5'6¾" tall and weighed 153 pounds. Both parents were deceased. In 1940, Pittman contracted venereal disease for the first time. Shortly after his induction at Camp Blanding on September 5, 1942, he was diagnosed with gonorrhea. The prosecution did not bother making an opening statement but went straight to the witnesses. Pittman pleaded not guilty, took the stand, but said nothing of significance. The court, with the same jury, finished at 11:50 p.m. – eighty minutes. The verdict was guilty and the punishment was death by hanging.

Colonel Damon M. Gunn, the JAG for the Second Corps, reviewed the cases on July 26. He saw no major problems in the outcome, summarizing:

"It is difficult to conceive of a more brazen manner in committing the offense. There are no circumstances shown which should warrant the commuting of this offense to life imprisonment. Purposely no discussion has been made of the influence which punishment adjudged in this case will have on the populace. This accused must be punished for what he has done. The fact that it is believed that it is necessary for our Army to be careful in its conduct especially at the beginning of a campaign has not entered into the case. However, this punishment should make all others aware of the seriousness of the offense. To commute this sentence to a life imprisonment would fit too well with the idea that a sentence to a penitentiary is soon commuted and is a way

of being relieved of the immediate dangers and hardships of combat service."

Lieutenant General Omar Bradley approved the sentences on July 27, 1943. Brigadier General Adam Richmond, the JAG for the North African Theater of Operations reviewed the cases on August 2, 1943 and found the records of trial to be legally sufficient, recommending the sentences be confirmed:

"The foregoing recommendation is based on the following considerations which so aggravate the offense as to warrant the most severe punishment. The act was committed on the soil of Sicily within a week after our first troops had set foot thereon and while our forces were still engaged with the enemy. It was accomplished in the home of and upon the person of an inhabitant of that island who was a mother and who, at the time, was following the peaceful pursuits of domestic life, in the presence of her husband and infant child. The act not only violates individual concepts of morality but also reflects upon our national honor, which is a combined national conscience of all of our people without regard to race, color or creed."

On August 4, 1943, General Dwight D. Eisenhower confirmed the sentences, but withheld the order directing the execution. A Board of Review (JAGs Samuel T. Holmgren, O.Z. Ide and Gordon Simpson) examined the cases between August 7 and 9, 1943, upholding the court's decision. The board observed the issue of the juries, offering that although the offenses were related, they were distinct and that the guilt of the accused was not inferable from the acts of the other soldiers, adding:

"It must be presumed that the defense, fully cognizant of the participation by the members of the court in the previous case, believed that the members were fully competent to try accused and that they would fairly determine his guilt or innocence solely upon the evidence presented at trial."

On August 24, 1943, General Eisenhower directed that the Provost Marshal of the NATO, Brigadier General Joseph V. DePaul Dillon would carry into effect the executions in accordance with the customs of the service. Not only would Brigadier General Dillon serve as the presiding officer, he would also be the actual executioner, when he cut the rope that released the trap door. Five days later, the Chief of Staff of the Second Corps, Brigadier General William Kean, stated that Bradley wished to have the executions carried out away from the Sicilian public, at a site, sheltered by hills, three miles south of Campofelice di Rocella.

At dawn on Monday, August 30, 1943, the general hanged Private Willie A. Pittman, Private Harvey Stroud, Private Armstead White and Private David White. In the fleeting moments of darkness, he assembled fellow Brigadier General Adam Richmond, the JAG of the NATO; Colonel Leon C. Boineau, Adjutant General of the Second Corps; Colonel Andrew T. McNamara, who had served as the President of the four General Courts-Martial and Colonel Marius S. Chattaignon, the senior Chaplain of the Second Corps. Lieutenant Colonel Alvin B. Welsh, of the Inspector General Office, Lieutenant Colonel F.W. Zies, Lieutenant Colonel Harrison D. Wilson, of the corps engineers, Lieutenant Colonel Claude O. Burch, Major Howard E. Snyder, a surgeon with the corps and Major Mitchell A. Mabardy (who had served as the investigating officer in the case) also stood in attendance. Five Chaplains accompanied the four condemned men. The husband of the rape victim was also present.

In the composition of the witnesses, General Dwight Eisenhower was sending a message to every American Army officer in North Africa. This was a stern communication to the senior Military Policemen, investigating officers, review-board lawyers and Presidents of courts-martial. The implication was that their responsibility did not end with a signature on a piece of paper, but could extend to witnessing the same man die. In this case, they would watch not one, but four young men lose their lives.

With two Brigadier Generals, three Colonels and four Lieutenant Colonels present, the trap door dropped from under the feet of Willie Pittman at 6:45 a.m.; at 6:59 a.m., doctors pronounced him dead. David White dropped through the trap door at 8:08 a.m.; a doctor pronounced him dead at 8:25 a.m. In between, Harvey Stroud and Armstead White met their deaths in the same manner. The officers watched as the bodies were wrapped in mattress covers for interment.

The Army originally buried the condemned men east of Caronia, Sicily, in the U.S. Military Cemetery #3, in graves designated General Prisoner 1, General Prisoner 2, General Prisoner 3 and General Prisoner 4, but the journey to their final resting places would be a protracted one. On April 25, 1947, officials reinterred the four at the U.S. Military Cemetery at Monte Soprano, in southern Italy. Buried in the General Prisoner plot – in coffins marked with crosses – David White lay in Grave 1, Harvey Stroud in Grave 2, Armstead White in Grave 3 and Willie A. Pittman in Grave 4. Later correspondence shows that the four men were to be reinterred at the U.S. Military Cemetery at Nettuno, Italy. The memo stated that concerning future paperwork:

"Disinterment directive will neither show rank nor use the terms 'dishonorable discharge' or 'General Prisoner' but will show name, service number and major component."

Officials disinterred Stroud from Monte Soprano on May 25, 1948 and two days later shipped his skeletal remains in a shroud to the Naples port morgue, placed them in a wooden casket on June 1, 1948 and moved them into temporary storage. The transfer to Nettuno never occurred. On October 7, 1948, a disinterment directive ordered that officials move Stroud's remains (presumably, the other three) as well from Monte Soprano to, "Land adjacent to World War I cemetery Fère-en-Tardenois, France."

On February 17, 1949, Army personnel placed all four remains on a train bound from Naples, Italy to Épinal, France. The "death train," undoubtedly kept secret from the civilian populations through the 800 miles in which it passed, arrived at Épinal, where the bodies again went into temporary storage. On April 4, 1949, an innocuous Army truck convoy transported the remains from Épinal to Fère-en-Tardenois. Officials reinterred the bodies at the American Military Cemetery at Oise-Aisne in Plot E. Willie A. Pittman is in Row 3, Grave 50; Armstead White is in Row 2, Grave 47; and David White is in Row 3, Grave 72. Harvey Stroud was originally buried in Row 2, Grave 2, but in 1951, cemetery personnel switched his grave to Row 2, Grave 26.[3]

*"You God-damn military pricks don't give a man to have a chance to have a good time."*

*"I will cut your damn throat."*

*"In order for drunkenness to affect the nature of accused's intent, it must be such as to cause him to lose control of his mental faculties."*

## 08  Private Charles H. Smith
36337437

Company A,
540th Combat Engineer Regiment
**Murder**
Hanged on September 6, 1943

Charles H. Smith was a rough man, a real badass born in Salem, Missouri on October 6, 1909. Smith had a lengthy criminal record, being arrested for speeding and fighting – he was fast with his temper and faster with his fists. Pocket-change offenses, but in 1930, Smith hit the big time, receiving a twenty-year sentence for an unarmed robbery in Granite City, Illinois. He did "seven years on the river" at the Chester, Illinois penitentiary before being released in 1937. Chester – later renamed Menard – Prison, located at the base of a limestone bluff a few hundred yards from the Mississippi River, was a rough old place. It had opened in 1878. From October through April – out in the exercise yard – the wind coming off the ice on "Ol' Man River" cut through a man's clothes to the bone. More than half the prison population worked in the stone quarries; it also had an asylum for insane convicts, although in this 122-acre frozen hellhole, everyone was a little bit crazy.

Smith was an inmate at Menard in early 1931, when Murley Johnson – a twenty-six-year-old broom-maker from Mattoon, Illinois – was executed in the electric chair located in the laundry building, for the murder of a woman and her two children. Murley's final words were "So long, boys." Menard topped that on December 11, 1931, when the state "fried" Hazel Johnson, Henry Pannier, Willie Green and James Jackson in a single day. Life was rough at Menard, where there was only one guard for every seventeen inmates; perhaps the Army would be a little easier. However, as Charles Smith would find out, after he was inducted at Camp Grant, Illinois on May 11, 1942, the Army could teach the boys at Menard a thing or two about playing rough.

Six months later, on May 7, 1943 at about 7:30 p.m., Private Smith – who had been drinking since 1:00 p.m. – visited the "Villa de Roses," a house of prostitution in Oran, Algeria. It was not exactly the Ritz; one of the other privates went inside, but said he "didn't like the looks of the girls" and departed. American MPs patrolled the bordello in case some of the troopers got a little too exuberant. Standing in line, Smith was getting too exuberant – waiting for an hour or two in front of a whorehouse did not bring out the best in a man's character. The ex-con had his knife out and was showing his fellow soldiers how sharp it was – when a Military Policeman guided him to the front entrance and told him "it was time he was going home." Smith replied, "You God-damn military pricks don't give a man to have a chance to have a good time."

Smith also told the MP, Private Sephus Joe Stinnett, if he came outside, Smith would cut his throat. About that time, another MP walked over, tapped Smith on the shoulder and started to lead him away from the establishment. The MP did not get far. In less than eight steps, Smith whipped out the knife and slashed Corporal William L. Tackett's throat.

U.S. Navy Pharmacist's Mate John F. Brookmeyer attempted to apply first aid to the stricken soldier, but the wound had severed both the jugular and carotid blood vessels. Smith started to run, but another soldier tripped him and down went the pair in the middle of the street. In the blink of an eye, two MPs of the 241st MP Company were all over Smith, and from the look of things, they got rough as well. The MPs manhandled Smith to the Office of Counter Intelligence; at that point, he had a bruise over his left eye, sported a bloody nose and had a brush burn on his left ear. A lieutenant examined the Smith's knife and found it tested positive for blood. The investigators took a blood sample from the accused and used the Simmons Laboratory standards for determining intoxication. Simmons classified 0.20 Blood Alcohol Content (BAC) as "drunk," 0.30 BAC as "drunk and disorderly" and 0.40 BAC as "dead drunk." Smith registered a 0.375 BAC.

For Colonel Edmund H. Leavey, Commander Mediterranean Base Section, the evidence was enough to go to a GCM, which convened at 8:30 a.m. on May 21, 1943 at the Headquarters, Mediterranean Base Section in Oran, Algeria. The prosecution presented several witnesses, including Private Stinnett, concerning the crime itself. Several technical witnesses discussed levels of intoxication.[1]

Inebriation was the only issue the defense raised. Private Smith testified in his own behalf, stating he had consumed ten or twelve glasses of red wine that evening. He added that he did not know whether he had struck the victim or even how he left the "Villa de Roses." He did remember, however, the butt whipping he took when he was down on the street. First Lieutenant Donald D. Casey and Sergeant Raymond McCoy of Smith's Company A of the 540th Combat Engineer Regiment testified that Smith was generally a good soldier, and that his "reputation as a whole is above average." The trial seemed to revolve around the potential answer to this quandary:

"In order for drunkenness to affect the nature of accused's intent, it must be such as to cause him to lose control of his mental faculties."

It appears as though the court struggled, as they did not render a decision until May 24, three days after the trial began. The court finally found Private Charles H. Smith guilty of murder, a violation of the 92nd Article of War.[2] The court then sentenced him to death. Lieutenant Colonel Claudius O. Wolfe, JAG for the Mediterranean Base Section, reviewed the record of trial on June 14, 1943 and found no significant errors. Colonel Leavey approved the finding and sentence and forwarded the trial records to the theater of operations. On July 21, 1943, General Dwight D. Eisenhower confirmed the sentence, but withheld the order directing the execution.

A Board of Review (JAGs Samuel T. Holmgren, O.Z. Ide and Gordon Simpson) examined the case and submitted its findings on August 2, 1943, upholding the court's decision to the Assistant JAG in charge of the Branch Office of The JAG with the NATO. The board stated that the record of trial supported the finding and sentence. Colonel Hubert D. Hoover, the Assistant JAG for the NATO, forwarded the results to General Eisenhower, stating that the general now had the authority to order the execution of sentence. Eisenhower so ordered the same day.

General Court-Martial Orders Number 20 directed that the execution would be conducted on August 14, 1943. Still a rough man, Smith perhaps attempted suicide, although he was more likely to have been injured in a fight with his guards sometime before that date and thus delayed the inevitable. A second decree, General Court-Martial Orders Number 27, dated September 3, 1943, changed the execution date to September 6, 1943. Brigadier General E.L. Ford, Chief of Staff of the North Africa Theater of Operations, noted in the latter order that General Prisoner Smith had "prevented by his wrongful act, the carrying into execution of the sentence on the date fixed." Charles Smith would now meet the hangman.

Major Arthur S. Imell, the Commander of the 2615th MP DTC, verified that the man in the death cell was really Charles H. Smith on September 5. On Monday, September 6, 1943, Major Imell organized nine commissioned officers as official witnesses for the hanging in Algiers. There is no record of Smith's last words or if he went to his death as jaunty as had Murley Johnson years before. Major Imell likely cut the rope that activated the trap door sometime around 7:00 a.m. Doctors pronounced Smith dead at 7:20 a.m.; the Army originally buried Smith in Oran, Algeria in the U.S. Military Cemetery in Plot U, Grave 1-2, but reinterred his body in 1949 at the American Military Cemetery at Oise-Aisne in Plot E, in Row 4, Grave 77.

Corporal William L. Tackett rests among the honored dead in the American Military Cemetery at Carthage, Tunisia. His remains are in Plot H, Row 19 and Grave 19.[3]

> *"I know I have committed a crime and should be punished for it but I didn't mean to kill anyone."*

> *"Either you do what I want you to do or you die."*

## 09 Private Lee A. Davis
### 18023362
**Company C, 248th Quartermaster Battalion**
**Rape and Murder**
Hanged on December 14, 1943

The accused sounded remorseful. Twenty-year-old Private Lee A. Davis provided a statement to Major Ferris U. Foster, investigating officer in the case, explaining that on September 28, 1943 he had been drinking beer, wine and scotch at several pubs. On his way home, he stopped to pick up his rifle and met two girls, asked them to walk over to some woods and then fired two or three times into the air, not meaning to hit anyone, but he did and the bullet killed Cynthia June Lay. He added:

> "I know I have committed a crime and should be punished for it but I didn't mean to kill anyone. I wasn't in my right mind then and it was an accident because I thought I had my gun in the air. All I ask of you all, will you spare my life. I am sorry I did what I did but I know it won't bring back the girl's life and I am sorry and I want all the Christians to pray for me."

What Davis did not say in his contrite statement was that he raped the other girl, a nurse, while her friend lay dying.

The evidence was sufficient for Colonel Charles O. Thrasher, Commander Southern Base Section, to order a GCM, which convened at Tottenham House, Marlborough, in Wiltshire, England on October 6, 1943. The rape victim testified that Davis had approached them just past 7:45 p.m. as they were walking to the Savernake Hospital. Halfway up a hill, the soldier approached them and asked where they were going. The young women replied that they were going to the hospital at which time the soldier dropped behind them as they moved on. A few minutes later, they heard a voice behind them saying words to the effect of "Stand still or I'll shoot." The two turned around and saw a "coloured" American soldier leveling his rifle at them. They tried to talk to him and then began running. The soldier fired; Cynthia June Lay fell. He caught up with the other girl and took her into the woods where he told her, "Either you do what I want you to do or you die."

Then he raped her. The following morning the victim reported the crime and an investigation began at the nearest American unit stationed at Iron Gates Camp. Someone found a pair of bloodstained trousers and shirt, and a carbine with serial number 1594722 in the mud near Hut 28. The clothing was marked with the first letter of the soldier's last name and the last four digits of his service number. Those numbers would lead to Private Lee A. Davis, a young man who was born on January 8, 1923 in Temple, Texas.

Davis had enlisted in the Army at Fort Huachuca, Arizona on March 25, 1941, as a rifleman for a period of three years – joining Company K of the 368th Infantry Regiment. He listed his home address as Phoenix, Arizona. Private Davis finished eight years of grammar school and one year of high school. He stood 5'9½" tall and weighed 135 pounds. He was married. He later transferred to Company C of the 248th Quartermaster Battalion, departing New York City for Europe on August 14, 1943 and arriving in Liverpool on August 21, 1943. Just five weeks later, he was involved in the crime.

The company commander assembled the entire unit and shortly afterward arrested Private Davis. The prosecution brought in Robert Churchill, the ballistics' expert, who testified that test cartridge cases from Davis' weapon matched those found at the site of the shooting. The Metropolitan Police Laboratory conducted forensic tests on the clothing found near the hut, and on other items of Davis' bloodstained clothing. The trial lasted two days and adjourned until October 26, in part – it was reported – because the rape victim suffered a nervous breakdown. According to a British newspaper, the Trial Judge Advocate summed up the case, in part, by saying to the panel:

> "The story of this little girl before you today would cause any man to scream at the thought of what she had to undergo that night."

Davis' remorseful statement was admitted as evidence, but it may have been overshadowed by his previous record – four courts-martial, twice for absent without official leave, once for disrespect to an officer and once for failing to obey a non-commissioned officer. The court found Davis guilty of murder and carnal knowledge, both violations of the 92nd Article of War.[1] It then sentenced him to be hanged by the neck until dead. *The Times of London* reported the death sentence the following day.

Colonel Thrasher approved the finding of guilty and the death sentence. Lieutenant General Jacob Devers, the Commanding General of the European Theater of Operations, confirmed the sentence for Private Lee A. Davis on November 13, 1943. Lieutenant General Devers issued General Court-Martial Orders Number 27 on December 4, 1943, directing that the execution occur on December 14, 1943 at Shepton Mallet.

Major James C. Cullens, Commandant, 2912th DTC, read the order directing the execution to Private Davis on December 8. At 12:01 a.m. on Tuesday, December 14, Major Cullens assembled those at Shepton Mallet Prison, who would be present at the execution. He read instructions to the seven personnel of official party and the thirteen additional witnesses. Cullens only needed five witnesses and it appears that he sensed a bit of squeamishness, as he added:

"I have thought it to be a very good idea to allow what people I can to retire to the ante room, but I believe the official witnesses should witness the execution. I will say this, if any of you are on the breaking point, you may retire as we have more than five witnesses, but I do want five to stay there."

The group adjourned until 12:47 a.m., when they reformed and moved to the execution chamber, arriving at 12:50 a.m. Cullens and a small group then went to Private Davis' cell; they returned at 12:55 a.m. According to one post-war source, as Davis entered the death chamber he looked at the noose and cried, "Oh, God, I'm going to die!" Major Cullens then read the entire General Court-Martial Orders Number 27 and asked the prisoner if he had a statement to make. Davis, now composed, replied,

"I want to thank all the officers and noncommissioned officers for being so kind to me and I want all of them to pray for my soul."

The Chaplain then asked the condemned if he had anything to say; Davis answered, "I want to thank you for everything you did for me and please ask them to pray for me."

The executioner, Thomas Pierrepoint, placed the hood over Davis' head and adjusted the rope; his assistant Alexander Riley then bound Davis' ankles with a restraining strap. The Commandant gave a silent signal, Pierrepoint bent down, removed the safety cotter pin and pushed the lever forward – activating the trap doors and Davis dropped to his death – the time was 1:00 a.m. Major Lewis F. Somers, the senior medical officer present, examined the body of Lee Davis at 1:10 a.m., but it appears that his heart was still beating, as Somers stated he could not make a pronouncement at that time. The medical officers re-examined Davis at 1:20 a.m. and finally pronounced him dead. Somers signed a form stating that the direct cause of death was "Suffocation (Asphyzia)."

The Army initially buried Private Lee A. Davis at Brookwood Cemetery in Plot X, Grave 1-3; in 1948, the Army transferred the remains to the American Military Cemetery at Cambridge, England. Officials reinterred his body in 1949 at the American Military Cemetery at Oise-Aisne in Plot E. He remains there in Row 3, Grave 61.[2]

*"If any of you other pricks move I'll mow you all down."*

*"I have not overlooked the fact that the accused is 23 years old and under some circumstances this fact is sufficient to weigh the balance in favor of commuting a death sentence. However, the entire command is composed of young men and every case coming to your attention will be that of a young man."*

## 10    Private Edwin P. Jones
15045804

Battery A,
    27th Armored Field Artillery Battalion,
    First Armored Division
**Attempted Murder and Murder**
Hanged on January 4, 1944

The Military Police had a thankless job during the war. They had to enforce regulations, break up fights, ensure order in certain unsavory civilian entertainment establishments and deal with thousands of soldiers who were armed – and by design – dangerous. Frequently these soldiers, who often were under great stress or under the influence of easily obtainable alcohol, cursed the military cops; often they spit on the MPs, sometimes they assaulted them, and in some instances, they killed them.

That is what happened at Assi Ben Okba, Algeria. Private Edwin P. Jones and Private Fred T. Bailey, two white soldiers of the 27th Armored Field Artillery Battalion, were armed, dangerous, intoxicated and looking to show some MPs "a thing or two." When it ended, one MP had his heart blown apart by a .45-caliber pistol round, while a second MP was clinging to life with a chest wound that went through his left lung and came out the middle of his back.

The fatal incident did not start that way; they almost never did. After deploying overseas, Edwin Jones wrote home on March 9, 1943 and April 28, 1943 saying that he was fine – but that was about to change. On August 28, 1943, Jones and Bailey met some friends at a bar in the village and drank a little wine and beer until it closed. They then took a bottle of wine with them, sat on a curb and continued drinking. At about 8:30 p.m., two MPs approached and told the group they would have to surrender the open container of alcohol. The soldiers asked if they could finish the wine first and the MPs agreed. The other artillerymen then went back to camp, while Jones and Bailey stewed in town – before deciding to return to camp "get our guns and see how they [the MPs] would act toward us." Private Jones pocketed his .45 automatic that he had bought from another soldier, but not before chambering

a round. Just before 10:00 p.m., the pair started making a disturbance back in the village. Sensing the precariousness of the situation, an MP went to a nearby town to get reinforcements to deal with the unruly pair. He returned with four other MPs; they found Jones and Bailey just after the 10:00 p.m. curfew. The MPs told the accused to get on the truck for a ride back to camp. It then got confusing – it was dark, the moon having set several hours after sunset; the MPs closed on the pair and grabbed them. Simultaneously, Private Jones drew his weapon and the big .45 erupted with three shots.

The first shot went wild. The second shot dropped Private Norman E. Hippert, after striking him in the chest. The third shot passed through Private Alfred E. Raby's heart. In the ensuing confusion, Jones escaped and hauled tail back to camp. Falling asleep, the next thing he knew the battery first sergeant was roughly waking him up and placing him under arrest.

Jones provided a sworn statement to First Lieutenant Henry W. Duncklee in the Criminal Investigation Division at Oran, Algeria the same day – August 29. By September 10, the investigating officer, Captain Charles H. Davis, concluded his work and on September 12, the charges were referred for trial. The case went to a GCM, which convened at 2:00 p.m. on September 21, 1943 in Oran, Algeria. The defense challenged one member of the panel, Lieutenant Colonel Jager, who was excused from the court.[1] Lieutenant Colonel Jager had been in the jury of a previous GCM that ended in a death penalty. However, another juror, Colonel Robert H. Bond, remained and this would be his second GCM, leading to the death penalty.

Private Edwin P. Jones and Private Fred T. Bailey received a joint trial, although Bailey was not charged with murder, but lesser charges. Both pleaded not guilty to all charges. The prosecution presented eyewitness testimony from Second Lieutenant Charles M. Hunter, who had been on duty with the MPs. Hunter's testimony was devastating to Jones, but it may have helped Bailey, when the officer stated that Bailey might have said at the instant of the shooting, "Stop. Don't shoot anymore. Realize what you are doing."

The prosecution then put three enlisted MPs on the stand to testify and followed that with Private Norman E. Hippert, who proved an excellent witness. They then introduced Private Jones' statement made the day after the incident. The defense made no case, and both accused soldiers desired to remain silent. The court found Private Edwin P. Jones guilty of murder and attempted murder, both violations of the 92nd Article of War.[2] The court sentenced Private Fred T. Bailey to confinement at hard labor for one year and nine months and a dishonorable discharge. After also considering two previous court-martial convictions for AWOL, the court sentenced Private Edwin P. Jones to be hanged by the neck until dead and adjourned at 8:45 p.m.

Edwin P. Jones was typical of many of the other defendants in this study. The son of a farmer in rural Henry County, Kentucky, Jones was born on February 16, 1920. The family led a hardscrabble upbringing despite their hardworking parents. Edwin was the oldest of eight children – four boys and four girls. Farming was tough on the bottomland and hilly farm country; the family sold cattle and hogs in Louisville and raised two or three dairy cows; they also had a small tobacco patch as well, but harvesting crops was difficult with a one-horse plow. The children attended the rural Collins' School, a one-room wooden structure. However, farming came first and Edwin Jones left school to help on his uncle's farm. It was backbreaking work and Edwin enlisted on September 5, 1940; he reported to Fort Knox, some 80 miles from home and soon became a cook.

The unmarried soldier's life changed on August 6, 1941. Home on pass, he and two brothers went to the nearby town of Lockport along the Kentucky River. There was a dance at the "Jenny Barn" establishment, and shortly after 11:00 p.m., a fight broke out. Edwin's younger brother Willie had a knife, while another brother Robert apparently picked up a golf club. Unfortunately, for the Jones boys, Earl "Pedro" Kistner – one of the other protagonists – wielded a pistol and fired two shots. One of the rounds killed Willie; the other passed through Robert's shoulder and struck Edwin, penetrating his lung. An ambulance rushed Edwin to a hospital; he survived. At the county examining-trial nine days later, Kistner said that he had no gun in the fracas until he felt one being pressed against his side at which time he grabbed the piece and fired the rounds. Judge F.C. Vance ruled that there was insufficient evidence for an indictment; others thought that the ruling was a travesty. In any case, Private Jones spent a month in the hospital. There was no evidence that this episode was ever mentioned at Edwin Jones' GCM.

Lieutenant Colonel Claudius O. Wolfe, the Judge Advocate at the Headquarters of the Mediterranean Base Section, reviewed the case on October 27, 1943. He found that the record of trial was sufficient to support the findings. Brigadier General Arthur R. Wilson, the Commander Mediterranean Base Section of the NATO concurred with his Judge Advocate and approved the finding and sentence, sending the trial records to the theater commander. On December 6, 1943, General Dwight D. Eisenhower confirmed the sentence, but withheld the order directing the execution. A Board of Review (JAGs Samuel T. Holmgren, O.Z. Ide and Gordon Simpson) examined the case and submitted its findings on December 23, 1943 – upholding the court's decision – to the Assistant JAG in charge of the Branch Office of The JAG with the NATO. The board stated that the record of trial supported the finding and sentence. Colonel Hubert D. Hoover, the Assistant JAG for the NATO, forwarded the review results to General Eisenhower. The same day the NATO Brigadier General E.L. Ford – for General Eisenhower – published General Court-Martial Orders Number 56, stating the execution occur thirteen days later.

Events began to accelerate and at 11:00 a.m. on January 3, 1944, an officer notified General Prisoner Edwin Jones that he would be executed in 48 hours. Chaplain Marvin D. Brown began furnishing spiritual aid the next day. On Wednesday, January 5, 1944, under the supervision of Colonel W.H. Jones, Jr., the Provost Marshal for the Mediterranean Base Section, the Army hanged Private Edwin P. Jones at Oran, Algeria at the Stockade of the Mediterranean Base Section operated by the 2615th MP DTC. Major Arthur S. Imell probably served as the executioner; records reveal that the trap door released at 7:47 a.m. and that a medical officer pronounced Jones dead at 7:59 a.m. The Army originally buried Edwin Jones at Oran in the U.S. Military Cemetery in Plot U, Grave 1-3.

Alfred E. Raby – the victim – was from Wayne County, Michigan; this study could not determine the location of his remains.

• • •

The day after the Army hanged Private Jones, Lewis D. Jones, an attorney in New Castle, Kentucky, wrote the Office of the Adjutant General about the soldier. In the letter, the attorney wrote:

"This boy has written his father that he has been in some serious trouble in Africa and that someday they would find out about it."

The family found out about the situation on January 11, 1944, when The Adjutant General's Office sent a letter to the parents of Edwin P. Jones. It stated that their son's death was due to his own willful misconduct. The Jones family held a memorial service at the Drennon Chapel in Drennon Springs, Kentucky on February 13, 1944. After the war, his mother wanted her son's remains to be returned home. That finally occurred in August 1949. On August 21, 1949, officials buried Edwin P. Jones next to his younger brother Willie in the family plot at the Drennon Chapel, after the church choir sang hymns at the family home and the Veterans of Foreign Wars organized the color guard. The night before, in the family's parlor, four former Army buddies of Edwin in North Africa, explained in hushed conversation to the men of the family exactly what had happened. The newspaper account of the funeral mentioned nothing of the murder or subsequent execution.[3]

*"Private Waters is an indirect or psychological casualty of war."*

*"Should any of you feel faint or feel that you are about to become ill do not hesitate to step from the execution chamber into the adjoining anteroom."*

## 11    Private John H. Waters
### 32337934
Engineer Model Makers Detachment
**Self-maiming,**
**Abandoning a Guard Post and Murder**
Hanged on February 10, 1944

The motive and crime were as old as the human race. Private John H. Waters, a white soldier, entered this world on October 1, 1905. He was stationed in a foreign country, at Phyllis Court, Henley-on-Thames, England. He was alone – on detached service with the British, making models of battle campaigns – and found a girlfriend, Doris May Staples, who was his same age. Waters thought he had a good six-month-old relationship brewing – at least she wasn't some of that "jailbait" running around – but that liaison was about to turn sour. Doris had been seeing other men. As the accused would later say:

> "If she went out with others and was a lady about it and told me I wouldn't have minded, but I don't like this lying stuff."

On July 14, 1943, John Waters left his guard post with a .38-caliber Smith & Wesson revolver, probably had a drink or two and went to see Miss Staples who worked at a tailor shop. He visited the shop three times. On the final visit, Staples had a few words with Private Waters just outside the shop and then turned to go back in. Waters followed her, pulled out the weapon and shot her three times. The victim fell to the floor at which time Waters shot her twice more. In all, two bullets struck her in the chest, one under the left armpit, one in the right knee and one in the right calf. The chest shots killed her.

Then Waters tried to kill himself. He stepped into the toilet in the rear of the shop, placed the pistol under his chin and pulled the trigger. The bullet passed through his chin, the floor of his mouth, his tongue and hard palate and lodged in the left frontal region of his brain. Police rushed Waters to the hospital. The bullet later moved to the left occipital region of the rear of his brain, where doctors surgically removed it. By the time of his trial, Waters suffered from partial blindness, convulsions and headaches, unable to remember significant events. A doctor stated that Waters likely

suffered "intellectual deterioration with the passage of time," including his ability to remember.

The following day, Staff Sergeant Edmund P. Crovo attempted to question Waters, but the accused fell asleep after twenty seconds. Crovo returned each of the following three days, but Waters was asleep at each visit. Finally, on July 19, the persistent investigator obtained a signed statement; in it, Waters detailed his relationship with the deceased to include, "One time she told me she was pregnant and I gave her money to straighten it out." Waters said he "had never thought of shooting her," but admitted firing the weapon. He could not recall how many times he shot or where the bullets hit. He could also not remember anything that happened afterward.

A board of officers convened on October 27, 1943 to determine the accused's sanity. The board found that Waters was sane and responsible for his actions "now" and on the day of the crime. Captain Jay Hoffman, 36th Station Hospital, completed a clinical abstract of Private Waters determined by the board. Waters had small pox, scarlet fever and pneumonia as a child. He completed the sixth grade at age fifteen, held back several times because of illness. He had been a model worker in plaster all his adult life. Married in 1925, he had one child; he separated from his wife in 1929. However, he may have abandoned this family and been sentenced to one and one-half years in jail, if later FBI fingerprint records are accurate. Waters had another child with a "common-law wife." He was Catholic, but not a frequent churchgoer. The *New York Times* wrote that he had lived in Chicago Heights, Illinois. He was inducted on May 16, 1942. He scored a 105 on the Army General Classification Test, which placed Waters in Category III.

The Eastern Base Section, Services of Supply, European Theater of Operations convened a GCM at Watford, Hertfordshire, England on November 29, 1943.[1] Private Waters pleaded not guilty to all charges. The prosecution presented two witnesses that had been in the tailor shop, and Private Waters' statement, which the defense did not contest. On cross-examination by the defense, one of the store employees testified that a short time before the incident she heard the victim tell the accused that two thousand more Yanks were coming to Henley and that she would not want him after they arrived. Waters supposedly replied, "We will see." The witness said that the victim had a bad reputation in town. Waters' company commander and first sergeant testified that Waters was a good soldier and a very good model technician. A witness mentioned that there was a smell of alcohol on Waters, but the defense did not raise the issue in mitigation.

Private Waters then took the stand. He said he did not remember going on guard duty, going to town, being in the tailor shop, seeing the victim or committing the shooting. He said he did not recall being questioned by Sergeant Crovo or providing a statement. He added that life had taken a hard turn for him and that several problems had made him significantly depressed. The court recalled Sergeant Crovo to the stand; he testified that Waters was able to give a "clear-cut picture of events" leading up to the shooting, but that it took "the best part of an hour" to obtain the statement. The court convicted Private Waters of three charges: murder, a violation of the 92nd Article of War; leaving his guard post, a violation of the 86th Article of War; and maiming himself, a violation of the 96th Article of War.[2] The court then sentenced him to death by hanging. Brigadier General Ewart G. Plank, Commander Eastern Base Section, approved the verdict and the sentence and forwarded the packet.

*The Times of London* reported the conviction and death sentence on December 1, 1943 as did the *New York Times*. However, the verdict and sentence did not sit well with the townspeople of Henley-on-Thames; 302 residents signed a petition for clemency. Days previously, thirty-five members of the Engineer Model Makers Detachment, including the commander and first sergeant, sent a letter to Lieutenant General Jacob Devers requesting that he change the sentence from death to imprisonment. The letter read, in part, "Private Waters is an indirect or psychological casualty of war."

Lieutenant General Devers was not moved. On December 24, 1943, he signed the order confirming the sentence for Private Waters, but withheld the order directing its execution. Then Lieutenant General Devers left to become the Commanding General of the NATO, to be replaced by General Dwight D. Eisenhower. In the meantime, the Branch Office of The JAG with the ETO reviewed the case on January 31, 1944. The three-man panel (Judge Advocates B. Franklin Riter, Charles M. van Benschoten, and Ellwood W. Sargent) ruled the court was legally constituted, had jurisdiction of the person and offenses, and committed no errors injuriously affecting the substantial rights of the accused; thus, the record of trial was legally sufficient to support the findings of guilty and the sentences imposed.

Then a very rare thing happened; Washington's representative weighed in and Brigadier General Edwin C. McNeil, the head of the Branch Office of The JAG with the ETO, wrote Brigadier General Edward C. Betts, the Judge Advocate for the ETO. General McNeil felt that "commutation of this sentence to life imprisonment would be justified." General Betts presented these views, along with the findings of the Board of Review, to General Eisenhower. "After full consideration and considerable discussion," General Eisenhower directed that General Court-Martial Orders Number 5 be published on February 4, 1944; it set the date for the execution for February 10, 1944 at Shepton Mallet Prison under the auspices of 2912th DTC.

Shortly after midnight, on February 10, 1944, Major James C. Cullens, Commandant of the 2912th DTC, addressed an assembly of seven officials and eleven witnesses at Shepton Mallet. He stated the expectations for all concerned. At the end of his address, Major Cullens remarked:

> "Should any of you feel faint or feel that you are about to become ill do not hesitate to step from the execution chamber into the adjoining anteroom."

The time was 12:38 a.m. The witnesses adjourned until 12:53 a.m., when Major Cullens led the group to the execution chamber, arriving at 12:55 a.m. Guards escorted the condemned man into the chamber one minute later. The Commandant asked Waters if he had a statement, to which Waters replied, "I thank you very much for what you have done for me and I am sorry."

The Chaplain asked the condemned if he wished to say anything to him. Waters repeated his previous statement. Thomas Pierrepoint placed the white hood over his head and adjusted the noose around his neck; his assistant, Alexander Riley, strapped Waters' ankles together. After Major Cullens gave a silent signal to the executioners, Pierrepoint bent down, removed the safety cotter pin, pushed the lever forward and Waters dropped to his death. The time was 1:00 a.m.

At 1:19 a.m., Major Thomas O. Otto and two other medical officers examined the body and pronounced John Waters dead. A graves registration officer, First Lieutenant Lynford G. Chase, signed for the body. The Army buried Waters at Brookwood American Military Cemetery in Plot X, Row 1 and Grave 4. In Grave 5 was J.C. Leatherberry. A cross of wood marked the grave; an identification tag fixed to the cross and a second one buried with the body. In 1948, the Army transferred the remains to the American Military Cemetery at Cambridge, England and reinterred Waters' body in 1949 at the American Military Cemetery at Oise-Aisne in Plot E. He remains there in Row 2, Grave 46.[3]

*"It is about time for us to come to a showdown. I have witnesses that say that you have been threatening to shoot me. I think it is about time to come to a showdown."*

## 12    Private Charles E. Spears
32337619

Company D,
    387th Engineer Battalion (Separate)
**Murder**
Hanged on April 19, 1944

Sometimes two soldiers, for whatever reason, just go at it day after day until the situation turns ugly. On December 17, 1943, the situation between Private Charles E. Spears of Company D and Private David Quick of Company A turned really ugly; when it ended, Private Quick lay dead of a gunshot wound and Private Spears began a four-month march to the gallows. It was not over some serious problem. It was not a racial confrontation – both soldiers were black – and it was not about women; Charles Spears killed David Quick over a lousy five bucks. The pair had a long history. Both men met in the guardhouse at Fort George Meade, Maryland (the battalion was formed at the post) in June 1942. The accused would later say that Private Quick borrowed some money, but refused to pay it back. Later, in Oran, Algeria, the two were again in confinement – sharing a pup tent. Private Spears was in the guardhouse again in Italy in 1943, during which time he gave Quick $5.00. In November, Private Spears broke out of confinement and found Private Quick; for a time their relationship was fine: drinking and talking about money.

On December 17, with the accused again absent without leave, the pair started drinking at a bar in Naples, Italy about noon. The two left at 2:00 p.m. after an argument over money, but at about 3:30 p.m. an Italian indicated to Private Spears that Private Quick was looking for him. Spears found Quick first, sitting at the home of Signore and Signora Rafael Di Orio (where Quick was picking up his laundry), and said: "Quick, I hear you have been looking for me and I am looking for you." After Quick asked why Spears was looking for him, Spears replied:

"It is about time for us to come to a showdown. I have witnesses that say that you have been threatening to shoot me. I think it is about time to come to a showdown."

The accused later claimed that Quick said, "If there is going to be any shooting, let's shoot," and then stuck his hand inside his jacket. Spears was faster and pulled his own pistol – that he had purchased a day or two before – and fired two close range shots. One of the bullets did horrific damage, entering the victim's chest above and to the right of his heart, fracturing the left first rib and perforating the windpipe and the principal blood vessel from the heart to the body. The bullet then turned downward exiting to the right of the sixth rib about three inches from the backbone. Quick grasped himself near his heart, staggered to his feet and tumbled down; he died where he fell. MPs found a small Italian Beretta pistol in his right hand pocket, but a witness would later testify that Quick had made no movement to his weapon and that his arms had been folded across his chest when he was shot. Spears fled and stayed at a place he termed "Lina's house," until the MPs arrested him – hiding on the roof – five days later.

The case went to a GCM on January 27, 1944 at the Peninsular Base Section (PBS) in Naples. Private Charles Spears pleaded not guilty to the charge. Mrs. Di Orio testified about the shooting, clearly identifying Private Spears as the killer and providing testimony that ruled out self-defense. The medical officer presented the cause of death and the prosecution presented a voluntary statement the accused had previously made after his arrest. The defense also presented a significant amount of testimony and called to the stand a soldier who had known Private Spears for a year. He testified that the victim carried a gun – which was corroborated by the MP report of the scene of the crime – and that Quick got "pretty nasty" when he was drinking. Then the soldier testified about an earlier encounter, which he personally witnessed, between the two:

"[Spears] asked Quick about his money and Quick said he wasn't going to give him his money and pulled out of his pocket a small pistol and said if he asked him about his money again something might happen to him."

Private Spears took the stand. He stressed that he did not intend to shoot Quick when he went to the house, but that he fired "because he [Quick] made an attempt to get his gun which I knew he had." The court returned a verdict the same day, finding Private Charles E. Spears guilty of murder, a violation of the 92nd Article of War.[1] The court then sentenced him to death by hanging.

Charles Spears had a checkered past. Born in Zanesville, Ohio on May 20, 1910, he stood 5'10" tall and weighed 154 pounds. He had three brothers and four sisters; his mother was also alive. In August 1942, a Special Court-Martial convicted him of AWOL and theft. In his defense of the charge of theft from a woman, he said:

"I took the money and watch just to play a joke on her. I wanted to see what kind of woman she was. I wanted to see whether or not she was playing me for a sucker."

That earlier court was not impressed and sentenced him to four months at hard labor. Missing several teeth, he broke his right hand while boxing in the stockade on August 29, 1942 (while in the stockade hospital for the injury, he was intoxicated and disorderly on September 19.) In February 1943, a second Special Court-Martial sentenced Charles Spears to six months at hard labor for going three AWOLs. A third Special Court-Martial sentenced him in April 1943 for six AWOL charges and sentenced him to another six months at hard labor. A fourth Special Court-Martial convicted him for escaping from confinement in the fall of 1943 – he received four months at hard labor, but obviously, those punishments failed to get his attention.

The Staff Judge Advocate reviewed the case on February 12, 1945 and found no significant errors. Brigadier General Arthur W. Pence, Commander Peninsular Base Section, concurred with his Judge Advocate and approved the verdict and sentence. On March 18, 1944, Lieutenant General Jacob L. Devers, the Commanding General of the NATO, confirmed the sentence, but withheld the order directing the execution. In mid-February, Colonel Harold D. La Mar, the JAG for the PBS, sent a letter to Colonel Hubert D. Hoover, Assistant JAG for the NATO, La Mar's higher JAG headquarters. Colonel La Mar spoke of forwarding some additional paperwork and the need for more court reporters to handle his large volume of cases. He wrote in part:

"Our volume of work over here has been particularly heavy. This comes about not only through the number of troops assigned to this headquarters of which approximately one-third are colored, but also of the close proximity of the other forces. The result of our location is that most any soldier who goes AWOL from his organization winds up in our territory. As soon as he runs out of money, he engages in theft, robbery, counterfeiting or some other illegal activity, which sooner or later leads to his apprehension. In view of the fact that most of his criminal activity has taken place in our territory the combatant organizations frequently ask us to try this case since all of the witnesses are here and consequently we try many cases of men who do not belong to us."

In this case, the 387th Engineer Battalion (Separate) did belong to the PBS but not for long. A "colored" service unit, it would greatly distinguish itself on January 22, 1944, when elements of the battalion would hit the beach on the first wave of the Allied sea invasion at Anzio, with three men winning the Silver Star.

Charles Spears would not be one of them, however. A Board of Review (JAGs Samuel T. Holmgren, O.Z. Ide and Donald K. Mackay) examined the case and submitted its findings on April 1, 1944, upholding the court's decision. The Headquarters, NATO, published General Court-Martial Orders Number 25 the same day. On Wednesday, April 19, 1944, the Army hanged Private Charles E. Spears at the Peninsular Base Section Stockade Number 1. Captain James McCadie and Captain Raymond E. Nelson pronounced Spears dead.

The Army buried Charles Spears in Naples, Italy in the General Prisoner Section, Grave 1-1, but reinterred his body was in 1949 at the American Military Cemetery at Oise-Aisne in Plot E. His body remains there in Row 1, Grave 18.[2]

Private David Quick is buried at the Long Island National Cemetery in Section H, Site 8860.

*"The murder was committed in cold blood in a violent and brutal manner."*

*"If there is no matter of policy that requires the death of Private Leatherberry to satisfy the British sense of justice, that his life be spared."*

## 13   Private J.C. Leatherberry
### 34472451
Company A,
  356th Engineer General Service Regiment
**Robbery and Murder**
Hanged on May 16, 1944

The taxicab driver, Harry Claude Hailstone, of Colchester, was a crippled man, with one foot described as contracted and whose hands were deformed. His face was smeared with blood and was severely bruised. He had thumb marks on his throat, indicating he had been strangled from behind. His thyroid cartilage was fractured; his windpipe was congested and there was hemorrhaging in his eyes. The bruises on his face were consistent with blows from a fist. He had abrasions on his shins and knees, indicative that the assailant(s) had pulled him backward over the driver's seat and his legs had thrashed against the lower dashboard, as he died gasping for air.

The motive was robbery – the stolen items were one cigarette lighter and a billfold, which had a value of just £2 (American currency equivalent $8.06.) What we know about this case is clouded by the fact that both of the accused soldiers lied in their testimony. What we do know is that Private J.C. Leatherberry and Private George E. Fowler of the 356th Engineer General Service Regiment were involved. Leatherberry, a black soldier, was born on January 19, 1922 in Hazlehurst, Mississippi; he later lived in Crystal Springs. He was married and was inducted on October 16, 1942. Medical records indicate that he had bouts of gonorrhea in 1940 and 1943. He stood 5'8" tall and weighed 160 pounds; he smoked one pack of cigarettes a day. Sentenced to fifteen days hard labor for AWOL at a previous court-martial, his previous service record was often "poor." At the time of the offense, Leatherberry was assigned to Company A. Private George Fowler, another black soldier, was in Company E.

At the beginning of December 1943, both men were in London, and both appear to have been AWOL. On December 7, they boarded a train from London to Colchester, where they took a cab – driven by Harry Claude Hailstone – and started for the Birch airfield, where their unit was bivouacked.

Halfway to their destination, they asked the cab driver to stop, saying they had to get out and urinate. At this halt, one or both of the accused strangled Hailstone, hid the body under a barbed-wire fence at the side of the road, drove the cab to within a quarter mile from their unit, abandoned the vehicle and returned to camp.

Much of what we know we owe to Detective-Superintendent G.H. Totterdell, of the Essex Police, who took charge of the case. Authorities found the abandoned cab on December 8 at noon; Totterdell deduced the assailant who had driven the cab could have been an American by the way it was abandoned on the right side of the road. A machinist found a cream-colored Canadian officer's raincoat on the side of the road the same day and turned it in to authorities; it had extensive bloodstains on it. Police found the victim's body at noon on December 9 and estimated he had been dead between thirty-six and forty-eight hours. Totterdell concluded that given the weight of the victim's body it would have required two assailants to move it from the cab. The raincoat had an officer's name in it and Totterdell tracked down the officer, who said a "coloured" American soldier had taken it. The soldier had left behind a gas mask, which had a name in it and the owner was traced to Company E, 356th Engineer General Service Regiment. When confronted, the owner said he was indeed missing the piece of equipment, having loaned it to Private Fowler.

Authorities questioned Fowler on December 12; after being advised of his rights – and after police found a pawn ticket for a Rolex watch that had been in the pocket of the raincoat – Fowler admitted to being part of the crime. However, he stated that he had not been the key participant; a Private J.C. Leatherberry had told him he was going to rob the cab driver. Fowler also said that he had been loaned the Canadian officer's raincoat – but had given it to Leatherberry to wear – and that Leatherberry had strangled the victim, after Fowler had stepped out of the cab to relieve himself. Fowler said that his only role had been to help dispose of the body – he also did not receive any portion of the victim's belongings. Investigators then turned to Leatherberry, who had been identified by Fowler on December 16 at an identification parade, and arrested him on December 18. Leatherberry also made a statement to investigators.

The Army tried the two men separately. Fowler cooperated with authorities, although Captain J.J. Webber, Royal Canadian Army Hospital, stated that Fowler had stolen his coat, when they had been drinking. Fowler received a sentence of life imprisonment.

The GCM for Private Leatherberry met on January 19, 1944 at the Town Hall, Ipswich, in Suffolk, England the same day and location as Fowler's, but in a different room.[1] The prosecution produced evidence that microscopic fibers, taken from under the fingernails of both accused, were similar to the fibers on the victim's jacket. Forensic evidence showed that the blood on the overcoat was the same type – the relatively infrequent AB – as the victim. They also found trace AB blood on the accused's underclothes, and postulated it came from Leatherberry wiping his hands off later. Blood was under the fingernails of the accused, but it was not in sufficient quantity to test. The court admitted both Fowler's and Leatherberry's statements.

Leatherberry claimed he had never met the victim, alive or dead. He said he had stayed in London until the morning of December 8, when at 10:45 a.m. he took a train to Colchester and rode a bus from there to camp. The prosecution presented evidence that the train trip alone would take two hours and twenty minutes, and that as Leatherberry's company commander saw him on December 8 between 12:30 p.m. and 1:00 p.m. his return could not have happened in the manner he described. The defense produced an alibi witness, Kay Peters, the manager of a café in London. She said that Leatherberry had been in her establishment with a girlfriend at 11:00 p.m. on December 7 and had eaten breakfast there at 10:00 a.m. on December 8. The prosecution attempted to discredit her testimony, introducing additional testimony that Kay Peters was "interested in every colored boy's welfare, who came into her café." The girlfriend testified Leatherberry had been with her until December 8; the prosecution tried to show she had been tainted in her testimony by reading about the crime in the newspaper before testifying. The prosecution produced a corporal, who testified that he saw Fowler "and another colored soldier" at about midnight on December 7 in camp.

Leatherberry's explanation of where he spent the night of December 7 differed in his court testimony from his original statement. Originally, Leatherberry said that Fowler had traveled with him back from London on December 8; on the stand, he said he had not traveled with Fowler at all. He also said he had been in a fight on the night of December 7, which accounted for the blood on his clothes. Leatherberry also denied wearing the Canadian officer's raincoat.

The court had taken a four-day recess at the request of the defense (to produce these alibi witnesses from London); on January 24, they issued their verdict at 11:00 p.m. and convicted J.C. Leatherberry of murder and robbery, both violations of the 92nd Article of War.[2] They then sentenced him to be hanged by the neck until dead, although the court record did not indicate that the vote was unanimous. *The Times of London* reported the sentence on January 25, 1944 as did the *New York Times* – on page three – under the title:

### "U.S. SOLDIER IS CONVICTED Leatherberry Is Sentenced in Britain to Die for Murder"

On February 6, 1944, Lieutenant Colonel William F. Butters, Staff Judge Advocate of the Eastern Base Section, Supply of Services, ETO, reviewed the case. He found that although there had been some hearsay statements admitted at the trial, they did not materially affect the outcome. He also noted that the defense had received one continuance (for four days) to produce witnesses; they hinted they might have other witnesses, but had never asked for another continuance. Butters added:

> "There was evidence of design and premeditation to commit the robbery. The murder was committed in cold blood in a violent and brutal manner. After the robbery, the body of the cab driver was left where death could be the only result had it not already occurred. The sentence is considered appropriate."

Colonel Roy W. Grower, Commander Eastern Base Section, approved the finding of guilty and the sentence of death. He forwarded the records of the trial to the theater commander. On March 4, 1943, the ETO JAG's Office reviewed the case. Captain H.R. Stadtfield noted that the credibility of the witnesses for the prosecution and defense was a matter entirely for the court and that Private Fowler – the prosecution's main witness – "testified in straight-forward and honest manner." He added that the Defense Counsel had recommended clemency based on conflicting testimony of witnesses and the fact that Fowler received a lesser sentence of life imprisonment. Brigadier General Edward C. Betts concurred with Stadtfield's report.

General Dwight D. Eisenhower did not buy the clemency argument and confirmed the sentence, on March 7, 1944, withholding the order directing the execution. On May 1, 1944, the ETO issued General Court-Martial Orders Number 26, ordering that the execution occur at Shepton Mallet Prison on May 16, 1944. Numerous Army organizations began preparations. In one extant note, it was observed that the executioner, Thomas W. Pierrepoint, had acknowledged his willingness to officiate at the proceedings. All in all, the note read, "For your info – I think everything is button-up."

Not every Army entity was so enthusiastic. On May 6, 1944, Major James C. Cullens, Commandant of the 2912th DTC, sent an unusual letter to General Eisenhower. In it, Cullens asked for the sentence to be commuted to life imprisonment. He noted that Private Fowler had received life imprisonment and asked, "if there is no matter of policy that requires the death of Private Leatherberry to satisfy the British sense of justice, that his life be spared." Cullens added that as the only "friend" of the condemned man in the ETO, he had no scruples against the death penalty for murder, nor would he flinch in carrying such sentences into execution, as Commandant of the 2912th DTC.

General Eisenhower did not commute the sentence. Ten days later, Major Cullens fulfilled his duty unflinchingly. Just after midnight, on Tuesday, May 16, Cullens assembled nine official party personnel and twelve witnesses at Shepton Mallet Prison. He told them what would happen over the next hour, adding, "This is no laughing matter and see that all of you conduct yourself with that in mind."

Everything seemed to be in order. The day before the execution, Thomas and Albert Pierrepoint had weighed and measured the condemned man; Albert noted in his ledger that J.C. Leatherberry stood 5'10" tall and weighed 174 pounds. From that data, the executioners calculated that a drop of 6'7" would be correct. With Army thoroughness, the base section engineer had previously sent Major James R. O'Grady to inspect the gallows, "To insure satisfactory mechanical condition at the prescribed time."

The witnesses adjourned until 12:50 a.m., when Major Cullens led the group to the execution chamber, arriving at 12:52 a.m. MPs escorted Private J.C. Leatherberry into the chamber three minutes later. The Commandant read General Court-Martial Orders Number 26 and asked Leatherberry if he had a statement to make. He replied:

"I have no statement to make, sir. I want to thank the guys for everything as they were so nice to me, the guards and everything."

The Chaplain then asked the Private Leatherberry if he wished to say anything to him. Leatherberry said, "Sir, I want to thank you for being so nice to me and everything you have done for me."

Thomas Pierrepoint placed the white hood over Private Leatherberry's head and adjusted the noose around his neck. His assistant, Albert Pierrepoint, simultaneously strapped Leatherberry's ankles together. After Major Cullens gave a silent signal to the executioners, Albert scurried off the trap doors as Thomas dropped to one knee, removed the safety cotter pin and pushed the trap door lever, sending Private Leatherberry to meet his maker. The time was 1:00 a.m. Eight minutes later, three medical officers, led by Major Louis Judelsohn, examined the body and pronounced Private J.C. Leatherberry dead. A graves registration officer, First Lieutenant Harold A. Myers, Brookwood Cemetery Detachment, signed for the body at 1:25 a.m. The Army buried Leatherberry at Brookwood American Military Cemetery in Plot X, Row 1 and Grave 5. His neighbors were John H. Waters in Grave 4 and Wiley Harris, Jr. in Grave 6. A sergeant fixed one identification tag to a wooden cross and buried a second one with the body.

• • •

On June 18, 1944, the War Department sent a classified message to the theater stating that a Federal District Court had recently ruled that all convictions of Article of War offenses, for which a death penalty was expressly authorized, must be by unanimous vote – that is, not only did the vote on the penalty have to be unanimous in the case of death, but also did the original guilty-not guilty vote. The message also stated that unless the trial record showed that the guilty vote was unanimous, the execution should be put on hold until the issue was resolved back in the Federal court system. On December 20, 1944, the Fourth Circuit Court of Appeals in *Stout v. Hancock* reversed the lower ruling, stating that the Army only needed to have a unanimous vote for the death penalty in the penalty phase, not in the guilty-not guilty vote.

On June 29, 1944, Major Theo F. Cangelosi, of the Branch Office of the JAG with the ETO, wrote a letter to the Office of The JAG in Washington, DC. The letter stated that two executions – including that of J.C. Leatherberry – in theater did not have death sentences <u>recorded</u> (underline in the original) as unanimous; Major Cangelosi requested that Washington provide a certificate showing what the <u>actual</u> (underline in the original) vote was. That actual vote could not be determined by this study.

• • •

In 1948, the Army transferred the remains to the American Military Cemetery at Cambridge, England. Authorities reinterred J.C. Leatherberry in 1949 at the American Military Cemetery at Oise-Aisne in Plot E. His remains rest in Row 4, Grave 86.[3]

*"I wouldn't have hit him but he came at me first."*

*"After the trap is actuated, it will be approximately eighteen to twenty minutes until the surgeons are able to pronounce the man dead and this twenty minutes is rather a gruesome affair."*

## 14    Private Wiley Harris, Jr.
6924547
626th Ordnance Ammunition Company,
  Fifteenth Corps
**Murder**
Hanged on May 26, 1944

Was stabbing a pimp seventeen times until he died – after the pimp first tried to trick a soldier out of $4.00 and then struck the soldier in the face – self-defense or murder? A GCM attempted to answer that question on March 17, 1944, as they weighed the fate of Private Wiley Harris, Jr.

Eleven days earlier, on the evening of March 6, Private Wiley Harris and his friend, Private Robert Fils, were on pass from the 626th Ordnance Ammunition Company in downtown Belfast, Northern Ireland. After having a few drinks at a pub on York Street, they went to the "Diamond Bar" on North Queen Street where they had a few glasses of *Guinness*. A local, Harry Coogan, approached Private Harris, a black soldier from Mayweather County, Georgia, who had entered the Army at Fort Benning, Georgia on May 21, 1937, and asked him if he wanted a girl. Harris pointed to one at the bar and then bought a round of *Guinness Stout* for the three. Coogan said the price would be £1 (about $4.00) and the trio went to an air raid shelter across the road. Harris paid the fee in coins and went into the shelter with the girl, while Coogan waited outside "in case the police would come."

Within a minute or so, Coogan indeed gave the alarm that the police were approaching, but when Private Harris and the girl went outside, there were no "coppers." Then things got dicey. Harris asked the girl to return to the shelter – she refused. Harris then asked Coogan to give back his money. Coogan refused. The girl started to run. Harris heard the sound of coins falling to the pavement. Stooping to pick them up, Harris received a blow in the face under his right eye by Coogan. Harris pulled out a "Boy Scout-type" knife, opened the folding blade and struck Coogan – seventeen times by the report of autopsy.

Private Harris, in a statement made three days later, then fled, threw away the knife and went to the "Red Cross Club" on James Street, where he cleaned off the blood and spent the night. He returned to his unit the next day, where MPs promptly arrested him. He stated that the incident was self-defense, offering, "I wouldn't have hit him but he came at me first." The ferocity of the wounds led authorities to recommend a GCM, which occurred ten days later. On March 17, 1944, the court found Private Wiley Harris, Jr. guilty of murder, a violation of the 92nd Article of War. The jury sentenced Private Harris to be hanged by the neck until dead; the record did not show, however, that the vote was unanimous. [1]

Wiley Harris was born in Greenville, Georgia on June 12, 1918. Plagued by a severe stuttering problem, he finished six years of grade school and then quit to become a common laborer. During his struggles in life, he had been shot in the groin. He later married and fathered a daughter, but found nothing positive in life, so he enlisted in the "old Army" on May 21, 1937. Standing 5'8" tall and weighing 130 pounds, he was assigned to the 24th Infantry Regiment, an all-black "Buffalo Soldier" unit at Fort Benning. Harris soon deserted. He received a GCM, but deserted again in December 1939 and remained away from the Army until October 9, 1942. This time, he remained in the service, but received another court-martial conviction in 1943.

The Fifteenth Corps Commander, Major General Wade H. Haislip, approved the sentence on March 23, 1944 – the same day that the JAG reviewed the case – and forwarded the record of trial to General Eisenhower, who confirmed the sentence, on April 12, 1944, but withheld the order directing the execution. On May 1, 1944, the ETO issued General Court-Martial Orders Number 32, which ordered that the execution occur on May 26, 1944 at Shepton Mallet Prison. The *New York Times* ran a story the day prior to the execution, informing the public of the event. Member of Parliament, Cecil M. Lowe sent a telegram to President Franklin Roosevelt, stating that 99% of the adult public was "indignant" of the verdict and suggested that the sentence be postponed to "cement Anglo-American friendship."

Roosevelt did not intercede. Just after midnight, on Friday, May 26, Major James C. Cullens, Commandant of the 2912th DTC, assembled nine official party personnel and seven witnesses at Shepton Mallet Prison. He told them what would happen over the next hour, noting as to their number:

"We have a very small party here tonight which pleases me very much because I never like to have the presence of the morbidly curious at an occasion like this."

Major Cullens continued:

"After the trap is actuated, it will be approximately eighteen to twenty minutes until the surgeons are able to pronounce the man dead and this twenty minutes is rather a gruesome affair."

The official party adjourned until 12:53 a.m., when Major Cullens led the group to the execution chamber, arriving at 12:54 a.m. The Commandant, Chaplain and guards (Corporal Andre Creed and Corporal George W. Pressey) escorted Private Harris into the chamber one minute later. The Commandant then read the entire General Court-Martial Orders Number 32 and asked Harris if he had a statement to make. The condemned replied, "I don't have any statement to make, sir." The Chaplain then asked Private Harris if he wished to say anything to him. Harris said:

"I appreciate what you did for me sir. I appreciate what everybody did and I want to wish everybody good luck."

Thomas Pierrepoint placed the white hood over Harris' head and adjusted the rope around his neck. His assistant, Alexander Riley, strapped Harris' ankles together. After Major Cullens gave a silent signal, Thomas Pierrepoint bent down, removed the safety cotter pin, pushed the trap door lever forward and Wiley Harris, Jr. dropped to his death. The time was 12:59 a.m. At 1:14 a.m., Major James G.M. Weyand pronounced Private Harris dead. A graves registration officer, First Lieutenant Lynford G. Chase, Brookwood Cemetery Detachment, signed for the body at 1:25 a.m. The *New York Times* ran a story on the execution (but did not mention the location) on May 27, 1944 titled, **"U.S. Soldier Hanged as Slayer."**

On May 31, 1944, Major General Haislip signed a letter of condolence to the brother of the victim. It read in part:

"The death of Harry Coogan, your brother, at the hands of an American soldier is regrettable. The punishment awarded will deter others from like action and evidence to you and your community the severe punishment which the military courts of the United States Army may award in cases involving such atrocious crimes committed by its personnel."

The Army originally buried Private Wiley Harris Jr. Brookwood American Military Cemetery in Plot X, Row 1 and Grave 6. In Grave 5 was J.C. Leatherberry. Marking the grave was a temporary wooden cross; an identification tag was fixed to the cross and a second one was buried with the body. In 1948, the Army transferred the remains to the American Military Cemetery at Cambridge, England. Authorities later reinterred the body at the American Military Cemetery at Oise-Aisne in Plot E. His body remains there in Row 4, Grave 92.[2]

On June 29, 1944, Major Theo F. Cangelosi, as he had in the Leatherberry case, requested that the Office of The JAG in Washington, DC provide a certificate showing what the actual (underline in the original) vote was in the Wiley Harris case. That actual vote could not be determined by this study.

*"Your worries are over now boys. I have shot the First Sergeant and I'll turn on the lights so I can show you."*

*"Those of you, who have not yet had your breakfast, may get it in our mess immediately following the execution."*

## 15   Private Alex F. Miranda
39297382

Battery C, 42nd Field Artillery Battalion,
   Fourth Infantry Division
**Murder**
Executed by Firing Squad on May 30, 1944

Until the last day of his life, Private Alex F. Miranda did not like sergeants. He did not like thin sergeants. He did not like fat sergeants. He did not like tall sergeants. He did not like short sergeants. He did not like English Police sergeants. He did not like American Army sergeants. He especially did not like his battery First Sergeant – so he killed him.

Shortly after midnight, on March 5, 1944 Private Alex F. Miranda, from Santa Ana, California, was urinating on (or near) a church in Honiton, Devonshire, England. He had been drinking. Shortly afterward, Miranda's opinion of sergeants immediately worsened as Special Sergeant Bill Durbin of the Devonshire Police arrested him and took him to the Honiton Police Station. During the encounter, Miranda said to Durbin:

"You are a fine fat sergeant. I would make you a top sergeant [First Sergeant.] Come on guard tomorrow night and I will give you a royal welcome."

While waiting for his unit to pick him up, Miranda saw a group of English constables. Miranda again vented his feelings toward non-commissioned officers, remarking, "I hope they [the policemen] rip their guts out." He then turned to Sergeant Durbin again and said, "I was not pissing in the street. You are lying. I will rip your guts out."

About 12:20 a.m., Corporal Joel Wehking arrived with a driver to escort Private Miranda back to the unit at Broomhill Camp. They returned to camp, arrived at the guardhouse and Corporal Wehking then allowed Private Miranda to return to his Quonset hut. It was dark and the battery First Sergeant, Thomas Evison of Port Norris, New Jersey was asleep in a top bunk near the door. Next to his bed was a weapons' rack with half a dozen carbines in it. Miranda made some remarks about the sleeping First Sergeant, saying that he snored too loudly. The First Sergeant told Miranda to go to bed. Within minutes, a shot rang out, followed by Miranda's laughing voice:

"Your worries are over now boys. I have shot the First Sergeant and I'll turn on the lights so I can show you."

When the lights came on, sure enough the First Sergeant lay dead, a bullet from one of the carbines having slammed through his forehead. Miranda's fellow soldiers apprehended him and the unit immediately tasked Major Francis A. Chilson to serve as the investigating officer. For Major Chilson it was an easy task; he recommended a trial by GCM.

Alex Miranda, a Mexican-American, had been born on July 23, 1923 in Santa Ana, California. Before his induction, he had gone to school for eight years, before becoming a pie-baker, earning $32 a week. Standing 5'8" tall and weighing 161 pounds, with brown eyes and black hair, Miranda was married and had one daughter.

The GCM met on March 20, 1944.[1] It was an open and shut case. The jury found Private Alex Miranda guilty of murder, a violation of the 92nd Article of War.[2] The jury sentenced Private Miranda to death by musketry. The Judge Advocate at the Fourth Infantry Division, Lieutenant Colonel White E. Gibson, Jr., reviewed the case on April 3, 1944; Gibson opined that the jury should not have determined the manner of death for the execution, stating that the opinion was irregular and not correctible, as hanging was more ignominious. Therefore, any change from death by musketry would technically be increasing the severity of the penalty. The Fourth Infantry Division Commander, Major General R.O. Barton, approved the sentence the same day and forwarded it to General Eisenhower. The Staff Judge Advocate at the ETO reviewed the case on April 15, 1944 and found no discrepancies. On April 20, 1944, General Dwight D. Eisenhower confirmed the sentence, but withheld the order directing the execution. On May 23, 1944, the ETO issued General Court-Martial Orders Number 33, which ordered that the execution for May 30, 1944 at Shepton Mallet Prison.

Shortly after 6:00 a.m. on Tuesday, May 30, 1944, Major James C. Cullens, Commandant of the 2912th DTC, assembled the official party personnel and witnesses at Shepton Mallet Prison. He noted that this was the first execution by shooting. He ended his instructions by saying:

"Now this is not an occasion for any levity or joking of any sort, and I would like to say that I appreciate utmost silence by the witnesses particularly during the proceeding. Those of you, who have not yet had your breakfast, may get it in our mess immediately following the execution."

The Commandant recessed the group until 6:58 a.m., when they gathered at the outer yard of Shepton Mallet. In the backdrop was a tall wall. The Commandant arrived at the location with the prisoner and asked him if he had anything to say. Miranda answered:

"Yes sir. I want to thank all the boys for their nice way of treating a prisoner on his way out and I guess I never met any better fellows until I came in this place, especially Sergeant Ahlers. I hope God has a place in heaven for him. I want to thank this other gentleman that is here [the Chaplain.] I am welcome that he came to accompany me."

Alex Miranda finally found a sergeant he did not hate. The Chaplain then asked Private Miranda if he had anything to say to him. Miranda answered:

"Yes, Father. Pray for me and may God have a place for you in heaven. I'll do the same for you."

The guards then tied Private Alex Miranda to a wooden post. Miranda declined to have a blindfold. At 7:00 a.m., the firing squad marched to a single rank facing the prisoner at a distance of twenty-five paces. The squad, under the command of First Sergeant Bert E. Ward, was composed of Tech Sergeant Thomas R. Clements, Tech Sergeant George M. Harris, Sergeant Donald B. Cunningham, Sergeant Ralph E. Devlin, Jr., Sergeant John H. Folger, Sergeant Marvin F. Richardson, Sergeant Donald P. Seigle and Sergeant Walter A. Woodka – all sergeants, perhaps to the chagrin of the condemned. The Commandant then barked the order, "Squad – Ready … Aim … Fire."

The eight sergeants, looking eye to eye with the doomed man, squeezed their triggers; several bullets passed through the prisoner, struck the wall and ricocheted into the air, but striking no witnesses or spectators, as officers ducked for cover. The time was 7:01 a.m. One minute later, three medical officers pronounced Private Alex F. Miranda dead from a gunshot wound. We do not know how many of the official party or witnesses then ate breakfast in the mess.

*The Times of London* reported on the execution on June 1, 1944. The Army buried Private Alex F. Miranda at Brookwood Cemetery in Plot X, Grave 1-7. In 1948, the remains travelled by truck to the American Military Cemetery at Cambridge, England. They went on the move again in 1949 to the American Military Cemetery at Oise-Aisne in Plot E and buried in Row 2, Grave 27.

First Sergeant Thomas Evison is buried among the honored dead in the American Military Cemetery at Cambridge, England, in Plot C, Row 5 and Grave 42.[3]

• • •

The *Santa Ana Register* carried a story on page one of the May 31, 1944 issue titled "Report of S.A. Man Executed for Army Slaying," which included Miranda's name and the name of the victim. On October 28, 1944, the Federal Bureau of Investigation sent a document to the Army, summarizing civilian arrests of Alex Martinez/Alex Flores Martinez/ Alex Miranda-Martinez/Alex Miranda/Alex Flores Miranda from 1940 to 1942 in the Chula Vista, Los Angeles and Santa Ana areas. The five crimes listed ranged from public intoxication to burglary; the document seems to indicate that fingerprints of each arrestee matched the fingerprints of Alex F. Miranda, taken when he entered the Army on May 18, 1943.

In 1989, Louis Martinez, a nephew of Alex Miranda, made a request for the Army to reverse the murder conviction and instead find him guilty of the lesser charge of manslaughter, based on his belief that Miranda was too drunk to realize the consequences of his actions. Martinez also requested that the body of his uncle be returned to the family. Government officials did not overturn the conviction, but did agree to release his remains. A witness to the exhumation stated that on November 15, 1990, officials commenced excavation of Grave 27 in Row 2 with the removal of the top copper portion of the casket by cutting carefully around the edge with an electric circular metal cutting disk. This operation lasted about twenty-five minutes, after which they removed the cover – revealing the remains wrapped in a GI blanket. Miranda's identification was verified by two metal identification disks pinned to the blanket. A witness at the exhumation took an unauthorized photograph, showing that there was very little deterioration of the remains after more than fifty-five years.

Louis Martinez paid $4,000 to the U.S. Government and the remains of his uncle arrived in California in November 1990. Alex F. Miranda's remains now rest in the Santa Ana Cemetery in Placentia, California. Back in France, the marker for Grave 27 lays on the ground at Plot E, but there are no remains under it – preserving the symmetry – and adding a little to the mystery – of the burial field.

*"Then I took out my pistol and pulled the trigger."*

*"There are no extenuating or mitigating circumstances, except perhaps the youth of the accused. In my opinion the age of 19 1/2 years is not a circumstance to warrant commutation of the sentence in this case."*

## 16  Private Robert L. Donnelly
13132982
Battery B, 36th Field Artillery Battalion
**Desertion and Murder**
Hanged on May 31, 1944

It was relatively easy for an American soldier to desert in Italy. Ease out of your unit, head to a big city like Naples, learn a little Italian, make friends with some of the locals, get a pistol so you could make a little money by robbing folks, and a man could stay out of the line of fire at the front for weeks or maybe even months. That is what Private Robert L. Donnelly, a nineteen-year-old white soldier did; in fact, he even purloined an MP brassard to slip on, just in case anyone got too nosey about what he was doing in the "City of Sun." However, Donnelly pushed his luck too far, when he thoroughly screwed up and killed a real Military Police soldier.

Donnelly's problems began at Venafro, Italy on the evening of December 16, 1943, when he absented himself from his unit. He made his way to Naples, living in different hotels by night and drinking in different bars by day. About January 6, 1944, MPs found Donnelly in a house of prostitution, confiscated his pistol ammunition, but for some reason returned his pistol to him and released him. On January 20, 1944, Donnelly – armed with a German Luger – walked down a side street near the *Via Roma* with the intention of robbing a civilian store. Two MPs drove by and suddenly stopped. They questioned the group – during which time Private Donnelly refused to provide his name or unit – and then loaded them into a truck and began driving. Suddenly, Donnelly pulled out the pistol, as one MP frantically yelled, "Look out, Barresi, he's got a gun!" As Robert Donnelly would later admit, "I took out my pistol and pulled the trigger."

MP Sergeant Barresi ran after Donnelly, who fled after the shot, but was unable to catch him. When the sergeant returned to the vehicle, he found his partner Technician Fifth Grade John P. Brown, Jr. lying dead some twenty feet away. Donnelly's bullet had struck him in the chest. Authorities apprehended Donnelly on January 27, 1944; he voluntarily made a statement admitting to the crime. After a quick investigation, the Commanding

General, PBS ordered a GCM, which began at Naples on March 14, 1944. Donnelly pleaded not guilty, but the prosecution had Donnelly's statement. The defendant refused to take the stand and the defense team presented no witnesses. The court found Private Donnelly guilty of desertion, a violation of the 58th Article of War and murder, a violation of the 92nd Article of War and sentenced him to hang by the neck until dead.[1]

Born in Pittsburgh, Pennsylvania on July 27, 1924, Donnelly was a laborer before his induction into the Army on October 24, 1942. He was slightly wounded in action on September 25, 1943 and sent to a hospital, which treated and released him two days later. On October 19, 1943, he was diagnosed with jaundice; on February 10, 1944, while in the stockade, he was diagnosed with a type of gonorrhea.

Brigadier General Arthur W. Pence, Commander PBS, approved the verdict and sentence. On April 18, 1944, Colonel C.B. Mickelwait, the Acting JAG for the NATO, reviewed the case. Mickelwait found that the court-martial had been carried out in a proper manner; there were no errors in the record prejudicial to the rights of the accused. Concerning other circumstances, Mickelwait wrote:

"There are no extenuating or mitigating circumstances, except perhaps the youth of the accused. In my opinion the age of 19 8/12 years is not a circumstance to warrant commutation of the sentence in this case."

On April 30, 1944, Lieutenant General Jacob L. Devers, Commanding General of the NATO, confirmed the sentence, but withheld the order directing the execution. The order came soon enough; on May 16, 1944, the North Africa Theater of Operations, published General Court-Martial Orders Number 32, proscribing that Private Donnelly would be executed in fifteen days. Captain William G. Wood was in command of the PBS Disciplinary Training Stockade and supervised the execution on Wednesday, May 31, 1944; five days previously, he had notified Donnelly of the upcoming execution. Sixty-five minutes before the hanging, Catholic Chaplain Patrick B. Fay arrived to provide Private Donnelly spiritual aid. Ten commissioned officers were present as official witnesses; the trap door dropped at 5:20 a.m. Captain William W. Huntress, a medical officer, pronounced Private Donnelly dead at 5:34 a.m. and the location of the death as being "near Aversa."

The Army buried Private Donnelly in the U.S. Military Cemetery in Naples, in the field for General Prisoners, Grave 1-5. Authorities reinterred his body in 1949 at the American Military Cemetery at Oise-Aisne in Plot E, in Row 4, Grave 95.[2]

His mother later wrote Army authorities; although she had received communications from them, she thought her son had been shot and killed. She was mistaken – it had been her son doing the shooting and killing.

*"Both the victim, *********, and her companion Private First Class Edward J. Heffernan testified that two colored soldiers were involved in the crime but neither was able to identify accused as the soldiers who committed the offense alleged. However, proof of the guilt of both accused was established by circumstantial evidence of the strongest and most convincing quality. Such positive evidence is often of a far more tangible value than casual personal identification of accused, which frequently may be deemed evidence of a rather frail nature, particularly when the identification of colored soldiers is involved."*

## 17     Private Eliga Brinson
34052175
4090th Quartermaster Service Company
**Rape**
Hanged on August 11, 1944

## 18     Private Willie Smith
34565556
4090th Quartermaster Service Company
**Rape**
Hanged on August 11, 1944

"Overpaid, oversexed and over here" was an uncomplimentary phrase used by many British civilians in describing their American "cousins" in military uniform on the island during the war. Sometimes the portrayal was done in jest, but in the cases of Private Eliga Brinson and Private Willie Smith there was no humor involved.

Both men seem to have constantly been in trouble. Two Summary Courts-Martial had convicted Eliga Brinson for absence without leave (AWOL), while a Special Court-Martial convicted him for unlawfully carrying a concealed weapon. Summary Courts-Martial had twice convicted Willie Smith for absence without leave. Their problems were only just beginning. According to the prosecution, a sixteen-year old English girl left a dance in Bishops Cleeve, Gloucester, England with an American soldier, Private Edward J. Heffernan, late on March 4, 1944. Shortly after midnight, the pair passed the "Kings Head Pub" at which point the young lady noticed two "colored soldiers" standing by the door; and more ominously, that the two soldiers had begun to follow them. Ten minutes later, the pair approached the couple, when suddenly one assailant struck Private Heffernan. The girl screamed; the second assailant grabbed her and put his hand to her throat. Heffernan jumped up off the ground and ran for

help. The girl was not so fortunate; both soldiers dragged her into a field, where both men raped her. After they departed, the victim got up and ran home, telling her mother when she finally arrived, "Oh mother, the blacks have had me and they have knocked me about terrible."

Shortly after, the victim's mother called a registered nurse to examine her daughter. The nurse found that the victim's lips were bruised and bloodied and that there were superficial scratches on her legs. She did not medically confirm, however, that the victim had been raped. The police responded quickly and within an hour English Constable William G. Hale, and Sergeant James O. Hall, 255th MP Company, began collecting evidence from the scene of the crime. Both investigators noticed two pairs of distinctive boot prints in the mud and noted that. Two hours later, the pair went to the 4090th Quartermaster Service Company and spoke with the commander, who apparently authorized them to conduct a search of the unit. Sergeant Hall found two pairs of boots in Tent #21; the soles appeared to match the boot prints at the crime.

After daylight, the investigation continued and led to Brinson and Smith. MPs warned both men of their rights, but did not tell them the specifics of the crime, only that it was very serious. Both men elected to make statements, indicating that the men had been drinking in several pubs that evening, but that both men had returned to their bivouac area about 11:00 p.m. on March 4. A bed check in the camp, made between 11:00 and 11:45 p.m., found that both men were absent. Private Benjamin Wilkerson testified that he went to bed at 11:30 p.m. and at that time Private Brinson was absent.

An investigating officer recommended to Lieutenant General John C.H. Lee, the Commander of Services and Supply, ETO – and the convening authority – that a court-martial be held. A GCM convened on April 28 at Cheltenham, England, to try the accused jointly.[1] The soldiers pleaded not guilty. The trial did not start well for the Trial

Judge Advocate. The victim was unable to identify the accused. She testified that she was not certain that the two soldiers outside the pub were the same soldiers who attacked her. Private Heffernan was also unable to identify the accused at the trial. Several American soldiers testified that the two accused were in the pub the night of the crime, but could not place them in the company of the victim. However, the prosecution brought in an expert witness, Dr. Edward B. Parks, Director of the Bristol Forensic Laboratory. Parks made two significant assertions. First, he concluded that the two pairs of boots that investigator Sergeant Hall had found in camp, subsequently linked to the accused, made the footprints at the scene of the crime. Parks' exact words were,

"With regard to Smith, I should say that it is nearing the realm of sheer impossibility for another heel to make the cast other than the heels of Smith … Of Brinson, it is possible, but a very, very unlikely possibility."

Dr. Parks also testified that the mud stains on the clothing of the victim and the clothing of both accused were of the same general type and character. He also stated he found seminal fluid on the victim's skirt and on the coat and trousers of both accused. The accused stuck by their stories. Private Smith also stated that he had been wearing the blouse of a soldier named Spivy on the night in question. Spivy testified Smith had not. Private Brinson took a similar tack and testified that a soldier named Odell was wearing Brinson's overcoat (the one that Dr. Parks had identified) on the night of the crime.

The trial lasted two days, with the jury convicting both men on April 29, 1944 of carnal knowledge, a violation of the 92nd Article of War.[2] The court then chose the death penalty. The *New York Times* reported the death sentences on April 30, 1944, while *The Times of London* did so the following day. An Alabama newspaper described the verdict under the headline, **"Negro Soldiers to Die for Attack in England."**

Lieutenant General Lee reviewed the case, approved the results and forwarded them to his superior. On June 9, 1944, General Dwight D. Eisenhower signed a letter confirming both sentences, but withheld the order directing the execution of the sentences. The Branch Office of The JAG with the ETO reviewed the case on July 13, 1944. The three-man panel (JAGs B. Franklin Riter, Charles M. van Benschoten, and Ellwood W. Sargent) ruled the court was legally constituted, had jurisdiction of the person and offenses, and committed no errors injuriously affecting the substantial rights of the accused; thus, the record of trial was legally sufficient to support the findings of guilty and the sentences imposed.

Meanwhile, United States Senator Claude Pepper of Florida, who also served on the Committee on Foreign Relations, wrote Major General Myron C. Cramer, the Army's JAG in Washington, DC. In his cordial letter, Senator Pepper wrote,

"My dear General, friends of mine from my home town of Tallahassee, Florida, have called to my attention the case of Eliga Brinson, who, according to information they have received, might possibly be under sentence of death for rape of a British girl in England. I do not know his outfit number over there, nor the name of his Commanding General, but I would appreciate your review of the case before final action is taken and a report made to me on it. Many thanks for your kind cooperation, and with best wishes to you, I am always."

Brigadier General Edwin C. McNeil forwarded Senator Pepper's letter through the legal office at the Headquarters, ETO. In the third paragraph of the letter, McNeil presented his view on the strength of the case:

"The evidence for the prosecution was ably presented by the Trial Judge Advocate, and accused were capably represented by Defense Counsel. The members of the court also performed their duties in a commendable manner. Special mention is made of the splendid efforts of Dr. Edward B. Parks, Director of the Bristol Forensic Laboratory, whose research and testimony materially resulted in the conviction of the accused, and of the prompt and efficient investigation of the crime by Sergeant James O. Hall, 255th Military Police Company and Police Constable William G. Hale of the British constabulary, stationed at Bishops Cleeve."

In the prior paragraph, McNeil dismissed the fact that none of the victims had been able to identify the assailants, a fact that observers might conclude was a weakness in the prosecution.

"Both the victim, *********, and her companion Private First Class Edward J. Heffernan testified that two colored soldiers were involved in the crime but neither was able to identify accused as the soldiers who committed the offense alleged. However, proof of the guilt of both accused was established by circumstantial evidence of the strongest and most convincing quality. Such positive evidence is often of a far more tangible value than casual personal identification of accused, which frequently may be deemed evidence of a rather frail nature, particularly when the identification of colored soldiers is involved."

Whatever McNeil meant by this letter, the judicial process continued. On August 4, 1944, the ETO issued an order directing that the executions of Brinson and Smith be carried out. Authorities transferred the prisoners to Shepton Mallet. In the early morning hours on Friday, August 11, guards walked the accused to the small brick execution chamber. Inside were Lieutenant Colonel James C. Cullens, Commanding Officer, 2912th DTC, and seventeen Army officials and witnesses. Two British civilians – Thomas Pierrepoint and another man – were present as well. They were the executioners. Although not mentioned in the report, but standard operating procedure, there was likely a second assistant executioner (a total of three) as well. The time was 12:58 a.m. Lieutenant Colonel Cullens read General Court-Martial Orders Number 62, directing that the executions of Brinson and Smith be carried out, and then asked the condemned if they had any last words. Private Brinson replied:

"Yes sir. I thank all the men here for how they treated me the way they did since I have been here. I thank the Chaplain for being with me."

Willie Smith was born in Birmingham, Alabama, the home of the jazz and blues club *Tuxedo Junction*, made famous by Glenn Miller. He would "swing" tonight, but there would be no music, as he made his statement:

"Yes sir. I want to thank you Colonel for being so kind to me while I was here and I thank you for what you did for me."

Brinson then directed some remarks to the Chaplain, saying:

"I beg your pardon Chaplain. I thank you for what you did to me. When I get there, I will tell the Father what you did for me and I will tell him about you."

Smith followed with:

"And you, father, I want to thank you for being with me and I am innocent to go to my divine savior."

The executioners then prepared the prisoners for a rare simultaneous hanging, with the assistant fastening the ankle straps on both prisoners and Thomas Pierrepoint placing the white hood on each and adjusting the noose on top of that around their necks. Lieutenant Colonel Cullens then gave a silent signal and Pierrepoint dropped down to one knee, pulled the safety cotter pin out of its slot and pushed the lever forward that released the trap doors. The time was 1:01 a.m. Major John C. Urbaitis, Major Morton J. Rossins and Captain August K. Zinn examined the bodies and declared them legally dead.

Eliga Brinson was born on February 21, 1919 in Tallahassee, Florida. A Protestant, he stood 6'1" tall and weighed 180 pounds. In the 1930s, he came down with malaria; he contracted gonorrhea in 1938; he would have several later reoccurrences of the disease. The same year, he was involved in an auto accident that damaged his knees. Another car wreck in 1940 injured his head. Brinson had two brothers and seven sisters. He was inducted on May 2, 1941 at St. Leonie, Florida. Willie Smith was born on June 30, 1933. He was married with one child. On January 9, 1943, he was inducted at Birmingham, Alabama.

*The London Times* reported the executions on August 12, 1944. Army personnel buried Smith and Brinson at Brookwood Cemetery in Plot X, Grave 1-9, but moved their bodies in 1948 to the American Military Cemetery at Cambridge, England. In 1949, the remains travelled to the American Military Cemetery at Oise-Aisne in Plot E. Eliga Brinson is located in Row 4, 93; Willie Smith is in Row 3, Grave 69.[3]

• • •

The rape victim's family later sent a letter that made its way to Brigadier General Edward Betts. In it, they requested that the Army pay the victim compensation for two week's lost wages. General Betts noted that the Army had already paid the victim "the usual witness fee for testifying before the court-martial." It does not appear that this additional money changed hands. One could only push the U.S. Army so far.

*"I am tired of your shit. I want a straight story."*

*"The Theater Commander has directed that I ascertain from you whether, in your judgment, the execution of the death sentence in this case is requisite to the ends of justice; or, whether the ends of justice would be as well served by his commutation of this sentence to imprisonment for life."*

## 19 Private Clarence Whitfield
### 34672443
240th Port Company, 494th Port Battalion,
  First Army
**Rape**
Hanged on August 14, 1944

The Army could be tough on soldiers who committed crimes. It could be very tough on soldiers who committed capital crimes. When a senior commander decided it was time to make an example to show the soldiers in his command what would not be tolerated, the Army could be extremely tough. For the convicted soldier, it was a matter of life and death; for everyone else, it was a matter of getting out of the way. In the case of Private Clarence Whitfield, Lieutenant General Omar Bradley, First Army, wanted to send an extremely tough message; for Bradley's superior, General Dwight Eisenhower, it was time to get out of the way.

The issue began at 6:30 p.m. on June 14, 1944 at Vierville Sur Mer, France, just eight days after the start of the Normandy invasion. Two young Polish women were pulling a small wagon toward a field of cows, intending to milk them. Four "colored" soldiers, who had been drinking in a bombed-out church, approached and pushed the wagon into the field. By sign language, the soldiers indicated they wanted some milk; they apparently were interested in something else. As described in the court records, one of the sisters walked to the field to herd the cows back. One of the soldiers followed and tried to rape her. After a few minutes, the other sister went to find her sibling and one of the girls was able to escape. Someone fired a shot. Then the accused raped the girl who remained.

The fleeing girl alarmed her brother-in-law, who immediately ran to two American Army officers, Second Lieutenant Walter S. Siciah and First Lieutenant James P. Webster, of the 3704th Quartermaster Truck Company. The pair sprang into action and took a jeep to the scene, some three-hundred yards away – Siciah spoke Polish. The two officers and husband of the victim found the woman and the accused in the field. The husband promptly struck the accused in the face. Second Lieutenant Siciah asked the accused what he was doing and Clarence Whitfield replied, "I am not doing anything here; I was passing through."

First Lieutenant Webster then questioned the accused; Whitfield said he "was getting something" and made a "back and forth" motion with his hand in front of his crotch. The officers then took Whitfield to the battalion for further questioning – no rights warning had been given nor would it be at the second session. The executive officer questioned the accused concerning who was involved. Whitfield answered, "there was about nine," and one of them was white. The exasperated officer said, "I am tired of your shit. I want a straight story."

Whitfield then replied, "Well, sir, there was about twelve of them." The officer then said, "Now you tell me the truth." The accused finally admitted that two men from the unit, "another colored boy" and himself, and one soldier he did not know, had been present at the farm.

The crime occurred on June 14; by June 16, charges had been preferred. On the following day, the investigating officer finished his work; the charges were forwarded to the commanding officer and approved; the charges were received by the Judge Advocate; and the charges were referred for trial. The single black soldier had been born in Wrightsville, North Carolina on February 7, 1924. Standing 5'0" tall and weighing 164 pounds, Whitfield had completed two years of high school; he then became a short-order cook, making $20 per week. He entered the Army on April 23, 1943. In October 1943, he went AWOL, receiving a Summary Court-Martial, which fined him $21 and restricted him for fifteen days. Six days later, he went AWOL a second time and received a second Summary Court-Martial on November 20, 1943 that restricted him for another fifteen days. Whitfield started the year off with a bang by going AWOL on January 1. A third Summary Court-Martial fined him $15 and restricted him for ten days. He received a Special Court-Martial for AWOL on an un-documented date. He had caught gonorrhea in 1939 and again in 1943; on February 6, 1944, he contracted syphilis from a prostitute in Manchester, England.

A First Army GCM convened at the Château Sisil, in Vierville Sur Mer, France (only one-hundred yards from the scene of the crime) on June 20, 1944.[1] The accused pleaded not guilty. The prosecution introduced Whitfield's previous statements, the two lieutenants testified, as did the victim and her sister. Two soldiers testified for the defense, implicating an additional soldier, who had never been identified. Private Whitfield, at his own request, took the stand. He said he tried to convince the victim to have intercourse with him, but had never touched her when she did not. The jury believed the victim, found Private Whitfield guilty of carnal knowledge, a violation of the 92nd Article of War, and voted for the death penalty.[2]

The JAG for the First Army had reviewed the case on June 22, 1944. He said the matter boiled down to two issues: "first whether the accused and ********** had sexual intercourse and, second, if so, whether she consented." Colonel Ernest M. Brannon believed the victim had been raped and that Whitfield had done it. Brannon found that the accused had admitted at the scene of the crime and again back at his company, that he had intercourse, but had not used force. Brannon opined that the introduction of these statements – even though they could not be considered voluntary – were proper as they did not amount to a confession, "merely admissions against interest." Colonel Brannon finished by writing:

"In my opinion the accused's conduct merits the extreme penalty imposed by the court. His act was vicious and without any extenuating circumstances. Such conduct not only brings disgrace on our Army but, if not checked will interfere with the good relations that must be maintained between our forces and the local populace. Under existing conditions, with a large force of troops congregated in a relatively small area where there are few women, stern measures are necessary to deter others. The accused's conduct justifies making an example in his case."

Four days later, Lieutenant General Omar Bradley approved the results and forwarded them to his superior General Dwight Eisenhower. On July 17, 1944, General Eisenhower signed an order confirming the sentence, but withheld the order directing the execution of the sentence. One day later, Brigadier General Edward C. Betts sent a letter to Lieutenant General Bradley. Betts asked the following:

"The Theater Commander has directed that I ascertain from you whether, in your judgment, the execution of the death sentence in this case is requisite to the ends of justice; or, whether the ends of justice would be as well served by his commutation of this sentence to imprisonment for life."

Lieutenant General Bradley sent a scorching reply on July 26. Bradley, backing his own Judge Advocate Colonel Brannon, wrote:

"This man was found guilty of rape and it is believed that the testimony justifies the finding. The sentence of death was therefore approved. It seems to me that if the Board of Review has any doubt as to the sufficiency of the testimony to justify this finding and sentence, the man should be found not guilty and released from confinement. On the other hand, if it is admitted that he is guilty it seems to me he should pay the extreme penalty. This is one of the most outrageous crimes that can be committed by an invading army, particularly when it is committed by force of arms. At the present time, we are having considerable difficulty because of the number of rape cases. All of this contributes to the bad name of the American Army. One way to discourage future cases is to make those convicted of this crime pay the extreme penalty."

The JAG Board of Review (JAGs B. Franklin Riter, Ellwood W. Sargent and Edward Stevens Jr.) for the ETO met on July 27. They found there were no serious errors in the trial, and no doubt as to the sufficiency of the testimony to justify this finding and sentence. So "Ike" got out of the way and on August 12, 1944, the ETO issued a General Court-Martial Orders Number 66, directing that the execution of Private Clarence Whitfield be carried out in two days. The day prior to the execution, at 6:05 p.m., Captain Ira Ravner, an MP, read the General Court-Martial Orders to the condemned man at St. Lô.

On Monday, August 14, 1944, at the imposing Château de Canisy, outside Canisy, the First Army sent a tough message. A detail from the 607th Graves Registration Company, led by Captain Whitman Pearson, took its position one-hundred and fifty feet from the execution site at 4:35 p.m. Five minutes later, a fifteen-man detail from Company B, 518th MP Battalion, under First Lieutenant Arthur F. Driscoll, took their guard posts. The executioner took his position. At 4:45 p.m., Colonel William H.S. Wright, the First Army Provost Marshal, assembled the eleven official witnesses. Among them were Colonel Ernest M. Brannon, the First Army Judge Advocate and Colonel Rosser L. Hunter, the First Army Inspector General. At 4:50 p.m., Colonel Wright led the condemned, along with a Chaplain and a guard detail, to the site. He then asked Private Whitfield if he had a statement to make, but Whitfield did not. The Chaplain then asked the prisoner if he had anything to say to him. The soldier replied, "What will you tell my mother?" The Chaplain replied that she would be told that he died in France. Whitfield then asked if his mother would get his insurance. Colonel Wright said that she would; we do not know if he was aware that she indeed would not receive her son's GI Life Insurance death benefit.

What followed next was highly unusual. The executioner then placed a hood over the prisoner's head followed by the noose. That was normal. However, the executioner was a British subject, Thomas W. Pierrepoint, who had performed numerous executions for American forces before, but all had been at Shepton Mallet Prison on English soil. Now he was operating in France; the crime had occurred in France; the victim was Polish; and the condemned man was American. The reason for Pierrepoint's appearance was a frantic message from the First Army to the ETO on August 9. It seems that the First Army had no hangman. However, Eisenhower's staff was prepared for this possibility and sent a letter to the First Army. It stated, in part:

"As requested in your cable of 9 August 1944 (Ref No A-33616), Mr. Thomas William Pierrepoint, a British civilian, is being sent to your headquarters and directed to report to the Provost Marshal, First United States Army, to assist in carrying out the act of execution. Mr. Pierrepoint will arrive by air transport on 13 August 1944. Upon completion of this service, he should be returned to the United Kingdom by the first available air transport."

The Chaplain said a quick prayer and at 4:59 p.m., Colonel Wright gave a silent signal to Mr. Pierrepoint, who pushed the trap-door lever forward; Private Whitfield dropped like a stone through the opening. Colonel William H. Amspacher, Medical Corps, pronounced Private Whitfield dead at 5:14 p.m. and the graves registration personnel took the body and buried Clarence Whitfield at the U.S. Military Cemetery at Marigny, Normandy in Plot Z, (a separate area graves for General Prisoners, apart from the graves of the soldiers honorably killed in action) Grave 1-1, but officials reinterred his body in 1949 at the American Military Cemetery at Oise-Aisne in Plot E. His remains are in Row 2, Grave 37.

On September 6, 1944, the 12th Army Group, under Lieutenant General Bradley, published a memo, "Courts-martial death sentence," which read in part:[3]

"Recently an enlisted man assigned to a unit of the First US Army was sentenced to death by hanging for the offense of rape committed on the continent. The execution took place on 14 August 1944. The exemplary punishment inflicted in this case will be published to the members of each unit of this command at the earliest opportunity."

• • •

In the mid-1990s, researchers from *After the Battle Magazine*, for an article entitled "Normandy Executions," travelled to Canisy, France, the site of Whitfield's execution. They located Monsieur Aimable Lehoux, who witnessed the execution of Clarence Whitfield. Lehoux took the visitors to the field where the execution took place; fifty years after the execution, the field was a vineyard. The old Frenchman made two remarkable observations. He stated that the day before the execution, Whitfield was brought to the scaffold and helped dig a pit beneath it. Second, on the day of the execution, again according to Monsieur Lehoux, Whitfield smoked a cigar enroute to the gallows. Neither observation is confirmed by the Army's judicial file.

• • •

The author visited Canisy in 2011 in preparation for this study. Although damaged during the 1944 invasion, the Château de Canisy certainly was still an imposing edifice on the day that Clarence Whitfield died in its gardens, which Canisy Mayor Etienne Viard pointed out. The massive structure started as a castle in 1588, but over the years became a four-story château. A later owner was friends with Alexis de Tocqueville – the distinguished historical analyst of America, who would have found much to consider at the hanging at the grand château – after two American military titans had wrestled over a man's fate.

*"I did the shooting and I'll take my medicine."*

*"I couldn't say he was drunk because I can't distinguish a drunk person."*

It looked like a scene out of the old American "Wild West." A group of soldiers stood at a bar along the *Via Roma* in the Secondigliano quarter of Naples, Italy. In the group was Private Ray Watson of Company B, 386th Engineer Battalion (Separate) and he had been drinking *Strega*, a type of Italian whiskey. Another black soldier saw that Watson was armed and was "threatening to shoot" and headed outside to find the MPs. The trooper found Private First Class Philip Tobeas and Private John Brockman, of the 112th MP Prisoner of War Detachment, walking patrol. Tobeas and Brockman took the complaint and strode across the street to the bar; both were wearing MP brassards – Tobeas carried a Thompson .45 submachine gun, while Brockman had a 12-gauge pump "Street-Sweeper" riot shotgun. As they crossed the street, they met with reinforcements, Private James Stewart and Private James Nichols, assigned to the 128th MP Battalion. Both carried sawed-off shotguns – the quartet had enough firepower to take on a kraut *panzer* division.

However, they were not facing slow-moving tanks. As the MPs approached Private Watson, the troublemaker suddenly whipped out a revolver and began firing. Chaos erupted in the room; a pistol bullet hit Tobeas, shattering his leg and he fell to the ground. Seconds later the shooter hit Brockman; the bullet entered the left side of his chest just below the collarbone, passed through the left lung, ripped into the aorta and then penetrated the fourth thoracic vertebra. As the battle spilled into the street, Stewart and Nichols each fired twice with their shotguns, hitting Watson in the left hand. Watson returned fire, but did not hit anyone else. Later testimony would be confusing concerning where each MP was standing when hit, but it seemed clear that the accused fired first and that his bullet killed Private Brockman, as no one else had a weapon of that caliber.

The accused ran several hundred yards, before finding a weapons carrier of the 316th Service Group, and flagged a ride. Heading out of town, Watson jumped off and the frightened weapons carrier crew drove back to Secondigliano and met more MPs, to whom they reported the incident. The MPs swarmed over the area and finally found Watson, but not the murder weapon. Hiding in some high grass, he was wounded in the hand and leg so MPs took him to a medical facility. The incident occurred at 1:45 p.m. on April 15, 1944. By 4:00 p.m., an investigation officer interviewed Private Ray Watson. The officer told the accused that anything he might say could be used as evidence against him in court and that he could remain silent, at which point Watson blurted out, "I did the shooting and I'll take my medicine."

Watson spent eight days in the hospital with the gunshot wound. A GCM, appointed by the Commander of the PBS, convened at Naples, Italy on May 30, 1944. There were two charges against Private Watson: murder and assault.[1] The twenty-year-old Watson, who was inducted on February 7, 1942, pleaded not guilty. Because of his admission of the crime and the fact that numerous witnesses testified against him, Watson's defense was that he was drunk and not in command of his actions. Private Obediah Johnson, of Watson's company, testified that he had been drinking with the accused for two hours that morning and that Private Watson was "pretty well intoxicated." The prosecution pressed Private Johnson, who finally stated, "I couldn't say he was drunk because I can't distinguish a drunk person." Private Ray Watson took the stand in his own defense. His testimony in part included:

"I was in the room drinking with some fellow. Somebody on the outside had hit him and I felt sorry for him and took him next door and bought him a drink and while we were in there drinking a fellow brought the MPs over and I turned around towards the door when they charged in. As they came in, I charged out the door with the gun in my hand – in my left hand. The only thing I remember was when I came out the door and was shooting. I don't know if I hit anybody or not."

The court did not buy Watson's defense, found him guilty of both charges and sentenced him to be hanged; they took into consideration that Watson had previously been punished by a court-martial for breaking curfew; the court probably did not know that Watson had been diagnosed with syphilis in February 1944. On June 8, 1944, the proceedings were reviewed at the PBS and approved by the commander Brigadier General Arthur R. Wilson. On July 17, 1944,

Lieutenant General Jacob L. Devers, Commander of the NATO, signed the confirmation of sentence. A Board of Review with the NATO examined the case on August 21, 1944. Judge Advocates Mortimer Irion, Donald Mackay and Henry Remick reviewed the trial transcript, going into great length to support the contention that the death of Private Brockman indicated that the accused had demonstrated willful opposition to force to lawful authority and that the accused manifested ill will toward personnel representing such authority. The three-member review panel concluded:

"The court was legally constituted. No errors injuriously affecting the substantial rights of accused were committed during the trial. A sentence of death or imprisonment for life was mandatory upon the court-martial upon conviction of accused of murder in violation of Article of War 92. In the opinion of the Board of Review the record of trial is legally sufficient to support the findings of the sentence."

On Tuesday, August 29, 1944 at Aversa, Italy, the Army hanged Private Ray Watson by the neck until dead. Temporarily buried at the U.S. Military Cemetery in Naples, in the General Prisoner Plot, Grave 1-6, his body was interred in 1949 at the American Military Cemetery at Oise-Aisne in Plot E, in Row 2, Grave 25.[2]

*"I do not remember ever seeing the girl who picked me out in the identification parade."*

*"It is definitely not a time for levity."*

## 21 Private Madison Thomas
38265363
**964th Quartermaster Service Company**
**Rape**
Hanged on October 12, 1944

Sometimes the character of the victim drove the momentum of the trial. Such was the case against Private Madison Thomas, who allegedly raped an older widow on July 26, 1944 at Gunnislake, Cornwall, England. She lived alone; her husband had been a member of the Royal Navy and died at the Battle of Jutland in 1916 in the First World War. He had been Chief Writer of the Royal Navy and was sailing on the *HMS Defence* – the Flagship of the First Cruiser Squadron – when it was struck by a hail of German battlecruiser shells and exploded, killing all 903 men aboard. Being a seafaring nation, England held her naval battles in high regard and those sailors of the Royal Navy, who died defending "King and Country," were the honored dead. To make matters worse for Private Thomas, the victim was the local chairperson of the British Legion. It would not help his defense either, when it was revealed later that she cared for an invalid brother at home. Everybody in Gunnislake knew her and many attended the dances she organized for the American troops in the area – troops she considered as helping England in her hour of need.

It appears that at 10:40 p.m. on July 26, 1944 that the last thing on Private Madison Thomas' mind was helping anyone in her hour of need. The victim at that hour was walking home, her duties as the local British Legion representative to the Wednesday dance completed. Suddenly a "colored soldier" approached her and asked if she had far to go to her home. She indicated she did not, and that he should hurry to catch his bus back to his company. The victim then stopped at the house of Miss Jean Elizabeth Blight, who was sitting in the summer air outside her home. The soldier went on and the two women talked for a while, when suddenly he returned and asked Miss Blight for a "kiss goodnight." She rejected the offer and for the second time the soldier disappeared.

The victim then departed the Blight residence and continued on her way home. It was a lonely road, ill lit, with hedges close to the pavement. At an isolated stretch of the road going up Albaston Hill, out of the dark for a third time came Private Thomas. Again, he asked her how far she had to go, but when she replied, he became aggressive, grabbed her, threw he over a hedge into a grassy field and began to rape her. She pleaded with her assailant, who had ripped her gold wristwatch off her arm and told her he would give it back later if she consented. The Royal Navy widow replied, "That will never be, boy."

An enraged Thomas then struck her a heavy blow on the side of the head and completed the crime, with a sharp knife held at her throat. She later testified that she tried to scream but that her attacker "clutched" her throat until she almost went unconscious. At some point during the ordeal, she tried to reason with her attacker, reminding him of what his parents would think. According to her, Thomas replied that he had no parents. The victim went to the local police and authorities arranged to have the entire American company, located at Whitchurch Down Camp, stand formation at 4:30 p.m. on July 27. Jean Blight positively identified Private Thomas as the soldier who had approached the two women. Later the victim confirmed the same. Dr. Frederick Hocking, Royal Cornwall Infirmary, examined the accused and found bloodstains on the front of his trousers of the same type of blood as the victim; the blood was not Thomas' type.

On August 2, 1944 at the Provost Marshal office at Raglan Barracks, Devonport, Devonshire, Special Agent S.T. Michaelson of the Criminal Investigation Division, interviewed the accused. After being warned that anything he said could be used against him and after being instructed that, it was his privilege to remain silent, Thomas made the following statement:

"I was inducted into the Army in November 1942 at Camp Beauregard, Louisiana. I have been with this unit since July 7, 1944.

I left camp without a pass on the first truck to Gunnislake, right after chow, 26th July 1944. We got into town about 6:30 p.m. and I went with the boys to the pub about 7:00 p.m. and had a couple of glasses of beer. We picked up one of our trucks and went down to the dance at the Legion Hall in Gunnislake. I stayed at the dance till it closed; after the dance closed about 11:00 p.m., I got on the first or second truck back to camp. I got back to camp about 11:30 p.m. and went to bed.

I used to wear glasses but they were broken about two weeks ago. I do not remember ever seeing the girl who picked me out in the identification parade. I have never seen Mrs. ********* who picked me out as the soldier who raped her. I did not know what is on the front of the trousers I was wearing as it must be paint as I do not know where I got blood on my trousers."

There was more to Madison Thomas. Born March 3, 1921 in Arnaudville, Louisiana, a few miles west of the Mississippi River, he did not attend school, was single and worked as a sharecropper. Thomas stood 5'6" tall and weighed 141 pounds. In both 1942 and 1943, he was diagnosed with gonorrhea. In 1943, his character and efficiency were rated as satisfactory, but this changed to a rating of poor character and unsatisfactory efficiency in 1944. Part of that may have stemmed from a Special Court-Martial that year for using threatening language, while accosting an English woman, when he said, "I'll shoot you if you don't stop." Thomas went on to ask her if she would be interested in making a couple of *pounds*; fortunately for the victim, this encounter did not lead to a rape. The encounter with that woman was at 10:30 p.m., the same as the recent attack. Now he was involved in a charge that could mean his life.

Private Thomas' statement did not stop the Southern Base Section of appointing a GCM to convene; it met at Plymouth, Devonshire at 10:15 a.m. on August 21, 1944.[1] Private Thomas maintained his innocence; both women maintained that he was the assailant. An expert witness, Dr. Frederick Hocking testified that he had found blood stains on the front of the accused trousers and that this blood was the same type as that of the victim, but was not the same type as that of the accused. We do not know exactly when the court became aware of Thomas' previous court-martial or the similarities of that crime to the current one. In any case, the court convicted Private Madison Thomas of rape and sentenced him to death by hanging.[2]

Brigadier General Charles O. Thrasher, Commander Southern Base Section, approved the finding of guilty and the sentence of death. General Dwight Eisenhower confirmed the sentence on September 12, 1944, but set no date for the execution. On October 5, 1944, he signed General Court-Martial Orders Number 85 and the stage was set. The hanging would be held at the 2912th DTC, located at Shepton Mallet Prison. The day before the execution, Thomas and Albert Pierrepoint weighed and measured the condemned man; Albert noted in his ledger that Madison Thomas stood 5'8¼" tall and weighed 156½ pounds. The executioners calculated that a drop of 7'2" would produce an instant death. Late that evening, the commandant of the DTC called the witnesses together and briefed them on the execution procedure that would soon happen. He reiterated that it was a solemn occasion and that, "It is definitely not a time for levity."

He explained how he would read the full court-martial order and ask the condemned if he wished to make any last statements. It was a small crowd, just six officers as witnesses and ten men serving in some capacity in the execution party. He then recessed the group until 12:55 a.m. on October 12. At that time the Commandant, Major Herbert R. Laslett began the procession to the execution chamber. He was followed by Chaplain Andrew J. Zarek, who held the rank of captain, and Tech Sergeant George M. Harris and Private John H. Folger who would serve as guards. Behind them were Thomas W. Pierrepoint and Albert Pierrepoint. The group arrived at the gallows at 12:57 a.m. Then the commandant, Chaplain and guards went to the cell holding Private Thomas, General Prisoner Number 919; it was a quick trip and the accused arrived at the execution chamber in just one minute. Major Laslett then read General Court-Martial Orders Number 85 in full, while Albert Pierrepoint bound the condemned man's arms and ankles. Private Thomas declined to make a statement to Major Laslett, but did make one to the Chaplain:

"Yes sir, father, look after my pictures in my cell and send them home for me. I would like you to write home and tell my mother about it and send my pictures home."

Thomas Pierrepoint then placed the white hood over the condemned man's head and face and adjusted the noose around his neck. Commandant Laslett gave the silent signal to Pierrepoint, who knelt down, quickly removed the safety cotter pin and pushed the lever forward, which actuated the trap door; the time was 1:01 a.m. Major John C. Urbaitis, Captain August K. Zinn and Captain John R. Whiteman descended from the platform, examined the condemned, and pronounced him dead of suffocation, judicial, by hanging at 1:07 a.m. Authorities buried Madison Thomas at the Brookwood Cemetery in Plot X, Grave 1-10, but in 1948, the Army transferred his remains to the American Military Cemetery at Cambridge, England. The Army moved the remains in 1949 to the American Military Cemetery at Oise-Aisne. His remains are in Plot E, in Row 4, Grave 76.

Shortly after the execution, United States Senator John Overton of Louisiana wrote the Army asking for details. On October 27, 1944, Brigadier General Robert H. Dunlop, Acting Adjutant General, replied and informed the senator that Army policy was not to furnish information on soldiers executed, except to an authorized member of the family.[3] Normally, a U.S. Senator was a powerful official, but in the fall of 1944, it was the U.S. Army that was the big dog on the porch.

*"One pack of cigarettes daily; 25 bottles of beer weekly; and one pint of whiskey monthly."*

*"It may be inferred that the force of the descriptive words used was lost in translation from French to English, as they were doubtless under-statements."*

*"I thank you and the Chaplain for what you have done for me. I thank the lieutenants and all the guards for the candy and stuff they brought me."*

## 22 Technician Fifth Grade James Buck Sanders
34124233

Company B,
29th Signal Construction Battalion
**Rape**
Hanged on October 25, 1944

## 23 Private Roy W. Anderson
35407199

Company B,
29th Signal Construction Battalion
**Rape**
Hanged on October 25, 1944

Sometimes it appeared that a court-martial panel had a fundamental misunderstanding of its responsibility and mission. Such was the case of the GCM of Technician Fifth Grade James B. Sanders and Private Roy W. Anderson of Company B, 29th Signal Construction Battalion. MPs had arrested the two for several rapes on June 22, 1944. After an investigation, Brigadier General Ewart G. Plank, Commander, Advance Section, Communications Zone, ordered that a GCM be convened. On July 17, 1944, the court met at Ste. Mere-Eglise, France; the trial lasted three days, longer than usual and perhaps indicative that there was some confusion during the proceedings. Sanders and Anderson were tried together – an example of a joint offenses proceeding – a Private Florine Wilson was also tried with them for one of the offenses. Three days later, the guilty findings included one count of threatening and holding with a gun (96th Article of War) and two counts of carnal knowledge (92nd Article of War).[1]

What had actually happened at the small village? Activated on April 10, 1942 at Camp Gordon, Georgia, the unit arrived at Normandy on June 17, 1944. The unit's mission was to lay telephone lines, telephone poles and wooden telephone towers. On the morning of June 20, Sanders and Anderson were walking through the countryside with some other soldiers, when they arrived at Neuville-au-Plain, just a few miles north of Ste. Mere-Eglise and came upon the home. They asked for water and cider (an alcohol drink made from apples) and then departed. A short time later, they returned (according to the soldiers) and paid money for two women at the location to have sex with them. The victims said it was non-consensual. During the affair, a third soldier sat outside. One of the soldiers then fired a shot between the legs of an adult French male.

At 2:30 p.m., a Private Pope arrived outside the home, saw the civilians under guard, and quickly departed, sensing something was amiss. He reported the incident to a Private Keely, who went to the house and attempted to get the accused to stop, telling them that the officers had gotten wind of what was going on and might be there shortly. There was another soldier with Keely, named McCutcheon, who may have had sex with one of the women. Later in the afternoon Sanders, Anderson and Wilson (the last had stood guard outside the house) went back to their bivouac area. Rape Victim One later identified James B. Sanders as one of her attackers, but could not identify the other two men, who she said raped her. Rape Victim One also identified Sanders as the attacker of Rape Victim Two. Rape Victim Two also identified James B. Sanders as her assailant. Private Keely would also later identify Sanders as the attacker of Rape Victim Two. Roy W. Anderson, by his own admission, had sex with Rape Victim Two, but as a reviewing Staff Judge Advocate later noted:

"There is no direct identification of Anderson as one of those who raped ********* [Rape Victim One]."

However, Private Keely would later testify that he heard Anderson state:

"I didn't get any of this meat and I'm going to get me some more of this pussy before I leave."

Army investigators had identified a third soldier, McCutcheon, who may have raped one of the women, but he was not prosecuted in this trial. It was all very confusing. Neither of the two rape victims spoke English, so the court relied on Technician Fifth Grade Robert J. Railland of Company C in the 707th MP Battalion. There were mixed reviews of this arrangement. A later opinion by the European Theater Staff Judge Advocate "commended" the Trial Judge Advocate and the Defense Counsel for the manner in which the trial was conducted, given that it was necessary to secure much of the evidence through an interpreter. However, in another part of the review, the Staff Judge Advocate opined about the victims' testimony:

"It may be inferred that the force of the descriptive words used was lost in translation from French to English, as they were doubtless understatements."

Moreover, the Staff Judge Advocate reviewing the case seemed to provide a point normally made by the Defense Counsel:

"The nature of the testimony, not to mention the fact that much of it came through an interpreter, indicates the civilians were extremely excited, and the possibility of error on their part cannot be discounted."

This Staff Judge Advocate did not go on to say that this "possibility of error" constituted reasonable doubt. The court had not found any such concerns and declared both Technician Fifth Grade James B. Sanders and Private Roy W. Anderson guilty of raping both women that carried a mandatory punishment of either life imprisonment or the death penalty. The court selected death and sent the verdict forward for review.

Then the eleven voting members of the court took a highly unusual step: they all signed a recommendation for clemency and forwarded that to the Commanding General, Advance Section, Communications Zone, Brigadier General Ewart G. Plank. Stating that it was the recommendation of all of the members of the GCM, the letter asked that the sentence be reduced for each of the two defendants to life imprisonment. A pen and ink change to the type-written letter struck the word "reducing" and replacing it with the word "commuting." Then the letters (one for each defendant) stated the reasons behind the recommendation.[2] There were two:

"Possibility of the accused being somewhat under the influence of alcohol; and [a] lack of understanding on the part of [Anderson/Sanders] of the French people and language."

The legal system did not agree with the court's recommendation for clemency. The initial legal review upheld the verdict and sentence on July 30. Brigadier General Plank approved the sentence on August 2. General Dwight Eisenhower confirmed the sentence on August 30, 1944, but withheld the order directing the actual execution.

• • •

That was because the U.S. Army in France had hundreds of thousands of soldiers, but did not have a single hangman. It all started on July 8, 1943 when the War Department sent a pamphlet on "Execution of Death Sentences." Buried in the pamphlet was the phrase:

"The trap will be actuated personally by the officer charged with the execution of the sentence."

In England, because of the Status of Forces Agreement designating that a British hangman would be used, the ETO was technically not in compliance with the directive, but for a valid reason. Once in France, however, theater officials were in a conundrum. Thomas Pierrepoint flew from England to Normandy on August 14, 1944 to hang Clarence Whitfield at Canisy, but that was really stretching the agreement concerning executions in England. The role of a hangman was not sitting well in the ETO. Despite Washington's directive, many commanders believed that it was not a fitting job for a commissioned officer.

The search thus began for a hangman. Leaving no stone unturned, the Judge Advocate section queried Lieutenant Choffel, the French liaison officer at the theater, concerning whether a French National could be designated as a hangman by the French Justice Department, but,

"He expressed doubt that a French National could be found as a hangman because hanging is not a method of execution in France."

Initially, it was a wild goose chase. The 4237th Quartermaster Sterilization Company, for example, identified a corporal, who stated that he had witnessed hangings and felt qualified to perform the duties of a hangman. The Army did not select him; it was not interested in lynchings. Then the theater queried the War Department on the availability of civilian hangmen in the United States. Perhaps the Army could transfer the man to Europe. That did not work either.

The Normandy Base Section finally informed the Commanding General of the Communications Zone that a soldier had been found with experience as a hangman. The reply, dated September 10, 1944 and signed by Lieutenant Colonel Allen C. Spencer – Adjutant General of the Normandy Base Section – read:

> "John C. Woods, 37540591, Company B, 37th Engineer Combat Battalion, 5th Engineer Special Brigade is reported as having been assistant hangman twice in the state of Texas and twice in the state of Oklahoma."

A few days later, the Judge Advocate recommended to the Provost Marshal that a full investigation determine if Woods was sufficiently experienced. No evidence exists that this occurred. The Normandy Base Section sent a message to the Theater Provost Marshal on October 2, 1944 that Private John C. Woods and Private First Class Thomas S. Robinson (554th Quartermaster Depot) would volunteer to act as hangmen.

Meanwhile, on September 21, 1944 the ETO designated that at a future disciplinary training center, which would be opened at Paris, engineers would construct a portable gallows. The Paris DTC opened two days later at the Caserne Mortier. On September 28, 1944, Major General Milton Reckord – the Theater Provost Marshal – notified Brigadier General R.B. Lord that the search to find a hangman was successful and that:

> "G-1 has promised to provide the grade recommended by me for the hangman in order to compensate him in a small measure for the work he is to perform. I am recommending the hangman be made a Master Sergeant and the assistant hangman a T/3 (Staff Sergeant)."

The issue finally made it to General Eisenhower. A note from the G-1 to the Provost Marshal through the Judge Advocate on October 12, 1944 summarized:

> "Subsequent to the dispatch of the cable mentioned above [11 October 1944] the Commanding General expressed a wish to use the soldiers whom we had located. Consequently, a cable was sent to the U.S.

cancelling the initial request for this purpose. Seine Section has been allotted the necessary grades. Request you take the necessary action to coordinate with the Adjutant General on the procurement and assignment of the hangmen to Seine Section."

General Dwight Eisenhower finally had his hangman.

The ETO further solidified the use of enlisted men as executioners in publishing Standing Operating Procedure (SOP) No.54 – Execution of Death Sentences Imposed by Courts-Martial on December 14, 1944. On page five, the SOP stated:

> "The officer charged with the act of execution will give the executioner a silent signal indicating that the trap is to be actuated …"

The new master sergeant, John Clarence Woods was getting closer to his first hanging.[3]

• • •

Technician Fifth Grade James B. Sanders was born on June 9, 1917 at Lockhart, South Carolina. At the time he was inducted on May 26, 1942 at Fort Jackson, South Carolina, Sanders lived in Pacolet, South Carolina, a small town southeast of Spartanburg. Single, he listed his civilian occupation as cooking roasted meats; he stood 5'3" tall and weighed 133 pounds. Shortly after his enlistment, Sanders received a diagnosis of gonorrhea. His disciplinary record was checkered; a Summary Court-Martial convicted him on December 22, 1942 for a two-day absence without official leave. A second Summary Court-Martial convicted Sanders on February 23, 1943 for urinating on the floor of the squad tent. A third Summary Court-Martial convicted him on July 8, 1943 for being drunk in uniform in public and for wrongfully wearing staff-sergeant chevrons.

Private Roy W. Anderson, a communication lineman, was born on September 22, 1917 in Jeffersonville, Indiana; he had been inducted at Columbus, Ohio on June 22, 1942. Anderson had six years of schooling; he stood 5'6" tall and weighed 144 pounds. A laborer by trade, he made $20 a week working at the Mansfield Tire and Rubber Company. His listed religion was Protestant. He had a traumatic youth. At age six, he was in a car accident that fractured his skull. In 1937, he was shot in the back; in March 1942, he was diagnosed with gonorrhea. After entering the Army, he initially had solid ratings of an excellent character and satisfactory efficiency, but in 1943/44 he received two court-martial convictions for being absent without official leave – "going over the hill" in soldier parlance. He later stated that there was insanity on his father's side of the family. Regarding his personal habits, Sanders stated that he consumed:

"One pack of cigarettes daily; 25 bottles of beer weekly; and one pint of whiskey monthly."

On October 21, 1944, General Court-Martial Orders Number 91 (Sanders) and 92 (Anderson) – signed by Brigadier General R.B. Lord (by command of General Eisenhower) – directed that the two executions would be carried out on October 25, 1944 at the Seine DTC in Paris, France, located at the French Caserne Mortier at 128 Boulevard Mortier. A letter of instruction through Brigadier General Pleas B. Rogers, then head of the Seine Base Section, directed that the commanding officer of the Seine DTC, Major Mortimer H. Christian, appoint "a qualified executioner" for the proceeding; it is likely that he designated Master Sergeant Woods to attend. Special Orders Number 1 of the Seine DTC directed that Christian read the order of execution to General Prisoner Sanders at 6:00 p.m. the day before the execution.

Early on October 25, 1944, Captain Edward M. Sullivan examined General Prisoner Sanders and found him to be in excellent physical and mental condition. The sequence of the orders meant that Sanders would be the leadoff man. At 10:01 p.m. on October 25, 1944, Major Mortimer H. Christian led a procession into the death chamber. Chaplain Harry S. Williams and General Prisoner James B. Sanders followed him. On either side of Sanders were guards Technical Sergeant Charles F. Edwards and Sergeant Edward P. McHugh. Following in the column were Captain Edward M. Sullivan (MC) and Captain Albert M. Summerfield (MP), who would serve as the execution recorder. There would be five witnesses: Colonel Robert Chard, Lieutenant Colonel Charles Day, Lieutenant Colonel Harry L. Gustafson, Major Paul Hitler and Major Benjamin Lehman. Already in the chamber were Monsieur Lambolley of the Prefect of Police, Department of the Seine and four junior personnel.

The group halted at the foot of the steps of the scaffold; the two guards bound the condemned man's hands behind him and then assisted him to climb the steps and stand on the trap door. The two guards then bound the ankles of the prisoner, while Major Christian asked if Sanders had any last statement to make. Sanders made no reply but began to pray. The Chaplain also asked if the condemned had a statement to make, but the hooded Sanders continued to pray and the

Chaplain offered a prayer. The report mentioned that the hood and noose were adjusted – this was probably done by Master Sergeant Woods. At 10:05 p.m., Major Christian faced about and cut a rope, releasing a weight that actuated the trap door.

Sanders dropped through the opening; his body swayed slightly but there were no "jerks, tremors or visible convulsions." At 10:12 p.m., Dr. Edward Sullivan moved to his position at the lower screened portion of the gallows and made his examination. Initially, he indicated, "life was not extinct" by shaking his head. He made another examination at 10:15 p.m., but Sanders still was not dead. Finally, at 10:19 p.m. the medical officer made a third inspection and pronounced the man dead. The witnesses departed and Captain Walter B. Bradley (Graves Registration Section) removed the body from the death chamber after the assistants (likely Woods and T/3 Thomas Robinson) "proceeded to cut the rope and remove the body from the lower screened portion of the scaffold." This was very likely the first execution in which Master Sergeant John C. Woods played a role, and as would happen in many others, the condemned man did not quickly die. Possibly this was a result of a faulty placement of the knot in the hangman's rope or an inadequate drop distance, but it was no time for Major Christian to investigate. The commandant had a brisk schedule to meet and at 10:31 p.m., a second procession entered the death chamber. All the aforementioned personnel were present, except that on this occasion the condemned was General Prisoner Roy W. Anderson; his guards were Sergeant Earl E. Mendenhall and Sergeant Richard A. Mosley. The procedure was the same; when asked if he desired to make a statement, Anderson said:

"I thank you and the Chaplain for what you have done for me. I thank the lieutenants and all the guards for the candy and stuff they brought me."

Anderson then thanked the Chaplain, at which point Chaplain Williams began to read a prayer. At 10:33 p.m., Major Christian faced about and cut the rope, which resulted in the trap door releasing. The doctor waited a little longer this time; after ten minutes, he began his examination and pronounced the condemned dead one minute later. Captain Bradley and his assistants removed this body as well. The Army buried Sanders and Anderson at the U.S. Military Cemetery at Solers, France. Officials transported both to the American Military Cemetery at Oise-Aisne in Plot E in 1949. James Sanders was buried in Row 3, Grave 58. Roy Anderson's remains are in Row 2, Grave 29.

The *New York Times* did not report the story of the executions until October 31, 1944, mentioning that Sanders lived in Pacolet, South Carolina and Anderson had resided in Jeffersonville, Indiana. Within the file on this case is a stamp stating that the Record of Trial was examined by the Board of Review with the concurrence of the Assistant JAG, Branch Office of The JAG with the ETO and found to be legally sufficient to support the sentence. The stamp is dated 31 October 1944 – six days after James B. Sanders and Roy W. Anderson were executed.

• • •

Unknown to the Army, there was a dark secret about John C. Woods. On December 3, 1929, he joined the United States Navy, reporting to the west coast. After initial training, he received an assignment for the *U.S.S. Saratoga*. Within months, Woods deserted. Authorities apprehended him in Colorado, returning him to California, where he received a GCM. After the conviction, a medical officer recommended that a psychiatric board examine Woods. This happened on April 23, 1930. The report read:

> "This patient, though not intellectually inferior, gives a history of repeatedly running counter to authority both before and since enlistment. Stigmata of degeneration are present and the patient frequently bites his fingernails. He has a benign tumor of the soft palate for which he refuses operation. His commanding officer and division officers state that he shows inaptitude and does not respond to instruction. He is obviously poor service material. This man has had less than five months service. His disability is considered to be an inherent defect for which the service is in no way responsible. [He] is not considered a menace to himself or others."

The report also provided a diagnosis for John Woods – Constitutional Psychopathic Inferiority without Psychosis. The Navy then discharged him and he slid into obscurity in Kansas. However, John Woods was not in Kansas anymore.[4]

*"His standing in the Army is satisfactory, and unsatisfactory, depending on his sobriety."*

*"Then Captain Grimson told me that with all such testimony it wasn't necessary for me to take the stand, so I didn't. Then they throw the rope at me."*

*"The toes of the shoes barely touched the floor, did not support any weight, but prevented the body from swaying."*

## 24     Private First Class Paul M. Kluxdal

36395076

Headquarters Battery,
200th Field Artillery Battalion
**Murder**
Hanged on October 31, 1944

In many death penalty cases, military psychiatrists, using intelligence tests, found that the accused were substantially below average. Such was not the case with Private First Class Paul M. Kluxdal. Born on July 17, 1907 in Merrill, Wisconsin, Kluxdal was a radio operator in his unit, an occupation that required some real skill. From November 19, 1924 to July 14, 1927, he had served in the Wisconsin National Guard; he also attended the University of Wisconsin for two years. Prior to enlisting, Kluxdal, who was white, was married and lived in Oak Park, Chicago, Illinois; he was a construction foreman, building commercial chimneys. His wife worked for the War Department in Chicago; the couple had no children. Then Private First Class Paul Kluxdal did two stupid things. For several months, he made threatening statements against his first sergeant. Then, on August 12, 1944, he shot and killed his first sergeant. Despite his intelligence, that combination of events would get him hanged.

The incident happened near Vire, France. Kluxdal's unit, in support of the Fifth Corps, was in a bivouac position and the men were digging foxholes. That evening First Sergeant Loyce M. "Robbie" Robertson – from Birmingham, Alabama – was making the rounds, ensuring that his soldiers were properly at work, when he found Private First Class Kluxdal in possession of a bottle of alcohol and his position not yet complete. Robertson took the bottle away from Kluxdal, telling him that he should complete his foxhole and later, if the battery commander gave permission, he would give the bottle back to Kluxdal. At 10:30 p.m., Kluxdal approached the first sergeant, who was then in a discussion with the battery commander, Captain Horace L. Hall. A moment later, Captain Hall left the area; it was dark. Witnesses stated they saw the two men standing face-to-face, two yards apart, and heard Kluxdal say "I'll shoot you Robbie," or "I'll kill you Robbie," just before a shot was fired. Soldiers rushed to the scene, attempted to save the first sergeant and disarmed his assailant. First Sergeant "Robbie" Robertson died quickly of a single .30 caliber carbine round through his chest.

The following day, Private First Class Kluxdal made a written statement that he had been talking to the first sergeant and started to turn away when he "sort of stumbled" and as he began to fall the carbine came into his hands and accidentally went off. He added that he did not know how his weapon was loaded; Kluxdal stated that he had been drinking earlier in the evening, but was not drunk at the time of the incident. Later that day, an officer informed Kluxdal that he would be charged with murder.

Kluxdal had an alcohol problem; police had twice cited him for being drunk. In the military, he received two Summary Courts-Martial which reduced him in rank. His battery commander submitted the following evaluation of the soldier:

> "Because of his lack of control when drinking intoxicating beverages, his suitability for military duties is limited."
>
> "His standing in the Army is satisfactory, and unsatisfactory, depending on his sobriety."

The unit conducted an investigation, during which several soldiers came forward with accounts that Private First Class Kluxdal had threatened harm to the first sergeant in the months leading up to the Normandy invasion. Captain Hall also wrote a letter to the Commanding General, Fifth Corps, concerning the volatile nature of the accused. He stated in part:

> "His overbearing disposition and his habit of becoming argumentative and vicious on numerous occasions caused fights within the battery."

In another fight in July 1942, he was kicked on the left side of his face that resulted in a damaged eardrum. Kluxdal had other physical problems. His medical records indicated that in 1918 his left ring finger was amputated in an accident; he was missing five lower teeth. He had healed fractures of the third, fourth, fifth and sixth anterior ribs, but his left knee was the problem. In October 1943, he severely sprained his medial collateral and anterior cruciate ligaments. That December, he was diagnosed with lateral instability and swelling in the knee. In April 1944, he suffered a moderately severe sprain of the lateral collateral knee ligament, with some "dislocation of the semilunar cartilage [torn meniscus.]" Kluxdal stood 6' tall and weighed 172 pounds. He qualified as a marksman with his .30 caliber carbine and deployed with his unit to Normandy on June 8, 1944.

Major General Leonard T. Gerow, the corps commander, ordered that a GCM be convened at Moussy le Vieux, France on September 4, 1944 – there was a single charge – murder, a violation of the 92nd Article of War.[1] The GCM began at 9:00 a.m. Private First Class Kluxdal pleaded not guilty and the government presented its case.[2] The defense emphasized that it had been too dark for witnesses accurately to see what occurred. Although the accused did not take the stand, the defense made no objection to his statement being introduced into evidence. To counter the assertions that Kluxdal had made threatening statements about the first sergeant in the past, the defense recalled the battery commander, Captain Hall, who testified that in his two years in command he did not know of any animosity between the accused and the victim, and that Kluxdal had been in line for a promotion. The defense also called a non-commissioned officer, who testified that he never noticed any animosity between the two men and that the relationship "seemed friendly enough." The defense moved for a finding of "not guilty," on the grounds that the prosecution had not proven guilt, but the motion was denied. The record of the trial does not show that any information, concerning the severity of Kluxdal's left knee injuries, was considered at trial.

The court convicted Paul Kluxdal of murder and sentenced him to death by hanging. The Fifth Corps Staff Judge Advocate reviewed the case on September 14, 1944 and found no substantial problems. The review characterized the testimony of the medical officer in a different light than he originally stated; Captain Marsh's original statement said that the terrain in the area was "rough." The review indicated that the terrain at the scene of the crime was smooth, with the

grass short. Such a discrepancy was crucial if Kluxdal's statement that he tripped and fell was to be believed.

Major General Gerow approved the sentence on September 17, 1944 and forwarded the record of trial to higher headquarters. General Dwight Eisenhower confirmed the sentence on September 30, 1944, but withheld issuing a date and location at which the execution would take place. The Branch Office of The JAG with the ETO reviewed the case on October 12, 1944 and found no major issues. Meanwhile, on September 8, the two Defense Counsels for the convicted Kluxdal sent a letter to Major General Gerow, requesting leniency on the grounds that the evidence supported a finding of accidental shooting, not murder. They also opined that statements made by the accused four or five months prior to the incident had no bearing on the incident and their admission was an attempt to prove malice.

Paul Kluxdal was also busy. Asking that legal officers meet with him in prison as he had additional evidence, Private First Class Paul Kluxdal also sent a letter to the corps judge advocate. In the missive, Kluxdal described that he had a trick knee that caused his fall and his weapon discharged, adding that he did not receive adequate counsel. Kluxdal stated that he had initially asked for two military lawyers by name, but that they had been unavailable for service – a point that was factually correct. He then asserted that he had met his lawyers – probably on August 21 – while he was being held in the stockade and that they told him that they would meet again. According to Kluxdal, they did not meet again until two weeks later – on the morning of the trial. Kluxdal also complained about the conduct of his defense during the trial. He said that as the prosecution was resting its case, he spoke with his lawyer:

"Now after all this confusing, contradictory statements, the prosecution rests and the Defense Counsel asks for a recess. Then Captain Grimson told me that with all such testimony it wasn't necessary for me to take the stand, so I didn't. Then they throw the rope at me."

The Army "threw the rope" at General Prisoner Paul W. Kluxdal at about 10:00 p.m. on Tuesday, October 31, 1944 – Halloween – at the Seine DTC in Paris, France. In a memo from Brigadier General Pleas B. Rogers, Commander of the Seine Section in the Communications Zone, Major Mortimer Christian was charged with the overall responsibility of the execution and was directed to appoint a qualified executioner. Major Christian had only one qualified man, Master Sergeant John C. Woods. The ETO published General Court-Martial Orders Number 94 on October 26, 1944 that set the time and place for the event. Early on Paul Kluxdal's last day alive, Captain Edward M. Sullivan, a surgeon, examined the condemned man as required and found him to be in excellent physical and mental condition.

At 10:01 p.m. on October 31, 1944, Major Christian entered the death chamber at the Caserne Mortier, the home of the Seine DTC, in eastern Paris. Closely following him were Chaplain Harry S. Williams, General Prisoner Kluxdal and two guards – Technical Sergeant Charles E. Edwards and Sergeant Richard A. Mosley. Five official witnesses were already in the room. At the bottom of the gallows, Major Christian and Chaplain Williams ascended the steps, while the guards bound the prisoner's arms behind his back and then assisted him up the steps. After directing the prisoner to stand on the top of the trap doors at 10:02 p.m., Major Christian asked him if he had any last words; Kluxdal replied, "No Sir, thank you for your consideration." The Chaplain asked him the same question and Kluxdal stated, "No sir; thank you."

Master Sergeant John Woods, perhaps helped by his assistant, adjusted the black hood over the head of the condemned man and finally slipped the rope noose around Kluxdal's neck. Major Christian then faced about and cut the rope that released the weight, which actuated the trap doors open at 10:03 p.m. Kluxdal's body hurtled through the opening, at which point the unthinkable happened – Kluxdal's shoes hit the ground, sounding like a single loud "toe tap" in a Nicholas Brothers dance routine. Perhaps Woods did not measure the height of the condemned man before the execution – and as Kluxdal was 6' tall, he was several inches taller than most of the other soldiers Woods would hang. Perhaps Woods did not stretch the rope the previous day by suspending a heavy weight from it. The report of execution minimized the impact of the event by stating:

"The toes of the shoes barely touched the floor, did not support any weight, but prevented the body from swaying."

That may have been the observation in the report, but when the medical officer entered the lowered screened portion of the scaffold to examine the body at 10:15 p.m., he found "that life was not extinct." The doctor waited six additional minutes and then determined that Paul Kluxdal finally was dead. Master Sergeant Woods cut the rope that released the body; Captain Walter B. Bradley signed for the remains. The Army buried the body of Paul Kluxdal at the U.S. Military Cemetery at Solers, France; Sergeant Emmett R. Bailey, Jr. later stated that he was part of the burial detail.

• • •

Woods was familiar with transporting remains by truck. In Kansas, he had worked as a truck driver for the Wichita Casket Company.

• • •

The *Chicago Tribune* reported the hanging on November 3, 1944 and attempted to interview Kluxdal's former landlady, but she denied that he had ever stayed at the apartment listed by the Army as his residence. The *Stars & Stripes* published its story the same day, but erroneously reported the date of the crime. The *New York Times* reported the execution on November 5, 1944. The Army notified the widow of Paul Kluxdal of his death on November 10, 1944. She wrote back stating that she had found out about her husband by reading the newspaper, an unsatisfactory situation.

In 1949, officials reinterred Kluxdal's body at the American Military Cemetery at Oise-Aisne in Plot E, in Row 2, Grave 35.[3]

First Sergeant Loyce M. "Robbie" Robertson, who was born on August 22, 1917, is buried at the Union #3 Baptist Church Cemetery in Ballplay, Etowah County, Alabama.

*"I must have gotten drunk because the next thing I knew I was in the yard with a Colonel, two Lieutenants and two MPs."*

It was unbelievable. Two junior enlisted men in "Georgie" Patton's Third Army broke into a farmhouse a few hundred yards from their company bivouac area, wounded two people with gunfire, raped a woman, after which, one fell asleep on the bloodstained bed. The next morning an Army colonel, leading a posse of MPs, found the soldier on that same bed and observed that the soldier's fatigue trousers were bloodstained and that his fly was open. That is exactly the situation that Private Joseph Watson and Technician Fifth Grade Willie Wimberly, Jr. found themselves to be in shortly after the rape occurred on the evening of August 8, 1944. Wimberly had enough presence of mind to leave the scene of the crime before the officers arrived, but the colonel later found his helmet liner on the steps and inside the liner was marked "W2154," the initial being the first of his last name and the four digits being the last four of his service number.

The facts of the case fit an uneasy pattern of some American troops in Normandy; small groups of soldiers left a bivouac area at night and once out of supervision of senior, disciplined non-commissioned officers went searching for liquor and began binge drinking, attempting to consume all of it before heading back to camp. That scenario occurred at 8:00 p.m. on August 8, 1944, when Private Joseph Watson and Technician Fifth Grade Willie Wimberly, Jr. found a two-story farmhouse occupied by a sixty-six-year-old farmer and his thirty-three-year-old unmarried daughter. The two black soldiers understood no French, but bartered for a liter of apple alcohol cider, which they consumed before leaving the nervous residents. The Frenchman barricaded the door. Five minutes later the soldiers returned and broke through the barrier.

Wimberly then hit the man on the back of his head with his Thompson submachine gun, while Watson pushed the woman into a chair. Mysteriously, the two troopers abruptly departed again. Terrified, the farmer and his daughter retreated upstairs, where they barricaded another door and affixed a double lock on the latch. At midnight, the two soldiers returned, stormed up the steps and began firing at least twenty .45-submachine gun rounds through the door, wounding both civilians; the woman's wounds were the worst, fracturing her left tibia. Over the next few minutes, her father hobbled quickly down the steps and ran for help. Unable to flee with him, the woman remained and later claimed that she had been raped by both men. She would testify that every time she attempted to scream one soldier would hold his hand over her mouth, while the other pointed his weapon at her head. At the trial, she was unable to identify either attacker; her father positively identified Technician Fifth Grade Wimberly from a lineup of six "colored soldiers," but was doubtful about Watson's identity.

After a few hours, the farmer found Colonel Thomas H. Nixon of the Ordnance Department in the Third Army headquarters. The "hard-boiled" Nixon was a West Pointer, had twenty-six years in the Army and a Bronze Star; he decided to take two lieutenants and lead the MPs to the farmhouse.[1] After arriving, Nixon found a helmet liner on the steps and blood all over the upstairs room. Roughly grabbing Private Watson, who "seemed a little dazed," off the bed, Colonel Nixon jammed the helmet liner on Watson's head and ushered him out, finding a second helmet liner under the bed and about two dozen expended cartridges.

Over the next several hours, MPs interviewed Watson three times and he changed his story just as often. He first stated he had been sent to the house by a sergeant to investigate a shooting. Then he said he had been at the house with one or two other soldiers. He finally stated that he had never been in the house at all. Colonel Nixon begged to differ. The second helmet liner, found under the bed, was Watson's; the evidence linked both men to the scene of the crime. Wimberly made a statement, but blamed the attack on Watson, stating that he was only trying to go back to the company. Watson made a written statement and wrote he had been at the farmhouse with Wimberly and that, "I must have gotten drunk because the next thing I knew I was in the yard with a Colonel, two Lieutenants and two MPs."

Justice was swift. A GCM convened at Poilley, France on August 17, 1944. The charges were lengthy: one count of carnal knowledge, two counts of assault and one count of breaking and entering.[2] One Trial Judge Advocate, Captain Edwin L. Mayall (JAG) spoke French; the two victims were not believed to speak English.[3] Colonel Clell B. Perkins, Colonel Robert E. Cummings, Colonel Clarence C. Park, Colonel James J. Weeks and Major Andre B. Moore – four of the officers on the panel – had just finished another death penalty case the day before for Charles H. Jordan and Arthur E. Davis and had sentenced them to be hanged. Due to Third Army's rapid advance, the trial was adjourned on August 18, 1944, resuming at St. Sabine, France the next day. The jury found both men guilty of all charges and sentenced them to hang.

Private Joseph Watson and Technician Fifth Grade Willie Wimberly, Jr. were typical of the condemned. Watson, twenty-five-years-old, was from Texarkana, Texas. He was single; he dropped out of grade school during the fourth grade. Prior to his induction in the Army on August 15, 1942, Joe Watson worked on a sugar beet farm in Montana, making $32 a month with free room. Medics diagnosed him with syphilis in February 1944. Willie Wimberly, one of a dozen children, was born in Macon, Georgia on September 21, 1912. He later moved to Chicago, Illinois. He stood 5'3" tall and weighed 126 pounds; he had black hair and brown eyes. He had been married but separated in 1936; he had no children. Wimberly quit school in the fifth grade; he worked as a machine operator at a tire company, making $22 a week. He was inducted on July 8, 1942 and arrived with his unit in Liverpool, England on December 15, 1943.

The Third Army JAG reviewed the case on August 28, 1944. General Eisenhower confirmed the sentence on September 23, 1944. The Branch Office of The JAG with the ETO conducted a Board of Review on October 11, 1944. On November 6, 1944, the ETO published General Court-Martial Orders Number 95. Brigadier General R.B. Lord – by command of General Eisenhower – directed that the two executions would occur on November 9, 1944 at the Seine DTC at the Caserne Mortier, Paris, France. On November 9, 1944 at 10:02 p.m., Major Mortimer H. Christian led a procession into the death chamber. Chaplain Harry S. Williams and General Prisoner Willie Wimberly, Jr. followed him; Technical Sergeant Charles F. Edwards and Sergeant Edward P. McHugh served as guards. In the rear were Captain Edward M. Sullivan, the medical officer, and Captain Albert M. Summerfield, the recorder. Eight officers served as witnesses and fourteen enlisted spectators stood near a wall about fifteen feet from the scaffold.

The group halted at the foot of the steps of the gallows; the two guards bound the condemned man's hands behind him, assisted him to climb the steps and positioned him on the trap door. The two guards bound the ankles of the prisoner, while Major Christian asked if Wimberly had any last statement to make. He said, "No sir" and gave the same reply, when asked the same question by the Chaplain. It is likely that Master Sergeant John C. Woods adjusted the noose and black hood, while the Chaplain began to read a prayer. At 10:05 p.m., Major Christian faced about and cut the rope that released a weight and released the trap door. Wimberly dropped through the opening; his body swayed slightly, but there was no movement. At 10:15 p.m., Dr. Edward Sullivan moved to his position at the lower screened portion of the scaffold and made his examination. He made another examination at 10:20 p.m., but Wimberly still was not dead. At 10:29 p.m., Sullivan made a third inspection and pronounced Wimberly dead. The witnesses departed and by 10:31 p.m., Captain Walter B. Bradley had removed the body.

At 10:37 p.m., a second procession entered the death chamber. All the aforementioned personnel were present except that the condemned was General Prisoner Joseph Watson. However, a person dressed as a captain attempted to get in for this execution just before the procession arrived. Officials told him that unless he had permission from Major Christian he could not remain. The individual departed, his identity never revealed. The procedure, once the procession halted, was the same; when asked if he desired to make a statement, Watson said,

"Well, yes sir. I am glad to leave this world in the condition I'm in. I think I am fit to go. And I certainly appreciate your kindness."

Watson also thanked the Chaplain in his statement, which was,

"No more than to say I hope to meet you in heaven and you too [nodding toward the recorder]."

The Chaplain began to read a prayer. At 10:40 p.m., Major Christian again faced about and cut the rope, which resulted in the trap door being actuated. The doctor began his examination at 10:47 p.m. and pronounced death one minute later. Captain Bradley removed this body by 10:51 p.m. The Army buried the bodies of both men at the Solers American Military Cemetery Number 1 and reinterred them in 1949 at the American Military Cemetery at Oise-Aisne in Plot E. Joseph Watson is buried in Row 1, Grave 17; Willie Wimberly, Jr. is buried in Row 2, Grave 34.

Eight days after the execution, Lieutenant General George S. Patton ordered that a letter be sent to the rape victim. The dispatch ended with the following paragraph:

"The Commanding General wishes to express his sincere regret that the unfortunate incident occurred and that a member of the United States forces was guilty of such disgraceful conduct."[4]

*"The interests of society will not be served, nor will the ends of military justice be furthered, in the reviewer's opinion, by the extension of clemency in this case and hence no clemency is recommended."*

## 27 Technician Fifth Grade Richard B. Scott
38040012

229th Quartermaster
Salvage Collecting Company
**Assault and Rape**
Hanged on November 18, 1944

Richard Bunney Scott struck some people is a man who stretched the truth. He told a psychiatric board, for example, that his troubles in life were caused by his wife and her family because of their noted ability to cast "spells." He also told the board that at nights, just before he fell asleep, he would hear a voice calling his name. He told the alleged victims that he was from San Francisco, when it appears that he was from Texas. He gave a statement to an investigator, and then later said that this statement had been false; that statement had claimed that he had been invited by a husband to have sex with his pregnant wife on the floor of his house – which raised more than one eyebrow.

What can be established as true is that Richard B. Scott was born on August 23, 1916 in Carrolton, Texas and lived there all of his civilian life; he was inducted at Dallas, Texas on March 7, 1941. Scott stood 5'11" tall and weighed 161 pounds; he was black. A Baptist – before joining the Army, he was a cook, earning $12 per week. He was married in 1935. Two years later, police arrested him for drunkenness and he spent thirty days in jail. He claimed that he never knew his father, who had died in 1916 of pneumonia, and stated that his mother had been married several times. He also said that a car struck him in 1939, causing serious head injuries and two broken legs, which continued to give him problems.

The mix of officers for the GCM was typical: Lieutenant Colonel Paul H. Googe (TC), Lieutenant Colonel William C. Hollis (TC), Major George W. Seckinger (IN), Major Raymond J. Lamar (CE), Major Eugene T. Shields (QM) and Law Member, Captain Dean A. Van Deventer (QM), Captain Henry D. Bonneau (SC), and First Lieutenant Meade C. Harris, Jr. (CE.) Serving as the Trial Judge Advocate was First Lieutenant Vincent P. Clarke (TC); Second Lieutenant Joseph A. Bruggeman (QM) assisted him. For the defense, was Captain Jean E. Pierson (TC), First Lieutenant Joseph L. Weiser (CE).[1] First Lieutenant Harris, of the 354th Engineer (General Support) Regiment, was a substitution just a few days before the trial. Originally, Second Lieutenant Abraham Lincoln Byars (QM), 4089th QM Service Company, was slated to serve on the panel. The substitution came in Special Orders Number 22 of the Headquarters, Normandy Base Section; it stated that the order came from Colonel Benjamin B. Talley, acting commander of the base section. First Lieutenant Harris was black and perhaps Colonel Talley was attempting to follow the Theater Commander's policy on minority officers on serious courts-martial.

The GCM came to order at 10:00 a.m. on September 7, 1944 at Cherbourg. The charges were one count of carnal knowledge, a violation of the 92nd Article of War, one count of assault with a bayonet, a violation of the 93rd Article of War and one count of threatening assault with a bayonet, also a violation of the 93rd Article of War.[2] Technician Fifth Class Scott pleaded not guilty to all charges and specifications. Both the prosecution and defense stipulated that Scott's company commander, Captain Joseph Emery Jr. (QM) would testify that the accused's service was satisfactory. The crux of the defense was that Scott had consensual sex with the victim and never threatened the two men. The rape victim, who at the time had three small children – and who was pregnant with her fourth child – testified the sex had not been consensual and the two Frenchmen testified they had been threatened and in one case jabbed with a bayonet. The events had occurred at 10:30 p.m. on July 20, 1944 at the home of the victims at "78 Rue Sadi-Carnot" in the town of Octeville – adjacent to Cherbourg. Private Scott had worked the day before and had the day off.

Scott took the stand in the trial, after being advised of his rights again. He stated the sex was consensual and that he did not have a bayonet with him that night. A later review would state that it had been somewhat difficult to visualize the events of the evening from the testimony of all concerned, but that the court could have observed the demeanor of the witnesses and "estimate their veracity." That review also summarized:

> "The story of the accused, that the husband of a pregnant woman would, after trying to prevent the accused from sleeping on a table, or on the floor, invite him to have intercourse with his wife on the floor and in his presence, is too incredible for belief."

86

The panel found Technician Fifth Class Richard Scott guilty of all charges and specifications and sentenced him to be hanged. Scott felt he did not have a fair trial; the three French witnesses had perjured themselves – according to him – and the aforementioned bayonet was not produced as evidence at trial. Captain Walter E. Schroeder in the Staff Judge Advocate Section of the Normandy Base Section, Communications Zone, reviewed the case on September 20, and found that everything was legally sufficient. Commenting on the veracity of Scott, Captain Schroeder opined:

"Accused is not a sincere, convincing witness for himself under the best of circumstances and that his story was disbelieved by the court."

Schroder continued concerning any possible clemency for the convicted:

"The interests of society will not be served, nor will the ends of military justice be furthered, in the reviewer's opinion, by the extension of clemency in this case and hence no clemency is recommended."

Colonel Benjamin B. Talley, Commander Normandy Base Section, approved the findings. October 20, 1944, General Dwight Eisenhower signed an order confirming the sentence. Judge Advocates Franklin Riter, Ellwood W. Sargent and Edward L. Stevens, Jr. of the Branch Office of The JAG with the ETO signed off as reviewing the case on November 4, 1944 and finding no significant irregularities. The record of trial was legally sufficient to support the findings of guilty and the sentence. Brigadier General Edwin C. McNeil added an enclosure for General Eisenhower. It stated that while the court had denied a defense motion that the accused be examined by medical authorities, and although that was a legal decision:

"However, as this question was raised during the trial, your attention is invited to the matter for whatever action you may deem desirable, prior to execution of the sentence."

Eisenhower was way ahead of the Brigadier and directed a board of officers at the 289th General Hospital examine Richard Scott on October 27, 1944. Because of a lack of civilian records available to the board, their information could only be derived by talking with the accused, but their findings included:

- The patient's family background was chaotic
- He was the only boy in his mother's first marriage
- His mother married twice more, both marriages ended in divorce
- The patient was enuretic until age thirteen
- The patient attended school through the sixth grade
- At age eighteen, he married a girl "out of pity" as she was pregnant by another man
- His wife was frequently unfaithful and would occasionally come home drunk
- He was court-martialed once for AWOL
- He was treated in 1941 at an Army hospital for gonorrhea
- Neurological tests were normal
- Psychometric tests indicate a mental level of a six year old

The board said there was no evidence that he could not distinguish right from wrong. The evaluation included this conclusion:

"The patient is of a very primitive, immature type of negro who has a large mass of superstitious beliefs."

General Court-Martial Orders Number 106, dated November 15, 1944, designated that General Prisoner Scott would be hanged in three days' time at Cherbourg, France. The weather was fair on the morning of November 18, 1944. Carpenters had erected a gallows in a flat area immediately behind the buildings at Fort Du Roule. The eight official witnesses stood in order of rank from right to left on the east side of the scaffold; they were at a distance of about twenty-two feet. All were commissioned officers, ranking from lieutenant colonel to second lieutenant. Fourteen authorized spectators formed on the south side of the gallows at a distance of thirty feet. Eight were French citizens, of whom one was a woman and another was the husband of the rape victim. His wife was not present.

Twenty men from the 707th MP Battalion guarded the area around the site of the execution. Captain William E. Boyden commanded the detail with assistance from First Lieutenant Cecil N. Hughes. A command car brought the condemned and guards, Sergeant Earl F. Mendenhall and Sergeant Richard Mosley, to ninety yards from the gallows. The three men exited the vehicle and joined a small military procession. Leading the column was Major Mortimer H. Christian; Captain Melvin C. Swann, of the African Methodist Episcopal

Church and one of the Army's few black Chaplains, immediately followed him. The condemned walked next, flanked on either side were the guards. At the rear of the column, marched Captain Julius C. Rivellese of the Medical Corps; he was a surgeon and would determine when the prisoner was deceased. The procession started at 10:01 a.m.

The march concluded quickly. The procession reached the scaffold; the guards bound the prisoner's hands behind him and assisted him to climb the steps; the Commandant asked Scott if he had a last statement to make – he didn't; the guards placed the prisoner on the trap door and bound his ankles; the Chaplain asked if Scott had any last statement – he did and said, "I know my soul is going to heaven; my trust is in the Lord."

The guards adjusted the noose and black hood; the Chaplain started to pray aloud; and the Commandant faced about to cut the rope. Scott dropped through the trap door without fanfare at 10:04 a.m. Everyone remained silent except the Chaplain, who continued praying another minute and two French civilians, who began conversing. After eleven more minutes, Christian directed the Surgeon to enter the lower screened-in portion of the gallows; Captain Rivellese confirmed that General Prisoner Scott had died at 10:17 a.m. on November 18, 1944: "The cause of death was Judicial Asphyxia (execution by hanging.)"

First Lieutenant Harold A. Myers took custody of the body. The 3050th Graves Registration Section initially buried Richard B. Scott at the U.S. Military Cemetery at Marigny in Plot Z, Grave 1-2. On November 20, 1944, the *New York Times* reported that the execution took place, but did not name the condemned man. The Army reinterred the remains in 1949 in the American Military Cemetery at Oise-Aisne; it is located in Plot E, Row 2 and Grave 45.[3]

• • •

The execution took place in what today is a small French military installation atop Fort Du Roule that overlooks the port and city of Cherbourg. The base is closed to public access, surrounded by a high, barbed-wire fence. Although it was not possible for the author to gain access to the site in 2011, it was evident from the surroundings that the scaffold stood at a point overlooking the city of Cherbourg and the magnificent blue water of the Atlantic Ocean as it stretched westward toward a homeland that Richard Scott would never see again.

*"Accused is in no way particularly impressive, either for vigor or weakness. He appears to be a slum product, conditioned adversely by environment and associates toward a life of crime."*

*"Take the ring off my finger, Chaplain, please. Send it home to my wife."*

| 28 | Private William D. Pennyfeather |
|---|---|

32801627

3868th Quartermaster Truck Company

**Rape**

Hanged on November 18, 1944

The citizens of Cherbourg must have thought that the "beloved" German *Wehrmacht* was back in town for a return engagement. First, Richard Scott raped a woman on July 20, 1944; then on August 1, Private William D. Pennyfeather was alleged to have raped a Frenchwoman in the same city. About midnight on the latter date, according to witnesses, "four colored soldiers" knocked on the outside door of a small apartment building and yelled, "Is there any girls?"

When a Frenchman opened a window to see what the disturbance was, the troopers motioned for him to come down. As he and two other residents of the building got to the door, the American soldiers burst through the entrance; they were armed with knives. Holding a knife to the Frenchman's chest, the soldiers stated that there were Germans in the building and ordered the Frenchmen to go upstairs. The soldiers followed closely behind. After they got to the third floor, the troopers went into one apartment, where Private Pennyfeather allegedly exposed himself to a woman and tried to rape her; his comrades stopped him. Pennyfeather then went to a second apartment and began struggling with another woman, biting her on the cheek; this time his two buddies stood guard with their knives. Perhaps Pennyfeather had forgotten the "Sex Morality Lecture" he had received in August 1943 or the "Sex Morality Course" he had attended earlier the same day as the offense.

However, as in the Watson/Wimberly case, the "cavalry" was on the way. Just after 11:00 p.m., Corporal Donald L. Sharshel and Private Arthur J. Thomas, both Military Policemen, observed "two colored soldiers" standing in front of the apartment building, trying to hide behind two Frenchmen. The MPs asked them some questions and the pair replied that they were waiting for a buddy. The MPs ordered them to return to their units, as it was after curfew; the MPs then went upstairs and found the rape in progress.

When one MP attempted to remove Pennyfeather, he replied, "I'm getting myself some pussy."

The next day Pennyfeather made a statement at the Criminal Investigation Division office at Cherbourg, after being advised of his rights. He stated that the sex was consensual, but his statement belied that: "She struggled a bit, but I held her down and had intercourse with her."

This statement, the observations of the two MPs and the accounts of the victim and several Frenchmen were enough for the Colonel Theodore Wyman, Jr., who was acting commander of the Normandy Base Section in addition to holding his regular position of the Cherbourg Base Commander, to appoint a GCM. The court members were the same as in the Scott case.[1] Again, First Lieutenant Meade C. Harris was a substitution for Second Lieutenant Abraham Lincoln Byars. The court met at 8:40 a.m. on September 2, 1944 at Cherbourg. Pennyfeather faced one charge and one specification: carnal knowledge, a violation of the 92nd Article of War.[2] He pleaded not guilty. The prosecution also presented evidence of a previous conviction by a Special Court-Martial in December 1943 for escape from restriction, breach of restriction, entering a restricted area and absence without leave for a period of four days. For this, he had served six months hard labor. Pennyfeather also had a previous court-martial conviction in September 1943 for AWOL. The jury unanimously voted to convict and voted for the death penalty; it was 3:20 p.m.

Captain Walter E. Schroeder in the Staff Judge Advocate Section of the Normandy Base Section, Communications' Zone, reviewed the case on September 14, and found that everything was legally sufficient. It appears that he also interviewed Pennyfeather, who had been inducted in New York City on February 11, 1943 – and was trained as a jackhammer operator – and found the following biographical information:

- Pennyfeather was born in New York on July 21, 1920
- He stood 5'7" tall and weighed 152 pounds
- His father died in 1943; he never knew his mother
- He was raised by his grandmother
- He attended school through the seventh grade

- He was arrested for felonious assault in 1937 but the charge was dismissed
- In 1938 he committed a strong-arm robbery (including assaulting the victim with his fists) and was sentenced to 1-30 years' incarceration
- He served twenty-one months in the Elmira Reformatory before being released
- He violated parole and served another year at Elmira; released on October 6, 1942
- His occupation was a rug cleaner, a job in which he made $16 a week
- He was married on July 20, 1943
- His unit arrived in Scotland on October 7, 1943

During the interview, Pennyfeather stated that he had received a fair trial and that he was satisfied with the Defense Counsel. Commenting in general on the condemned, Captain Schroeder opined:

"Accused is in no way particularly impressive, either for vigor or weakness. He appears to be a slum product, conditioned adversely by environment and associates toward a life of crime."

Schroder continued concerning any possible clemency for the convicted:

"There is nothing in this case, in the reviewer's opinion, which indicates that society or the interests of military justice and discipline would benefit by the extension of clemency in this case, and hence no clemency is recommended."

Schroder was not understating Pennyfeather's performance. Throughout his service, Pennyfeather displayed a "poor" character and "unsatisfactory" performance of duty; he also failed to qualify with his rifle in 1943.

Colonel B.B. Talley, now in command of the Normandy Base Section, approved the sentence and forwarded the trial record. On October 4, 1944, General Dwight Eisenhower signed an order confirming the sentence. Judge Advocates Franklin Riter, Ellwood W. Sargent and Edward L. Stevens, Jr., Branch Office of The JAG with the ETO, reviewed the case on November 4, 1944, finding no significant irregularities. General Court-Martial Orders Number 103, dated November 15, 1944, designated that William D. Pennyfeather would be hanged at Fort du Roule in Cherbourg on November 18, 1944.

A command car brought the condemned and his guards, Sergeant Earl F. Mendenhall and Sergeant Richard Mosley to a spot approximately ninety yards from the scaffold at 10:29 a.m. (twelve minutes after Scott had died.) The three men exited the vehicle and joined a small formation. Other than the condemned, all participants had been at Richard Scott's execution. Leading the procession was Major Mortimer H. Christian, followed by Chaplain Melvin C. Swann. The condemned walked next; a guard flanked him on either side. At the rear of the column marched Captain Julius C. Rivellese (MC.) The procession started at 10:30 a.m. As spectators were seven French civilians, including the rape victim. The group reached the gallows; the guards bound the prisoner's hands behind him and assisted him to climb the steps; Christian asked Pennyfeather if he had a last statement to make. The prisoner replied, "The Lord is with me; that's about all." The guards placed the prisoner on the trap door and bound his ankles; the Chaplain asked if Pennyfeather had any last statement; he did and said, "Take the ring off my finger, Chaplain, please. Send it home to my wife."

The Chaplain reached around to comply with this request, but could not get the ring off Pennyfeather's finger. The Commandant assured the condemned that the Chaplain would later take care of the ring. The guards adjusted the noose and black hood; the Chaplain started to pray aloud; and Christian faced about to cut the rope at 10:33 a.m. Pennyfeather dropped through the trap door without flourish. All was silent, except for the Chaplain, who continued praying until 10:34 a.m. At 10:48 a.m., the Commandant directed the Surgeon to enter the lower screened-in portion of the scaffold; "Doc" Rivellese reported that Pennyfeather was dead.

First Lieutenant Harold A. Myers (Graves Registration Section) took custody of the body and buried William D. Pennyfeather at the U.S. Military Cemetery at Marigny in Plot Z, Grave 1-3. On November 20, 1944, the *New York Times* reported that the execution took place, but did not give the name of the condemned man. The Army reinterred his remains in 1949 at the American Military Cemetery at Oise-Aisne in Plot E; it lies in Row 3, Grave 66.[3]

*"Maxie, don't do this. Don't do the woman like that."*

*"She made a mistake. I didn't rape nobody."*

## 29    Private Curtis L. Maxey
34554198
3277th Quartermaster Service Company
**Rape**
Hanged on November 18, 1944

When Private Curtis L. Maxey and Private L.B. Hollingsworth of the 3277th Quartermaster Service Company came ashore on the southern coast of France with the invading Seventh U.S. Army as part of "Operation Dragoon," they were not contemplating liberating Europe from Nazi tyranny; for them there would be no "Crusade in Europe." The pair had much less lofty aspirations in mind and within hours of setting foot on French soil, they had terrorized several French civilians and raped a French woman.

The facts of the case were all too familiar. Two soldiers left their unit without permission. Their platoon had landed on "Yellow Beach" not far from Saint Tropez, France at 11:00 a.m. on August 15, 1944. By 5:00 p.m., the two troopers appeared at a farm and requested some wine. They began drinking, but only stayed for ten minutes. At 10:00 p.m., they returned to the house, firing their rifles; they then entered the dwelling. According to the Frenchman and his wife who lived there, the two soldiers began searching through the house. The couple had an infant child; another woman also lived in the house. Then events turned ugly; Private Curtis Maxey, age twenty-two, grabbed the woman by the arm and dragged her outside. She screamed and her husband charged Maxey, who then struck the farmer on the shoulder with the butt of his rifle. Hollingsworth kept his rifle pointing at the Frenchman, while Maxey raped the woman.

The woman then ran back into the house, which distracted Hollingsworth; the farmer pushed his wife inside, closed and bolted the door and carried his wife upstairs. The two soldiers remained outside for thirty minutes, firing their weapons. Then they departed; at 11:00 p.m., the two soldiers appeared at a small château about three-hundred yards away. They entered and asked for wine. The owner led them to a small house adjacent to the château, where other American soldiers were sleeping. Later, Maxey told one of them that he had sex with a woman earlier in the night. After dawn, the men returned to their company at 8:30 a.m.

The farmer reported the incidents to authorities and investigators found that Maxey and Hollingsworth had been missing from their company during the time when the crimes were committed. MPs organized a lineup of six "colored" soldiers, each wearing a helmet or helmet liner. The French couple identified Maxey and Hollingsworth from the row of men. They also stated that Maxey had worn unusual gold rings and those rings were later found on the soldier. They also recounted, as did the third adult at the farm, that when the two soldiers first came in the house, Maxey showed them some photographs of his family; the MPs found the photographs in Maxey's wallet and the French woman identified them. On August 21, 1944, Criminal Investigation Division agents interviewed Private Hollingsworth, who spilled the beans. He stated that Maxey had shot his rifle at the house and that Maxey had raped the woman. He emphasized that he tried to stop Maxey, but that Maxey cut him by hitting him with his weapon. He also described said that Maxey had an MP insignia on him during the night in question and was trying to pretend that he was an MP. Hollingsworth stated of his cohort, "He told me he was going to get this woman or else." Hollingsworth also said he told the other man, "Maxie, don't do this. Don't do the woman like that. These people ain't bothering us none."

One of the agents examined Hollingsworth's rifle and concluded that it had not been recently fired. The agents also interview Private Maxey. He denied everything: he didn't drink alcohol; he didn't go to the farm; he had never seen the French farmer before; he didn't fire his rifle; that the other soldiers at the château were not "colored" but were white soldiers "drinking gin or something."

On August 22, 1944, Captain Alfred O. Ludwig, a psychiatric consultant, examined the two accused. He found Hollingsworth to be illiterate. Curtis Maxey had been born in Deatsville, Alabama on June 16, 1922. He was inducted at Fort Benning, Georgia on November 9, 1942. Concerning Maxey, Ludwig wrote:

"He appeared to have average intelligence. There was no evidence of neuro-psychiatric disease. This man knows the difference between right and wrong, and must be considered to be fully responsible for his acts both at the present time, and to have been so at the time of the commission of the alleged offense."

A GCM met at St. Tropez, France on September 4, 1944. The two defendants were tried jointly, based on the nature of the crime.[1] The witnesses testified for the prosecution. Private Maxey elected to remain silent and not take the stand. Hollingsworth elected to make an unsworn statement. The Law Member directed that the statement could only be used concerning the accused Hollingsworth. However, Hollingsworth's initial statement to the CID was admitted as Exhibit K, and there does not appear to be any instructions limiting its use. Hollingsworth's lieutenant testified that the soldier was of good character. The panel found Private Hollingsworth guilty of rape and sentenced him to a dishonorable discharge and life imprisonment to be served at the U.S. Penitentiary at Lewisburg, Pennsylvania. They found Private Curtis Maxey guilty of carnal knowledge, a violation of the 92nd Article of War. The court then sentenced Curtis L. Maxey to death by hanging.[2]

Seventh Army legal officials reviewed the trial transcripts on September 14, 1944 and found no significant errors. Lieutenant General Alexander M. Patch, Commander Seventh Army, approved the finding of guilt and the sentence of death. Lieutenant General Jacob L. Devers, the Commanding General, NATO, signed the order confirming the death sentence on October 17, 1944. A Board of Review by the Branch Office of The JAG with the NATO reviewed the case as well. They found on October 31, 1944 that the trial had no major errors.

The Army hanged Private Curtis L. Maxey at the Peninsular Base Section Stockade Number 1 near Aversa, Italy on November 18, 1944 and buried him at the U.S. Military Cemetery in Naples, in the General Prisoner Plot (Grave 1-7.) In 1949, officials reinterred the remains at the American Military Cemetery at Oise-Aisne in Plot E, where they lay in Row 3, Grave 71.[3]

*"About a week later I stole a car and got sentenced to from 1-10 years in San Quentin, suspended, and 6 months in the county jail and 3 years' probation ... I stole another car and got 1-10 years in San Quentin, suspended, and 10 months in county jail."*

## 30  Private Theron W. McGann

39332102

Company A,
    32nd Signal Construction Battalion
**Rape**
Hanged on November 20, 1944

After the war, interviews with Army prison officials indicated that many offenders in the ETO had criminal records in civilian life. Some had been guilty of robbery, larceny, burglary and other felonies; most of the officers believed that such personnel had been of little value to the service. In fact, according to one study, some 4,441 men went directly from American penal institutions into military service in World War II.[1] However, the problem went much deeper. During its initial screen of personnel for induction into the service, one out of every eight young men was excused "for reasons other than physical." According to author William B. Huie:[2]

"These were not the boys with bad hearts, bad eyes, or bad feet, but the boys with bad minds: their number was 1,532,500 – the temperamentally unstable, the maladjusted, the sexually perverted, and the overly nervous."

As the war went on, "Uncle Sam" gave these "maladjusted" a second look, and as losses rose, inducted many, including Private Theron W. McGann. The white soldier, assigned to Company A in the 32nd Signal Construction Battalion of the First Army, entered the home of two French women and raped one, while threatening both women with a pistol, on August 5, 1944 at Quibou, France. While he was not one of those felons, who went directly from prison to platoon, he was characteristic of those personnel with prior significant criminal records who had been of little value to the Army – one of the "bad minds."

Born in Portland, Oregon on June 25, 1921, McGann had two previous Summary Court-Martial convictions; one was for being absent without leave, while the second was for loitering on his post. He previously served in the 162nd Infantry Regiment of the Oregon National Guard, but a civil court conviction led to a discharge. Married, he was inducted into the Army on May 21, 1943 at Portland.

McGann was twenty-three-years-old, married, had finished eighth grade and was employed as an electrician and a truck driver, making $20 per week. Standing 5'9" tall and weighing 141 pounds, he had an Army General Classification Test score of 118, which made him a Class II. While he might have had a high IQ, McGann was known as a prevaricator in his unit. His character of service prior to the offense was listed as unsatisfactory, but a doctor had classified him as "constitutional psychopathic."

The two women made a complaint to American authorities the day after the incident. He was apprehended on August 7, 1944. On August 8, 1944, Private McGann signed a statement confessing that he had sex with the victim; the investigation finished on August 11, 1944. On August 16, 1944, the Commander, First Army, referred the charges for trial by GCM, which tried McGann on August 28, 1944 at Fougerolles du Plessis, France. It convened at 1:35 p.m. The charge was carnal knowledge, a violation of the 92nd Article of War.[3] McGann pleaded not guilty.[4] He did not take the stand; the defense challenged no jurors and offered no evidence on his behalf. The French women positively identified him as the brown-haired, blue-eyed American who raped her and his previous statement came in as evidence. The panel found him guilty of rape and sentenced him, "To be hanged by the neck until dead." The time was 4:00 p.m., 145 minutes after the opening gavel.

On September 19, 1944, the accused wrote a letter to review authorities. In it, he made several informative statements. He admitted the crime:

"On August 5, 1944, I did commit the crime of rape, and I pleaded guilty to it at my court-martial. I did not take the stand, as I didn't think it would help me any, as all I could say would tend to incriminate me more."

McGann also explained his checkered past:

"I soon left home and went to California, Los Angeles, to work for an Uncle. I didn't like the work so I quit. About a week later I stole a car and got sentenced to from 1-10 years in San Quentin, suspended, and 6 months in the county jail and 3 years' probation ... I went to work for my stepfather for a couple of years, then joined the National Guard, Headquarters

Company, 162nd Infantry, Captain Hook, Commanding Officer. After about 6 months, I went AWOL to California. I stole another car and got 1-10 years in San Quentin, suspended, and 10 months in county jail."

Toward the end of the letter, Private McGann mentioned his fondness for drink:

"All the time I have been in the Army, from May 21, 1943 to the time I was incarcerated I was always looking for something to drink."

The case was reviewed by the First Army Staff Judge Advocate, Colonel Ernest M. Brannon, on September 21, 1944; Brannon found no reversible errors. Lieutenant General Courtney H. Hodges approved the sentence on September 25, 1944 and forwarded the record of trial to the ETO. On October 26, 1944, the Staff Judge Advocate at the Headquarters, ETO reviewed the case. Brigadier General Edward C. Betts found no errors in the trial and recommended that no clemency be shown to the defendant. General Dwight Eisenhower signed the order confirming the sentence on October 27, 1944. On November 7, 1944, the Board of Review Number 1 of the Branch Office of The JAG with the ETO reviewed the case. Judge Advocates Riter, Sergeant and Stevens found no serious errors with the case. On November 15, 1944, the ETO published General Court-Martial Orders Number 104. Brigadier General R.B. Lord – by command of General Eisenhower – directed that the execution occur on November 20, 1944 under the direction of the Commanding Officer, Seine DTC. This officer signed for Private McGann at Mortier Caserne on November 15, 1944 and had him transferred to St. Lô.

The weather on November 20, 1944 in Saint Lô, France was cloudy with intermittent light rain. The Commandant, Seine DTC, Major Mortimer H. Christian had selected a location for the execution in a courtyard off the main highway in the northern section of the city. The building adjacent to the gallows revealed that it had been heavily bombed or shelled and only the walls were left standing; it was a grim tableau. A high hedge screened the northern side of the gallows; a stonewall enclosed the area at the rear. Ten officers stood as official witnesses for the execution, eighteen feet from the gallows. Twenty-eight authorized spectators were present as well, including eleven officers, seven enlisted men and ten French officials. Eight soldiers from Company B of the 793rd MP Battalion guarded the roads to the place of execution to prevent unauthorized spectators. At 9:59 a.m., a command car eased down the main highway to the entrance to the driveway. General Prisoner Theron W. McGann dismounted with his two guards, Sergeant Earl F. Mendenhall and Sergeant Richard Mosley. Major Christian formed the official party into a column and began marching to the gallows. Captain Anthony R. Feeherry, the Catholic Chaplain, followed him – then walked the condemned and the two guards. Following that trio was Captain Julius C. Rivellese, a medical officer. Captain Albert M. Summerfield, the recorder, joined the procession along the route.

At 10:00 p.m., the formation reached the bottom of the scaffold steps; the guards bound McGann's hands behind him and assisted him up the steps. While the condemned stood on the trap door and the guards bound his ankles, the Commandant asked if he had any last words. The condemned replied that he did not. The Chaplain then asked the prisoner if he had any last statements and McGann replied, "Pray for my soul." The Chaplain then began to pray the last rights at 10:02 a.m. and, after the black hood and noose were adjusted, the Commandant faced about at 10:03 a.m. and cut the rope, which released the weight that actuated the trap door. At 10:16 a.m., Captain Rivellese and Captain Summerfield entered the lower screened portion of the gallows to examine the prisoner. One minute later, Captain Summerfield announced, "I pronounce …" At that precise instant, the wall of the bombed-out building to the south of the gallows began to collapse. Spectators shouted a warning and all personnel scurried to avoid the falling debris. The Surgeon composed himself and announced, "I pronounce this man dead."

Major Christian dismissed the official witnesses and spectators. The assistants (possibly Master Sergeant John Woods) cut the rope, lowered the body to the ground under the gallows, removed the hood and unbound the deceased's hands. The Chaplain entered the area and performed the last rites. First Lieutenant Louis B. Weiss of the 3047th Quartermaster Graves Registration Company signed for the remains. The Army temporarily interred McGann at the U.S. Military Cemetery at Marigny, France in Plot Z in Grave 1-4 at 9:00 a.m. on November 21, 1944. An embossed identification tag accompanied the body; above the grave was a small white cross; to McGann's left was Private William Pennyfeather. After the war, the McGann family arranged for his remains to be transferred to Oregon.

On December 8, 1944, the First U.S. Army sent a letter to the chief of police at Quibou informing him that the offender had been hanged by the neck until dead and that the Commanding General expressed his regret that the offense was committed in the Quibou community, with the hope that such offenses would not recur in the future.[5]

• • •

According to Professor J. Robert Lilly, "Military Executions," in Clifton D. Bryant's *Handbook of Death and Dying*, Sergeant Emmett N. Bailey, Jr. observed the proceedings and recalled the fall of the wall. Sergeant Bailey also recalled that the rape victim attended the hanging, although the report of execution does not mention her presence. Professor Lilly also wrote that on December 11, 1944 the First U.S. Army wrote a letter of regret to the victim.

## 31 Private Arthur Eddie Davis
36788637

3326th Quartermaster Truck Company
**Assault and Rape**
Hanged on November 22, 1944

## 32                 Private Charles Henry Jordan
14066430

3327th Quartermaster Truck Company
**Assault and Rape**
Hanged on November 22, 1944

It was all about speed in Lieutenant General George S. Patton's Third Army. No plodding offensives for that outfit; get around the German's flank, make a dash for the vulnerable enemy logistical rear area and the Nazi front would collapse. The same need for speed was apparent in Third Army judicial proceedings; if there had been a "rocket docket" in World War II, it would have been "Georgie's" guys. Just ask Charles H. Jordan and Arthur E. Davis; from when they committed an assault and a rape until the time they appeared before a GCM was a scant six days.

The offense occurred on August 10, 1944 at La Rouennerie en Montour, France. The rape victim would later testify that at 6:30 p.m. two soldiers came to her farm, asking for cognac, but departed after none was found. Two hours later, they returned, demanding cognac and young unmarried girls. When told that none was available, the soldiers fired a rifle over her husband's head. The woman produced some cognac at which point the soldiers grabbed her. Her husband, meanwhile, fled and returned with a male neighbor. One of the soldiers began firing at both men, who escaped to call police. The two soldiers took the victim to a field two-hundred yards away, where both soldiers repeatedly raped her for two hours. Military Police arrested the two soldiers shortly thereafter in the vicinity of the farm. The MPs determined that both weapons recently had been fired; one weapon had no magazine – both soldiers denied that they had recently fired their weapons. Both had been drinking; one had a dead rabbit; one had his pants open at the fly.

The next day, one of the Frenchmen, who had been fired on, identified the two soldiers. A medical officer confirmed that the victim had been raped and had abrasions and cuts on her legs. Officials preferred charges against the pair on August 13;

the same day the investigating officer completed his work and Lieutenant General Patton made the decision that evening to convene a GCM. It was an easy decision for Patton. The general had been worried a long time about soldiers. In 1940, in a tent in Louisiana, a pensive Patton shared his thoughts on the war he knew would come to the country:[1]

"I'm worried because I'm not sure this country can field a fighting army at this stage in our history. We've pampered and confused our youth. We've talked too much about rights and not enough about duties. Now we've got to try and make them attack and kill. A big percentage of our men won't be worth a goddam to us. Many a brave soldier will lose his life unnecessarily because the man next to him turns yellow. We're going to have to dig down deep to find our hard core of scrappers. That takes time and time is short."

The GCM convened at 1:15 p.m. on August 16, 1944 at Poilley, France; the defense made no motion to sever the trials to try each man separately.[2] Both men pleaded not guilty to carnal knowledge, a violation of the 92nd Article of War, attempted murder, a violation of the 93rd Article of War and assault, a violation of the 96th Article of War.[3]

Both soldiers were black. Arthur Davis had been inducted on November 8, 1943 in Chicago, Illinois; he had been born in Cleveland, Ohio on August 8, 1919. Davis finished eighth grade; he stood 5'7½" tall and weighed 132 pounds. After moving to the south side of Chicago, he drove a bread delivery truck, making $35/week. Davis was separated and had a daughter. He contracted gonorrhea in 1936 and 1937 and suffered from hemorrhoids. Davis had no known court-martial convictions. Charles Jordan was born in Monticello, Georgia on October 9, 1920. Also known as Charlie Wilson, he finished two years of high school, before becoming an egg truck driver, making $15 a week. His first bout with gonorrhea occurred in 1940. Later an elevator operator, Jordan was married in 1939 and had two sons and a daughter. He enlisted on January 6, 1942 at Fort McPherson, Georgia. Assigned to Camp Croft, South Carolina the following month, he again contracted gonorrhea and syphilis. He developed a third case of the disease at Fort Benning, Georgia on May 25, 1942. Jordan stood 5'9" and weighed 150 pounds. He had a Summary Court-Martial conviction for AWOL and another Summary Court-Martial conviction for Breach of Restriction. He also had a Special Court-Martial conviction for taking and using a lieutenant's vehicle and for Breach of Restriction. Lastly, he had a Summary Court-Martial conviction for Breach of Restriction, using an unauthorized alias and unlawfully carrying a concealed weapon. His chain of command rated his character and efficiency as satisfactory. Jordan fractured his right hand on December 19, 1943, after falling out of a barracks window as he was attempting to wash it. He broke his leg in March 1944.

The defendants elected to remain silent at the trial. Defense counsels introduced no evidence on their behalf. The court admitted statements they had previously made; the victims identified the defendants as the two perpetrators. The rape victim identified unique identification bracelets that each man wore; she also mentioned seeing the rabbit, when she was talking to the men. Both men had been carrying M1 carbines; during the incident, a magazine fell from one of the weapons. The next day the victim's son located it at the scene of the crime; prosecutors introduced the magazine into evidence. The jury found both soldiers guilty of all three charges, although the court struck attempted murder from the charge, due to doubt concerning intent. The court unanimously voted to sentence both men to hang. The court adjourned at 6:30 p.m. The witnesses each received one-hundred *francs* for attending the trial.

The Third Army Staff Judge Advocate, Colonel Charles E. Cheever, reviewed the case with his assistant on August 11, 1944. They found no issues that adversely affected the rights of the accused. On September 23, 1944, Brigadier General Betts signed off on a review of the case by his own staff. He agreed that the record of trial was sufficient to support the verdict and sentence. Betts felt the need to comment on the speediness of the trial:

"The charges were served on the accused at 2100 on 13 August 1944 and the trial was held at 1315 on 16 August, less than five days later. While this was contrary to the policy of the JAG, no military necessity having been affirmatively shown, it appears that there has been substantial compliance in that ample opportunity was afforded for the preparation of their defense."

Addressing clemency, the review stated:

"There was no recommendation for clemency in this case, and none is here recommended in view of the brutality of the attack made upon a defenseless Frenchwoman who, aided by her husband and a neighbor, made every effort to resist."

General Dwight Eisenhower signed the order confirming the death sentences of Private Arthur E. Davis and Private Charles H. Jordan. The Board of Review Number 2 of the Branch Office of The JAG with the ETO reviewed the case on November 2, 1944. Judge Advocates Van Benschoten, Hill and Sleeper reviewed the trial records and found the record was legally sufficient to support the findings of guilty and the sentence. The ETO published General Court-Martial Orders Number 105 on November 15, 1944. By command of General Eisenhower, Brigadier General R.B. Lord directed that the Commanding Officer, Seine DTC carry the sentence into execution on November 22, 1944 at Montours, Ille-et-Vilaine, France.

It was. It is likely that under the direction of Major Mortimer A. Christian, the Army executed General Prisoner Jordan about 10:04 a.m. Fragmentary execution records indicate that General Prisoner Davis climbed the steps of the gallows and Sergeant Mendenhall and Sergeant Mosley guided him to the trap door at 10:31 a.m. One minute later, the Chaplain began to pray and at 10:33 a.m., the executioner – possibly Master Sergeant John C. Woods, actuated the trap door. At 10:45 a.m., Captain Carroll T. Adriance, a medical officer, examined the body; one minute later, he pronounced Arthur Davis dead. The executioner cut the body down at 10:48 a.m. and graves registration personnel removed it from the area by two minutes later. Twenty-four U.S. military personnel and ten French *Gendarmes* attended the executions as witnesses; five French civilians also attended. Captain Poole Rogers, 610th QM Graves Registration Company, signed for both bodies.

The Army interred both men's remains at the U.S. Military Cemetery at Marigny in Plot Z (in Graves 1-5 and 1-6) at 9:00 a.m. on November 24, 1944. In 1949, officials transferred both to the American Military Cemetery at Oise-Aisne to rest in Plot E. Arthur E. Davis is located in Row 4, Grave 82. Charles H. Jordan's remains are in Row 2, Grave 40.[4]

The mother of Charles Jordan requested that her son's remains be returned to the United States; they were not. A sister continued to write the Army until 1983 to request the life insurance money for her brother's death. It does not appear to have ever been paid, according to the regulations concerning the policy.

• • •

The author visited Montours, France in 2011 in preparation for this study. A man, who had lived in the village during the war, took the author to the area next to the village church, where the executions took place.

> *"This case was well tried. The evidence for the prosecution was ably presented by the Trial Judge Advocate and accused was capably represented by Defense Counsel."*

## 33 Private First Class James E. Hendricks

33453189
3326th Quartermaster Truck Company
**Breaking and Entering,
Attempted Rape and Murder**
Hanged on November 24, 1944

Some men seemed to have been born under an evil star. Private First Class James E. Hendricks certainly fit that bill. His mother died during his birth in Drewry, North Carolina on April 29, 1923. Nicknamed "Jack," he had a tough early life; many remembered that he had "violent temper tantrums." After finishing ninth grade, Hendricks went to Washington, DC looking for work; he got a job with the Government Printing Office. Hendricks faked an illness to avoid the draft, but the Army finally drafted him in February 1943; he was inducted at Fort Meyer, Virginia and soon reported to Camp Van Dorn, Mississippi. Assigned to the 272nd Quartermaster Battalion, he was 5'7½" tall, weighed 140 pounds and had two bouts of gonorrhea.

At 10:00 p.m. on August 21, 1944, a black soldier wearing a helmet and raincoat and carrying a rifle went to a home in Plumaudan, France and asked for a mademoiselle. He followed the French woman there around tried and to kiss her. To get rid of him, the family gave him two chicken eggs. The soldier crossed the road to the home of Victor Bignon. When no one answered, he fired a shot through the door, which brought Victor and his wife Noémie to the inside of the door, where they held it shut. The soldier fired a second shot through the door that fatally wounded Victor in the head; Noémie was injured. The soldier entered the home and grabbed the Bignon's eighteen-year-old daughter. The soldier and the three surviving members of the Bignon family then walked across the street to the Bouton home. In this residence, the soldier attempted to rape a woman but was unsuccessful.

First Lieutenant Donald Tucker, a black officer in command of Hendricks' unit, heard the shots. Assembling a detail, he went down the road a quarter of a mile to a farmhouse with the lights on. Nearby, Tucker and his men heard a noise. Out of a hedge, ten yards from the Bignon home, stepped Private First Class James E. Hendricks. Hendricks had been in the 3326th just eleven days. Tucker asked the trooper what he was doing and Hendricks replied

with the first of many lies, claiming that he was on a water detail, but the truck had left him. Then Hendricks introduced a new story – he had been walking back to camp with two privates. Lieutenant Tucker went to the Bignon home, where he found the slain man and the two bullet holes in the wooden door. The officer then examined Hendricks' rifle; five cartridges were in the magazine and the rifle smelled as though it had just been fired. At that point, Hendricks stated he knew nothing about what had happened – his third lie.

Tucker then asked Hendricks if he wanted to say anything, warning him that whatever he said could be used against him at a court-martial. Hendricks was now shivering – probably from fright, when his commander made him look at the two bullet holes and the body. Hendricks said he had gotten lost, found the house and began knocking. When no one answered, Hendricks fired a round through the door, knocked again and fired a second round. He stated he did not remember what happened after that until he met the lieutenant.

Tucker found two spent cartridges outside the door. Lieutenant Tucker now knew he had a big problem on his hands and took Hendricks to an MP station, where MPs observed blood on his raincoat. Private First Class Hendricks, witnessed by an officer at the station, signed a typewritten statement. He admitted to firing his rifle, but said it was an accident,

> "I walked up to the door to find out where my camp was and as I got to the door I stumbled and one shot went off into the door. After the first shot, I reached to pull the safety on but was nervous and the second round went off, and the door came open. I saw a man lying on the floor and head and jaw was covered with blood."

The accused ended his statement with, "I certify that I make this statement of my own free will and that this may be held against me." This final statement was his fourth lie since the incident. The investigation of the case lasted one day and arrived at the corps headquarters two days later. It was more than enough for Colonel Cyrus H. Searcy, the Eighth Corps chief of staff, who – for the commander – verbally approved a GCM. A GCM convened at Morlaix, Finistere, France at 9:05 a.m. on September 6, 1944. Private First Class James E. Hendricks pleaded not guilty to the two charges of murder, a violation of the 92nd Article of War, breaking and entering and assault – both violations of the 93rd Article of War.[1]

His statement was finally admitted as evidence, although the Defense Counsel fought the process, positing that the accused was under duress when talking to his company commander. None of the French civilians could positively identify Hendricks, although they were able to say that the soldier who visited both houses was the same man. Private First Class Hendricks, with agreement by his Defense Counsel, decided not to take the witness stand. The jury bought the connection that Hendricks had shot and killed Victor Bignon, while in the process of looking for a French woman to rape. By a unanimous vote on September 7, 1944, the members of the court found the accused guilty and unanimously sentenced him to be hanged.

That disturbed two members of the court. Lieutenant Colonel Juan A.A. Sedillo and Captain Frederick L. Orr signed a recommendation for clemency, requesting that the death penalty be commuted to life imprisonment, although they could have voted for that punishment themselves. The letter went to Major General Troy H. Middleton. The request did not provide any reasons for the clemency. It may have included the apparent experience gap between the two primary legal officers. Second Lieutenant Ralph M. Fogarty, the Defense Counsel and an Infantry officer, graduated from the John Marshall Law School in Chicago in 1940, but was not yet a member of the bar. Second Lieutenant Joseph D. Greene, the Judge Advocate attended law school at Fordham and had been admitted to the bar in 1931.[2]

The Staff Judge Advocate for the Eighth Corps reviewed the case on September 18, 1944. He found no significant problems and noted that two members of the court had requested clemency to the extent of commutation of the sentence to life imprisonment. He then reminded the corps commander that the reviewing authority was not authorized to commute sentences; that function could only be done by the Theater Commander as confirming authority. Major General Middleton, Commander of the Eighth Corps, approved the sentence on September 20, 1944 and forwarded the record of trial to the ETO.

The Staff Judge Advocate at the ETO reviewed the case. In the review, Major David J. Harman noted that there were several irregularities, but that none adversely affected the accused's rights. Harman also noted:

"This case was well tried. The evidence for the prosecution was ably presented by the Trial Judge Advocate and accused was capably represented by Defense Counsel. The Law Member and the other members of the court also performed their duties in a commendable manner."

Major Harman concluded his review by recommending against clemency for the following reason, "Great violence was used without any provocation whatsoever." General Dwight D. Eisenhower confirmed the sentence on October 27, 1944, but withheld the order directing the execution. On November 15, 1944, the ETO published General Court-Martial Orders Number 109. Brigadier General R.B. Lord directed that the execution occur on November 24, 1944 at Plumaudan, Côtes-du-Nord, under the direction of the Commanding Officer, Seine DTC.

The weather on November 24, 1944 in Plumaudan was miserable, with a continuous cold, light rain. Château La Vallée, a fourteenth-century manor house, stood down the road from the small village church. Deserted for many years, its walls appeared unstable and the windows were long gone; what it did have possess was a courtyard the size of an American baseball field, where early that morning American soldiers were noisily constructing a scaffold. Around the perimeter of the yard ran a low, stone, wall. Nine officers stood as official witnesses for the execution eighteen feet from the gallows. Seventeen authorized spectators were present as well, including eight officers, four enlisted men and five French officials. The murder victim's family declined to attend. Soldiers from the 795th MP Battalion guarded the area.

At 10:58 a.m., a cargo truck rolled up to the entrance of the chateau and backed into the yard. General Prisoner James E. Hendricks dismounted with his two guards, Sergeant Earl F. Mendenhall and Sergeant Richard A. Mosley. Major Mortimer H. Christian, the Commandant of the Seine DTC, formed the official party into a column and began marching to the gallows. To his rear were Captain Robert J. Sanders, a black Baptist minister, Hendricks, Mendenhall and Mosley. Behind that trio was Captain Norman Duren, a medical officer and Captain Albert M. Summerfield, the recorder.

At 10:59 p.m., the procession reached the bottom of the gallows steps; the guards bound Hendricks' hands behind him and then assisted him walk up the steps, after the Commandant and Chaplain Sanders had reached the top of the scaffold. Captain Duren took his position in front of the witnesses. While the condemned stood on the trap door and the guards bound his ankles, the Commandant asked if he had any last words. Hendricks replied that he did not. The Chaplain then asked the prisoner if he had any last statement and Hendricks replied, "Thank you for what you've did for me. Tell all the boys not to do what I did."

Chaplain Sanders then began to pray; after someone – perhaps Master Sergeant John Woods – adjusted the black hood and noose, the Commandant faced about at 11:04 a.m. and cut the rope, which released the weight that actuated the trap door. Hendricks' body showed no muscular movement and only slightly swayed at the end of the rope. There was some audible conversation among a few French civilians, who had stopped at a distance to watch. At 11:14 a.m., Captain Duren and Captain Summerfield entered the lower screened portion of the gallows to examine the prisoner. One minute later, Summerfield announced, "I pronounce this man dead."

Major Christian dismissed the official witnesses and spectators. The executioner cut the rope, lowered the body to the ground under the gallows, removed the hood and unbound the deceased's hands. Captain Poole Rogers, 610th Quartermaster Graves Registration Company, received the remains of the prisoner. According to an account by Professor Alice Kaplan in *The Interpreter*, at the conclusion of the execution, Sergeant Emmett N. Bailey, Jr., who was in graves registration, wrapped the body of James Hendricks in a mattress cover, after which the guards carried the body on a stretcher to an awaiting truck. The Army interred Hendricks at the U.S. Military Cemetery at Marigny in Plot Z, Grave 1-7. Officials transferred the remains to the American Military Cemetery at Oise-Aisne in 1949, where they are located in Plot E in Row 1, Grave 13.[3]

A few weeks after the court-martial, Major General Middleton wrote a letter of commendation for First Lieutenant Tucker. In the letter, General Middleton wrote, in part:

"Were it not for the exemplary initiative which you displayed and the competency of the timely action which you took on the occasion referred to above, the guilty soldier might never have been so clearly connected with the crimes and identified as the perpetrator thereof … Your alertness, judgment and ability reflect the greatest credit both upon yourself and upon the military of the United States."

On December 12, 1944, Colonel C.C.B. Warden, the Adjutant General of the Eighth Corps wrote a letter to Madam Bignon, stating that Private First Class Hendricks had been tried, convicted, sentenced and executed. He also expressed the corps deepest regrets and sympathies.

• • •

Two weeks after the Hendricks trial, Colonel Claud T. Gunn sat on another GCM involving a rape, as did Captain John Silbernagel. They convicted the seven defendants and sentenced them to life imprisonment. As found by Professor Alice Kaplan, Major General Middleton, the convening authority, was so disgusted that the accused had not received the death sentence that he sent a letter castigating the court, which was required to be read by Colonel Gunn to all court members – it was a real "dressing down." Part of the letter stated:[4]

"As officers of the United States Army I would have expected a far clearer recognition of duty and the dictates of justice from the members of the court…Nevertheless, the court saw fit – and in so doing stultified itself to a regrettable degree – to impose the lightest sentences permissible under Article of War 92. I have approved the sentences with the most extreme reluctance and only to the end that the accused will not go entirely unpunished … Unfortunately, the provisions of Article of War 19 and 31 prevent me from ascertaining which members of the court were responsible for the adoption of life sentences rather than death sentences. However, those members who were guilty of such gross failure to vote for adequate punishments will themselves recognize the application of the foregoing reprimand."

Middleton would never again serve as a convening authority that resulted in a conviction for a capital crime and resulting execution.

• • •

In September 2011, during a visit to Plumaudan, the author interviewed Monsieur Louis Massard, who as a young man in the village had been a witness at Hendricks' execution. He recalled that there were about fifty French civilians at the event, standing some twenty yards from the scaffold. He stated that an American officer had read a lengthy document in English at the scaffold – this was probably the GCM Order – beginning before the prisoner arrived. Then a truck backed into the yard of the Château La Vallée. In an interesting recollection, Monsieur Massard stated that the condemned man sat in the back of the truck with two "large American Military Policemen," who allowed him to smoke a last cigarette, while the officer finished reading the document.

Monsieur Massard was undoubtedly recalling Sergeant Mendenhall, who stood 6' tall and weighed 180 pounds. Sergeant Mosley dwarfed him. Hailing from Pineville, in hardscrabble eastern Kentucky, Mosley was 6'5" tall, weighed 203 pounds, had a 46" chest and a 34" waist. His imposing countenance was topped off with a long scar down the left side of his face, but beneath this powerful outer presence, he was a troubled man.

On October 30, 1944 – just five days after his first duty escorting prisoners to their deaths – Mosley woke up in the middle of the night with severe pain in his kidneys and bladder; he also had involuntarily urinated in his bunk. His guts were killing him. Hendricks was the last execution Sergeant Mosley could endure; he was promoted to Tech Sergeant on January 17, 1945 and formally applied for a transfer the next day; it occurred shortly thereafter.

The big MPs and several American officers then escorted the prisoner from the truck to atop the gallows. Hendricks stood straight on the scaffold and did not appear to be afraid. Monsieur Massard then saw a black officer speak to the condemned – this was Chaplain Robert J. Sanders, the black Baptist minister – but the French civilians could not hear what Hendricks said as his final words, although no one in the crowd was talking. Monsieur Massard remembered that all the French had been silent and respectful; he offered his opinion that many may have been in shock that a soldier was being hanged in their village. After the execution, he saw the Americans dismantle the gallows and take the wood away.

Monsieur Massard ended his recollection by stating that the victim's eighteen-year-old daughter at the time, who had been grabbed by Hendricks during the incident, was still alive and living in the village. He then took the author to the scene of the crime. The Bignon home is still in existence as is the Bouton family house a few yards away; even more amazing is the fact that both bullet holes remain in the door. One hole is just below the handle of the door, while the other is fourteen inches higher. Both appear to have been firing straight into the door, not at an upward angle that Hendricks implied in one of his explanations that he had stumbled and that his weapon accidentally had fired.

*"Get back in the hut before I kill you."*

*"Squad: Ready … Aim … Fire."*

## 34    Private Benjamin Pygate
33741021
960th Quartermaster Service Company
**Murder**
Executed by Firing Squad on
  November 28, 1944

On the evening of June 17, 1944, Private Benjamin Pygate, a thirty-five-year-old black soldier assigned to the all-black 960th Quartermaster Service Company, was angry. He had just gone into his unit's recreation hall at Drill Hall Camp at Westbury, Wilshire, England to grab a beer, but found that the bar had closed for the evening. Pygate, all 5'1½" and 122 pounds of him, stalked off to his barracks, where he promptly got in an argument with four other soldiers. Pygate seemed to be more of an observer at this point, but all that was about to change, when he said to Private First Class James E. Alexander, "Get back in the hut before I kill you."

Shortly thereafter, Benjamin Pygate kicked Alexander in the groin, backing him into the door. That type of behavior happened sometimes with a guy who had had his fingerprints taken fourteen times by law enforcement agencies and had spent time at such garden spots as Rikers Island and Sing Sing. Alexander, in his pain, knew nothing of Pygate's past. Then the accounts got fuzzy; Pygate half-closed the door, reached around to his back pocket – removing a knife with his right hand – and went toward Alexander, probably stabbing him in the throat. Seconds afterward, Pygate supposedly put the knife back in his pocket – although a later examination that night could find no blood traces in Pygate's pockets – and then pushed Alexander into the hut and shut the door. Pygate then walked around the hut to the rear. An autopsy showed that Alexander died of the throat wound; the examination also showed that he had inhaled a great deal of blood into his lungs before he died.

The company first sergeant immediately sent Private First Class Wilson to the hut with instructions to restrict everyone. Wilson followed his orders and then observed Private Pygate walking out the back door with his hands under his field jacket. Pygate walked toward the latrine as his left hand moved from underneath the jacket. A later search behind the hut found a knife – in fact, the search discovered several knives at the same location.

Benjamin Pygate was born in Dillon, South Carolina on February 2, 1909. In addition to his small frame, he had poor eyesight – 20/200 in his right eye and 20/70 in his left. He only finished eight years of grade school before moving to Washington, DC. In the nation's capital, he worked as a common laborer, making $25 per week. He also started getting into trouble; a court sentenced him to three years' incarceration at the Lorton Reformatory in northern Virginia. Single with no children, Pygate moved to New York City, where he again had numerous brushes with the law. On May 5, 1943, he was inducted at Fort Meyer, Virginia and sent to anti-aircraft training. The following month at Camp Stewart, Georgia, he was diagnosed with gonorrhea. His unit deployed to Scotland, arriving on March 11, 1944. Several weeks later in April, while working at a depot, he was involved in an accident, where several boxes fell on his head resulting in a "moderately severe" laceration of the scalp.

After the stabbing, authorities arrested Pygate immediately and placed him into military confinement on June 18. Charges were preferred the next day. The investigation concluded on June 22. On June 30, the commander of the Southern Base Section, Brigadier General Charles O. Thrasher, ordered that a GCM try Pygate on July 15, 1944 at Tidworth, in Wilts, England. The court convened at 10:10 a.m.[1] Private Pygate, who had no previous court-martial convictions, pleaded not guilty to murder (92nd Article of War).[2] Captain George Schwarz and Major Beatty, who had examined the deceased, said that a knife, such as the one introduced as evidence to the court, could have caused the fatal wounds. Schwarz added only that a pointed instrument with sharp edges produced the wound. Several soldiers testified that they believed Pygate stabbed Alexander.

Private Benjamin Pygate elected to take the stand and recounted that he was trying to be the peacemaker in the affair and that his mind went "dark" about the time of the stabbing. He added that he had not owned a knife since coming to the organization, although he had once borrowed one, and that he had never before seen the knife that was introduced to the court. A defense witness testified that Pygate did push the victim into the hut, but when asked if the accused stabbed the victim, the witness – a Private First Class Burton Lucas – stated, "I couldn't say; he pushed him that's all." Lucas also testified that he saw a Private Dempsey strike at the deceased with a poker, but the blow missed and hit the door of the hut. Captain Schwartz testified for the defense that the previous April he had treated Pygate for a head injury that required ten stitches, but in the doctor's opinion, there was no brain injury from that accident. He said it was possible, but not probable, that this injury would have caused lapses of memory, which the accused was claiming happened on the night of the incident. The jury convicted Private Pygate of murder and sentenced him: "To be shot to death with musketry." Then the court adjourned; the time was 2:10 p.m., four hours after the opening gavel.

The Staff Judge Advocate of the Southern Base Section examined the court's findings on August 5, 1944 and found them sufficient for both the conviction and the sentence of death by musketry. Brigadier General Thrasher concurred, approved the results and forwarded the trial records to the ETO on the same day. On August 31, 1944, General Dwight Eisenhower confirmed the sentence, but withheld the date of execution. The Branch Office of The JAG with the ETO reviewed the trial records on September 16, 1944 and found nothing improper. Judge Advocates Riter, Sargent and Stevens opined that the record of the trial was legally sufficient to support the findings of guilty and the sentence.

Pygate reported to the 96th General Hospital for evaluation in mid-September. Captain George Tepper diagnosed Pygate with a "constitutional psychotic state, emotional instability." About the same time, a battery of mental tests indicated that Private Pygate had a vocabulary level of a ten-year-old and an IQ of 78. A three-physician panel met on September 26, 1944 to determine the sanity of Benjamin Pygate. The proceeding – at which Pygate appeared, as did his records – determined the following:

"That he did at the time of the alleged wrongful act on 17 June 1944, have the necessary degree of mental normality to warrant his being held responsible for his actions.

That he did have sufficient mental capacity to justify his being brought to trial on 15 July 1944.

He does have the proper appreciation of right and wrong."

On November 22, 1944, the ETO published General Court-Martial Orders Number 111 – pertaining to General Prisoner Benjamin Pygate. Brigadier General R.B. Lord – by command of General Eisenhower – directed that the execution occur on November 28, 1944 at the 2912th Disciplinary Training Center, located at Shepton Mallet Prison.

Shortly before 9:00 a.m. on November 28, 1944, Major Herbert R. Laslett briefed seven officers who were assigned as official witnesses for the execution. Shortly afterward, a column of men marched to the outer yard of the prison. In the procession was Major Laslett, Chaplain Andrew J. Zarek, the condemned and guards: Technical Sergeant Luther S. Moore, Technical Sergeant Thomas R. Clements, Sergeant Frank S. Butler, Sergeant Pete W. Milner, Sergeant Walter A. Woodka and Sergeant Jack A. Youngblood. Major Laslett then read General Court-Martial Orders Number 111 and addressed the prisoner, "Private Benjamin Pygate, are you Benjamin Pygate?"

Pygate indicated that he was and Major Laslett him if he had any last remarks; Pygate responded in the negative. The Chaplain asked the prisoner the same question. Pygate did, but the words were spoken so softly that only Chaplain Zarek could hear them. The guards tied General Prisoner Pygate to the post. After the Miranda execution, authorities constructed a large wooden box filled with earth behind the execution post to preclude a repeat of dangerous ricochets. One of the personnel then placed a black hood over Pygate's head and – if he followed official Army procedure – pinned a four-inch diameter white target on Pygate's uniform over his heart. At 9:00 a.m., the firing squad, under the command of Captain Philip J. Flynn, marched to its assigned place in a single file about twenty-five paces from the prisoner. In the firing squad were some veteran troops. First Sergeant Bert E. Ward was in charge. Other members of the detail were: Technical Sergeant George M. Harris, Sergeant Raymond F. Dent, Sergeant Ralph E. Devlin, Sergeant William G. Goppold, Sergeant John J. Markiel, Sergeant Louis B. McKinley, Sergeant George O. Watkins, Corporal Albert H. Grizzard and Corporal Kenneth H. Derr, who was listed as the supernumerary and may not have had to take part in the firing. Ward, Harris, Dent, Devlin and Grizzard were career soldiers. Captain Flynn then readied the squad and at 9:03 a.m. gave the following order, "Squad: Ready … Aim … Fire."

There were no reports of ricochets. Major John C. Urbaitis, Captain David R. Capson and Captain John R. Whiteman approached the prisoner, who was slumped at the post. They examined the body and at 9:06 a.m. pronounced him dead; the three agreed that the cause of death was "gunshot wound (rifle), judicial." An enlisted man from graves registration signed for the body and transferred it to the Brookwood Cemetery in Plot X, Grave 1-11 on November 30, 1944. In 1948, authorities transferred the remains to the American Military Cemetery at Cambridge, England. Officials reinterred Benjamin Pygate's remains at the American Military Cemetery at Oise-Aisne in 1949 and placed them in Plot E. They are located in Row 4, Grave 85.

Private First Class James E. Alexander is buried among the honored dead at the Cambridge American Cemetery at Cambridge, England in Plot B, Row 3 in Grave 39.

• • •

On October 22, 1944, Benjamin Pygate typed two letters. One went to a brother and sister in Washington, DC and the other went to a cousin in Little Rock, Arkansas. Each summarized his situation, with Pygate emphasizing that he had been having mental lapses for some time and that he could not remember what had happened the night he was accused of murdering James Alexander. As Pygate wrote, "I couldn't say anything to defend myself, because I didn't know what had happen."

He also told his family that after the trial he had been sent to a military hospital (it was the 96th U.S. General Hospital) where he received "some kind of treatment to my Spine." Since that time, his head, nerves and vision became better. What the treatment was remains unknown. However, the problem was not with Pygate's head, his vision, his nerves or his spine. Benjamin Pygate, very likely unknown to the Army, was a hardened criminal. On February 6, 1945 – several months after his execution – the Army finally received a transcript from the FBI listing the incidents in which Pygate had been arrested and fingerprinted. The offenses included:

| July 19, 1927 | Washington, DC | Assault with a Dangerous Weapon |
| June 10, 1929 | Washington, DC | Assault |
| August 26, 1930 | Washington, DC | Assault with a Dangerous Weapon |
| September 11, 1933 | Washington, DC | Public Intoxication |
| September 11, 1935 | New York City | Moral Turpitude |
| October 11, 1936 | Little Rock, AR | Vagrancy |
| February 5, 1937 | New York City | Depositing a Slug in a Coin Box |
| November 26, 1937 | Washington, DC | Assault |
| July 1, 1938 | New York City | Burglary of a Residence |
| July 20, 1938 | New York City | Public Loitering |
| February 16, 1939 | New York City | Felonious Assault |
| February 18, 1939 | New York City | Attempted Assault 2nd Class |

The report added that for the final charge, Benjamin Pygate received a sentence of two years and six months to five years imprisonment at Sing Sing Prison. That made it very likely that Benjamin Pygate entered the Army immediately after his release from that institution.[3]

*"She reminded me of a person I have already seen that has been questioned by the Gestapo."*

*"I am awful sorry for everything I did. If I wasn't drunk, I would not have done it. God bless all you boys. God bless the Army."*

## 35     Technician Fifth Grade Leo Valentine, Sr.

32954278

396th Quartermaster Truck Company
**Rape**
Hanged on November 29, 1944

## 36     Technician Fifth Grade Oscar N. Newman

35226382

712th Railway Operating Battalion
**Rape**
Hanged on November 29, 1944

Glenn Miller's *In the Mood* was popular on Armed Forces Radio, but along the Red Ball Express, nobody was in a good mood. The rapes were getting more violent. A sergeant and two technicians fifth grade lured a seventeen-year-old French girl into a military vehicle, drove away and raped her in the back of the truck. The girl escaped, found a civilian riding his bicycle and appealed for help. The soldiers soon found them, chased the Frenchman off, and drove to a secluded spot; then they raped her again, before finally releasing her. They beat her severely, even though she had prayed for them to stop during the attack. The three men then drove away, but MPs arrested them at a checkpoint. The French physician that examined the victim said, "She reminded me of a person I have already seen that has been questioned by the *Gestapo.*"

The incident took place at Fromontiers in the Champagne district on September 18, 1944. Accused were a white soldier, Technician Fifth Grade Oscar N. Newman, and two black soldiers, Sergeant Johnnie E. Hudson and Technician Fifth Grade Leo Valentine, Sr. Hudson and Valentine were members of the 396th Quartermaster Company; Newman was assigned to the 712th Railway Operating Battalion. The 396th was assigned to the Third Army, but as Patton was dashing across France, the Third Army requested that the Advance Section, Communications Zone, take over the proceedings; this occurred without incident.

Hudson, showing remorse, cooperated and in testimony raised some doubt as to whether he actually raped the victim – his information helped convict the others. Hudson would not escape punishment; he received a sentence of life imprisonment at Lewisburg, Pennsylvania Federal Penitentiary. In 1958, the Secretary of the Army authorized the remission of the unexecuted portion of his confinement. Newman and Valentine would not be so fortunate.

Captain Donald H. Martin, the commanding officer of the 396th Quartermaster Truck Company stated that Valentine had been an assistant to the unit supply sergeant, that he was thoroughly to be trusted and that his work was of the highest caliber. Valentine was twenty-four years old, hailing from Gastonia, North Carolina; he was inducted at Fort Dix, New Jersey on July 16, 1943. He was married and had two children; at the time of the trial, his wife was expecting their third child. He had worked in a shipyard and had been a truck driver, a job that brought in $20 a week. Valentine left school after the seventh grade. After the court-martial, an interviewer wrote of him, "He expressed no regrets for his conduct but did have concern for the welfare of his wife."

Oscar Newman was born in Macon, Ohio on July 19, 1918; he had been inducted at Columbus, Ohio on August 13, 1943. A Lutheran, he had been married in Kentucky in 1940; he stood 6'0" tall and weighed 150 pounds, with blue eyes and brown hair. He graduated from high school and had some college. He had a Summary Court-Martial conviction for a one day unauthorized absence. Before entering the Army, Newman worked for a railroad company as a telegraph operator, making $200 a month. He had arrived in France on August 16, 1944.

A single GCM met at Reims, France on October 3, 1944. Each defendant pleaded not guilty. The Army would try each defendant on his own charge of carnal knowledge.[1] Each defendant submitted an unsworn statement to the court, which could only apply to that individual and not against the other defendants. Valentine admitted having sex with the girl. Newman admitted having sex, but said Valentine forced him to do so by pointing his carbine at him. Newman said that Valentine had slapped the victim. The victim testified through an interpreter. The panel unanimously found Valentine and Newman guilty and sentenced them to death by hanging. Four-fifths of the board found Johnnie Hudson guilty; he thus received life imprisonment.[2]

On October 12, 1944 the Office of the Staff Judge Advocate of the Advance Section, Communications Zone reviewed the case, finding that many of the Trial Judge Advocate's questions were leading, but did not see any major issues. The reviewer characterized the attacks as "fiendish acts" and "grossly appalling." Brigadier General Ewart G. Plank, the Commander of the Advance Section of the Communications Zone, approved the sentences on October 17, 1944. General Dwight Eisenhower confirmed the sentences on November 5, 1944, but withheld when or where the sentence would occur. The Branch Office of The JAG with the ETO reviewed the trial records on November 18, 1944 and found nothing improper with the case.

In addition to the events in the judicial system, the chain of command began to put the heat on the leadership of the units to which the convicted men belonged. Colonel Jefferson E. Kidd, on behalf of Brigadier General Plank, wrote a letter to Newman's commander. In it was the following sentence, "The failure of a Commanding Officer to supervise the activities of members of his command is indicative of neglect of duty and lack of leadership."

The company commander wrote back stating that Newman was off duty at the time of the incident; no evidence is on file of any follow-up to that explanation. The Chaplain for the 712th Railway Operation Battalion wrote a letter seeking clemency for Oscar Newman to Brigadier General Plank on November 8, 1944. He wrote that Newman was not the criminal type and showed every indication that he was repentant. The letter also said that Newman's parents were nearly seventy years old and that he was married. The letter of clemency produced nothing.

On November 25, 1944, the ETO published General Court-Martial Orders Number 114 – pertaining to General Prisoner Leo Valentine, Sr. – and General Court-Martial Orders Number 115 – pertaining to General Prisoner Oscar N. Newman. Brigadier General R.B. Lord – by command of General Eisenhower – directed that the two executions would occur on November 29, 1944 at the French village of Beaunay. The weather on November 29 at Beaunay was fair, but engineers constructed the execution scaffold in the interior of a large barn on the edge of the village in case the afternoon weather soured. The large openings of the barn, facing to the north and south, permitted a dozen officials and twenty-five authorized spectators to see the two hangings scheduled for the day. Four "colored" and four "white" organizations had been invited to have a representative at the execution. Newman was ready; a medical officer had previously found him to be in excellent physical and mental condition.

On the north side of the barn, about thirty-five feet from the gallows stood the spectators; included in the count were ten French citizens. Two were members of the victim's family. The official witnesses stood on the opposite side, a little closer at about twenty feet. Soldiers from Company C of the 391st MP Battalion guarded the roads to the place of execution. At 2:55 p.m., a weapons carrier approached the barn and stopped 100 yards away. General Prisoner Leo Valentine, Sr. dismounted with his two guards, Sergeant Alfonso Girvalo and Sergeant Robert V. Childers. A third guard, Sergeant Thorrolf P. Dyro carried a collapse board. Should the condemned faint or offer resistance, the sergeants would strap his body to the board and carry him to the scaffold and even up the steps to the trap door should that prove necessary. Lieutenant Colonel Henry Peck, Commanding Officer, 2913th DTC, formed the official party into a column. Behind him was First Lieutenant Sanford N. Peak – a black, Baptist Chaplain – then the condemned and the guards. Following that trio was Captain Ernest J. Haberle, serving as the recorder and then three medical officers, Major Lenpha P. Hart, First Lieutenant Paul B. Jarrett and First Lieutenant Jack E. Keefe.

At 2:58 p.m., the procession reached the bottom of the gallows steps; the guards bound Valentine's hands behind him and then escorted him up the steps. While the condemned stood on the trap door, the Commandant asked if he had any last words. General Prisoner Valentine replied, "See that my wife and children are taken care of." The Chaplain then asked the prisoner if he had any last statement and although Valentine replied in the affirmative, he did not say anything else. Chaplain Peak began to pray aloud. Master Sergeant John C. Woods placed the black hood over Valentine's head and then followed with the noose, adjusting it snugly. Meanwhile, his assistant Technician Third Grade Thomas F. Robinson bound the prisoner's ankles. Then the Commandant faced about and cut the rope, which released the weight that actuated the trap doors. The time was 3:00 p.m. Ten minutes later, the medical officers entered the screened in lower portion of the gallows. General Prisoner Leo Valentine, Sr. was pronounced dead at 3:11 p.m. of Judicial Asphyxia.

The same procedure applied to General Prisoner Oscar N. Newman, who arrived at the scaffold at 3:36 p.m. When asked if he had a final statement, Newman replied:

"I am awful sorry for everything I did. If I wasn't drunk, I would not have done it. God bless all you boys. God bless the Army."

The condemned man then asked if Chaplain Peak would say a prayer with him. The executioner adjusted the noose and hood, and at 3:40 p.m., the Commandant cut the rope, releasing the trap doors. Doctors pronounced General Prisoner Oscar N. Newman dead of Judicial Asphyxia at 3:51 p.m. The Army interred the remains of both men at the U.S. Military Cemetery at Solers, France and reinterred them in 1949 at the American Military Cemetery at Oise-Aisne: Oscar Newman in Plot E, Row 4, Grave 80; and Leo Valentine, Sr. in Plot E, Row 2, Grave 41.

• • •

Serving as the hangman was not what Henry Peck signed up for when he became a commissioned officer. The son of Russian-Jewish immigrant parents, Peck grew up on the multi-ethnic streets of New York City. Perhaps it was the stories that his parents – Peck could read and write Hebrew – told of turn of the century Russian and its *pogroms*; perhaps it was his study of history at Columbia University. Henry Peck did not like cutting the rope that released a weight that opened the trap door. That was a job for a non-commissioned officer. His unit received a Master Sergeant John Woods, who supposedly hanged a few men in Texas and Oklahoma. Woods, and his assistant Thomas F. Robinson, were in in Beaunay with Lieutenant Colonel Peck, but the execution report states that Peck initiated the trap door.

• • •

On December 7, 1944, the Commander, 712th Railway Operating Battalion, Lieutenant Colonel F.R. Doud, wrote a letter to the mayor of Fromontiers, Monsieur Jules Babiot. He concluded the communication by stating,

"We wish to express our deepest sympathy to all concerned in the incident and our profound regret over the commission of the crime for which the above soldier paid the supreme penalty."

The War Department sent a Battle Casualty Report authorizing that the mother of Oscar Newman, who was residing in Columbus, Ohio, be informed of her son's death. The report said that her son:

"Died in non-battle status due to his own misconduct. Judicial asphyxiation per GCMO 115, HQ ETOUSA, 25 Nov 44."

The report was dated February 27, 1945 – almost three months after Oscar Newman was hanged. The War Department also wrote the Prudential Insurance Company with information concerning Oscar Newman's death. At the top of the letter was the admonition: "**Not To Be Given To the Public.**"[3]

• • •

In 2011, the author visited Beaunay and spoke with Michel Jacquesson, owner of a Champagne winery in the small village. Monsieur Jacquesson, who was born after the war, interviewed several people in the village, who had been alive during the conflict. They recalled the execution and identified the site on the edge of the village. The barn is no longer standing, but during the war, the village mayor owned it and allowed American authorities to use it for the execution. They also recalled that the mayor, as well as the father and mother of the victim, attended the hangings.

*"I think I shot that woman."*

*"They are both Negro men, one of whom is quite young, and both appear to have the usual meager education of ordinary southern Negroes. This tends to give them less control of their emotions and to make them more subject to the strain and stress of unusual excitement."*

## 37 Private First Class William E. Davis

33541888

3121st Quartermaster Service Company
**Attempted Rape and Murder**
Hanged on December 27, 1944

The morning of December 27, 1944 in Brittany, France was cool and crisp. Frost covered the grass and low shrubs in a hedge-rowed field near Guiclan, Finistere, France – thirty miles northeast of Brest. Hundreds of miles to the east, the Fourth Armored Division was breaking the German encirclement of Bastogne during the "Battle of the Bulge." That was a real, live shooting war against the enemy. Today, they had gathered to hang one of their own, who had tried to rape a woman. When neighbors tried to stop the attack, the soldier started shooting and killed the victim. The psychiatrist had written that the guy, William E. Davis had only one "winter" of school and could only read and write at the third grade level. He had an IQ of between 70 and 80. The "shrink" had said he had some "dulling." The trooper had pleaded not guilty, but had already given the MPs a statement admitting that he did it! What were they thinking in Washington letting guys like this in the Army in the first place? They already had enough gold-brickers.

• • •

Take the Army General Classification Test, for example. In 1939, the enlisted strength of the Army stood at 187,000. But with the signing of the Selective Service Act on September 16, 1940, the Army began to expand in a quick – some said too quick – manner; in just one month in 1942, some 514,000 men joined the Army's ranks. To put the right man in the right job – a task that was often scoffed at throughout the Army using numerous examples of mal-assignments – the service developed the Army General Classification Test (AGCT), which allegedly measured inherent intelligence, occupational experience and the ability to learn. Those soldiers who scored a 130 or higher were designated Class I; Class II encompassed scores of 110 to 129. Class III comprised soldiers who had scored 80 to 109, while Class IV was reserved for soldiers with AGCT

scores of 70-89. Bringing up the rear was Class V – soldiers scoring 69 or less. Most officer candidates and potential non-commissioned officers came from Class I and II. Within the part of the service known as the Army Ground Force, in December 1943 – for example – Class IV and V comprised 37% of the total strength. Within the Army Service Force (such as engineers, ordnance, signal and quartermaster), 35% of the soldiers were in Class IV and V.[1] The ACGT did not seem to correlate to education level. According to Army sources as reported in the *Stars & Stripes* on October 27, 1944, the median education level for the U.S. soldier in the war was the second year of high school. About 27.4% of soldiers had not finished grade school; 23.3% of military personnel had finished high school; and 1% of personnel in the military had four or more years of college.[2]

• • •

Engineers constructed the scaffold in a field twenty-five yards from the nearest road. The execution site was two-hundred yards from the actual spot of the murder in compliance with command guidance that when possible, executions should be carried out near to where the crime was committed. In addition to the official party, five official witnesses, eleven authorized U.S. spectators and three French observers gathered. No townspeople were present, nor were any family members; in fact, the village had requested that the execution not be held in their community.

Around the field, twenty-seven men of Company A of the 795th MP Battalion, under the immediate command of Captain William G. Fleming, guarded the site. A covered personnel carrier brought the prisoner to the edge of the field, where he dismounted with his guards and joined the official procession. At 10:54 a.m., the procession started in this order: Lieutenant Colonel Henry L. Peck, Major Gerald P. O'Keefe, the Chaplain, General Prisoner William E. Davis, guards flanking Davis and immediately behind him, Sergeant Dino A. Cavicchioli, Sergeant Thorrolf P. Dyro, and Sergeant Alfonso Girvalo. Captain Milton Asbell, the recorder; and medical officers Captain Walter V. Edwards, Captain Chapin Hawley and Captain Thomas B. Baer brought up the rear.[3] Standing on the gallows were Master Sergeant John C. Woods and Technician Third Grade Thomas S. Robinson – they would be Davis' executioners.

The procedures at the gallows followed all the previous ones; by this time, the Army had the routine down to a science. Lieutenant Colonel Peck read General Court-Martial Orders Number 146 in its entirety. The condemned made no statements; at 11:00 a.m., Woods adjusted the black hood over Davis' head and the rope noose around his neck. At 11:01 a.m., the Commandant signaled Woods, who cut the rope that released the weight and actuated the trap doors. Ten minutes later, Peck ordered the medical officers to examine the prisoner. At 11:13 a.m., they pronounced William Davis dead. Woods cut the rope and removed the body from the lower screened understructure of the scaffold. Captain Poole Rogers of the 610th Graves Registration Company signed for the body and removed it to a truck.

The story began almost thirty years before. Private William E. Davis had been born in Richmond, Virginia on March 8, 1915. An only child, his father died when he was young; his mother died in 1943. A Catholic, he attended school through the fourth year; at age ten, he began working in a store and later worked on a farm. He took a common-law wife in 1943; Davis was inducted on October 7, 1943 in Richmond, Virginia. The Army recorded his height at 5'5½" and his weight as 141 pounds. Back in 1940, William Davis suffered severe frostbite in both feet that resulted in both his big toes being amputated. That could have led to a 4F classification and no military service, but the Army needed men.

Now the scene had shifted to France and the attempted rape and murder. The crime occurred on August 22, 1944. The Army had two suspects; both soldiers denied being at the scene of the crime. Then, on August 28, 1944, Private First Class Davis made a voluntary statement to investigators. He admitted that he and the other trooper, Private First Class Potts had gone to a farmhouse after drinking some cider, had seen a woman, and then had tried to bribe the victim into having sex with them. He said a group of eight Frenchmen burst into the house and one tried to grab his weapon. He stated he then ran out of the house and started shooting at the fleeing Frenchmen, adding that that he saw the woman fall. Davis finished by stating that he told Potts, "I think I shot that woman."

The Army formally arrested Private Davis on August 31, 1944. A GCM convened at Morlaix, France on September 23, 1944; it would last two days. It was one of the first major cases for the newly activated Ninth Army and everyone wanted to get off on a good foot. Private Davis had requested that First Lieutenant Phillip Schiff, of the 3860th Quartermaster Supply Company, be appointed as Defense Counsel. The charges against the defendants were one count of murder, a violation of the 92nd Article of War, and one count of assault, a violation of the 93rd Article of War.[4]

Both accused pleaded not guilty. Several witnesses testified against the two; Davis had already admitted the crime in his earlier statement. Both sides stipulated that the victim had died of a gunshot wound on August 23 and that the wound had been inflicted the day earlier. During the pre-trial investigation, MPs took three of the Frenchmen through three different quartermaster companies, where they positively identified the two defendants. There was no collusion between the witnesses. The MPs had separated the Frenchmen and each toured the three companies by himself. All three came up with the same results. Davis' defense took the strategy that he had only been trying to defend himself against the Frenchmen that he thought were going to attack him. The panel did not buy it. The GCM convicted both men, sentencing Private First Class Potts to life imprisonment at the United States Penitentiary at Lewisburg, Pennsylvania. It sentenced William Davis to death by hanging.

Some officers, though, wanted to spare Davis' life. The Trial Judge Advocate, Major Benjamin S. Morris, had served in the office of a District Attorney for four years before entering the Army and had been a Trial Judge Advocate for a year and a half before deploying to Europe. He wrote a letter to the reviewing and confirming authorities recommending clemency for both Davis and Potts. In his argument, Major Morris wrote:

> "They are both Negro men, one of whom is quite young, and both appear to have the usual meager education of ordinary southern Negroes. This tends to give them less control of their emotions and to make them more subject to the strain and stress of unusual excitement… and are both wholly devoid of the tendencies that distinguish the true criminal."

The request achieved no results. On October 6, 1944, the Office of the Staff Judge Advocate for the Ninth Army – which had been the convening authority – reviewed the case records. It found no major discrepancies. Lieutenant General William H. Simpson – "Big Simp" – a tall Texan, approved the verdict and sentence; then he sent the files up to his boss. General Dwight Eisenhower signed the order confirming the sentence of Private First Class William Davis on October 27, 1944. A Board of Review by the Branch Office of The JAG with the ETO reviewed the case on November 29, 1944. Judge Advocates Riter, Sargent and Stevens found no serious problems at the trial, although they found that the investigator did not inform the two accused of their rights before they made their oral statements to him; he did inform them of these rights before they signed subsequent written statements (over the objection of the defense.) The Board stated that the victim, Madame Pouliquen, appeared to suffer great pain from the time she was shot until she died hours later. The review found no problem with her deathbed statement, "The blacks have killed me."

On December 21, 1944, the Headquarters of the European Theater published General Court-Martial Orders Number 146. Brigadier General R.B. Lord – by command of General Eisenhower – directed that the execution would occur six days later. At 10:00 a.m. on December 26, 1944, Major Harry M. Campbell read the order directing the execution to General Prisoner Davis, who was then in the Brittany Base Section Guardhouse. At 8:45 p.m. that evening, Captain Thomas Baer of the 49th Field Hospital examined the condemned man and found him in excellent physical and mental condition.

That led to the execution the following morning. The Army temporarily interred General Prisoner Davis' body in Plot Z, Grave 1-8 at the U.S. Military Cemetery at Marigny and reinterred it in 1949 at the American Military Cemetery at Oise-Aisne in Plot E, Row 1, in Grave 19.

However, something was bothering Lieutenant Colonel Peck. On December 29, 1944, he sent a memorandum about the execution through the Commanding General of the Brittany Base Section to General Eisenhower. In it, Peck raised a point concerning the protracted suffering of the prisoner that had not been mentioned in his earlier *pro forma* execution report. Peck wrote:

"It is recommended that paragraph 11a, Standard Operating Procedure 54, as above, be rescinded. Reading the GCM Order in its entirety on the scaffold prolongs the suffering of the condemned man, increases the tension of all present and encourages complete collapse of the condemned. It is believed that paragraph 6a of the same Standard Operating Procedure adequately covers legal requirements. Paragraph 11a is inconsistent with the portion of 7a, said Standard Operating Procedure, as reads: 'Every precaution will be taken to prevent the protracted suffering of the prisoner.'"

The official execution report had not mentioned the "complete collapse" of General Prisoner Davis. Perhaps the reporting officer had decided not to make mention of the final condition of the prisoner before the hood was slipped over his head. On the other hand, perhaps Lieutenant Colonel Peck was the only man close enough to see the terror in Davis' eyes as the GCM Order was being read.

On March 12, 1945, the War Department sent a Non-Battle Casualty Report stating that William E. Davis had died in a non-battle status due to his own misconduct. The message authorized that Davis' wife in Onancock, Virginia be notified that her husband had died on December 27, 1944 at Finistere, France. She was unsatisfied with the message and enlisted the assistance of U.S. Representative Schuyler Otis Bland, a long-serving Member of Congress from the 1st Congressional District of Virginia. Representative Bland wrote the Army and on June 15, 1946, Colonel E.C. Gault wrote Davis' wife, stating in part,[5]

"You may rest assured that your husband was given a fair and impartial trial by a legally constituted court and that the record of same and the sentence imposed were reviewed and approved by the proper authority.

• • •

Decades after the war, Professor Alice Kaplan found two witnesses to the execution, who recalled that the town crier in Guiclan stood on the cemetery wall after Sunday Mass, and announced that the soldier wound be hanged the next day. She also wrote that the older people in the town began calling the field of execution "black man's field" after the hanging.

*"I know I am guilty of rape but so far as murder is concerned I didn't do it."*

## 38   Corporal Ernest Lee Clark
33212946

306th Fighter Control Squadron,
9th Air Defense Command
**Rape and Murder**
Hanged on January 8, 1945

## 39   Private Augustine M. Guerra
38458023

306th Fighter Control Squadron,
9th Air Defense Command
**Rape and Murder**
Hanged on January 8, 1945

The U.S. Army had a significant problem with alcohol consumption in the war, especially in the European and Mediterranean Theaters. The natural abundance of alcohol in these societies, combined with the ability to purchase it in bars, cafés or from private citizens at their homes meant that just about any unsupervised soldier could get loaded. Some commanders began to think that Glenn Miller's *Little Brown Jug* must be a song about their own unit. This drinking problem can be seen in the case of Corporal Ernest Lee Clark and Private Augustine M. Guerra of the 306th Fighter Control Squadron. On the afternoon of August 22, 1944, the pair left camp and did not return until 11:00 p.m. They obtained a ride into the small English town of Ashford on the camp water truck, but it was not water that Clark and Guerra were after.

After watching a movie at the local cinema, which ended at 6:00 p.m., the two went to the "Locomotive Pub," where each had two Scotch whiskeys and two glasses of beer. After thirty minutes, they left and walked to the "Denmark Arms Pub." Each drank another two Scotch whiskeys and one glass of beer. The pair then went to a third pub – the name of which they could not recall – and each had a light ale. The young men proceeded to the "Smith Arms Pub" and drank a glass of beer apiece. They then went to the "Alfred Arms Pub" and quaffed some light ale. Not quite satisfied with their intake, Clark and Guerra continued up the street to the "Albion Public House," where they switched to consuming two gins and one light ale each. Then they began to backtrack and returned to the "Alfred Arms," where they had one light ale apiece. From there, it was back to the "Smith Arms," where they drank "a couple of beers."

Then the pair left the pub scene, found a fifteen-year-old girl, and raped and killed her. They then returned to camp and hit the hay. A railroad employee found the girl's body the next morning. There had not been too many Americans in town the previous evening, which narrowed potential attackers; the police gathered descriptions of the two. A white corporal [Clark] became one suspect, while the other was described by a witness in the "Smith Arms":

"He was very dark, more like a half-caste, with black hair, swarthy complexion, thick lips and snub nose. I knew this last man by sight as he was often in the Smith Arms."

One might forgive the witness for being emotional in describing Augustine Guerra, who was Hispanic (Mexican-American); the witness was the father of the dead girl. The next afternoon, he visited the unit of the accused and identified them as the pair he saw at the "Smith Arms." Three days later, officials read Clark his rights and he made a detailed statement. He said that both men raped her and that Guerra had held his hand over the victim's mouth to silence her – but that the victim was still breathing when the soldiers departed. As Clark said to one of the investigators after making his statement, "I know I am guilty of rape, but so far as murder is concerned I didn't do it."

An English physician, Dr. Frederick J. Newall, took hair samples from the accused to compare with hair samples that he found on the victim's body. The Army initially decided to try both men jointly, but the defense made a motion to sever; the Army agreed, and both received separate trials. Private Augustine M. Guerra went first, on September 22, 1944. His charges were one count of murder and two counts of carnal knowledge, all violations of the 92nd Article of War.[1] Guerra pleaded not guilty. This study did not find the record of trial, but it probably progressed similar to Corporal Clark's trial two weeks later. The panel convicted Private Augustine M. Guerra and sentenced him to death.

The second GCM convened at Ashford, Kent, England on October 6, 1944 at 9:30 a.m.[2] Corporal Ernest Lee Clark faced one count of murder and two counts of carnal knowledge, all violations of the 92nd Article of War.[3] Clark pleaded not guilty, but the evidence was overwhelming. Pathologist Dr. Keith Simpson testified that he compared the various hairs that Dr. Newall had collected and stated that the hairs found on the body corresponded with the hairs taken from the suspects. Clark did not testify at the trial, but the court admitted two statements he made under oath during the investigation. The defense presented a witness, who testified that he was a good worker but "could not hold his liquor." Clark had a previous Summary Court-Martial in 1943 for being absent without leave for ten days; the court considered this. On October 9, 1944, the panel, which convened at the Ashford Police Station, convicted him on all specifications (but determined the rape was not pre-meditated) and sentenced him to death by hanging. The *New York Times* reported the results next day:

### "Soldier Doomed to Hang American Convicted of Murder of English Girl, 15"

Private Clark, who was born on August 10, 1920 in Clifton Forge, Virginia, was inducted at Roanoke, Virginia on September 17, 1942. He stood 5'11" tall and weighed 185 pounds; he dropped out of high school after two years. Clark was single and had been employed as a professional baseball player, making $90 a month. Records show that both his parents were deceased; an FBI fingerprint report indicates that he may have been arrested in 1938 in West Virginia and spent ten days in jail for "train-riding." In 1939, he was involved in a serious auto accident; he had another car wreck in July 1943 and suffered a concussion. His service record indicated that his character and efficiency were rated as excellent in 1943. Augustine Guerra was born in Cibolo, Texas on May 4, 1924, but lived in San Antonio before being inducted on April 5, 1943. A U.S. citizen, he stood 5'4" tall and weighed 136 pounds; the Army classified him as white. Guerra attended school for four years; he was a laborer and made $90 a month. An FBI fingerprint record indicated that he had been arrested in San Antonio: for drunkenness on September 20, 1942; for theft on November 19, 1942; and for vagrancy on January 7, 1943. Guerra went on sick call a lot – in fact, he "rode" sick call like a rented mule, although his service record showed his character as excellent and his efficiency as satisfactory.

On October 23, 1944, the Staff Judge Advocate of the Ninth Air Force Services Command reviewed the trial records, finding nothing substantial. It did mention that the Staff Judge Advocate, who was conducting this review, had been called as a prosecution witness reference the chain of custody of a police document, but that this did not disqualify him from reviewing the case. Brigadier General Myron R. Wood, commander of the Ninth Air Force Service Command, approved the sentences on October 26, 1944. General Dwight Eisenhower signed the order confirming the death sentences for Ernest Lee Clark and Augustine M. Guerra on December 4, 1944. On December 14, the Board of Review Number 2, of the Branch Office of The JAG with the ETO found that the trial was legally sufficient. On December 30, 1944, the ETO published General Court-Martial Orders Number 151 – pertaining to Augustine M. Guerra and General Court-Martial Orders Number 152 – pertaining to Ernest Lee Clark. Brigadier General R.B. Lord – by command of General Dwight Eisenhower – directed that the executions would occur on January 8, 1945 at the 2912th DTC located at Shepton Mallet Prison.

The day before the execution, Thomas and Albert Pierrepoint weighed and measured the condemned men. Albert noted in his execution ledger that Augustine Guerra stood 5'5½" tall and weighed 147½ pounds, while Ernest Clark was 5'11½" and weighed 189 pounds. The hangmen calculated a drop of 7'8" for Guerra and 6'2" for Clark would produce instant death.

At 12:46 a.m., January 8, 1945, the execution party entered the execution chamber at Shepton Mallet Prison. In the lead was Major Herbert R. Laslett, the Commandant of the 2912th DTC, followed by Major John C. Urbaitis, Captain David R. Capson and Captain Forrest R. LaFollette, all medical officers. Chaplain Andrew Zarek walked in, as did Tech Sergeant George M. Harris, Technician Third Grade Harry P. Ross and Private First Class George W. Pressey, serving as guards. There were eight other commissioned officers in the chamber serving as official witnesses. Thomas and Albert Pierrepoint were already inside the chamber. At 12:50 a.m., the two prisoners arrived at the chamber. The Commandant read both General Court-Martial Orders. Both men made the same last statement to the Commandant, "I am proud to pay for my crime." To the Chaplain, General Prisoner Ernest Lee Clark then stated, "I want to thank you for coming here with me, and what you did to teach me the way to really live." General Prisoner Augustine M. Guerra stated to Chaplain Zarek, "I want to thank you for everything you have done for me."

The Pierrepoints adjusted the hoods and nooses. With double trap doors, it would be a simultaneous hanging side-by-side. The Commandant gave a silent signal and at 1:01 a.m., the two men dropped to their deaths. Medical officers pronounced Clark dead at 1:13 a.m. and Guerra dead at 1:15 a.m. The Army buried the bodies at Brookwood Cemetery (Clark in Plot X, Grave 2-1 and Guerra in Plot X, Grave 2-2.) In 1948, officials transferred the remains to the American Military Cemetery at Cambridge, England and in 1949, reinterred them at the American Military Cemetery at Oise-Aisne in Plot E. Augustine M. Guerra rests in Row 2, Grave 44. Ernest Lee Clark's remains are in Row 3, Grave 68.

Undertakers buried the murder victim in an unmarked grave in Willesborough, England.[4]

*"Three of the other boys got picked out with Cooper, but I wasn't."*

*"The trap mechanism did not function properly due to faulty construction. The quick action and ingenuity of the executioner and his assistant in overcoming the mechanical failure of the trap brought the suspense and delay to a very minimum. However, the body was catapulted to the lower portion of the scaffold clearly and hung suspended with a slight swaying due to the mild breeze, but, with no sounds or muscular movement."*

| 40 | **Private First Class John David Cooper** |
|---|---|

34562464
3966th Quartermaster Truck Company
**Assault, Breaking and Entering, and Rape**
Hanged on January 9, 1945

| 41 | **Private J.P. Wilson** |
|---|---|

32484756
3966th Quartermaster Truck Company
**Assault, Breaking and Entering, and Rape**
Hanged on February 2, 1945

The U.S. Army was always thinking of everything. In anticipation of potential executions in the field, the War Department published Pamphlet 27-4, *Procedure for Military Executions* shortly after the Normandy invasion. This pamphlet prescribed everything needed to conduct either an execution by hanging or an execution by musketry – a firing squad. That was important, because as every soldier knew, in everything in life there was, "The right way, the wrong way, and the Army way."

The instructions included building a scaffold, nineteen feet in overall height, with the platform and trap door standing ten feet above the ground. The design envisioned ten steps from the ground to the platform; around the platform were two wooden railings, the tallest 3'6". The trap door measured 2'6" by 3'. The trap door release mechanism could be either a lever or a counterweight held by a rope that when cut would spring the trap. The manual also discussed equipment. Concerning the hood:

"The hood will be of black sateen material, split at the open end so that it will come well down on the prisoner's chest and back. A draw string will be attached to secure the hood snugly around the neck."

Of course, the most important item was the rope itself. Therefore, the War Department weighed in on that piece of equipment:

"The rope will be of manila-hemp, 1½ inches in diameter and approximately 20 feet in length. The rope will be stretched to eliminate any spring. After the hangman's knot is tied, the rope will be treated with wax, soap, or grease to insure a smooth sliding action through the knot."

The manual advised that where available, the Corps of Engineers should be employed in the construction of the gallows, but when not available, other troops or civilians could be employed. The manual stressed that preliminary tests be conducted to ensure the strength of the rope and the stability of the scaffold construction.[1]

Even so, sometimes the equipment just didn't work quite the way the Army manual had intended. Such was the case one cold Friday morning of February 2, 1945 at a rock quarry on the Route de Chonville, just southwest of Lérouville, Meuse, France. Behind the gallows stood a shear eighty-foot high rock wall, jutting upward to the blue sky. Heavy sledgehammers and sharp steel chisels had scarred the dark, gray rock with gaping fissures – a rapacious assault against nature in the otherwise pristine, rustic landscape.

Maybe the cold caused the problem; a two-inch blanket of snow and ice covered the quarry; the area was slippery with slush. The weather was clear with a slight breeze. The crowd was huge for an execution: seven officials, five official witnesses and fifty-nine authorized spectators – sixteen of them were French. They were all present to see General Prisoner J.P. Wilson drop through a trap door, swing at the end of a rope for a few minutes and be pronounced dead; and it almost didn't happen. For his part, J.P. was ready; a medical officer at 8:30 p.m. the previous evening in Commercy had declared that Wilson was in excellent physical and mental condition.

MPs formed the official witnesses into a single rank, ten paces from the east side of the gallows and then herded the spectators to a distance of twenty paces from the scaffold on the south side. This last group formed in three ranks; everyone had an unobstructed view. A command and reconnaissance ¾-ton vehicle brought the condemned and his guards at 10:50 a.m. to a position about one-hundred yards from the scaffold; Wilson would walk the last three-hundred feet. Lieutenant Colonel Henry L. Peck, Commandant of the Loire DTC, led the way at a brisk pace. They arrived at the gallows and MP guards Sergeant Russell E. Boyle, Sergeant Kenneth L. Breitenstein and Sergeant Alfonso Girvalo efficiently tied his Wilson's hands behind him at 10:52 a.m. They then assisted him climb the steps of the gallows. Peck read General Court-Martial Orders Number 30 that was dated January 26, 1945; the prisoner had no last statement to make. At 10:59 a.m., the executioner adjusted the noose and hood on the condemned and the Commandant signaled the executioner to spring the trap door. The recorder described what happened next:

"The trap mechanism did not function properly due to faulty construction. The quick action and ingenuity of the executioner and his assistant in overcoming the mechanical failure of the trap brought the suspense and delay to a very minimum. However, the body was catapulted to the lower portion of the scaffold clearly and hung suspended with a slight swaying due to the mild breeze, but, with no sounds or muscular movement."

The hangman was Master Sergeant John C. Woods, who – with the help of his assistant, Technician Third Grade Thomas Robinson – finally caused the trap door to open. Major Andrew J. McAdams, Captain Ralph S. Blasiele and Captain William H. Devinelli pronounced Wilson dead at 11:19 a.m. No one seemed to be shocked at the malfunction; perhaps they were numb by the weather or the actual crime itself.

No one had cried when J.P. Wilson and his accomplice John David Cooper had been convicted of one of the worst crime sprees of the war, a two-night assault in which two fourteen-year-old girls, one eighteen-year-old girl and one forty-year-old woman were violently raped. Two of the rapes took place on September 19, 1944 at Lérouville; the second two rapes happened two nights later on September 21, 1944 at Ferme de Marville. The accused also committed an assault and wrongfully imprisoned several Frenchmen in a cellar.

Authorities tried to find the attackers. It appears that of the eight French civilians involved in the incident, only three could provide strong identifications, as they had a difficult time identifying the two "colored" soldiers. However, they were better at identifying uniforms, ribbon bars and uniform decorations – the problem was, the rank insignia and medals that were being described fit no possible suspect. Then investigators got a break and found a duffle bag in Wilson's tent that had a shirt with the higher rank, driver's medal, expert shooting medal with four bars and a brass whistle and chain, all of which had been described by the victims. Wilson initially would not tell his company commander that he owned the shirt, but later admitted ownership of the garment and duffle bag to an investigating officer. MPs arrested Wilson on September 26 and Cooper the following day. Cooper made a statement saying he had sex, but that it was consensual. He implicated Wilson in the events.

The Third Army convened a GCM at Nancy, France on October 25, 1944 and tried the men jointly. The charges included four counts of carnal knowledge, violations of the 92nd Article of War; and two counts of breaking and entering, violations of the 93rd Article of War; and two counts of assault, two counts of breaking and entering, and one count of wrongful imprisonment, all violations of the 96th Article of War.[2] Both defendants pleaded not guilty, but the court convicted them and sentenced them to death by hanging.

Born in Dover, Georgia on June 11, 1922, John David Cooper was inducted at Fort Benning, Georgia on December 26, 1942. His parents were still alive. As a civilian, he had driven a coal truck, earning $25 a week. J.P. Wilson had been born in Columbus, Mississippi on January 24, 1918; his religion was listed as Protestant; he stood 5'11" tall and weighed 185 pounds. Records indicate that he contracted gonorrhea in 1938 and again in September 1943. He was married, with an 18-month-old son; he entered the Army on December 26, 1942 at Fort Dix, New Jersey. Wilson had three previous courts-martial for absent without official leave. Both men were black.

The Third Army JAG reviewed the case on November 9, 1944. He found no serious errors in the case and noted that Cooper's company commander had submitted a letter stating that the soldier had been obedient and efficient and that the sentence should be reduced to twenty years imprisonment. Lieutenant General George S. Patton, Commanding General of the Third Army, approved the sentences for both soldiers on November 15, 1944. General Dwight Eisenhower signed the order confirming both sentences on December 14, 1944, but withheld the exact execution location and date.

Then came a hitch; J.P. Wilson escaped from the stockade. He later wrote a letter to General Eisenhower professing his innocence and claiming that he attempted to return to the villages where the crimes were committed to talk to the victims – whom he stated made a mistake identifying him – but as events transpired he had not been able to find them. The wheels of justice continued to grind, however, and on January 3, 1945, the ETO published General Court-Martial Orders Number 2. Major General Royal B. Lord, acting for General Eisenhower, set a date of six days later for the execution of Private Cooper.

While Wilson was loose, the Army executed John David Cooper on January 9, 1945 at the same quarry that Wilson would later be taken. The day before Cooper's execution, Lieutenant Colonel John K. Martin examined the condemned man and found him in excellent physical and mental condition. The medical officer wrote, "This man is very stable at the present time."

There was a drizzling snow the day of the Cooper's execution; the sun tried to peep through the clouds and the silence was only broken by the sound of aircraft. The night before Private Cooper had slept under guard nearby in the local "Bastille" at Commercy, three miles southeast of the gallows. Two of the rape victims attended as spectators. All of them signed a roster verifying their attendance. Lieutenant Colonel Henry Peck supervised the event; Sergeant Alfonso Girvalo, Sergeant Dino Cavicchioli and Sergeant Thorroff Dyro served as guards. Cooper had no final words, everything went according to plan and Master Sergeant John C. Woods hanged him at 11:07 a.m. The *Stars & Stripes* reported on January 19, 1945:

### "Two U.S. Soldiers Hanged"
"Two American soldiers have been hanged in France, one for murder, the other for rape. The first execution was at Lérouville on January 9, the second at Beaufay yesterday. Both sentences were reviewed and confirmed by Gen. Eisenhower. The soldiers' names were not given."

Colonel Warren Hayford III, Commanding the Central District of the Brittany Base Section, interviewed Wilson on January 27, 1945, after he was apprehended. Wilson felt he was unjustly tried. He also stated he had alibi witnesses that could prove he was in camp on at least one night in question. He mentioned that he first saw his Defense Counsel about one day before the GCM. He mentioned to Colonel Hayford that at one of the lineup identification parades, no one identified him, stating, "Three of the other boys got picked out with Cooper, but I wasn't."

Wilson's letter and interview changed nothing and he had his own date with the hangman on February 2, 1945. The Army interred both bodies at the U.S. Military Cemetery Number 1, Limay, in Meurthe-et-Moselle, France, re-interring them at the American Military Cemetery at Oise-Aisne in Plot E in 1949. J.P. Wilson is located in Row 1, Grave 9. John David Cooper's body is in Row 4, Grave 81.

On February 24, 1945, the Army notified J.P. Wilson's wife of his death. However, John D. Cooper's mother did not receive notification of her son's death until June 24, 1945. In the Non-Battle Casualty Report concerning Cooper, The Adjutant General's Office remarked, "Unit concerned has been directed to furnish explanation for delay submission of casualty report."

Wilson's father, after receiving a letter from the Adjutant General in 1948 that his son had been convicted of rape and hanged, wrote the War Department on October 26, 1948. He stated that as his daughter in law had been told in early 1944 that her husband had been killed in action in Germany, he wanted to know if his son was missing in action or dead.

J.P. Wilson was neither killed in action nor missing in action. The Army knew exactly where he was – buried in an unnamed grave in an inaccessible cemetery.[3]

## 42       Private Walter James Baldwin

34020111

574th Ordnance Ammunition Company
**Murder, Assault,**
**Absenting Himself from His Unit**
Hanged on January 17, 1945

The morning of January 17, 1945 in the village of Beaufay, Sarthe, France was cool with a steady drizzle of rain. Snow blanketed the ground of the one-hundred by sixty-yard rectangular hedge-rowed field on the farm of Adolpha Drouin. Drouin was not present; an American soldier had murdered him the previous August. Thirty-six U.S. military personnel and fourteen French civilians were present to see a man hang. Earlier, military carpenters erected a temporary gallows twenty-five yards from the entrance to the field. A detail of twenty-five enlisted men, under the command of First Lieutenant Paul G. Lincavage, from Company A, of the 795th MP Battalion, stood on guard. Conditions were crowded; the spectators stood twenty paces from the west side of the scaffold, twenty paces from the east side and five paces from the south side; all had an unobstructed view. Even so, several French civilians craned their necks and attempted to get a closer view of the proceedings, but the MPs held their ground and kept the crowd back.

Shortly before 11:00 a.m., a ½-ton, 4x4 command-and-reconnaissance car drove to the edge of the field, and from it, guards assisted Private Walter J. Baldwin – the condemned man who had killed Monsieur Drouin – from the vehicle. At 10:57 a.m., the official procession headed by Lieutenant Colonel Henry L. Peck, and including a Chaplain, General Prisoner Baldwin, three guards (Sergeant Russell E. Boyle, Sergeant Kenneth L. Breitenstein and Sergeant David E. Miller) and four official witnesses, marched to the gallows at a crisp pace, lasting only half a minute. The procession halted and the guards tied the prisoner's hands behind him, while Peck and the Chaplain ascended the platform. One minute later, Baldwin – assisted by the guards – climbed the steps, stood on the trap door and had his ankles bound. The time was 10:59 a.m.; thirty seconds later, the Commanding Officer read the GCM Order and asked the prisoner if he had a statement to make, before the order directing the execution was carried out. The prisoner replied, "No, I have nothing to say to you Colonel."

Baldwin had nothing to say to the Chaplain either, and at that point, the executioner adjusted the hood and noose. The time was 11:03 a.m.; the Chaplain started intoning a prayer. Seconds later, Peck silently signaled the executioner, who cut the rope, which released the weight that actuated the trap. The mechanism operated without fault and the prisoner dropped cleanly through the trap door, remaining motionless – no sounds, swaying or muscular movement were heard or seen. In the chilly air, no witnesses showed visible or audible reaction, including Monsieur Drouin's twenty-one-year-old daughter, who attended. Ten minutes later, Peck signaled four medical officers to examine the body; they entered the lower screened understructure of the scaffold and at 11:19 a.m., Lieutenant Colonel D.H. Waltrip emerged and reported, "Sir, I pronounce this man officially dead." As Captain Milton B. Asbell, the official recorder of the proceedings, noted:

"Each official performed his task in a highly efficient manner. The proceedings were conducted with dignity, solemnity and military precision."

That is what the official report said. Only that may not be what actually happened. A small execution checklist, buried deep in Walter Baldwin's personnel file, tells another story. It lists that the medical officers made their first pronouncement on Baldwin's condition at 11:19 a.m., but then made a second examination about a minute later. This clearly indicates that Baldwin was not dead at 11:19 a.m. – another botched execution.

What led Private Baldwin to his death half a world away from his home in Mississippi? A board of medical officers' report from September 8, 1944 indicated that Walter J. Baldwin was born October 8, 1922 in Shellmound, Mississippi. A black soldier, he was the oldest of four children; his mother left home when he was three, his father died at age forty-nine of a heart attack. Baldwin had no history of hereditary mental disorders; he had the usual childhood diseases. He finished the sixth grade, leaving to become "an engineer of a train." Police arrested him once as a civilian for stealing fruit; he suffered from gonorrhea. Baldwin stood 5'11" and weighed 168 pounds on induction; he was later listed as 6'2" and 210. The railroad life did not pan out, and Baldwin worked as a furniture truck driver at $9 per week. He was inducted on March 10, 1941, at Camp Shelby, Mississippi. The medical board remarked that during the examination, the patient was quiet, well behaved and cooperative, with many positive attributes. However, they noted:

"He did not seem to realize the seriousness of his crime. He had a superior attitude, regarding himself. He often had a silly smile on his face … He admitted to three court-martials. For AWOL twice and once for misconduct … Mental age of 14 years on the Kent E.G.Y. and Vocabulary tests, 12 years on the revised Binet Simon test."

Baldwin had previously faced at least five courts-martial. In October 1942, his superiors noted his mental deficiency and ordered a psychopathic evaluation. The opinion came back:

"It is my impression that this patient is a constitutional psychopath with emotional instability and inadequate personality and should be discharged from the service under the provisions of Section VIII as he is too inadequate to ever become a soldier."

He was not discharged and Private Baldwin went with his unit to France, assigned in the Communications' Zone. According to the "Report on Charges preliminary to trial," Baldwin went AWOL on August 18, 1944. Five days later, at about 3:30 p.m. on August 23, Baldwin entered the barnyard of Adolpha Drouin. There was a struggle just outside the Drouin home, during which Baldwin fatally shot Adolpha Drouin (he would die later that day), and wounded his wife Madame Louise Drouin in the thigh. Later that day, Baldwin walked in to an American unit bivouacked nearby and admitted that he had just shot a Frenchman.

On August 26, 1944, investigator John Poust interviewed Private Baldwin and submitted a summary of that interview. Baldwin stated he did not wish at that time to make a written statement; Poust stated that he informed the defendant of his

rights. Poust recalled that Baldwin said that he had been captured on August 18 by a German soldier wearing a U.S. uniform. The German took Baldwin's weapon and held him prisoner at the Drouin farm, questioning Baldwin about his unit, depot locations and other military "skinny." Strangely enough, Baldwin said that for three days he rode on a motorbike with the German, even visiting a U.S. Army depot, but made no attempt to escape until August 21, when the motorbike skidded and crashed, knocking the German unconscious. Baldwin did not take the German into custody, nor would he report it to superiors, until after he was arrested.

A second investigator, Agent Harvey M. Fisher, read Baldwin his rights and pressed for a written statement that Baldwin provided. Baldwin omitted the portion of his story about the German, concentrating on the shooting. He first stated that the farmer approached him with a pitchfork, and that he fired a round from his carbine deliberately at the Frenchman's foot. The victim continued to approach with the pitchfork raised; Baldwin put his weapon between the prongs of the pitchfork and during the struggle, the carbine went off. Baldwin added that he yelled for help, and that sometime during the incident a third shot was fired.

Major Charles T. Shanner, the Assistant Staff Judge Advocate for the Loire Section Communications' Zone ETO, weighed the evidence in this preliminary hearing and on September 12, 1944 recommended that the matter be tried by GCM. Lieutenant Colonel Dean E. Ryman, the Staff Judge Advocate, concurred, and a GCM convened on October 6, 1944 at the Palais de Justice, Le Mans. Three officers served on the prosecution: First Lieutenant Roscoe C. Nelson (JAG), Second Lieutenant John H. Earle (QM) and Second Lieutenant Elmer B. Collins (QM.) Three officers served on Baldwin's defense team: Major Howard L. Watson (FA), Captain James J. Leitch (OD) and First Lieutenant Albert T. Declert (OD.) The jury included: Colonel Charles H. Cunningham (CE), Colonel George A. Ford (TC), Colonel James A. Doyle (FA), Lieutenant Colonel Joseph H. Edgar (FA), Lieutenant Colonel Rudolph C. Blankenburg (CE), Major Benjamin H. Schoolnik (MC), Major Joseph A. Thornton (SC), Captain Harold A. Gerrish (OD), Captain Edward M. Mertel (QM), First Lieutenant Charles R. Smith (CE) and First Lieutenant Benjamin C. Smith (CE).[1] First Lieutenants Charles R. Smith and Benjamin C. Smith were black; Baldwin and his defense team successfully challenged both off the panel, for reasons we will never really know, although his Defense Counsel explained the decision in this manner:

"The accused feels that this member of the court [Benjamin C. Smith], due to the unusual diction of the accused, would be prejudiced in the event that the accused elected to take the stand. I might say in explanation to the court that this man has a very unusual diction for a colored person ..."

Baldwin pleaded not guilty to all charges. Madame Louise Drouin and her daughter testified for the prosecution as did the criminal investigators and a Lieutenant Flanders, to whom Baldwin reported the incident. Baldwin did not testify in his own defense. The court convicted Baldwin of one count of murder, a violation of the 92nd Article of War; one count of absenting himself from his unit, a violation of the 61st Article of War; and one count of assault, a violation of the 93rd Article of War.[2] On October 7, 1944, the court sentenced Walter J. Baldwin to hang.

On November 4, 1944, Lieutenant Colonel Dean E. Ryman, the Staff Judge Advocate for the Loire Section, reviewed the case and found many problems, from the statement of the criminal investigators, to the hearsay nature of the testimony provided by the Drouin daughter. He also found the challenge of the two black panel members to be unusual, as both were added to the panel by vocal order of the commanding general two days before arraignment. Lieutenant Colonel Ryman explained that the additions of the two officers came because,

"... the accused being a colored soldier and the offense a capital one, and a limited number of colored officers, becoming unexpectedly available for court-martial duty ..."

Lieutenant Colonel Ryman opined that the court's dismissal of the two first lieutenants was not harmful to the accused. However, Ryman blasted the conduct of the proceedings, writing:

"I have been reading records of courts-martial and the proceedings of Boards of Officers with considerable frequency for over a quarter of a century, but do not recall another one which shows such a lack of comprehension by all concerned of what the tribunal had to do, or how to go about doing it ... however, I am of the opinion that (despite all the fumbling) the correct result has been obtained ..."

Brigadier General Leroy P. Collins, Loire Section Commander, approved the verdict and sentence on November 4. On January 10, 1945, the ETO issued General Court-Martial Orders Number 10, directing that the execution be carried out. Lieutenant Colonel R.A. McWilliams, the Assistant Adjutant General, signed a second set of orders – to be hand-delivered to the Commanding Officer, Loire DTC – directing that the execution occur at Beaufay, on January 17. The proceedings would follow Standing Operating Procedure Number 54, "Execution of Death Sentences Imposed by Courts-Martial." The courier officer was unnamed. Lieutenant Colonel Henry Peck received the directive and sprang into action. On January 15, the DTC Adjutant, First Lieutenant K.M. Cashion, Jr. published a set of orders authorizing Peck and six other personnel from the organization to proceed to Beaufay the following day to "carry out the instructions of the Commanding General, Brittany Base Section. The list included Master Sergeant John Woods and Technician Third Grade Thomas Robinson.

On January 16, 1945, Captain Ernest A. Weizer, a medical officer, examined Robinson and found him to be "in excellent physical and mental condition." That took Private Walter J. Baldwin to that cold, rainy morning of January 17, 1945 in the village of Beaufay, where the proceedings were then conducted with "military efficiency." The *Stars & Stripes* reported the execution and its location, but did not give the name of the condemned man nor any details concerning the procedure.

The Army initially buried Baldwin at the U.S. Military Cemetery at Marigny in Plot Z in Grave 1-9 and in 1949, re-buried the remains at the American Military Cemetery at Oise-Aisne in Plot E, Row 2, in Grave 43.[3]

Captain Frank N. Ford, commander of the 574th Ordnance Ammunition Company, wrote a letter of condolence to Baldwin's mother on March 27, 1945. In it, he stated, "He was one of our best ammunition handlers."

• • •

The author visited Beaufay in September 2011 and located the Drouin farm, finding that the old farmhouse was no longer in use, but still standing as it had in 1944. Several people recalled that shortly after Private Baldwin had been arrested, French Resistance fighters had found a German soldier. They hanged him at a barn about one mile from the Drouin farm site – the villagers who spoke with the author had no idea if this was the same German soldier that Baldwin had mentioned in one of his explanations of his whereabouts at the time of the crime.

*"If Farrell has to hang, I will see to it that you are a witness to the execution."*

*"I do not think that I got a fair deal. The guilty one, who confessed to this crime, and who received natural life sentence, is the one who is guilty, although I must pay the penalty by hanging."*

## 43  Private Arthur J. Farrell
32559163

Troop C,
  17th Cavalry Reconnaissance Squadron
**Rape**
Hanged on January 19, 1945

Sometimes significant activities took place after the court-martial and before the execution. Such was the case of Private Arthur J. Farrell, a combat veteran of the 17th Cavalry Reconnaissance Squadron. On September 24, 1944 in Brittany, he and Corporal Wilford Teton raped a fifty-seven-year-old French woman. The victim and two other French civilians identified Farrell, who was tall and white, and Teton, who was a Shoshone Indian and short. The Commander, Brittany Base Section, Communications Zone ordered that a GCM convene at Rennes, France on October 16, 1944.

The court met at 10:30 a.m. that day.[1] Although Teton and Farrell were charged separately with one count of carnal knowledge, it was a joint trial.[2] As the trial showed, Farrell actually committed the rape, while Teton assisted in holding down the victim and ensuring no one interrupted them. The pair fled and almost immediately, First Lieutenant Maurice C. Reeves of the 1391st Engineer Forestry Battalion – who had received a report of a disturbance – apprehended Farrell, just seventy-five yards from the scene of the crime. Teton then escaped, but not for long. Both accused testified at trial that they were at the home of the victim to get something to drink, but denied any knowledge of sex or a rape. The panel sentenced Farrell to death by hanging and Teton to life imprisonment at Lewisburg, Pennsylvania.

Arthur J. Farrell was born in Jersey City, New Jersey on November 20, 1906. His parents separated when he was about eighteen, his mother moving to Pennsylvania. He had one brother and a sister. Farrell drooped out of high school after sophomore year and held a variety of jobs. He was married in 1927, but left his wife after three months due to her infidelity. He married again in 1932; the couple had no children. In a job as a Standard Oil truck driver, he accidentally backed over a woman and killed her. In the 1920s, he served three years in the New Jersey National Guard as an engineer. Two

Summary Courts-Martial convicted him twice in 1944 for being absent without official leave. Farrell stated he had started drinking at age fourteen and had smoked a pack of cigarettes a day since he was sixteen. He had a large bulbous nose and a florid complexion, with two lower front teeth missing. His superiors characterized his service as "Poor." He was a rifleman with the scouts.

The legal review on October 28, 1944, by the Staff Judge Advocate of the Brittany Base Section, found the record of trial was legally sufficient to support the findings of the court and the sentence was free from any injurious errors affecting the rights of the accused. The reviewing authority – Commander Base Section, Colonel Roy W. Grower – approved the sentence the following day. Judge Advocates Riter, Sargent and Stevens of The Branch Office of The JAG with the ETO reviewed the case on November 29, 1944 and found no significant errors. Meanwhile, on November 19, 1944, General Dwight Eisenhower signed an order confirming the sentence. He withheld the order directing the actual place and time of execution.

Then events began to get sticky. During a routine inspection on December 18, 1944 at the Brittany Base Guardhouse, Farrell asked to speak privately with Major Harry M. Campbell, the Commandant of the Guardhouse. Farrell stated that he was innocent of the rape, but knew who the guilty party was and that this individual had agreed to tell the true story if Farrell's death sentence was commuted. Major Campbell then talked to Private Teton, who was concerned about the ramifications of testifying and a possible death sentence. First Lieutenant John F. Curran, a JAG officer, walked in and opined that Teton could not receive a harsher penalty than life, at which point Private Wilford Teton told investigators, "I raped the woman." Teton continued that he had made no deal with Farrell concerning his admission. However, there was a problem. At several times during the interview, Major Campbell appeared to exert pressure, stating, "If Farrell has to hang, I will see to it that you are a witness to the execution." This was too much for Brigadier General Grower (he had been promoted), who immediately ordered that Major Harry P. Cousans, of the Inspector General Office, conduct an in-depth investigation. Cousans produced a highly-detailed report, concluding that Farrell was doing everything he could to stop his execution; that Teton had lied; and that Major Campbell had made threatening statements to Teton so effectively that Teton was willing to agree to anything.

On January 10, 1945, the ETO published General Court-Martial Orders Number 11. Brigadier General R.B. Lord – by command of General Eisenhower – directed that the execution occur on January 19, 1945 at St. Sulpice, Ille-et-Vilaine, France. The following day, January 11, 1945, the Staff Judge Advocate sent a memo to the Branch Office of The JAG with the ETO stating that Brigadier General Grower had personally considered the additional information of Private Teton's confession and the Inspector General's investigation, and ordered the sentence of General Prisoner Arthur J. Farrell to be executed. "Artie" Ferrell wrote a final letter to his mother on January 18, 1945. In it, he stated:

"I do not think that I got a fair deal. The guilty one, who confessed to this crime, and who received natural life sentence, is the one who is guilty, although I must pay the penalty by hanging."

Farrell told his mother that two soldiers, Cowen and Hayden, had disposed of Teton's bloody clothes after they returned to the unit after the rape. Later on January 18, Captain Henry H. Kalter examined Farrell and found him to be in excellent physical and mental condition.

Engineers constructed a gallows in the courtyard of a school in the village of St. Sulpice de la Forét. The little square, which may have served at one time as a playground, was bordered on its southern side by a fence; on the opposite side was a thick hedge. The schoolhouse formed the third side of the square. A small shed was located on the last side. On any other day, the scene may have been charming to visitors and tourists; on this day, it was not. A frigid blanket of slush covered the ground; many of the spectators would get wet feet this morning of January 19, 1945. Although the sun was shining, a northerly winter wind was blowing, making it seem even colder than it was. Thirty-five officials, witnesses and authorized spectators packed the little square, which was no bigger than twenty by sixteen yards. French civilians of the town declined to attend, although they had been invited. The execution was not going to plan. The three medical officers were ninety minutes late and no military hanging could proceed without them. Finally, the docs arrived and the schedule could finally get underway. At 12:08 p.m., a covered

personnel carrier brought the condemned man to an alley next to the schoolyard. He descended and joined a procession for the death march into the courtyard. At the head was Lieutenant Colonel Henry Peck, Commandant of the Loire DTC. Chaplain Gerard F. O'Keefe walked to Peck's left; they were followed by the condemned and three guards: Sergeant Russell E. Boyle, Sergeant Kenneth L. Breitenstein and Sergeant David E. Miller. One of the NCOs carried a brace-board in case the prisoner grew violent or fainted. In that case, the NCOs would place the condemned on the 6'6" long by 7" wide hardwood board, and buckle three leather straps to pinion him to the rigid frame. Captain Milton B. Asbell followed; he would serve as the recorder of events. The prisoner halted at 12:09 p.m.; the guards tied his hands behind his back, while Lieutenant Colonel Peck read the GCM Order. Farrell then climbed the steps; the guards bound his ankles, as he stood on the trap door. He had no last statements, as the noose and black hood slipped around his neck and head. Peck gave the silent signal to Master Sergeant John C. Woods, who cut the rope that released a weight, springing the trap door at 12:13 p.m. Three medical officials, Captain Isadore G. Manstein, Captain Charles E. Cassady and Captain Charles E. Thompson, pronounced the Farrell dead at 12:26 p.m. Army personnel interred Farrell's remains at the U.S. Military Cemetery at Marigny, Manche, France in Plot Z, Grave 1-10 on January 22, 1945.

On March 16, 1945, Arthur Farrell's mother wrote a letter to General Eisenhower. A reply was sent to her on May 30, 1945, that stated in part:

"General Eisenhower took deep personal interest in the tragic case of your son. Immediately prior to the date originally set for his execution, in order that no stone be left unturned, he directed a stay of execution and ordered a new investigation, in the sincere hope that some circumstance might be revealed thereby which would justify clemency – the exercise of which was his heartfelt desire."

On September 5, 1945, Senator Francis J. Myers of Pennsylvania wrote a letter to Major General Myron Cramer, requesting information on the Farrell case. Major General Cramer replied to the Senator on September 13, 1945, in part reproducing the May 30 letter to Farrell's mother. On October 9, 1945, Arthur Farrell's mother wrote a letter to General Eisenhower, stating that Eisenhower did not give her son a fair trial. Brigadier General Edward C. Betts wrote a return letter to the mother. He began by stating, "The anguish you expressed in your letter over the tragic case of your son is most sympathetically understood." Then General Betts added:

"You are assured that final action in your son's case was not taken until after the evidence had been carefully and thoroughly reviewed and the question of clemency given every consideration."

Wilford Teton left prison in June 1955. Arthur J. Farrell is buried at the American Military Cemetery at Oise-Aisne in Plot E, Row 1, and Grave 21.[3]

*"The son-of-a-bitch threatened me so I just plugged him."*

## 44   Private James W. Twiggs
### 38265086

Company F, 1323rd Engineer
  General Service Regiment
**Murder**
Hanged on January 22, 1945

In an intense argument, you could say a lot about another man before the discussion came to blows. However, once you talked about another soldier's mother, anything could happen – including murder. A later review by the Normandy Base Section Staff Judge Advocate of the actions by Private James W. Twiggs on the afternoon of September 20, 1944 revealed just that:

> "The argument was about whether illegitimate children took the name of their father or their mother. Twiggs mentioned that he had been in jail. Adams said that if he was, it was for stealing. Twiggs replied that if he was in for stealing, Adams' mother was there, too."

Private Adams took offense, left the area and returned with his carbine. He pointed it at Private Twiggs and said if he did not retract his statement, Adams would shoot him. Twiggs retracted the statement and Adams left. About three and a half hours later, Private Twiggs was cleaning his weapon, when he observed Adams walking in the vicinity; Twiggs took aim, fired a round and watched as it smashed into the victim's chest, exiting his upper right arm. Private William Adams died within minutes. Moments later, the company commander confronted Private Twiggs about the shooting. Twiggs, not yet twenty-five, replied, "The son-of-a-bitch threatened me so I just plugged him."

That was enough for the chain of command. Within five days, they recommended to Major General Lucius D. Clay, the Commander of the Normandy Base Section, Communications Zone, that a GCM try the soldier. Clay concurred. A GCM met on October 25, 1944 at 9:00 a.m. at the Omaha Beach Section in Laurent, France.[1] Twiggs pleaded not guilty to one charge of murder, a violation of the 92nd Article of War.[2] His strategy was that it was self-defense and that he had meant only to stop Private Adams from shooting him. Private Twiggs took the stand and said, in part, "He [Adams] said, 'Twiggs, I still don't like what you said and I'm going to get you.'" The court ruled that Private Twiggs had lain in wait for the victim and that it had been a premeditated ambush. They convicted Twiggs and sentenced him to death.

James W. Twiggs, who was black, was born in Topeka, Kansas on January 4, 1920, but moved to Grand Lake, Arkansas and also lived in Leland, Mississippi. He entered the Army on December 3, 1942 at Camp Wolters, Texas and initially went into the Infantry. Private Twiggs later served at Camp Swift, Texas, where he was convicted by a Special Court-Martial for being absent without official leave; a Summary Court-Martial convicted him of being drunk on duty as a driver. He would later tell a physician that he neither smoked nor drank alcohol. He did chase women, however. An $11 fling with a prostitute at a tavern in Taylor, Texas left Private Twiggs with a bad case of gonorrhea; it was his second bout with "the clap."

The Staff Judge Advocate of the Normandy Base Section reviewed the case file for sufficiency on November 18, 1944. Major General Clay approved the sentence on November 21, 1944. General Dwight Eisenhower signed the confirmation order, confirming the sentence of death, but stated no place or date of execution. The date of the confirmation order was December 16, 1944; Eisenhower's mind that day may have been elsewhere, as early that morning the Germans slashed through American positions at the beginning of the "Battle of the Bulge." On January 13, 1945, the ETO published General Court-Martial Orders Number 16. Brigadier General R.B. Lord – by command of General Eisenhower – directed that the execution would occur on January 22, 1945 at the Loire DTC in Le Mans.

• • •

Known to many GIs as the "Continental Stockade," the Loire DTC – which officially opened on December 5, 1944 – was a rough place, because it had rough inmates, some 1,605 on January 25, 1945. The Army believed that anything less tough and many GIs would prefer to ride out the war in the rear in comparative safety – "three hots and a cot" – rather than face the rigors of combat. The stockade administration ensured that each prisoner worked eight hours per weekday; three hours of that consisted of hard labor. Incarcerated troopers also participated in thirty minutes of physical training and thirty more minutes of close-order drill every weekday; to "improve" morale, they sometimes had choir practice. Soldiers lived in two-man pup tents; center administration worked in red brick buildings. During fights, MPs used tear gas to break-up the warring parties. As it was often difficult to determine who hit whom first, authorities could employ mass punishments to discourage bad behavior that included exposure to freezing weather on a windy hill and confining hard-core bad actors to a six by ten foot "hole" – actually confining fifteen prisoners to the same hole for thirty-six hours – until they got the message. Many of the MPs assigned to the DTC were "big city" policemen. General Prisoners, convicted of murder or rape, lived separately from all other prisoners – "a cage within a cage." The condemned stayed on this death row for approximately two weeks prior to their execution.

Two days before an execution, Master Sergeant Woods would visit the supply room, where the supply sergeant, Thomas Ward, would measure the hemp rope "from one wall to the other" and cut it. Then Woods would pull a black hood from a spool of pre-maid hoods and cut it to the appropriate length. Often, he would use the same hood for two hangings. Woods would then put the coiled rope and black hood under his Army-issue green trench coat and carry them across camp – hidden, so that he would avoid the jeers and catcalls of the prisoners.[3]

• • •

James Twiggs wrote a letter to General Eisenhower on January 12, 1945, requesting clemency. Eisenhower directed that Colonel Harold D. Jones, an Inspector General, to visit the condemned man and interview him. On January 15, 1945, Colonel Jones sat down with General Prisoner Twiggs and conducted a lengthy, ninety-six-question interview. Twiggs maintained that he acted in self-defense; he also said that his company commander had mischaracterized his service. As to whether he thought he received a fair trial, Twiggs answered, "No sir, not in getting the rope. I don't believe that I deserve to get that, sir."

However, a week later that is exactly what he would receive. On January 21, Master Sergeant John C. Woods drove an Army flatbed truck to a ravine just outside the northwest corner of the Loire DTC at Le Mans. On the truck was a portable scaffold; Woods, engineers and a prisoner detail removed the gallows from the truck and set it up just outside the barbed wire fence. Woods tested the trap door that afternoon and the following morning. At 2:00 p.m. on January 21, Captain Ernest A. Weizer, a medical officer, examined Twiggs and found him to be "in excellent physical and mental condition."

At 10:45 a.m. on January 22, 1945, officials, witnesses and official spectators gathered at the site. It was a large crowd of sixty-seven personnel; for the first time this included eight General Prisoners – four black and four white – who would witness the death of a fellow prisoner. The other witnesses stood in several ranks; Army personnel wore Class B uniforms. The General Prisoners stood in a single rank behind the stockade barbed wire, twenty yards behind the other spectators. Fifty-one enlisted men of Company C, 389th MP Battalion – under the command of First Lieutenant Roland B. Dixon, guarded the site.

This was the first hanging at the Loire DTC, and one witness recalled that on the morning of an execution, the mood in the center would turn ugly. As the condemned man was taken from his cell, other prisoners on the death row would strike their aluminum mess kits against the bars and shout obscenities in protest of the event. The condemned would then climb into a vehicle – during the process, all prisoners in the camp stood at attention by their tents, to prevent unrest. On this day, there were increased guards at the DTC, in case unrest boiled over to a riot. One non-commissioned officer and three privates stood at the main gate, denying access to everyone but a few authorized personnel. Four additional privates patrolled the catwalks, keeping all prisoners at least ten feet from the fence. One NCO and three privates, armed with M3 Sub-machineguns, guarded the eight prisoner-witnesses, ensuring they stood at "Parade-Rest" and remained silent. At the gallows, one NCO and four privates kept the area around the structure free of unauthorized personnel. Eight guard patrols outside the wire, each with one NCO and two privates, ensured that no one would come within twenty-five yards of the fence. In the event of any disturbance inside the camp, the patrols would cover every possible avenue of escape.

A command and reconnaissance car brought the General Prisoner Twiggs to a position about twenty-five yards from the gallows. Here he met Lieutenant Colonel Henry L. Peck, the Commandant, Chaplain James M. Maudy and guards Sergeant Russell E. Boyle, Sergeant Alfonso Girvalo and Sergeant Robert V. Childers. Captain Milton B. Asbell, who served as the recorder, brought up the rear. Other than these personnel, no one approached within twenty-five yards of the prisoner. Twiggs halted at the base of the scaffold at 10:58 a.m. The guards tied his hands behind his back and assisted him up the thirteen steps, while the Commandant read the GCM Order. Standing on the trap door, the condemned made no last statements. The executioner adjusted the noose and hood at 11:02 a.m. and Chaplain Maudy began to recite a prayer. A few seconds later Lieutenant Colonel Peck nodded to Master Sergeant John C. Woods, who then cut the rope that released the weight and actuated the trap door. Ten minutes later, the three medical officers entered the lower section of the scaffold, which was screened by green canvas to prevent view by the spectators, and examined the condemned, but he was not yet dead; his neck was apparently not broken. About eight minutes later, they checked again and Lieutenant Colonel Harry Butler, of the 166th General Hospital, pronounced James Twiggs dead at 11:22 a.m. The witnesses departed and Master Sergeant Woods and his assistant cut the rope, releasing the body.

Captain Poole Rogers of the 610th Graves Registration Company signed for the remains of James E. Twiggs and buried them the following day at the U.S. Army Cemetery at Marigny in Plot Z, in Grave 1-11. The Army reinterred his body in 1949 at the American Military Cemetery at Oise-Aisne in Plot E, Row 4, in Grave 88.[4]

*"Each accused is not only clearly guilty of one of the most detestable of crimes in its most cruel form but their actions reveal human brutality and savagery degrading to a contemptibly low level."*

*"May I see the rope?"*

## 45    Private Mervin Holden
38226564
646th Quartermaster Truck Company
**Assault and Rape**
Hanged on January 30, 1945

## 46    Private Elwood Johnnie Spencer
33739343
646th Quartermaster Truck Company
**Assault, Sodomy and Rape**
Hanged on January 30, 1945

You could never tell what you might hear from a condemned man moments before his death in response to the question, "Do you have a statement to make before the order directing your execution is carried out?" Often the condemned man said nothing at all; another might simply say "No." Frequently the prisoner would mention something about his family. In the case of General Prisoner Mervin Holden, he answered the question by the Commanding Officer of the Loire Disciplinary Center by posing a question of his own: "May I see the rope?"

This time the rape victim was a gray-haired lady, fifty-one years old and living in Namur, Belgium. At about 11:00 p.m. on October 24, 1944 two soldiers – one described as a small "mulatto" and the other as a tall "Negro," rang the doorbell at the home of a Belgian couple, declaring that they were from the police. The two soldiers, who had been drinking and were looking for a whorehouse, entered; somewhat later, a neighbor heard the victim cry out for help. The following day, the couple went to American authorities; an American doctor examined her, but could not determine if a rape had been committed.

The victim and her husband identified both men at a line-up of soldiers at Military Police headquarters on October 25, 1944. Presumably, the line-up consisted entirely of black soldiers, but the conduct of the inspection is not mentioned in the files; MPs arrested both troopers at that time. Private Elwood J. Spencer made a statement to investigating agents on October 26, 1944, stating that both he and Private Holden had sex with the woman, but

implied that it was consensual, although according to Spencer, the lady had said "no." Spencer also said that Holden held a long knife in front of the husband of the woman. Holden made his own statement; he stated that Spencer had pushed the woman against the wall and corroborated that the woman said "no" when asked if she wanted sex. He said that the husband also said "no."

Mervin Holden was born on October 1, 1920 in Robeline, Louisiana. He was inducted on September 24, 1942 at Shreveport, Louisiana. His parents were living, but had separated when he was nine years old; he had three brothers and a sister. Holden completed the fourth grade of school, finishing that grade at age twelve. At age seven, he became sick with typhoid fever. He had one previous Special Court-Martial conviction for failure to obey a lawful order by a superior. Holden weighed about 210 pounds and was 6'1" tall. Before the war, he had been involved in several knife fights and had four knife scars on his body.

Elwood Spencer was born in Gastonia, North Carolina on December 4, 1924. His mother and father separated and then remarried; both were still living. At age seven, he was sick with pneumonia. He had four sisters and two brothers and completed seventh grade, leaving at age fifteen to go to work in Washington, DC as a laundry steam-press operator. He was inducted at Fort Myer, Virginia on April 6, 1943 and immediately reported to Fort Meade, Maryland. Spencer stood 5'7" tall and weighed 142 pounds; records show that he was missing six teeth. He had one previous Special Court-Martial conviction in February 1944 for disobeying an order; his punishment was a reduction from Technician Fifth Grade. In a neuropsychiatric examination on November 5, 1944, Lieutenant Colonel Roscoe W. Cavell stated, "Private Spencer is literate and of dull normal intelligence with an IQ of approximately seventy-five."

The GCM met at 9:00 a.m. on November 14, 1944, a joint trial with separate charges.[1] Spencer faced one count of carnal knowledge, a violation of the 92nd Article of War, and a charge of sodomy and a charge of assault, both violations of the 96th Article of War. Not charged with sodomy, Holden faced the other two violations.[2] Both defendants pleaded not guilty, took the stand and stated that all actions were consensual. The victim testified that both men had held a knife to her during the actions.

The court-martial panel convicted both defendants on all specifications and charges and sentenced both to death by hanging.

The Ninth Army JAG reviewed the trial record for Private Spencer on November 24, 1944, finding no irregularities. On November 27, 1944, Lieutenant General William H. Simpson, Commander Ninth Army, approved the sentences of Private Elwood Spencer and Private Mervin Holden. The ETO JAG's office reviewed the trial records on December 21, 1944 and found no serious problems. Writing the opinion was Captain Robert K. Bell, who opined:

> "Each accused is not only clearly guilty of one of the most detestable of crimes in its most cruel form but their actions reveal human brutality and savagery degrading to a contemptibly low level."

General Dwight Eisenhower confirmed the sentence of death for Spencer and Holden on December 23, 1944. The Board of Review Number 1, consisting of Judge Advocates Riter, Sargent and Stevens, of the Branch Office of The JAG with the ETO reviewed the two cases on January 11, 1945, finding no serious problems with the trial. On January 20, 1945, the ETO published General Court-Martial Orders Number 21. Brigadier General R.B. Lord – by command of General Eisenhower – directed that the execution of Private Spencer and Private Holden occur on January 30, 1945 at Namur, Belgium. The evening before, at 8:30 p.m., Major John Wilson examined both men and found them in excellent physical and mental condition.

The execution site for Spencer and Holden was perhaps the gloomiest of any used by the U.S. authorities in Europe – not that any location for a hanging or firing squad could be considered cheery. Fort d'Orange, the Citadel of Namur – also called The Devil's Castle – perched atop a hill two miles southwest of the Belgian city of Namur and overlooking the frigid Meuse and Sambre Rivers, had once been the scene of heavy bombardment by German siege guns in World War I. Surrounding the fort was a dry moat fifty feet deep. The entrance to the citadel was across a strong, wooden bridge ninety feet long that spanned the deep moat. The courtyard inside the high walls, shaped as an irregular hexagon, measured forty yards by twenty yards. Surrounding the space were thick, dreary gray walls in the Vauban style, stretching to a height of twenty to fifty feet. A wooden gallows stood in the center of this courtyard, with the wooden steps facing west. Three inches of snow blanketed the entire area; it was a January cold,

accompanied by a slight, but "crisp," wind and paltry snow flurries. Present were one-hundred and eight officers and men. It was one of the biggest execution crowds of the war and in the small confines, men were packed together. With typical Army efficiency, each spectator provided his signature on a sign-in roster. Eighty-three spectators were enlisted men, representing dozens of different units; it was clear that the Ninth Army wanted to get the word out of what happened to rapists in the command.

At 11:00 a.m., an Army jeep approached and halted ten yards from the bridge. Guards assisted General Prisoner Mervin Holden from the vehicle. At 11:01 a.m., the official procession began, headed by Lieutenant Colonel Henry L. Peck, Commanding Officer, Loire DTC, and including Chaplain Lorenzo Q. Brown (a black, Methodist minister), General Prisoner Holden, three guards (Sergeant Russell E. Boyle, Sergeant Kenneth L. Breitenstein and Sergeant Alfonso Girvalo), Captain Milton B. Asbell (Recorder) and six official witnesses (Captain Harry H. Turney-High, Major James E. Brewster II, Major Alden C. Russell, Captain Paul S. Davis, Captain Harlan J. Wills and First Lieutenant Martin A. Agather). The procession marched in a straight line over the bridge, the soldiers' boots making a crunching sound in the snow. Holden sang a spiritual hymn that could be heard by the spectators. The group passed through the entrance archway, executed a column half-left and halted at the foot of the scaffold at 11:02 a.m. The executioner's assistant bound the condemned man's hands behind his back and then assisted him up the wooden steps. Standing on the trap door, as the executioner's assistant bound his ankles, Holden listened to Lieutenant Colonel Peck read the GCM Order. The prisoner had no statement to make to the Commandant; to Chaplain Brown he simply said, "Pray for me. He's got a place for me." Mervin Holden then asked his strange last question to the Commanding Officer, to which Lieutenant Colonel Peck replied, "It is forbidden."

Master Sergeant John C. Woods adjusted the hood and noose. The time was 11:05 a.m.; Chaplain Brown started intoning a prayer. Thirty seconds later, the Commanding Officer silently signaled the executioner, who cut the rope, which released the weight that actuated the trap. Holden had continued singing until he started to fall. The trap mechanism operated without fault and the prisoner dropped cleanly through the trap door, remaining motionless – no sounds or muscular movement were heard or seen; the body swayed slightly in the breeze. In the chilly air, no witnesses showed visible or audible reaction; they were just shivering in the cold. Ten minutes later, the Commanding Officer signaled the three medical officers (Major John S. Wilson, Captain Thomas C. Hankins and Captain Charles J. Tommasello) to examine the body; they entered the lower screened understructure of the gallows and at 11:19 a.m., the senior medical officer emerged and reported, "Sir, I pronounce this man officially dead."

Graves's registration personnel signed for the body, as Master Sergeant Woods cut it down. It was almost time for the second execution. At 11:53 a.m., an Army jeep halted ten yards from the bridge, and from it, guards assisted General Prisoner Elwood Spencer from the vehicle. At 11:54 a.m., the official procession began, headed by Lieutenant Colonel Peck, and including Chaplain Brown, General Prisoner Spencer, the same guards, Captain Asbell and the same official witnesses. The procession marched in a straight line over the bridge, passed through the entrance archway and halted at the foot of the scaffold at 11:56 a.m. The executioner's assistant bound the condemned man's hands behind his back and then assisted him up the wooden steps. Standing on the trap door, the condemned man had his ankles bound, while he listened to Lieutenant Colonel Peck read the GCM Order. The prisoner had no statement to make to Peck; to Chaplain Brown he simply said, "Explain it to my Mother, that's all."

Master Sergeant John C. Woods adjusted the hood and noose. The time was high noon; Chaplain Brown started intoning a prayer. Thirty seconds later, the Commanding Officer silently signaled Woods. The trap mechanism operated without fault and the prisoner dropped cleanly through the trap door, remaining motionless, the body swayed slightly in the breeze. Again, no witnesses showed visible or audible reaction. Ten minutes later the Commanding Officer signaled the three medical officers to examine the body; they entered the lower screened understructure of the gallows and at 12:13 a.m., the senior medical officer emerged and reported, "Sir, I pronounce this man officially dead."

That ended the two executions. The Army initially buried the remains of the two men at the U.S. Military Cemetery at Andilly, France. The Army reinterred the remains in 1949 at the American Military Cemetery at Oise-Aisne in Plot E. Mervin Holden's remains are in Row 1, Grave 8. Elwood J. Spencer's body is in Grave 33 of Row 2.[3]

> *"If the death penalty is ever to be imposed for desertion it should be imposed in this case, not as a punitive measure, nor as retribution, but to maintain that discipline upon which alone an army can succeed against the enemy."*

## 47     Private Eddie Slovik
### 36896415

Company G, 109th Infantry Regiment,
   Twenty-Eighth Infantry Division
**Desertion**
Executed by Firing Squad on
   January 31, 1945

The U.S. Army had two purposes to issue death penalties during the war. First, and most obvious, was to punish those soldiers who committed heinous acts. Additionally, the function of the death penalty was to serve as a significant warning to other soldiers to stay in line, obey the orders of their superiors and soldier with their comrades through the war's end, when everyone finally could go home. Private Eddie Slovik was not the only deserter in the ETO – not by a long shot – but he was the only deserter to be executed, in part because he was at the confluence of several firestorms. First, he committed the crime. Second, he stated he would desert again, if sent back to the front. Third, he was assigned to a unit that had experienced severe losses and in some leader's eyes was close to breaking. Finally, Eddie Slovik, was deemed a "loser" in both civilian and military life, and was assessed to have no redeeming social value.

Therefore, Eddie Slovik became an example of deterrence. Do you want to go over the hill? You'll end up tied to a post on a freezing January morning like Eddie Slovik, with eleven rounds of rifle fire smashing through your chest. Maybe it was made worse because of the unit he was in – the Twenty-Eighth Infantry Division. As one historian said of the unit:[1]

> "A big, tough, hard-luck, meat-grinding outfit that the people of the United States had organized, trained, equipped, paid, and sent to France for only one purpose: to kill Germans."

Brigadier General Edwin C. McNeil, the head of the Branch Office of The Adjutant General with the ETO, wrote the best summary of what transpired in Eddie Slovik's desertion:

"This soldier performed no front line duty. He did not intend to. He deserted from his group of fifteen when about to join the infantry company to which he had been assigned. His subsequent conduct shows a deliberate plan to secure trial and incarceration in a safe place. The sentence adjudged was more severe than he had anticipated, but the imposition of a less severe sentence would only have accomplished the accused's purpose of securing his incarceration and consequent freedom from the dangers which so many of our armed forces are required to face daily."

A GCM, appointed by the Commanding Officer, Twenty-Eighth Infantry Division, convened at Rötgen, Germany at 10:00 a.m. on November 11, 1944. The panel included: Lieutenant Colonel Guy M. Williams (FI) – who had presided at more than one hundred General Courts-Martial in the division, Major Orland F. Leighty (DC), Major Herbert D. White (AG), Major Robert D. Montondo (IN), Captain Benedict Kimmelman (DC), Captain Arthur V. Patterson (IG), Captain Stanley H. French (MC), Captain Clarence W. Welch (IN) and First Lieutenant Bernard Altman (IN) – a lawyer who also served as the Law Member. Captain John I. Green (JAG) was the Trial Judge Advocate; First Lieutenant Harold C. Patrick (AG) assisted him. The Defense Counsel, Captain Edward P. Woods (IN), was not a lawyer, but had defended twenty serious offenders and was able in court; many of his clients had been found not guilty.[2] None of the officers held combat leadership positions, because on that day every combat officer in the division was under enemy fire at the front. The accused faced the following charge and specifications:

**Charge: Violation of the 58th Article of War.**
*Specification 1*: In that Private Eddie D. Slovik, Company G, 109th Infantry, did, at or near Rocherath, Belgium, on or about 25 August 1944, desert the service of the United States by absenting himself without proper leave from his organization, with intent to avoid hazardous duty and to shirk important service, to wit: action with the enemy, and did remain absent in desertion until he was delivered to United States military authorities by Canadian military authorities at or near Brussels, Belgium, on or about 4 October 1944.

*Specification 2*: In that Private Eddie D. Slovik, Company G, 109th Infantry, did, at or near Elbeuf, France, on or about 8 October 1944, desert the service of the United States by absenting himself without proper leave from his organization, with intent to avoid hazardous duty and to shirk important service, to wit: action with the enemy, and did remain absent in desertion until he surrendered himself at or near Rocherath, Belgium, on or about 9 October 1944.

Private Slovik pleaded not guilty. The prosecution presented several witnesses that stated that Slovik had been in the unit, but had left. Prosecutors admitted into evidence, over no objection by the defense, Slovik's handwritten confession, which ended with, "And I'll run away again if I have to go out their [sic.]" The prosecution's case lasted fifty minutes. Private Slovik declined to take the stand. A psychiatric evaluation of Private Slovik had found nothing wrong with him. The defense rested; a buddy of Slovik, John Tankey, might have been able to shed light on the first incident of desertion, but Tankey was wounded on November 5, 1944 and was unavailable. The prosecution made a closing argument. The defense declined to do the same. The panel then took a vote and found Slovik guilty of both specifications and the charge. The Trial Judge Advocate read a statement that described Slovik's age, pay and service data. The court adjourned, while the panel took a secret written ballot. Lieutenant Colonel Williams insisted on three ballots. The first was unanimous for death. He then suggested that the panel take a cigarette break. The panel returned and took a second vote. Again, it was unanimous for death. Finally, Williams told the group, "Well, gentlemen, this is serious. We've got to live with this the rest of our lives. Let's take a third ballot." Again, the panel voted and again the vote was unanimous. The court returned to session and Private Slovik heard the court's decision for him:

"To be dishonorably discharged from the service, to forfeit all pay and allowances due or to become due, and to be shot to death with musketry."

The court adjourned at 11:40 a.m. The first GCM resulting in a death penalty for desertion in the U.S. Army since the 1800s had taken just one-hundred minutes. The verdict must be examined in light of what was going on around "Dutch" Cota's division. The Twenty-Eighth was fighting in the Hürtgen Forest. The division's shoulder patch was a red keystone-shaped symbol (It was often called the "Keystone Division"); because of the losses of the unit, the division had acquired the disagreeable nickname of "The Bloody Bucket." Infantry line companies were often less than fifty percent strength. In the first two weeks of November, the division reported 5,684 battle and non-battle losses. One regiment lost 167 men killed, 431 missing in action, 232 captured by the enemy and 719 wounded. Commanders were throwing everyone into the line; the division could not afford even one malingerer.[3]

The morning after his conviction, Private Slovik swept out the guardhouse, so the other soldiers, who had received lesser punishments in other cases by the court-martial, could catch a few more winks of "shut-eye." Two days later, he arrived at the Seine Base Section Stockade in Paris. On November 26, 1944, the Staff Judge Advocate of the division, Lieutenant Colonel Henry J. Sommer, reviewed the findings; before the court-martial, Lieutenant Colonel Sommer had interviewed Private Slovik and had offered to suspend judicial proceedings if Slovik would return to his unit at the front and start to soldier. Slovik declined the offer. The review found that the record of trial was legally sufficient. However, it did note:

"While the essential elements of proof of desertion to avoid hazardous duty are fully established, the record leaves much to be desired so far as proof of details concerned."

This was because the unit never "picked up" Slovik in August on the company Morning Report and thus the company had no document showing he was later absent. The Trial Judge Advocate thus had to ask leading questions to refresh the memories of several witnesses in the chain of command, who had been in almost continuous combat. Even then, the company commander could not remember the exact name of the town in Belgium, where Slovik deserted.

Now a second boot dropped on Eddie Slovik, and it was a heavy one. The FBI furnished Lieutenant Colonel Sommer with Slovik's civilian criminal record; it was damning; he had six civilian convictions. Major General Norman Cota approved the sentence on November 27, 1944, but only the actual death sentence. Why this was done remains in dispute. Sommer would later say that the other words were superfluous, although Cota would later state that he had always assumed that the next of kin received the insurance and accumulated pay and allowances. The ETO Staff Judge Advocate reviewed the case on December 23, 1944. Major Frederick J. Bertolet wrote that the original trial was sufficient. He then opined on potential clemency,

"If the death penalty is ever to be imposed for desertion it should be imposed in this case, not as a punitive measure, nor as retribution, but to maintain that discipline upon which alone an army can succeed against the enemy."

General Dwight Eisenhower confirmed the sentence on December 23, 1944, but withheld establishing a date and location; he reportedly told Brigadier General Edward C. Betts that the decision pained him greatly, as he had wanted to equal General John Pershing's record in World War I for having no soldiers shot for desertion. On January 6, 1945, the Branch Office of The JAG with the ETO reviewed the case. In a lengthy review, Judge Advocates Riter, Sargent and Stevens found no significant problems. On January 23, 1945, the ETO published General Court-Martial Orders Number 27. Major General R.B. Lord directed that the execution occur on January 31, 1945 at the 109th Infantry Regiment area in France. The division designated Ste. Marie aux Mines as that location.

Slovik was still in Paris, where on December 9, 1944, he wrote to General Eisenhower (misspelling his name Eisenhowser) requesting clemency, but did not write that if given the opportunity he would go to the front lines. That seemed true to form. Born on February 18, 1920 in Detroit, between 1932 and 1937, Eddie Slovik received five convictions by the Juvenile Court of Detroit; four offenses were breaking and entering; one was assault and battery. In each case, he received parole. Then authorities caught him embezzling; a trial sentenced him to six months to ten years in prison on October 1, 1937. He first went to state "joint" at Jackson, but due to his age, authorities transferred him to the Michigan Reformatory at Iona, where he served one year. In 1939, a court convicted him of unlawfully driving away in an automobile and sentenced him to 2½ years to 7½ years. Slovik later said he spent a total of five years in jail. According to historian William B. Huie, General Eisenhower never read Slovik's letter.

On January 30, 1945, General Eisenhower directed that immediately upon the cessation of hostilities by armistice or otherwise all unexecuted sentences to death for purely military offenses – such as desertion – would be stayed and that appropriate orders be presented for his signature to commute them to life imprisonment. According to Brigadier General Betts, Eisenhower's rationale was that:

"Exemplary punishment of such offenses would, then, no longer serve a purpose requisite to the accomplishment of the Army's mission."

The same day, men from the 103rd Engineer Combat Battalion constructed a six-inch square wooden post and a heavy six-foot by six-foot wooden backstop panel in the courtyard of 86 *Rue du General Bourgeois* in Ste. Marie aux Mines, France. The same day, a four-man MP detail in Paris escorted Slovik in a weapons carrier the 227 miles to the French village, located northwest of Colmar, France. Because of the snowstorms, Slovik arrived at 7:30 a.m. on January 31, 1945; he then spent two hours in a small room with a Chaplain. No civilians were present; the unit had temporarily evacuated occupants of the residence. A seven and a half-foot high wall surrounded the premises. Snow on the ground measured fifteen inches. Men shoveled several paths through it, so the execution could proceed. At 9:50 a.m., fifty-two witnesses, led by Major General Cota, assembled in the courtyard. Most were members of the Twenty-Eighth Infantry Division. "Dutch" Cota was sending a message. At 9:55 a.m., guards entered the room of Private Slovik and tied his hands behind his back. Military Police Sergeant Frank J. McKendrick, of Philadelphia, whispered to Slovik, "Try to take it easy, Eddie. Try to make it easy on yourself – and on us," to which, Slovik replied,

"Don't worry about me; I'm okay. They're not shooting me for deserting the United States Army – thousands of guys have done that. They're shooting me for the bread I stole when I was twelve years old."

The Director of Execution, Major William Fellman II, led the execution party at the slow-step out of the building. Chaplain Carl P. Cumming followed, along with the condemned (escorted by six men of the division headquarters' MP platoon) and Lieutenant Colonel Sommer, who would serve as the recorder. To assist Major Fellman were First Lieutenant Zygmont E. Koziak and Second Lieutenant John J. Hucker. Four medical officers were present: Major Robert E. Rougelot, Major Donald W. Lyddon, Captain Marion B. Davis and Captain Charles E. Galt. It was cold and someone draped a GI blanket over Slovik's shoulders. The firing squad, already in the yard, was from the 109th Infantry Regiment, the men personally selected by the regimental commander on January 28, 1945. They included:

Sergeant Albert H. Bruns (in command),
    Company F
Private Aaron Morrison, Headquarters Company,
    1st Battalion
Private James K. Baker, Company A
Private First Class Oscar R. Kittle, Company D
Private Frist Class Earl Y. Williams, Company B
Private John J. James, Company F
Private Clarence M. Revlet, Company F
Private Robert A. Irons, Company G
Private Charles E. McDaniel, Company G
Private First Class Trinidad Sanchez,
    Headquarters Company, 3rd Battalion
Private Cass W. Carper, Headquarters Company,
    3rd Battalion
Frank Nawrocki, Headquarters Company,
    3rd Battalion
Thomas E. Keresey, Headquarters Company,
    3rd Battalion

• • •

Aaron "Pappy" Morrison hailed from West Virginia. After his father had died in a car wreck when Aaron was thirteen, he worked in a coal-company store to support his mother. Inducted at age eighteen, during the fighting in the Vosges Mountains, he guided mule teams loaded with rations and ammunition to resupply the forward companies – while under enemy fire. On January 28, he was playing poker with several of his buddies, when the company first sergeant walked up and notified him that he would be on a firing squad for a deserter. One of Morrison's buddies spoke up and said:

"What the hell they need those eleven other guys for? Old Pappy here ain't missed a squirrel's head at a hundred yards since he was six years old! Those other guys'll just be wasting ammunition."

"Pappy" was not so exuberant and went to his company commander to see if he could get out of the detail. The captain replied, "Not unless you want to take his place." Morrison would later state that emotions among the firing squad were mixed. Some were reluctant to be there, but another soldier stated:

"I got no sympathy for the sonofabitch! He deserted us, didn't he? He didn't give a damn how many of us got the hell shot out of us, why should we care about him? I'll shoot his goddam heart out. If only one shot hits him, you'll know it's mine."

• • •

The execution party reached the post at 9:57 a.m. Major Fellman read the GCM Order, as Private Slovik looked up at the gray, overcast sky and moved his lips in prayer. Eddie Slovik had no last statement to make to either Major Fellman or Chaplain Cumming. Fellman then ordered, "Prepare the condemned for execution." MPs secured Private Slovik to the execution post with straps around his chest and shoulders; other MPs wrapped a strap just above his knees and tied his ankles to the post with a rope. After placing a black hood – which had been sewn from cloth by a local French seamstress the day before – over his head, the execution party moved out of the line of fire. At 10:01 a.m., the firing squad marched into position – a single rank about twenty paces from the condemned man. Almost immediately, Major Fellman commanded: "Ready-Aim-Fire." The twelve-man detail immediately fired; one rifle had been loaded with a blank, while the other eleven for live rounds, but because of the negligible recoil of a blank round, each of the riflemen knew if he had fired it or not. According to the execution report:

"The body stiffened at the impact of the bullets. Blood and pieces of flesh splattered from the prisoner's back on to the board panel behind the post and the body then slumped forward, supported by the straps."

The document stated that about five seconds after the shots, the body straightened up, with the head and shoulders raising a foot and then dropping down. Three seconds later the body again raised six inches. The medical examiners would later say that both movements were involuntary muscle reflexes, but some of the witnesses were not too sure. "Pappy" and his comrades had seen better days on the rifle range. According to the examination, the rounds struck the following points on Slovik's body:

Two rounds: left sub-clavicular region,
    one inch apart
One round: one inch above left nipple
One round: one inch to the right of the left nipple
One round: adjacent to the sterno-manubrial
    junction, left side
One round: lower right sternum
One round: below fifth interspace, two inches from
    sternum (probably fatal wound)
One round: seventh interspace, right side,
    two inches from sternum
One round: graze of deltoid region, left shoulder
One round: upper left arm, shattering bone

The chief medical officer rushed over and heard a heartbeat, as he examined Slovik with a stethoscope. Seconds seemed to be hours and Major Fellman ordered the squad to reload, in case they needed another volley. The Chaplain yelled at Fellman to give Slovik another volley if he liked it so much. Major Fellman ordered the medical officer to either pronounce Slovik dead or else stand back so another volley could be fired. The medical officer replied, "The second volley won't be necessary, major. Private Slovik is dead."

The medical officers, Major Robert E. Rougelot, Captain Marion B. Davis, Jr. and Captain Charles E. Galt, officially pronounced Eddie Slovik dead at 10:08 a.m. An hour later, troopers burned the wooden firing post and brace board near the site. Army personnel placed the body of Private Slovik in a mattress cover and initially buried him at a temporary U.S. military cemetery at Épinal, France. The Army reinterred the remains at the American Military Cemetery at Oise-Aisne in Plot E, where his body lay for thirty-eight years in Row 3, Grave 65.

• • •

If the Army thought the sentence would influence other would-be deserters not to desert, it was sadly mistaken, as there was almost no mention of it. On February 7, 1945, the *Stars & Stripes* had this snippet of the event on page four:

**"GI Deserter Shot"**
"An American deserter has been executed by a firing squad at St. Marie-aux-Mines, France, for desertion, SHAEF announced today, without disclosing the soldier's name."

After Private Slovik's death, the 109th Infantry Regiment commander, Lieutenant Colonel James E. Rudder – who at Normandy had heroically led U.S. Army Rangers at Pointe du Hoc – sent a message to his soldiers that read:

"Today I had the most regrettable experience I have had since the war began. I saw a former soldier of the 109th Infantry, Private Eddie D. Slovik, shot to death by musketry by soldiers of this regiment. I pray that this man's death will be a lesson to each of us who have any doubt at any time about the price that we must pay to win this war. The person who is not willing to fight and die, if need be, for his country has no right to life. According to record, this is the first time in eighty years of American history that any United States soldier has been shot to death by musketry for deserting his unit and his fellow men."

• • •

After the war, Major General Cota granted an interview to author William Bradford Huie in 1953. In it, General Cota reflected on the Slovik case:

"I can't honestly assert that I was surprised by the action of the theater commander. After I approved the sentence, I thought the accused would ultimately be shot. I'll admit I was surprised – maybe a little irritated – at first when I learned that the theater commander was sending the soldier up for me to shoot. I had thought the execution would be performed back at the DTC, where many of the murderers and rapists were executed. But as soon as I thought it over, I conceded the logic in the theater commander's action: a deserter should be shot by the outfit he deserts."

Panel member, Benedict B. Kimmelman, wrote of his experiences in the case in: "The Example of Private Slovik," *American Heritage*, in September 1987. Kimmelman had anguished over the verdict since the war. The gist of his concern was that he had seen multiple instances of surrender and desertion during the "Battle of the Bulge" and no one had been punished. He went on to conclude that because Slovik's Defense Counsel was inexperienced, that amounted to a failure to give Slovik the full benefit of his day in court. To Kimmelman, a non-lawyer, this amounted to Slovik not receiving a fair trial.

In 1987, Eddie Slovik's remains returned to Detroit's Woodmere Cemetery in the Ferndale Section. Like so many events in his life, there was a problem and the airlines initially "lost" the remains in the airport in San Francisco, enroute from France to Michigan, but finally located them, and they continued on their way. The casket initially had an American flag, but a protest from the local chapter of Veterans of Foreign Wars led to removal of the flag and the addition of red, white and blue flowers. John Tankey – Eddie Slovik's buddy from the war – told reporters, "They wanted to make an example out of somebody, and Eddie was it." Eddie Slovik's current tombstone reads, "Honor and Justice Prevailed."[4]

Because his current gravestone indicates he was a private, but has no mention that he was executed as a deserter, it is decorated by volunteers each year on Memorial Day with an American flag. On the other hand, maybe they do know.

*"The evidence in this case indicates that the accused committed a series of crimes, unparalleled in this locality for their exhibition of savagery and bestiality. His past record of drunkenness and sexual crimes from his earliest youth to the present date demonstrates clearly that he is devoid of a sense of moral responsibility, as well as of personal discipline. All indications are that he is definitely a menace to society."*

*"Sir, we do not find this man dead."*

## 48 Private Waiters Yancy
37499079
1511th Engineer Water Supply Company
**Assault, Rape and Murder**
Hanged on February 10, 1945

## 49 Private Robert L. Skinner
35802328
1511th Engineer Water Supply Company
**Rape**
Hanged on February 10, 1945

The United States military conducted a worldwide effort during World War II. While history has generally credited the nation with fighting a two-front war (Europe and Pacific), the country actually was fighting on many more fronts, including the China-Burma-India Theater, Alaska and North Africa. The U.S. Navy and Merchant Marine fought a bloody struggle against Hitler's U-boats in half the world's oceans and against the Japanese navy in the other half. The "Arsenal of Democracy" produced the weapons and supplies of war, not only for the United States, but for many of her allies as well. These efforts required millions of men from every walk of life and strata of society. By the third year of the war, the United States was clearly winning the conflict. However, the brutal fact was that by 1944, the United States was running out of men.

The country turned to the nation's women to fill hundreds of thousands of positions in key armaments industries and certain positions in the military. The country also drafted and accepted as volunteers more black soldiers. From the Tuskegee Airmen to the 761st Tank Battalion, some 125,000 black soldiers fought overseas during the war. However, these additional sources were still not enough and by 1943, the Army began to relax standards for induction.[1] In the case of Private Waiters Yancy and Private Robert L. Skinner of the 1511th Engineer Water Supply Company, the Army actually scraped the bottom of the barrel.

On the night of August 1, 1944 at 10:30 p.m., the two soldiers walked into the tiny three-house hamlet of Hameau-Pigeon, France, looking for cider. A nineteen-year-old girl went to a shed to get some of the alcohol; Private Skinner attempted to grab her, but she broke free. Waiters Yancy, meanwhile, threw another woman to the ground and beat her on the head with his helmet and fists. Yancy then shot Xaver M. Hébert, in the arm. As two more Frenchmen approached the scene, Waiters shot one in the stomach at a distance of seven yards and shot the other twice in the back. Waiters then jumped on one man and hit him with the stock of his carbine so hard that it broke both the stock and the victim's arm. The soldier then turned toward the girl and struck her in the face with his damaged carbine, fracturing her cheek. The two soldiers, having crushed all resistance at the house, grabbed the girl, took her to a nearby orchard and raped her. Auguste Lebarillier, the victim with the stomach wound, received treatment at the 101st Evacuation Hospital at Saint-Sauveur-le-Vicomte, France, but died shortly thereafter. Seven weeks earlier, Lebarillier had hidden several American glider soldiers of the One Hundred and First Airborne Division from the enemy in the first days of the invasion.

All witnesses concerned described the two soldiers as "colored", one standing 5'4" or 5'5" and the other 5'8" or 5'9" (Waiters was 5'3" and 149 pounds; Skinner was 5'9" and 162 pounds.) Investigators found several expended cartridges with the same lot-number marking; the 1511th Engineer Water Supply Company was the only unit in the vicinity with that same number. Investigators also found several pieces of splintered stock; one of the pieces of wood had the initials "F.Y." The company supply sergeant reported his weapon was missing. The company commander then searched the unit garbage pit and found a bundle of uniform items and a disassembled carbine. Yancy's name was on two of the uniform items; he also was the assistant to the supply sergeant and slept in the same tent as this NCO. Yancy had thrown the stock of his own weapon away, stolen the sergeant's carbine, switched the stock and thrown the receiver into the garbage pit. Investigators never found the remaining pieces of Yancy's assigned weapon.

Yancy initially denied involvement, until MPs found a bloody field jacket in his duffel bag. He confessed on August 4, 1944 that he had shot three Frenchmen during the incident and raped the girl. He stated that Private Robert L. Skinner was with him and that Skinner had raped the girl first. The rape victim later identified Yancy. The next day, Skinner made a voluntary statement concerning his role in the incident and admitted having sex with the girl. Later, Private Yancy made a second written statement, stating his earlier admission had been correct, but that some of the details were sketchy because he was drunk at the time, adding,

"I just lost all control of myself. It seems that every time I get to drinking that I get like this and want to be with a woman. That alcoholic beverage seems to do this to me and if I can't be with a woman, I masturbate. This is something natural, I take after my father and I can't help. In two previous court-martials I had was due to me being under the influence of intoxicating liquors and being with women. I think I should be put under the care of a medical doctor or have him look into my case to see if he can't break me of this habit."

A board of medical officers at the 298th General Hospital examined Private Yancy on October 3, 1944; he had been in the hospital under observation since September 18. Lieutenant Colonel John M. Sheldon, Major Moses M. Frohlich and Captain Herbert T. Schmale found that Yancy, born in 1923, had five brothers and sisters and that his parents were separated. His father came home occasionally, usually after drinking excessively. Yancy was a bed-wetter until age ten. He began drinking alcohol at an early age and dropped out of school at age fifteen – he had repeated the fourth grade. He told the panel he began masturbating at age eight and intercourse at age fourteen. Police caught Yancy at age eighteen having sex with a fifteen-year-old girl and charged him with statutory rape. A year later, he assaulted an older black woman, after she refused to have sex with him, using a rock to hit her in the head; he also admitted trying to rape her. Yancy considered Chicago as his home. He was inducted at Fort Leavenworth, Kansas on January 23, 1943. A Special Court-Martial sentenced him once for refusing to go on guard duty. A Summary Court-Martial sentenced him for being drunk, allowing some girls to ride in his truck, and then driving his vehicle off a road into a swamp.

Private Robert L. Skinner was also under observation at the 298th General Hospital. The same panel found that Skinner was born on May 20, 1924 in Paris, Tennessee. Skinner's father died shortly after his son's birth and that much of Skinner's life was spent living with a cousin. His foster mother died when he was fourteen; he then lived with his mother in Chicago and Dayton, Ohio; he graduated from high school in Murphysboro, Illinois and later attended a trade school in Chicago. Just after his fifteenth birthday, Skinner received probation for two years for petty larceny. Three years later, police arrested him at a crap game and gave him the ultimatum of jail or the Army. He reported for induction on May 21, 1943 at Fort Thomas, Kentucky and later went to Fort Leonard Wood, Missouri for engineer training. He later went absent without official leave, receiving fifteen days restriction from a Summary Court-Martial. Skinner was not married. The panel wrote that Skinner was evasive and refused to participate in a psychometric examination, refusing to answer questions about the activities of his mother. In civilian life, Skinner went by the name Robert Lee Scofield.

The Army tried the men separately. The GCM of Private Waiters Yancy met at 9:00 a.m. on November 7, 1944 at Cherbourg.[2] Private Yancy pleaded not guilty to all charges and specifications, which included murder and carnal knowledge, both violations of the 92nd Article of War, and three counts of assault in violation of the 93rd Article of War.[3] There was some concern during the trial about the psychiatric examination. The Defense Counsel introduced it, but it was a two-edged sword, as Yancy also admitted to previous sexual crimes, two previous courts-martial and included:

"On questioning he [Yancy] goes into considerable descriptive detail which generally coincides closely to his alleged confession."

Nevertheless, as the examination was admitted by the defense, it was allowed. The defense then tried to show that the defendant was a person of low mentality, but that did not work either. The jury suspended the trial late on November 7, so that key participants could begin the Skinner trial. The Yancy panel reconvened on November 9, 1944 and unanimously found Yancy guilty on all counts; they sentenced him to death by hanging and adjourned at 10:43 a.m.

On November 8, 1944, Robert L. Skinner's trial began at the same location at 9:05 a.m. Second Lieutenant Joseph A. Bruggeman again served as the

Trial Judge Advocate. Captain Jean E. Pierson (TC) sat as Defense Counsel; he was assisted by First Lieutenant Joseph L. Weiser (TC.) On the court-martial panel were Lieutenant Colonel Paul H. Googe (TC), Lieutenant Colonel William C. Hollis (TC), Major Raymond J. Lamar (CE), Major Eugene T. Shields (QM), who also was the Law Member, Captain Oliver K. Jones, Jr. (TC), Captain Henry D. Bonneau (SC) and Captain Capers G. Bradham (CE.)[4] Googe, Hollis, Lamar, Shields and Bonneau had previously been members of General Courts-Martial that convicted and sentenced to death in separate trials Richard Scott and William Pennyfeather in September. Captain Capers G. Bradham was black.[5] Bruggeman had successfully prosecuted Scott and Pennyfeather; over the next day, he would add two more death penalty convictions to his resume. Pierson and Weiser, on the other hand, had lost as Defense Counsels in the Scott and Pennyfeather cases and would lose in the Skinner and Yancy cases.

The prosecution attempted to introduce Skinner's statement, but the Law Member excluded it. An NCO, who had been present when Skinner made the statement, received permission to testify; he stated that the accused had admitted he was with Private Yancy during the incident and that the rape victim had bitten his hand. The rape victim testified that Skinner had hit her three times in the face with his hand. Skinner declined to take the stand and the defense called no witnesses. The panel unanimously found Skinner guilty of carnal knowledge and sentenced him to death.[6] The court adjourned at 11:15 a.m., after taking two hours and ten minutes.

On November 21, 1944, the Staff Judge Advocate for the Normandy Base Section reviewed the trial records of Private Robert L. Skinner and found that the proceedings had been sufficient. It also opined that the Law Member should have allowed Skinner's statement into evidence. The review also stated:

"Considering the violent and gross nature of the offense committed by accused, the adverse effect it had and will have on relations with the local civilian population, the injury to the victim which necessitated treatment for a period of five weeks, and the absolute lack of anything in accused's background which would merit the extension of clemency in this case, none is hereby recommended."

On November 25, 1944, the Adjutant General of the Normandy Base Section sent a letter to the victims stating that the soldiers, who committed the acts, had been found guilty by a GCM and had been sentenced to death. The same day the Staff Judge Advocate for the Normandy Base Section reviewed the trial records of Private Waiters Yancy and found that the proceedings had been sufficient. Concerning clemency, the review pulled no punches:

"The evidence in this case indicates that the accused committed a series of crimes, unparalleled in this locality for their exhibition of savagery and bestiality. His past record of drunkenness and sexual crimes from his earliest youth to the present date demonstrates clearly that he is devoid of a sense of moral responsibility, as well as of personal discipline. All indications are that he is definitely a menace to society."

Colonel Eugene M. Caffey, the Commander of the Normandy Base Section, approved both sentences on November 26, 1944 and forwarded the records of trial up the chain of command. General Dwight D. Eisenhower signed the order confirming the death sentence for Private Robert L. Skinner on December 14, 1944. The Staff Judge Advocate for the ETO also reviewed Yancy's case, publishing their findings on December 22, 1944. Brigadier General Edward C. Betts concurred with the report that stated there were no major errors in the trial, although he found it curious that Yancy's written statement was not admitted into evidence, even though it was available. This review also introduced an assessment that Private Yancy had the mental age of nine years and eight months.

General Dwight D. Eisenhower signed the order confirming the death sentence for Private Waiters Yancy on December 23, 1944. The Staff Judge Advocate for the ETO reviewed Skinner's case on December 29, 1944. The board concluded that the trial had been sufficient. Their ruling had actually come fifteen days after General Eisenhower signed the confirmation order for Private Skinner's death sentence, but did not affect the validity of it. On January 16, 1945, Private Robert L. Skinner wrote a short letter to General Eisenhower, stating he was not guilty of the rape. Eisenhower designated that Colonel Caffey select an officer to interview the condemned; the task fell to Colonel Warren Hayford III, Commanding Officer of the Central District in the Brittany Base Section. Hayford interviewed Skinner on January 25, 1945. Skinner brought up two points: he first met his Defense Counsel just one day before the trial and that the victim had lied on the witness stand – the sex had been consensual. The transcript of the interview went to the Supreme

Commander. Transmittal and receipt stamps show that the Assistant Adjutant General at the ETO saw the interview transcript on February 5 and forwarded it to the Board of Review for the JAG for the ETO on February 6, 1945. The same day as Skinner's letter, the Branch Office of The JAG with the ETO weighed in. Board of Review No.1, with Judge Advocates Riter, Sargent and Stevens, found no significant problems with the record of trial.

On February 3, 1945, the ETO published General Court-Martial Orders Number 33. Brigadier General R.B. Lord – by command of General Eisenhower – directed that the execution of Private Waiters Yancy would occur on February 10, 1945 at Bricquebec, France. Captain Louis J. Baronberg, a medical officer, examined the men at about 7:30 p.m. the evening before the execution to ensure that each was in appropriate physical and mental health; they were.

On the cold, rainy morning of February 10, 1945 at Bricquebec, France, seven officials, five witnesses and sixteen authorized spectators stood near a wooden gallows located in a hedgerowed orchard, named La Ferme des Galeries, off the Avenue Matignon. Although the area was studded with trees, none was in the immediate area of the scaffold. Nine of the spectators were French citizens, including the living victims, headed by the rape victim. At approximately 9:58 a.m., a covered 2½-ton truck approached the field and halted fifty yards from the single entrance through the trees. A procession formed and marched from the vehicle to the scaffold. In the lead was Lieutenant Colonel Henry L. Peck, Commanding Officer of the Loire DTC. To his left was Chaplain Kilian R. Bowler. Next, walked General Prisoner Yancy Waiters, who was flanked by two guards and trailed by a third guard, who carried the brace-board. These three enlisted men were Sergeant Clyde R. Perkins, Corporal Albin S. Paprocki and Private First Class George B. Weber. Captain Milton B. Asbell and five official witnesses followed the guards.

The party halted at the steps of the gallows at 10:02 a.m.; the guards bound the arms of the condemned behind him and escorted him up the steps. At 10:04 a.m., Lieutenant Colonel Peck read General Court-Martial Orders Number 33, while the guards bound the prisoner's ankles, and then asked the prisoner if he had any final words. Waiters Yancy replied, "Thank you for everything." Chaplain Bowler then asked Private Waiters Yancy the same question, to which the prisoner replied, "Thank you for all that you've done."

Master Sergeant John C. Woods, adjusted the hood and rope at 10:07 a.m., and the Chaplain began to intone a prayer. Thirty seconds later, the Commanding Officer gave a silent signal to Woods, who cut the rope that released the weight and actuated the trap door. Everything functioned smoothly and at 10:18 a.m., Lieutenant Colonel Peck ordered the three medical officers to examine the prisoner. Captain Louis J. Baronberg, Captain Bernard S. Betherick and Captain Louis J. Guardino walked into the screened-in portion of the lower gallows and reported at 10:20 a.m., "Sir, we do not find this man dead." Peck ordered an additional five-minute wait. They did so, examined the body and pronounced Waiters dead at 10:27 a.m. The executioner then cut the rope and removed the body from beneath the gallows.

The witnesses stood in the cold intermittent rain for another twenty-five minutes for the second execution. Once again, a vehicle pulled up to the entrance of the field and General Prisoner Robert L. Skinner dismounted. Everything occurred in the same sequence, with Lieutenant Colonel Peck reading General Court-Martial Orders Number 32 at 10:58 a.m. He then asked the prisoner for his last words, which were, "Thanks very much." It was the Chaplain Bowler's turn to speak to the condemned man, who answered, "Thank you very much, Chaplain." Again, the trap door slammed opened, the prisoner dropped and by 11:17 a.m., the three medical officers pronounced the condemned dead.

The Adjutant General's Office in Washington, DC notified the mothers of Yancy Waiters and Robert L. Skinner on February 24, 1945 of their deaths by hanging. The Army initially buried the bodies of Waiters Yancy and Robert Skinner at the U.S. Military Cemetery at Marigny in Plot Z (Yancy in Grave 1-12 and Skinner in Grave 1-13) on February 12, 1945. Officials reinterred the remains in 1949 at the American Military Cemetery at Oise-Aisne in Plot E. Waiters Yancy's remains are in Row 2, Grave 31. Robert L. Skinner's body is in Grave 64 in Row 3.[7]

• • •

Citizens later inscribed Auguste Lebarillier's name on a monument in nearby Quettetot, France on May 8, 1989, as a victim of war.

• • •

In 1994, staffers for *After the Battle Magazine* visited Hameau-Pigeon and found that Monsieur Xavier Hébert was alive and still living in the tiny village. Monsieur Hébert recalled some of the events concerning the execution, saying that he rode in an American jeep to the execution site. He observed that there were hundreds of black American soldiers in attendance, guarded by a large number of MPs. Hébert continued in his interview by stating that some French villagers approached the area to see what was happening, but MPs, firing their weapons in the air, chased them away. He finally said that it had taken Yancy six minutes to die and that Skinner was present and observed this. This last assertion seems faulty, as records indicate that Skinner did not arrive at the site until well after the first execution. And Yancy had taken almost twenty minutes to die.

● ● ●

In 2011, the author visited the scene of the crime and the subsequent executions. The site of the hangings is today a series of sports fields a half-mile northwest of the center of Bricquebec. The Avenue Matignon is now a pedestrians-only walkway. Four miles to the west is the crime scene – the tiny hamlet of Hameau-Pigeon. The old farm buildings remain intact. Xavier Hébert passed away several years ago, but his family still occupies it. Hameau-Pigeon is so small and isolated that this is probably the reason why the execution was held in Bricquebec (a deviation from standard operating procedures) – so additional French civilians would be aware of the price American soldiers would pay if convicted of murder or rape.

*"I am really not guilty."*

*"The house to which I was conducted on the 24th of September 1944 was the same one which I visited on the night of the 20th of August 1944 and at this place I shot and killed Eugene Tournellec."*

## 50 Private William Mack
32620461
Battery A, 578th Field Artillery Battalion
**Assault and Murder**
Hanged on February 15, 1945

In some of the 96 death penalty sentences, it is obvious that the accused must have thought that his interrogators and the officers appointed over him were idiots. There seems to be no other explanation for a reasonable observer to explain how a defendant could change his story, often under oath, so many times and continue to believe that no one would figure out that he had to be lying.

August 20, 1944 was a Sunday; Private William Mack had the day off. At about 8:00 p.m., he told his fellow soldiers he was leaving the battery area to "get some cock." Armed with his M1 .30 caliber carbine, he had been drinking. Three hours later, he entered the home of Eugene Tournellec, about one and one-half miles from his unit. Mack demanded cognac, wine and cider and initially tried to kiss Tournellec's oldest daughter, Catherine. Eugene left the house to get help, during which time Mack fired a round through the door and then opened it, firing outside five or six times. One of the shots hit Eugene Tournellec in the forehead, which proved mortal. Mack then turned his attention to Catherine Tournellec, age sixteen, dropped his pants and touched her with his "private part." Mack then departed the house and Catherine fled. The next morning, she found the body of her father outside the door.

Meanwhile, at 11:50 p.m., August Jeanne, age nine, ran into the bivouac area of the 578th Field Artillery Battalion screaming that the Germans were murdering her father and mother. Second Lieutenant Alfred E. Kayes, Battery A, went to the scene and found four expended cartridges and one live round; he subsequently turned them over to an Ordnance officer, who directed that the weapons in the unit be test fired, concluding that firing marks on the expended rounds test-fired in Private Mack's weapon were similar to those found at the scene of the crime.

Private William Mack was a cook in Battery A. A black soldier, he had been born in St. George, South Carolina on September 21, 1910. He lived with his family, until his father died in 1924; he then lived on his own in St. George until 1937, finishing the sixth grade at age eighteen. He later worked for the Peoria Paper Box Company and the Burr Metal Company; in these jobs, he made $23 a week. In New York City, police arrested him for carrying a blackjack; a court gave him a suspended sentence. In another incident, police arrested him for being disorderly. Married with three children, Mack was inducted on November 7, 1942 at Fort Dix, New Jersey. Mack stood 5'8" tall and weighed 150 pounds; on the Army General Classification Test, he scored 59, making him a Class V. In 1937 and 1940, doctors diagnosed him with venereal disease. He had a previous Summary Court-Martial for missing training for one day.

On September 8, 1944, investigators read Private Mack his rights and then took his statement. Mack identified a weapon as his assigned carbine. He said that on the night in question he did not leave camp and kept his weapon with him the entire time. He added that he heard about a rape and murder the following day, and subsequently an officer test-fired his carbine. He finished by stating that he was not drunk on the day of the crime. Nevertheless, the evidence mounted against him. On September 23, 1944, Private Mack made a statement to Colonel R.E. Bower, the Inspector General of the Eighth Corps. He said he had remained in the battery area, and had consumed a small amount of wine that morning. He told Colonel Bower that although this was his day off, he had been helping his comrades clean some pots. Mack said that near evening, he left his weapon in his tent and walked to the front gate of the battery area, staying until it was almost dark. At 9:30 p.m., he went to bed and slept with his carbine. During the questioning, Mack remarked:

"That would be the last thing I would think of doing is killing somebody; something that I never wanted to have to do. That is why I hated it so bad to come in the Army, because I never believed in killing anybody."

Then Mack made a remarkable statement; he told the colonel that earlier in the campaign four soldiers in his unit raped some French women and that he had been present and had tried to stop the soldiers. Mack added that none of the four soldiers ever received a court-martial for the incident, that the battery commander knew of it, and that the "punishment" was for each of the men to pay $10 to the husbands of the victims. Because of his knowledge of the previous incident, Mack insinuated that he was being framed for the recent attack. Toward the end of his 24-page statement, Private William Mack concluded, "I am really not guilty."

Two days later, Private Mack requested to make another statement to Colonel Bower. He said that the day before – after he had first talked to the colonel – his memory started becoming a little clearer. Mack rambled for six pages of testimony, mostly stating that although he could not remember details, he must have been the person who had killed Eugene Tournellec, although he added, "I don't remember firing a gun." Private Mack mentioned that he kept hearing a man moaning, but that he did not recall seeing any adults, only a baby in a crib. On October 2, 1944, the accused changed his story once again. At Rennes, France, Major A.D. Brittingham, the officer assigned to investigate the overall case, interviewed Private Mack. He showed Mack the testimony that would be presented against him and the list of witnesses that would testify against him in court. The major then asked Mack if he wished to present any witnesses on his own behalf or cross-examine the witnesses against him. Mack gave a negative answer to both questions. Then Mack gave the following statement of his own volition, which read:

"The house to which I was conducted on the 24th of September 1944 was the same one which I visited on the night of the 20th of August 1944 and at this place I shot and killed Eugene Tournellec. I do not remember seeing any girl at the house – only the old man and a baby."

On October 6, the accused reported to the 127th General Hospital for observation. On October 27, 1944, Major Melvin F. Blaurock, a neuro-psychiatrist, wrote that the soldier had a mental age of eleven, but that in his opinion Private Mack was not psychotic or feeble-minded and: "Therefore if he is guilty, he can be punished as the court sees fit."

A GCM convened at Morlaix, France at 10:30 a.m. on November 23, 1944. The charges against Private William Mack included murder, a violation of the 92nd Article of War, and assault, a violation of the 93rd Article of War.[1] Private Mack pleaded not guilty to all charges and specifications. Captain George A. Schoberlein, Jr. served as the Defense Counsel; both his Assistant Defense Counsels were absent, but the defendant stated he had no objection to this.[2] Three soldiers testified that Private Mack had departed the battery area the night of the incident. They also stated that he had been drinking Calvados and wine. One soldier testified that he did not see Private Mack back at the battery until 2:00 a.m. on August 21. Surviving members of the Tournellec family could not identify the accused as the man who had perpetrated the crime. Pierre Tournellec, age fifteen, testified that after the first shot, he heard his father fall. The Law Member ordered that test firing conducted in the unit to determine which weapon had fired the rounds at the incident be stricken as hearsay. However, the prosecution brought in an expert witness, Ordnance officer Second Lieutenant Raymond A. Dortenzo, who testified that he fired the accused's weapon the night prior to the trial and that the expended rounds appeared to him to be the same as those found at the scene of the crime. The Defense Counsel made no objections to this testimony. Colonel Bower testified concerning his interviews of the accused, although the typewritten transcript was not entered into evidence. The Defense Counsel made no objection. Private Mack elected not to take the stand. The Defense Counsel introduced that Private Mack had been heavily drinking, inferring that he was not responsible for his actions. The court did not agree. It voted unanimously to convict Private William Mack of all specifications and sentenced him to hang.

On December 5, 1944, the Staff Judge Advocate of the Brittany Base Section, Lieutenant Colonel Dean E. Ryman, reviewed the record of trial. The review declared that the record of trial was legally sufficient to support the finding of the court and that the death sentence was free from any errors injuriously affecting the substantial rights of the accused. The reviewing officer also concluded that the evidence clearly showed that the accused was the perpetrator of the crime. The next day Colonel Roy W. Grower, the Commander of the Brittany Base Section, approved the sentence for Private William Mack and forwarded the records of trial up the chain of command. General Dwight D. Eisenhower signed the order confirming the death sentence for Private William Mack on January 2, 1945, but withheld the order to execute the sentence.

The Board of Review Number 1, consisting of Judge Advocates Riter, Sargent and Stevens, of the Branch Office of The JAG with the ETO, reviewed the case on January 30, 1945, finding no serious problems with the trial. On February 9, 1945, the ETO published General Court-Martial Orders Number 40. Brigadier General R.B. Lord – by command of General Eisenhower – directed that the execution of Private William Mack would occur at Plabennec, France on February 15, 1945. Doctors examined General Prisoner Mack the day before to ensure that he was in appropriate physical and mental health to be executed the next day – he was.

The site of the execution was an athletic field just outside the village of Plabennec, about eight miles north of Brest. A bright sun was shining about noon this February 15, 1945; the weather was mild and clear for that time of year, with a slight wind blowing. Seven officials attended; there were also five official witnesses, twenty-three military spectators and seven French observers. Among these seven were the daughter, cousin and grandmother of the murder victim. At 12:58 p.m., a covered 1½-ton truck halted sixty yards from the scaffold. Out stepped the condemned man, William Mack. He joined a foot procession led by Lieutenant Colonel Henry Peck, Commandant of the Loire DTC, and Chaplain John E. Sjanken. Flanking Mack were two guards, Staff Sergeant Charles R. Brinker and Sergeant John R. Hands. Behind, carrying a brace-board was Private Jay D. Pease. A recorder, First Lieutenant Lawrence Slon came next, followed by six official witnesses. Fifteen men, under command of First Lieutenant Allan H. Toole, of the 795th MP Battalion guarded the perimeter of the field.

The procession stopped at the gallows, where guards bound the prisoner's hands behind his back; they then assisted him up the wooden steps, positioned him on the center of the trap door and tied his ankles. Lieutenant Colonel Peck read General Court-Martial Orders Number 40 and then asked Mack if he had any final words. Private Mack responded:

"I'm proud to say that I've made my peace with the Lord. I've nothing to fear because I am on my way to peace and glory. I hope that the war will soon be over and everyone will return home to the ones that we love. Good Lord, take care of my family. Lead them and keep them on the straight and narrow path to glory. This is thy faithful servant talking."

Chaplain Sjanken then asked William Mack if he had anything to say; the prisoner replied, "See that those pictures are kept together and are sent home with those letters I wrote." The Chaplain then began to pray, while hangman Woods, adjusted the hood and rope. At 1:07 p.m., Lieutenant Colonel Peck gave a silent signal to Woods, who cut the rope that released a weight, springing the trap door. At 1:17 p.m., Peck directed that Captain Frederick W. Hall, Captain George G. Lenk and Captain Thomas Baer, examine the condemned. They did, but reported that William Mack was not dead yet. Five minutes later the three officers re-entered the lower screened understructure of the scaffold, examined the prisoner and pronounced the man officially dead. The three medical officers signed a certificate that stated that at 1:25 p.m. on February 15, 1945 William Mack died of judicial asphyxis (execution by hanging.) The *Chicago Tribune* reported the hanging on February 17, 1945 under the heading, **"U.S. Army Hangs Yank for Murder Near Brest."** The article gave no names or details of the offense or court-martial. On March 5, 1945, The Adjutant General's Office in Washington, DC notified the wife of William Mack in Brooklyn, New York of her husband's death by hanging.

The Army initially interred the body of William Mack on February 19, 1945 at the U.S. Military Cemetery at Marigny in Grave 1-14 in the General Prisoner section (Plot Z.) Officials reinterred the body in 1949 at the American Military Cemetery at Oise-Aisne in Plot E. William Mack's remains are in Row 3, Grave 63.

In the GCM file of Private William Mack is a checklist with twenty-six actions to be completed in the proceeding. Most deal with mundane issues such as if an "In" is stamped on the record, if a copy of the record had been withdrawn for the judicial file or if a record of trial has been entered on Form #19. In item twenty-five – "Examined by Clemency Section" – a date and notation is written in pencil. The date is "9/26/45" and the notation reads, "Death sentence already executed."[3]

• • •

By now, there appears to have been some concern about Master Sergeant Woods from his chain of command. Perhaps it was the high number of botched hangings; perhaps it was just his demeanor. On February 13, 1945, Lieutenant Colonel Peck wrote a letter to the War Department requesting confirmation of Woods' service in the Navy. Something just was not right; Count Basie could play *One O'Clock Jump* faster than Woods could hang a man.

*"I asked the Negro soldiers in a nice way to pay for their drinks."*

*"You got no business in these people's house;
you don't go in white people's houses in the States."*

*"These niggers are no good and let's shoot them."*

## 51    Private Otis B. Crews
### 14057830
3423rd Quartermaster Truck Company
**Murder**
Hanged on February 21, 1945

The U.S. Army had elements of organizational and individual racism in World War II. It was segregated – in part, because many officers throughout the years believed that black soldiers were inferior to white soldiers. Another reason for segregation was that both civilian and military leaders were convinced that black and white soldiers serving together would fight each other, because of prejudices each group had toward the other. Army bureaucratic forms often required information on whether a soldier was "white" or "colored." While we cannot accurately measure how the bureaucracy used that racial information, the mere fact that race was mentioned raised the possibility that it could be used in a negative or improper way.

This should not come as a surprise. The Army has always been a reflection of society and to a great degree America in the 1940s was a segregated nation – both in the north and the south. Nevertheless, not every accusation of racism in the U.S. Army – institutional or individual – during the war could be proven, nor were many even based on fact. That uncertainty, concerning racist accusations, sometimes crept into the court-martial arena – and there is no better example of this ambiguity than the case of Private Otis B. Crews.

At about 7:00 p.m. on January 16, 1944 at a wine shop at 53 *Via San Donato*, in Orto D'Atella, Italy, Private Crews, who was black, was drinking wine with two other black soldiers. They had asked the owner of the establishment, which was about ten miles north of Naples, if there were any women available. The woman, Rafaella del Prete, told them "no." After the soldiers drank three glasses of wine, they asked for more and Signora del Prete began to get nervous. About that time, Master Sergeant John A. Ganobcik and Master Sergeant James E. Collier, both white and assigned to the 334th Quartermaster Depot Company, entered the café, accompanied

by an Italian deaf-mute, who was dressed in an American uniform and who worked in their supply dump. Ganobcik later made a statement that soon after he entered the bar one of the soldiers – who turned out to be Crews – made a remark, "No one better fuck with me."

Master Sergeant Collier later stated that the deaf-mute made some sort of gesture at the three troopers and with that, Crews became belligerent, asking about the man. Collier answered and Crews then stated, "I don't care who he is, but he had better stop that or else I'll kill his ass before daylight." The two NCOs sensed that trouble was brewing and departed the café with their Italian companion. Signora del Prete sent a Signore Della Corte, who spoke English and was a translator at an American supply dump, to get some Military Policemen. He did and summoned Private Milton K. Ziegler and Private Wilbur Bryant, who were on patrol nearby with the 2651st MP Company.[1] Private Wilbur Bryant was twenty years old and hailed from West Virginia; he carried a .30 caliber carbine, while Ziegler was unarmed. The pair of MPs went into the café. Exactly what was said next remains unclear, but as Ziegler moved forward to search the men, Private Otis Crews began firing a .45 caliber U.S. Army pistol at the MPs, fatally wounding Private Bryant. The three soldiers fled; Ziegler initially pursued them – after picking up Bryant's weapon – but heard Bryant crying for help and returned to assist him. The autopsy of Private Bryant, who died twenty-six hours after being shot, indicated that he had been wounded with three shots; one to the left chest, one to the spleen and kidneys and a third to the buttocks.

The Military Police attempted to investigate but had no leads and within a few months, the case grew cold. On June 4, 1944, the Criminal Investigation Division assigned Agent Victor L. Dobrin and Agent Bernard Lipinski to pick up the investigation. The two agents canvassed witnesses and developed descriptions for all three men, sending this information to every unit that had black soldiers in the Peninsula Base Section and the entire Fifth U.S. Army. That generated a list of forty suspects. The pair contacted every unit with black soldiers and asked them to report the name of every soldier who was absent without leave on the day of the incident. They then requested a report on all confiscated .45 caliber U.S. pistols over the previous six months. The intrepid officers winnowed through all the information, which had begun to indicate that the three men were in the 28th Quartermaster Battalion. The two agents drove to the unit and after a discussion with the chain of command, fingerprinted the entire battalion. As the three soldiers in question had left the fingerprints on their glasses at the café, a match developed and on July 30, 1944, MPs arrested Private Otis Crews. Private Crews, who was born on March 17, 1917 in Carnegie, Georgia – a small town in western Georgia near Lake Eufaula, had enlisted on July 10, 1941.

Investigators interviewed the surviving MP, Private Milton K. Ziegler on August 1, 1944. Ziegler stated that while on patrol an Italian man had approached him saying that three "colored" soldiers were in his wine shop and had refused to pay for their drinks. The MP added that he had no weapon, but his partner had a .30 caliber carbine in his hands and the two went to the café in question. Private Ziegler continued:

"I asked the Negro soldiers in a nice way to pay for their drinks. One of them, a tall, light-browned, mustachioed Negro, who had his right hand in his field jacket pocket, made a movement as if gripping a pistol. I warned Bryant: 'Watch it' and to the colored soldiers, I said, 'Put your hands up. You've got to be searched.'"

Private Ziegler stated further that Bryant never spoke during the incident but held his weapon at the ready as if he expected trouble. Earlier on August 1, he had identified a prisoner at the Criminal Investigation Division, so he finished his statement by stating the results of that session, "I positively identify this soldier as the tall soldier of the three who fired at Bryant." Investigators questioned Private Richard W. Coleman, one of the three soldiers at the café, on August 2, 1944. Coleman stated that he did not know that Private Crews was armed. He also stated that both MPs carried carbines over their shoulder and that one MP did all the talking, saying, "These niggers are no good and let's shoot them." Coleman, who did not identify which MP had made the statement, then added that the two MPs then took their weapons off their shoulders and Private Crews began shooting. On August 4, 1944, investigators interviewed Private David Morris, the other of the two soldiers with Crews. He stated that he did not have a weapon nor did he know that Crews had one. Morris stated that when the two

MPs came into the café, one had a "Tommy gun" and the other had a .45 pistol. Morris stated that not much was said except that one of the MPs asserted that the three men had not paid for their drinks. He added that as one of the MPs stepped toward Private Crews, the accused gave him a little push and started firing, stating, "I saw Crews do the shooting." Private Crews also voluntarily made a statement that he had shot the MP, but fired in self-defense after he heard Bryant state, "Let's don't argue with them. Let's kill them." Crews also stated that Private Bryant had said, "You got no business in these people's house; you don't go in white people's houses in the States."

On August 25, 1944, Colonel John W. Huyssoon, the JAG for the PBS, provided his advice to the Commander of the PBS concerning how to dispose of the case:

"In my opinion, a *prima facie* case exists justifying trial upon the Charge and Specification as drafted. In my opinion the accused had no legal justification for the killing and there was no reasonable cause under the circumstances to believe that his life was in danger or for him to have been so provoked by the unseemly language employed as to warrant a finding that he killed in the heat of passion and was guilty of manslaughter only – a lesser included offense."

Brigadier General Francis H. Oxx, Commanding General, Peninsula Base Section in Italy, concurred and ordered a court-martial. A GCM met at Naples, Italy at 9:11 a.m. on September 26, 1944.[2] Private Otis Crews pleaded not guilty to the charge of murder, a violation of the 92nd Article of War.[3] The court weighed all the statements, found Crews guilty of murder and sentenced him to death by hanging. Brigadier General Oxx approved the sentence and forwarded the trial records up the chain of command. Lieutenant General Joseph T. McNarney signed the order on January 18, 1945 confirming the death sentence for Private Otis B. Crews, but withheld the order to execute the sentence. The Branch Office of the Judge Advocate General with the Mediterranean Theater of Operations (MTO) reviewed the case on February 13, 1945. Judge Advocates Sargent, Irion and Remick found that no errors injuriously affecting the substantial rights of the accused occurred during the trial. They also added that the record of trial was legally sufficient to support the findings and sentence. Concerning possible racial provocation and possible self-defense, the review stated:

"The evidence as to accused's claim of self-defense was conflicting. Ziegler testified that he spoke 'in a nice way' to the soldiers and that, neither he nor deceased used abusive language or threatened them. His testimony was corroborated by that of [Sanso] Giuseppe who testified that the military policemen spoke 'calmly, not threateningly' to the accused and his companions, and did not threaten them by any motions, although Bryant carried his weapon in readiness. Accused and Coleman testified that deceased quickly pulled his 'Tommy gun' from his shoulder and that he (accused) heard the safety click. The question of the credibility of witnesses, as well as the question of fact as to whether accused acted in self-defense was for the determination of the court."

The review did not state that Sanso Giuseppe, who had been in the café, did not speak English, but apparently, the court decided he was a credible witness concerning demeanor. The same day, the MTO published General Court-Martial Orders Number 28. Major General George D. Pence – by command of Lieutenant General Joseph McNarney – directed that the execution of Private Otis B. Crews occur at Aversa, Italy on February 21, 1945.

On February 19, 1945, Major W.G. Neiswender read General Court-Martial Orders Number 28 at 9:00 a.m. at the stockade to General Prisoner Crews. Major Neiswender told him that his execution would be at 8:00 a.m. on Wednesday, February 21, 1945. That morning eight commissioned officers assembled at the place of execution. They included: Colonel Kirk Broaddus (CAV), Major Arthur S. Imell (IN), Major Tex Davis (OD), Captain John J. Stringfellow (MP), First Lieutenant Paul S. Logan (MP), First Lieutenant T. Schintz (MP), First Lieutenant Edward T. Clunan and First Lieutenant Benjamin Mondragon (IN.) Twenty years earlier, Colonel Broaddus had been a young lieutenant in the 10th Cavalry Regiment, one of the original "Buffalo Soldier" regiments, at Fort Huachuca, Arizona. Major W.G. Neiswender served as the officer in charge of the execution. Spiritual assistance to Private Crews came from Chaplain William T. Watts. Everything remained on time and the trap door opened precisely at 8:00 a.m. Captain Samuel Penchansky, a medical officer with the 262nd Station Hospital, pronounced Private Crews dead at 8:09 a.m.

The Army initially interred Otis B. Crews' body at the U.S. Military Cemetery in Naples, in Plot GP (General Prisoner), Row 1 and Grave 8. His remains are now buried at the American Military Cemetery at Oise-Aisne in Plot E – in Row 2, Grave 30.

Major W.G. Neiswender sent a letter of condolence on April 12, 1945 to the mother of Private Otis Crews. It read in part:

"Your son, Otis, died at this station on the 21st of February, 1945 and was buried in Southern Italy. The funeral was under the auspices of an Army Chaplain … You have the sympathy of the officers and men of this organization in your bereavement … May I express my own personal sympathy in your loss, which is made so much more difficult by the time and distance which has separated you from your son."[4]

## 52     Private William Clifton Downes

**33519814**

597th Ordnance Ammunition Company
**Breaking & Entering, and Rape**
Hanged on February 28, 1945

It was another incident of a home invasion culminating in multiple rapes in Normandy. On July 12, 1944, three black soldiers in the 597th Ordnance Ammunition Company, Private James R. Parrott, Private Grant U. Smith and Private William C. Downes, allegedly broke into a home in Étienville and raped a sixty-two-year-old woman and her fifteen-year-old daughter. They then returned to their company bivouac area. Two weeks later, the three soldiers – who had not yet been apprehended for the first attack – allegedly went on the prowl again, broke into a home in the village of Renouf (two miles from Étienville) and raped a middle-age widow. Her two children escaped and found First Lieutenant Michael Sorbello of the 795th Anti-Aircraft Artillery Automatic Weapons Battalion. The quick-thinking officer summoned three enlisted men and had the children lead them back. Near the home of the attack, he found the three men and began asking them questions, while the latest rape victim identified the men as her attackers. They had struck her on her face and one eye, which would later bruise.

Officers arrested the three soldiers on July 28, 1944. After a thorough investigation, the Commander of the Normandy Base Section determined that the three men would be tried jointly in a GCM. The court met at Cherbourg on November 22, 1944. The three men pleaded not guilty to three counts of carnal knowledge, a violation of the 92nd Article of War, and two counts of breaking and entering, in violation of the 93rd Article of War.[1] The court weighed the testimony of the victims, especially the degree of certainty with which they could – or could not – positively identify the three accused. All three defendants took the stand and denied all specifications. Downes testified that he had been on detail all day long on July 12; concerning the events of July 26, Downes claimed that the three men had been in the village looking for cognac, but finding none, they were in the process of returning to their company area. When earlier questioned by First Lieutenant Sorbello, Downes testified that, "We told him we got lost from our area or we wouldn't been out that late."

The jury found Private William C. Downes guilty of all charges, but determined that Private James R. Parrott and Private Grant U. Smith were only guilty of the charges and specifications related to the attack on July 26, 1944. Private Smith had two previous Special Court-Martial convictions for being absent without official leave; Private Downes also had a Special Court-Martial conviction for the same offense. The jury then sentenced all three men to death by hanging.

Then the Army's judicial review process weighed in and higher commanders played a role to which they were entitled. First, the Staff Judge Advocate of the Normandy Base Section opined in his review concerning the admissibility of some of the evidence concerning the identification of the accused by various French civilians, identification he termed extra-judicial. Brigadier Henry S. Aurand considered his Staff Judge Advocate's review and approved the sentences, but concerning Specification 2 of Charge II, struck that portion of the specification concerning "burglariously." He then forwarded the matter to General Dwight Eisenhower, whose Staff Judge Advocate reviewed the case on December 18, 1944. Eisenhower confirmed the sentences, but then cited "special circumstances" and commuted the sentences of Parrott and Smith to dishonorable discharges from the service, forfeiture of all pay and allowances and confinement at hard labor for life at the United States Penitentiary at Lewisburg, Pennsylvania. He signed the confirmation order, confirming the sentence of death for Private William C. Downes, on January 14, 1945, but stated no place or date for the execution. William Downes was born on January 27, 1915 in Copeland, Virginia. He was inducted on December 17, 1942 at Norfolk, Virginia.

On February 9, 1945, the Branch Office of The JAG with the ETO reviewed the case. Judge Advocates Riter, Sherman and Stevens concluded that the record of trial was sufficient, but disagreed with the Staff Judge Advocate of the Normandy Base Section in his opinion concerning the admissibility of some of the identification evidence. The Board of Review mentioned that Eisenhower invoked special circumstances, but did not elaborate on what exactly these were. On February 23, 1945, the ETO published General Court-Martial Orders Number 50. Brigadier General R.B. Lord directed that the execution of Private William C. Downes occur at Étienville on February 28, 1945. On February 24, 1945, a set of orders from the Normandy Base

Section directed three medical officers to attend the execution. Their mission would be straightforward, "Pronouncement of the extinction of life."

A second set of orders, from the Loire Disciplinary Center, directed that Master Sergeant John C. Woods, Technician Third Grade Thomas F. Robinson and Technician Fifth Grade Herbert A. Kleinbeck proceed to Étienville two days before the execution. Their implied missions were to prepare the gallows for the event, conduct the hanging and dismantle the gallows after the execution. The same set of orders directed that General Prisoner William Downes be taken on February 27, 1945 to Cherbourg. It is presumed that he was confined that evening at Fort du Roule and then transported to Étienville early on February 28.

At 9:45 a.m., on February 28, 1945, seven officials, five military witnesses, five military observers and five French civilians – including one of the rape victims – met at a gallows constructed in an open field three-hundred yards south of Étienville. Low hedgerows surrounded the field, like many others in the war-torn region. The gallows faced south. An intermittent rain was falling that winter day, with the sky slightly overcast. A detail from Company A of the 384th MP Battalion, under the command of First Lieutenant David J. Duff, guarded the site. At 9:58 a.m., a closed 2½-ton, 6x6 truck slowly approached the field and halted fifty yards from the scaffold. The condemned man debarked and took his place in a column of men. At the head was Lieutenant Colonel Henry L. Peck, Commandant of the Loire DTC, followed by the prisoner and Chaplain Augustus G. Spears – a Methodist, who was one of the Army's few black Chaplains. Three guards surrounded the prisoner: Sergeant Russell E. Boyle, Sergeant Kenneth L. Breitenstein and Sergeant Alfonso Girvalo. Recorder, First Lieutenant Lawrence Slon and five officials followed.

The procession marched to the foot of the steps of the scaffold and halted at 10:00 a.m. The guards bound the condemned man's arms behind his back and assisted him to climb the gallows. As Woods bound the prisoner's ankles, Lieutenant Colonel Peck read General Court-Martial Orders Number 50. The prisoner elected to make no final statement, nor did he make a statement to Chaplain Spears. After Master Sergeant John C. Woods adjusted the black hood and rope, the prisoner said a prayer aloud for one minute. The Commandant gave a silent signal to Woods, who cut the rope that released the weight, which actuated the trap door. The body dropped and after reaching its lowest point, swung in a slight motion. At 10:19 a.m., the Commandant ordered the examination of the prisoner. Captain Robert L. Kasha, Captain Louis J. Baronberg and Captain Louis J. Guardino entered the lower screened understructure of the scaffold, examined the prisoner and pronounced him dead.

The Commander of the Normandy Base Section wrote a letter of regret to the Mayor of Étienville on March 10, 1945. He expressed his regret and informed the mayor that one of the convicted had been executed and the other two soldiers were sentenced to life imprisonment. The War Department notified an aunt of William Downes on March 15, 1945 that he had died in a non-battle status due to his own misconduct.

The Army initially interred the body of William Downes at the U.S. Military Cemetery at Marigny on the day of his death. Buried in Grave 15 of the General Prisoner section, to his left was William Mack. Officials reinterred the remains 1949 at the American Military Cemetery at Oise-Aisne in Plot E, where they are in Grave 16 of Row 1.[2]

• • •

During the author's visit on September 15, 2011 to the village of Étienville – which has a population of 332 – Mayor Georges René, who was a small boy during World War II, pointed out the house where the crime occurred and the nearby field, where William Downes was executed several months later. The house is still standing; the site of the execution is now a cornfield.

*"The Defense Counsel told us we was going to get a raw deal. He said he didn't think that court would give us a fair trial and sentence us to be hung."*

*"I beg the court to live; beg mercy from the court to let me live, sir."*

## 53     Private Amos Agee
34163762

644th Quartermaster
  Troop Transport Company
**Rape**
Hanged on March 3, 1945

## 54     Private John C. Smith
33214953

644th Quartermaster
  Troop Transport Company
**Rape**
Hanged on March 3, 1945

## 55     Private Frank Watson
34793522

644th Quartermaster
  Troop Transport Company
**Robbery and Rape**
Hanged on March 3, 1945

Private Amos Agee, Private John C. Smith and Private Frank Watson arrived in France on August 30, 1944 to begin their roles in the grand endeavor to liberate Europe from Nazi tyranny. Three days later, on September 2, they reported to their new unit, the 644th Quartermaster Troop Transport Company at about 11:00 a.m. Within an hour, the trio ate "chow" and began hitting the "hooch," the unit chain of command having failed to assimilate the new soldiers in a proper manner. At 3:00 p.m., the three young men visited the village of Le Noyer, where they visited a French family and asked for more alcohol. After a half hour, the soldiers returned to their unit, ate supper and again went out on the countryside to find something to drink. At about 11:00 p.m. – in what may have been an ignominious record for new soldiers in the theater – Private Watson robbed two Frenchmen and all three soldiers raped a French woman. The trio subsequently returned to camp, played cards for a while and then went to sleep.

They awoke the next morning to find several French civilians in consultation with Captain Isidor Lazar, their company commander. Lazar then ordered part of his company to fall in, but the victims could not find Private Watson. Agee

and Smith, as they were on a work detail. Two days later, five French civilians returned and identified all three soldiers, repeating the identification, after Lazar rearranged the line-up. MPs then arrested the three black soldiers. Authorities confined the three soldiers at the U.S. Army Prisoner of War Stockade at Trévières on September 3. On September 9, 1944, Captain Abraham J. Swiren, the investigating officer in the case, explained to the three men their rights; all three elected to make statements. Captain Regnard Robert (MC) examined the female victim and found abrasions and bruises on her. Given all the evidence, Captain Swiren recommended to the Commanding General, Advance Section that the case should go to a GCM. The commander agreed.

On October 18, 1944, the GCM began at Rambouillet, outside of Paris. Two officers served on the prosecution: Captain Vincent F. Kelley (QM) and First Lieutenant George F. Kerby (QM.) Two officers served on the defense team: Captain Justin R. Howard (QM) and First Lieutenant Alexander Doran (QM.) The all-Quartermaster Corps jury included: Lieutenant Colonel Thomas B. Kellum, Major Anthony T. Campbell, Major Paul B. Roesch, Major Edward Warren, Jr., Captain Clifford M. Beasley, Captain Clarence A. Witzal, Captain Isidor Lazar and First Lieutenant Yancey Griggs; First Lieutenant Griggs was black.[1] The author did not find if Captain Lazar remained on the panel. The three accused pleaded not guilty to all charges. The prosecution presented the female victim, who testified that all three men, armed with a rifle, took turns holding her down and raping her. Her husband corroborated her testimony under oath. A neighbor testified that he saw three "colored soldiers" at the victim's home that afternoon, but he could not identify the accused in court. A maid at a nearby hotel identified all three men as drinking at the hotel that afternoon. Captain Isidor Lazar testified about the line-up after the crime; the court admitted the medical officer's examination into evidence.

All three accused submitted sworn statements in which they admitted going to the house that afternoon, but all three stated they had nothing to do with the events of later in the evening. Amos Agee was the first defense witness to take the stand. He said he had been so drunk that he could not remember everything that happened. When asked if he had anything else to tell the court, Agee answered, "I beg the court to live; beg mercy from the court to let me live, sir." John C. Smith testified next. He substantially told the same story, although he indicated that the three had gone drinking after supper, but that he had nothing to do with any women that night. Frank Watson testified last; he stated he was "pretty high," but did not recall visiting the victim's home the evening of the crime. The court did not buy their explanations. It convicted Private Watson of two specifications of the 93rd Article of War for robbery and all three men of the more serious charge of carnal knowledge.[2] On the trial's second day, the jury chose death by hanging for all three soldiers.

Amos Agee was born on February 16, 1916 in Linden, Alabama, fifty miles south of Tuscaloosa. Standing 5'8" tall and weighing 174 pounds, he was inducted on November 19, 1941 at Fort McClellan, Alabama. Medical forms indicate that the single soldier suffered from syphilis and gonorrhea. Agee attended high school for three years, before quitting and becoming a steel worker for $20 per week. Agee had been convicted three times before at a court-martial, once for failure to obey the order of a superior officer (and drunk and disorderly) and twice for AWOL.

John C. Smith was born on September 20, 1917 in Bedford County, Virginia, one of ten children. A Baptist, he left school after just four years and became a farmer. He was single and entered the Army on October 14, 1942 at Roanoke, Virginia. Smith later went to Fort George Meade, Maryland; he subsequently reported to the 70th Ordnance Battalion at Fort Huachuca, Arizona. In the service, he was diagnosed with syphilis. Smith's mother lived in Roanoke, Virginia.[3] Frank Watson, born in Florida in 1923, was inducted at Camp Blanding, Florida on September 29, 1943. Watson's father lived in Oneil, Florida; Watson had lived in Baltimore, Maryland.[4] Neither Watson nor Smith had any previous military convictions.

The Commanding General, Advance Section, Brigadier General Ewart C. Plank approved the sentences on December 4, 1944. On January 14, 1945, General Dwight D. Eisenhower signed a letter confirming all three sentences, but withheld the order directing the execution. Private Watson wrote a letter to General Eisenhower on January 16, stating that he did not think he received a fair trial. Eisenhower referred the letter to Colonel Warren Hayford III, the Commander of the Central District of the Brittany Base Section. Hayford visited Private Watson in the stockade on January 25 to find out more information. Watson told the colonel,

"The Defense Counsel told us we was going to get a raw deal. He said he didn't think that court would give us a fair trial and sentence us to be hung."

Colonel Hayford tried to get Watson to name which member of the defense team, Captain Howard or First Lieutenant Doran had made the remark. Watson seemed to indicate that it was Doran. Hayford then asked Private Watson what was unfair about the trial, specifically, "Do you think the other witnesses were lying?" Watson replied, "I know they was." Hayford asked the question another way, "You think the civilian witnesses were lying, is that it?" Watson again answered, "Yes, sir." Watson said he had been fairly represented by counsel. Hayford closed the interview by stating, "All right, this will be sent up and considered by the proper authorities."

The Branch Office of The JAG with the ETO reviewed the case on February 14, 1945. The three-man panel (Van Benschoten, Hill and Anthony Julian) ruled the court was legally constituted, had jurisdiction of the person and offenses, and committed no errors injuriously affecting the substantial rights of the accused; thus, the record of trial was legally sufficient to support the findings of guilty and the sentence imposed. There is no mention of Colonel Hayford's interview of Private Watson. If another "proper authority" considered Watson's claim, it changed nothing. On February 26, 1945, the ETO issued three orders: General Court-Martial Orders Number 52 directed the execution of John C. Smith, General Court-Martial Orders Number 53 directed the execution of Amos Agee and General Court-Martial Orders Number 54 directed the execution of Frank Watson. The same day Brigadier General Edward C. Betts wrote to Private Smith – who had written the theater commander – that General Eisenhower would not commute the sentences. Lieutenant Colonel Herman De Feo examined all three men about 7:00 p.m. on March 2 and found all to be in excellent physical and mental health.

The Army executed Private Agee first. On Saturday, March 3, 1945, Lieutenant Colonel Henry L. Peck, Commanding Officer, Loire DTC, assembled twelve Army officials and witnesses, three French Gendarmes and fourteen French civilians – including the husband of the raped woman, the Mayor and the Deputy Mayor. The party stood before a temporary gallows in a hedge-rowed orchard in the village of La Saussaye, Commune de Bure, two and one-half miles east of Le Mêle-sur-Sarthe. The weather was cool, clear and sunny as the military observers stood in a single rank, twelve paces from the northern side of the gallows, while the French observers stood twenty paces from the western side. First Lieutenant William Malkenson and twenty men from Company B, 389th MP Battalion provided the guard force.

At 11:00 a.m., a ½-ton, command-reconnaissance vehicle approached, drove to the entrance to the field, and from it, guards assisted Amos Agee. At 11:02 a.m., Lieutenant Colonel Peck led the execution procession, consisting of himself, Chaplain Kilian R. Bowler, the prisoner, three guards (Sergeant Russell E. Boyle, Sergeant Alfonso Girvalo and Sergeant Kenneth L. Breitenstein), and the recorder, Captain Milton B. Asbell. The procession reached the foot of the south side of gallows, at which point Lieutenant Colonel Peck and the Chaplain ascended the steps. During the half-minute march, Agee repeated:

> "Lord Jesus have mercy … through the Valley of Death … Lord have Mercy … Thy rod and Thy staff … O Lord have mercy."

The guards bound his hands behind his back at 11:03 a.m., led him up the steps and positioned him on the trap door. Thirty seconds later, Peck read General Court-Martial Orders Number 53. This was the order directing the execution. The executioner's assistant bound Agee's ankles. The time was 11:04 a.m. The Commanding Officer and then the Chaplain asked the condemned if he had any last words. Agee replied to Peck, "Thank you for everything." To the Chaplain he replied, "Father, I thank you for everything." After a moment, the Chaplain began the Lord's Prayer. The time was 11:07 a.m. The prisoner then asked, "Let me pray a little; Chaplain, let me look at you once more." The executioner, Master Sergeant John C. Woods, adjusted the noose and the hood. A "little" lasted ninety seconds, when Peck silently signaled Woods, who cut the rope that released the weight that actuated the trap. The mechanism operated without fault and the prisoner dropped cleanly through the trap door and hung suspended in the lower screened recess of the scaffold. The witnesses stood silent without reaction, as the Chaplain performed the last rites; the time was 11:09 a.m.

At 11:20 a.m., the Commanding Officer ordered the three medical officers to examine the body. The trio made their examination, emerged, and returned to their original positions. Lieutenant Colonel Herman F. De Feo, reported, "Sir, we pronounce this man officially dead." The time was 11:23 a.m. Peck temporarily dismissed the gathering a minute later, while the executioner cut the rope and removed the body. First Lieutenant Hardy C. Derx of the

3058th Graves Registration Company signed for the remains. The time was 11:25 a.m.

Private John C. Smith was the next to die. At 11:40 a.m., the ½-ton, command-reconnaissance vehicle approached and returned to the entrance to the field, this time carrying Private Smith. The proceedings followed the same sequence as before, until 11:45 a.m., when Lieutenant Colonel Peck asked the condemned if he had anything to say. Private Smith replied, "I want to shake hands with you." Peck complied with the request and then said to Smith, "Good luck, son." The prisoner replied, "See you all somewhere." Peck then asked if Private Smith had anything to say to the Chaplain. Smith answered, "Write to my mother; see that she gets everything." The trap door actuated at 11:47 a.m. That's when something went wrong. Smith's body dropped and made no sound or muscular movement, but the fall apparently did not break his neck. When the medical officers entered the lower screened understructure of the gallows at noon, Lieutenant Colonel DeFeo examined Smith for two minutes and announced, "Sir, this man is not dead." It was another SNAFU for the hangman. Peck ordered a five-minute wait. At 12:10 p.m., the medical officer reported, "Sir, I pronounce this man officially dead." Master Sergeant Woods cut the rope and removed the body, and First Lieutenant Derx signed for it in just one minute, half the time the two procedures took in the first execution – the reason for this promptness was that one more man still needed to be hanged.

That man was Private Frank Watson. At 12:35 p.m., the ½-ton, command-reconnaissance vehicle returned to the entrance to the field with Watson. Again, the same procedures were followed; Watson made no statement to the Commanding Officer, but to the Chaplain he said, "All I want you to do is pray for me." At 12:44 p.m., Woods released the trap door; this time there were no problems and by 1:00 p.m. the senior medical officer had pronounced Watson dead. The recorder prepared three separate reports of the proceedings. In each report, he ended with:

> "Each official performed his task in a highly efficient manner. The proceedings were conducted with dignity, solemnity and military precision."

Chaplain Ernest Kistler fulfilled Private Smith's wishes and wrote his mother in Roanoke. The Chaplain conveyed his condolences, but did not mention that her son had been hanged. Chaplain Kilian R. Bowler wrote the Agee family on August 8, 1945. He stated that Private Agee had converted to the Catholic faith.

Army personnel interred all three bodies on March 5, 1945 at the U.S. Military Cemetery at Marigny in Plot Z, Graves 1-16, 1-17 and 1-18. In 1949, officials reinterred them at the American Military Cemetery at Oise-Aisne in Plot E; Amos Agee is located in Row 1, Grave 14; John C. Smith's body lays in Row 3, Grave 67; and Frank Watson's remains are in Row 3, Grave 55.[5]

• • •

The author visited La Saussaye in September 2011. However, no one in the tiny village knew exactly where the executions had taken place. Concerning this incident in history, the area's collective memory is lost.

> *"The woman that Cubia and I had intercourse with did not scream nor object to our actions when we were with her."*

## 56      Private Cubia Jones
### 34563790
Company A,
    1698th Engineer Combat Battalion
**Rape**
Hanged on March 17, 1945

## 57 Corporal Robert L. Pearson
### 38326741
Company A,
    1698th Engineer Combat Battalion
**Rape**
Hanged on March 17, 1945

Cubia Jones and Robert Pearson were typical of those soldiers, who were the products of hardscrabble backgrounds, but until a serious incident occurred, they would not have been thought capable of a major crime. Cubia Jones was born in Thomson, Georgia on May 12, 1919. An only child, Cubia Jones' mother died when he was eight. His father – a sharecropper – died of tuberculosis when Cubia was thirteen. By that point, the youngster had dropped out of school at the age of twelve, still in the third grade; he moved in with an aunt. Later intelligence examinations would conclude that Jones had the mental level of a child nine to eleven years old. At age fourteen, Jones, who was black, began work as a sawmill worker and truck driver, earning $12 per week. He had various illnesses and maladies: mumps in childhood, pneumonia at age ten, gonorrhea at age fourteen (he told a physician that he first had intercourse at age ten), gonorrhea again at age twenty-three (which caused a three-month hospital stay) and syphilis at age twenty-five. He also came down with measles in April 1944. Jones began drinking daily at age sixteen and began smoking marijuana. His last incident with marijuana was in November 1944. Cubia Jones was arrested at age sixteen for being drunk and disorderly. Cubia Jones had been inducted on December 29, 1942. At his induction physical, he did thirty sit-ups, six pull-ups and ran the shuttle run in sixty-three seconds, all of which put him in the "poor condition" category. Originally, in the Field Artillery, he was transferred into the Combat Engineers and served as an ammunition carrier and a laborer. A Summary Court-Martial convicted him in June 1943 for being absent without leave, when he overstayed a weekend pass because his aunt was ill. He received company punishment in August 1943

for being drunk. A Special Court-Martial convicted him in November 1944 for being absent without official leave when he went home to visit his wife before going overseas. Cubia Jones was married on June 5, 1944; he and his wife had no children. He stood 5'7½" tall and weighed 150 pounds.

Corporal Robert L. Pearson, also black, was born on May 30, 1923 in Mayflower, Arkansas. His mother died when he was four years old; two of his brothers died in infancy. His father was still living, a retired railroad worker. Robert Pearson graduated from high school at age eighteen and then worked in a shoe-repair shop, a drug store and finally as a porter at a bus station, where he earned $14 a week; he was Baptist. Unlike Jones, Pearson regularly attended church. He did not gamble or use much alcohol, nor was he married. Intelligence tests indicated that he had a mental age of about twelve. He moved to Muskogee, Oklahoma and entered the Army on December 30, 1942 at Fort Sill. Pearson was initially assigned to the Army Air Corps, but in February 1943 transferred to the Field Artillery; he stood 5'7" tall and weighed 168 pounds. His unit converted to the Combat Engineers and Pearson became an assistant squad leader and received a promotion to corporal on April 5, 1943. According to available information, Pearson had been an excellent soldier prior to this incident.

Both men were assigned to Company A of the 1698th Engineer Combat Battalion stationed at Chard, England; they had embarked in New York City on October 29, 1944 and had arrived in England on November 11, 1944. On December 3, 1944, they left camp to walk downtown. The evening was dark and before too long they met a young woman walking in their direction. They began talking with her and ended up in a muddy field adjacent to the street, where both soldiers had sex with her. Both men would later claim that the relations were consensual; unfortunately, for them, she would claim otherwise.

Shortly after the incident, the woman ran into a friend and reported that she had been assaulted. The two then went to the Somerset Constabulary station and reported the incident. Witnesses later stated that she looked distressed, pale and crying, with her lip bruised and nose slightly swollen. British law enforcement authorities quickly notified U.S. authorities; the two soldiers had returned to camp at 9:15 p.m.; at 11:30 p.m., the company commander held an inspection of his men, looking for muddy clothing. MPs immediately arrested Pearson, as he had mud on his trousers. They arrested Private Jones was arrested at 1:30 p.m. on December 4. Private Jones signed a statement that day at 5:15 p.m. He said that when he and Pearson asked if they could have sex with her, she said that she would with one but not with both. Jones began the act, but quickly stopped, after which Pearson began. Jones then said he would try again, but according to Jones, the woman said, "No, I am feeling bad; I cannot do it anymore." With that, Jones said he stopped. The two talked with the woman for a short time during which, according to Jones, she said, "I will meet you there tomorrow night." Corporal Robert L. Pearson also made a statement. He said that the woman initially told them that if they did not kill or hurt her she would tell them where more ladies were. According to Pearson, she told them that she had children at home and that when the sex began she pulled up her dress. Pearson added that when he was having sex with the woman she hugged and kissed him. He stated that he did not carry a knife and did not see Private Jones carry a knife that evening. Pearson concluded by stating, "The woman that Cubia and I had intercourse with did not scream nor object to our actions when we were with her."

The accounts of Pearson and Jones did not match that of the victim. On December 5, 1944, she made a sworn statement and answered questions by an investigator. She said that the men approached her on the night in question; she said she became frightened and told them to leave her alone. She said she told them that she was married and was nine months pregnant. When she started to shout, she said that the men put their hands over her mouth and nose and that she began losing consciousness. She added that the pair started to pull her toward a gate, but she could not recall how she got in the muddy field. She added that the taller of the two men waved a knife in her face, and that if she said anything about the encounter, they would shoot her. Major Albert M. Keenan, who was investigating the incident, then asked her several questions, the more important of which follow:

"Did you give consent to the act of intercourse by either of the soldiers at any time? *Certainly not.*

Was the act of intercourse committed with or against your will by both soldiers? *Against my will, absolutely.*

Did you assist in the act in any manner? *Of course not.*

Did you pull your dress up? *No, they did, of course.*"

On December 11, 1944, Major John C. Urbaitis, a medical officer, examined Cubia Jones and inquired about the incident. Jones said that the woman appeared to have had sex previously with someone else and agreed to have sex with him. He also denied using any violence or threats. Finally, Jones stated that the investigating agents assured him that if he signed a statement he would be allowed to return to his unit. He added that he had lost his knife on the evening in question and that the woman showed him his knife, when she confronted him on December 5. Major Urbaitis also interviewed Robert Pearson. Pearson said that the incident was consensual and added after the act she told the two soldiers to go over the fence first to get to the street so that they would not be seen together. Pearson said that Major King accompanied the woman to identify the accused and did not insist that she answer Pearson's questions. The corporal added that she was unable to explain at the time how she got in the field, where the acts took place.

Major General Frank W. Milburn, Commanding General of the Twenty-First Corps, decided to convene a GCM. The court met at Chard, Somerset, England on December 13, 1944. The Trial Judge Advocate was Major James E. Henderson (JAG); his assistant was Captain Clay Brazil (CE.) Major William D. Sommers (IG) served as the Defense Counsel; he was assisted by Second Lieutenant Myron L. Borawiak (OD.) On the panel were: Lieutenant Colonel Vincent C. Frisby (CE), Lieutenant Colonel Sam W. Russ (JAG), who was the Law Member, Lieutenant Colonel Thurman S. Doman (CE), Lieutenant Colonel John A. Allgair (CE), Major Bernard A. McDermott (CE), Major Charlie E. Morgan (CE), Major Robert S. Burrus, Jr. (CE), Captain William W. Whatley (CE), Captain Edward C. Telling (CE), First Lieutenant John A. Elder (CE), First Lieutenant Roy E. March (CE) and Second Lieutenant George T. Flynn (CE.)[1]

The plethora of Corps of Engineer officers presented an interesting dynamic. Allgair and Burrus were assigned to the 282nd Engineer Combat Battalion, while McDermott and Telling were officers in the 290th Engineer Battalion. Morgan, Whatley and Marsh were members of the 1257th Engineer Combat Battalion, while Elder and Flynn were assigned to the 1256th Engineer Battalion. Normally, this was not desired, due to the thought that there might be some implied pressure in the jury room to vote the same way. The statements of the accused entered into evidence, as did the statement of the victim and statements by investigators. The knife became an exhibit. The victim was unable to identify either defendant. The Law Member instructed the court that the statements given by each defendant could not be considered against the other defendant, only the individual who uttered it. Both accused declined to take the stand. The Defense Counsels did not introduce any evidence. The jury found each defendant guilty of carnal knowledge, a violation of the 92nd Article of War.[2] The court then decided to sentence Jones and Pearson to death by hanging.

The Staff Judge Advocate reviewed the case and found no reversible error. Major General Milburn concurred and forwarded the records of the trial up the chain of command. General Dwight Eisenhower signed the order confirming the sentences of Corporal Pearson and Private Jones on February 12, 1945, but did not state when and where the executions would take place. The Branch Office of The JAG with the ETO reviewed the case on March 5, 1945. JAGs B. Franklin Riter, Malcolm C. Sherman and Ellwood W. Sargent ruled the court committed no errors affecting the rights of the accused; thus, the record of trial was legally sufficient. On March 11, 1945, the ETO published General Court-Martial Orders Number 67. Brigadier General Royal B. Lord directed that the two executions occur on March 17, 1945 at Shepton Mallet Prison. It would be a rare simultaneous double execution, with both men hanged at the same time.

Major Herbert R. Laslett, Commandant of the 2912th DTC, briefed the assembled officials and witnesses shortly after midnight on Saturday, March 17, 1945, just outside the execution chamber at Shepton Mallet. He told them this was a solemn occasion and to conduct themselves properly. At 12:47 a.m., Major Laslett led Chaplain John R. Berkstresser, two guards and two civilian executioners – Thomas W. Pierrepoint and Herbert Morris – followed by six official witnesses, toward the execution chamber, where they arrived at 12:50 a.m. The condemned men arrived under guard at the chamber at 1:01 a.m. Major Laslett read General Court-Martial Orders Number 67. He then asked Corporal Pearson if he had any final words. Pearson replied, "I just want to say, sir – I just want to speak to Cubia Jones. I just want to say to Cubia, that I hope we meet in Heaven." Private Jones replied, "So do I. I hope we all meet in Heaven." Chaplain Berkstresser then asked the men if they wished to say anything to him. Private Jones replied, "Nothing, except that I hope you will pray for me that I may reach – that I get up there to Heaven." Corporal Pearson then added, "I want to say, sir that I'm glad you stood by with us; that is all I have to say. May God bless you and protect you."

The executioners then placed the hoods over the men's heads and adjusted the nooses. The Commandant gave a silent signal and Thomas Pierrepoint bent down, removed the safety cotter pin and quickly pushed the lever forward, activating the trap doors; the time was 1:05 a.m. Major John C. Urbaitis, Captain David R. Capson and First Lieutenant John E. Deardorff examined the two bodies and declared the men dead at 1:22 a.m. It would be a busy day; Major Laslett received a promotion to lieutenant colonel later that afternoon.

On March 26, 1945, the War Department sent a telegram to the next of kin of Robert L. Pearson informing her that he had died in non-battle status due to his own misconduct. The same day another telegram went to the wife of Cubia Jones. Chaplain Berkstresser wrote to the wife of Cubia Jones on March 20, 1945. In his letter, he said that Private Jones had been executed and that Berkstresser had been present. He ended the missive by stating that Cubia Jones "went to his death like a man." The Army initially buried Jones and Pearson Brookwood Cemetery in Plot X, Grave 2-3 and Grave 2-4 on March 18, 1945, but transferred them to the American Military Cemetery at Cambridge, England in 1948. Officials reinterred their remains at the American Military Cemetery at Oise-Aisne in Plot E in 1949. Robert L. Pearson is located in Row 1, Grave 22. Cubia Jones' body lays in Grave 15 of Row 1.[3]

*"I shot him three times, and I'm all right now."*

*"Considering all the circumstances in this case, it is my opinion that the sentence should be confirmed and commuted to dishonorable discharge, total forfeitures and confinement at hard labor for the term of his natural life."*

## 58    Private John W. Taylor
### 37485128
Company D, 371st Infantry Regiment,
  Ninety-Second Infantry Division
**Murder**
Hanged on March 20, 1945

The U.S. Army's GCM system could be very fast from the time of the commission of the offense until the trial of an accused. In a way, it had to be. The tempo of war was difficult to predict. Units could be in one location on one day and thirty miles away on the next. Witnesses could later be wounded or killed, depriving the court of critical testimony. The stress of war could cloud the memories of the witnesses who did survive – time was of the essence.

Such was the case of Private John W. Taylor of the Ninety-Second Infantry Division in Italy. Private Taylor, a black soldier, shot and killed one of his fellow soldiers in Company D at about 7:00 p.m. on January 23, 1945 in the Italian coastal village of Pietrasanta about twenty miles north of Pisa. Officers immediately arrested Taylor and later that night, preferred charges against him. On January 24, 1945, Captain Fred A. Brewer of the 371st Infantry Regiment assumed duties as the investigating officer; he jumped to it and finished his investigation the same day. Brewer forwarded the investigation to the regimental commander, Colonel James Notestein, who recommended a GCM and forwarded the packet to the JAG of the Ninety-Second Infantry Division, Lieutenant Colonel Ralph L. Neary.[1] Neary received the packet on January 25, 1945. He examined the information on January 26 and recommended to the division commander, Major General Edward M. Almond that a GCM be convened. General Almond probably made his decision the next day on January 27, 1945, referring the charges for trial on January 28, 1945; at this point, legal authorities appointed Defense Counsels and the Trial Judge Advocate. The GCM met on January 30, 1945 at 7:25 p.m. – an overall time of just a few minutes over seven days.

One factor helping to accelerate the judicial timeline was the simplicity of the crime. Private John W. Taylor and Private First Class Earl Johnson had been having trouble, punctuated by several arguments, for about a week. After their most recent

disagreement, Johnson had jumped up, grabbed his rifle, pointed it at Private Taylor and clicked the safety off. Two other soldiers took the rifle away, which seemed to calm the situation – but only for about thirty minutes. Then Private Taylor, in his own statement, concluded:

"I thought about the way Johnson had been acting and I decided that I might as well get rid of him for if I didn't he would probably kill me."

Taylor acted on his thoughts, went downstairs, loaded his rifle, returned to the scene and shot Johnson once. He then told another soldier to get out of the way, after which Private Taylor pumped two more rounds into Private First Class Johnson's prostrate body for good measure.

The court met at the Rear Echelon Headquarters of the Ninety-Second Infantry Division.[2] Private John W. Taylor pleaded not guilty to the charge of murder, a violation of the 92nd Article of War.[3] The court admitted Taylor's confession into evidence, as well as a statement by the company commander, Captain Robert E. Moock, who told the court that minutes after the shooting, Taylor said, "I shot him three times, and I'm all right now." The defense presented one witness, Private James W. Alexander, of Company G. Alexander testified that there had been a previous argument and that Private First Class Johnson had reached up and grabbed a rifle, but that two other soldiers subdued him. Private Taylor elected to remain silent. The panel voted, found Private John W. Taylor guilty of murder and sentenced him to death by hanging.

The process continued quickly after the trial. From January 31 to February 2, clerk-typists transcribed the minutes of the trial; the President of the Court (Lieutenant Colonel Crozier), the Trial Judge Advocate and the Defense Counsel read and authenticated the resulting official transcript. The results went forward to the Ninety-Second Infantry Division Staff Judge Advocate on February 3. He reviewed them on February 4, agreed with the findings of the court and sent them to the commander. Major General Almond approved the sentence on February 6, 1945 and sent the packet on February 7, 1945 to the Office of the Theater Judge Advocate for the MTO. The packet probably took several days to reach this last destination, which was at Caserta, Italy, just north of Naples. At this point, a review began to take a little time to determine all the facets of the case. Brigadier General Adam Richmond, the Theater Judge Advocate, had no major concerns with the conduct of the trial. He did think, however, that there was a matter of extenuation, considering the previous threat by the victim. He wrote,

"Considering all the circumstances in this case, it is my opinion that the sentence should be confirmed and commuted to dishonorable discharge, total forfeitures and confinement at hard labor for the term of his natural life."

Lieutenant General Joseph T. McNarney disagreed with the recommendation of Brigadier General Richmond and signed the order confirming the death sentence for Private John W. Taylor on February 26, 1945, but withheld the order to execute the sentence. A Board of Review from the Branch Office of The JAG with the MTO examined the case on March 8, 1945. Judge Advocates Mortimer Irion, Ellwood W. Sargent and Henry Remick reviewed the trial transcript, concluding that the court had been legally constituted and that no errors injuriously affecting the substantial rights of accused were committed during the trial. The MTO published General Court-Martial Orders Number 38 on March 8, 1945. Major General George D. Pence – by command of Lieutenant General Joseph McNarney – directed that the execution of John W. Taylor would occur at Aversa, Italy on March 20, 1945. On March 18, 1945, Major Neiswender read General Court-Martial Orders Number 38 to John W. Taylor at the stockade; Chaplain William T. Watts arrived the same day to provide constant support to the prisoner through the execution. The commander asked General Prisoner Taylor if he had anything to say or to make any requests – Taylor replied that he did not. Taylor then received a complete change of clothing and walked to a new and separate cell.

On March 19, 1945, the headquarters of the PBS Stockade Number 1 published Special Orders Number 42 that proscribed how the execution would be conducted. Major W.G. Neiswender, commander of the PBS Garrison Stockade Number 1, would supervise all three hangings. First Lieutenant Victor N. Formica had the mission of preparing and testing the scaffold that would be used to hang three men in succession. Military Police officers First Lieutenant John W. Daschner, First Lieutenant William Vassil and Second Lieutenant Durey G. Ranck received

the order that they would operate the mechanism to spring the trap door – which would make them the official hangmen for the execution. First Lieutenant Victor E. Hipkiss was to head a special guard detail of twenty enlisted men from the 54th MP Company to guard the area. One of the officers at the stockade, First Lieutenant Clifford A. Payne, was to select twenty-five trainees and have them in formation at the place of execution at 7:30 a.m. on the date of the hanging. First Lieutenant Payne would then lead the guard detail of Sergeant David V. Hamilton, Sergeant Arthur Lee, Sergeant Harold F. Weber and Private Harry A. Timmerman that would escort the three condemned men to the place of execution, arriving no later than 7:55 a.m. Eight officers served as official witnesses on the morning of execution. All the junior officers performed their missions precisely. The trap door of the scaffold released at 8:18 a.m. on March 20, 1945. Major Andrew M. Jamison, Jr., a medical officer from the 262nd Station Hospital, pronounced the prisoner dead at 8:33 a.m.

An Army Chaplain later conducted a funeral service at the U.S. Military Cemetery at Naples, where Private Taylor was interred in Plot GP, Row 1, in Grave 12. Officials exhumed the remains in 1949 and transferred them to the American Military Cemetery at Oise-Aisne in Plot E. Taylor's remains are in Row 1, Grave 24.

On April 3, 1945, the War Department sent a telegram to John W. Taylor's next of kin. The message notified her that he had died in a non-battle status at Aversa, Italy due to his own misconduct.[4] Letters from the family to the Army requesting payment of the soldier's insurance continued until 1962.

Private First Class Earl Johnson, who entered the service from Alabama, is buried among the honored dead at the American Military Cemetery at Florence, Italy in Plot C, Row 2, in Grave 12.

*Defense Question:* *"After you heard the first shot and turned around, did the deceased at any time make any movement toward the accused?"*

*Witness Answer:* *"No, sir, he was not armed."*

An old axiom in trials is that when cross-examining a witness never ask a question that does not support your case. In the case of Kinney Jones, the selection of questions asked at the GCM flew in the face of not only conventional wisdom, but also straight common sense. To be fair, the defense had a tough mountain to climb. On January 1, 1945, First Lieutenant Leonard S. Morgan determined that Private First Class Kinney Jones, a black soldier, who was born on March 15, 1914 in Greenville, South Carolina, was drunk. The officer decided that Jones would move out of the platoon building live in a pup tent for a while. About 8:00 a.m., the next morning, Corporal Milton Winstead ordered Jones to put his gear in the pup tent and then to go relieve another soldier, who was guarding a nearby bridge. Moments later, several witnesses heard loud talk and then observed the accused fire nine or ten shots at the victim from point-blank range, mortally wounding him. Private First Class Jones would later say that Corporal Winstead had told him, "You son of a bitch, come on. I'm going to work hell out of you today."

Jones did not admit committing the crime. The GCM met at 7:10 p.m. on January 17, 1945.[1] Private First Class Kinney Jones pleaded not guilty to murder.[2] The defense cross-examined many of the prosecution witnesses with questions that certainly did not help their own case. The following are a sample:

To Technician Fifth Grade Benjamin H. Belcher, witness to the crime:

**Defense Question:** "After you heard the first shot and turned around, did the deceased at any time make any movement toward the accused?"
**Witness Answer:** "No, sir, he was not armed."
**Defense Question:** "Are you absolutely certain it was this man [pointing to the accused] who did the shooting?"

**Witness Answer:** "Yes, sir."
**Defense Question:** "You could recognize the accused from where you were?"
**Witness Answer:** "Yes, sir."

To Private Ellis Beard, witness to the crime:

**Defense Question:** "At the time you heard the accused and the deceased talking together, did you at any time hear Corporal Winstead speak in a threatening manner toward the accused?"
**Witness Answer:** "No, sir."

The prosecution rested after presenting five witnesses. The accused declined to take the stand. The defense presented no witnesses. The trial probably took no longer than three hours; the panel unanimously voted to convict Kinney Jones of murder and sentence him to death by hanging.

The next day, January 18, the Ninety-Second Infantry Division Staff Judge Advocate reviewed the case and found no significant issues. Major General Edward M. Almond approved the sentence on January 21, 1945. The Office of the Theater Judge Advocate for the MTO reviewed the Jones' case on February 12, 1945; Brigadier General Adam Richmond opined that the sentence was legal and justified. On February 19, 1945, Lieutenant General Joseph T. McNarney signed the order confirming the death sentence for Private Kinney Jones, but withheld the order to execute the sentence. The Branch Office of The JAG with the MTO reviewed the case on March 3, 1945 and found no real issues. The MTO published General Court-Martial Orders Number 36 on March 3, 1945. Major General George D. Pence – by command of Lieutenant General Joseph McNarney – directed that the execution of Kinney Jones occur at Aversa, Italy on March 20, 1945.

On March 18, 1945, Major Neiswender read General Court-Martial Orders Number 36 to Kinney Jones at the stockade; Chaplain William T. Watts arrived the same day to provide spiritual support to the prisoner through the execution. The commander asked General Prisoner Jones if he had anything to say or to make any requests – Jones replied that he did not. Kinney Jones then received a complete change of clothing and marched to a new and separate cell.

The eight officers from the previous hanging were still present as official witnesses on the morning of execution: Lieutenant Colonel Paul T. Gerard (MP), Lieutenant Colonel George A. Tischner (MC), Major Arthur S. Imell (IN), Captain John E. Fleming (DC), First Lieutenant Edward T. Clunan (IN), First Lieutenant William L. Reed (FA), First Lieutenant Carl I. Mercer (MP) and First Lieutenant Lyle N. Nichols (MP.) The trap door of the scaffold released at 9:00 a.m. on March 20, 1945. Major Andrew M. Jamison, Jr. pronounced Kinney Jones dead at 9:17 a.m. An Army Chaplain later conducted a funeral service at the U.S. Military Cemetery at Naples, at Plot GP, Row 1 and Grave 12. The Army exhumed the remains in 1949 and buried them at the American Military Cemetery at Oise-Aisne in Plot E. His remains are in Grave 42 of Row 2.

On April 3, 1945, the War Department sent a telegram to the cousin of Kinney Jones. The correspondence stated that Jones had died at Aversa, Italy on March 20, 1945 of "Judicial Strangulation" and he had died in a non-battle status, due to his own misconduct. Major W.G. Neiswender wrote on April 19, 1945 stating that the officers and men of the unit shared in her sympathy and bereavement, but he did not provide details of his death, other than an Army Chaplain had been present at Kinney Jones' funeral in southern Italy.

Corporal Milton W. Winstead, who was born on August 1, 1925, is buried among the honored dead at Arlington National Cemetery in Section 12, Site 5733.[3]

*"I shot the old man and the little girl ran out. I then shot the woman, [and] then chased after the little girl. I followed her about 200 yards and when I was close enough I shot her."*

*"I made that other statement because they made me. They didn't threaten me. They didn't touch me. They didn't make any promises. They just kept saying things and then I said those things after them. I don't know why I signed it."*

## 60  Private John H. Mack
### 34042053
Battery C, 599th Field Artillery Battalion,
Ninety-Second Infantry Division
**Three Murders**
Hanged on March 20, 1945

Although sworn statements made by accused soldiers included the fact that the accused rights were explained to him, it becomes clear that many soldiers did not fully understand that their admissions of committing the crime would come back to literally hang them. Such appears to have been the case of Private John H. Mack, assigned to Battery C of the 599th Field Artillery Battalion in the Ninety-Second Infantry Division.

On December 31, 1944, at about 2:00 a.m., an American soldier gunned down three members of the Lombardi family – father, mother and fourteen-year-old daughter – in Pietrasanta, Italy. At daylight, Italian police began to investigate; witnesses – extended-family members who also lived in the house – had seen the soldier before at the home and U.S. authorities joined in. Battery C was close to the site of the incident. One witness picked Private John H. Mack from a group of soldiers; MPs immediately took him into custody. Agent Weston Hoffmann interviewed Mack and read Article of War 24 to the accused, which included:

"To warn a soldier that if he makes a statement, he makes it of his own free will, voluntarily; too, he does not have to make a statement, and in making it, anything incriminating can be used against him."

Agent Hoffmann would later testify that he was sure that the accused understood the explanation, "I asked him, and broke it down for him. I asked if he understood it." Mack said he understood, made the statement and signed it. It his account of the facts, Private Mack concluded:

"I shot the old man and the little girl ran out. I then shot the woman, [and] then chased after the little girl. I followed her about 200 yards and when I was close enough I shot her."

In what probably caused his defense lawyer to scratch his head, during his statement, Private Mack offered, "I have been awarded an Expert Medal for firing the M1 rifle."

John Mack was born in Menlo, Georgia – a north Georgia village on the Alabama line – on May 11, 1910. His father died at age fifty-one and a sister died at age twenty-six in an accident. Standing 5'11" tall and weighing 180 pounds, he worked as a reel operator in a tannery; he was black. He initially served at Camp Livingston, Louisiana and then left the Army, but returned to the service on January 23, 1942 at Fort Oglethorpe, Georgia and later reported to the 599th Field Artillery Battalion at Fort Huachuca, Arizona. While there, he fractured his ankle. The unit moved to Camp Polk, Louisiana, where Private Mack suffered appendicitis.

On January 2, 1945, Mack changed his tune and requested to make another statement. In this recollection, Mack stated that he had been in the house (scene of the crime) previously, but not on the night in question. He also explained away some blood evidence on his uniform. Most importantly, Mack said of the original statement:

"I made that other statement because they made me. They didn't threaten me. They didn't touch me. They didn't make any promises. They just kept saying things and then I said those things after them. I don't know why I signed it."

The Staff Judge Advocate reviewed the charges several days later and Major General Edward M. Almond, the Ninety-Second Infantry Division's commander, ordered that a GCM convene on January 18, 1945. The court met at 7:10 p.m. at the division rear headquarters.[1] Private Mack pleaded not guilty to three counts of murder, violations of the 92nd Article of War.[2] The Trial Judge Advocate submitted various witness statements, including both of Private Mack's. They also submitted photographs of the dead bodies that were taken by an Army photographer. The defense objected, stating that there was no evidence that the particular photos were taken at the place of the alleged crime, but the Law Member overruled this. The court voted unanimously to convict Private John Mack of murder and sentenced him to death by hanging.

The Staff Judge Advocate of the Ninety-Second Infantry Division reviewed the case and found everything to be in order on January 21, 1945. On January 23, 1945, Major General Almond approved the sentence and forwarded the paperwork to the MTO. The Staff Judge Advocate at the MTO reviewed the case on February 14, 1945 and found that there were no major irregularities. Lieutenant General Joseph T. McNarney signed the order confirming the death sentence for Private John H. Mack on February 19, 1945, but withheld the order to execute the sentence. On March 6, 1945, the MTO published General Court-Martial Orders Number 37. Major General George D. Pence – by command of Lieutenant General Joseph McNarney – directed that the execution of Private John Mack would be carried out at Aversa, Italy on March 20, 1945. The Branch Office of the JAG with the MTO reviewed the case on March 6 and found no significant problems.

On March 18, 1945, Major Neiswender, commander of the PBS Garrison Stockade Number 1, read General Court-Martial Orders Number 37 to John Mack at the stockade; Chaplain William T. Watts arrived the same day to provide support to the prisoner. The commander asked Mack if he had anything to say or to make any requests – Mack replied that he did not. General Prisoner Mack then received a complete change of clothing and he moved to a new cell.

The same eight officers from the previous execution served as official witnesses. The trap door of the scaffold released at 9:48 a.m. on March 20, 1945. Major Andrew M. Jamison, Jr. pronounced General Prisoner Mack dead at 10:01 a.m.

An Army Chaplain later conducted a funeral service at the U.S. Military Cemetery at Naples, where Private John H. Mack was interred in Plot GP, Row 1 and Grave 10. In 1949, officials reinterred the body at the American Military Cemetery at Oise-Aisne in Plot E. His remains are in Row 1, Grave 4.

On April 3, 1945, the War Department sent a telegram to the mother of John H. Mack. The correspondence stated that he had died at Aversa, Italy on March 20, 1945. The cause of death was "Judicial Strangulation" and the deceased had died in a non-battle status due to his own misconduct. Representative Malcolm C. Tarver of the 7th Congressional District of Georgia, after contact with the family, wrote the Adjutant General in Washington, DC. The Army sent a more-detailed letter to the mother, informing her that her son had killed three people. The family continued corresponding with the Army through 1950, concerning death benefits for their son.[3]

*"I went to bed about 2300 [11:00 p.m.] in the presence of Corporal Foster, Corporal Ballard and Private Worthey."*

## 61   Private Lee A. Burns
38520648

792nd Ordnance (LM) Company,
   Ninety-Second Infantry Division
**Rape**
Hanged on March 27, 1945

Timing is everything, and nowhere is that time-honored adage truer than in the rape case of Private Lee A. Burns. Police accused him of raping a fourteen-year-old girl in Italy on November 27, 1944. Based on the evidence, the girl was clearly raped; both the victim and her mother would later positively identify Burns out of a five-man lineup. However, the timeline of the crime was close to exonerating the defendant – some might conclude it actually did.

Private Lee Burns, and several other black soldiers, were out on the town with the "General's jeep" on the evening of November 27. At 10:00 p.m., the accused, accompanied by Private Aldene Worthey and a Private Jones of the Division Headquarters Company, were at the home of an Italian couple, drinking wine. Present was the couple's daughter. Captain Cecil B. Morris, Burns' company commander, and Corporal Dewey Lewis drove up to the home and ordered the men to return with them to the company area – a distance of about two blocks. The group arrived at camp at 10:15 p.m. Morris then told the accused to remain in his quarters the rest of the night. Private Ben Esther, who slept next to the accused, testified that he saw the accused enter his sleeping quarters at 10:30 p.m. He said that he later awakened during the night and saw the accused asleep, but could not pin down a time. Corporal Dewey Lewis testified that he saw the accused enter his quarters at 10:40 p.m. Private Burns, in a sworn statement, said:

> "I went to bed about 2300 [11:00 p.m.] in the presence of Corporal Foster, Corporal Ballard and Private Worthey."

Private Aldene Worthey, in a statement made on December 26, 1944, said that he saw Burns get undressed and go to bed. The victim and her mother would later testify that at 10:45 p.m. the accused, with three or four companions, came to the house, claimed they were Military Police, searched the house and departed. At approximately 11:15 p.m. – according to the two witnesses – the accused

returned alone. Over the course of the next ninety minutes, the accused terrorized and raped one of the females. These times differed slightly from those made by the mother in a statement on December 4, 1944. On that earlier statement, she said that Burns returned at 11:00 p.m. and remained in the house until 12:10 a.m. This study could not find testimony by Corporal Ballard, which might have corroborated Burns' claim that he went to bed at 11:00 p.m. Given the fact that it would have taken the accused at least fifteen minutes to quietly get out of bed, get dressed, slip out of camp and walk two blocks to the scene of the crime, every minute counted.

Lee Burns, born in Homer, Louisiana on November 9, 1913, was inducted on September 12, 1943. Private Burns had two previous courts-martial. On November 19, 1943 a Summary Court-Martial found him guilty of being absent without official leave for an eleven-day period; on August 21, 1944 a Special Court-Martial convicted Burns of wrongfully appearing in uniform wearing technician fourth grade chevrons.

The GCM for Private Burns met in the Ninety-Second Infantry Division Rear Area on January 19, 1945. Burns pleaded not guilty to the charge of carnal knowledge, a violation of the 92nd Article of War.[1] Sitting on the court were Lieutenant Colonel Henry C. Britt (IN), who was also the Law Member, Lieutenant Colonel John J. Phelan (IN), Major Samuel A. Montgomery (MC), Major John A. Campbell (CE), Major Harry K. Bayless (FA), Captain Frank Rinaudo (IN) and Captain Harold L. Lastrapes, Jr. (IN.) Major Harry B. Lane (FA) served as the Trial Judge Advocate; he was assisted by Major Alvin D. Wilder, Jr. (CE.) Major Daniel B. Vancourt (QM) was the Defense Counsel, with Captain Chester C. Heizer (IN) as Assistant Defense Counsel.[2] Britt, Phelan, Montgomery and Campbell had been on the jury that sentenced Kinney Jones to death two days previously. Burns elected to remain silent; it does not appear that the defense questioned the timeline. Coming to order at 7:05 p.m., the court finished two hours and forty minutes, finding him guilty and sentencing him to death by hanging.

Two days later, the division Staff Judge Advocate reviewed the case, finding no major errors. Major General Almond approved the sentence on January 25. The Office of the Theater Judge Advocate for the MTO, under Brigadier General Adam Richmond, had no major concerns with the conduct of the trial; this review occurred on February 12, 1945. On February 19, 1945, Lieutenant General Joseph

T. McNarney signed the order confirming the death sentence for Private Lee A. Burns, but withheld the order to execute the sentence. A Board of Review from the Branch Office of The JAG with the MTO examined the case on March 17, 1945. Judge Advocates Ellwood W. Sargent, Mortimer Irion and Henry Remick concluded that the court had been legally constituted and that no errors injuriously affecting the substantial rights of accused occurred during the trial.

The MTO published General Court-Martial Orders Number 51. Major General George D. Pence directed that the execution of Lee Burns occur at Aversa, Italy on March 27, 1945. Major W.G. Neiswender, Commander of the PBS Garrison Stockade Number 1, read General Court-Martial Orders Number 51 to the condemned man at 5:00 p.m. on March 26, 1945 at the stockade. The prisoner had nothing to say and received a change of clean clothing. He then marched, under guard, to a new, separate cell, with a twenty-four-hour deathwatch. A Chaplain would provide support during the night. Major Neiswender presided over the execution of General Prisoner Lee A. Burns at Aversa, Italy on March 27, 1945. Eight commissioned officers served as official witnesses; three officers released the trap door at 12:59 p.m. and Captain Joel J. McCook – a medical officer – pronounced Burns dead at 1:14 p.m.

The Army initially buried his remains at the U.S. Military Cemetery at Naples, in the General Prisoner plot in Grave 2-15. In 1949, the Army transferred the remains to the American Military Cemetery at Oise-Aisne in Plot E. His remains are now in Row 4, Grave 74. On April 12, 1945, the War Department sent a telegram to Lee A. Burns' mother, notifying her that he had died in a non-battle status at Aversa, Italy due to his own misconduct.[3]

*"Either you give me that money today or I will spray your tent with gas."*

*"I picked up my rifle and shot him."*

## 62    Private Abraham Smalls
34512812

Company L, 370th Infantry Regiment,
  Ninety-Second Infantry Division
**Murder**
Hanged on March 27, 1945

In some cases, it is obvious that the counsels for the defense attempted to mount vigorous cases, given the limitations of the system. Most of the Defense Counsels were not lawyers; in fact, all of them had "regular" jobs that had significant professional demands. Because of the speedy nature of military judicial proceedings during the war, Defense Counsels often did not initially meet their defendants until a few days before the actual trial – sometimes the day before the trial. Locating witnesses for the defense was difficult as was traveling to the actual scene of the crime, so the Defense Counsel could develop alternative theories of what transpired, was often nearly impossible.

Captain Alonzo W. Farr (IN) and his assistant Second Lieutenant William T. Josey (IN) mounted the best defense they could in the case of Abraham Smalls. It was an uphill fight. On the morning of February 4, 1945 Company L of the 370th Infantry Regiment bivouacked in a rest area near Viareggio, Italy. Private Abraham Smalls and Private First Class George W. Jones got into an argument over a bar of soap, but trouble between the two had been brewing for some time. As Jones reached down to pull up the front pins on the accused's tent, Private Smalls picked up his M1 rifle and fired a round at the victim; then he fired five or six additional shots at Jones for good measure, which would soon put his two Defense Counsels behind the eight-ball. Private Smalls, a married black soldier with four children, had been wounded on September 29, 1944 by grenade shrapnel in his ankle, although the incident was caused by another American soldier carelessly handling a hand grenade.

The GCM for Abraham Smalls met at 9:40 p.m. on February 17, 1945. Sitting on the panel were the following: Lieutenant Colonel James C. Horne (IN), Lieutenant Colonel Louis G. Osborne (AG), Major William M. Campbell (MP), Major Jerome A. Vesely (SC), Major Robert E. Brown (MC), Captain Raymond B. Ochsner (AG), Captain Wendell Price (DC) and First Lieutenant Paul B. Lewis (IN.) Lieutenant Colonel Gaston M. Wood (IN) served as

the Trial Judge Advocate.[1] It was the fourth court-martial ending with a death penalty for Lieutenant Colonel Osborne, the third for Major Campbell and Captain Price, and the second for Lieutenant Colonel Horne and Captain Ochsner. Previously, Lieutenant Colonel Wood had successfully prosecuted Mack, Grant and Taylor. Second Lieutenant Josey had been the Assistant Defense Counsel in the Mack, Grant and Taylor cases.

Private Abraham Smalls pleaded not guilty to the charge of murder, a violation of the 92nd Article of War.[2] The defense immediately asked for a two-day continuance in order to allow for a psychiatric examination of the accused. They received the extension and the following day Captain Holloman, the Ninety-Second Infantry Division Psychiatrist, interviewed Private Smalls. He stated that he found nothing wrong with the defendant. However, Holloman added that it was division policy for a board of officers (not a single officer) to make such an examination; he thus did not feel free to submit a formal report on his findings. Back in session, the Trial Judge Advocate called a witness, who was present at the crime; they followed by calling the battalion surgeon, who testified that the cause of death was gunshot wounds.

Then the defense team went to work. They first called First Sergeant John Graves. Graves testified that the victim was 5'8" or 5'9" tall and weighed 165 to 170 pounds. This line of questioning was probably to establish that the victim was much larger than the accused. Then the defense called Private Cicero Clark. Cicero testified that in December, Private First Class Jones pointed a rifle at Private Smalls and threatened to kill him. Clark added that Jones then struck Smalls several times. This testimony was designed to show that Jones had been the aggressor in the relationship, had previously threatened to kill the accused and had actually consummated physical violence against the accused – in other words, the accused was in fear for his own safety. Captain Farr then called Private First Class Walter Hills, who testified that he had seen Jones "picking on" Private Abraham Smalls "very much." Hills added that he had not paid much attention to the matter. The nature of the last portion of his testimony was probably designed by the defense to show that no one in the company was coming to Smalls' aid and that he finally had to take matters into his own hands. The defense then had Private Smalls submit an unsworn statement to the court. He described how the day before the incident Jones had threatened to set the accused's tent on fire. He then stated that Jones threatened him on the day of the incident by saying, "Either you give me that money today or I will spray your tent with gas." Smalls added that Jones then started kicking him in the feet. Smalls told Jones to stop. When Jones did not, Smalls said, "I picked up my rifle and shot him."

The court convicted the accused of murder and sentenced him to death by hanging. Smalls had been born on October 31, 1910 in Adams Run, South Carolina. Standing 5'5½" tall and weighing 135 pounds, Smalls had worked as a cook at *Henry's Hotel* and *Realy's Cafeteria* in Charleston, South Carolina, making $20 per week. He had finished six years of school. He entered the Army in November 1942 and reported to the 828th Tank Destroyer Battalion at Fort Huachuca, Arizona. Smalls advanced to the rank of Tech 5, when his Army career took a turn for the worse, after he was caught committing a lewd act with a fellow male enlisted soldier. That scheduled GCM never occurred, due to a conflict of statements; a board of officers convened and recommended that Smalls be discharged from the service, saying he was "unfit to associate with enlisted men." However, someone higher in Smalls' chain of command overrode this recommendation and transferred him to Fort Hood, before an assignment to the Ninety-Second Infantry Division.

The division staff judge advocate reviewed the case on February 24, 1945 and found no major errors in the trial. Major General Edward Almond approved the sentence on February 28, 1945. Lieutenant General Joseph T. McNarney signed the order confirming the death sentence for Private Abraham Smalls on March 12, 1945, but withheld the order to execute the sentence. The Branch Office of the Judge Advocate General with the MTO reviewed the case on March 19, 1945. Judge Advocates Sargent, Irion and Remick found that no errors injuriously affecting the substantial rights of the accused had been committed during the trial. They also added that the record of trial was legally sufficient to support the findings and sentence. As to the issue of provocation, they opined:

"Even assuming this to be true, such harassing conduct on the part of deceased and the degree of violence used against accused shortly before the shooting, as he described it, did not, under the circumstances established by the evidence in the case, justify his resort to the firearm, and did not amount to legal provocation."

The MTO published General Court-Martial Orders Number 52 on March 19, 1945. Major General George D. Pence – by command of Lieutenant General Joseph McNarney – directed that the execution of Abraham Smalls would occur at Aversa, Italy on March 27, 1945. Major W.G. Neiswender, Commander of the PBS Garrison Stockade Number 1, read General Court-Martial Orders Number 52 to the condemned man at 5:17 p.m. on March 26, 1945 at the Headquarters' Building of the Garrison Stockade. The prisoner stated he had nothing to say and received a change of clean clothing. He then marched, under guard, to a new, separate cell, with a twenty-four-hour deathwatch. Chaplain William T. Watts would provide religious support during the night.

Major Neiswender presided over the execution of General Prisoner Abraham Smalls at Aversa, Italy on March 27, 1945. Eight commissioned officers served as official witnesses; the trap door released at 1:35 p.m. and Captain Joel J. McCook – a medical officer – pronounced General Prisoner Smalls dead at 1:47 p.m. Army personnel buried Private Abraham Smalls at the U.S. Military Cemetery at Naples, in the General Prisoner plot in Grave 2-13. Authorities transferred his remains to the American Military Cemetery at Oise-Aisne in Plot E. His remains are in Row 1, Grave 23.

On April 3, 1945, the War Department sent a telegram to Abraham Smalls' second cousin, who he designated as a contact in case of an emergency. The message notified her that he had died in a non-battle status at Aversa, Italy due to his own misconduct.[3]

Private First Class George W. Jones is buried among the honored dead at the American Military Cemetery in Florence, Italy.

*"No evidence was introduced by the defense and accused elected to remain silent."*

## 63        Private First Class General L. Grant

34557976

Company D, 366th Infantry Regiment, Ninety-Second Infantry Division

**Murder**

Hanged on March 27, 1945

By the spring of 1945, it was clear that there were problems in the Ninety-Second Infantry Division. With the Private First Class General Lee Grant case, each line regiment in the 92nd – the 366th, 370th and 371st – suffered through a capital case and each regiment now had a soldier executed. The type of crime was all too common: a soldier visited a home and asked for wine; the owner of the home appeared reluctant to serve him and the accused opened fire with his .45 pistol, killing the nephew. The accused, General L. Grant, would later make a statement saying that he had shot his pistol, but only after the man – and two women and a white American soldier sitting in the room – had grabbed him and started punching him. The accused then ran.

The incident happened on January 8. Later that day, Captain Thurston E. Jamison, Grant's company commander, interviewed him, but Grant's answers did not elicit suspicion.[1] However, the following day, MPs apprehended Grant and he elected to make a statement. He admitted being at the scene of the crime, but claimed self-defense – that he had fired the weapon to make the people turn him loose. Somehow, he received a wound in the left thumb during this period and went to the Peninsular Base Stockade Hospital on January 10. Authorities preferred charges against Private Grant on January 23. Major General Edward M. Almond, the division commander, decided on February 1 that a GCM was in order.

The GCM met at the division rear area at 7:10 p.m. on February 8, 1945. Sitting on the panel were Lieutenant Colonel James C. Horne (IN), Lieutenant Colonel Louis G. Osborne (AG), who was also the Law Member, Major William M. Campbell (MP), Major Frederick Krug (DC), Captain Harold A. Butler (IN) and Captain James L. Glymph (IN.) Lieutenant Colonel Gaston M. Wood (IN) served as the Trial Judge Advocate. Captain Francis L. Robinson (MC) was the Defense Counsel; he was assisted by Second Lieutenant William T. Josey (IN.)[2] Osborne and Glymph had previously been members of the juries on the Mack and Taylor cases. Campbell

had been on the Mack case. Krug had served on the Taylor panel. Lieutenant Colonel Wood had won convictions in the Mack and Taylor cases. Captain Robinson and Second Lieutenant Josey had been on the losing end of both.

Private First Class Grant pleaded not guilty to the charge of absenting himself without leave – a violation of the 61st Article of War – and to murder – a violation of the 92nd Article of War.[3] The two white soldiers testified for the prosecution; they indicated that there had been no attack against the accused. The defense just seemed to sit there, if the review records are accurate. The Branch Office of the JAG with the Mediterranean theater of Operations later found, "No evidence was introduced by the defense and accused elected to remain silent."

The court found Grant not guilty of the first charge of being absent without leave. They voted unanimously to convict on the murder charge. General L. Grant was born on May 25, 1921 in Union Point, Georgia and later resided in nearby Greensboro; he dropped out of school at an early age and worked as a janitor before he landed a job planting kudzu at $30 a month. Grant was inducted on November 27, 1942; he was 5'11" tall and weighed 166 pounds. He was involved in a barracks fight on May 22, 1943 at Fort Devens, Massachusetts, in which another trooper bit him on the face and left index finger. He contracted gonorrhea in 1944; that October, he dislocated his knee. Private Grant had qualified for the Good Conduct Medal and the European-African-Middle Eastern Campaign Medal; he also qualified for the Expert Infantryman's Badge. The panel voted to give Private First Class General L. Grant death by hanging. The court took in account that Grant had received a Summary Court-Martial in February 1944 for a thirteen-day absence without leave in January 1944.

The division SJA reviewed the case on February 12, 1945 and found no serious flaws in the proceedings. Major General Almond approved the sentence three days later. Lieutenant General Joseph T. McNarney signed the order confirming the death sentence for Private First Class General L. Grant on February 28, 1945, but withheld the order to execute the sentence. A Board of Review from the Branch Office of the JAG with the MTO examined the case on March 10, 1945. Judge Advocates Ellwood W. Sargent, Mortimer Irion and Henry Remick concluded that no errors injuriously affecting the substantial rights of accused were committed. The review concluded that, "The possibly impetuous nature of his act was not a defense." Colonel Hubert D. Hoover advised Lieutenant General McNarney that he now had the authority to order the actual execution. The MTO published General Court-Martial Orders Number 49 on March 16, 1945. Major General George D. Pence, the Chief of Staff, directed that the execution of General L. Grant would occur on March 27, 1945.

Major W.G. Neiswender, Commander of the PBS Garrison Stockade Number 1, read General Court-Martial Orders Number 49 to the condemned man at about 5:00 p.m. on March 26, 1945 at the headquarters hut. The prisoner stated he had nothing to say and received a change of clean clothing. Guards then marched him to a new, separate cell, with a twenty-four-hour deathwatch. A Chaplain would remain the entire night.

Major Neiswender presided over the execution of General Prisoner General L. Grant at Aversa, Italy on March 27, 1945. Eight commissioned officers served as official witnesses; the trap door released at 2:09 p.m. and Captain Joel J. McCook – a medical officer – pronounced General Prisoner Grant dead at 2:24 p.m.

The Army interred the body of General L. Grant at the U.S. Military Cemetery at Naples, in Plot GP, Row 2 in Grave 14. Officials reinterred his remains in 1949 at the American Military Cemetery at Oise-Aisne in Plot E. Originally, the remains were in Row 3 and Grave 11; in 1952, a memo from the American Battle Monuments Commission explained that the final burial site had been changed to Row 3 in Grave 59.

On April 12, 1945, the War Department sent a telegram to General L. Grant's wife. In the message, the department notified her that he had died in a non-battle status at Aversa, Italy due to his own misconduct. The family continued correspondence with the government – requesting a correction to the record – until 1980 concerning his death, to include a letter to President James Earl Carter.[4]

*"I and Chester Coet left when the fuss began. We left Williams there alone."*

*"I don't know whether Olin went up the steps, but I know he wanted to go up to have relations with the woman because he said so."*

## 64    Private Olin W. Williams
### 34649494
4194th Quartermaster Service Company
**Rape and Murder**
Hanged on March 29, 1945

When the accused has a distinguishing facial mark, acts guilty in a lineup and has two fellow soldiers swear that they left him at the scene of the crime, many juries would conclude that he had just swung on a third strike. That was the case of Private Olin W. Williams. Williams, a black soldier with black hair and a dark complexion, was born in Elloree, South Carolina on September 16, 1921. He attended grade school for five years and worked in a laundry company for $12 a week. He was inducted on March 20, 1943. Williams stood 5'8" tall, weighed about 150 pounds and had a medium build; he suffered from multiple bouts of gonorrhea and had a fused third finger on his left hand. More significantly for him on September 24, 1944 was that he had an upper front left tooth missing. At about 8:30 p.m. on September 23, Private Williams – missing tooth and all – arrived at the house of Albert Lebocey in the village of Le Chene Daniel, near Chérence-le-Héron, France. With him were two other soldiers. The men drank some cognac; thirty minutes later the accused tried to grab a woman, but she eluded him. Williams' two companions left the house. Private Odell Austin, one of the men, would later make a sworn statement that he observed the woman start crying and the owner start arguing with the accused. As Austin would state, "I and Chester Coet left when the fuss began. We left Williams there alone."

Private Coet had his own statement to make. He confirmed that Williams had been in an argument with the homeowner and corroborated Austin's account that the two men left Williams in the house. He also added this damning opinion, "I don't know whether Olin went up the steps, but I know he wanted to go up to have relations with the woman because he said so."

Coet also added that, as he and Austin were getting ready to go to sleep in a barn after leaving Williams, Coet – referring to Williams and the couple's young daughter – said to Austin, "A man was a fool trying to touch a little girl like that." Three days later, Private Williams made his own sworn statement. He did not mention any argument and stated that he left the house at the same time that Austin and Coet; he also said that Coet, "this light boy," was not telling the truth. However, by this time, the statements were just icing on the Trial Judge Advocate's case.

Hours after the crime, a soldier woke First Lieutenant Gus N. Bacalis, the commander of the 4194th Quartermaster Service Company, Williams' unit. The soldier informed the officer that a Frenchman had been shot and killed. Bacalis acted quickly. Grabbing an interpreter, he went to the scene of the crime, found the dead man and began searching for possible witnesses. He found the deceased man's wife at her mother's house; the distraught woman explained what happened and said that an American soldier had raped her. She added that she thought she could recognize him, as he was missing a front tooth. Bacalis returned to his company and immediately held a formation to determine if any soldiers were missing. No one was. Later that morning, criminal investigators arrived at the company with the rape victim. Lieutenant Bacalis held a formation and ordered every soldier to open his mouth, as the woman walked by, so she could see the soldier's teeth. When she arrived at Williams, he closed his mouth and had "a very queer look" on his face. First Lieutenant Bacalis ordered him to open his mouth and when he did, the victim positively identified him. However, Bacalis wanted to make sure. After the inspection was completed, the agents and the victim went to another formation of soldiers and Bacalis slipped Williams into that formation as well. When the victim approached Private Williams, she again identified him.

The investigation continued until October 10. A few days later, the commander of the Normandy Base Section decided a GCM should handle the matter. By this time, however, the unit had moved far to the east and was now in Belgium; in the confusion of the front, it was not possible to begin the trial until December 15, 1944, when the witnesses were brought back to Granville, France. The court convened at 1:30 p.m. that day.[1] Williams pleaded not guilty to one count of murder and one count of carnal knowledge, both violations of the 92nd Article of War.[2] The prosecution presented the witnesses linking Williams to the scene of the crime, as well as that of the rape victim. Private Williams elected to take the stand. He said he had been in the couple's house on three different nights; on the night of the crime, he maintained that he left with his two companions and did not return. The defense called two additional witnesses, who stated that they saw Williams in the company area at 11:30 p.m., but this did not establish an alibi, as the crime occurred three hours later. The court found Private Williams guilty of both specifications of the charge and sentenced him to be hanged by the neck until dead.

The next day, the German Army smashed through thinly defended American lines in the Ardennes Forest, an action that became known as "The Battle of the Bulge." The German attack seemed to delay a review of Williams' case. The Staff Judge Advocate of the Normandy Base Section did not review the trial record until January 23, 1945, with Brigadier General Henry S. Aurand, Commanding General of the Normandy Base Section, approving the sentence the same day. General Dwight Eisenhower signed the order confirming the sentence of Private Williams on March 4, 1945, but did not state when and where the execution would take place.

The Branch Office of The JAG with the ETO reviewed the case on March 14, 1945. The three-man panel (JAGs B. Franklin Riter, Ellwood W. Sargent and Malcolm C. Sherman) ruled the court was legally constituted, had jurisdiction of the person and offenses, and committed no errors injuriously affecting the substantial rights of the accused. Therefore, the record of trial was legally sufficient to support the findings of guilty and the sentences imposed. On March 24, 1945, the ETO published General Court-Martial Orders Number 85. Brigadier General R.B. Lord – by command of General Eisenhower – directed that the execution would occur near Le Chene Daniel, France on March 29, 1945. The day before the event, Captain Henry K. McHarg, the Commander of the Beach District Guardhouse, read the order of execution to Private Williams at the Granville Stockade at 9:00 a.m. That evening, medical officer Captain Lawrence B. Kuhlmann examined the condemned man at 8:30 p.m. and found him to be in excellent physical and mental condition.

At 9:48 a.m. on March 29, 1945, Lieutenant Colonel Henry L. Peck, the Commanding Officer, Loire DTC, assembled seven officials, five official witnesses, ten authorized military spectators and three authorized French spectators (including the mayor and the brother of the murder victim) in a hedgerowed field along Route N 799.

Peck then read General Court-Martial Orders Number 85 and instructed them on proper conduct. This reading of the order was slightly different from previous executions; earlier, the commanding officer waited until the condemned was present before reading the document. Today's procedure would speed up the process by a minute or two. The weather was cool, with a slight breeze. The ground was soggy, covered with a lush blanket of grass; previous rainfall made the men's footsteps spongy. In the corner of the field, twenty-five yards from the scene of the crime, stood a freshly built gallows. General Prisoner Olin W. Williams had been there once before. Eleven enlisted men of the 387th MP Battalion and the Beach District Guardhouse watched over the area; there were no disturbances. At 10:00 a.m., an Army 1½-ton, 6x6 covered personnel carrier pulled up to the field's entrance and Williams dismounted. He joined a procession led by Lieutenant Colonel Peck, Chaplain Raymond W. Parker – a black Presbyterian minister – and guards: Sergeant Russell E. Boyle, Sergeant Alfonso Girvalo and Sergeant Jack D. Briscoe. Behind the guards walked Captain Milton B. Asbell (the recorder) and five official witnesses. Briscoe was as sick as a dog; he had been running a 100° fever. The group arrived at the gallows at 10:02 a.m. The guards then bound the prisoner's hands behind his back, led the prisoner up the steps and oriented him on the trap door. At 10:03 a.m., the executioner's assistant, Technician Third Grade Thomas F. Robinson, bound the ankles of the prisoner.

Both Lieutenant Colonel Peck and Chaplain Parker asked the prisoner if he had any last statement, but Williams remained silent. Master Sergeant John C. Woods then placed the black hood over the condemned man's head and put the noose around his neck; the time was 10:05 a.m. Thirty seconds later, Peck gave a silent signal to Woods, who then cut the rope, which released the weight and actuated the trap. Everything worked correctly, although there was some muscular movement of the condemned, and at about 10:19 a.m. Captain Lawrence B. Kuhlmann, Captain Robert S. Randall and First Lieutenant Carlos B. Brewer pronounced Williams dead. Peck dismissed the witnesses and spectators. Woods cut the rope and First Lieutenant Milliard R. Jones, 3059th Graves Registration Company, took possession of the body and buried it at the U.S. Military Cemetery at Marigny in Plot Z, Grave 2-21.

On April 9, 1945, the Commanding General of the Normandy Base Section sent a letter of regret to the rape victim. The letter stated that the soldier concerned and been tried, sentenced to death and executed. It ended with, "Your cooperation and assistance in bringing the offender to justice is appreciated." On April 10, 1945, the War Department sent a telegram to Olin Williams' mother, communicating that her son had died in a non-battle status at Le Chene Daniel, Chérence-le-Héron, France, due to his own misconduct.

Private Olin W. Williams is now buried at the American Military Cemetery at Oise-Aisne in Plot E. His remains are in Row 1, Grave 20.[3]

• • •

The author visited Chérence-le-Héron in September 2011. One-half mile south is the tiny hamlet of Le Chene Daniel, consisting of a few houses at the intersection of D999 and D81. The location where Olin Williams was hanged is now a cornfield.

*"I want you to understand, Sir, I am innocent. I had nobody to talk to. If I could get out of the stockade. I went from the cell to the mess hall. I never had a chance. I had five non-coms to prove it."*

*"Sir, there is still some evidence of life."*

## 65     Private Tommie Davison

34485174

427th Quartermaster
Troop Transport Company
**Assault, Attempted Assault against
an Official, and Rape**
Hanged on March 29, 1945

People were afraid of Tommie Davison. Maybe it was his appearance; one witness would say that he had a "nasty look" with "bad eyes." A black soldier, he stood 5'11" and weighed a solid 180 pounds. Maybe it was his demeanor. Another soldier would later swear that at the scene of the crime – a brutal rape at the village of Prise Guinment, France on August 23, 1944 – Davison was yelling, "I ought to shoot this mother-fucker!"

Maybe it was his age. Born on August 10, 1914 in West Point, Mississippi, he was older than most of the other soldiers. Perhaps it was his upbringing. After his first wife died, Tommie Davison married a sixteen-year-old girl, but he never designated her as a beneficiary for his Army allotments. He had no formal education and could neither read nor write. However, Tommie could brawl and police soon arrested him for fighting. His brushes with authority continued after he was inducted at Camp Shelby, Mississippi on December 2, 1942; he had three previous court-martial convictions. Davison took quartermaster training at Camp Lee, Virginia, arrived in England in September 1943 and deployed to Normandy on June 10, 1944.

It seemed to be a complex case, until one understood that the French witnesses were reporting what happened in French time (sun-time), two hours earlier than U.S. Army time for the region. In mid-afternoon on August 23, 1944, the accused came to a farm in the hamlet of Prise Guinment. He asked for and paid for a chicken. Three other "colored" soldiers were present; one of them warned Henri Duqueroux that the accused was dangerous. Private Davison began yelling, made suggestive gestures, and asked Duqueroux for a mademoiselle, showing him five-hundred *francs*. The French people became afraid and locked themselves inside the house. Davison temporarily left, but returned

about 5:00 p.m. French time (7:00 p.m./1900 hours, U.S. Army time), waved his pistol (a captured German P-38) and raped the woman.

One of the Frenchman reported the incident to American authorities and the 427th Quartermaster Troop Transport Company formed up for an inspection. Davison, who had been drinking heavily, was one of the last to "fall-in" for the formation. One of the Frenchman spotted Davison and informed Chief Warrant Officer (CWO) Earl E. Lane, Jr., the unit personnel officer. Lane approached Davison, when suddenly Davison put his hand in his pocket and started to withdraw a pistol, pointing it at the warrant officer. A scuffle ensued to disarm him, which involved CWO Lane and the company First Sergeant. Private Davison would say that he cooperated; others said they had to knock him down to get his weapon.

With all this evidence, the commander of the Normandy Base Section decided a GCM would handle the matter. The court met at 1:30 p.m. on December 9, 1944 at Granville, France. Sitting on the panel were: Lieutenant Colonel George R. Anderson (QM), Major Samuel H. Berry (JAG), who was also the Law Member, Major George M. Seckinger (TC), Major Ray H. Fentriss (CE), Captain Phillip H. Carlin (OD), First Lieutenant Jason R. Gray (TC), First Lieutenant Lafayette Parker (QM), First Lieutenant Lloyd R. Hagen (AG) and First Lieutenant Francis Harkins (FI.) Captain Robert G. Hisey (IN) sat as the Trial Judge Advocate; he was assisted by Second Lieutenant John R. Davis (OD.) Captain Carl W. Miller (IN) served as the Defense Counsel. He was assisted by Second Lieutenant Michael P. Murphy (TC.) All of the officers, except Major Fentriss and Second Lieutenant Davis, had served on the Olin W. Williams' GCM six days before.[1]

Private Tommie Davison pleaded not guilty to the charge of carnal knowledge, a violation of the 92nd Article of War, a charge of assault, a violation of the 93rd Article of War and an attempted assault of a warrant officer, a violation of the 65th Article of War.[2] The prosecution presented the testimony of the French witnesses and three U.S. soldiers, who had been at the farm and had seen the accused when he first arrived. Tommie Davison elected to take the stand. He said that he had never asked for a chicken and had not seen the three soldiers, who had been at the farm and testified for the prosecution. He stated that he returned to camp at about 5:30 p.m. or 6:00 p.m. (U.S. Army time.) The defense called two witnesses, Technician Fifth Grade Stivers and Technician Fourth Grade Thompson, who testified that Davison brought eggs, not a chicken, back to camp and that they saw him at 6:15 p.m. (U.S. Army time.) The times given did not preclude Davison from going back to the scene later. Testimony varied as to whether Davison had his pistol in his holster during the incident. The court found Davison guilty of all three charges – making a few minor changes to the lesser charges. The panel then sentenced him to be hanged by the neck until dead.

On January 25, 1945, the Staff Judge Advocate of the Normandy Base Section reviewed the trial records. Lieutenant Colonel Franklin H. Berry, the Staff Judge Advocate, occurred with the opinion that the trial had no significant error. The report did provide one interesting insight. Technician Fifth Grade Richmond of the 427th Quartermaster Troop Transport Company testified somewhat inconsistently; the review made the following conclusion, but never stated the basis for doing so: "… It can also be considered that Richmond would naturally tend to favor the accused wherever possible."

Shortly afterward, Brigadier General Henry S. Aurand, Commanding General of the Normandy Base Section, approved the sentence. The Branch Office of The JAG with the ETO reviewed Davison's case on March 14, 1945. The three-man panel (JAGs B. Franklin Riter, Ellwood W. Sargent and Malcolm C. Sherman) ruled the court was legally constituted, had jurisdiction of the person and offenses, and committed no errors injuriously affecting the substantial rights of the accused. Therefore, the record of trial was legally sufficient to support the findings of guilty and the sentences imposed. On March 24, 1945, the ETO published General Court-Martial Orders Number 86. Brigadier General R.B. Lord – by command of General Eisenhower – directed that the execution would occur on March 29, 1945 near Prise Guinment (near Barenton), Manche, France.

The day before the execution, Captain Henry K. McHarg, the Commander of the Beach District Guardhouse, read the order of execution to Private Davison at the Granville Stockade about 9:00 a.m. That evening, medical officer Captain Lawrence B. Kuhlmann examined the condemned man about 8:30 p.m. and found him to be in excellent physical and mental condition. At 2:45 p.m. on March 29, 1945, Lieutenant Colonel Peck assembled seven

officials, five official witnesses, ten authorized military spectators and three authorized French spectators – including the Frenchman that Davison tried to shoot – in a hedgerowed field near Prise Guinment. Lieutenant Colonel Peck had been a busy man that day – early that morning he had supervised the execution of Olin W. Williams and then drove twenty-five miles to this next mission.

The weather was cool and clear. The ground was soggy, covered with a blanket of grass and a few trees. A freshly built scaffold stood in the southeast corner of the field. The six enlisted men of the 387th MP Battalion and five enlisted men of the Beach District Guardhouse observed the area. Peck read aloud General Court-Martial Orders Number 86 and instructed the witnesses and spectators on proper conduct. At 2:59 p.m. an Army 1½-ton, 6x6 covered personnel carrier pulled up to the field's entrance and General Prisoner Tommie Davison dismounted. He joined a procession led by Lieutenant Colonel Henry L. Peck, Chaplain William B. Crocker – a minister in the Negro Baptist Church – and guards: Sergeant Russell E. Boyle, Sergeant Alfonso Girvalo and Sergeant Jack D. Briscoe. Behind the guards walked Captain Milton B. Asbell (the event recorder) and five official witnesses to the gallows. The guards then bound the prisoner's hands behind his back, led him up the steps and placed on the trap door. At 3:01 p.m., Technician Third Grade Thomas F. Robinson bound the ankles of the prisoner. Lieutenant Colonel Peck asked the prisoner if he had any last words and a torrent of words poured out of the condemned man's mouth:

"I want you to understand, Sir, I am innocent. I had nobody to talk to. If I could get out of the stockade. I went from the cell to the mess hall. I never had a chance. I had five non-coms to prove it."

Peck made no reply. No one was afraid of Tommie Davison now. No one cared if it was U.S. Army time or French time; it was just time for Tommie Davison to die. Chaplain Crocker asked the prisoner if he had any last statements to make, but Davison remained silent. The executioner then placed the black hood over the condemned man's head, followed by the noose around the man's neck; the time was 3:02 p.m. Thirty seconds later, Peck gave a silent signal to Master Sergeant John C. Woods, who then cut the rope, which released the weight and actuated the trap. Everything worked correctly and at about 3:14 p.m., Captain Lawrence B. Kuhlmann, Captain Robert S. Randall and First

Lieutenant Carlos B. Brewer marched in a single file to the understructure of the scaffold and examined the body. They returned to their positions and the senior officer reported, "Sir, there is still some evidence of life." Peck directed the men to wait; at 3:21 p.m., they made a second evaluation; this time they found that the prisoner was officially dead. Peck then dismissed the witnesses and spectators and Woods then cut the rope. First Lieutenant Milliard R. Jones of the 3059th Graves Registration Company took possession of the body and signed a hand receipt for the same at 3:25 p.m. The Army took the remains to the U.S. Military Cemetery at Marigny and buried them in Plot Z in Grave 2-22.

On April 9, 1945, the War Department sent a telegram to Tommie Davison's seventy-two-year-old father in West Point, Mississippi. His son had died in a non-battle status at Prise Guinment, France, due to his own misconduct; there was no mention that it took Davison eighteen minutes to die from the time the trap door was actuated.

General Prisoner Tommie Davison is now buried at the American Military Cemetery at Oise-Aisne in Plot E. His remains are in Row 3, Grave 60.[3]

*"I'm worried about my present predicament."*

## 66 — Private William Harrison, Jr.

**15089828**
2nd Combat Replacement Crew Center
**Rape and Murder**
Hanged on April 7, 1945

William Harrison, a white soldier from Ohio, raped and strangled to death a seven-year-old Irish girl, Patricia Wylie on September 25, 1944 at Killycolpy in Northern Ireland. Harrison had persuaded her father to allow her to accompany him to "Dorman's Pub" to get the family a present about 4:00 p.m. Harrison later attacked the child near a haystack in a field, raped her and strangled her to death. He then proceeded to the pub, where he drank until 10:00 p.m. He returned to base, ate at both the enlisted and the officers' mess, and slept in the officers' mess until early morning, when he departed and spent the rest of the night in a jeep. Military Police arrested him and noticed blood and abrasions on the soldier. Harrison admitted choking the girl, but was unsure about the sex. A medical board examined William Harrison on October 24 and found him sane to stand trial. His GCM originally convened on November 6, 1944 to address the following charges:[1]

**Charge: Violation of the 92nd Article of War.**
*Specification 1:* In that, Private William Harrison, Jr., Headquarters and Headquarters Squadron, 2nd Combat Crew Replacement Center Group, did, at Killycolpy, Stewartstown, County Tyrone, Northern Ireland, on or about 25 September 1944, with malice aforethought, willfully, deliberately, feloniously, unlawfully, and with premeditation kill one Patricia Wylie, a human being, by strangulation.
*Specification 2:* In that, Private William Harrison, Jr., Headquarters and Headquarters Squadron, 2nd Combat Crew Replacement Center Group, did, at Killycolpy, Stewartstown, County Tyrone, Northern Ireland, on or about 25 September 1944, forcibly and feloniously against her will, have carnal knowledge of Patricia Wylie.

It was a lengthy trial, convening November 6, 7, 17 and 18, and finishing on December 2, 1944. Seventeen witnesses appeared for the prosecution. Nine witnesses, including two psychiatrists, appeared for the defense. Thirty-six pages of the trial transcript

record Harrison on the stand. He claimed that on the day of the crime, he had consumed fifteen beers, fifteen gins and two glasses of port wine. When asked why he choked the victim, instead of denying the act, he stated, "I don't know." The defense wrapped up its case with the following statement:

"Our defense boils down to simply a question of whether or not he had the intent – whether or not he did premeditate to do this crime, whether or not he knew what he was doing when he committed it. I submit for those reasons he is not guilty as charged and I don't hesitate to leave the matter further in your hands."

On November 18, the court sentenced Harrison "in such manner as the reviewing authority may direct to suffer death." This finding was not specific enough and the court reconvened on December 2, 1944, when jurors sentenced him to death by hanging. The *New York Times* reported on the verdict the following day, but Irish newspapers had been all over the story since the beginning, with headlines such as:

"Tyrone Murder Charge: U.S. Soldier on Trial,"
   *Belfast Telegram*, November 6, 1944
"Patricia Wylie Murder,"
   *Belfast Telegraph*, November 7, 1944
"Dramatic Statement Read at Court-Martial,"
   *Irish Daily Telegraph*, November 8, 1944
"Tyrone Murder Trial,"
   *Belfast Telegraph*, November 17, 1944
"Accused Gives Evidence,"
   *Belfast Telegraph*, November 18, 1944
"Death Sentence on American Soldier,"
   *Belfast Telegraph*, November 19, 1944

William Harrison, Jr. was born in Ironton, Ohio on July 22, 1922. As a child, he was anemic and contracted mumps. He graduated from high school and became a motor mechanic, earning $20 per week. An only child, Harrison had a cousin, who was epileptic; his father was crippled, having both legs amputated following a motorcycle accident. William Harrison stood 5'7" tall and weighed 136 pounds. In 1940, he contracted gonorrhea. In 1941, Harrison injured his right hand and remained in the hospital for fifteen days. He enlisted on February 4, 1942 in the Army Air Corps. Harrison had five court-martials – three Summary and two Special – for being absent without official leave. More alarmingly, he exhibited an unstable mental condition.

On April 24, 1943, while assigned to the 93rd Bomb Group, doctors diagnosed Harrison with "constitutional psychopathic state, inadequate personality." The diagnosis, made at the 2nd Evacuation Hospital, also mentioned that he suffered from hysteria and amnesia. A board, however, found that although he was an inadequate individual, who has resorted to the use of alcohol, he had no definite mental disease and recommended that he return to duty. In June 1944, Harrison attempted suicide. The diagnosis at the 79th General Hospital included "constitutional psychopathic state, inadequate personality, manifested by periodic alcoholism." A Special Court-Martial convicted him of AWOL and sentenced him to six months at hard labor and confinement. That punishment was to end on December 26, 1944. However, on September 23, 1944, Colonel P.D. Coates, Commander of Army Air Force Station 238, signed an order remitting the remainder of Harrison's sentence. Two days later, Harrison committed the crimes.

Brigadier General Morris Berman, Commander of the Base Air Depot Area, approved the sentence on December 6, 1944. General Dwight D. Eisenhower confirmed the sentence on January 2, 1945. The Branch Office of The JAG with the ETO, Board of Review Number 1, reviewed *United States v. Private William Harrison, Jr.* Judge Advocates Riter, Sargent and Stevens found that the record of trial was legally sufficient. Over the next month, Congressman Edward McCowen, 6th Congressional District of Ohio, inquired if the sentence could be commuted to life imprisonment. Dr. Douglas Lothian, Down Mental Hospital, got into the act and wrote Harrison's mother on December 9, 1944. He had testified for the defense at trial and as he wrote in the letter, "His [Harrison's] responsibility for his acts was not full responsibility, but only partial." The request went unapproved, but it confused the issue and the Army forwarded the case to the White House for final decision by the President. The JAG office was beside itself. A short, hand-written, caustic note to Colonel R.E. Kunkel, the Chief of the Military Justice Division, initialed by "J.B.S.," stated:

"Colonel Kunkel,
  The AG [Adjutant General] did not do so well here, but nothing we can do now will help or make this silly kid any better-off or happier."

The situation required finesse; the Army's Military Aide at the White House approached the President on March 23, 1945 and explained that if the President took the option to intervene, there could be an avalanche of other presidential requests. Roosevelt agreed and told the aide that he "would not even consider reviewing said case." The JAG radioed General Eisenhower and told him to proceed with the case, while Major General Myron C. Cramer informed Congressman McGowan that the President had declined to intervene. On March 30, 1945, the ETO published General Court-Martial Orders Number 88. By command of General Eisenhower, Major General R.B. Lord set the date of execution as April 7, 1945.

Shortly after midnight on April 7, Major Philip J. Flynn, Commandant of Guardhouse Overhead Detachment Number 6833, assembled the official witnesses and participants in the scheduled execution and briefed them. He asked the officers if there were any questions, but no one replied in the affirmative. Major Flynn then recessed the assembly until 1:50 a.m. At that time, the group re-assembled and moved to the execution chamber. Major Flynn, Chaplain John Berkstresser and two guards, Tech Sergeant Luther S. Moore and Sergeant Bruno T. Anello, marched to the death cell of William Harrison, Jr. Meanwhile, civilian executioner Thomas W. Pierrepoint and his assistant Herbert Morris ensured that all was in order on the gallows. At 1:59 a.m., the procession arrived at the chamber. Major Flynn read General Court-Martial Orders Number 88 in its entirety, while Herbert Morris bound the ankles of the condemned man. Major Flynn asked Harrison if he had any last statement to make. William Harrison replied, "Yes sir. I would like you to try and see my mother and father and I am happy to pay for my crime." The Chaplain asked Harrison the same question, to which the prisoner responded, "Only that you try to see my mother and father and explain things to them."

Thomas Pierrepoint then placed a white hood over the head of the condemned and adjusted the rope. At 2:02 a.m., the Commandant gave a silent signal to the Pierrepoint, who pushed the lever forward, releasing the trap doors. The Commandant subsequently stated, "I believe this man is dead," at which point the three medical officers descended the steps to examine the body. Major John Urbaitis later signed a certificate, stating that Harrison died of Judicial Strangulation at 2:22 a.m.

Graves' registration personnel originally buried Harrison and his two identification tags at the Brookwood Cemetery in Plot X, Grave 2-5. In 1948, the remains were transferred to the American Military Cemetery at Cambridge, England. General Prisoner William Harrison, Jr. is now buried at the American Military Cemetery at Oise-Aisne in Plot E. His remains are in Row 3, Grave 62.

On April 8, 1945, Chaplain John E. Berkstresser of the U.K. Base Guardhouse wrote the parents of William Harrison. In the letter, he mentioned the death of the soldier, but did not mention the manner or circumstances surrounding his death. The War Department sent a Non-Battle Casualty Report, concerning Private Harrison, to his family on April 16, 1945. The telegram stated that the soldier had died of Strangulation – Judicial.[2]

## "Dear Sir, I was tried for mudder and the court find me guilty and sences me to be hong."

In very few of the 96 death penalty sentences is the quality of remorse evident. There are a handful of exceptions, where the condemned expressed repentance at his execution, but we cannot determine whether this emotion was a genuine feeling, or fear and trepidation. Private Benjamin Hopper was an exception; he understood that he had done wrong and paid the ultimate price anyway, despite some, who thought his sentence should have been commuted.

Private Benjamin F. Hopper wanted to be a good soldier, but he needed help. Born on August 20, 1920 in Hickory, North Carolina, one of eight children, he needed a father, but his father left the home – headed for New York City – and his mother raised him. Hopper listed his occupation as loading trucks and washing dishes. He stood 5'7" tall and weighed 160 pounds. Educated through the fourth grade, the black soldier had a limited ability to read and write, relying on others to assist him. He often did not receive this help, as shown in his post-conviction letter to General Dwight Eisenhower seeking clemency:

"Gen. Eisenhower
Dear Sir, I was tried for mudder and the court find me guilty and sences me to be hong Sir. And Sir I am asking you to please Sir look in to this mader close Sir for me because I have made a great mucstake Sir and wont you to give me another chanch in the armey."

Benjamin Hopper told General Eisenhower that he had never been in trouble before in the Army; that was not exactly true. A Special Court-Martial in Georgia had convicted him for being absent without official leave. Early in 1944, a Summary Court-Martial convicted Hopper of being in Liege, Belgium without a pass. Hopper may not have been lying; he may have genuinely had a faulty memory. A psychiatric evaluation, which on November 21, 1944 determined that Benjamin Hopper had an IQ of 50, also found, "He has a mental age of approximately 9 years, bordering on mental deficiency." Private

Hopper told the psychiatrist that during his argument with Private Jackson, Jackson pointed his rifle at him and threatened, "Goddamn it, I'll shoot you."

The case was straightforward and an excellent example of stupid situations that soldiers could get themselves into, if they had been drinking and did not consider the consequences of their actions. Private Hopper and four other soldiers were in the "Maison Des Huiets Heures Café" in Welkenraedt, Belgium – just outside Liège – on October 28, 1944, a few minutes after midnight. Hopper and Private Randolph Jackson, Jr. started arguing. The other three troopers, apparently used to these kinds of verbal exchanges, paid little attention, even as the pair expressed a desire to shoot one another. Private Jackson then offered his own weapon to Private Hopper, perhaps a dare to the other man. It was a dumb decision. Hopper took the weapon, fired multiple rounds and killed Jackson. Hopper then placed the murder weapon on top of Jackson's fallen body and refused to help transport the dying man to a medical facility, saying, "You didn't see nothing."

MPs arrested him the same day. His GCM convened at 10:00 a.m. on November 23, 1944 at Soumagne, Belgium, the location of the First Army Headquarters.[1] Private Benjamin Hopper pleaded not guilty to the charge of murder, a violation of the 92nd Article of War.[2] He elected not to testify and his defense presented no evidence on his behalf. The jury found him guilty and sentenced him to be hanged. Court records then went to the staff judge advocate at the First Army. Lieutenant Colonel John W. Bonner wrote that there were no significant errors, but raised issues concerning premeditation, opening the window to life imprisonment. Colonel Ernest M. Brannon, First Army Staff Judge Advocate, concurred and made this recommendation to his commander. Lieutenant General Courtney H. Hodges, Commander First Army, signed his recommendation as the convening authority on December 22, 1944. Part of it read:

"In the foregoing case of Private Benjamin F. Hopper, 32720571, 3170th Quartermaster Service Company, the sentence is approved, but it is recommended that it be commuted to the dishonorable discharge of the soldier, forfeiture of all pay and allowances due or to become due him, and confinement at hard labor for the term of his natural life."

Private Hopper's letter followed to General Eisenhower. On January 25, 1945, Colonel Warren Hayford III, the Commander, Central District, Brittany Base Section, interviewed General Prisoner Hopper on direction of General Eisenhower. Hopper told the colonel that he wanted to go to the front and soldier, and that he would never get into trouble again. Colonel Hayford attempted to ascertain if the convicted man had received a fair trial; Hopper said he did not think so. Benjamin Hopper said that he wanted to tell the jury what happened, but:

> "My Defense Counsel said he was going to tell them. Told me to stay silent. So, he got up and told them I wasn't guilty. He didn't say much else."

Hayford pressed Hopper, asking him if he had wanted to testify and if so, what had his lawyer told him. Hopper replied, "He said it didn't make much difference. Said it would be better for me to sit silent." Colonel Hayford pressed harder, asking Hopper if he recalled whether the Defense Counsel told the court what the defendant's story was. Hopper replied, "No, he didn't tell them. He said someone would ask him questions and he would say – he didn't explain it to the court."

MPs transferred Hopper to the Loire DTC, while the ETO Judge Advocate reviewed the case. Brigadier General Edward C. Betts recommended to General Eisenhower no clemency. Eisenhower concurred with Betts. On February 12, 1945, General Dwight D. Eisenhower signed an order confirming the sentence of Private Benjamin F. Hopper, but withheld directing execution. The Branch Office of The JAG with the ETO reviewed the case on April 4, 1945. JAGs Van Benschotten, Hill and Julian ruled the court committed no errors injuriously affecting the substantial rights of the accused; thus, the record of trial was legally sufficient to support the findings of guilty and the sentence imposed.

On April 7, 1945, the ETO published General Court-Martial Orders Number 107. Major General R.B. Lord directed that the execution would occur on April 11, 1945 at the Loire DTC at Le Mans. The night before at 7:00 p.m., Major Ernest A. Weizer, a medical officer, examined General Prisoner Hopper and found him to be in excellent physical and mental condition.

At 10:42 a.m. on April 11, 1945, the Commanding Officer, Loire DTC assembled six other officials, five official witnesses and thirty-five authorized military spectators – in a ravine in the northwestern corner of the Loire DTC at Le Mans. Included in the spectators were eight General

Prisoners: Bernard Diamond, Milton Hodge, Joseph Carr, Willie Johnette, Charles Lee, Albert Williams, Edward Allen and Adron Sayler. Four were white soldiers and four were black. The official witnesses stood in a single rank twenty paces from the south side of the gallows. The military spectators were in a single rank, ten paces behind the witnesses. Twenty yards to the rear, were the General Prisoners, under guard and behind a barbed-wire enclosure.

The weather was clear, bright, warm and sunny. Twenty-five enlisted men of the 389th MP Battalion, under the immediate command of First Lieutenant Rolan B. Dixon, guarded the site. Lieutenant Colonel Henry L. Peck, read aloud General Court-Martial Orders Number 107 and briefed the witnesses and spectators on proper conduct. At 10:58 a.m., an Army ½-ton, 4x4 covered reconnaissance car pulled up to the ravine and General Prisoner Benjamin F. Hopper dismounted. He joined a procession led by Lieutenant Colonel Peck, Chaplain Andrew Zarek and guards: Sergeant Russell E. Boyle, Sergeant Alfonso Girvalo and Sergeant Jack D. Briscoe – who carried a brace-board. Behind the guards, walked Captain Milton B. Asbell, the event recorder, and the five official witnesses. The group quickly arrived at the scaffold. The guards then bound the prisoner's hands behind his back, led the prisoner up the thirteen steps and positioned him on the trap door. At 11:00 a.m., the executioner's assistant bound Hopper's ankles. Lieutenant Colonel Peck asked Hopper if he had any last words and Hopper replied, "Pray for me." Lieutenant Colonel Peck replied, "God bless you son." However, Peck could not help Benjamin Hopper now. Chaplain Zarek asked the prisoner if he had any last statements to make, to which Hopper replied, "Father, I would like you to write to my mother."

The Chaplain then began to intone a prayer. The executioner, Master Sergeant John C. Woods, then placed the black hood over the condemned man's head, put the noose around the man's neck and adjusted them both; the time was 11:01 a.m. Seconds later, Peck gave a silent signal to Woods, who released the weight and actuated the trap. Everything seemed to work correctly, the body slightly swayed in the breeze, and at 11:13 a.m., Major Roy Campbell, Captain Daniel Thaw and Captain Francis O. Lamb marched in a single file to the understructure of the gallows and examined the body. They returned to their positions and the senior officer reported, "Sir, this man is not dead." Lieutenant Colonel Peck replied, "Make your second examination in five minutes."

At 11:24 a.m., the officers made a second evaluation and found that the prisoner was officially deceased. Peck dismissed the witnesses and spectators and the executioner then cut the rope. Captain Benjamin D. Lucas, of the 3045th Graves Registration Company, took possession of the body and signed a hand receipt for the same. The Army buried Benjamin Hopper's body at the U.S. Military Cemetery at Marigny in Plot Z, Grave 1-19; Sergeant Emmett N. Bailey, Jr. was a member of the burial detail. Officials reinterred the remains at the American Military Cemetery at Oise-Aisne in Plot E in 1949. They are located at Row 1, Grave 7.

On April 18, 1945, the War Department sent a telegram to Benjamin Hopper's father. The message stated that Hopper was deceased through execution by judicial hanging. Chaplain Zarek fulfilled Hopper's request and wrote his mother on July 4, 1945. In the letter, the Chaplain mentioned that shortly before his death, her son converted to Catholicism and that before his death, "He showed unusual courage and was not afraid to die."[3]

## 68     Private John Williams
32794118
434th Port Company, 501st Port Battalion
**Murder and Rape**
Hanged on April 19, 1945

## 69     Private James L. Jones
34221343
434th Port Company, 501st Port Battalion
**Murder and Rape**
Hanged on April 19, 1945

## 70     Private Milbert Bailey
34151488
434th Port Company, 501st Port Battalion
**Murder and Rape**
Hanged on April 19, 1945

The 434th Port Company, an all-black unit based at Maghull, England, deployed to France. On October 11, 1944, Private John Williams, Private James L. Jones and Private Milbert Bailey stabbed and killed a man and then raped his nineteen-year-old daughter at La Pernelle, Hameau Scipion, on the Cherbourg Peninsula. MPs apprehended the three soldiers on October 16, 1944. On December 14, 1944, a GCM found all three guilty and sentenced them to death.[1]

Details of the case are scanty, as complete GCM files for all three soldiers, were not present at the U.S. Army Clerk of Court. James L. Jones was born in Reform, Alabama (thirty miles west of Tuscaloosa) on December 12, 1912; he later lived in Millport, Alabama. He entered the Army on May 6, 1942 and went overseas in May 1944. He had a previous court-martial conviction. Milbert Bailey also had previous court-martial convictions. Bailey, who was born in Louisiana on September 6, 1914, had attended grammar school. Prior to entering the service, he worked at a shipyard in Pascagoula, Mississippi. He was inducted at Jacksonville, Florida on September 20, 1941. Bailey stood 5'7" tall and weighed 140 pounds; his medical record indicated that he smoked fifteen cigarettes a day and consumed a pint of alcohol every week. Ten days after his induction, Private Bailey injured his head, receiving several sutures on his scalp. He had gonorrhea, stating that he caught the disease from a New Orleans prostitute during an $11.50 fling.

Private Bailey told physicians he had first contracted the illness in 1935. On May 16, 1943, Milton Bailey's mother died. Sometime that summer, Private Bailey was involved in an automobile accident in Florida. In February 1944, while assigned to the 649th Tank Destroyer Battalion, he received a diagnosis with Post-Traumatic Syndrome, due to the concussion he received in the accident. He may not have received further treatment for this.

John Williams was born in Orlando, Florida on March 8, 1917. Standing 5'6½" and weighing 118 pounds, he finished five years of grade school. He later married, had a child and became a longshoreman, but was later divorced. He enlisted on February 6, 1943 in New York City. Private Williams then reported to the 28th Cavalry Regiment at Camp Lockett, California. The 28th was an all-black regiment and was the last cavalry regiment in the Army to be horse-mounted. Private Williams contracted malaria, while in the regiment, as well as two cases of gonorrhea. A Special Court-Martial convicted him in July 1943 for AWOL; a second court-martial convicted him in February 1944 for AWOL, during maneuvers in Louisiana. Re-assigned to the 434th Port Company, 501st Port Battalion, he arrived in France July 4, 1944. By that time, his service record listed both his character and efficiency as unsatisfactory.

The ETO published General Court-Martial Orders Number 116 on April 15, 1945. It stated that Private Bailey, Private Jones and Private Williams would hang on April 19, 1945 at La Pernelle, Hameau Scipion, France. On April 18, 1945, three events occurred. First Lieutenant David J. Duff, a Military Police officer with the Beach District Guardhouse, read General Court-Martial Orders Number 116 to each of the condemned at the guardhouse about 9:55 a.m. Minutes later Chaplains William L. Bell, Rufus A. Cooper and Carlos M. May arrived at the guardhouse to act in their official capacity for the three men through the execution the next day. All three Chaplains were black; two were members of the African Methodist Episcopal Church and one served at the African Methodist Episcopal Zion Church. Finally, about 10:45 a.m., Major Samuel H. Boyer, a medical officer in the 1349th Engineer Regiment, examined all three prisoners and found them to be in excellent physical and mental condition. It is likely that all three condemned men, and the Chaplains, spent that last night at the Beach District Guardhouse at Cherbourg.

On the morning of April 19, the village of La Pernelle was warm, as the sun was shining and the weather clear. A blanket of grass, dotted with an occasional tree, covered the ground of a hedgerowed field, one-hundred yards long by thirty-five yards wide, located two-hundred yards east of road GC 125. Adjacent to the field was the victim's house; justice was coming home. The scaffold, on the southwestern corner of the field, faced east – the condemned men would experience the sun on their faces one last time before they died. At 9:55 a.m., Lieutenant Colonel Henry L. Peck, Commander of the Loire DTC, gathered seven official witnesses, five additional witnesses, twelve authorized military spectators and two French civilian spectators. One was the brother of the murdered man. The event started late, as the military spectators were thirty minutes tardy.

Lieutenant Colonel Peck read General Court-Martial Orders Number 116 to the assembly and gave them instructions on proper decorum. The official witnesses moved to a position ten paces from the side of the gallows; the others were slightly further away, except for the medical officers, who had the best view, just eight paces from the stair-side of the scaffold. Ten men of the 387th MP Battalion and five soldiers from the Beach District Guardhouse, under the immediate command of First Lieutenant David J. Duff, guarded the area. At 10:08 a.m., an open ½-ton, 4X4 truck brought General Prisoner Milton Bailey to the field and halted twenty yards from the gallows. At 10:09 a.m., a procession began from the truck to the scaffold; in the lead was Lieutenant Colonel Peck with Chaplain Carlos M. May to his left. They were followed by Bailey, flanked on each side and to the rear by Sergeant Russell E. Boyle, Sergeant Alfonso Girvalo and Sergeant George M. Harris. Harris was new to this type of work; Boyle and Girvalo had been to this rodeo before.

As the group reached the gallows, Peck and May climbed the steps, while the guards bound Jones' hands behind his back and then assisted him up the steps. During the climb, the recorder gave the command "Attention." As Bailey stood on the trap door, the assistant executioner bound his ankles 10:10 a.m. Peck and the Chaplain then each asked the condemned man if he had a statement to make, but he did not. Chaplain May then started intoning a prayer and Master Sergeant John C. Woods adjusted the black hood and noose at 10:11 a.m. Peck then signaled Woods, who cut the rope, releasing the weight and actuating the trap. Bailey "precipitated" through the open trap door and hung suspended in the lower recess of the scaffold, with no sounds or muscular movements. The recorder

gave the command "Parade Rest" and the assembly began the first interminable wait until 10:26 a.m., when Lieutenant Colonel Peck directed the medical officers to make their examinations. Lieutenant Colonel Fred G. DeBusk – the senior medical officer – reported at 10:28 a.m., "Sir, we find this man deceased."

First Lieutenant Milliard R. Jones of the 3055th Graves Registration Company, signed for the body. Then a second waiting period began. At 10:50 a.m., an open ½-ton, 4X4 truck brought General Prisoner James Jones to the field, halting twenty yards from the gallows. At 10:51 a.m., the procession began; in the lead was Lieutenant Colonel Peck with Chaplain William L. Bell to his left. The prisoner, flanked on each side and to the rear by Sergeant Russell E. Boyle, Sergeant Alfonso Girvalo and Sergeant George M. Harris, followed. Harris was now a veteran with one execution under his belt; Boyle had now done fourteen and Girvalo had seventeen.

The group reached the scaffold; Lieutenant Colonel Peck and the Chaplain climbed the steps, while the guards bound Jones' hands behind his back and then assisted him up the steps. The recorder again gave the command "Attention." Once on the trap door, the assistant executioner bound Jones' ankles bound at 10:53 a.m. Jones also had no statements to make. Chaplain Bell then started intoning a prayer and Woods adjusted the black hood and noose at 10:54 a.m. The Commanding Officer signaled Woods, who cut the rope that released the weight and actuated the trap. The prisoner dropped through the open trap door and hung suspended in the lower recess of the gallows. The recorder again gave the command "Parade Rest" and the assembly began a third waiting period until 11:09 a.m., when Lieutenant Colonel Peck directed the medical officers to make their examinations. They did, and the Lieutenant Colonel Fred G. DeBusk reported at 11:11 a.m., "Sir, we pronounce this man officially dead." First Lieutenant Milliard R. Jones then signed for the second body.

It was time for the next execution and at 11:27 a.m. an open ½-ton, 4x4 truck brought General Prisoner John Williams to the same spot as the others. Thirty seconds later the procession began from the truck to the scaffold; in the lead was Lieutenant Colonel Peck with Chaplain Rufus A. Cooper to his left. Then walked the prisoner, flanked on each side and to the rear by Sergeant Russell E. Boyle and Sergeant Alfonso Girvalo and Sergeant George M. Harris. Harris might now have been experiencing the heebie-jeebies. The group reached the gallows; Lieutenant Colonel Peck and the Chaplain climbed the steps, while the guards bound Williams' hands behind his back and then assisted him up the steps – during the climb, the recorder again gave the command "Attention." Once he was on the trap door, Technician Third Grade Thomas F. Robinson, the assistant executioner, bound his ankles at 11:29 a.m. Lieutenant Colonel Peck then asked the prisoner, "Private Williams, do you have a statement to make to me before the order directing your execution is carried into effect?" Private Williams replied, "No sir … only thing is I prayed to the Lord and He answered my prayers. I leave to a heavenly rest. You may take my body but not my spirit; the Lord is with me." Lieutenant Colonel Peck replied, "Amen."

Chaplain Cooper then asked the condemned man if he had anything to say to him as the Chaplain. Williams replied, "Thank you. May God bless you." The Commanding Officer then said, "May the Lord have mercy on you."

Chaplain Cooper started intoning a prayer as the executioner adjusted the black hood and noose at 11:29 and thirty seconds. The Commanding Officer then signaled Master Sergeant Woods, who – for the third time that morning – cut the rope, releasing the weight and actuating the trap at 11:30 a.m. The prisoner fell through the open trap door and hung suspended in the lower recess of the gallows, the body slightly swaying. The recorder then gave the command "Parade Rest" and the assembly waited one last time until 11:45 a.m., when Lieutenant Colonel Peck directed the medical officers to make their examinations. At 11:47 a.m., Lieutenant Colonel Fred G. DeBusk reported, "Sir, we pronounce this man officially dead."

First Lieutenant Jones took possession of the morning's third body. The Army buried them at 10:00 a.m. on April 20, 1945 in the U.S. Military Cemetery at Marigny in Plot Z, Grave 1-20 (Bailey), Grave 2-23 (Jones) and Grave 2-24 (Williams); Sergeant Emmett N. Bailey, Jr. was part of the burial detail for all three men. Later, officials reinterred the remains at the American Military Cemetery at Oise-Aisne in Plot E. Milbert Bailey's remains are in Grave 90; James L. Jones' body is in Grave 84; and John Williams' remains are in Grave 94, all in Row 4.

The Adjutant General sent a telegram on April 27, 1945 to the mother of James L. Jones, stating that the cause of death of her son was execution pursuant to an approved sentence of a GCM and that he died of judicial strangulation. On the same day, a similar telegram went to the wife of Private Williams, although she had already written a letter to President Roosevelt in March 1945, asking for assistance. In the missive, she wrote the following sentence concerning the crime – undoubtedly communicated to her by her husband, "He [Private Williams] did not kill the French fellow; Private James Jones is the one who committed that." She made no mention of the rape. Then, after the White House forwarded her letter to the Army, correspondence became muddled. She had received the telegram concerning her husband's death on April 27, 1945; a second report of death followed on May 3, 1945; and a third special registered letter to her went out on April 27 from the Army, stating that her husband's death was due to his willful misconduct. On May 9, 1945, Major General J.A. Ulio, The Adjutant General, signed a letter to Mrs. Williams that could only have added to the confusion. In it, Major General Ulio wrote, "I realize there is little comfort to be offered you at the present time but you may be assured of my deepest sympathy for the anxiety caused by your husband's confinement."

Nowhere in the letter did the letter mention the death of Private Williams. However, he was not confined; he had been executed twenty days before, but the Adjutant General's office had not caught the implied error. Down at the 434th Port Company, Captain Herbert J. Skelton at least got the sequence correct and wrote a letter of condolence to the wife of his deceased soldier on May 3, 1945. He stated that her husband had "contributed materially to the success of the War Effort" but that he had died not in the line of duty. Captain Skelton added no further details.[2]

• • •

Major General J.A. Ulio, finally received Lieutenant Colonel Peck's letter concerning Master Sergeant Woods and wrote the Chief of Naval Personnel on April 22, 1945, stating that the Secretary of War requested verification of Navy service for John C. Woods. The reply indicated that Apprentice Seaman John C. Woods of Wichita, Kansas had enlisted for four years on December 3, 1929. The reply included that Woods had been absent without leave from February 24, 1930 to March 7, 1930 and had received an ordinary discharge under honorable conditions on May 15, 1930.

• • •

In September 2011, Monsieur Daniel Bellamy, the Mayor of Le Pernelle, pointed out to author the house that had been the scene of the crime, the field in which the executions occurred and the grave of the murder victim in the Le Pernelle Cemetery, overlooking the Atlantic Ocean. The mayor also mentioned that the rape victim was still alive and lived in another town in Normandy – almost sixty-seven years after that horrible day.

_"Although I have approved the sentence, I feel that under all the circumstances in this case, the death sentenced should be commuted to life imprisonment or confinement for a term of years."_

**71**

# Corporal Shelton McGhee, Sr.

34529025

3823rd Quartermaster Truck Company,
133rd Quartermaster Battalion

**Attempted Assault Against an Officer and Murder**

Hanged on May 4, 1945

Corporal Shelton McGhee, Sr. grew up in difficult circumstances. Born in Holly Springs, Mississippi on May 8, 1916, he left school in the ninth grade to go to work. His father was killed by police when Shelton was thirteen. His work record was good and he had no brushes with the law. He became a Pullman Porter, married and divorced. McGhee, a black soldier, was inducted at Camp Forest, Tennessee on February 5, 1943; he was 5'9" tall and weighed 175 pounds, with black hair and brown eyes. He scored 87 on the Army General Classification Test, Category IV.

At 11:00 a.m., on December 15, 1944 at Livorno, Italy, Corporal McGhee started for town, but his attention quickly turned to a craps game at the guard tent. The men shared a bottle of cognac. All but two of the players, McGhee and Technician Fifth Grade George W. Brown, dropped out of the game. An argument ensued, with McGhee saying, "No man takes nothing from me." Brown, a black soldier and a friend of the accused, replied by waving the money he had won in front of Corporal McGhee. The pair stopped playing, after McGhee had lost all of his money and began walking away. Moments later, McGhee repeated the phrase and took a German P-38 pistol from his pocket. His first shot dropped the victim and McGhee fired several more rounds hitting Brown in the lungs, kidney, liver, small intestine and large intestine; he then walked twenty-five feet to the prostrate Brown and kicked him twice in the head. As McGhee walked away from the scene, he said to onlookers, "I'm going to kill everybody."

Witnesses rushed the victim to medical care, but he died shortly thereafter. A few minutes later, First Lieutenant James A. Green, commander of the 3823rd Quartermaster Truck Company, asked him what happened. McGhee responded: "No mother-fucker is going to take this gun from me. I killed one man and I'll kill you." McGhee raised the gun and Lieutenant Green, figuring that discretion was the better part of valor, turned and ran. From the side of his eye, he saw the accused pull the trigger.

Officials preferred charges against Corporal McGhee on December 23, 1944; in eight days, the investigation was complete. Brigadier General Francis H. Oxx, Commander of the PBS, referred the charges for trial by GCM on January 11, 1945. On January 24, 1945, psychiatrists examined the accused, finding him to have a well-integrated personality, with good morale and motivation. The report was quite positive and included their observation, "Speech is fluent, relevant, coherent, and he expresses himself in a logical and orderly manner."

The GCM met at Livorno, Italy at 9:30 a.m. on February 3, 1945.[1] The accused pleaded not guilty to the charge of murder, a violation of the 92nd Article of War and to an attempted assault against a commissioned officer, a violation of the 64th Article of War.[2] Two enlisted men testified that the accused and the victim had been on friendly terms. Second Lieutenant Robert C. Schaut testified for the defense and stated that Corporal McGhee had been an excellent soldier prior to the incident. McGhee elected to testify on his own behalf, stating that he thought Brown had a gun and was going to shoot him. None of the witnesses supported that theory. Corporal McGhee had one previous Summary Court-Martial for entering an off-limits house of prostitution on April 28, 1944 that resulted in a twenty-dollar fine and reduction to the rank of private; he later worked his way back to corporal.

The panel found Corporal McGhee guilty of both charges, all jury members voting for the death penalty. The trial lasted two hours and fifteen minutes. The legal section at the PBS reviewed the case on March 26, 1945. Colonel Claudius O. Wolfe, Staff Judge Advocate of the PBS, opined that given the previous positive record of the accused, imprisonment for life would be an adequate punishment and that this recommendation be made to the confirming authority. On March 30, 1945, Brigadier General Oxx wrote a letter to the Commander, MTO, stating that he had approved the sentence of death for Corporal McGhee, stating,

"Although I have approved the sentence, I feel that under all the circumstances in this case, the death sentenced should be commuted to life imprisonment or confinement for a term of years. The accused undoubtedly was influenced in his actions by anger."

Not only was General Oxx opening the door to life imprisonment, but also that imprisonment could be for less than that. However, General Joseph McNarney confirmed the death sentence on April 14, 1945, after seeing the review of the theater staff judge advocate. In the review, Brigadier General Adam Richmond stated that the evidence supported the charges and that there was no extenuation or mitigation. On April 21, 1945, Judge Advocates Sargent, Irion and Remick reviewed the case at the Branch Office of The JAG with the MTO. They found no major errors and did not address commutation. The MTO published General Court-Martial Orders Number 67 the same day, setting the date of execution for May 4, 1945 at Aversa, Italy. Chaplain John C. Bain arrived at the stockade on May 3 to provide spiritual assistance.

On May 4, 1945, the Army hanged General Prisoner Shelton McGhee, Sr. Under the direction of Major W.G. Neiswender, commander of the PBS Garrison Stockade Number 1, the trap door dropped at 8:12 a.m. and doctors pronounced McGhee dead at 8:25 a.m. Three lieutenant colonels and two majors served as official witnesses. The Army buried McGhee at the U.S. Military Cemetery at Naples, in the General Prisoner plot in Grave 2-16. Exhumed in 1949, Shelton McGhee, Sr. is currently buried at the American Military Cemetery at Oise-Aisne in Plot E. His remains are in Row 1, Grave 6.[3]

• • •

In 1996, the son of Shelton McGhee, Sr. turned to his Congressman to find where his father was buried. The Member of Congress wrote the Army with this request. On March 18, 1997, an officer at the U.S. Army Reserve Personnel Center wrote back, providing the judicial file on Private McGhee to the Congressman, but wrote, "No specific information concerning his burial is contained in those documents." The author contacted this family member in 2012. It appears that the Congressman never forwarded any of the information to the son, who knew no details about his father's death or where he was buried.

*"Therefore I conclude that he cannot be held responsible for his action."*

## 72 Private George E. Smith, Jr.
33288266

784th Bombardment Squadron,
466th Bombardment Group,
96th Combat Bombardment Wing (Heavy),
Second Air Division
**Murder**
Hanged on May 8, 1945

Sometimes at trial, it was easy to determine whether the accused had actually committed the crime. However, when the psychiatrists got involved concerning the mental state of the accused at the time of the crime, matters in the courtroom could take a painful turn. When there were three psychiatrists and their opinions were not identical, it could get so painful that at the end of a four-day trial – everyone involved was ready for a "Section VIII," not just the accused.

The basic facts of the crime were easy to follow. At about 1:30 p.m. on a cold December 3, 1944, Private George E. Smith, Jr. and Private Leonard S. Wojtacha, two white soldiers, left Attlebridge Airdrome, near Honingham, England. They were going hunting and each carried an M1 .30 caliber issue carbine and ammunition. Walking through the fields, Wojtacha – who was from Detroit, Michigan – noticed that Smith fired at an oil drum, then a cow and finally a squirrel. Private Smith was happy and laughing as he shot; by 2:15 p.m., they found themselves in a wooded area. The owner of the woods, sixty-year-old Sir Eric Teichman – a British diplomat – heard the shots and growled to his wife, "I'm going to stop this damned poaching."

Unarmed, he then wandered out of his house to see exactly who was disturbing the tranquility of his 3,000-acre estate. He came upon Private George E. Smith, Jr. and Private Teichman. Smith yelled to his compatriot, "Watch out. There is an old man behind you." Sir Eric asked the pair, "Just a minute. What are your names?" Private Smith replied in two ways. First, he shouted, "Get back, Pop." Then Smith shot the diplomat in the face.

Smith and Wojtacha quickly left the scene. They passed near an old man walking a dog and according to Wojtacha, he told Smith that was the same old

man they had encountered earlier, to which Smith replied, "I must have missed him. I should have shot him again." The men arrived at their barracks at 2:50 p.m. The next morning, all the airmen in the unit received the command to turn in their weapons. A day later, Smith walked up to Wojtacha at the mess hall and in a low voice said, "Don't say anything. Let them find out for themselves." Meanwhile, the base Provost Marshal investigated the crime scene. MPs had found ten empty M1 carbine cartridges and two wads of chewing gum fifty yards away, which indicated Americans might be involved. They took plaster casts of footprints at the area of the shooting. In a separate facet of the investigation, agents – after another airman came forward and said he saw the pair leave the base – determined that Private Smith and Private Wojtacha had gone hunting the afternoon of the shooting. The Provost Marshal confronted Private Leonard Wojtacha with what he knew; Wojtacha became scared and made a full statement.[1] On December 7, 1944, MPs informed Private George Smith that he would be charged with murder. As the police officer began reading him his rights, Smith interrupted him, stating, "I shot him."

Smith then made a complete written confession. That afternoon, both accused soldiers took investigators to the scene of the crime and reenacted what had occurred. Dr. Henry Smith, a firearms expert and Director of the Home Office Laboratory in Nottingham, examined the bullet taken from the body of deceased and a bullet fired from the murder weapon and said he was satisfied beyond reasonable doubt that the accused's carbine had fired the death bullet.

The *Chicago Tribune* was the first to jump on the case in the U.S. on December 6, 1944, with the headline on page one:

**"Hunt for Briton's Slayer Turns to Yank Airdrome"**

The "Trib" would publish six articles on the case. The *New York Times* also was on top of the case, featuring six articles on the murder, beginning December 8, 1944 and ending with a report on the execution several months later. To the prosecution, it looked like an open and shut case – until the psychiatrists muddied things up. Major Thomas A. March, a neuro-psychiatrist, examined the accused and made the following report on December 9, 1944:

"Psychiatric examination discloses this man to be an Inadequate Personality of a Constitutional Psychopathic State. The above condition indicates that this man has an immature emotional system, which makes him subject to inadequate control of his actions and faulty judgment. Said enlisted man is not mentally ill and is cognizant of the difference between right and wrong. His actions, however, as indicated above, are subject to poor control and faulty or immature judgment."

Major Leo Alexander, Chief of Psychiatric Section, 65th General Hospital, examined George Smith and he diagnosed Smith's condition as,

"Constitutional psychopathic state, with inadequate and immature personality, emotional instability, schizoid traits, and explosive (poorly repressed) primitive-sadistic aggressiveness; severe. Mental deficiency, borderline, mental age nine years. In older psychiatric terminology … Mentally defective, homicidal degenerate."

An English psychiatrist got into the act as well. Dr. John V. Morris, Superintendent of the Norfolk County Mental Deficiency Institution, examined the accused. Dr. Morris concluded that Smith suffered from Schizophrenia and might at times be able to distinguish right from wrong, but if he had an impulse to do something wrong, he would not possess enough reasoning power or control to resist. Smith was subject to uncontrollable impulses; he was an anti-social type, without regret of killing, and whose permanent restraint was necessary. Morris also concluded that Smith's brain was diseased and that he suffered from early Schizophrenia. The doctor concluded: "Therefore I conclude that he cannot be held responsible for his action."

Who was George E. Smith, Jr.? Born on April 14, 1918 in Pittsburgh, Pennsylvania, his score on the Army General Classification Test score was 67, Class V, which placed him in the lower 20 percent of his organization. Smith was inducted on August 13, 1942 at Pittsburgh; on that date, he was already on parole from the Huntingdon Reformatory in Pennsylvania, serving a lengthy sentence for auto theft. He had previously worked for the Carnegie Steel Mills for two years. Although his sentence was to run until 1948, the state waived parole supervision, as Smith was going into the Army. The son of a steelworker, he had six previous convictions by courts-martial: two Summaries and four Specials, including absent without leave, attempt to escape from a city jail, failure to obey a lawful command from his commanding officer, wrongfully taking and using an automobile and disorderly in uniform in a public place. Smith stood 5'5" tall and weighed 165 pounds.

The GCM convened on January 8, 1945 at the Attlebridge Airdrome camp chapel.[2] Private Smith pleaded not guilty to the charge of murder, a violation of the 92nd Article of War.[3] His lawyer stated that Smith's confession was made under duress. Private Smith elected not to take the stand; the defense argued that he was insane. The court-martial lasted four days, due to repeated hospitalization of the defendant. After listening to all the evidence, much of it pertinent to the mental state of the accused, the jury unanimously found him guilty and voted unanimously for the death penalty. On January 12, 1945, the *New York Times* ran an article about the assessed mental age of the accused; the following day the newspaper reported on the conviction and sentence. The *Times* stated that Smith had admitted he had eight courts-martial since 1942 and that he had consumed fifteen cups of beer the day of the murder. The newspaper also reported that Smith wrote an essay in the guardhouse, which included, "My name should have been Trouble, not Smith."

The paper also reported Smith as a "happy-go-lucky homicidal degenerate," and recounted that during the penalty phase of the trial, Defense Counsels had Smith disrobe to show the jury he had tattoos from his neck to his knees – to include a baby face and an upside-down "13" – in an effort to show that he was mentally unbalanced. The *Stars & Stripes* ran several stories about the trial and the accused. One article stated that Smith liked to read, "Comics like Superman and Terry and the Pirates."

Appeals to commute the sentence began. Smith's assistant Defense Counsel wrote to the General Eisenhower, requesting that the sentence be commuted to life imprisonment. Perhaps more significantly, Lady Teichman appealed to Eisenhower and the U.S. Ambassador in London to spare Private Smith's life. The Second Air Division JAG reviewed the case on February 7, 1945. On April 3, 1945, General Eisenhower signed an order confirming the sentence of Private George E. Smith, Jr. The order withheld directions concerning the execution. On April 26, 1945, the Board of Review Number 1 of the Branch Office of The JAG with the ETO reviewed the case. Judge Advocates Riter, Burrow and Stevens concluded that questions of evidence were properly resolved. The board then addressed the mental competency of the accused, stating:

"It is not for the Board of Review to weigh evidence, and in view of the record, it must conclude that the court properly found on the competent evidence adduced, that the accused was legally sane."

Major Philip J. Flynn, Commanding Officer of the United Kingdom Base Guardhouse, had an unenviable duty early on May 8, 1945. On the continent, people were celebrating VE Day, the day that the Allies formally accepted the unconditional surrender of the armed forces of Nazi Germany. The warring parties had signed the actual surrender document the day before; it would be ratified in Berlin, Germany on May 8. In a few hours in London, hundreds of thousands of joyous people would mass on Trafalgar Square and up The Mall to Buckingham Palace. The crowds would cheer King George VI and Prime Minister Winston Churchill for their perseverance in a fight that the British came close to losing in 1940.

There would be no cheering, however, at Shepton Mallet Prison. Major Flynn briefed the nine official witnesses for the execution of General Prisoner George E. Smith that there would be no demonstrations or "unseemly" conduct. Cheering fell into that category. The witnesses arrived at the execution chamber at the prison at 1:57 a.m., May 8. Two minutes later, General Prisoner George E. Smith, Jr., Major Flynn, Chaplain George E. Montie, and guards Sergeant John A. Dunwoody and Technician Third Grade Harry P. Ross, entered the chamber. Major Flynn then read General Court-Martial Orders Number 128 in its entirety and then asked General Prisoner Number 1915 whether he had any last statement to make. Smith replied:

"Well sir, I would like to have you give my regards to your boys; you were really swell, and the Chaplain and the Lieutenant, what you call him, you were really swell."

Chaplain Montie asked the prisoner the same question to which Smith began repeating the Catholic Act of Contrition. Civilian executioner Thomas Pierrepoint, and his assistant Herbert Morris, prepared the prisoner by binding his ankles and adjusting the rope and hood. Major Flynn gave Pierrepoint a silent signal and at 2:03 a.m., the executioner actuated the trap door. Colonel Harry H. Hammel, Major John C. Urbaitis and Captain David R. Capson pronounced Private George E. Smith, Jr. dead at 2:25 a.m. The *New York Times* announced the execution on May 11, 1945:

## "U.S. Private Is Hanged; Pays Penalty for Having Shot Briton Who Challenged Him"

On May 22, 1945, Brigadier General Walter R. Peck sent a letter of regret to Lady Teichman, expressing his deepest sympathy and informing her that the accused had been executed. George E. Smith, Jr. was originally buried at Brookwood Cemetery in Plot X in Grave 2-6. In 1948, the remains were transferred to the American Military Cemetery at Cambridge, England. In 1949, his body was exhumed and transferred to the American Military Cemetery at Oise-Aisne in Plot E. His remains are in Row 3, Grave 52. Sir Eric Teichman is buried at the Honingham Churchyard, Honingham, England.[4]

• • •

On August 24, 1949, the Pennsylvania Board of Parole received a letter from law enforcement authorities in California, stating that they had apprehended George E. Smith, Jr., who was on parole from the state of Pennsylvania. Superintendent G.I. Giardini, supervisor of the Keystone State board, wasted no time and fired off a letter that same day to the War Department, requesting that they advise Pennsylvania whether Smith had been hanged, and if so the date, or whether his case was reviewed and his sentence reconsidered. The Army took its time in replying, but finally, on October 10, 1949, Colonel E.C. Gault, of the Adjutant General's Division, responded, saying that George E. Smith, indeed, had been executed on May 8, 1945. Colonel Gault added, "This information is confidential and should be so considered by your office."

There are no further copies of correspondence between Pennsylvania and California in George Smith's personnel file. The trail simply ends. The most-likely explanation is that California police arrested someone that they believed was George E. Smith, Jr., but was in fact, someone else. Because, if in 1949, California police arrested the same man that killed Sir Erich Teichman, then whom did the Army execute on May 8, 1945 and who lies buried under grave number 52 in the fifth field at the American Military Cemetery at Oise-Aisne?

## 73 Private George Green, Jr.
38476751

998th Quartermaster
Salvage Collecting Company
**Murder**
Hanged on May 15, 1945

Living in cramped conditions day after day, performing menial tasks hour after hour could put many soldiers in a bad mood. When your corporal, after you accidentally knocked over a can of urine, grabbed you by the shirt collar and told you to clean it up, you might feel like lashing out, but when you were married and had a one-year-old baby, you had to think twice about the ramifications of your actions if you pulled a trigger.

George Green, Jr., a black soldier born in New Boston, Texas and assigned to the segregated 998th Quartermaster Salvage Collecting Company, probably did not consider the repercussions that morning of November 18, 1944, when he shot and killed Corporal Tommie Lee Garrett, a black non-commissioned officer in the unit. The result was the shooting death of Corporal Garrett, the execution of George Green, the loss to a wife of her husband, the loss to a mother and father of their son and the loss of a father for a one-year-baby.

What happened was truly stupid. At about 7:30 a.m., George Green accidentally knocked over a urine-can – used at night by the soldiers – in the corner of his barracks at Champigneulles, France. Corporal Garrett asked Private Green if he had knocked the can over to which Green replied that he had, but that Garrett should not talk "so big" about the incident. Garrett grabbed Green by the collar and told him to clean it up; Garrett had a small pocketknife in his hand, but did not appear to threaten Green with it. Green festered over the incident and about forty-five minutes later was overheard to say that he was "going to get" someone At 8:30 a.m., Corporal Garrett, Private Green and the rest of the men in the platoon were at a salvage dump, sorting a pile of olive drab clothes. Several witnesses then saw Private Green raise his M1 carbine to eye level, and deliberately fire a round that struck its target twelve feet away. That target was Corporal Garrett's heart and the non-com was dead within minutes. Witnesses also heard the accused respond to a question of why he had just done such a thing, by saying that he had intended to kill Garrett, because Garrett had pulled a knife on him. The bystanders had seen no knife in the hands of the

deceased nor was a knife seen near him. There had been no verbal altercation. Private Green was not a known troublemaker; in fact, his platoon sergeant characterized Green as efficient and a good soldier.

The event had been so out of character. Green was born in Steven, Arkansas on May 10, 1924 and later moved to East Texas, where he completed the tenth grade. He then took on the job of a house mover, earning three dollars a day before getting a job as a janitor at the Red River Ordnance Plant in Texarkana, Texas at $65 a month. His supervisor would later submit a sworn statement about the character of George Green at the plant that included:

"He was a loyal and an American citizen of the United States, and that he made a good employee with the war plant while employed with them, and as far as I know to my personal knowledge or by hearsay never was intoxicated or arrested and that his reputation was good."

George Green entered active duty on April 19, 1943; he joined the 998th Quartermaster Salvage Company on January 8, 1944. Green stood 5'10" tall and weighed 140 pounds; he was described as slender with black hair and brown eyes. He was married in 1943; he and his wife had a son. While Private Green had one Summary Court-Martial for being drunk and disorderly, he had no civilian convictions. He underwent an appendectomy in August 1943.

The GCM convened at 3:30 p.m. on December 9, 1944 at Nancy, France.[1] Private George Green, Jr. pleaded not guilty to the charge of murder, a violation of the 92nd Article of War.[2] Private Green elected not to take the stand. The Trial Judge Advocate presented overwhelming evidence that the accused committed the crime. Numerous witnesses testified that the earlier argument about the "urine-can" did not look serious and that Corporal Green had not threatened Private Green with the pocketknife. The jury voted unanimously to convict the accused and sentenced Private Green to be hanged by the neck until dead.

The Third Army Staff Judge Advocate received the court-martial records on December 11, 1944. Because the "Battle of the Bulge" began just five days later, he did not review the case until December 28, 1944 – being caught up in Patton's counter-attack into Luxembourg. The review found no significant errors and recommended that the approving authority approve the findings and sentence, and that no clemency be recommended. Lieutenant General Patton was unavailable for most of the period; he finally approved the findings and sentence on January 9, 1945. Two weeks later, George Green wrote to General Eisenhower. He stated that he had shot the victim, but had not intended to kill him. Green requested, "Sir if it is that I might die let me do it, Sir, in the Service of my Country."

The legal section at the Headquarters, ETO examined the records of the trial on February 25, 1945. The reviewing officer found that the record of trial was legally sufficient to support the findings and sentence, and that no clemency should be extended in this case. General Dwight D. Eisenhower signed the order confirming the sentence for Private George Green, Jr. on the same day, but withheld the order directing the execution of sentence. On March 12, 1945, the wife of George Green wrote General Eisenhower. She knew about her husband's court-martial conviction and asked, "Please, Sir, give my husband another chance and I am praying to God that you give him clemency (Sp) please."

On May 1, 1945, Brigadier General Edward C. Betts wrote to Private Green stating that General Eisenhower had rejected the bid for clemency. The same day, the ETO issued General Court-Martial Orders Number 129. Major General Thomas B. Larkin directed that the execution occur at the Loire DTC at Le Mans on May 15, 1945. The day before the execution, Major Roy Campbell, a medical officer, examined the condemned man and found him in excellent physical and mental health. That afternoon, Master Sergeant John C. Woods drove an Army flatbed truck to a ravine just outside the northwest corner of the Loire DTC at Le Mans. Woods, engineers and a prisoner detail removed a portable scaffold from the truck and set it up just outside the barbed wire fence. Woods tested the trap door twice.

The weather in Le Mans on May 15, 1945 was warm, clear, bright and sunny. At 10:43 a.m., the Commandant, Loire DTC, gathered five authorized witnesses and forty-five authorized spectators to the location of the gallows. Eight of the spectators were General Prisoners – four black and four white – under guard behind the camp's barbed wire fence. Lieutenant Colonel Peck briefed everyone on the proper conduct at the event and read General Court-Martial Orders Number 129. At 10:58 a.m., a command and reconnaissance car, ½-ton, 4x4 halted in the ravine thirty-five yards from the gallows. Out stepped General Prisoner George Green, Jr. and his guards. Green promptly joined a procession that marched toward the scaffold a minute later. Peck led the way, followed by Chaplain Alfred S. Kramer, the prisoner, guards Sergeant Russell E. Boyle, Staff Sergeant Charles R. Brinker and Tech Sergeant Frank

Landi. The recorder, First Lieutenant Lawrence Slon, followed. The procession reached the foot of the gallows at 10:59 a.m. Peck and Kramer ascended the thirteen steps, while the guards bound Green's hands behind his back. They then assisted the condemned man up the steps and positioned him on top the trap door. The executioner's assistant then bound Green's ankles. Lieutenant Colonel Peck then asked the prisoner if he had any last statements to which Green replied:

"Yes Sir, I have. I don't have any hard feelings toward you for this. Pray for everyone. I hope that if you are not a Christian that you become one. I have no fear. A person has no fear of death if he is right with God. Death is an honor. Jesus died for a crime he did not commit. I really did a crime, a bad crime. I believe that the Good Lord has forgiven me for what I did. I hope that the Lord forgives all of you for what you are doing here today. I hope God blesses all of you."

Lieutenant Colonel Peck replied, "May the Lord have Mercy on you, son." Chaplain Kramer asked if he had any last words. Green replied, "You have been very nice to me. I wish that you would keep on being nice to people. I want to say a word of prayer." The prisoner then began a short voluntary prayer that lasted about one minute. He was allowed to finish, at which point Chaplain Kramer began intoning a prayer, while the executioner adjusted the hood and noose. At 11:05 a.m., Peck signaled Master Sergeant Woods, who cut the rope that released the weight and actuated the trap. Everything "operated perfectly"; the condemned man hung motionlessly and made no motion or sound. According to Sergeant Thomas Ward, the noise of the trap door slamming open could be heard in the "chow line" outside the mess hut in the middle of the camp. The recorder then gave the command of "Parade Rest." At 11:19 a.m., Peck directed that Major Roy Campbell, Captain Daniel Thaw and Captain Robert E. Hansen examine the body. They promptly declared that the prisoner was dead. Peck dismissed the formation. The executioner cut the rope and removed the body from the lower part of the gallows. Captain Hardy C. Derx, 3058th Quartermaster Graves Registration Company, signed for the body at 11:25 a.m. and removed it for later interment at the U.S. Military Cemetery at Marigny in Plot Z in Grave 2-25. The official report stated that the site was efficiently guarded by twenty-five men of Company C in the 389th MP Battalion, under the command of Captain Roland B. Dixon. After the crowd dispersed, Master

Sergeant Woods had the construction detail load the gallows on the Army flatbed truck and drove the vehicle back to its storage location at the motor pool.

On May 26, 1945, the War Department sent a telegram to the wife of George Green, Jr. It informed her that her husband died in a Non-Battle status due to his own misconduct and that the cause of death was "judicial axphyxiation (execution by hanging.)"

The Army exhumed George Green, Jr. in 1949; he is now buried at the American Military Cemetery at Oise-Aisne in Plot E. His remains are in Row 2, Grave 36.[3]

Corporal Tommie L. Davis is buried among the honored dead at the Lorraine American Cemetery at St. Avold, France, in Plot B, Row 18 in Grave 48.

*"The Commanding Officer, at 11:15 a.m. ordered the Recorder to instruct the French civilians, who were conversing among themselves, to maintain silence until they were dismissed."*

## 74   Private First Class Haze Heard

34562354
3105th Quartermaster Service Company
**Murder**
Hanged on May 21, 1945

Private First Class Haze Heard shot and killed a French woman on October 13, 1944 at Mesnil-Clinchamps. That evening, he entered the home of a French couple, near a large American ammunition depot, leaving after drinking two glasses of alcohol. He returned and demanded he be given the young woman. The family pushed him outside and locked the door, but Heard fired two rounds through the window, killing the woman and then fired two more through the door. He broke through the door, but neighbors were enroute to help. After a struggle, Heard escaped, remaining at large for two months. Brigadier General Henry S. Aurand, Commander Normandy Base Section, ordered that a GCM be convened for the following:

**Charge: Violation of the 92nd Article of War.**
*Specification:* In that Private First Class Haze Heard, 3105th Quartermaster Service Company, did, at Mesnil-Clinchamps, France, on or about 13 October 1944, with malice aforethought, willfully, deliberately, feloniously, unlawfully, and with premeditation kill one Madame Berthe Robert, Mesnil-Clinchamps, Villiage Le Bosc Benard, Calvados, a human being, by shooting her with a 1903 Model Calibre .30 U.S. Army Rifle.

On January 25, 1945, a GCM convened at Granville, Manche, France, convicted him of murder and sentenced him to death by hanging. Brigadier General Aurand approved the sentence on February 24, 1945 and forwarded the record of trial up the chain of command. General Dwight D. Eisenhower confirmed the sentence on March 18, 1945. Meanwhile, Heard's wife wrote President Franklin Roosevelt asking for clemency. Haze Heard was born on Toccoa, Georgia – a small town on the border with South Carolina – on June 7, 1922. He had five brothers and sisters, was married and had a son. Heard was inducted on December 18,

1942. Shortly after entering the service, he contracted gonorrhea in 1943 at Fort Leonard Wood. He had no previous court-martial convictions.

On May 11, 1945, the ETO published General Court-Martial Orders Number 137, stating that Haze Heard would be executed on May 21, 1945 at Mesnil-Clinchamps, Calvados, France. First Lieutenant Charles H. Andrews, Jr., a medical officer, examined Heard the day before the execution and found him in excellent physical and mental condition. Earlier that day, Captain Henry McHarg III read General Court-Martial Orders Number 137 to the condemned man. The site of the execution was an apple orchard belonging to Monsieur Eugene Roberts, one-half mile south of Mesnil-Clinchamps, Calvados, France – some five miles west of Viré. A low hedgerow surrounded the orchard on three sides, with farm buildings in the north completing the rectangular farmyard. The scaffold stood in the center, facing south. It was a miserable day to die – the weather was overcast, cool with a light intermittent rain. At 10:45 a.m., Lieutenant Colonel Henry L. Peck, the Commanding Officer, Loire DTC, gathered eleven witnesses, ten authorized military spectators and six French civilians (all relatives of the deceased, including her husband, a son and a daughter.) He read them GCM Order 137 and gave instructions on their expected conduct. The attendees then assembled near the scaffold.

At 11:00 a.m., a 1½-ton 6x6 personnel carrier arrived and halted twenty yards from the gallows. The prisoner descended and formed with a small group to complete his march to the gallows. Leading the way was Lieutenant Colonel Peck, with Chaplain Emanuel L. Briggs. They were followed by the prisoner, who was escorted by guards Staff Sergeant Charles R. Brinker, Sergeant George M. Harris and Sergeant Jack D. Briscoe. The recorder, First Lieutenant Lawrence Slon followed. Shortly after 11:01 a.m., the procession halted at the foot of the gallows; the Commandant and the Chaplain walked up the steps, while the guards bound the wrists of the condemned man and helped him up the steps. Both Peck and Briggs took their positions and asked Heard if he had any last words, to which he replied "No, Sir." The Chaplain then started intoning a prayer and Master Sergeant John C. Woods slipped the hood over Heard's head and adjusted the noose. At 11:04 a.m., Peck nodded to Woods, who cut the rope that released a weight that actuated the trap and the prisoner "precipitated through the opened trap door." Heard's body hung suspended. There was a slight muscular action and a slight swaying motion. The military personnel stood silent, awaiting the pronouncement of death, but:

> "The Commanding Officer, at 11:15 a.m. ordered the Recorder to instruct the French civilians, who were conversing among themselves, to maintain silence until they were dismissed."

At 11:19 a.m., Peck ordered the medical officers to examine the body. They did and pronounced him "officially dead." After Master Sergeant Woods cut the rope and removed the body from the gallows, First Lieutenant Milliard R. Jones, 3059th Quartermaster Graves Registration Company, removed the body. Soldiers interred Heard originally at the U.S. Military Cemetery at Marigny in Plot Z in Grave 2-26. Sergeant Emmett N. Bailey, Jr. was a member of the burial detail. Officials reinterred Heard at the American Military Cemetery at Oise-Aisne in Plot E in 1949. Haze Heard's remains are in Row 2, Grave 38.[1]

• • •

The author visited the scene of the events in September 2011, south of Mesnil-Clinchamps, about one-half mile south of highway D524. The Deputy Mayor and the Secretary to the Mayor provided the town's registrar for the day of the murder and led a visit to the scene of the crime and subsequent execution. There, they met the grandson of the murder victim, who showed the author where the scaffold had been located. He also told the author that his mother – who was the daughter of the victim – lived with him in the same house where the event had started. She had told her son that the American soldier had first spotted her – she was seventeen at the time – in front of the house and had then approached the family for the alcohol.

The grandson also told the author that there were still two bullet holes from the incident in the armoire inside the home, but that for reasons of privacy for his mother, the author did not go inside. The grandson stated that at the execution about one-hundred French civilians witnessed the event, including the entire family of the deceased victim. They were led to believe that the man executed was a civilian because he wore no military insignia, not realizing that stripping the condemned man of all rank and patches before execution was standard Army procedure.

*"Defense counsel dwelt at length on racial tendencies of the negro. Even assuming the correctness of his statements, it is clear that we should not apply different sets of conduct rules."*

## 75      Private First Class William J. McCarter

34675977
465th Quartermaster Laundry Company
**Murder**
Hanged on May 28, 1945

Gambling has been a problem in most armies since before Roman soldiers rolled dice at Golgotha. It seemed that every GI thought he was the best gambler in the Army and if he didn't win that could only mean two things – somebody was cheating or stealing. When that happened, the situation could turn ugly.

Circumstances turned ugly early on the morning of February 1, 1945 at the barracks of the 465th Quartermaster Laundry Company – an all-black unit – at Thionville, France. A crap game was the action and by 2:30 a.m., there were only three troopers left in the game – Private First Class William J. McCarter, Private Charles P. "CP" Williams and Private James F. Hunt. To make matters worse, all had been drinking. The dice turned cold for McCarter, who then accused the other men of stealing his money. The two denied the claim and offered to let McCarter search them, but he declined and left – heading for the mess hall to get some "chow."

Private First Class William McCarter was inducted on June 22, 1943 at Fort Bragg, North Carolina; he had been born on October 22, 1906 in Charlotte, North Carolina; he then moved to High Point. A Protestant, he stood 5'2" tall and weighed 122 pounds. He had attended school for seven years, before becoming a waiter. He left that job and learned how to clean clothes, gaining employment at the Kent Clothes Cleaners in Greenville, South Carolina earning $25 a week. McCarter's wife had died; he had a son in Philadelphia. He also had a sister and a brother. He was a laundry machine operator in the 465th Quartermaster Laundry Company.

At about 3:00 a.m. Private First Class McCarter walked by the guardhouse and asked if any of his fellow soldiers were out of the company area. The guard replied that only Private Williams had not returned. McCarter answered, "I'll get him; he got my money." Fifteen minutes later, the guard heard Private First Class McCarter in the dark say, "Is that you, Williams?" The guard then heard Private Williams reply, "Yes, it's CP."

A carbine then barked and "CP" fell with shots to his neck, left buttock, left foot and three to his back – he was struck six times, all from behind. The guard recalled that McCarter then uttered, "I got him." McCarter made the same statement to Corporal Thomas Williams a few minutes later and subsequently made another voluntary statement in which he said, "The reason I shot Williams is because he stole my pocketbook and because he had threatened to kill me a few weeks ago."

It was an open and shut case. Officials preferred charges against Private First Class William J. McCarter on February 4; the investigation finished on February 5; Major General Walton H. Walker, Commander Twentieth Corps, ordered on February 7 that a GCM would handle the case. The GCM convened in Thionville, France at the headquarters of the Twentieth Corps at 1:30 p.m. on February 16, 1945.[1] William McCarter pleaded not guilty to the charge of murder, a violation of the 92nd Article of War.[2] The evidence against the accused was overwhelming and the jury quickly convicted him of murder and unanimously voted for the death penalty. The court adjourned at 4:45 p.m.

Colonel Frank P. Corbin, Jr., the Staff Judge Advocate of the Twentieth Corps, reviewed the case on February 27, 1945. He stated that the trial was conducted correctly and that the verdict was appropriate. In an additional comment, he remarked about race:

> "Defense counsel dwelt at length on racial tendencies of the negro. Even assuming the correctness of his statements, it is clear that we should not apply different sets of conduct rules."

Colonel Corbin showed some sympathy for the accused, stating that company officers thought well of him, that he was a "good and industrious worker" and that the accused had definite salvage value as a soldier, "were it not for the nature of this offense." On March 1, 1945, Major General Walker approved the sentence and forwarded the trial record to General Eisenhower. Brigadier General E.C. Betts reviewed the record of the trial at the headquarters of the ETO on March 27, 1945; he found no major problems with the trial, but did note that the company commander of the accused had requested leniency. General Betts also remarked that the court-martial panel made no recommendation for clemency, nor did the convening authority, nor would General Betts. General Eisenhower signed the confirmation order of the sentence for Private First Class McCarter, on March 29, 1945. He withheld the order directing the execution of sentence. The Branch Office of The JAG with the ETO reviewed the case on May 3, 1945. The three-man Board of Review Panel Number 2 (Van Benschoten, Hill and Julian) ruled the court was legally constituted, had jurisdiction of the person and offenses, and committed no errors injuriously affecting the substantial rights of the accused – therefore the record of trial was legally sufficient to support the findings of guilty and the sentence imposed.

On May 12, 1945, the ETO issued General Court-Martial Orders Number 138. Major General Thomas B. Larkin – by command of General Eisenhower – directed that the execution occur at the Loire DTC at Le Mans on May 28, 1945. At 6:40 p.m. on May 27, 1945, a medical officer examined the prisoner and found him to be in excellent physical and mental condition. Master Sergeant John C. Woods wheeled an Army flatbed truck from the motor pool to a ravine outside the northwest corner of the Loire DTC. On the truck was a portable scaffold; Woods directed soldiers to remove the gallows from the truck and set it up just outside the barbed wire fence. Woods tested the trap door that afternoon and would test it again the following morning.

On the morning of May 28, 1945, the sister of Private First Class McCarter sent a letter to General Eisenhower saying that she had not been informed of the imprisonment of her brother. She added that if there was anything under the sun the general could do to help her brother to do so. By then it was too late. That morning the weather in Le Mans was warm; the sun occasionally broke through the light clouds in the generally overcast skies. At 10:43 a.m., Lieutenant Colonel Henry L. Peck gathered five authorized witnesses and forty-two authorized spectators near the gallows. Eight of the spectators were General Prisoners, who were under guard behind the camp's barbed wire fence, twenty paces behind the other onlookers. Peck read General Court-Martial Orders Number 138. At 10:58 a.m., a command and reconnaissance car, ½-ton, 4x4 halted thirty-five yards from the scaffold. Out stepped General Prisoner William McCarter. He promptly joined a procession that marched toward the scaffold a minute later. Peck led the way, followed by Chaplain Alfred S. Kramer, the prisoner, guards Sergeant Russell E. Boyle, Sergeant Alfonso Girvalo and Tech Sergeant Frank Landi. The recorder, First Lieutenant Lawrence Slon, followed to the rear. The procession reached the foot of the gallows a shade after 10:59 a.m. Peck and Kramer ascended the steps, while the guards bound McCarter's hands behind his back. They then assisted the condemned man up the thirteen steps and positioned him on the trap door. The executioner's assistant then bound McCarter's ankles. Peck asked the prisoner if he had any last statements. McCarter replied:

"I am ready to die, Sir. The Chaplain and I have prayed together. I believe that Jesus listened to me. I believe that I am forgiven. I fear nothing, I am satisfied that I am forgiven."

Then the Chaplain asked if he had any last words. McCarter replied:

"Chaplain Sir, I am glad that you were with me. You being with me gave me spirit and you and Smith praying with me, I got more out of it. Thank you for what you have done."

Master Sergeant John C. Woods then adjusted the hood and rope over the condemned man's head. Chaplain Kramer began to intone a prayer; at 11:03 a.m., the Commandant signaled the executioner, who cut the rope, which released the weight and actuated the trap. Everything worked well; the condemned man made no motion or sound, after he fell. The recorder then commanded, "Parade Rest." The witnesses and spectators stared at the green canvas, surrounding the lower portion of the scaffold. Behind the opaque fabric, the deceased hung at the end of the rope for four minutes when suddenly Captain Carl Patrick, an official witness, became ill and left the area unsteadily. Thirteen days earlier Patrick had watched George Green hang.

At 11:18 a.m., Peck directed Major Ernest A. Weizer, Captain Daniel Thaw and Captain Robert E. Hansen to examine the body. They declared that the prisoner was dead at 11:20 a.m. Peck dismissed the formation. The executioner cut the rope and removed the body from the lower part of the gallows. Captain Hardy C. Derx removed the body for interment. Twenty-five men of Company C in the 389th MP Battalion, under the immediate command of Captain Roland B. Dixon, had efficiently guarded the area. The Army temporarily interred William J. McCarter at the U.S. Military Cemetery at Marigny in Plot Z in Grave 2-27. Exhumed in 1949, his remains are now buried at the American Military Cemetery at Oise-Aisne in Plot E, in Grave 91 of Row 4.

On June 26, 1945, the War Department sent a telegram to William McCarter's sister, stating that her brother died by execution by judicial hanging; it added that the death was in a non-battle status, due to his own misconduct. Chaplain Kramer sent a letter of condolence to the family on July 24, 1945, but gave no details of the execution. [3]

Private Charles P. Williams is buried among the honored dead in the Luxembourg American Cemetery at Luxembourg City, Luxembourg. He rests in Plot G, Row 8, Grave 3 – only about five-hundred feet from the grave of General George S. Patton.

## 76    Sergeant Clete Oscar Norris

37082314

**3384th Quartermaster Truck Company**
**Murder**
Hanged on May 31, 1945

Sergeant Clete O. Norris, a black soldier in the segregated 3384th Quartermaster Truck Company, shot and fatally injured his company commander – Captain William E. McDonald – on January 6, 1945, shortly after being ordered out of a café by the sergeant of the guard. When confronted by the non-commissioned officer, Sergeant Norris pointed a weapon at him. Norris and a companion left the establishment, when they were then confronted by Captain McDonald, who took their weapons. A short while later, Norris found anther pistol on the side of the road, as he and another group of soldiers were heading back to camp. Armed with the weapon, Norris returned to the café. As he approached, a flashlight shined and a voice in the night called "Halt"; in return, Norris fired a shot. The flashlight fell to the ground, as did a helmet about fifteen feet away from the accused; more importantly, so did Captain McDonald.

MPs arrested Norris the following day. He stated that he was drunk on the night of the incident; he also admitted shooting at somebody outside the café, after the person flashed a light on him and said, "Halt." He said that he did not know that it was Captain McDonald, who was serving as the Officer of the Day for the guard force. MPs then confined Sergeant Norris to the 3rd Replacement Depot Stockade. Captain McDonald died on January 9, 1945. On February 9, 1945, at 1:30 p.m., a GCM convened at St. Trond, Belgium. Sergeant Norris pleaded not guilty to the following:[1]

**Charge: Violation of the 92nd Article of War.**
*Specification*: In that Sergeant Clete O. Norris, 3384th Quartermaster Truck Company, did, at or near Boehle, Belgium, on or about 6 January 1945, with malice aforethought, willfully, deliberately, feloniously, unlawfully, and with premeditation kill one Captain William E. McDonald, a human being, by shooting him with a gun.

In addition to the two appointed Defense Counsels, Second Lieutenant Benjamin D. Tissue – by request of Sergeant Norris – defended the accused. Lieutenant Tissue had earned the Silver Star for gallantry in action with the Eightieth Infantry Division for actions on September 12, 1944. Fourteen witnesses appeared at court for the prosecution. After a six-hour trial, the court convicted Sergeant Norris of murder and sentenced him to death by hanging, adjourning at 9:15 p.m. The Staff Judge Advocate of the Advance Section, Colonel Edward A. Levy, reviewed the trial records on February 24, 1945 and found no significant problems. Brigadier General Ewart G. Plank approved the sentence the next day and forwarded the record of trial. On April 2, 1945, Major Frank McNamee reviewed the case with the Staff Judge Advocate for the ETO. McNamee stated that nothing indicated premeditation, nor had prosecutors established a motive. He did state that malice could be inferred by the use of a deadly weapon and the knowledge that the act would likely cause death. Brigadier General Betts confirmed this opinion. General Dwight Eisenhower confirmed the sentence on April 3, 1945, but withheld issuing the order for the execution. The Branch Office of The JAG with the ETO, Board of Review No.2, examined the case files for *United States v. Sergeant Clete O. Norris*, but that changed nothing.

The ETO issued an order on May 26, 1945. By command of General Eisenhower, Deputy Chief of Staff, Major General T.B. Larkin stated that Clete Norris would hang on May 31, 1945 at the Loire DTC. Major Ernest A. Weizer, a medical officer, examined General Prisoner Clete Norris at 6:30 p.m. on May 30, 1945 at the Loire DTC. Dr. Weizer found the prisoner to be in excellent physical and mental condition, the only condition that could be designated on the pre-printed form.

Sergeant Clete Norris was born in Palestine, Texas on March 1, 1918. He attended elementary school for seven years and then became a waiter earning $45 a week. He moved with his mother to South Kinlock Park, Missouri and entered the Army at Jefferson Barracks, Missouri on September 25, 1941. At that time, he stood 5'5½" tall and weighed 132 pounds. He was later married in Los Angeles, California. He appears to have been a good soldier and rose to the rank of staff sergeant. On June 29, 1943, a Special Court-Martial convicted him for using an Army truck for personal work (and getting in a vehicle accident) and sentenced to six months at hard labor and reduction in rank. The GCM occurred too long in the past to be admissible.

At 9:45 a.m., May 31, 1945, Lieutenant Colonel Henry C. Peck, assembled six officials, five official witnesses and nineteen authorized military spectators in a ravine in the northwestern corner of the Loire DTC at Le Mans. Two General Prisoners, Berry W. Sims and Raymond H. Stimson, watched the proceedings, under guard. The scaffold was placed at a squared leveled area approximately fifteen yards on each side. It was cut out of the northern embankment in a position that the steps faced the ten-foot tall "cut" of the northern embankment. The official witnesses stood in a single rank about twenty paces from the south side of the scaffold. The military spectators were in a single rank another ten paces behind the witnesses. The medical officers stood ten paces from the north side of the gallows.

The weather was clear, bright, warm and sunny. Twenty-five enlisted men of Company C of the 389th MP Battalion, under the immediate command of Captain Roland B. Dixon, were guarding the execution site. Lieutenant Colonel Peck read aloud General Court-Martial Orders Number 174 and gave instructions to the witnesses and spectators on proper decorum. At 9:57 a.m. an Army command-and-reconnaissance car, ½-ton, 4x4 pulled up to the ravine and out stepped General Prisoner Clete Norris with his guards: Sergeant Russell E. Boyle, Sergeant Alfonso Girvalo and Technical Sergeant Frank Landi. One minute later, the men joined a procession, led by Peck with Chaplain Charles O. Dutton, then the condemned and the guards, followed by the official recorder of events, First Lieutenant Lawrence Slon.

The group arrived at the gallows at 9:58 a.m. They had walked thirty-five yards. While Peck and Kramer ascended the steps, the guards bound the prisoner's hands behind his back, led him up the steps and placed him on the trap door. At 10:00 a.m., the executioner's assistant bound the ankles of the prisoner. Lieutenant Colonel Peck asked the prisoner if he had any last words, but Norris did not. The Chaplain asked the prisoner if he had any last statements to make; again, Norris had nothing to say. Chaplain Dutton then began to intone a prayer. Master Sergeant John C. Woods placed the black hood over the condemned man's head, then put the noose around the Norris' neck and adjusted them both; the time was 10:01 a.m. Seconds later, Peck gave a silent signal to Woods, who then cut the rope that released the weight and actuated the trap. The recorder then commanded, "Parade Rest."

At 10:11 a.m., Peck ordered Major Ernest A. Weizer, Captain Daniel Thaw and Captain Robert E. Hansen to make their examination. The three officers marched in a single file to the understructure of the scaffold and examined the body. They returned to their positions and the senior officer reported at 10:13 a.m. that death had not yet occurred. A five-minute wait ensued, the officers repeated the process and at 10:20 a.m., Major Weizer reported, "Sir, we pronounce this man officially dead." Peck dismissed the medical officers; before they departed, they signed a certificate stating the time of death as 10:20 a.m. and the cause of death as judicial asphyxis (execution by hanging.) The recorder called the witnesses and the spectators to attention. Peck then dismissed everyone and Master Sergeant Woods cut the rope. Captain Hardy C. Derx took possession of the body and signed a hand receipt for the same at 11:23 a.m., interring Clete Norris at the U.S. Military Cemetery at Marigny on June 1, 1945 in the section for General Prisoners in Grave 2-28. Sergeant Emmett N. Bailey, Jr. was a member of the burial detail. Exhumed in 1949, Norris is now buried at the American Military Cemetery at Oise-Aisne in Plot E. Clete O. Norris's remains are in Row 4, Grave 79.[2]

Captain William E. McDonald, who was born on February 21, 1918 and who had entered the Army from Ohio in October 1941, rests among the honored dead at the Henri-Chapelle American Cemetery at Henri-Chapelle, Belgium. His grave is located in Plot C, Row 7, in Number 21.

*"What did you kill those MPs for?"*

*"We have, some of us, death sentences and being put to death by rope or firing squad won't help end the war."*

## 77 Private First Class Alvin R. Rollins

34716953
**306th Quartermaster Railhead Company**
**Two Counts of Murder**
Hanged on May 31, 1945

February 23, 1945 was a bad day for twenty-year-old Private First Class Alvin R. Rollins, of the 306th Quartermaster Railhead Company. The all-black unit had previously been stationed at Boughton, Northamptonshire, England – just seventy-two miles from London. Now, they were at Troyes, France. Troyes was OK, but it wasn't London. That morning, Rollins and the other soldiers in his barracks room received the bad news that they were restricted that evening, because the room had not met inspection standards. The soldiers worked hard in their job to operate a railhead, unloading railcar after railcar and ensuring the food and fuel moved off the railhead as soon as possible, so it wouldn't become a target for any enemy plane. Rollins worked in the mess hall that afternoon and he was going out on the town no matter what it took. He borrowed a field jacket from a friend and returned to his room to wash windows. He cut his thumb in the process, but he bandaged that up, put on his uniform and a borrowed jacket – which showed a rank higher than his own – and left the company area for downtown. He had in his pocket a German Luger pistol. That resulted in Alvin Rollins' day getting a lot worse.

Private First Class Rollins went to a café, but soon left. He stopped at a second café, called "Café Number 27" – it was off limits, but at that moment, Alvin Rollins really didn't care, nor did his drinking buddy, Private D.C. Williams. They soon would care, however. A jeep drove up outside the café and the dreaded cry went up: "MPs!" Sergeant Royce A. Judd, Jr. and Corporal Victor Paul strode into the joint and spotted Rollins, heading toward a back door. They stopped him and after a short discussion, in which the MPs told him they couldn't give him a break, the four men walked outside to the jeep and got in. That put five soldiers in the vehicle. At the steering wheel was Civil Affairs Division Private First Class John H. Hoogewind; to his right – in the center of the front seat – sat Private Williams. On the far right in the front seat was Corporal Paul. In

the back seat on the far left – behind the driver – was Sergeant Judd. Sitting on the right side of the rear seat was Private First Class Rollins – and his Luger.

It does not appear that the MPs searched either man for weapons, an omission that would prove fatal. As the vehicle started to move, there were several explosions inside – they were actually gunshots. The first struck Sergeant Judd in the right side of his neck and exited the left; the autopsy would later state that the bullet destroyed the jugular vein. The second and third shots struck Private First Class Hoogewind; one entered the right side of his head and exited the left front of his skull; the other shot entered his right shoulder in the back, exiting just underneath the clavicle. A later medical investigation would show the presence of powder burns at the entrance site of the wounds, evidence that the shots came from very close range.

Corporal Paul, sensing the slaughter unfolding, tried to jump from the jeep, but his foot caught under the dashboard and he was dragged for about twenty feet, until the vehicle – absent a conscious driver – hit a wall opposite the café. Paul recalled that as he jumped, another shot came from behind and whistled by his head. Rollins and Williams ran down the street; moments later, Williams asked his friend, "What did you kill those MPs for?" According to Williams, Rollins replied that he was already on restriction and that he was not going to do ninety more days constrained in the barracks. The two men stopped a block from the wrecked jeep; at this point, two more MPs rushed up and ordered them to halt. Two additional shots sounded. Williams ran back to the camp, but split from Rollins one-hundred yards from the entrance. Meanwhile, Corporal Paul was fighting to save his friends' lives. He flagged down another jeep and the rescuers took Sergeant Judd and Private First Class Hoogewind to the hospital; the time was just after 10:00 p.m. An hour later, Corporal Paul returned to the wrecked jeep and found two empty cartridges inside. In a second search, he found two more empty cartridges on the floor of the back of the jeep.

The next morning was a busy one. An officer found a spent bullet, across the street from the crime, with blood on it. A Luger could have fired it. Investigators also found two live rounds on Rollins. A later examination showed that the cartridges could have cycled through the Rollins' weapon. The

196

same morning, the soldier that had lent his field jack to Rollins found that jacket returned to his bed. The morning ended with Rollins telling Williams, "Don't say nothing about what happened last night."

Alvin Rollins had been born on December 5, 1924 in Chattanooga, Tennessee; he was inducted on June 15, 1943 at Camp Forrest, Tennessee. With no previous convictions, his chain of command said he was an excellent performer; he was entitled to wear a battle star. Corporal Paul picked him out of a lineup on two different occasions the day after the murder.

Rollins elected to make a sworn statement. He said that in the café, one MP pulled a gun from his holster, but the MPs had not told him that was under arrest, when they went to the jeep. He did not recall Williams getting into the jeep. He said that he did not see who fired the shots in the jeep. Rollins stated that Williams had a revolver-type pistol on the night in question and that Williams fired at the MPs, who told them to halt after they fled the jeep. Williams stated that Rollins had fired these last shots. Rollins said he had been drinking alcohol, but could not remember how much he had consumed. MPs took Rollins into confinement on February 24, 1945. Officials preferred charges on March 1, 1945. The investigation finished the next day and the JAG forwarded the legal packet to the convening authority on March 3, 1945. Brigadier General Charles O. Thrasher referred the case the next day for action by a GCM.

A GCM convened at Rheims at 9:22 a.m. on March 13, 1945.[1] Private First Class Alvin Rollins pleaded not guilty to two charges of murder; both were violations of the 92nd Article of War.[2] Confusion existed at trial whether or not Private First Class Rollins stated that he had fired his pistol on the day of the crime. Initially, he said he could not remember. On cross-examination, when asked if he had a gun on that night, Rollins stated, "I am not so sure." Later, he told the court that he had told other soldiers, "I fired one or two shots on February 23rd." On re-direct examination, the Defense Counsel asked Rollins why he had his gun that night and why he had broken restriction. Rollins replied that he left camp to meet a man to sell the gun to him. He also testified that he had suffered blackouts ever since he had been in the stockade. Corporal Paul and Private Williams positively identified Private First Class Rollins as the soldier in the rear of the jeep.

The defense attempted to show that Williams had fired at the second pair of Military Policemen and that Rollins was not familiar with his German Luger. The prosecution, in rebuttal, introduced testimony of the company commander and an investigating agent, who both watched Rollins disassemble and re-assemble the pistol. The agent then asked him, "Is that the gun?" To which Rollins replied, "That is the gun." The court unanimously voted to convict the defendant and sentenced him by another unanimous vote to hang by the neck until dead. The court adjourned at 3:50 p.m.

The Staff Judge Advocate section of the Oise Section reviewed the record of trial and published its findings on March 28, 1945. The reviewing officer found no discrepancies or significant errors in the proceedings. The same day Brigadier General Thrasher approved the sentence and forwarded the record of trial up the chain of command. Private First Class Rollins didn't want to wait for the results and on April 16, 1945, wrote General Eisenhower a letter. He did not state that he was innocent of the offense or that he had received an unfair trial, only that he and a lot of the other soldiers at the detention training center wanted another opportunity to soldier. As Rollins put it, "We have, some of us, death sentences and being put to death by rope or firing squad won't help end the war." On April 25, 1945, the Staff Judge Advocate at the ETO signed off on a review of the case that one of his majors had conducted. This review found no discrepancies, except to note that where a printed form was used:

"Where a printed form is used in the record of trial proper and part of it is not used, it is preferable to cross out the unused portion and thereby achieve a degree of completeness and accuracy that we strive to maintain in the administration of military justice."

It is not known if General Dwight D. Eisenhower actually read the entire judicial review – including the comments on "degree of completeness. Perhaps the theater senior lawyer, Brigadier General Edward Betts, simply briefed him. In any case, General Eisenhower signed the order confirming the death sentence in the case of Private First Class Alvin R. Rollins on April 29, 1945. On May 18, 1945, Board of Review Number 1 of the Branch Office of The JAG with the ETO reviewed the case. Judge Advocates Riter, Burrow and Stevens found that the record of trial was sufficient and that no significant errors had been made. They declined to comment on proper paperwork.

On May 26, 1945, the ETO published General Court-Martial Orders Number 180. The order stated that General Prisoner Alvin R. Rollins would be executed on May 31, 1945 at the Loire DTC. The evening before at 7:00 p.m., a medical officer examined Rollins and found him to be in excellent physical and mental health. At 10:45 a.m., on May 31, 1945, Lieutenant Colonel Henry C. Peck, assembled six other officials, five official witnesses and nineteen authorized military spectators at the northwestern corner of the DTC. The official witnesses – all commissioned officers – stood in a single rank about twenty paces from the south side of the gallows. Military spectators stood in a single rank ten paces behind the witnesses. The medical officers stood ten paces from the north side of the gallows.

The weather was clear, bright, warm and sunny. Twenty-five enlisted men of Company C of the 389th MP Battalion, under the immediate command of Captain Roland B. Dixon, guarded the execution site. Lieutenant Colonel Peck read aloud General Court-Martial Orders Number 180 and briefed the witnesses and spectators on proper conduct. At 10:57 a.m. an Army command-and-reconnaissance car, ½-ton, 4x4 pulled up to the ravine and out stepped General Prisoner Rollins with his guards: Sergeant Russell E. Boyle, Sergeant Alfonso Girvalo and Technical Sergeant Frank Landi. One minute later, the men joined a procession led by Lieutenant Colonel Peck with Chaplain Alfred S. Kramer, then the condemned and the guards, followed by the official recorder of events, First Lieutenant Lawrence Slon. The group quickly arrived at the scaffold at 10:58 a.m. While Lieutenant Colonel Peck and Chaplain Kramer ascended the thirteen steps, guards bound the prisoner's hands behind his back and then led Rollins up the steps and placed him on the trap door. At 10:59 a.m., the executioner's assistant bound the ankles of the prisoner. Peck asked the prisoner if he had any last words and Rollins replied, "I am glad to know that I have met Jesus." The Chaplain asked the prisoner if he had any last statements to make, to which Rollins replied at 11:00 a.m., "I like to say that I am glad that you were with me. You helped me to see God."

Chaplain Kramer began to intone a prayer. Master Sergeant John C. Woods, placed the black hood over the condemned man's head, then put the noose around the man's neck and adjusted them both; the time was 11:01 a.m. Seconds later, Peck gave a silent signal to Woods, who then cut the rope, which released the weight and actuated the trap. The recorder then commanded "Parade Rest." Everything worked correctly and at 11:16 a.m., Major Ernest A. Weizer, Captain Daniel Thaw and Captain Robert E. Hansen marched in a single file to the understructure of the gallows to examine the body. They returned to their positions and the senior officer reported at 11:18 a.m., "Sir, we pronounce this man officially dead."

Lieutenant Colonel Peck dismissed the medical officers; before they departed, they signed a certificate stating the time of death as 11:19 a.m. and the cause of death as judicial asphyxis (execution by hanging.) The recorder called the witnesses and the spectators to attention and Peck dismissed them at 11:20 a.m. The executioner then cut the rope. Captain Hardy C. Derx took possession of the body and signed a hand receipt for the same at 11:23 a.m.; his unit buried Alvin R. Rollins at the U.S. Military Cemetery at Marigny on June 1, 1945, in the section for General Prisoners, in Grave 29. To his left was Clete Norris. Rollins is now buried at the American Military Cemetery at Oise-Aisne in Plot E: Row 3, Grave 51.

On June 7, 1945, the War Department sent a telegram to the mother of Alvin R. Rollins in Chattanooga, Tennessee, listing the cause of death as "Judicial axphyxiation" and that the soldier died in a Non-Battle Status due to his own misconduct. On July 21, 1945, Rollins' company commander, First Lieutenant Mahlon C. Feinberg wrote a letter of condolence to the parents of the deceased, stating,[3]

"Prior to 31 May 1945 your son did a commendable job as a checker with this organization issuing rations to American troops in France."

Private First Class John H. Hoogewind is buried among the honored dead at the Épinal American Cemetery in Plot A, Row 36, Grave 40.

*"The condemned man cried, whimpered and faltered during the march to the gallows."*

## 78   Private First Class Matthew Clay, Jr.

38490561

3236th Quartermaster Service Company
**Murder and Assault**
Hanged on June 4, 1945

It was a long way for Private First Class Matthew Clay, Jr., a black soldier, born in Avery, Louisiana to Fontenay-sur-Mer, France. Born July 26, 1920 in the city known as, the "Tabasco Capital," Clay finished the sixth grade, leaving to work for two years on a farm and later for the Myles Salt Company. Clay had been married for five years; his wife and three-year-old daughter lived at Galveston, Texas. As he stated in a letter to General Dwight Eisenhower on April 7, 1945, his mother was dead. He had no brothers or sisters and was his wife's only support. He was inducted on December 11, 1943 at Lafayette, Louisiana, joined the Quartermaster Corps, and deployed to Europe, after the Normandy invasion.

At 9:30 p.m. on October 9, 1944, Clay was walking down a road "with 3 or 4 other colored soldiers" a mile from where his unit was bivouacked. By his own admission, Clay had already consumed about a quarter of cider alcohol. He stopped at a small bakery in the village of Fontenay-sur-Mer, the home of Monsieur Victor Bellery, his wife Augustine and their two children, aged six and eight. The prosecution presented the theory that Clay kicked in the door, and when the family awoke, he demanded more cider. When Monsieur Bellery refused, Clay stabbed him with a bayonet in the back and neck, and then struck Madame Bellery three times on the wrist and left shoulder, with the same weapon. He then ran away. Victor Bellery succumbed to his wounds later that night.

At 10:45 p.m., a Frenchman informed Lieutenant S. Aber of the One-Hundred Fourth Infantry Division, at the airstrip at Fontenay-sur-Mer that nearby someone had been murdered. At almost the same time, Aber noticed a figure thirty yards away. The officer approached and determined the soldier was drunk. When asked what he was doing, the soldier replied that he too was looking "for the criminal." The accused dropped a flashlight and a bayonet that appeared to be bloody. Aber turned the soldier over to the MPs.

Things started to get complicated. On October 10, Technical Sergeant Joseph P. Denove, of the Investigation Section, 505th MP Battalion, obtained a statement from the accused. There were three problems with this interview and statement. A John Louis signed the statement, not Matthew Clay Jr. "Louis" stated that he could not write well, so asked the investigating sergeant to "take it down as I told it." Clay stated that he signed the statement only after Denove threatened him with violence. Clay stated that he gave the false name of "John Louis" because he had been scared. The statement was enough to arrest Clay on October 11. Agent Robert E. Fuller, of the 17th Criminal Investigation Section, went to the Normandy Base Stockade, interviewed the accused on October 13 and obtained a second statement – which later was admitted into evidence.

A GCM convened at 11:00 a.m. on January 20, 1945 at Cherbourg to hear the case. Three officers served on the prosecution: First Lieutenant Vincent P. Clarke (TC), First Lieutenant Joseph A. Bruggeman (TC) and First Lieutenant Sydney Weitzer (TC.) Three officers served on Clay's defense team: Captain John F. Kottnauer (QM), First Lieutenant Joseph J. Bartle (IN) and First Lieutenant Morris Beizer (TC.) The jury included Lieutenant Colonel William C. Hollis (TC), Lieutenant Colonel Edward E. Benson (CE), Lieutenant Colonel Raymond F. Hufft (CAC), Major Robert B. Schofield (QM), Major Eugene T. Shields (QM), Major Albert D. Levin (TC), Captain Dean A. Van Deventer (QM), Captain Henry D. Bonneau (SC) and First Lieutenant Hugh A. De Lean (TC.)[1] It was the fourth GCM that that ended with a death sentence, resulting in execution, for Hollis, Shields and Bonneau and the third for Van Deventer.

Clay pleaded not guilty to all charges. Madame Bellery testified for the prosecution, as did the two agents. Clay was the sole defense witness. The defense team took a two-prong strategy: Clay was intoxicated – he admitted drinking a quart of cognac on the day in question – and he struck Monsieur Bellery in self-defense, after Bellery first hit him on the head with a wooden mallet. Concerning inebriation, the court determined that he was not so sufficiently intoxicated that he did not have the necessary intent to constitute murder; they said that he could remember details of the killing, obeyed orders when stopped by Lieutenant Aber and gave a false story, which showed that he knew that "he had committed a reprehensible act." The problem with self-defense was that *A Manual for Courts-Martial, U.S. Army* clearly stated that,

> "To avail himself of the right of self-defense, the person doing the killing must not have been the aggressor and intentionally provoked the difficulty."

Plainly, by breaking into a home of sleeping occupants, Clay was the aggressor who provoked the difficulty. If any additional justification was needed, Clay stated in one instance that the pair of adults hit him, but then said at another point that no one had struck him in the head with the mallet. The court convicted Clay of murder, a violation of the 92nd Article of War, and of assault, a violation of the 93rd Article of War.[2] The court sentenced Private First Class Matthew Clay Jr. to death by hanging.

The Normandy Case Section JAG reviewed the case on February 19, 1945. On March 29, 1945, General Dwight D. Eisenhower signed a letter confirming the sentence but withheld the order directing execution. Clay wrote a letter to General Eisenhower on April 7, 1945, stating that he committed the crime in self-defense. The Branch Office of The JAG with the ETO reviewed the case on May 18, 1945. The three-man panel (Van Benschoten, Hill and Anthony Julian) ruled the court committed no errors injuriously affecting the substantial rights of the accused – in short that the record of trial was legally sufficient. On May 27, 1945, the ETO issued General Court-Martial Orders Number 185, directing that the execution occur.

On Monday, June 4, 1945, the sun beamed down on a glorious French morning in an orchard one-half mile southeast of Fontenay-sur-Mer. It was clear, sunny, warm and bright. The war had been over for about a month. Millions of people around the world were happy, but it was not a happy day for Matthew Clay, Jr. For Matthew Clay, it was judgment day. Army carpenters had constructed a temporary gallows in the orchard. Just after 10:34 a.m., the Commanding Officer, Loire DTC, Lieutenant Colonel Henry L. Peck, assembled nineteen U.S. Army officials and witnesses, and one French civilian – the mayor of Fontenay-sur-Mer – and read General Court-Martial Orders Number 185, directing the execution of Private First Class Matthew Clay, Jr. Peck then gave precautions concerning the proper conduct at this formation.

Peck, assisted by an eleven-enlisted man guard detail – led by First Lieutenant William C. McKinney – from Company A, 387th MP Battalion, led the personnel to their proper positions. The silent formation stood in single ranks, ten yards from the south and north of the scaffold and fifteen yards from the west. At 11:00 a.m., a 1½-ton, 6x6 personnel carrier approached, drove to a point twenty yards from the scaffold and guards assisted Private First Class Matthew Clay Jr. to dismount. At 11:02 a.m., Peck led the execution procession, consisting of himself, a Chaplain, the prisoner, three guards (Sergeant Russell E. Boyle, Sergeant Alfonso Girvalo and Sergeant Thomas J. Doyle), and the recorder, First Lieutenant Lawrence Slon, who noted, "The condemned man cried, whimpered and faltered during the march to the gallows."

At 11:03 a.m., the procession reached the foot of the gallows, at which point Peck and the Chaplain ascended the steps. Clay burst into tears and wrapped his arms around his head, imploring, "Lord, have mercy on me." The three guards forcibly tied Clay's hands behind him, and provided physical assistance to him, as he haltingly climbed the steps. At the top, the guards led him to the center of the trap door and helped tie his ankles. The time was 11:04 a.m. The Commanding Officer and then the Chaplain asked the condemned if he had any last words. In both instances, Clay responded in the affirmative, but could not get any words out. After a moment, the Chaplain began intoning a prayer and the executioner adjusted the hood and the noose. The time was 11:05 a.m. Thirty seconds later, Peck silently signaled Master Sergeant Woods, who cut the rope, which released the weight that actuated the trap. The prisoner dropped cleanly through the trap door and hung suspended in the lower screened recess of the gallows. The body swung in a circular motion; the witnesses stood silent without reaction. Fifteen minutes later, Peck ordered the three medical officers to examine the body. The trio marched in single file to the understructure, made their examination and returned to their original positions. Captain Peter W. Chernenkoff, then reported, "Sir, we pronounce this man officially dead."

The time was 11:22 a.m. The Commanding Officer then dismissed the gathering, while the Master Sergeant Woods cut the rope and removed the body, which was then signed for by Captain Robert E. Berry of the 3059th Graves Registration Company. The time was 11:25 a.m. As First Lieutenant Slon noted, "Each official performed his task in a highly efficient manner. The proceedings were conducted with dignity, solemnity and military precision."

The Army buried Matthew Clay, Jr. in the U.S. Military Cemetery at Marigny in Grave 2-30 in the General Prisoner section; to his left was Alvin Rollins. Sergeant Emmett N. Bailey, Jr. was a member of the burial detail. Exhumed in 1949, Clay is now buried at the American Military Cemetery at Oise-Aisne in Plot E – Row 1, Grave 3.

On June 12, 1945, the War Department sent a telegram to the wife of Matthew Clay, Jr., stating that her husband had died at Fontenay-Sur-Mer, Manche, France on May 27, 1945 of "Judicial Axphyxation (execution by hanging)" and that he had died in a non-battle status due to his own misconduct.[3]

*"We came into the restaurant and we pulled out the gun,
and I was sort of waiting around."*

**Private Werner E.
Schmiedel**
7041115

503rd Replacement Company,
18th Replacement Battalion
Absent Without Official Leave,
Armed Robbery and **Murder**
Hanged on June 11, 1945

Most of the soldiers sentenced to death had committed a single incident of mayhem. Private Werner E. Schmiedel was an exception; he went on a multi-month crime wave. Schmiedel, also known as "Robert Lane," was the leader of the "Lane Gang" that terrorized Italian shopkeepers and travelers in 1944. The gang killed a café owner in a robbery and waylaid the chauffeur for a Polish general. Even *Time* picked up the story:

"In Italy the Army suddenly had a crime wave on its hands. Soldiers on leave in Rome swapped rumors of robbery and murder. Bandits had held up the chauffeur of Polish Lieutenant General Wladyslaw Anders when he was returning in the general's super-Cadillac from delivering the general to the airport. Military supplies were stolen. A cafe owner was shot to death. Nervous citizens stayed out of alleys, wondered what would happen when the weather got colder and hungry desperadoes grew more desperate."

Schmiedel's story began on September 2, 1944, when he was confined at the Disciplinary Training Stockade near Aversa, Italy. A white soldier, he escaped and made his way through war-torn Italy to Sparanise, twenty miles northwest of Naples. On September 7, he and gang compatriots, Private James W. Adams and Private Anthony Tavolieri robbed an Italian man of 150,000 *lire*. The men moved to Formia and robbed two MPs of their pistols and brassards on September 17, 1944. Later that day, the trio and two other gang members robbed Polish Lieutenant General Anders' driver near Capua. The men moved to Rome, where on October 10, 1944, they robbed a café and killed a man. Over the next two weeks, authorities arrested numerous members of the gang around Rome. Tavolieri died in a confrontation; finally, on November 3, 1944, authorities arrested Werner Schmiedel at "Rocky's Bar" in Rome.

Schmiedel's birthdate was May 4, 1919, November 16, 1923 or September 30, 1924, depending on his mood. He entered the Army on June 18, 1940, serving at Fort Knox, before going overseas. He listed his occupation as a farmer. His parents were still alive and lived together in Breinigsville. Werner had at least two brothers and two sisters. In 1942, he deserted. Authorities apprehended him and he served four months of hard labor. He went AWOL in 1943; after conviction at another court-martial, he received a sentence of one month at hard labor. Schmiedel stood 6' tall and weighed 155 pounds; he suffered from gonorrhea.

In 1944, Schmiedel hit the big leagues, going AWOL from May 20, 1944 to June 2, 1944. He escaped from the guardhouse on June 13, 1944 and remained at large for three days. He escaped again on June 21, 1944 and remained absent until June 30, 1944. On August 19, 1944, a GCM found him guilty of violating the 61st Article of War and sentenced him to twenty years, but Brigadier General Francis H. Oxx reduced the period of confinement to ten years. In thanks, Schmiedel escaped confinement on September 2, 1944 and his last crime wave began.

Firearms experts tested Schmiedel's weapons and found them consistent with the one that fired the bullet that killed the Italian. It appears that Private James Adams remained at large until February 16, 1945. Authorities decided to try Schmiedel and Jones together. Brigadier General Francis H. Oxx, the Commander, PBS, determined that a GCM was appropriate, based on the seriousness of the charges. The court convened on March 26, 1945. General Prisoner Werner E. Schmiedel and Private James W. Adams pleaded not guilty to a long list of charges that included murder, a violation of the 92nd Article of War, several counts of armed robbery, violations of the 93rd Article of War, and absent without leave, a violation of the 61st Article of War.[1] The Trial Judge Advocate was Captain Anthony J. Albert; Captain Philip J. Corso served as Defense Counsel.[2] During the investigation, Private Adams had made a statement that the shooting was accidental by Schmiedel and at the trial, both made unsworn statements that effect. Schmiedel stated:

"We were walking down the street and we decided to go into this restaurant. We came into the restaurant and we pulled out the gun, and I was sort of waiting around."

The jury did not buy the explanation, unanimously voted for conviction and for the death penalty on March 27, 1945 – the second day of the trial. According to the *Chicago Tribune*, the jury deliberated the issue of guilt for twenty minutes and the question of punishment for another twenty minutes, before reaching their consensus, which was read by the President of the Court, Colonel Walter L. Medding.

The PBS JAG reviewed the trial on April 6, 1945 and found everything correct. Brigadier General Oxx approved the findings of the court and sent the trial record up the chain of command. Then the Commander of the MTO weighed in as the confirming authority. On April 21, 1945, General Joseph McNarney upheld the sentence of death against Schmiedel, but reduced the sentence of Adams to life imprisonment. On May 26, 1945, a Board of Review from the Branch Office of The JAG with the MTO examined the records; Judge Advocates Irion, Sessions and Remick found no significant errors.

The MTO published General Court-Martial Orders Number 82 on May 28, 1945. It stated that General Prisoner Werner E. Schmiedel would be hanged at Aversa, Italy on June 11, 1945. Schmiedel was duly executed on that date. The *New York Times* reported the execution on June 12, 1945 with the article headline, **"U.S. DESERTER HANGED; Convicted of Having Murdered Italian during Hold-Up."**

On June 25, 1945, the War Department sent a telegram to Werner Schmiedel's mother stating that her son had died in Italy, as a non-battle casualty, due to his own misconduct, listing the cause of death was "Judicial Strangulation." The Army buried Schmiedel at the U.S. Military Cemetery at Naples, the General Prisoner plot, in Grave 2-17.

Exhumed in 1949, Werner Schmiedel is buried at the American Military Cemetery at Oise-Aisne in Plot E. His remains are in Row 3, Grave 53. The Canadian Army tried Canadian Private Harold Joseph Pringle, who had been a member of the "Lane Gang," sentenced him to death and executed him by a firing squad on July 5, 1945. Pringle is buried at the Caserta War Cemetery in Plot VII, Row B, in Grave 11.[3]

*"In view of this subhuman conduct, to keep the accused alive would mean the preservation of a continual menace to society."*

*"There is every reason to believe that he achieved the fundamental purpose of life and saved his soul."*

## 80 Private First Class Aniceto Martinez

38168482

Headquarters Detachment,
  Prisoner of War Inclosure Number 2

**Rape**
Hanged on June 15, 1945

Most GCM convictions for rape appear to have occurred when the jury disbelieved statements made by the accused that the act was consensual. Forensic evidence was in its infancy, compared to today, but in the case of Private First Class Aniceto Martinez, both his own words and criminal science played a role in sending this Mexican-American soldier from New Mexico to the gallows.

The rape victim, a frail, 112-pound, seventy-five-year-old woman, lived in Rugeley, Staffordshire, England. At 3:15 a.m. on August 6, 1944, she observed a man breaking into her house. Although she screamed and sprained her thumb in the resistance, her assailant completed his attack; she suffered a black eye and bruises, during the assault. Unknown to Martinez, his unit – Prisoner of War Inclosure Number 2 – conducted a bed check several hours before the attack – and Private First Class Martinez was the only man in the organization not present.

There were a lot of things that Private First Class Martinez did not know; born May 30, 1922 in Vallecitos, New Mexico, he had eight years of schooling, but did not know how to read or write well. Martinez spoke English (but no Spanish) and received a classification of white; he stood 5'8" tall and weighed 145 pounds. He had a light complexion with brown hair and brown eyes; he also wore glasses much of the time. Previously a farm laborer – he was a U.S. citizen – on October 19, 1942, he was inducted at Santa Fe, New Mexico and reported to Fort Bliss, Texas. He was single and became a military policeman. However, Aniceto Martinez failed his driver's aptitude test, so could not drive any MP vehicles. He transferred to the 793rd MP Battalion, stationed at Fort Custer, Michigan, before departing New York on May 27, 1943 for Europe; he arrived in the United Kingdom on June 2, 1943. That same year his service record shows that his character and efficiency were satisfactory.

Armed with the information that pointed toward Martinez, Police Inspector Horace J. Brooks, of the Staffordshire County Police, interviewed the accused soon after the crime. During this session, Martinez stated:

"I did go in the house. I did not break the door open. I had connections with a woman. She was not forced. It was at a little house at the bottom of the hill near the pub. It happened last night. I had some drink. I was not drunk. I was sick near the house."

The investigation located the service cap that Martinez had borrowed from a friend and worn on the night in question. A thorn sticking to the cap was similar to thorns on the six-foot-high Hawthorne bush that surrounded the victim's house. Blue fibers on the hat were similar to fibers from the blue portion of the quilt found on the victim's bed. Cloth fibers found around the bottom two buttons of Martinez's uniform were consistent with cotton fibers and threads of the victim's nightdress. The lower portion of his shirt contained a seminal stain. The U.S. investigators took over. In a statement made to authorities, Private Martinez could not recall hitting the victim. He did state that before the sex, the woman stated, "Let's get it over so you can go back home."

Then unforeseen problems – situations known to the troops of the day as FUBAR – raised their ugly head. Authorities placed investigation statements and other trial material in a case file and forwarded that by train to the Theater Provost Marshal Office, which was then in London. The packet disappeared, never to be located. The investigation had to be done again, delaying a court-martial for months.

A GCM finally convened at Whittington Barracks in Lichfield, Staffordshire, England on February 21, 1945. Private First Class Aniceto Martinez pleaded not guilty to a charge and specification of carnal knowledge.[1] Martinez testified at the court-martial, stating that he thought the building that he entered was a house of ill repute. Martinez also denied that the hat, trousers and shirt – previously admitted into evidence – had been worn by him on the night in question. The jury voted unanimously to convict the accused. There was no evidence of previous court-martial convictions; the jury then unanimously voted to sentence him to be hanged by the neck until dead.

The Staff Judge Advocate for the United Kingdom Base Section, Colonel Edward J. Kotrich, reviewed the case on March 2, 1945 and found no significant errors, although he did note that in the instructions given to the accused with respect to testifying, no mention was made of the weight that the jury might give to an unsworn statement. He recommended the following to the base section commander:

"In view of this subhuman conduct, to keep the accused alive would mean the preservation of a continual menace to society."

Brigadier General Harry B. Vaughan, Jr., commander of the United Kingdom Base Section, approved the findings and forwarded them up the chain of command. A Board of Review from the Branch Office of The JAG reviewed the case on May 29, 1945 and found no substantial errors. Judge Advocates Sleeper, Sherman and Dewey agreed with the findings of the court. The JAG of the ETO also found no substantial errors; he did note that due to darkness, the convicted soldier probably did not know the age of his victim, an opinion that did not seem to resonate with his boss. On April 15, 1945, General Dwight Eisenhower had signed a letter confirming the sentence for Private First Class Martinez, but withheld the order directing the execution of sentence. General Court-Martial Orders Number 204 would publish that information on June 9, 1945 and specified the location of execution as the United Kingdom Base DTC at Shepton Mallet Prison and the date as Friday, June 15, 1945.

The day before the execution, Thomas and Albert Pierrepoint weighed and measured the condemned man; Albert noted in his ledger that Aniceto Martinez stood 5'8¼" tall and weighed 167 pounds. From that data, the executioners calculated that a drop of 6'10" would produce instantaneous death. Shortly before 10:00 p.m. on June 15, the commanding officer, Major Philip J. Flynn briefed nine official witnesses on the proper conduct at an execution. Accompanied by Chaplain George E. Montie, guards First Sergeant William R. Nelson and Private First Class James L. Bradley, and Thomas W. Pierrepoint and his assistant Albert Pierrepoint, Major Flynn led the way to the execution chamber, arriving at 10:20 p.m. He then went to get General Prisoner Martinez, General Prisoner Number 1377, and returned four minutes later. Flynn then read General Court-Martial Orders Number 204 and asked Martinez if he had any last statement to make. The 22-year-old replied:

"Yes sir. Goodbye Major Flynn, I think you have treated me pretty swell while I was here, I would like to say goodbye to everybody, and I would like to thank the father for all he had done for me and I want you father, to say a prayer for me. I would like to say goodbye to everybody."

The prisoner and Chaplain Montie then repeated the Act of Contrition. Thomas Pierrepoint then put the white hood and rope over Martinez's head under the direction of Major Flynn, while assistant Albert Pierrepoint bound the prisoner's ankles with a restraining strap. Flynn then gave a silent signal to Thomas Pierrepoint, who bent down, quickly removed the safety cotter pin and pushed the trap door lever forward, sending Aniceto Martinez to eternity. The time was 10:28 p.m. Fifteen minutes later Major Flynn stated, "I believe this man is dead." Lieutenant Colonel D.T. Chamberlain, Lieutenant Colonel Douglas F. Heuer and Major John C. Urbaitis descended the steps to examine the prisoner, pronounced him dead and stated that the cause of death was "strangulation, judicial." The Army interred Martinez at Brookwood Cemetery in Plot X in Grave 2-7. The next day Chaplain Montie wrote a letter to Aniceto Martinez's mother. He did not explain the circumstances of the death, but did write that he was present with her son when he died. He concluded by saying, "There is every reason to believe that he achieved the fundamental purpose of life and saved his soul."

On June 28, 1945, the War Department sent a telegram to the father of Aniceto Martinez, stating that his son had died at Shepton Mallet, Somerset on June 15, 1945 of "Strangulation – Judicial" and that he had died in a non-battle status, due to his own misconduct. The following day, the United Kingdom Base Section sent a letter to the victim. In it, the Assistant Adjutant General stated that the Commanding General wished to express his deepest regrets for the unfortunate occurrence.

In 1948, officials transferred Aniceto Martinez's remains to the American Military Cemetery at Cambridge, England. One year later, they exhumed the remains and reinterred them at the American Military Cemetery at Oise-Aisne in Plot E. Aniceto Martinez's remains are in Row 2, Grave 39.[2]

*Prosecution: I am not attempting to get any discussion of race on the record.*
*I simply wanted the accused, and to show in the record, that the accused himself*
*personally is aware of his rights to have a colored officer on the court,*
*if he wants him on the court.*

## 81 Private Victor Ortiz-Reyes

30405077
3269th Quartermaster Service Company
**Murder**
Hanged on June 21, 1945

By early morning on January 28, 1945, Private Victor Ortiz had been pulling guard on and off at his unit's fuel point for twenty-four hours – in a cycle of four hours on duty and eight hours off. Eating arrangements were catch-as-catch-can of grabbing a cold sandwich here and there, but for the millions of American soldiers, who pulled guard, there was nothing unusual about that. As for actually missing "chow," that could lead to trouble. When it was time to go on guard duty again, Ortiz tried to get someone to go in his place; his sergeant of the guard, Sergeant Ramon E. Ortiz, took him to the orderly room to see the company commander, Captain Ignacio Bonit. Captain Bonit was not sympathetic and said, "You got to do the guard, because you are in the Army now." Private Ortiz would later claim that Bonit stated:

"Well, you have to go on guard; if you don't go on guard, I myself will drag you, or the Sergeant or both of us we will take you on guard."

Ortiz then left the room. At 1:20 a.m., the lights to the orderly room flicked on and at almost the same instant, someone fired several shots; both Captain Bonit and Second Lieutenant Israel I. Sylvan had been asleep in the room. In a moment, Bonit was dead and Sylvan observed Ortiz standing in the doorway with a carbine in his hand. Ortiz departed the room. The company first sergeant later found him sitting on his bunk with the carbine in his hands; Ortiz told the NCO, "The thing I have done is done."

Victor Ortiz-Reyes came from extreme poverty. Born on January 6, 1914 in Coamo, Puerto Rico, he left school after first grade, an illiterate. At an early age, he began swinging a pick and shovel, building roads. During the harvest season, he cut sugar cane for six dollars a week. He and his mother later lived in Salinas. Victor Ortiz volunteered for Army service on April 28, 1941 at Fort Buchanan, Puerto Rico; he had served with the 3269th Quartermaster Service Company since he enlisted. His service was excellent. Ortiz scored a 53 on the Army General Classification Test, taking the test in Spanish, which placed Ortiz in Category V. Private Ortiz stood 5'5" tall and weighed 118 pounds.

While awaiting trial, Ortiz stayed in confinement at a prison in Roubiax, outside Lille. Prison guards reported that his behavior was excellent in incarceration. A GCM convened at Lille, France on March 1, 1945 at 1:30 p.m.; the trial lasted three days, which was unusually long. Ortiz faced a murder charge, a violation of the 92nd Article of War.[1] It was a typical jury panel. However, due to the nature of the defendant's Spanish language upbringing, First Lieutenant Jose Hernandez-Borch sat as the interpreter, in case this skill was needed.[2] The defense used its authorized peremptory challenge to pull First Lieutenant Stanford A. Wright, who was assigned to the 4091st Quartermaster Service Company – an all-black, segregated unit – from the jury. The prosecution then asked for a short recess, which was granted. When the court went back into session, a remarkable exchange took place:

**Prosecution:** For the purpose of the record of trial, I would like to have it brought out that the accused himself is personally fully apprised of his rights as to having a colored officer on the court, if he desires one. The accused will state to the court himself personally that he understands his rights and does not want the member excused on the court, or does want him excused. I would appreciate it.

**Defense:** The position of the Defense Counsel in this matter is that the accused is not a Negro.

**Prosecution:** I am not attempting to get any discussion of race on the record. I simply wanted the accused, and to show in the record, that the accused himself personally is aware of his rights to have a colored officer on the court, if he wants him on the court.

**Law Member:** Subject to objection of the court, I will exclude that whole thing. I don't think it has any bearing.

**Prosecution:** The prosecution would like to state this, that it simply has been introduced in an effort to carry out what is believed in the opinion of the prosecution to be Theater policy, subject to your ruling.

The accused and his Defense Counsel went on to indicate that they objected to no member of the court then present and First Lieutenant Wright departed. Admitted into evidence was a description and sketch of the wounds on the deceased made by Captain Walter E. Marchand, Group Surgeon with the 558th Quartermaster Group. The drawing supported the prosecution theory that the victim was in the prone position, when struck by the bullets. Bonit's body lay on the floor next to his cot with his head toward the door to the orderly room. The defense maintained that Private Ortiz believed that Captain Bonit was going for a pistol during the incident and that Ortiz fired his M1 carbine in self-defense. Private Ortiz testified on the stand, stating that he had been sick and in his final confrontation with the victim, Captain Bonit reached for his pistol and stated, "Get out of here before I start shooting at you." The jury did not buy the defense's claim of self-defense; they voted to convict the Private Victor Ortiz and sentenced him to death.

On March 22, 1945, the Staff Judge Advocate of the Channel Base Section reviewed the record of trial. He found sixteen irregularities worthy of mention. He also addressed the issue of race in the composition of the court, stating:

"The Trial Judge Advocate stated into the record that the accused had a right to have a Negro as a member of the court. As a matter of law, the court had the jurisdiction regardless of whether a Negro was sitting as a member of the court or not. The Defense Counsel took the position that it was immaterial whether a Negro was sitting since the accused was not a Negro. The Law Member properly excluded the whole matter from the record."

The Staff Judge Advocate concluded that the record was legally sufficient to support the findings of the court. Brigadier General Fenton S. Jacobs, Commander Channel Base Section, Communications Zone, approved the sentence and forwarded the record of trial on March 25, 1945. On May 6, 1945, General Dwight D. Eisenhower signed a letter confirming the sentence of death for Victor Ortiz, but withheld the order directing the execution. The Branch Office of The JAG with the ETO reviewed the case on June 8, 1945. The three-man panel (Riter, Burrow and Stevens) ruled the court was legally constituted, had jurisdiction of the person and offenses, and committed no errors injuriously affecting the substantial rights of the accused – in short that the record of trial was legally sufficient to support the findings of guilty and the sentence imposed. On June 16, 1945, the ETO issued General Court-Martial Orders Number 213. Major General Thomas B. Larkin – by command of General Eisenhower – directed that the execution be carried out at the Loire DTC at Le Mans on June 21, 1945.

On the morning of June 20, 1945, Lieutenant Colonel Peck, accompanied by First Lieutenant Robert Celaya, read General Court-Martial Orders Number 213 to General Prisoner Ortiz. To ensure complete understanding, Lieutenant Celaya translated the document into Spanish. Within hours, Master Sergeant John Woods drove an Army flatbed truck to a ravine just outside the northwest corner of the Loire DTC. Woods, engineers and a prisoner detail removed the gallows from the truck and set it up just outside the barbed wire fence. Woods tested the trap door that afternoon and the following morning. That evening at 6:30 p.m., Major Ernest A. Weizer examined the condemned man and found him to be in excellent physical and mental condition.

The morning of June 21 was cool and overcast; a light wind blew from the north. At 10:40 a.m., Lieutenant Colonel Henry L. Peck gathered five official witnesses and twenty-three authorized spectators at the gallows. Here, he briefed them on the proper conduct at the event and read General Court-Martial Orders Number 213. At 10:58 a.m., a command and reconnaissance car, ½-ton, 4x4 halted thirty-five yards from the scaffold. Out stepped General Prisoner Victor Ortiz. It was a lot colder in France than in Puerto Rico at this time of year. Back home, Puerto Ricans were getting ready to celebrate the *Fiestas Patronales de San Juan Bautista* – the annual holiday honoring Saint John the Baptist, the patron saint of San Juan. There was no celebration at this ravine, though – no hot *Pastelillos de Carne* and no cold rum on the rocks.

Private Ortiz quickly joined a procession that marched toward the scaffold a minute later. Peck led the way, followed by Chaplain Kilian R. Bowler, the prisoner, guards Tech Sergeant Frank Landi, Sergeant Alfonso Girvalo and Tech Sergeant Vincent J. Martino. Then marched First Lieutenant Lawrence Slon (the recorder) and Private Alfred Portillo, who would serve as interpreter, if required. The procession reached the foot of the gallows seconds before 11:00 a.m. Lieutenant Colonel Peck and Captain Bowler ascended the steps, while guards bound Ortiz's hands behind his back. They assisted the condemned man up the thirteen steps and positioned him on the trap door. The executioner's assistant then bound Ortiz's ankles. Peck then asked the prisoner if he had any last statements. Ortiz replied that he did not, at which point the Commandant asked if Ortiz fully understood what he had said. Ortiz replied that he did, and then Chaplain Bowler asked if he had any last words. Ortiz replied, "I ask for your prayers and the prayers of the Lord." With no need for an interpreter, Private Portillo departed the gallows. Master Sergeant John C. Woods and his assistant then adjusted the hood and rope over the condemned man's head. Chaplain Bowler began to intone a prayer; at 11:03 a.m., the Commandant signaled the executioner. who cut the rope, which released the weight and actuated the trap. Everything worked well; the condemned man made no motion or sound. At 11:18 a.m., Lieutenant Colonel Peck directed that Major Ernest A. Weizer, Captain Daniel Thaw and Captain Henry H. Kalter examine the body. They did so and promptly declared that the prisoner was officially dead. Peck then dismissed the formation. The executioner cut the rope and removed the body from the lower part of the scaffold. Captain Hardy C. Derx signed for the body and removed it for later interment. The official report stated that twenty-five men of Company I of the 156th Infantry Regiment, under the command of Captain Charles E. Williams, efficiently guarded the site.

The Army temporarily interred Ortiz at the U.S. Military Cemetery at Marigny in Plot Z in Grave 2-31. Exhumed in 1949, Victor Ortiz is buried at the American Military Cemetery at Oise-Aisne in Plot E. His remains are in Grave 87 of Row 4.

On June 26, 1945, the War Department sent a telegram to Victor Ortiz's mother in Salinas, Puerto Rico. The message stated that Private Victor Ortiz was deceased through execution by judicial hanging. It further stated that he died in a non-battle status due to his own misconduct. Chaplain Bowler wrote Ortiz's mother, saying that her son had asked him, "to tell you not to worry about him as he said that he died a child of Mary."

The Army initially buried Captain Ignacio Bonit in France. Officials reinterred his body on January 26, 1960; it rests in Plot C571 in the Puerto Rico National Cemetery in Bayamón, Puerto Rico.[3]

• • •

That evening was a good time for a beer. Master Sergeant Woods and Sergeant Ward, as they often did, went to a bar in downtown Le Mans for a few cold ones. According to Sergeant Ward, Woods never talked about his past and constantly reminded Ward that the hangings at the DTC should never be discussed in public.

*"I put her on the road so that her feet were near the side of the road and her head near the middle of the road. Then I drove the truck over her."*

*"This young adult, colored soldier with a constitutionally inadequate personality and a mental deficiency of moron level."*

## 82      Private Willie Johnson
38270465
3984th Quartermaster Truck Company
**Murder**
Hanged on June 26, 1945

Private Willie Johnson had some serious mental problems, problems that not only affected his life, but ones that a jury had to assess to determine if the maladies would have prevented Willie from not only understanding right from wrong, but also if he could even comprehend the ramifications of making a confession.

Because that confession was a whopper. The situation was this: at 8:30 p.m. on August 23, 1943, three French women on the outskirts of Rennes, France flagged down a passing U.S. Army gasoline tanker truck and inquired if they might catch a ride to their home village of Antrain, some twenty-five miles away. The driver, Private Willie Johnson – a twenty-two-year-old black soldier from Idaville, Oklahoma – indicated he was going in their direction and the three women climbed into the cab of the truck. As the vehicle approached Antrain, Johnson repeatedly placed his right hand on the knees of two of the women. They asked him to stop the truck, but Johnson refused. All three began to scream, as one attempted to grab the steering wheel; Johnson then slowed and stopped the vehicle for a brief moment. One woman jumped clear of the vehicle, but the other two only got as far as the running board on the passenger's side, before Johnson gunned the engine. After a short time, one of the women summoned the courage to spring from the moving vehicle – breaking her right leg in the effort – which left Madame Julien Fontaine still standing on the running board of the truck from hell.

The next morning villagers of Equilly – some eighteen miles from Antrain – found the dead body of Madame Fontaine lying in the road. Her head was "broken" and the calves of her legs were "completely crushed." A drying stream of blood a meter long flowed from her head; there were tire marks across her legs. The investigation began to implicate Private Willie Johnson. Johnson and his

750-gallon deuce-and-a-half tanker truck had been part of a convoy, but he left the column and was still missing at 2:00 a.m. on August 24, 1944. He finally showed up, shortly before reveille. Soon after, he showed a buddy, Private First Class Leon P. Reed, also in the segregated 3984th Quartermaster Truck Company, a small red bag with white flowers on it. The bag contained six or seven jars of face cream and belonged to the woman, who had broken her leg; Johnson told Reed that the night before, he had "clipped a woman."

Johnson and Reed then prepared the truck for movement of the unit. Later on their way toward Rennes, they passed the body of a dead woman on the road, guarded by MPs. Reed then observed blood on the trousers and sleeves of the accused; after arriving at the unit's new location, Private First Class Reed inspected the entire vehicle and found blood on the running board gas can, the rifle rack and the passenger's seat. The information made its way up to the company commander. Incredibly, Johnson was not finished boasting of his escapades; later that morning he showed Reed a small knife, which the dead woman's daughter would later identify as belonging to her mother.

Second Lieutenant Paul E. Pauly of the Criminal Investigation Division received the case and by the end of September, through solid detective work, he pieced together the unit most likely involved in the incident. Pauly finally located Private Johnson, who after being advised of his rights, made a statement on October 7, 1944 that he did, indeed, pick up the three women, but that they had all jumped off his truck and he returned to his unit. Johnson said he discovered the little red bag and the knife in the cab of his truck, but he could not explain the blood evidence on the vehicle. Two days later, after having been advised of his rights once again, he made a full written confession. In it, he said that the last woman jumped off the vehicle ten miles after the second one did and had badly hurt her head. He stopped, put the badly injured woman on the back of his vehicle and drove around for two and a half hours, at which point he decided to have sex with her. After that, Johnson wrote:

"I heard her groan some. I decided to keep her from telling anybody so I dragged her out and put her in front of the right rear wheel. I don't know whether she was alive when I put her there but she was warm, I know that. I put her on the road so that her feet were near the side of the road and her head near the middle of the road. Then I drove the truck over her."

Brigadier General Henry S. Aurand, Commanding General of the Normandy Base Section, had read enough of the investigation to decide to convene a GCM, which would meet at Granville on January 27, 1945. Willie Johnson's defense team knew their client was in deep trouble and that his confession could well be fatal, so they agreed to an insanity examination. A board of medical officers convened at the 165th General Hospital on January 23, 1945. Their findings were startling. Born on December 25, 1921, Johnson had a history of five periods of unconsciousness, following head injuries. While there was no evidence of skull fracture, he did have bleeding from his nose and mouth. Johnson had attended school only for six months; he could not read or write. He was enuretic to age twenty-one and contracted gonorrhea at age twenty-two. Inducted in September 1942, Johnson could not complete the road marches and was unable to qualify with a weapon. Using the Kent Emergency Test, doctors found him to have a mental age of eight years. The officers were unsure as to whether or not he had encephalopathy. They described Johnson as, "This young adult, colored soldier with a constitutionally inadequate personality and a mental deficiency of moron level."

The doctors also said that Johnson was slow, dull and had poor judgment, but was cooperative, rational, and had a good memory. He was 5'11" tall and weighed 172 pounds. Married with one child, Johnson worked as a farm laborer, until inducted. Initially assigned to the 354th Engineer General Support Regiment, he deployed to England in July 1943, transferred to his current unit and landed in France in July 1944. It does not appear that Johnson had a civilian criminal record; he did have two Summary Court-Martial convictions, for being absent without leave.

The court met at 9:20 a.m. on January 27, 1945. Private Johnson pleaded not guilty to murder, a violation of the 92nd Article of War.[1] The following officers sat on the panel: Lieutenant Colonel George R. Anderson (QM), Lieutenant Colonel Joseph H. Edgar (FA) who was also the Law Member, Major Don B. Conley (FI), Major Robert H. Verhage (TC), Major Mead Hartwell (QM), Captain William C. Martin (QM), Captain Phillip H. Carlin (OD), First Lieutenant Jason R. Gray (TC), and First Lieutenant Lafayette Parker (QM.) First Lieutenant Vincent P. Clarke (TC) served as the Trial Judge Advocate. He was assisted by First Lieutenant Joseph A. Bruggeman (TC) and First Lieutenant Sydney Weitzer (TC.) Captain John F. Knottnauer (QM) filled the position of Defense Counsel. He was assisted by First Lieutenant Morris G. Beizer (TC) and First Lieutenant Joseph J. Bartl (IN.)[2] It was the third court-martial to adjudicate a death sentence that was later carried into execution for Lieutenant Colonel Anderson, Captain Carlin, First Lieutenant Gray and First Lieutenant Parker; the second for Lieutenant Colonel Edgar. The defense objected to a statement that prior to the crime, the accused told his buddies that, "If a woman don't give me what I want, I will just kill her."

However, the court admitted the statement. The defense also objected to the admission of Johnson's statement to investigators, arguing that it amounted to a confession, involuntarily made. Johnson then took the stand for the limited purpose of stating that threats of physical violence were used to coerce him to confess. The defense introduced the findings of the board of medical officers, stating that this showed that the accused did not have sufficient intelligence to understand the warning given to him, with respect to his rights under Article of War 24. The court then called the investigating agent to the stand, who stated that he had carefully explained the accused's rights to him and used no improper influences to induce the accused to make a statement. The Law Member ruled the statement had been voluntary and admitted it into evidence.

The accused's company commander and platoon sergeant testified for the defense that Johnson had an excellent character and military efficiency. That opened up a line of cross-examination, when they stated that the accused had the ability to understand orders and had always appeared capable of carrying out normal military duties and responsibilities. The jury weighed the evidence and unanimously voted to convict Private Willie Johnson of murder and sentenced him to be hanged by the neck until dead.

The Staff Judge Advocate for the Normandy Base Section reviewed the trial record on February 17, 1945. Lieutenant Colonel Franklin H. Berry found that there were no reversible errors; he added:

"The conduct of the accused in assaulting the deceased, forcing her to leap from his moving vehicle, attacking her while she was bleeding and unconscious condition, and in subsequently disposing of her by crushing her with his truck, show conclusively that his acts were premeditated, cold-blooded, and brutal in the extreme."

General Dwight D. Eisenhower signed the order confirming the sentence for Private Willie Johnson on March 29, 1945. The order withheld the date and place of execution. The Board of Review Number 2 of the Branch Office of The JAG with the ETO reviewed the case on June 11, 1945. Judge Advocates Sleeper, Sherman and Dewey found that the trial conformed to standard and that there were no serious errors in the proceedings. Meanwhile, on March 22, 1945, Private Willie Johnson wrote General Dwight Eisenhower a letter asking for his consideration and requesting an opportunity for the convicted man to redeem himself, by worthy service to the country. Eisenhower reviewed the letter and gave it to Brigadier General Edward C. Betts. Betts wrote Private Johnson on June 23, 1945, stating that General Eisenhower could not grant the plea, but did say of the Commanding General, "He invokes God's forgiveness and mercy on you." On May 30, 1945, Brigadier General Betts wrote a letter to Private Johnson's mother, stating that her son had requested that the Army inform her of his situation. General Betts stated that a GCM tried Private Johnson on January 27, 1945 for murder, found him guilty and sentenced him to death. He ended with, "You may be sure that the facts and circumstances in your son's case will be fully examined before final disposition of the case."

On June 21, 1945, the ETO issued General Court-Martial Orders Number 218. Major General Thomas B. Larkin – by command of General Eisenhower – directed that the execution occur at the village of Le Haye Pesnel on June 26, 1945. At 11:00 a.m. the day prior, First Lieutenant David E. Duff, Military Police, read General Court-Martial Orders Number 218 to General Prisoner Willie Johnson. Later that day, a medical officer found the prisoner to be in excellent physical and mental health.

The morning of June 26 was clear, bright, warm and sunny. It was now time for the "final disposition of the case." At 10:40 a.m. Lieutenant Colonel Henry L. Peck, Commandant Loire DTC, gathered five authorized witnesses and twelve authorized spectators at a rock quarry one-half mile from the village of Le Haye Pesnel. Five of the spectators were French officials from the village. The quarry provided cover for three sides of the gallows; a hedge and bushes shielded the fourth from view. The scaffold faced south. The personnel stood between ten and fifteen yards from the scaffold. Lieutenant Colonel Peck briefed the gathering on the proper conduct at the event and read General Court-Martial Orders Number 218. At 10:58 a.m., a 2½-ton 6x6 covered cargo vehicle approached, halting fifty yards from the gallows. Out stepped General Prisoner Willie Johnson. It had been a 2½-ton truck with which he had committed murder and it would be a 2½-ton truck in which he would have his last ride.

Johnson quickly joined a procession that marched toward the scaffold seconds later. Peck led the way, followed by Chaplain William L. Bell, the prisoner and guards Sergeant Thomas J. Boyle, Sergeant Alfonso Girvalo and Technician Fifth Grade Vincent J. Martino. First Lieutenant Lawrence Slon followed in the rear. The procession reached the foot of the gallows seconds before 11:00 a.m. Peck and Bell ascended the steps, while the guards bound Johnson's hands behind his back, assisted him up the steps and positioned him on top the trap door. The executioner's assistant then bound Johnson's ankles. The Commandant asked the prisoner if he had any last statements. Johnson replied "No." Chaplain Bell then asked if the prisoner had any last words. Johnson again replied "No." Master Sergeant John C. Woods and his assistant Technician Third Grade Thomas F. Robinson adjusted the hood and rope over the condemned man's head. The Chaplain began to intone a prayer; at 11:01 a.m. the Commandant signaled Woods, who cut the rope which released the weight and actuated the trap. Everything worked smoothly; the condemned man made no motion or sound after falling. At 11:16 a.m., Lieutenant Colonel Peck directed that Captain Nelson J. Dente, Captain Marion F. Whitten and Captain Frank J. Gallagher examine the body. They marched to the understructure of the gallows, made their examinations and promptly declared that the prisoner was officially dead; they would later state that the cause of death was judicial asphyxis. Lieutenant Colonel Peck dismissed the formation. Master Sergeant Woods cut the rope and removed the body from the lower part of the scaffold. First Lieutenant Milliard R. Jones signed for the body and removed it. The official report stated that the site was efficiently guarded by 11 men of Company B of the 387th MP Battalion, under the immediate command of First Lieutenant Harry Bender.

On July 9, 1945, the War Department sent a telegram to Willie Johnson's father, stating that his son had died in a non-battle status due to his own misconduct; the cause of death was "judicial asphyxiation." The postal service could not locate the recipient and never delivered the letter. The Adjutant General of the CHANOR Base Section wrote a letter to the mayor of Equilly, expressing regret over the murder of a citizen in the community. The letter explained that the perpetrator was executed and that, "Such conduct is not tolerated in the Armed Forces of the United States."

Chaplain C.L. McGee of the 46th Quartermaster Group (TC) wrote a letter to the family on August 7, 1945. He provided no details concerning Private Johnson's death, but did state that he was a good soldier and his performance was excellent. Meanwhile, the family sought information concerning their son's death, writing The Adjutant General on October 26, 1945; Colonel Albert W. Johnson provided the grieving mother with a detailed response on December 12, 1945 that included:

> "The records of this office disclose that on 27 January 1945, Private Willie Johnson was found guilty by a GCM convened at Granville, Manche, France, of the crime of murder, in violation of Article of War 92. He was sentenced to be hanged. The reviewing authority approved the sentence and the record of trial was forwarded for action under Article of War 48. On 29 March 1945, the sentence was confirmed by the Commanding General, ETO. The record of trial was then examined in a branch office of The JAG as required by the statutes of the United States and was held to be legally sufficient to support the findings of guilty and the sentence. The sentence was carried into execution at Le Haye Peshnel, France, on 26 June 1945."

Willie Johnson's mother wanted details, but the Army did not provide some of them. The letter did not state that that her son had taken three women on a lengthy unpleasant ride in his vehicle. It did not say that he groped two of the women. The colonel did not say that one of the women broke her leg trying to escape from the moving vehicle. He did not say that the murder victim jumped from the vehicle and was brought back unconscious, raped by her son, and run over by her son in a 2½-ton truck, crushing her legs and "breaking" her head. The letter also did not mention that the murder victim was a mother with a daughter.

The Army initially buried Private Johnson at the U.S. Military Cemetery at Marigny at 3:00 p.m. on July 12, 1945, in Field GP (General Prisoner) (Z), in Row 2, in Grave 32. At that time, his grave was marked with a cross. To his right, in Grave 33, lay Tom Gordon. Officials later reinterred Willie Johnson at the American Military Cemetery at Oise-Aisne in Plot E. His remains are in Row 2, Grave 28.[3]

*"Get in the house, or I'll blow your head off."*

*"The place, time, and circumstances were such as to exclude any reasonable doubt as to their identity."*

## 83    Private Fred A. McMurray
38184335

177th Port Company
**Two Rapes and Murder**
Hanged on July 2, 1945

## 84    Private Louis Till
36392273

177th Port Company
**Two Rapes and Murder**
Hanged on July 2, 1945

From the manner in which Private Louis Till spoke and the way he carried himself, you might think that he was a small-time gangster from Chicago. Fear was Till's game. He had terrorized his wife, terrorized his fellow soldiers and terrorized local Italians, who did not cooperate with him. Unfortunately, for Private Till, one of his co-conspirators was not afraid of him and agreed to testify against the tough guy from the "Windy City" in return for a recommendation of clemency in his own case.

It started on June 27, 1944 near Civitavecchia, Italy – along the Mediterranean coast northwest of Rome – with Till, Private Fred A. McMurray and Private James Thomas, Jr. – from the all-black, segregated 177th Port Company – accompanied by an unidentified British soldier, looking to find some wine. They ran across a Navy sailor, James E. Carter at an Italian civilian's house, doing his laundry. The four men approached and after a brief conversation the tallest soldier, who appeared to be 6' tall, weighing 200 pounds, with a dark complexion, struck Carter three times in the face, shoved a small pistol into his back and robbed him, taking a .45 caliber Model 1911 U.S. Service pistol from Carter. Carter was pretty well battered, when his assailant yelled, "I'm going to kill the mother-fucking son of a bitch."

Till then fired a shot, but the pistol jammed and the startled sailor, realizing that this might be his only chance at safety, jumped in his jeep and took off. Carter would later report the incident. Military Police would escort him through several all-black units in the area, but he did not find his assailants. They were approaching an Italian house and struck the man of the house to show him who was in charge. Till and McMurray raped two women,

striking one of the women in the head and face, and pushing her to the floor. She was two and one half months pregnant; several days after the attack, she suffered a miscarriage. She later said that the men were all wearing masks. The two men also assaulted the other woman, hitting her in the head and face. She was over eight months pregnant. The men then went to a second house and tried to force their way in. They opened the door and when Signora Anna Zanchi started to close it, the soldiers started shooting. Hit in the stomach, she died several hours later at a U.S. Army hospital. John Masi, an Italian, who had lived several years in the United States, was in the house and later stated that the two men were black, wore masks; the taller man was about 5'10" and weighed 175 pounds, while the shorter soldier was 5'5" and stocky. Masi said the taller man told him, "Get in the house, or I'll blow your head off." Masi also stated that the taller man also spoke Italian with a Neapolitan accent. Masi later watched as MPs recovered empty .45 and .32 shell cases by the front door of the home. Masi also found a green fatigue cap at the front entrance. More damningly, MPs found a soiled airmail envelope nearby, with the following address:

"Pvt. Fred McMurray,
379th Port B.N.T.C.,
APO 765, c/o Postmaster,
New York, N.Y. 177th Port Co."

Private James Thomas, Jr. made a statement on July 8, 1944. It was fairly detailed, concerning the assault of the sailor, but stated that he and the English soldier went back to camp, where they remained the rest of the night. That was not true and on July 12, 1944, investigators pressed Thomas for more information, at which time he made a second statement that the four men took twenty minutes to plan the home invasion of the first Italian house. He stated that Till and McMurray had sex with two women, as did the English soldier. Thomas claimed that he did not engage in sex, as he had a chancre sore. He also said the men had worn U.S. Navy weather masks as disguises.

MPs arrested the accused on July 19, 1944. After having his rights read to him, McMurray made a written statement. He stated that during the incident with the sailor, Till appeared with a .45 caliber pistol and asked Thomas how it operated. As the two were examining it, the weapon accidentally discharged. The group proceeded to get drunk, when the local air raid siren started to wail and anti-aircraft guns began shooting. At this point, according to McMurray, Till said, "Everybody follow me: If anybody turns back I'll blast him." The group, by McMurray's account, went to the first Italian house where Till struck an old man. McMurray said that the sex acts were consensual. As he put it, "Till, Thomas and the English soldier all got some tail, but I didn't." Then Thomas and the English soldier went back to camp. Till and McMurray went to the second Italian house, where Till threatened he would shoot. According to McMurray, he begged Till not to shoot, but Till fired a shot into the house anyway.

Authorities confined Fred McMurray and Louis Till at the Peninsular Case Section Stockade on July 19, 1944. Officials preferred charges on September 8, 1944, but because of shoddy processing, the final investigation report did not reach the chain of command until November 3, 1944. On December 27, 1944, Brigadier General Francis H. Oxx, the Commander of the PBS, determined a joint GCM was appropriate for Till and McMurray. Prosecutors had an ace up their sleeves. Because of the discrepancies in Private Thomas's statements, the PBS Trial Judge Advocate talked to Thomas about testifying for the government in the cases of Till and McMurray. Private Thomas faced two counts of rape, but would have a separate trial. Captain Eugene J. Ralston offered to recommend clemency, if Thomas would make a statement and repeat it in court if necessary. Thomas agreed.

Louis Till was from Madrid, Missouri, reportedly growing up an orphan. An amateur boxer, he worked at the Argo Corn Company in Argo, Illinois – close to Chicago. He married Mamie Carthan on October 14, 1940; both Till and his wife were eighteen years old. On July 25, 1941, they had a son, Emmett. The couple separated in 1942; according to some sources, he had attacked his wife so violently that she defended herself by throwing a pan of boiling water on him. On July 9, 1942, Till was inducted at Chicago, Illinois – according to a source, it was the Army or jail from a judge, who was tired of Till violating restraining orders. Till had two previous Summary Courts-Martial. One was in August 1943, for being absent without leave; the second, in December 1943, was for disobeying a standing order. In 1944, medics diagnosed him with syphilis. Till could speak Italian with a Neapolitan accent.

Fred A. McMurray was born on February 25, 1920 in Ruston, Louisiana. He was married in September 1941 and was inducted at Camp Livingston, Louisiana on June 30, 1942. McMurray had four previous Summary Courts-Martial. In March 1944, he went absent without leave and did the same in April. In May 1944, he wore his identification tags improperly and again was absent without leave. Later that month he was absent again. Medics diagnosed McMurray with syphilis in September 1943, which he said he got from a clandestine prostitute.

The court convened at Livorno, Italy on February 17 at 9:45 a.m.; it included the following officers: Colonel Roger W. Whitman (QM) Law Member, Lieutenant Colonel Charles H. Dobbs (IN), Lieutenant Colonel Leo S. Strawn (MC), Major John M. Sanders (OD), Captain Lloyd J. Roberts (AG), Captain Gerald D. Bertram (QM) and First Lieutenant Morris W. Meullier (CAC.) Second Lieutenant Mervin R. Samuel (QM) would have to serve as the Trial Judge Advocate as the assigned officer was away on official business. First Lieutenant John W. Wynn (CAC) would sit as the Defense Counsel as the primary counsel was also officially absent.[1] It was the third death sentence – that was later carried out – awarded by Colonel Whitman, Lieutenant Colonel Strawn, Lieutenant Colonel Dobbs, Major Sanders, Captain Bertram and Captain Roberts.

Till and McMurray faced a joint trial – neither objected – and both pleaded not guilty to one charge of murder and two charges of carnal knowledge, violations of the 92nd Article of War.[2] Thomas testified for the prosecution. The Trial Judge Advocate introduced statements by the various Italian witnesses; John Masi testified that the tall soldier fired two shots into the house and the shorter soldier fired one. It was not clear what caliber bullet killed Anna Zanchi, although that did not really matter. The rape victims could not positively identify the faces of their attackers, although Private Thomas did. The accused had their rights as a witness explained to them and both elected to remain silent. Meanwhile, their Defense Counsel was busy, objecting to the introduction of Private McMurray's statement, saying it had been made involuntarily. The Law Member overruled this objection, but instructed the court that the statement could only be used concerning McMurray. First Lieutenant Wynn objected that the identity of the accused had only been established by an accomplice to the crime. The Law Member overruled that objection as well. After hearing the evidence, the jury voted unanimously to convict. They then read evidence concerning prior court-martial convictions for each of the accused and voted unanimously to sentence both defendants to be hanged by the neck until dead.

The Staff Judge Advocate of the PBS did not complete his review of the case files until April 18, 1945. Colonel Claudius O. Wolfe reported that the record of trial was legally sufficient to support the findings of guilty. Concerning the victims' inability to identify their attackers, Wolfe stated that, "The place, time, and circumstances were such as to exclude any reasonable doubt as to their identity." On April 20, 1945, Brigadier General Oxx approved the findings and forwarded the record of trial up the chain of command. On May 14, 1945, Colonel Adam Richmond, the Mediterranean Theater Judge Advocate, reviewed the case. He, too, found no significant discrepancies and recommended that the sentence for each man be confirmed. On May 17, 1945, General Joseph T. McNarney, Commanding General of the MTO, signed the order confirming the sentences for both men; the order withheld the date and place of execution. Judge Advocates Irion, Sessions and Remick of the Branch Office of The JAG with the MTO examined the trial records on June 13, 1945. They found the trial to have been satisfactory and commented on the use of testimony by a confederate, quoting *A Manual for Courts-Martial, U.S. Army*:

"A conviction may be based on uncorroborated testimony of an accomplice, but such testimony is of doubtful integrity and is to be considered with great caution."

The review board stated that Thomas' testimony had been corroborated in most of its important aspects. The MTO published General Court-Martial Orders Number 88 the same day. Major General George D. Pence, under the authority of the theater commander, set the time and location of execution for both men. On July 1, 1945, at 9:00 a.m. at the Headquarters' Building, PBS Stockade Number 1, Captain Glenn A. Waser, the stockade commander, in the presence of eight commissioned officers, read the General Court-Martial Order for the execution to General Prisoner Fred A. McMurray. He read a similar order to Louis Till shortly afterward. Chaplain William C. Strother – a black, Methodist minister – stayed with McMurray from 8:30 a.m. through the execution the next day.

• • •

The Army conducted executions in Italy differently than it did in the rest of Europe. There were no hangings conducted near the scene of the crime. Instead, MPs transferred all the condemned to a stockade near Aversa, Italy for execution of sentence. The Peninsular Base Section Stockade Number 1 was a seven and a half acre facility enclosed by barbed wire fences and four guard posts on the corners. The headquarters consisted of wooden huts. Guards and prisoners lived in tents. The stockade was situated just to the west of *Strada Statale 7bis* (the Naples to Aversa road), some two miles south of Aversa. Locals called the area *Fondo San Felice*. At the rear of the stockade was a rifle range, surrounded on all sides by an earthen berm. Known as "the pit," this was the site for all firing squads.

Within the stockade was a large, permanent gallows, unlike the smaller, transportable versions used in France and Belgium. The sturdy structure conformed to Army requirements with the addition of one unique feature. Beneath the gallows platform stood three soldiers; each soldier operated a four-foot-long wooden lever. Upon a silent signal, initiated by the commandant (and probably relayed by another officer), each of the soldiers pushed his lever forward, which pulled a rope downward. Passing from above through pulleys, all three ropes were connected to the same single release pin, which when pulled released the trap doors. The system provided sufficient uncertainty to the three operators that none of the men could be sure whose lever initiated the final release of the pin. Above, two soldiers held the shoulders of the condemned man to ensure that as he fell through the center of the trap door opening, he did not strike the edge of the doors. Indications of this arrangement first appear in executions on March 20, 1945, but were not confirmed until unofficial photographs, in private hands, surfaced for the Till and McMurray executions. Additionally, condemned men in Italy had their hands handcuffed behind their back, instead of their wrists tied with rope, and that the handcuffs were already on when the condemned marched to the gallows.

• • •

On July 10, 1945, the MTO sent a confidential telegram to the War Department, stating that the Army hanged Private Fred A. McMurray at the PBS Stockade Number 1 at Aversa, Italy on July 2, 1945. Lieutenant Colonel Joseph R. Hrado, Major John S. Cole, Major Ralph M. Rowley, Major John J. Hazel, Captain Daniel R. Scholes, Captain William C. Schreve, Captain Frank Rinando and

First Lieutenant Clyde R. Thorn served as official witnesses. Photographs show that an Army jeep brought McMurray close to the gallows, which was located in a grove of fruit trees. Chaplain William C. Strother walked in front of McMurray, who was handcuffed and flanked by two guards. The execution detail wore summer, tan cotton uniforms and overseas caps; McMurray, bareheaded, wore dark green work fatigues sans shoes laces and belt to prevent a suicide during his last night alive. The flanking guards held the prisoner by his arms.

The procession passed a group of armed guards in white helmets, standing at attention. McMurray's eyes looked slightly upward, probably at the noose on the gallows a few yards away. The guard formation contained both black and white soldiers. Private McMurray climbed the steps of the gallows, where Captain Glenn A. Waser would officiate the proceeding. The second photo shows McMurray standing on the trap door, as an MP binds his legs close to the knees with a uniform belt. Waser is shown in the photograph reading the GCM order; two other MPs are holding McMurray's arms, while he stares straight ahead. The photographer is standing at the base of the steps. Chaplain William C. Strother then began to read scripture. Two soldiers put the black hood over the condemned man's head and followed that by slipping the noose around his neck. On a silent signal by Captain Waser, the three soldiers (two of whom appear to be lieutenants) under the gallows pushed their levers forward. The three men were combat veterans, all having the Combat Infantryman's Badge. McMurray plunged through the trap door at 8:49 a.m. The third photograph shows him hurtling downward; the rope is not yet taut; the knot is horizontal to the ground and directly over McMurray's left shoulder. The senior observer is not looking at the body lunging downward, not complying with his official orders that proscribed that action. In fact, he has one hand on the rail to the steps and appears to want to begin walking downward. Major Paul W. Kabler, a medical officer, pronounced McMurray dead at 9:08 a.m. The fourth photograph shows the officer examining the deceased with a stethoscope. McMurray's handcuffed wrists show no sign of a struggle. The knot of the rope is in front of his chin, probably causing his neck to break.

The Army hanged Louis Till a few minutes later, using the same procedures. Four photographs exist of this execution as well. The first photograph shows Till enroute to the gallows. He is wearing a one-piece coverall; his boots are also devoid of laces. Staring straight ahead, Till has a small moustache just under his nose. Photograph two shows General Prisoner Till staring straight ahead on the trap door,

as Captain Waser reads the order. The officer to the right of the prisoner has his hand on Till's right shoulder, steadying him. In the third photograph, the senior observer seems in even a greater hurry to get off the scaffold, as Till plummets downward in a black hood. The final photograph shows two medical officers examining the deceased hanging from the rope. The knot of the rope is directly behind Till's head; his hands show no bruising or abrasions. On July 11, 1945, a second confidential telegram to the War Department announced that Private Louis Till had been hanged.

Chaplain Strother officiated at McMurray's funeral in Naples at the U.S. Military Cemetery. His remains were in the General Prisoner plot at Grave 2-19; Louis Till was buried in Grave 2-18. On July 13, 1945, the War Department sent two telegrams, one to the wife of Louis Till and one to the mother of Fred McMurray. Both communications informed the next of kin that the service-members died on July 2, 1945 in Italy; both the deaths were in non-battle status, due to the misconduct of the soldiers. The cause of death for each was judicial asphyxiation. The Army exhumed the bodies of Louis Till and Fred A. McMurray in 1949 and buried them at the American Military Cemetery at Oise-Aisne in Plot E. Till's remains are in Row 4, Grave 73; McMurray's remains are at Row 1, Grave 2.[3]

• • •

In *Fighting for America: Black Soldiers – The Unsung Heroes of World War II*, Christopher Paul Moore stated that Louis Till's wife said that, although she had received her husband's personal effects: "the Army had never told her the cause of her husband's death."[4] However, the telegram that she received listed the cause of death as "Judicial Asphixiation," [spelled incorrectly on the document] due to his own misconduct in Italy on 2 July 1945. What the telegram did not state was that her separated husband had killed one woman and raped two other women, which resulted in one miscarriage.

His crimes had received some public notoriety. American expatriate, critic and poet, Ezra Pound had moved to Italy from England in 1924, enamored with Mussolini's fascism. He made hundreds of radio broadcasts from Italy criticizing the United States. American forces apprehended him at the end of the war and placed Pound in a military detention camp in Pisa, Italy. During his time in custody – after returning from incarceration in Italy he would be held in St. Elizabeth's Federal Hospital for the Insane in Washington, DC; he began to write *The Pisan Cantos*, a work that would later win him acclaim. In the cantos, Pound wrote,[5]

"Pisa, in the 23rd year of the effort in sight
of the tower
   And Till was hung yesterday
   For murder and rape with trimmings."

Pound spent time in the MTO DTC, three miles outside of Pisa and had met Louis Till. While the soldier had indeed been hanged, Pound took some artistic license, when he mentioned Pisa, as Till had died in Aversa.

The Army returned Louis Till's silver ring, bearing the initials "LT," to his estranged wife in Chicago. In 1955, she let her son, Emmett take the ring to visit relatives in Mississippi, where he was soon murdered, resulting in a civil rights case that gained lasting national attention. Authorities identified Emmett's mutilated body, in part, through the distinctive ring.

*"I said don't kill me. The soldier said that he would if I did not let him do as he wished so I let him do as he wished because I was afraid the soldier would kill me."*

*"The court should have been advised not to consider the statements insofar as they involved the acts of the accused who was not the author of the statement."*

## 85    Private Henry W. Nelson
### 35726029
Company A, 371st Infantry Regiment,
    Ninety-Second Infantry Division
**Robbery, Assault and Rape**
Hanged on July 5, 1945

## 86          Private John T. Jones
### 38315973
Battery B, 599th Field Artillery Battalion,
    Ninety-Second Infantry Division
**Robbery, Assault and Rape**
Hanged on July 5, 1945

When the jury in the robbery, assault and rape case against Private Henry W. Nelson and Private John T. Jones returned a verdict of guilty, Defense Counsel First Lieutenant Frank R. Taylor, probably saw a ray of hope in the result. Two of the jury members voted to acquit. First Lieutenant Taylor hoped that those that had voted not guilty would subsequently vote for the lesser penalty of life imprisonment, because he knew that the death penalty required a unanimous vote. However, even military juries could be fickle and this was the Ninety-Second Infantry Division, which executed more soldiers than any other division in World War II.

The crime was all too familiar. On January 29, 1945, two American soldiers started drinking and went to an Italian home at Massa Macinaia, Italy – twelve miles northeast of Pisa. Identifying themselves as police, they entered, looked around and broke into the attic. Then they went outside and shot an Italian man in the eye. Taking the victim inside, one of the soldiers slapped an Italian woman, who was screaming, and pushed her to the floor. After threatening her, and possibly putting a knife to her throat, the soldier raped the woman. The second soldier then had sex with the woman. The two soldiers went to a second home, where they stole a watch, two rings and two bicycles. MPs arrested Private Henry Nelson, who made a statement concerning the incident, in which he admitted to shooting a man in the eye, stating that he fired to scare the man. He also admitted having sex with the female victim. Private John Jones also made a statement, but admitting to only stealing the items in the second house and made no mention of the rape. He said that Nelson was armed and fired his weapon, but did not say that Nelson hit anyone.

A joint GCM convened at Lucca at 2:10 p.m. on March 17, 1945. It included the following officers: Lieutenant Colonel James C. Horne (IN), Lieutenant Colonel Thomas S. Gasiorowski (FI), Major Jerome A. Vesely (SC), Major Frederick R. Krug (DC), Captain James L. Glymph (IN), Captain Wendell L. Price (DC) and First Lieutenant Paul B. Lewis (IN.) Lieutenant Gaston M. Wood (IN) served as the Trial Judge Advocate, while the aforementioned First Lieutenant Taylor (QM) was the Defense Counsel. Thirteen other officers were excused from the jury pool by vocal orders of the commanding general. It was the fifth court-martial resulting in an execution on which Captain Glymph and Captain Price sat; the fourth for Lieutenant Colonel Horne and Major Krug; and the third for Lieutenant Colonel Gasiorowski, Major Vesely and First Lieutenant Lewis.[1]

Both defendants pleaded not guilty to carnal knowledge, a violation of the 92nd Article of War, and specifications of robbery and assault, both violations of the 93rd Article of War.[2] At trial, both accused elected to make unsworn statements to the court. Nelson said that both men drank a great deal, but denied shooting the man. He made no mention of the rape, but did say the pair stole the two bicycles. Jones' statement was similar, but admitted to stealing the bicycles. Their Defense Counsel objected to the admittance of their original statements, made shortly after being arrested. First Lieutenant Taylor argued that neither man had been advised of his rights, before making the statements. A lieutenant that witnessed Private Jones sign the statement testified that he never heard the sergeants warn him of his rights. He added that no threats were made, promises given or force used. The Law Member overruled the motion. All Italian witnesses stated that both soldiers had been "colored." The rape victim's daughter "unequivocally" identified Jones as one of the assailants, testifying,

"I said don't kill me. The soldier said that he would if I did not let him do as he wished, so I let him do as he wished because I was afraid the soldier would kill me."

Signore Luigi Decanini, the owner of the stolen property, and his wife identified in court Private Jones as one of the soldiers involved in the theft of their property. Five of the seven panel members voted to convict both soldiers. In the penalty phase of the trial, the jury was unanimous in sentencing both defendants to be hanged.

Henry W. Nelson was born in East St. Louis, Illinois on March 28, 1924. Missing seven teeth and racked with syphilis and gonorrhea that were now sulfonamide resistant, he stood 5'11" tall and weighed 157 pounds. Nelson made it through one year of high school, before becoming a sheet metal worker for $25 per month. He was single. In 1943, he was assigned to the 28th Cavalry Regiment at Camp Lockett, California. He had a Summary Court-Martial conviction for speeding and three absences without leave: one from June 30, 1944 to July 7, 1944, a second from August 26 to August 30, 1944 and a third from November 24, 1944 to February 1, 1945.

John T. Jones was born on August 11, 1912 in Silvercreek, Mississippi. He attended seven years of grade school, before dropping out to work as a railroad freight car loader – moving lumber from one car to another. Jones stood 5'11" tall and weighed 166 pounds. He received $20 per week for this backbreaking work. He entered the Army on November 3, 1942 and after training reported to Fort Huachuca, Arizona; there he contracted gonorrhea and began to accumulate two summary court-martial convictions for AWOL. Records indicate his mother was already deceased; Private Jones was married. His service record indicated that his character was unsatisfactory, but his efficiency was satisfactory.

Lieutenant Colonel William T. Thurman, the Ninety-Second Infantry Division Judge Advocate, reviewed the case on March 29, 1945. He found no substantial errors. Brigadier General Adam Richmond, the Mediterranean Theater Judge Advocate, reviewed the case on April 13, 1945, finding that the trial record was legally sufficient to support the findings and sentence, but recommended that the punishment be commuted to a dishonorable discharge, total forfeitures and confinement at hard labor for life. On April 21, 1945, General Joseph T. McNarney, Commanding

General of the MTO, signed the order confirming the sentences of Private Nelson and Private Jones. General McNarney withheld the order, however, directing the execution of the sentences. He also did not follow the recommendation of Brigadier General Richmond that the punishments be commuted to life imprisonment – General McNarney was going all the way on this one. On May 11, 1945, a Board of Review from the Branch Office of The JAG with the MTO reviewed the trial transcripts. Judge Advocates Sargent, Irion and Remick found that the accused had received a fair trial. They did note, however:

"The court should have been advised not to consider the statements insofar as they involved the acts of the accused who was not the author of the statement."

In a cover letter for the review, Colonel Hubert D. Hoover, Assistant JAG of the Branch Office made a note that two-thirds of the members of the court concurred in the findings of guilty. The MTO published General Court-Martial Orders Number 95 on June 22, 1945. It stated that the executions of Private Henry Nelson and Private John Jones would occur at Aversa, Italy on July 5, 1945. At 8:30 a.m., the day prior to the execution, Chaplain Douglas Hall arrived at the stockade and remained with Private Jones and Private Nelson for that day and the following morning. Hall was a black minister with the Negro Baptist Church.

Captain Glenn A. Waser, the Commanding Officer of the PBS Stockade Number 1, officiated at both executions. The trap door dropped at 8:44 a.m. for General Prisoner Henry W. Nelson. Captain George R. Lee, a medical officer at the 32nd Station Hospital, pronounced Nelson dead at 8:57 a.m.; Captain Joseph Dalgin assisted him. The trap door released at 9:20 a.m. for General Prisoner John T. Jones. Captain George R. Lee pronounced Jones dead at 9:35 a.m. Eight official witnesses had been present at the proceeding, including three U.S. Navy Chief Petty Officers. Representatives of the 3044th Quartermaster Graves Registration Company removed the remains removed from the area.

On July 15, 1945, the War Department sent a telegram Henry W. Nelson's mother. In it, she discovered that her son died of "death by hanging" on July 5, 1945 in Italy in a non-battle status, due to his own misconduct. A similar telegram went to the mother of Private John T. Jones on July 23, 1945. She enlisted the support of Congressman James E.

Morrison of Louisiana to obtain more information on the death of her son and the death benefits from the GI Insurance Plan. She received additional information. However, as in the case of every other family of the executed, no monetary benefits were ever received.

Henry W. Nelson and John T. Jones were originally interred at the U.S. Military Cemetery at Naples, in the General Prisoner (GP) plot in Graves 2-21 and 2-22, respectively. John Jones was buried in a white cotton mattress cover at 1:30 p.m. on July 5; presumably, Henry W. Nelson was interred minutes before. Exhumed in 1949, both are now buried at the American Military Cemetery at Oise-Aisne in Plot E. Nelson's remains are in Row 1, Grave 1. Jones' remains are in Row 2, Grave 48.[3]

## 87 — Private Charles H. Jefferies

33181343

Company F, 366th Infantry Regiment,
Ninety-Second Infantry Division

**Assault and Murder**

Hanged on July 5, 1945

A squad of infantry in Company F of the all-black 366th Infantry Regiment, attached to the Ninety-Second Infantry Division, was billeted with an Italian family at Barga, Italy – fifteen miles north of Lucca. Private Charles H. Jeffries stood outside the building and without warning began firing his weapon; he later said he was test firing it. That prompted Staff Sergeant Joe Wynn, the squad leader, to take the weapon from the soldier. The veteran NCO sensed that something was "queer" about Jeffries and notified the platoon leader. Soon after, Staff Sergeant John A. Williams came from the platoon command post to get Jeffries, who was given back his rifle. Jeffries began arguing with Private First Class James Livingston, raising his rifle. Staff Sergeant Wynn – sensing trouble – slapped Jeffries, took his rifle and emptied it of ammunition, returning the weapon to Jeffries, who departed for the command post.

An hour later, as the squad finished supper, Jeffries burst in the room and began shooting, hitting Private First Class John B. Walker in the shoulder, Private First Class Livingston in the arm and leg and Private First Class Mansee Bonnett in the leg. Italian civilian Silvana Bechelli suffered wounds in both knees and the stomach, Giaconda Bonini in the right hip and Alda Bonini – a baby – a slight flesh wound. Far worse, a round went through the heart of Alfredo Bechelli, a small boy, instantly killing him. Staff Sergeant Williams fired one shot in defense; Private Jeffries ran off, but the company soon found him.

Jeffries later made a statement, saying he surrendered his weapon at the platoon command post; then Lieutenant French, his platoon leader, marched him to the scene of the crime, as Jeffries had his hands behind his back. Jeffries claimed that French fired a round and then told him to run for his life. After reaching the house, according to Jeffries, First Sergeant Parkman knocked him down and kicked him, before taking him to Captain Harold J. Barnett, the company commander.

Charles Jeffries was born in Coatesville, Pennsylvania on July 15, 1923. Jeffries finished the 8th grade of school. He stood 5'3" tall and weighed 130 pounds. His father and mother were deceased; he had four brothers and three sisters. Jeffries was inducted on April 13, 1942. He had fractured his skull in a truck wreck in April 1941 and a medical classification board in 1943 recommended that he transfer to a limited service unit. In August 1944, an English truck sideswiped Jeffries, cutting his left hand and bruising his leg and chest. Jeffries concealed the scope of these injuries, as he wanted to serve, but his chain of command in the 366th Infantry Regiment noticed his inabilities and scheduled a board of officers to begin in January. Every witness stated Jeffries should not be in the Infantry, as Jeffries testified, "I feel that my services are useless." The board recommended his release to the 366th Infantry Regiment's commander, Lieutenant Colonel Howard D. Queen, a black officer. Colonel Queen approved the finding.

A GCM convened at 7:25 p.m. on February 28, 1945. The following officers made up the panel: Lieutenant Colonel Clement W. Crockett (FA), Major John J. Hazel (IN), Major John W. Halterman (IN), Major Nicholas E. Piccione (CE), Major Rocco F. Meconi (FA), Captain Vernon C. Might (IN), Captain Lester H. Brownlee (FA), First Lieutenant Frederick M. Coles (IN) and Second Lieutenant Claude M. Richardson, Jr. (FA.) Captain Howard F. Luther (IN) sat as the Trial Judge Advocate. He was assisted by First Lieutenant Frederick E. Bentley (IN.) Captain Clifford R. Moore (FA) served as the Defense Counsel; his assistant was Second Lieutenant Eldrich N. Hammond (QM.) Major Halterman had previously served on a jury that resulted in a death sentence; Captain Brownlee and Second Lieutenant Richardson were black.[1]

Private Jeffries pleaded not guilty to murder, a violation of the 92nd Article of War, and not guilty to six specifications of assault, violations of the 93rd Article of War.[2] He elected not to take the witness stand. Witnesses positively identified him as the shooter. The jury voted to convict and unanimously voted to sentence Private Jeffries to be hanged. Lieutenant Colonel Alonzo G. Ferguson, a black officer who had replaced Colonel Queen in mid-December 1944, approved the findings.

The Mediterranean Theater Staff Judge Advocate reviewed the record of trial on April 8, 1945. He concluded that no direct evidence showed that the murder weapon was a rifle, but that there were no serious errors in the conduct of the trial. He ended with, "There are no mitigating or extenuating circumstances."

On April 21, 1945, General Joseph T. McNarney, Commander of the MTO, signed the confirmation order in the case of Private Charles H. Jeffries. He withheld the order designating the time and location for the execution. On May 2, 1945, a Board of Review from the Branch Office of The Adjutant General with the MTO reviewed the case and found that the record of trial was legally sufficient. The MTO published General Court-Martial Orders Number 94 on June 22, 1945; the execution would occur at Aversa, Italy on July 5, 1945. The day prior, Captain Glenn A. Waser, commander of the PBS Garrison Stockade Number 1, read General Court-Martial Orders Number 94 to General Prisoner Jeffries and asked him if he had anything to say or request. Jeffries had nothing to say; he received a fresh change of clothes and moved to a new cell that was under a 24-hour deathwatch. Chaplain Douglas Hall remained with the prisoner during the day. At 8:10 a.m. on July 5, 1945, with five Army officers and three Navy Chief Petty Officers as official witnesses, the trap door dropped, sending Charles Jeffries to his death. At 8:23 a.m., Captain George R. Lee certified that Jeffries was dead.

The War Department sent a telegram to an aunt of Charles Jeffries on July 16, 1945, informing her that her nephew had died in Italy on July 5, 1945 of "judicial strangulation" and that he died in a non-battle status, due to his own misconduct. A second letter, dated August 18, 1945 to the aunt, mentioned that her nephew had been convicted of murder and executed.

Soldiers initially interred Charles H. Jeffries at the U.S. Military Cemetery at Naples, in the General Prisoner plot in Grave 2-20. Exhumed in 1949, he now is buried at the American Military Cemetery at Oise-Aisne in Plot E. His remains are in Row 4, Grave 78.[3]

> "Although no witness testified that he saw accused actually fire the first shot, the Board of Review believes that competent, substantial evidence establishes beyond any doubt that the accused fired the shot which caused Corporal Broussard's death."

## 88 Private Tom E. Gordon
34091950
3251st Quartermaster Service Company
**Absent Without Official Leave,**
**Assault and Murder**
Hanged on July 10, 1945

It was not usual for the Trial Judge Advocate, nine days after obtaining a conviction and a sentence of death against an accused, to write a letter to a lieutenant general requesting clemency in the case, but that is exactly what happened in the case of Private Tom Gordon. On February 22, 1945, First Lieutenant John E. Walsh, JAG, wrote the following to the Commanding General of the Seventh Army, Lieutenant General Alexander M. Patch:

> "The evidence adequately proves all of the specifications and charges and under such a set of facts the court was probably justified in imposing the death penalty. However, in view of the low standard of mentality of the accused and the question as to the sobriety of the accused at the time the offenses were committed, there is some doubt as to whether or not a full intent existed at the time the offenses were committed. It is believed by the undersigned that the interests of military justice will be served if the reviewing authority, in his discretion, recommends commutation of the sentence to life imprisonment. I therefore recommend leniency in this case and request a recommendation by the reviewing authority that the death penalty imposed herein be commuted to life imprisonment."

That Tom Gordon had been drinking was never in dispute. About 1:30 a.m. on November 12, 1944, he walked into his barracks, after a night of drinking, and proceeded to make a lot of noise, yelling and cursing. Among other things, Gordon yelled, "I wish I had a pistol; I'd kill all of these rotten mother-fuckers." Then Private Gordon added, "I'm going to kill the first son of a bitch that raises hell with me, and I bet it will be Broussard." Unfortunately, Private Gordon did not have a pistol; he had a Springfield Model 1903 rifle. No one else in the room was armed. Moments later two shots rang out; Corporal Laurence Broussard lay

dying and Private Willie Best was shot through the thigh. The certificate of death said that Broussard died at 7:10 a.m. on November 18, 1944 and that the cause of death had been the gunshot wound he received six days earlier; it had cut part of his pancreas and passed through his left kidney.

A GCM met at Lunéville, France at 9:00 a.m. on February 13, 1945.[1] Private Gordon pleaded not guilty to one charge of murder, a violation of the 92nd Article of War, one charge of assault, a violation of the 93rd Article of War, and one charge of absent without leave, a violation of the 61st Article of War.[2] A witness for the defense stated that an hour before the incident he had been drinking with Gordon; Gordon was "drunk and staggering"; his talk did not make sense; and that when he left, Private Gordon was lying across a weapons carrier vehicle. First Sergeant Otto McQueen testified that the accused had been drinking, but his speech was clear and he knew what he was doing. Major Alfred O. Ludwig gave Private Gordon a psychiatric evaluation and found that he had a mental age of about nine years; Ludwig stated that the accused knew the difference between right and wrong and was not a "moron." Private Gordon elected to make an unsworn statement at the trial. He said he received a pass, went to three bars and could not remember anything about the night until he woke up on November 13, went to the MPs, who then told him he had shot somebody. The jury did not buy his defense and voted to convict him of murder. They unanimously voted to sentence Private Tom Gordon to be hanged by the neck until dead.

Private Tom Gordon, a black soldier, was born on March 7, 1915 in Greenville, South Carolina. He left school at age thirteen and became a truck driver making $13 a week. He liked hunting and fishing; his religion was Baptist. In the Army, Tom Gordon had been overseas for thirty months and had been a dockworker for much of the time – and unfortunately had been racking up trouble. A Summary Court-Martial convicted him on October 1, 1943 for being off-limits in the street and for resisting arrest. Nineteen days later, a second Summary Court-Martial convicted him for entering an off-limits house of prostitution at 26 *Rue de Nail* in Oran, Algeria sentenced him to thirty days of restriction. On December 9, 1943, a third Summary Court-Martial slammed him for wrongfully entering 26 *Rue de Nail* a second time and gave him another thirty days restriction. Obviously, Private Gordon liked something at this location. A Special Court-Martial later convicted him for being absent without leave from March 8-25, 1944 and sentenced him to six months confinement at hard labor. Private Gordon went to the hospital May 7 to June 13, 1944 for a hernia that had been caused the previous November, while he was lifting heavy crates at the port.

On March 30, 1945, the Staff Judge Advocate for the Seventh Army reviewed the case file. He found no significant errors and noted that the Trial Judge Advocate had recommended clemency, shortly after the trial. However, Colonel Pinckney G. McElwee recommended no clemency to Lieutenant General Patch. Colonel McElwee did state:

"In the present case there are some mitigating circumstances, namely that a colored soldier of low mentality, though not drunk, under the stimulus of liquor 'ran amuck in his barracks.'"

Lieutenant General Alexander M. Patch, Commander Seventh Army, approved the sentence of death in the case of Private Tom Gordon on April 3, 1945 and forwarded the record of trial up the chain of command. General Dwight D. Eisenhower signed the order confirming the sentence for Private Tom Gordon on May 6, 1945. Days earlier, Private Gordon wrote the Supreme Commander a letter, stating he did not remember what had happened and requested a pardon. General Eisenhower withheld the order directing the time and place of execution. Board of Review Number 1 of the Branch Office of The JAG with the ETO took the case up for review on June 20, 1945. Judge Advocates Riter, Burrow and Stevens stated that:

"Although no witness testified that he saw accused actually fire the first shot, the Board of Review believes that competent, substantial evidence establishes beyond any doubt that the accused fired the shot which caused Corporal Broussard's death."

Meanwhile, other JAGs were weighing in on First Lieutenant Walsh's recommendation for clemency. Captain Donald K. Carroll added:

"No doubt appears to exist that accused had been drinking, and I feel that the liquor had much to do with his crimes. It no doubt helped to make him 'mean' and put him in a killing mood, but he seems to have been in sufficient control of his facilities to give the impression to the prosecution witnesses that he was not drunk."

However, Colonel Franklin Riter hand-wrote his opinion on the document:

"I do not recommend any consideration of clemency. It was a cold-blooded killing. I am satisfied the accused knew exactly what he was doing."

On June 29, 1945, the ETO published General Court-Martial Orders Number 235. Major General Thomas B. Larkin – by command of General Eisenhower – directed that the execution be carried out at the Loire DTC on July 10, 1945. On July 2, 1945, General Omar Bradley signed a telegram to the War Department stating that the date of execution for Private Tom Gordon would occur on July 10, 1945. At 2:00 p.m. on July 9, 1945, Captain Henry H. Kalter, a medical officer, examined the condemned man and found him to be in excellent physical and mental condition. Master Sergeant John C. Woods drove an Army flatbed truck to a ravine just outside the northwest corner of the Loire DTC. Woods, engineers and a prisoner detail removed the portable scaffold from the truck and set it up just outside the barbed wire fence. He tested the trap door that afternoon and the following morning.

The morning of July 10, 1945 was overcast and cool; a light rain fell on Le Mans. At 10:45 a.m., Lieutenant Colonel Henry L. Peck, now Executive Officer – formerly Commandant – Loire DTC, gathered five authorized witnesses and sixteen authorized spectators at the site of the gallows; now that the war was over there seemed to be fewer attendees at the executions. Peck briefed them on the proper conduct at the event and read General Court-Martial Orders Number 235; then the attendees moved ten to twenty paces from the gallows. At 10:59 a.m., a command and reconnaissance car, ½-ton, 4x4 halted thirty-five yards from the scaffold. Out stepped General Prisoner Gordon.

The condemned man quickly joined a procession that marched toward the scaffold. Peck led the way, followed by Chaplain James F. Donald, the prisoner, guards Tech Sergeant Frank Landi, Sergeant Alfonso Girvalo and Tech Sergeant Vincent J. Martino. The recorder, First Lieutenant Lawrence Slon brought up the rear of the column. The procession reached the foot of the gallows at 11:00 a.m. Lieutenant Colonel Peck and First Lieutenant Donald ascended the steps, while the guards bound Gordon's hands behind his back, assisted him up the steps and positioned him on top of the trap door. The executioner's assistant then bound the prisoner's ankles. Lieutenant Colonel Peck then asked the prisoner if he had any last statements. Gordon replied, "Thank you for everything you have done." Peck replied, "The Lord have mercy on you." Chaplain Donald then asked Gordon the same question to which he replied: "Will you read the 51st Psalm to me?"

The Chaplain started reading the 51st Psalm, while the executioner adjusted the hood and noose at 11:02 a.m. Thirty seconds later, Lieutenant Colonel Peck gave a silent signal to the Master Sergeant John C. Woods, who cut the rope, which released the weight and actuated the trap. Everything worked well; the condemned man made no motion or sound. At 11:18 a.m., Peck directed that Lieutenant Colonel Arthur J. Gavigan, Captain Daniel Thaw and Captain Henry H. Kalter examine the body. They did, and promptly declared that the prisoner was officially dead – the cause of death was judicial asphyxis. Peck then dismissed the formation. Woods cut the rope and removed the body from the lower part of the gallows. Captain Hardy C. Derx signed for the body and removed it for later interment. The official report stated that twenty-five men of Company I of the 156th Infantry Regiment, under the immediate command of First Lieutenant Charles W. Fritz, guarded the site efficiently.

On July 20, 1945, the War Department sent a telegram to Tom Gordon's mother, stating that her son had died at the Loire DTC in France on July 10, 1945 in a non-battle status, due to his own misconduct. The communication stated that the cause of death was judicial axphyxiation. The Army initially buried Private Gordon at the U.S. Military Cemetery at Marigny on July 12, 1945 at 3:00 p.m. He was buried in Field GP (Z), Row 2 in Grave 33. At that time, over his grave stood a cross. To his left, in Grave 32, lay Willie P. Johnson. Tom E. Gordon was exhumed in 1949 and reinterred at the American Military Cemetery at Oise-Aisne in Plot E. His remains are in Row 1, Grave 10.[3]

*"True, human life seems cheap when there is a war on, but it can never be so cheap that the nearest of kin of the accused person should be denied the right to move heaven and earth to obtain a reprieve or a commutation."*

## 89      Private Robert Wray
34461589
3299th Quartermaster Service Company
**Murder**
Hanged on August 20, 1945

There was no doubt that Private Robert Wray shot and killed Private First Class Billy Betts on December 17, 1944 at the "Café Moderne" in Golbey, France – a suburb of Épinal. The bullet entered the front of Private Betts' neck and exited the rear left shoulder; he was dead on arrival. What was at issue was exactly what went on in the bar before the shooting, which was complicated, in that some of the soldiers were black – including the perpetrator, some were white – including the victim, and some were Puerto Ricans, speaking Spanish. The witness statements varied as to what was said and done and that was only those observers who remained in the café; other potential witnesses skedaddled out the door with the accused, never to be seen again.

Private First Class Charles Carey, a white soldier, later stated that he heard someone in the café say, "Don't anyone move or I'll shoot." Carey also said that he saw a white soldier walk toward a "colored" soldier, when a shot was fired. Carey said that the "colored" soldier had a gun in his hand. The "colored" soldier then left the establishment. Sergeant Ismael Torres, a Puerto Rican in the Sixty-fifth Infantry Regiment, later stated he saw a "colored" soldier and a white soldier wrestling in the corner of the room and the "colored" soldier had a pistol in his hand that looked like a German P-38. The white soldier escaped and ran out of the café and the soldier with the pistol slammed the door closed, turned around and yelled, "Everybody keep quiet, because I'm going to kill everybody here." Sergeant Torres continued that a second "colored" soldier then stood next to the trooper with the P-38. This unidentified trooper pulled out a revolver and pointed it at the crowd. A white soldier then started toward the black soldiers and the trooper with the P-38 fired a shot that felled him. According to Sergeant Torres, "The colored soldiers then opened the door and then ran away."

Sergeant Torres picked Private Robert Wray out of a small lineup of two soldiers. The non-commissioned officer recognized Wray by the scars on his face. Private First Class Victor Piechnik, a white soldier and a friend of the victim, later testified that accused came up to him in the café and asked for one-hundred *francs*. Piechnik stated that he replied, "I don't know you well enough to give you a hundred *francs*." Private First Class Piechnik went on to say that, the accused then reached for his hip and pulled out a ".45" and pointed it at him. Piechnik then stated he told Wray that he could have all the money and Piechnik left the café; outside he heard the shot. Robert Wray made a statement on December 23, 1944; he saw events a little differently. He stated had had borrowed the P-38 because earlier in the evening, some guys in the 424th Engineers had told him they were going to "whip my ass." At the bar, Wray stated that a white soldier started calling him a "nigger" so Wray hit him in the chest with his fist. The white soldier jumped up and hit Wray in return and an old-fashioned bar fight ensued. Another soldier grabbed Wray and someone else hit him in the head. Wray broke free from the soldier, pulled out his pistol and stated, "Don't come no further." As Wray was backing toward the door, a white soldier advanced to a yard away and Wray fired his pistol. He then returned to camp and gave the P-38 to the soldier, who had loaned it to him in the first place.

Robert Wray was born on March 27, 1921 in Shelby, North Carolina. He was inducted on November 7, 1942 at Fort Bragg, North Carolina. His company commander, Captain John J. Harkins (QM) described Wray's character and efficiency as "poor." However, Wray's section sergeant stated that the accused gave him no trouble and that his efficiency was good. A corporal in the section stated that Private Wray was always a good worker and was always courteous to superiors. In September 1943, a Summary Court-Martial convicted Wray of violating standing orders. Another Summary Court-Martial convicted him in December 1943 for going absent without leave. In January 1944, a third Summary Court-Martial convicted him of smuggling five gallons of cognac and other intoxicating liquor into the company. Finally, in July 1944, a fourth Summary Court-Martial convicted him another incident of absence without leave. Private Wray was single, with a fifteen-year-old brother at home and a married brother in the Navy. Medics diagnosed him in June 1944 with syphilis.

On March 22, 1945, Dr. Malcolm J. Mann conducted a psychiatric examination of Robert Wray. He found that the subject was illiterate and uneducated, but showed no sign of pre-existing mental illness. Dr. Mann concluded that Wray was sane and knew the difference between right and wrong. He also stated the Wray told him that on the night in question at the café, a white soldier had called him a "Nigger" and that he had then slapped the soldier, which resulted in everyone ganging up on him. The soldier that Wray had slapped then approached and Wray shot him with a P-38 pistol.

The GCM convened the next day at Lunéville, France. Private Wray pleaded not guilty to the charge of murder, a violation of the 92nd Article of War.[1] After being advised of his rights, Private Wray elected to take the stand. He changed his story and said that when he entered the café, a Puerto Rican soldier pulled out a .45, but Wray took it away from him. The Puerto Rican ran out the door, at which time everyone wanted to jump on Wray, so he pulled out the P-38 and shot the victim, as he approached Wray. In answer to a question, Wray stated that he thought the Puerto Rican, who had pulled the .45, was the same man that advanced toward him. In response to a question by a court member, if he was mad at the Puerto Rican, Wray answered, "If I pulled a gun on you, you would be mad at me, wouldn't you, Sir? If I was aiming to shoot you?" The jury did not buy his claim of self-defense and voted to convict Private Robert Wray. The jury then unanimously sentenced him to be hanged by the neck until dead.

On May 6, 1945, the Staff Judge Advocate of the Seventh Army reviewed the case file of the trial. Colonel Pinckney G. McElwee concluded that the findings were justified. He concluded by stating, "This type of person is of no value to the Army or society, and is in fact, dangerous to all with whom he is in contact." The Staff Judge Advocate for the ETO reviewed the case on June 19, 1945. Betts also concluded that the trial was complete and that the evidence justified the outcome. On June 26, 1945, General Omar N. Bradley, then in command of the ETO, signed the order confirming the sentence. General Bradley withheld issuing the order directing the time and place of execution. A Board of Review in the Branch Office of The JAG with the ETO examined the case on August 3, 1945. Judge Advocates Sleeper, Sherman and Dewey found the record of trial sufficient to support the finding of guilty and the sentence of death. On August 11, 1945, the ETO published General Court-Martial Orders Number 319. It stated that Robert Wray would be executed on August 20, 1945 at the Loire DTC. On August 19, 1945, Master Sergeant John Woods drove an Army flatbed truck to a ravine just outside the northwest corner of the Loire DTC at Le Mans, removed the scaffold from the truck and set it up just outside the barbed wire fence. Woods tested the trap door twice.

August 20, 1945 was overcast and cool; a light northeasterly wind was blowing. At 10:48 a.m. Lieutenant Colonel Henry L. Peck, the Executive Officer of the Loire DTC, gathered five authorized witnesses and ten authorized spectators at the site of the gallows. Four of the spectators were General Prisoners. Peck briefed them on the proper conduct at the event and read General Court-Martial Orders Number 319; the attendees formed ten to twenty paces from the scaffold. The General Prisoners, under guard, formed in a single rank, twenty paces behind the spectators. At 10:59 a.m., a command and reconnaissance car, ½-ton, 4x4 halted thirty-five yards from the scaffold. Out stepped General Prisoner Robert Wray, who quickly joined a procession that marched toward the gallows. Peck led the way, followed by Chaplain Charles O. Dutton, the prisoner, guards Sergeant Russell E. Boyle, Sergeant Alfonso Girvalo and Tech Sergeant Vincent J. Martino. The recorder, First Lieutenant Lawrence Slon, brought up the rear of the column, which reached the foot of the gallows at 11:00 a.m. Peck and Dutton ascended the steps, while the guards bound Wray's hands behind his back, assisted the condemned man up the steps and positioned him on top of the trap door. The executioner's assistant then bound the prisoner's ankles at 11:01 a.m. Lieutenant Colonel Peck then asked the prisoner if he had any last statements. Robert Wray replied, "Thank you for what you have done," to which Peck then replied, "May the Lord have mercy on you." Chaplain Dutton then asked the condemned man the same question, but Wray said nothing. Lieutenant Colonel Peck then said, "Let us pray."

The Chaplain started intoning a prayer, as Woods adjusted the hood and noose at 11:02 a.m. Thirty seconds later Lieutenant Colonel Peck gave a silent signal to the executioner, Master Sergeant John C. Woods, who cut the rope, which released the weight and actuated the trap. Everything worked well; as the report stated:

> "The body hung suspended with no sounds but a slight muscular action of the shoulders and knees and a slight swaying motion that lasted for three to four minutes."

At 11:17 a.m., Lieutenant Colonel Peck directed that Captain Daniel Thaw, Captain Theodore E. McCabe and Captain Forrest R. LaFollette examine the body. Two minutes later, they declared that the prisoner was officially dead; they would later write that the cause of death was judicial asphyxis. Peck then dismissed the formation. Woods cut the rope and removed the body from the lower part of the scaffold. First Lieutenant Milliard R. Jones signed for the body and removed it for later interment. The official report stated that twenty-five men of Company I of the 156th Infantry Regiment, under the immediate command of First Lieutenant Frank K. Kozoil, had efficiently guarded the site.

On September 6, 1945, The Adjutant General's Office sent a telegram to the mother of Robert Wray, stating that her son had died at the Loire DTC in France on August 20, 1945 in a non-battle status due to his own misconduct. The communication stated that the cause of death was judicial axphyxiation. The Army originally buried Robert Wray at the U.S. Military Cemetery at Marigny in Plot Z in Grave 2-34, exhumed his remains and reinterred them in 1949 at the American Military Cemetery at Oise-Aisne in Plot E. They rest in Row 4, Grave 75.[2]

Private First Class Billy Betts, of the 568th Railhead Company, entered the Army from California. He is buried among the honored dead at the Épinal Military Cemetery at Épinal, France. It is located in Plot B, Row 17 and Grave 72.

• • •

On September 11, 1945, Wray's mother wrote to Major General Edward F. Witsell at the War Department. She complained that she had never received detailed information on her son's situation and that the brief information contained in the War Department's telegram was inadequate, and by that time, did not allow her to ask for a reprieve. As she stated in her letter:

"True, human life seems cheap when there is a war on, but it can never be so cheap that the nearest of kin of the accused person should be denied the right to move heaven and earth to obtain a reprieve or a commutation."

*"In fairness to the accused and in vindication of the processes of military justice, I recommend that he be subjected to a careful psychiatric examination."*

*"OK for exam but unless insane I think they ought to hang him."*

*"I'm no doctor, but I don't think he's sane."*

## 90 Private Henry C. Philpot
39080069

234th Replacement Company,
    90th Replacement Battalion
**Murder**
September 10, 1945

The crime was straightforward. On March 30, 1945, at Bad Neuenahr, Germany, Private Henry Philpot was drunk in the mess hall. His company commander told Second Lieutenant John B. Platt, the Officer of the Day, to arrest Philpot and take him to the stockade. As the lieutenant attempted to do this, Private Philpot pointed his M1 rifle at the officer and fired a single round that severed the lieutenant's spine and killed him. The Sergeant of the Guard immediately clubbed Philpot over the head, rendering him unconscious, and authorities hauled him to jail. Several witnesses were on hand; the facts were not debatable. Whether or not Henry Philpot was insane was another matter.

Henry Philpot was born in Redding, California on June 22, 1917. An "American Indian," he was married in 1936, but – according to him – after catching his wife cheating and catching gonorrhea and syphilis from her, he gave her the boot and separated in 1938. He quit high school after one year and became a logger. Philpot was inducted on May 7, 1941 at Sacramento, California. Described as stocky, he stood 5'7 ⅜" tall and weighed 155 pounds. In June 1943, a GCM convicted him of drunkenness. A Summary Court-Martial, in October 1944, convicted Philpot of disrespect to an officer; two months later, a Special Court-Martial convicted him of being absent without leave and for drunk and disorderly.

Brigadier General Ewart G. Plank determined on April 10, 1945 that a GCM would handle the case. It convened at Marburg, Germany at 9:50 a.m. on April 23, 1945.[1] Private Henry C. Philpot pleaded not guilty to the charge of murder, a violation of the 92nd Article of War.[2] Witnesses described what happened; no witnesses appeared on behalf of the accused. After his rights were explained to him, Private Philpot elected to take the stand, saying that he had been under the influence of alcohol and was unable to give a clear account of what happened. He did not know if he pulled the trigger. The court voted to convict him of murder and unanimously voted to sentence him to death. Their work done, the court adjourned at 2:50 p.m. on April 23, 1945 – just four hours after the start of the proceedings.

The Staff Judge Advocate in the Advance Section, Colonel Edward A. Levy, reviewed the case on April 7, 1945 and found no serious irregularities in the trial documents. Brigadier General Ewart G. Plank, the commander of the Advance Section of the Communications Zone, approved the sentence on May 10, 1945 and forwarded the record of trial. General Dwight D. Eisenhower signed the order confirming the sentence on June 7, 1945, but withheld the order directing the execution of the sentence.

On June 26, the Board of Review Number 1 of the Branch Office of The JAG with the ETO reviewed the case. Judge Advocates Riter, Burrow and Stevens found no major errors or omissions in the legal process, but all three commented on the accused. Captain Donald K. Carroll, a junior JAG in the office, started the ball rolling by writing a memo that included, "Assuming sincerity in his testimony, accused seems to me to be a psychopath of some sort …" Major Edward L. Stevens and Colonel Franklin Riter concurred. Lieutenant Colonel William F. Burrow added, "OK for exam but unless insane I think they ought to hang him."

Brigadier General Edwin C. McNeil, the chief of the Branch Office of The JAG with the ETO, added a cover memo to summarize the board's thoughts:

"Assuming the accused was and is of normal mentality, there is not a shadow of excuse to be offered in palliation of his crime. However, his testimony is a strange conglomeration of statements of fact and explanations of his emotional life. It is clearly indicative that he possesses some degree of education, but inherently bespeaks him as 'a man of very strange sensitivities.' In fairness to the accused and in vindication of the processes of military justice, I recommend that he be subjected to a careful psychiatric examination."

A Board of Officers met at the 235th General Hospital, and examined the accused. Philpot told them of an additional court-martial for drunkenness he had in 1942. He mentioned that he had spent six months in the stockade in England for being drunk and disorderly. He told the board that he had not lived with his father and mother, both half-blood American Indians, because they both drank heavily. He ran away from home at age sixteen, because his aunt would get drunk and beat him. Philpot finished his first year of high school. He told them of the dream in which he was "hung." Major Lester W. Flake, the commander of the Delta DTC in which the accused was confined, spoke to the board. He said that Philpot was not in complete control of his faculties. When asked if he felt the accused was crazy, Major Flake responded, "I'm no doctor, but I don't think he's sane."

The board, however, declared that Private Philpot was sane and had been sane at the time of the incident; he was also able to distinguish right from wrong. That set the final legal ball rolling and on August 30, 1945 the U.S. Forces, European Theater published General Court-Martial Orders Number 365. In it, Lieutenant General Walter Bedell Smith, the Chief of Staff – acting by command of General Eisenhower – directed that the execution occur on September 10, 1945 at the Loire DTC. An NCO escorted General Prisoner Philpot from the Delta DTC – outside Marseilles – to Le Mans on September 6, 1945.

On September 9, 1945, Master Sergeant John C. Woods drove an Army flatbed truck to a ravine outside the northwest corner of the Loire DTC at Le Mans and removed the potable scaffold from the truck, setting it up just outside the barbed wire fence. Woods tested the trap door that afternoon and the following morning. At about the same time, Lieutenant Colonel Henry L. Peck met with the condemned man and read him the General Court-Martial Order in its entirety. At approximately 8:00 p.m., Captain Daniel Thaw examined the prisoner and found him to be in excellent physical and mental condition.

September 10, 1945 at Le Mans was clear, bright, warm and sunny; summer was ending on a high note, but not for Henry Philpot. He had experienced a bad dream "about getting hung." Today that nightmare would come true. At 10:49 a.m., Lieutenant Colonel Peck, the Executive Officer of the center, gathered the authorized witnesses and spectators at the gallows site; six of the latter were General Prisoners. Peck briefed them on the proper conduct expected at the event and read General Court-Martial Orders Number 365 in its entirety; the attendees stood ten to twenty paces from the gallows. The six General Prisoners, under guard, formed in a single rank, twenty paces behind the spectators.

At 10:59 a.m., a command and reconnaissance car, ½-ton, 4x4 halted thirty-five yards from the gallows. Out stepped General Prisoner Henry C. Philpot, who joined a procession that marched toward the scaffold. Peck led the way, followed by Chaplain Charles O. Dutton, the prisoner, guards Sergeant Russell E. Boyle, Sergeant Alfonso Girvalo and Tech Sergeant Vincent J. Martino, who carried the brace-board, followed by the recorder, First Lieutenant Lawrence Slon; it reached the foot of the scaffold at 11:00 a.m. Peck and Dutton ascended the steps, while the guards bound Philpot's hands behind his back, assisted him up the steps and positioned him on top of the trap door. The executioner's assistant then bound the prisoner's ankles at 11:01 a.m. Lieutenant Colonel Peck asked the prisoner if he had any last statements. Henry Philpot replied, "I guess it's too late to say I am sorry, but I am sorry." The Chaplain then asked the condemned man the same question and Philpot replied, "I hope that the Lord will forgive me for my sins."

Chaplain Dutton started intoning a prayer and the executioner adjusted the hood and noose at 11:02 a.m. Thirty seconds later, Peck gave a silent signal to Master Sergeant John C. Woods, who cut the rope that released the weight and dropped the trap door. Everything worked well. At 11:17 a.m., Peck directed that Captain Daniel Thaw, Captain Theodore E. McCabe and Captain Forrest R. LaFollette examine the body. Two minutes later, they declared that the prisoner was officially dead and that the cause of death was judicial asphyxis. Peck then dismissed the formation. Master Sergeant Woods cut the rope and removed the body from the lower part of the gallows. Captain Hardy C. Derx signed for the body and removed it for later interment. The official report stated that twenty-five men of Company I of the 156th Infantry Regiment, under command of First Lieutenant Francis O. Center, had efficiently guarded the site. At the messhall, the cooks heard the trap door slam open.

Chaplain Dutton wrote the family on September 12, 1945. The War Department sent a telegram on September 25, 1945 to the half-brother of Henry Philpot stating that he had died on September 10, 1945 at the Loire DTC due to his own misconduct. It stated that the cause of death was judicial axphyxiation. The Army originally buried Henry C. Philpot at the U.S. Military Cemetery at Marigny in Plot Z in Grave 2-35. Officials exhumed his remains and reinterred them in 1949. They rest at in the American Military Cemetery at Oise-Aisne in Plot E, Grave 89 in Row 4.[3]

Second Lieutenant John B. Platt, who was from Wisconsin, is buried among the honored dead at the Ardennes American Cemetery at Neupre, Belgium. His remains are in Plot R, Row 32 in Grave 12.

## 91 Private Charles M. Robinson

38164425

667th Quartermaster Truck Company,
Sixty-Sixth Infantry Division

**Murder**

Hanged on September 28, 1945

On March 6, 1944, the Headquarters of the ETO, under the direction of General Dwight D. Eisenhower promulgated a policy designed to have significant impact on military justice in the theater by introducing an additional element of fairness. It directed that whenever practicable, one or more "Negro officers" would be detailed as members of certain courts-martial – that tried serious, violent crimes – before which were to be tried "Negro personnel." Courts-martial that dealt with crimes involving "interracial sensibilities" also fell into this category.

The GCM of Private Charles M. Robinson was tailor-made for this directive. The offense was murder – obviously a violent crime; Robinson was black and the victim was a white French woman – one could make an argument that "interracial sensibilities" might be involved. The convening authority looked inside the division, looked throughout western France – where the division was operating – and even went to the Twelfth Army Group to find just one black officer to sit on the court-martial. When none was deemed available, the trial occurred anyway.

The crime was as old as mankind. Charles Robinson's French girlfriend came to camp at Messac – fifteen miles southwest of Rennes – on the evening of March 31, 1945, entered the tent in which Robinson lived, jumped into bed with another soldier named "Jimmy" and remained with him until the next morning. She was a real *Minnie the Moocher*, as Cab Calloway would say. Robinson went out on a convoy the next morning and returned to camp in the afternoon. A witness saw him talking with the girlfriend – prosecutors would later establish that the victim had been a hooker at the "Café Des Sport" in Rennes. The joint wasn't exactly the "cat's meow." The woman was friendly, but Robinson appeared very angry and told her to "go and fetch Jimmy." As she turned, not more than four or five feet from the accused, he pulled out a .45 pistol and shot her one time. The bullet penetrated her head above the right ear, exited above the left ear and she dropped dead. One witness saw Robinson pull the trigger, while another witness saw him standing over the body looking at it, and saw him conceal the pistol under

his jacket. Soldiers found the weapon two hours later in a mud hole, ninety feet from the incident; a witness would testify that he saw the accused near the hole. Other witnesses saw the accused walking quickly through the company area. Fifteen minutes later he appeared in a tent; the acting company commander was playing a piano inside, with his back to the opening, and was unaware of Robinson's presence, but others saw him.

Charles M. Robinson was born on April 4, 1923 in Houston, Texas. He was inducted on July 2, 1942 at Fort Sam Houston, Texas and wound up in the segregated, all-black 667th Quartermaster Truck Company. He was Protestant, had never been married, stood 5'8" tall and weighed 150 pounds. Private Robinson had attended eight years of grammar school and two years of high school; he then became a truck driver and also worked as a cement finisher. As a youth, he broke his right arm; he had also been hit on the head with a baseball bat. Dental records showed he was missing six upper teeth. On June 3, 1943, he sprained his ankle. Robinson's mother and father were still married; he had one sister and two brothers. He scored a 68 on the Army General Classification Test, placing him in Category V. Private Robinson had a previous Special Court-Martial conviction, but later rose to Technician Fifth Grade, before being busted again. His company commander stated that his leadership was very poor and he had a tendency to lie; his military fitness was poor, attitude was poor and his general suitability as a soldier was poor. The commander wrote, "Soldier shows a tendency to ignore existing regulations, shows no enthusiasm to work and has a 'smart aleck' attitude."

After the investigation, Major General Herman F. Kramer – the commander of the Sixty-Sixth Infantry Division – decided that a GCM was the appropriate venue to decide the case. On April 12, 1945, a neuro-psychiatric examination of Charles M. Robinson revealed some other information. Major Sidney L. Sands, the Sixty-Sixth Infantry Division Neuropsychiatrist, found that Robinson's father had been unemployed for many years due to a head injury suffered in World War I and that his mother was chronically ill due to high blood pressure. Robinson persistently denied his guilt in the killing to the doctor, stating that the witnesses had misidentified him and that he was not at the scene of the crime. Dr. Sands concluded that Private Robinson was sane and could assist in his defense.

Meanwhile, the Sixty-Sixth Infantry Division was attempting to find a "Negro officer" to sit on the jury. Failing to locate any, the Division Staff Judge Advocate wrote the Twelfth Army Group Judge Advocate, Colonel C.B. Mickelwait for help. Colonel Mickelwait replied, stating that the division had complied with the spirit, as well as the letter, of the policy concerning ensuring that there was a "Negro" officer on the panel of all serious courts-martial. He wrote:

"It is my view that it is not the purpose of the subject letter to obstruct the expeditious administration of military justice, and that, because of the present tactical situation, the delay which would be caused by further efforts on your part to secure Negro officers for the court in the case would obstruct such administration to an extent which would be incompatible with the underlying purpose of the enforcement of disciplinary measures in such cases."

The GCM convened – without any minority juror on the panel – at Ploërmel on April 18 and 19.[1] Private Charles M. Robinson pleaded not guilty to the charge of murder, a violation of the 92nd Article of War.[2] The defense presented a vigorous case and showed that one of the witnesses, another French woman, had identified the accused, but that he was the only person in the lineup. The shooting occurred at 3:15 p.m. Robinson was apprehended at 3:30 p.m., but another witness for the defense stated that Robinson had entered the company commander's tent at 3:10 p.m.

After being advised of his rights, Private Robinson elected to take the stand. He testified that he had returned from the convoy at 2:45 p.m., had drawn his Post Exchange rations, gone to his tent for ten minutes and then gone to the tent where the lieutenant was playing the piano and stayed there twenty to thirty-five minutes. Robinson went on to say that after he was arrested by the Military Police, he was taken to the scene of the crime, where the MPs struck him with their fists in the stomach and over the ear in an attempt to make him confess. He was taken to the French Gendarmes office where – according to Robinson – he was beaten again by the MPs. Robinson said he had not seen the victim in his tent on the night of March 31. He also stated that he had only seen her twice before and did not even know her name. A photograph of Robinson – which had been torn from a larger group photograph – had been found in the deceased's purse; he said that he did not know how she had come in possession of it, as it as it given it to the proprietress of the "Café Des Sport." He said that on the convoy mission he had carried a carbine and not a pistol and said he had

never owned the pistol that had been introduced as evidence. He denied shooting the victim and denied placing a pistol in a mud hole.

A witness for the prosecution said that at no time on the convoy had he seen Private Robinson with a carbine, but he did see a pistol in the waist of the accused's trousers, just before he and the accused saw the victim and another female. The same witness stated that he saw the accused near the mud hole after the shooting. A different witness stated on the stand that he saw the accuse raise the pistol, take aim, and fire. No witnesses could be found to corroborate the accused's story about sitting in the back of the tent, while the lieutenant was playing the piano. At the conclusion of the trial, the French woman, who had been with the victim for part of the afternoon, picked out the accused from a lineup of thirteen "similarly-dressed colored soldiers." The two MPs, who had apprehended the accused, denied striking or threatening him. The jury voted to convict Private Robinson of murder and unanimously voted to sentence him to hang by the neck until dead.

The Sixty-Sixth Infantry Division Staff Judge Advocate reviewed the trial transcript, concluding that the document showed that the evidence amply established – beyond a reasonable doubt – the guilt of the accused. He noted that many of the questions in the trial were leading and that the Trial Judge Advocate was perhaps "overzealous" in eliciting facts. The Staff Judge Advocate opined:

"Expediency also often requires the propounding of leading questions to colored witnesses, who generally either are evasive and reluctant, or too voluble, enthusiastic and unresponsive, having difficulty in finding language to express accurately their thoughts and knowledge, and who often misconceive the purpose of the question."

Major General Kramer approved the sentence and forwarded the record of trial up the chain of command on May 6, 1945. General Dwight D. Eisenhower signed the order confirming the sentence for Private Robinson on June 15, 1945. He withheld the order directing the execution of the sentence. On September 1, 1945, the Board of Review Number 2 in the Branch Office of The JAG with the ETO reviewed the case files. Judge Advocates Van Benschoten, Hepburn and Miller found no serious errors in the conduct of the trial. They did not comment on the lack of a black officer for the jury. On September 17, 1945, the U.S.

Forces, European Theater, published General Court-Martial Orders Number 416, setting the execution for General Prisoner Charles Robinson at the Loire DTC on September 28, 1945.

On September 27, 1945, Master Sergeant John Woods transported the venerable portable scaffold from the motor pool to a ravine just outside the northwest corner of the Loire DTC. Woods, engineers and a prisoner detail removed the gallows from the truck and set it up just outside the barbed wire fence. Woods would test the trap door twice.

The weather was clear, bright, warm and sunny on Friday, September 28, 1945; summer had changed to fall on the calendar, although not in the air. At 10:43 a.m., Lieutenant Colonel Henry L. Peck, now back in command of the training center, gathered seventeen authorized witnesses (and six General Prisoners) near the gallows. The war had ended and procedures were changing. Although the victim in this case had been French, no French officials were present. Peck briefed them on the proper conduct expected at the event and read General Court-Martial Orders Number 416 in its entirety; the witnesses then aligned themselves twenty paces from the gallows. The GPs, under guard, formed a single rank, twenty paces behind the witnesses; they still had a good view, which was the whole point of their attendance.

At 10:59 a.m., a command and reconnaissance car, ½-ton, 4x4 halted thirty-five yards from the scaffold. Out stepped Charles M. Robinson, who joined a procession that marched toward the gallows. Peck led the way followed by Chaplain Charles O. Dutton, the prisoner, guards Sergeant Cleon Seeber, Sergeant Alfonso Girvalo and Tech Sergeant Vincent J. Martino (one of the guards carried the brace-board.) First Lieutenant Lawrence Slon, brought up the rear of the column, which reached the foot of the gallows at 11:00 a.m. Peck and Dutton ascended the steps, while the guards bound Robinson's hands behind his back, assisted the condemned man up the steps and positioned him on the trap door. The executioner's assistant bound the prisoner's ankles at 11:01 a.m. Peck asked the prisoner if he had any last statements. Robinson replied, "All I can say, Sir, is that they are taking the life of an innocent man." Chaplain Dutton then asked the same question and Robinson responded, "I hope the Lord forgives and receives me." The Chaplain started intoning a prayer as Woods adjusted the hood and noose seconds later. Peck then gave a silent signal to Woods, who cut the rope, which released the weight and actuated the trap. Everything worked as planned. At 11:16 a.m., Lieutenant Colonel Peck directed that Major Melvin H. Blaurock, Captain

Daniel Thaw and Captain Forrest R. LaFollette examine the body. They did, and two minutes later declared that the prisoner to be officially dead of judicial asphyxis. Peck then dismissed the formation. Woods cut the rope and removed the body from the lower part of the gallows. Captain Hardy C. Derx signed for the body and removed it for later interment. Twenty-five men of Company I of the 156th Infantry Regiment, under the immediate command of First Lieutenant Richard H. Stetler, had efficiently guarded the site. As the recorder noted, "Each official performed his task in a highly efficient manner. The proceedings were conducted with dignity, solemnity, and military precision."

The War Department sent a telegram on October 9, 1945 to the mother and father of Charles Robinson, stating that he had died at the Loire DTC on September 28, 1945, due to his own misconduct. It stated that the cause of death was judicial axphyxiation. On November 30, 1945, Member of Congress Albert Thomas sent a note to Major General Edward F. Witsell asking for information concerning the case; this study did not find any reply sent to the Congressman.

Army personnel interred Charles M. Robinson at the U.S. Military Cemetery at Marigny in Plot Z in Grave 2-36. The Army reinterred the remains in 1949 and they now rest at the American Military Cemetery at Oise-Aisne in Plot E, in Grave 70 of Row 3.[3]

*"While a creditable combat record does not endow the individual with any special immunity, neglect to give it due weight is equally an injustice and an impairment of public respect for the Army's administration of military justice."*

*"His shooting of Martha Gary is inexplicable except that he was an Indian with too much liquor."*

## 92     Private First Class Blake W. Mariano
38011593

Company C, 191st Tank Battalion,
  Forty-Fifth Infantry Division
**Rape and Murder**
Hanged on October 10, 1945

The accused could not remember a thing, but five witnesses – including several Germans, who until just days before had been enemies – testified that Private First Class Blake W. Mariano had raped two women and killed a third. The incident happened on April 16, 1945 in Lauf, Germany, a town on the Pegnitz River in northern Bavaria. According to them, early that morning at least fourteen German civilians had found refuge in an air raid cellar of a castle, when American soldiers burst in. The accused, pointing his rifle, took one woman outside, where he raped her. Some twenty minutes later, the accused returned alone to the cellar and approached a forty-one-year-old woman, who stated she was Swedish. He motioned for her to undress; during that process he became angry and shot her – she died in the cellar several hours later. The accused then took a third woman outside the cellar and raped her.

Blake W. Mariano, a full-blooded Navajo Indian named *Hoska-Yith-Ela-Wood*, was born near Gallup, New Mexico on April 4, 1916. As a child, he attended a Navajo school for six years and had completed the third grade at the age of thirteen. Mariano had an Army General Classification Test score of 51 (deep within Class V), scored a mental age of eleven years on the Kent Emergency Scale. A medical board classified him as a "high grade moron." He was married with three children, but was later divorced. Before going into the Army, Mariano dug irrigation ditches. Mariano entered the service on March 8, 1941 at Santa Fe, New Mexico. He departed the United States to go overseas on August 6, 1942. His mother was living, as was a sister; his father was dead. He also had a wild side. In 1940, he caught gonorrhea; he contracted syphilis from a prostitute, while in Newcastle, England in January 1943. He caught another dose on October

28, 1943 from a French prostitute at Tlemcen, Algeria, while assigned to the 804th Tank Destroyer Battalion. Despite his shortcomings, Blake Mariano could fight – one of Patton's scrappers. In the 191st Tank Battalion at Anzio, he served as a gunner on a Sherman tank. Near Épinal, France, on September 23, 1944, shrapnel wounded him in the left hip.

An investigation began several days later and the finger of blame began pointing in the tank gunner's direction. On May 1, 1945, Mariano, after having been advised of his rights, made a sworn statement. In it, he explained that he was not carrying a weapon on the night of April 15, 1945, but after going into a cellar in Lauf – eight miles northeast of Nürnberg – he drank so much cognac that his mind went completely blank. He said his personal weapon was a Thompson, but he did not recall carrying it that on that night. Authorities did not formally arrest Mariano until May 8, 1945, by which time the Forty-Fifth Infantry Division was long gone from the Nürnberg area. Two days later a board of officers of the division met at Munich to assess the mental fitness of Private First Class Blake W. Mariano. Listening to numerous witnesses and the accused, the board determined that he was mentally balanced. He was very calm under enemy fire.

Division commander Major General Robert T. Frederick assessed the evidence and ordered that a GCM handle the case. One convened at Munich on May 25, 1945. Private First Class Blake Mariano pleaded not guilty to one charge of murder and two specifications of carnal knowledge, all violations of the 92nd Article of War.[1] After receiving a rights warning, Mariano elected to take the stand. He recalled going into a cellar filled with Polish and Russian people and said that while in the town he drank "very much" cognac and schnapps. He finished by stating that he could remember nothing else until the next morning (April 17) when he found himself in the turret of his tank. For the defense, a German physician testified that he had examined one of the rape victims on May 1 and in his opinion, she had never had sexual intercourse. That forced a modification to the first specification to change to committing an assault with the intent to rape. The prosecution introduced all witness testimony, the observations of a board of officers and the testimony of the accused's company commander, who had stated that Mariano was a calm soldier in combat, but when drinking, "he seems to go wild." A tank driver testified that when the accused starting drinking he would chase after women, "to get in their pants."

On May 26, 1945, the jury found Private First Class Mariano guilty of the charge and unanimously sentenced him to death by hanging. The Forty-Fifth Infantry Division Staff Judge Advocate reviewed the trial transcripts, as did Major General Frederick, who approved the sentence and forwarded the trial records up the chain of command. Meanwhile, a friend of Blake Mariano's mother wrote the Office of the Adjutant General, expressing deep concern. Mariano had written his mother earlier stating, "This dam people they told the Army I kill one woman and myself I didn't know about that ... even they told me I be hang." The wheels of justice continued to grind. General Dwight D. Eisenhower signed the order confirming the sentence of Blake W. Mariano on August 4, 1945. He did not direct the execution of sentence. On September 6, 1945, the Board of Review Number 3 of the Branch Office of The JAG with the European Theater reviewed the trial record. They found everything in order and stated that there were no serious errors in the conduct of the trial. Then Brigadier General Edwin C. McNeil, Assistant JAG, weighed in with two points in support for his recommendation that General Eisenhower commute the death sentence. McNeil quoted a July 21, 1945 War Department letter on the subject of courts-martial, which read:

"While a creditable combat record does not endow the individual with any special immunity, neglect to give it due weight is equally an injustice and an impairment of public respect for the Army's administration of military justice."

Then Brigadier General McNeil stopped quoting regulations and stated his personal reasons for recommending that Eisenhower commute Mariano's death sentence to life imprisonment: "His shooting of Martha Gary is inexplicable except that he was an Indian with too much liquor."

However, General Eisenhower did not change his mind. In a memo back to Brigadier General McNeil it was noted that:

"The Theater Commander gave personal consideration to this matter on 28 September 1945 and directed that the Sentence as confirmed and approved be carried into execution."

So, on October 6, 1945, the United States Forces, European Theater issued General Court-Martial Orders Number 458, stating that General Prisoner Blake W. Mariano would be hanged by the neck until dead on October 10, 1945 at the Loire DTC. On October 8, 1945, Brigadier General R.B. Lovett, the Adjutant General at the theater, signed a set of orders titled "Designation of Officer Courier." In them, he tasked Second Lieutenant Robert D. Aubry with the following:

"You are hereby designated as officer courier for the purpose of delivering the sealed envelopes [CZ-13672] identified on the reverse side hereof to the Adjutant General at the Headquarters specified [Commandant, Loire DTC, Le Mans, France.] All documents entrusted to you as officer courier will be kept in your personal custody at all times until such documents are delivered to the Adjutant General of the addressee or as authorized in paragraph 3, below. It is your direct responsibility to take all steps necessary to safeguard the documents in your custody and to prevent any unauthorized person from possession thereof of access thereto at any time."

On October 9, 1945, Master Sergeant John Woods drove the now-familiar Army execution truck to a ravine outside the Loire DTC at Le Mans. A prisoner detail, under Woods' watchful eye, removed the scaffold from the truck and set it up just outside the barbed wire fence. Woods tested the trap door that afternoon.

The weather was clear, bright and sunny on the morning of October 10, as fall was finally hitting Le Mans. At 10:39 a.m., Lieutenant Colonel Henry L. Peck gathered five witnesses and eight spectators at the ravine, where the gallows was located. Six of the spectators were General Prisoners. Although two of the victims in this case had been German, no persons from that defeated nation were present; this was an all-American event. Peck briefed the personnel on the proper conduct expected at the event and read General Court-Martial Orders Number 458 in its entirety; the witnesses, dressed in Class B uniforms less web equipment, then aligned themselves twenty yards from the gallows; the spectators stood ten yards behind them. The GPs, under guard, formed in a single rank, twenty yards behind the spectators; at fifty yards from the gallows, the GPs could not hear what was being said, but still had a good view – which would serve as a deterrent factor for their own conduct.

At 10:59 a.m., a command and reconnaissance car, ½-ton, 4x4 halted thirty-five yards from the gallows. Out stepped General Prisoner Blake W. Mariano, who joined a procession that marched toward the scaffold. Lieutenant Colonel Peck led the way; he was followed by Chaplain Charles O. Dutton, the condemned, guards Sergeant Russell E. Boyle, Sergeant Alfonso Girvalo and Sergeant Howard C. Jones. The recorder, First Lieutenant Lawrence Slon, brought up the rear of the column, which reached the foot of the gallows at 11:01 a.m. Peck and Dutton ascended the steps, while the guards bound Mariano's hands behind his back, assisted him up the steps and positioned him on top of the trap door. The executioner's assistant then bound the prisoner's ankles at 11:02 a.m. Peck finally asked the prisoner if he had any last statements. Mariano shook his head no.

The Chaplain then asked the condemned man the same question and again Mariano shook his head negatively. Chaplain Dutton began intoning a prayer and the black hood and noose were adjusted a few seconds later. Peck gave a silent signal to Woods, who released the trap door. Everything worked as planned. However, one General Prisoner became sick; MPs allowed him to sit down. The proceedings continued. At 11:19 a.m., Peck directed Major Melvin H. Blaurock, Captain Theodore E. McCabe and Captain Forrest R. LaFollette to examine the body. They did and two minutes later emerged from under the gallows, assumed their original positions and declared that the prisoner was officially dead; they would later write that the cause of death was judicial asphyxis and the time of death was 11:21.5 a.m.

Lieutenant Colonel Peck then dismissed the formation. Master Sergeant Woods cut the rope and removed the body from the lower screened part of the scaffold. Captain Hardy C. Derx signed for the body and removed it for later interment, which occurred on October 11, 1945 at the U.S. Military Cemetery at Marigny in the General Prisoner Plot, Grave 36. To his left were the remains of Charles Robinson, in Grave 37. The official report stated that Captain Charles W. Fritz had efficiently guarded the execution site with twenty-five men of Company I of the 156th Infantry Regiment.

On October 25, 1945, the War Department sent a telegram to Blake Mariano's mother, stating that her son had died at the Loire DTC on October 10, 1945 due to his own misconduct. It stated that the cause of death was judicial axphyxiation. Mrs. Mariano also had in her possession a letter from Chaplain Dutton. Officials reinterred the remains in 1949 and buried them at the American Military Cemetery at Oise-Aisne in Plot E – in Row 1, Grave 12.[2]

## 93    Private Woodrow Parker
34561139

163rd Smoke Generator Company,
One-Hundredth Infantry Division
**Rape and Murder**
Hanged on October 15, 1945

## 94    Private Sydney Bennerman, Jr.
34174757

163rd Smoke Generator Company,
One-Hundredth Infantry Division
**Rape and Murder**
Hanged on October 15, 1945

The two accused entered a Polish refugee camp and broke into a barracks on April 15, 1945, as the One-Hundredth Infantry Division was in Germany and moving from Heilbronn toward Stuttgart. A Polish girl asked an elderly Polish man for protection, but the two soldiers crushed the man's skull. After dragging the girl outside the barracks, they both raped her; at some point in the assault, they fractured her skull, causing death. Authorities apprehended the two accused on April 17, 1945 – days after the segregated, all-black 163rd Smoke Generator Company had greatly assisted the division's crossing of the Neckar River, while under enemy fire. Their GCM, on order of the division commander, Major General Withers A. Burress, convened on April 28, 1945.

At the GCM, held at Bad Cannstatt, just outside of Stuttgart, the men faced two specifications of murder and one of rape.[1] The jury convicted both men and unanimously sentenced them to death by hanging. Major General Burress approved the sentences on May 26, 1945 and forwarded the trial records up the chain of command. General Dwight D. Eisenhower confirmed the sentences for Woodrow Parker and Sydney Bennerman, Jr. on August 4, 1945. On October 10, 1945, the United States Forces, European Theater, published General Court-Martial Orders Number 479, in which Lieutenant General Walter Bedell Smith, Chief of Staff – by command of General Eisenhower – specified that the convicted men would be shot on October 15, 1945.

Sidney Bennerman, Jr. was born on January 31, 1918 in Wilmington, North Carolina. He was inducted at Fort Bragg, North Carolina in November 1941; he stood 5'11" tall and weighed 160 pounds. He was listed as a staff sergeant earlier in his career. Bennerman received a conviction in a Special Court-Martial on February 28, 1944 in Italy for disobedience of, and insubordination to, a non-commissioned officer, receiving confinement at hard labor for six months; the order mentioned that Bennerman had a previous court-martial conviction. A year earlier, medics diagnosed him with syphilis. Bennerman was married and had two children. His family later lived in Gadsden, Alabama. Before deploying overseas, he was stationed at Camp Siebert, Alabama. Private Bennerman was authorized to wear a star on his European-African-Middle Eastern Campaign Medal for the "Southern France" campaign. Private Woodrow Parker was born in 1918 in Alabama. He was single, attended grammar school and resided in Tallapoosa County in Alabama. On December 12, 1942, he was inducted at Fort Benning, Georgia.

On September 20, 1945, MPs transferred General Prisoners Parker and Bennerman to Camp Miami near Reims, France, part of the Assembly Area Command. A firing squad, under the direction of the center commander, executed Woodrow Parker and Sydney Bennerman, on October 15, 1945 at the Delta DTC at Les Milles, Bouches du Rhone (Bouches-du-Rhône), France. Chaplain Charles R. Storer wrote Mrs. Bennerman on July 21, 1945, while Major Edward F. Witsell, Acting Adjutant General of the Army did so on October 30, 1945.

Officials originally interred the deceased at the U.S. Military Cemetery at Marigny. In 1949, authorities transferred the remains of Woodrow Parker and Sidney Bennerman to the American Military Cemetery at Oise-Aisne in Plot E. Parker's remains are in Row 3, Grave 56. Bennerman's remains are next to him in Row 3, Grave 57.[2]

The author could not locate the GCM files for either soldier at the U.S. Army Clerk of Court for this study. The personnel file for Sydney Bennerman exists at the National Archives and Records Administration (Military Personnel Records Center) in St. Louis. On the front page are the words: "This is a vault case." Woodrow Parker's personnel file was missing at the time of this study. While the Army sent the usual telegrams to the family of Sidney Bennerman, his wife wrote several letters seeking additional information, including a letter to President Truman on March 26, 1946, stating that her husband had been executed for treason, which, of course, was not the case.

> *"If my son was shot by U.S. government a grave mistake was made as my son was of unsound mine & stay in Insane Hospital 5 years."*

## 95 Private Mansfield Spinks

36793241
Company I, 366th Infantry Regiment,
    Ninety-Second Infantry Division
**Rape and Murder**
Executed by Firing Squad on
    October 19, 1945

Most judicial proceedings involving the death penalty in the European and the North African/Mediterranean Theaters of Operation were expeditious in nature. From the time an accused committed the offense, until the time he was executed, usually ranged from six weeks to four or five months. In the case of Mansfield Spinks, however, several events came together in such a way that a full nine months elapsed from the night of the crime, until Spinks met his end in front of a firing squad. However, when one of the defendants escapes during the trial and the other claims the crime was a murder for hire – with sex as the payment – timing goes out the window.

Almost immediately after the murder on January 16, 1945, the delays began. Military authorities arrested Private Spinks four days later. The following day, after being advised of his rights, he made a lengthy statement, stating that he and Private Charlie Ervin, Jr. had been drinking. They walked into several houses at Forte Dei Marmi, Italy – fifteen miles southeast of La Spezia; in the last house, they said they wanted to spend the night and the Italian family gave them chairs and blankets, before departing the room. Then Spinks and Ervin hatched a diabolical plan. Spinks' rifle had a mechanical problem and after firing one round, it would jam. So the two decided they would roust the Italians out of bed and when they were in the room, Spinks would fire a round into the fireplace and then set his weapon down. The Italian would probably then pick up the weapon to urge the two soldiers to leave; at that point, Ervin would shoot the man, claiming self-defense.

The actual murder happened in just this fashion, after which the two soldiers and the deceased's wife left the building; both later had sex with her, which was classified as rape. But was it? In Spinks' statement, he mentioned that the Italian woman had earlier told Ervin that she didn't much care for her husband. That's not what **she** said. The rape victim made a statement to MPs the same day as Spinks. She confirmed that the soldiers were staying there, but said that in the middle of the night, after her husband had gone downstairs, she heard two shots. Then the two soldiers rushed her out of the house, raped her and left her in the dark. She made it home at 7:20 a.m. the next morning. Police were at the home and she gave them her version of events. One of the two soldiers visited her on January 18, 1945 in a possible attempt to convince her to keep silent. On January 19, 1945, she was able to identify one of her attackers in a large line-up at a nearby American camp – he had a scar on the left side of his face. She mentioned nothing about her relations with her husband.

On February 1, 1945, Major General Edward M. Almond, Commanding General of the Ninety-Second Infantry Division, determined that a GCM would handle the case. One convened on February 7, 1945. Private Mansfield Spinks, a black soldier, who was born on November 7, 1924 in Chicago, pleaded not guilty to murder and carnal knowledge, both violations of the 92nd Article of War.[1] Ervin was not present, having entered the 170th Evacuation Hospital on February 6.

Things did not go well for the Trial Judge Advocate, who attempted to introduce the statement made by Private Spinks on January 21, but the Defense Counsel, at the time Captain Clifford R. Moore, asked questions so accurately that it became apparent that Spinks' may not have been informed of his rights. Then the Trial Judge Advocate called the rape victim to the stand. She identified the accused as one of her attackers, but did not see the other – the soldier who had raped her first. That was because Private Charlie Ervin was not there, having escaped from the hospital on February 17, 1945; it had been the Army's desire to try both men jointly, but when Ervin skipped out, Mansfield Spinks was left holding the bag and was tried alone.

The rape victim testified that she had never seen either man before; that and the absence of Ervin meant that any idea the defense had of raising the issue of murder for hire went out the window. Then the defense called Sergeant Weston Hoffman of the Criminal Investigation Division, who had helped conduct the investigation, Captain Moore was able to get Sergeant Hoffman to state that initially Private Spinks did not want to make any statement and that he knew nothing of the crime. Hoffman stated that when confronted by evidence and the rape victim's statement, Spinks "broke down and confessed." The Defense Counsel elicited from Sergeant Hoffman that it had been Private Ervin, who had shot the victim, and that Spinks did "not directly" kill the man. There was one additional problem for the Trial Judge Advocate; the medical officer, who had examined the deceased, was nowhere to be found. Faced with these multiple hurdles, the Trial Judge Advocate requested and received a continuation of the case to change the first specification (murder) and to find the medical officer; perhaps he would get lucky and even locate Charlie Ervin.

The Army did located Ervin, but almost six months later, after he had committed several additional serious crimes (see **96 – Charlie Ervin, Jr.**) Meanwhile, after the convening authority withdrew the Charge and Specifications from the original court and referred them to another GCM, a new trial for Spinks, which met on April 28, 1945. This second court convicted Private Spinks of the Charge and both Specifications; then it sentenced him to death by musketry. There was no issue of double jeopardy.

On May 2, 1945, Allied Force Headquarters at Caserta, Italy sent a message to the War Department stating that Mansfield Spinks received a sentence of death by musketry for murder and rape. On May 24, 1945, the headquarters transmitted a message to Washington that the appropriate commander approved Spinks' death sentence. General Joseph T. McNarney, Commander of the MTO, signed an order on June 20, 1945 confirming the sentence for Private Mansfield Spinks; he withheld the order directing the execution of that sentence. The next day, Allied Force Headquarters sent a message to the War Department, stating that the death sentence had been confirmed. On July 18, 1945, a Board of Review with the Branch Office of The JAG with the MTO reviewed the case. Judge Advocates Sargent, Irion and Remick found no serious errors.

General Court-Martial Orders Number 106, published by the MTO on July 30, 1945, stated that General Prisoner Spinks would be executed on August 10, 1945. However, the Army needed him as a material witness in the GCM of Charlie Ervin, Jr., now facing his own legal problems in court. Spinks later appeared at Ervin's court-martial, which began August 22, 1945.

It was almost the end of the line for Private Mansfield Spinks. Life had been hard on the mean streets on the south side of Chicago. Years later, the area would see the construction of the crime-ridden Robert Taylor Homes public housing project. Spinks, who stood 5'5" and weighed 130 pounds, quit school after the third grade; he later got a job carrying steel, earning $30 per week to help support his six brothers and sisters. He had been inducted on June 2, 1943 in Chicago. On October 4, 1945, the MTO published General Court-Martial Orders Number 122. It stated that Mansfield Spinks would be shot at Aversa, Italy on October 19, 1945. In a twist of fate, Charlie Ervin would join him in front of the firing squad that day, for other crimes Ervin committed. At 10:00 a.m., on October 18, 1945, five officers met at the headquarters building of the PBS Garrison Stockade Number 1. In the presence of Mansfield Spinks, one of the officers read General Court-Martial Orders Number 122 to the condemned and then asked him if he had any final requests. Spinks made a final request – which was honored – but there is no mention of it in his file. The condemned man received a new change of clothing and walked to a new, separate cell, under a twenty-four-hour deathwatch. It is believed that Chaplain Douglas F. Hall, a black officer of the Baptist faith, remained with him during these final hours.

First Lieutenant Clyde R. Thorn, the Acting Commander of the PBS Garrison Stockade Number 1, was in charge of the execution. The day prior to the event, his headquarters issued Special Orders Number 116, delineating the upcoming event. The following men comprised the firing squad: First Sergeant Howard Laux, Corporal Irving Spinney, Private First Class Edward G. Anderson, Private First Class Walter J. Bryk, Private First Class Jack R. Freeman, Private First Class James E. Hatfield, Private Edward J. Deveau, Private Calvin C. Gardner, Private John S. Gardner, Jr., Private Clyde R. Harrington, Private Charles H. Orwig and Private John H. Torpor. The men wore wool serge uniforms with ties, overseas' caps and web belts, and carried M-1 rifles. First Sergeant Laux was a prototype top kick. Tall and rugged, he sported a two-inch scar on his left cheek, perhaps a souvenir of an encounter in which his opponent likely took a far worse beating. Even on this morning, Laux's uniform sported crisp creases. Laux would have this squad fully prepared and ready for the two executions they would conduct this morning.

At 7:30 a.m., officers assembled twenty-five trainees in formation at the execution site; they would serve as spectators. The execution area measured some twenty-five feet wide by fifty feet long, dug into the earth, surrounded on all sides by an earthen berm. At the impact end of the "the pit," soldiers had constructed a wall on top of the berm, four sandbags high – to catch any "Maggie's Drawers" shots. Surrounding the depression was a grove of mature fruit trees. Ten feet in front of the impact end stood a four-inch-by-four-inch wooden post sunk several feet into the ground. Its top rose about seven feet above the base of the excavation.

For executions, guards tied the condemned man to the stake, using a belt just above the knees and another strap at shoulder level. The bands secured the prisoner in such a way that he would not sag toward the ground, after being struck by the gunfire, but rather remain upright, so a medical officer could more easily confirm his death. The range lay oriented from the east, where the impact wall was located, to west, where the firing squad stood. Spinks would face one last time toward his sweet home Chicago, while the early morning sun would shine into the eyes of the firing squad.

Second Lieutenant Richard B. Hoffer led a special guard of a dozen men from the 138th MP Company. At 7:55 a.m., First Lieutenant Thorn, accompanied by Staff Sergeant Hubert Aschenbrenner and Staff Sergeant Julian S. Foster – serving as special guards – arrived at the site with Private Mansfield Spinks. Captain Charles F. Willis was present as the medical officer. The guards tied General Prisoner Spinks to the wooden-post; the firing squad then marched into positions, faced the prisoner, raised their weapons and on command fired. The time was 8:12 a.m. Captain Willis pronounced Mansfield Spinks dead at 8:17 a.m.

On October 20, 1945, First Lieutenant Edgar L. Hunt, the acting commander that day for the PBS Garrison Stockade Number 1 wrote a letter of condolence to the Spink's mother. He did not mention the cause of death for her son. The Adjutant General's Office prepared a "Report of Death" on Mansfield Spinks on November 8, 1945. The day before, the War Department sent a telegram to Mrs. Spinks stating that her son had died in a non-battle status due to his own misconduct. She received the telegram, announcing her son's death, and wrote letters later in November to the Office of The Adjutant General and the President of the United States Harry Truman, respectively. In both letters, she stated that she had received no money after his death and that nothing her son had done was his fault, because his mind was not right. She mentioned that for five years, beginning at age twelve, her son had been a patient in the Dixon State Hospital in Illinois, under the care of a Dr. Murray. Later in the letter, she wrote:

"If my son was shot by U.S. government a grave mistake was made as my son was of unsound mine & stay in Insane Hospital 5 years."

Colonel Albert Johnson, Acting Chief of the Military Justice Division, wrote a letter to Mrs. Spinks. He thanked her for her letters to the Adjutant General and the President of the United States, requesting information about her son. Colonel Johnson explained that Mansfield Spinks received a death sentence for murder and rape, confirmed on June 20, 1945. Various reviews had examined the case. Colonel Johnson ended the letter by stating:

"However, you may be assured that he received a fair and impartial trial and that he would not have been tried and convicted had he not been considered mentally responsible for his actions."

Mansfield Spinks' mother continued correspondence with the government for several years. The Army originally buried Mansfield Spinks at the U.S. Military Cemetery at Naples, in the General Prisoner Plot, Row 2, Grave 23. Exhumed in 1949, he now is buried at the American Military Cemetery at Oise-Aisne in Plot E. His remains are in Row 3, Grave 49.[2]

*"Frank jumped off the truck on the ground and
I shot the one who throwed the box. I shot twice."*

## 96  Private Charlie Ervin, Jr.
34042926

Company I, 366th Infantry Regiment,
  Ninety-Second Infantry Division
**Assault and Murder**
Hanged on October 19, 1945

After Private Charlie Ervin, Jr. skipped out of his unit to avoid being tried for murder and rape, along with Mansfield Spinks, he remained on the lam for several months. However, it was hard to break old habits, and in July 1945, Ervin returned to assault and murder – with an accomplice. Charlie "Tony" Ervin, Jr. apparently liked the coast of Italy, because his final crime was at Pietrasanta. On the night of July 30-31 an Italian truck, operated by civilians and loaded with lemons bound for Genoa, broke down outside Pietrasanta. That was easy pickings for Ervin; about 4:30 a.m., he and Private Elmer "Frank" Sussex, who was absent without leave from Company F of the 371st Infantry Regiment, came upon the vehicle and decided to shake down the truck operators. They began by asking the Italians for their identity passes; during the exchange, Sussex struck one of the Italians with a long knife; two gunshots exploded in the dark and struck two of the Italians. As events would prove, "Frank" did the cutting and "Tony" did the shooting.

Unfortunately, for "Tony," one bullet hit Pietro Testini in the lower abdomen and within two hours, he lay dead. The two black soldiers raced from the scene, while the surviving Italians sought medical help. MPs stepped up their search and on August 2, 1945, MPs arrested Private Charlie Ervin, Jr. and Private Elmer Sussex, while they were asleep in a school building – next to two carbines. A ballistics expert with the Criminal Investigations Division later concluded that an assailant had fired one of the carbines at the crime scene, based on cartridges found there. Agents explained legal rights to both suspects; each subsequently made a statement. Sussex admitted cutting one of the men and said, "When I jumped on the ground Ervin fired two shots." Private Elmer Sussex later clarified his own role in the crime:

"While I was on the side of the truck I did make several stabbing motions at the civilians with my knife, but I did not actually stab or cut anyone until the lemon box was thrown at me."

Private Charlie Ervin also implicated himself in his statement, "Frank jumped off the truck on the ground and I shot the one who throwed the box. I shot twice."

Major General Edward M. Almond, Commanding General of the Ninety-Second Infantry Division, ordered a GCM to convene. It met at the Mediterranean Theater DTC in Pisa, Italy at 2:05 p.m. on August 22, 1945 On the court were the following officers – all from the Ninety-Second Infantry Division: Lieutenant Colonel James C. Horne (IN), Lieutenant Colonel William M. Campbell (MP), Major Bennett G. Gray (FA), Major Joseph W. Henry (GS) who was also the Law Member, Captain Maxwell W. Vails (IN), Captain Clyde A. Worthen (IN), First Lieutenant William V. Childs (SC) and First Lieutenant James M. Kidd (IN.) Captain Maxwell Vails and Captain Clyde Worthen were black; Worthen had just received a Silver Star for "Gallantry in Action."[1] Captain John L. Duggan (FI) and First Lieutenant Douglas F. Osborne (JAG) shared duties as the TJA. Captain Francis L. Robinson (MC) served as the Defense Counsel; he was assisted by First Lieutenant Frank R. Taylor (QM.)

It would be the final GCM in Europe, ending with an execution, for crimes occurring before VE Day, given that Charlie Ervin had actually started his crime spree in January 1945. The jury was an experienced one. It was Horne's fifth GCM that ended with a sentence of death and an execution and Campbell's fourth. It was a joint trial and both defendants pleaded not guilty to one charge of murder, a violation of the 92nd Article of War, and two specifications of assault, violations of the 93rd Article of War.[2] No witness to the shooting identified either defendant at trial, but the Trial Judge Advocate had the incriminating statements of both men. The jury convicted both men. The court sentenced Private Elmer Sussex to life imprisonment and unanimously voted to sentence Private Charlie Ervin, Jr. to be shot to death with musketry.

The Ninety-Second Infantry Division Staff Judge Advocate reviewed the case on September 1, 1945. Major General Almond approved the sentences for both men and designated that Sussex would serve his sentence at the U.S. Penitentiary at Lewisburg, Pennsylvania. General Joseph McNarney confirmed the sentences on September 20, 1945; he withheld the order directing the execution of Private Ervin. On September 22, 1945, the Board of Review from the Branch Office of The JAG with the MTO reviewed the case. Judge Advocates Irion, Sessions and Remick found no substantial errors in the proceedings.

Charlie Ervin, Jr. was born on February 18, 1919 in Lexington, Tennessee; he later lived in Tiptonville in northwest Tennessee. After leaving school, he became a farm laborer, earning $7 a week. Ervin stood 5'7" tall and weighed 132 pounds. He was inducted at Fort Oglethorpe, Georgia on April 23, 1941; dental records show he was missing six upper teeth. Ervin's record in the Army was less than stellar. In January 1942, a Summary Court-Martial convicted him for being absent without official leave, sentencing him thirty days confinement with hard labor. He spent eighteen days in the hospital in May-June 1942 for gonorrhea. Another Summary Court-Martial convicted him in April 1943 of AWOL and fined him twenty dollars for this infraction. In July 1943, he reported sick with syphilis. In February 1944, a third court-martial convicted him of breaking restriction. That was followed on March 29, 1944 by a Summary Court-Martial conviction that resulted in thirty days confinement at hard labor for allowing a civilian to ride in his military truck. In May 1944, his syphilis flared up again.

However, Charlie Ervin had a positive side as well. He received a wounded to the thigh on December 31, 1944 and received a Purple Heart several days later. On January 10, 1945, Ervin was authorized a Combat Infantryman's Badge. He was also authorized the European-African-Middle Eastern Campaign Medal with two campaign stars. Then his life again changed for the worse with the murder and rape on January 16, 1945, the escape from the hospital and the second murder on July 31, 1945. "Tony" Ervin's bad habits were about to kill him. The MTO published General Court-Martial Orders Number 121 on October 4, 1945. Major General Lyman L. Lemnitzer, acting for the theater commander, designated that Ervin would be shot by a firing squad on October 19 at Aversa.

On October 18, 1945, officers read General Prisoner Ervin the General Court-Martial Order, asked him if he had any last words and issued him a clean uniform – minus any insignia. First Lieutenant Clyde R. Thorn supervised the execution by firing squad at the PBS Garrison Stockade Number 1 at Aversa, Italy on October 19, 1945. Five photographs exist in private hands that appear to show the execution of Charlie Ervin, Jr., although it is likely that one or more are of the Spinks' execution that occurred minutes earlier. The first two photographs show the condemned man, as he is tied to the post; an officer is reading the General Court-Martial Order to him. The third photograph shows the condemned, with his head slumped forward, under the black hood, as a medical officer is checking for a pulse.

The fourth photograph shows two men carrying an empty stretcher as they approach the post; the condemned man is still tied to it and upright. The last photograph portrays the two stretcher-bearers departing the area, with a deceased under a sheet on the stretcher. The firing squad members pulled their triggers at 8:26 a.m., just nine minutes after the previous execution of Mansfield Spinks. Physician Charles Willis pronounced Charlie Ervin, Jr. dead at 8:29 a.m.

It was the final execution in Europe for capital crimes committed before VE Day. As the smoke from the rifle rounds drifted away, the thoughts of First Sergeant Laux, the men in the firing squad and those soldiers who took part in other roles during the execution began to turn toward home, where executions were just something you read about every now and then in your hometown newspaper. For big Clyde Thorn, however, the visions of this day would never truly go away. Although he seldom talked of them, his experiences during the war often haunted him over the next forty-seven years, until he passed away in rural Arkansas.

The Army originally interred Private Ervin in the U.S. Military Cemetery at Naples, in Plot GP, Row 2 in Grave 24. He was reinterred in 1949 and is now buried at the American Military Cemetery at Oise-Aisne in Plot E. His remains are in Row 3, Grave 54.[3]

# PART III

## A Closer Look

# View from a Potential Defense Counsel or Trial Judge Advocate

*"It is your problem because you, as Staff Judge Advocates, can do more to see that appropriate and just sentences are imposed in the first instance, or corrected by the reviewing authority, than any other officers in our Army. It concerns you, and the officers exercising courts-martial jurisdiction, whom you represent, because you and they will be judged not only by the fairness and legality of your trials, but upon the equality with which you administer justice between different persons convicted of substantially the same offenses."*[1]

Originally, this section was to have been titled "Reversible Error?" However, both the author and lawyer T.G. Bolen concluded that this description would have been too presumptuous, as our reviews of the cases did not include an examination of various legal precedents. However, there were *avoidable errors* – caused by the compression of available time, inexperience of court members and sometimes an apparent overall lack of attention to detail. While these factors adversely affected some cases, they provide excellent opportunities for future Judge Advocates to learn from the mistakes made by others. Here are several examples – in which an experienced lawyer meticulous reviewed the files, noting procedures and errors that perhaps could have been avoided.

## 1 – David Cobb

*Asking the Right Questions and Following Up*

This case illustrates clearly the difficulty in conducting a trial, when none of the questioners has had professional experience conducting an examination of witnesses. It is frustrating to read the record of the questioning of the witnesses and find that discrepancies or glaring omissions occur in the testimony, but no one seems to take any notice of the problem.

The accused was walking guard when a lieutenant and a corporal approached him and the accused objected to the lieutenant regarding the amount of time he had on guard duty. The lieutenant advised him that he, the lieutenant, had nothing to do with that and he must walk his post as ordered. A corporal, who was the sergeant of the guard, approached the accused to take his rifle. The accused refused to give it up and ordered the corporal to halt, whereupon the corporal backed away. The lieutenant again demanded that the accused give him his rifle. Over the next few minutes, there is conversation between the lieutenant and the accused, which deals with the accused refusing to give up the rifle, because he says it would be a violation of General Orders to give up his rifle while on guard duty. The lieutenant apparently takes another step toward the accused and reaches for the rifle, at which point the accused fires, hitting the lieutenant with a fatal shot in the chest.

This case turns on one central dispute – whether the accused knew that the lieutenant was the Officer of the Day – or, did he feel that he was being tested and asked to violate a General Order, by surrendering his rifle, while on guard duty? It is not a case with a possibility of manslaughter or reckless homicide. The defendant either reasonably believed that he was not allowed to surrender his weapon and took the action he understood was required of a soldier walking guard, in which case he is innocent, or he was irritated at walking guard and when the lieutenant did not relieve him, he simply killed him in cold blood.

This is what makes it so necessary to find out what each witness saw or heard (in their own words.) Unfortunately, just the opposite takes place. The witnesses very rarely describe anything in their own words. To understand this, we must place ourselves in the time and situation that existed when this court-martial was taking place. It is clear that the accused and the other enlisted men who were present at the scene and were called as witnesses were all black and that the dead lieutenant was a white officer. We must remember that in 1942, black soldiers, particularly those who grew up in the South, understood the line that they walked with respect to their contact with a white soldier. This is magnified when the witnesses are enlisted men and the questioner is an officer. The chances that one of these witnesses would testify on the stand in answer to a question, "You are wrong about that, Sir," is, in my opinion, almost a non-existent possibility. As you read the testimony, it is more reminiscent of an officer conducting a quiz than it is of witness testimony in a capital case.

The first witness was Corporal William Mason, Jr., sergeant of the guard on the day in question. The witness stated that the accused started his duty at twelve and got off at eight. He is then asked if that is twelve midnight, and he replies, "12 midnight." He then testifies that the accused was supposed to have eight hours off and the officer asks, "That would be noon, is that right?," and the witness answers, "Yes, Sir." Obviously, there is some confusion in the times, but that is never made clear. It is a rare occurrence when the witness's answer contains more than eight words. Page nine of the trial record contains nineteen questions and replies, only two answers contain more than eight words. The same situation continues on page ten. The standard reply to the questions asked the witness is "Yes, Sir." That is the entire answer six times on page ten, plus one answer of "No, Sir." On page eleven, which contains eighteen questions and answers, the answer in its entirety is either "Yes, Sir" or "No, Sir" to ten of the questions. The questions are leading; at no point does the witness ever give a lengthy discussion of what he saw and heard. This is the standard throughout the entire court-martial. A short examination by the court and Lieutenant Spears asks the witness three questions, which the witness answers as follows:

"Q. Does the rifle which shot the lieutenant have a safety?
A. Yes, Sir.
Q. How do you carry the safety on guard?
A. Locked.
Q. Did you see him pull the safety off?
A. I didn't until I heard a shot."

It is hard to imagine anything less clear with respect to whether or not the witness actually saw the accused pull the safety off. A great deal of time is spent examining witnesses with respect to the weapon, the position of the safety, and when the rifle was at port arms versus when it was not. The real question of the trial, namely, did the Officer of the Day identify himself and did the accused acknowledge it and did the accused order him to halt and explain why he couldn't surrender his weapon is very rarely examined. One of the witnesses to the occurrence is asked:

"Q. Did you go in the jeep with the body?
A. No, Sir."

It is difficult to see what significance that had to anything at issue. At one point, the witness is asked if he saw the accused's finger on the trigger, to which the witness replies, "Yes, Sir." The next question is, "Were you pretty close?" The answer is, "Well, no." We do not know how close he was. It simply is left unexplained. There is also an examination of some length about the clothing worn by the deceased and the pistol carried by the decedent, and the witness is asked if it shows any sign of being fired, to which the witness answers, "No, Sir." He is then asked if he is in a position to judge if the gun was fired a short time before that, and his answer is, "I couldn't say that I could." Again, none of this has any probative value at all, as there is never any suggestion by anyone that the deceased fired his pistol, nor is there disagreement that the accused, David Cobb, shot the deceased, Lieutenant Cobner, from a distance of a few feet, firing a fatal shot into the lieutenant's chest. The question as to whether or not the accused knew the deceased was the Officer of the Day could be illustrated by whether or not there was a formal guard mount, when the Officer of the Day would be announced. It is unclear from the record whether there was a formal guard mount.

Witness Private Cashie Mason, is asked if he is sure that it was the accused that shot the lieutenant, to which Mason replied, "Yes, Sir. I was there and saw it." Again, this is a fact that is not at issue. There is no question about who shot Lieutenant Cobner. After the shooting, no one took the accused's weapon away. They took the body in a jeep to the hospital, but no one seems to have notified any authorities or asked for MPs to arrest Cobb. Even more unbelievable is the conduct of the accused. A private has just killed a lieutenant and the private simply goes back to his guard post and continues walking guard for another fifteen minutes?

This brings us to the question as to whether or not David Cobb received a fair trial and a proper verdict and penalty. The actions of Cobb and Cobner leave one with the feeling that they both handled the situation very poorly. Cobb had been on active duty for one year, and Cobner probably not much longer. Both were in a situation that neither had the experience to handle, if something went wrong. Cobb's reaction to the facts, even taking them at his best, was completely improper if not irrational. If he thought he was being tested for his performance on guard duty, a warning shot or other procedures were available – not killing the officer.

Lieutenant Cobner should have been aware of the volatility of the situation. When the corporal backed away from Cobb, Cobner asked him if he was afraid. It would seem that being a few paces from an irrational individual with a loaded rifle, pointing it at your chest, being afraid would be a sensible reaction.

The lieutenant then did the most dangerous thing he could have done, namely he approached Cobb and attempted to take his rifle. Once again, actions as a result of poor judgment cannot remotely justify what happened in this case.

We are thus left with trying to determine Cobb's motive. Cobb appears from the record to have been very upset and angry that he was not going to be relieved. It is difficult to believe the conclusion that some of that anger was not directed to the lieutenant who refused to relieve him. If the court-martial board believed that Cobb acted with that motive involved in the shooting of Lieutenant Cobner, which they certainly would have been justified in believing from the record, then the guilty verdict seems to be appropriate. I think that a reviewing court in this case would be reluctant to upset the verdict based on the entirety of the evidence, even though it is less clear than you would hope in a capital case.

The Army was confronted with a private who shot and killed an officer with a very cloudy rationale for doing so. Does the enlisted man, who kills an officer, start with an uphill battle in a trial? Of course, he does; so does a defendant in a civilian court who has killed a police officer, unless the proof of the defendant's innocence is very clear and convincing. Given those circumstances, what is it the Army should have done in this situation? Ideally, two skilled and experienced criminal lawyers would be called upon to prosecute and defend the case; there probably were none in this category immediately available. Should they have sent Cobb and all the witnesses back to the United States for trial? In today's wars we might, but not in that existential conflict.

My conclusion is that everyone did the best they could under a very difficult set of circumstances and that Cobb was not prejudiced by the manner in which the trial was conducted or by his Defense Counsel, who clearly was not any less-skilled than the officer conducting the prosecution. Is the result irrational and imperfect? No, the members of the court-martial board took on a heavy duty, gave the duty their best efforts and were rational in the verdict. To criticize the result from a distance of seventy years, knowing the advances and improvements made in both a military courts-martial and a civilian criminal trial procedure, is patently unfair. However, they could have asked better questions and followed up on the answers.

## 2 – Harold A. Smith

*A Strong Investigation Leads to a Strong Case*

This case is not reviewed because of what went wrong, but rather of what went right. The first is the statement taken from the accused, which is filed in full by photocopy in the file. The statement could stand as an example of how to take an incriminating statement from an accused party. It consists of nine and a half handwritten pages, which Harold Adolphus Smith signs after the first paragraph, saying his rights have been explained to him, and then signs at the bottom of every page, and again at the end of the statement we find the accused's handwriting saying, "I have read my statement of 9 pages and 6 lines and it is all true."

Again, his signature, Harold Adolphus Smith, appears immediately below his handwritten sentence. The statement catalogs the accused's movements for a number of days prior to the incident. It explains his theft of the murder weapon and it gives what the accused evidently believes is a defense for his actions, but it serves to incriminate him in his own words. The accused, absent without leave, returned to another company late at night, ate a sandwich and slept at the company. The next afternoon, he shot a guard in cold blood, fired two shots at a witness that came to try and help the victim and then fled the scene. The victim died shortly thereafter of several gunshot wounds, including a fatal shot in the back. The accused does not deny firing the shots, but attempts to allege self-defense, when none of the facts, or even his statement, are sufficient for such a defense.

There is no question about the verdict and very little with respect to the death sentence. This case is a pleasure to read because of the review by Lieutenant Colonel J.M. Pitzer, who was the Assistant Staff Judge Advocate. The review consists of five single spaced legal sized pages in which the reviewer recites all the facts in the case, including the detailed medical reports, the accused statements, and the defense evidence. In paragraph seven, entitled "Comments on Irregularities in the Proceedings," the reviewer takes seven items, which occurred during the trial regarding which some objection might be raised. The reviewer explains in detail what constituted irregularity and why, in his opinion, all the other corroborative evidence is so substantial that none of the seven items constitutes substantial prejudice to the defendant, nor do any of them singly, or taken together, warrant not affirming the judgment. In paragraph eight, entitled "Opinion of the Staff Judge Advocate," he reviews the record and gives a review of the facts and law, which can only be described as admirable. Like the statement taken from the accused, this document could well be used for instruction in a legal class.

One of the frequent criticisms of the military court-martial system is that trials are rushed and that the amount of time between the incident and the execution is far too short. In this case, the offense occurred January 9, 1943; the charges were brought January 27 and signed by the Judge Advocate on February 11. The trial did not occur until March 12 and the record reflects, as required, the reason for the delay, which it says was for preparation of the case. The case concluded on March 22, was reviewed by the Staff Judge Advocate on April 23; the report of the Board of Review was dated May 20 and filed on June 5, and the execution occurred on June 25, more than five months after the incident. The entire file could stand as a model.

## 4, 5, 6 & 7 – Willie A. Pittman, Harvey Stroud, Armstead White & David White
*Why Severed Cases Require Separate Juries*
This court-martial involves four privates charged with the rape of a civilian Italian woman, with each of them individually performing the rape while the other three waited. This case is the type that causes lawyers to shake their head in dismay, while non-lawyers shake their head in dismay at the lawyers being dismayed. This is one of the strongest prosecution cases that could be built and one of the worst conducted hearings imaginable. The proof is overwhelming. The four privates broke into the residence of the victim and held her husband (and their baby) in a chair by standing next to him with a rifle. Another of the defendants stood outside the door with a rifle, while each of the four defendants went in the bedroom, had forcible intercourse with the victim, as her husband and baby sat nearby, and the three other defendants remained armed to prevent any interruption.

The statements given by the defendants all indicate that this is what happened and each one admits participating. No one ever states that the sex was consensual. They all acknowledge the act. It is hard to imagine any prosecution of this case that would not be successful. The dismaying part for a lawyer is the court that tried the case. The four trials occurred on the same day, one after the other, with a court composed of officers from the corps headquarters. On one case, a second lieutenant was excused, leaving a court consisting of seven officers, all from the same unit, including one captain, one major and six lieutenant colonels and colonels. The Trial Judge Advocate is a major from the same unit; the Defense Counsel was also a major from the same unit. This is, to say the least, a potentially unhealthy situation. Even worse is the fact that the same jurors hear each of the four cases one after the other, obviously knowing what was said in the previous case and knowing that a previous defendant involved the other defendants in each subsequent hearing. In the last case, all the jurors know that the three co-defendants were found guilty and sentenced to death. The chances of a different result for the fourth defendant, even if he could mount a reasonable defense, are almost zero. This is far beyond improper. To have one court-martial board hear four consecutive related cases on the same day is completely unacceptable from an image perspective.

Further, the review of the cases leaves much to be desired. In a review by Colonel Damon M. Gunn, his final paragraph states that the necessity for the Army to be careful in its conduct with Italian civilians has not entered into the case. The fact that the paragraph deals with that situation makes it very obvious that it did enter into the case. As an indication of how this case was handled, Gunn also states in the review that:

"Furthermore, the members of this court were all part of the American military force which had made one of the naval landings for the invasion of Sicily on 9-July 1943. They could thus properly take judicial notice of certain facts. This act was committed in the zone of combat not many miles from the front line where rifles are carried loaded and ready for instant action. The population was frightened by the fighting as the lines had passed their houses. The feelings of this family were something with which the court was familiar, but are not subject to accurate description."

That the court may not take judicial notice of any of the items Colonel Gunn cites is again an indication of the fact that the members of the court did take notice of items which were not judicially before them and basically functioned as a group to put these men to death. There is no question but that the death penalty was a proper one in this case, but the procedural aspects are simply shocking, particularly in a capital case.

## 24 – Paul M. Kluxdal

*Weighing Contradictory Testimony*

This is a troubling case. The occurrence itself is not in dispute, as all witnesses and the accused state that the accused, Paul Kluxdal, was talking to First Sergeant Loyce M. Robertson. It is undisputed that the two men were a few feet apart and that a carbine, held by the accused, discharged, with the bullet striking Robertson in the chest, with death resulting in a few minutes. The question before the court was whether the accused acted deliberately or whether he accidentally discharged the weapon.

The most damaging prosecution evidence comes from Private Roland Noble. According to the review documents, Noble testified that at the time of the shot, the accused held the carbine in both hands with the butt of the weapon under his right arm, barrel horizontal and pointed forward. However, his actual statement was actually quite weak: "He must have been in that position, (as Noble showed the court by holding the carbine), like that somewhere." No one else offered any evidence about the position of the weapon at the time of the shot. The reviewers could not see a photo of how Noble was holding the carbine; they could only speculate. The accused stated that he was holding the carbine and that it fired the shot that killed Robertson. The accused offered two theories how the incident occurred. He stated that he "stumbled" and the weapon went off accidentally. He stated that he had a problem with his knee, frequently causing him to stumble, and that the ground in the area was uneven and the combination – rough terrain and a trick knee – caused him to stumble.

The weakest point in the accused's testimony is his explanation for the weapon being in his hands and apparently pointed at Robertson – "I sorta stumbled and my carbine came into my hands as I proceeded to fall and it went off." Obviously, there is no reconciling the accused's testimony that the carbine fell into his hands when he stumbled and Noble's testimony that he saw the accused with the butt of the carbine under his right arm and the barrel horizontal.

It is, therefore, important to examine the accused's two theories as to why he stumbled. The court and its opinion seemed to pay little attention to the testimony about the knee, but Captain George W. Marsh (Medical Corps) testified that he had previously examined the accused and that the accused's knee ligament fluctuated and at times could not give good support. Marsh testified that he had sent the accused to the hospital several times, but that it had been several months since those incidents. There is no contradiction of this officer's testimony that the accused had a knee ligament problem. More troubling, concerning Marsh's testimony, is the question of whether the ground was level or rough. At the court-martial, Captain Marsh stated, "that the terrain was smooth, grass short, it was an apple orchard." Captain Marsh had previously made a statement to First Lieutenant Brown, the investigating officer, on August 14, 1944. In that sworn statement, Marsh described asking the accused to walk and describes what followed, "Kluxdal's walking was straight and well-coordinated considering the rough terrain and darkness." [author's underline]

Which description of the terrain was accurate? The trial never clarified that. The other evidence in the record is that some of the witnesses testified to overhearing a conversation between the accused and the decedent. The opinion of the court states that the conversation "in substance" amounted to a demand for the return of the accused's bottle of alcohol and a threat "I will shoot you" and a reply by the Sergeant, "Never do that," whereupon the accused fired his gun. Although that may be the conversation in what the court describes as in substance, the actual statement of the accused is the essence of the prosecutor's case and needs to be proved with no dispute as to its content.

The court described the conversation in the following language, which it said was heard by at least two witnesses. The court stated the accused said, "I'll shoot you" or "I'll shoot (or kill) you, Robbie." Although witnesses frequently cannot describe an incident in exactly the same detail, one would hope that the proof, which is used to determine deliberate action by the accused, of a three-word threat would be the same language by all the witnesses. Either the witnesses did not hear the statement clearly or did not remember the statement because the testimony is that it may have been "I'll shoot you" or it may have been "I'll kill you" or "I'll shoot you, Robbie."

It is very disturbing that the parties were not in agreement with what is the critical statement by the accused with respect to the incident itself. A substantial part of the evidence dealt with the testimony of several witnesses to the effect that there was animosity between the accused and the First Sergeant. It is very difficult to find any probative value in this testimony. The court solved this problem by using the standard excuse that the evidence was admissible and the only question is the weight that should be given it. The better test is whether the probative value of the evidence is sufficient to outweigh its prejudicial damage to the accused. It seems clear in this case that the testimony regarding a problem between the accused and the First Sergeant is so innocuous that its only purpose is to blacken the accused.

Even more damaging to the prosecution is the testimony of Captain Hall (the battery commander), who was recalled, and testified that no animosity between the accused and Robertson was ever called to his attention. This is further bolstered by the testimony of Sergeant Reber, who was recalled, and testified that although he had been in the battalion for over two years and knew the accused, he never noticed any animosity between the accused and Robertson and their relationship seemed friendly enough. This testimony stands not only in contradiction to the testimony of the witnesses about the accused complaining with respect to Robertson but it directly contradicts and refutes their testimony. The testimony of the witnesses with respect to difficulty between the accused and Robertson seems no more than the standard complaining of a private against one of his superiors.

The fact that the court ignored the problem with the bad knee and the condition of the terrain, while apparently accepting without question a damning three-word statement of two different sets of words, adds sufficient doubt to impose the death penalty. It is difficult to understand how the reviewing board could have issued the opinion that it did. I believe that considering all the testimony, one might conclude that it is more likely than not that the shooting might have been deliberate, but to say that no other reasonable conclusion is possible from the testimony is not borne out by the record.

## 33 – James E. Hendricks
### Taking the Stand as a Defendant
This is a court-martial charging the accused with murder and also unlawful entry of a dwelling and assault upon a female person, both with the intent to commit rape. The facts show that the defendant was approximately one-fourth of a mile from the company area when the incident occurred. The undisputed facts are that a soldier came to the house of the Bouton family, that he entered the house and asked for a "mademoiselle." He tried to kiss a woman, at which point her sons gave him two eggs that he put in his pocket, left the house and crossed the road. Two to three minutes after he left the Bouton house, two shots and a shriek erupted from the Bignon home across the road. Twenty minutes later the same soldier returned to the Bouton house,

along with three French civilians from the Bignon home across the street. At this point, the soldier attempted a sexual assault on one of the women and shortly thereafter, the soldier left the house.

Upon hearing the two shots, Lieutenant Frank Tucker left his company area and went to the area from which the shots had come. Tucker and a detail of men heard noises in a hedge, whereupon they fired their weapons and the accused came forward from the hedge. This occurred about ten yards from the Bignon house in which a Frenchman lay dying of a gunshot wound. Tucker asked the defendant what he was doing in the area and the defendant said that he had been on the water detail and the truck had left him. Tucker then told the accused that he knew that he had not been on the water detail and he was lying. The defendant then said he was out working with two privates and trying to get back to camp.

Lieutenant Tucker then took the accused's rifle which contained five shells, smelled the chamber, which revealed that it had been recently fired. Standing orders in the company were that rifles contain seven rounds of ammunition; that discrepancy was soon explained. Upon observing the deceased's body in the house, the accused stated that he had gotten lost and found this house. He had knocked on the door, and when no one answered, fired a round through the door. When no one answered again, he fired a second round through the door. An inspection of the house showed that two shots had been fired through the front door at an upward angle, striking the victim in the head and killing him. Hendricks' further statement was that he didn't remember anything afterward until he saw Lieutenant Tucker.

The defendant was then taken to a Military Police station where he told the MPs that he went to the murder house to get directions, and as he approached the door, he stumbled, dropped his rifle and it went off, and when he reached down to put the safety on, it went off again. The MPs found eggs in the pocket of the defendant's raincoat and there was blood on the left side of the collar.

Unless you are willing to assume that Lieutenant Tucker perjured himself with respect to all the occurrences with the defendant, it is clear that the defendant was just ten yards from a murder victim, that he had a recently fired rifle with two rounds of ammunition missing, that he was unable to explain why he was in the area, and then told several contradictory stories about what had happened. Based on the defendant's statement, there is no reason to assume that he did not fire the two shots through the door. The question that remains is what offense was committed by his firing the shots? Premeditation is not required. If the death occurred when the defendant intended to commit a felony, under those circumstances a prior intent to kill is not a necessary element of murder. The same rule would apply in civilian courts where a killing occurred during the commission of a felony, which would allow every participant in the commission of the felony to be charged with murder.

The sole argument to acquit Private First Class Hendricks would be that the soldier with a recently fired rifle with two rounds missing and an egg in his pocket and blood on his uniform collar was a different black soldier than the one who fired the two shots through the house door, assaulted the women and took the eggs and then disappeared. I believe it is entirely reasonable on the evidence to find that James Hendricks was at both homes and killed the victim.

One of the reasons for criticism of the Hendricks case is that the charge, drafted by the prosecution, should be much more specific than it is. The fact that the charge, as drafted, deals with the premeditated murder would be much better had it explained that the charge arose from a death, which occurred in the commission of a forcible felony. If I were on a reviewing court, I would not find this sufficient to reverse the conviction, but it is something that should be remembered in future cases in that murder in the commission of a felony when the specifications state "with malice aforethought" is confusing when the charge does not explain that malice aforethought is imputed by the killing in the commission of a felony. The reviewing authorities cite a number of times in which procedures were not followed in exact detail. Again, as a reviewing authority, I would find this worthy of note, but again, not prejudicial to the defendant in any degree to require a reversal of the conviction supported by the amount of evidence in this case. This is something to which future prosecution officers should pay greater attention.

Is there any evidence that the court convicted James Hendricks of a charge he did not commit? The answer is absolutely not. Civilian reviewing courts continually do not reverse in cases where minor errors occurred, but only where substantial error makes proof of guilt less than clear and convincing. A defendant is entitled to a fair trial, not a perfect trial. It is my opinion that James E. Hendricks received a fair trial.

## 56 & 57 – Cubia Jones and Robert L. Pearson

*"But at the mouth of one witness he shall not be put to death"*

The Pearson-Jones trial shows the difficulty of applying what sounds like a simple standard to the concept of reasonable doubt. In this case, an English woman accused the two defendants of raping her. Like most forcible rape cases, there was no other independent evidence of anyone who observed the incident. Consequently, the court-martial became what is now commonly referred to as a "he said, she said" case. That is, you have a person who claims to be the victim of a forcible rape. You have two defendants who say that is not what occurred. The defense in many criminal cases that the wrong defendant has been charged is rarely the defense in rape cases. The standard defense is that the accuser and the accused did in fact have sex, but it was consensual on the accuser's part. At this point, the evidence becomes circumstantial to support one side or the other.

When you have the testimony of a victim that she was brutally raped by two individuals, and the defendants' case consists of a denial of force, you believe the victim's horrific testimony, or you do not. This dilemma is as old as the scripture and as current as today's headlines. In the seventeenth chapter of the Old Testament Book of Deuteronomy, the text prescribes that, the punishment for the commission of a wicked act is death by stoning. The text then addresses specifically the problem of two conflicting witnesses. It provides, "At the mouth of two witnesses or three witnesses shall he that is worthy of death be put to death but at the mouth of one witness he shall not be put to death." That is about as succinct a treatment of the problem in a forcible rape case as can be illustrated.

What is the situation in this case? The accuser states that she was walking alone in the late evening when the two defendants approached her, asked her to go with them and each defendant took one of her arms. They walked some distance to a field and they assisted her in getting over a gate. They went to a location that was out of sight of general passersby and she says that both defendants then raped her. She indicates that while one soldier had intercourse, the other soldier held her down, that she asked them to stop and attempted to resist. In her statement, she says:

"It was then I noticed the taller one undid his coat or something. I thought he might have a knife or something and was going to kill me … While this soldier was doing the act of intercourse, the taller one held a knife over my face where I could see it."

She then has a cross-examination by Major Keenan, who asks eleven leading questions, essentially adding nothing to the case. She tells Major Keenan that the knife was held over her face so that I could see the blade. Her statement ends with, "I got over the gate and went home." To support her version, the evidence consists of the testimony of Frederick Bandy, a friend and neighbor to whom she complained of the assault. He notified the police, and a doctor came to her house. According to the report by the Board of Review, Mr. Bandy, the police officer and the doctor testified she was crying, pale and in a very distressed condition; her lip was bruised, her nose appeared to be slightly swollen and her Mackintosh was mud stained. The doctor testified that she had recent intercourse. This point is not in dispute, as the defendants admit that fact. Unfortunately, we cannot see any condition of the victim; no other evidence exists about her bruised lip or swollen nose. In her statement, she never mentions any physical injury, other than the intercourse and the fact that a knife was held over her face.

At this stage, an investigation was made of the defendants' quarters and the defendant Pearson displayed his trousers, the knees of which were wet and muddy. The defendant Jones on the following day identified a pair of trousers, bearing stains on both knees and mud, as his. That substantiates only the fact that they were present in the muddy field, which neither one of them denied. Pearson further testified that during the intercourse she hugged and kissed him. Jones further states that she agreed to meet him at a pub the next night. Jones identified a pearl handled knife and admitted it was his. The knife was in the possession of the victim and there is no explanation why she had possession of the knife following the occurrence. The defendants indicate that they made a statement in which they admitted the act of intercourse with consent because they were told by the investigators that if they made a statement, they could return to their unit quicker. This is even more serious, because the victim could not identify either of the defendants. Consequently, the only proof against the two defendants is the statement of the victim combined with circumstantial evidence that she had bruises to

her face. No one states that the defendants caused the bruises and the defendants do not admit to that.

What we have are two defendants who admit having intercourse with a woman and a woman who told three persons what had happened. The reviewing board points out that the fresh complaint can be considered in a rape case. The better rule is that the lack of a fresh complaint is more important in determining innocence than a fresh complaint is of determining guilt.

The reviewing board takes great liberty with the testimony. Giving weight to the muddy condition of the defendants' trousers and the identification of the knife as belonging to Jones, very little weight need be given to those facts as the defendants never denied being in the muddy field. There is no explanation as to why a victim, who was threatened by the knife in her face, left the scene with the knife in her possession. An indication of how the board strains to affirm the conviction is given in paragraph 7B, where the Defense Counsel requested that any reference in each statement to the accused other than by the maker of the statement be deleted – certainly not an unreasonable request. The Law Member overruled the request and the statements were read to the court without deletion. The review board points out that afterward the Law Member instructed the other members of the court that: "The statement Jones made concerning Pearson shall not be considered against Pearson and the statement Pearson made or any reference he made concerning Jones shall not be considered against Jones." The board then decides that reading of the statements without deletion was free from error. This is over reaching at best.

In cases such as this, it is important to investigate the reputation of the parties involved. Both have a routine personal history with Jones having three AWOL incidents of three days each, none of which appeared of a serious nature, while Pearson had no military offenses at all. Pearson is found to be sociable and attends church almost every Sunday. Both defendants have a mental age of about ten years. The reports would indicate that Jones had very little criminal difficulty and Pearson had none. Given their earlier background, both men seem to have been as successful in civilian employment. Nothing in the report suggests serious criminal behavior. Since this offense occurred in the community where the accuser lived, standard procedure would now cause an investigation to be made as to the woman's general reputation in the community, both for chastity and truthfulness. Apparently, this may not have occurred and it leaves a serious gap in the prosecution's case.

Based on this set of facts, the court found both defendants guilty of rape and imposed the death penalty. To say that no reasonable doubt exists that these two defendants raped the accuser requires giving the testimony of the alleged victim total weight and the testimony of the two accused no weight at all. While it may very well be that the accuser told the truth in her testimony, to feel so confident of that as to impose a death sentence, I believe, is in error and that the sentence should have been life imprisonment. The case can stand as a perfect example of how reasonable doubt requires more doubt to acquit when the crime is a brutal, horrific one than it would in most other criminal cases.

## 85 & 86 – Henry W. Nelson and John T. Jones
*Inside the Jury Room*

The review of this case does not deal with the trial or to proof. The proof may not be as strong as one would like, but it seems to be sufficient to sustain a guilty verdict. The serious question arises because the record shows that only two-thirds of the jury voted to convict. Since this was a jury of seven members, two of them apparently voted to acquit. In the system then in place, the jury took two votes, first for guilt, in which two-thirds of the jury must concur, and a second vote shortly thereafter on the question of penalty, which required a unanimous verdict for the death penalty. Perhaps further research can clarify this.

According to the record in this case, on the first vote concerning guilt, two members of the jury thought the defendants were not guilty beyond a reasonable doubt; five voted to find the defendants guilty. That should have precluded receiving the death penalty in the next page. Shortly thereafter, the second vote was taken and these two jurors who felt they could not find the defendant guilty, voted to execute him; it was unanimous for death. This is a very difficult vote to understand. The only rationale that seems conceivable, but not reasonable, is that the two jurors, who voted that the defendants were not guilty, minutes later took the position that since the majority thought they were guilty, that that would conclude they were in fact guilty and felt that death was an appropriate penalty for the offense. That rationale seems tortured at best.

What happened in that jury room? Were the two jurors, in question, on their first death penalty jury? Were they seasoned veterans of the judicial procedures? Was the specter of command influence raised? Were the perceived desires of the approving authority discussed? While the counsels for the defense are obviously not allowed in the jury room, they need to ensure that they remind the jury in closing arguments that they should not be improperly influenced by these forces. The Defense Counsel in this case had two jurors ready to lean to a lesser sentence, as minutes before they had demonstrated they had reasonable doubt as to whether the defendants even committed the offenses – and he lost them in the jury room.

## 91 – Charles M. Robinson
*Fair and Impartial Juries*

The reason for this review is not because of the procedure, which occurred during the trial itself, but rather because of a general problem, which existed at that time and still remains of how to constitute a fair and impartial jury. The problem surfaces with General Eisenhower's letter, which directed that whenever practical, one or more "Negro" officers will be detailed as members of all court martials before which are to be tried "Negro" personnel for more serious crimes, including cases of violence and disorder and those of interracial sensibilities. The accused in this case was black; the charge was a serious crime. Therefore, every effort had to be made to obtain a black officer to serve on the court martial panel.

One of the concerns is that such a letter required that the court-martial panel not be composed by people chosen at random, but at least one member has to be chosen because of race. Any attempt to compose a jury, even for this reason, in order to give a defendant an advantage is an improper way to assemble a jury. The basis of assembling a jury of one's peers is to call them at random from a large group. In these cases, the members of the panel were selected by a higher-ranking officer to serve; unfortunately, we have no knowledge of what went into his decision to select any specific member of the court. In considering this letter, it is necessary to realize that in 1945 not only the military, but also the entire country was gingerly beginning to approach the problem of de-segregation and its results throughout everyday life. One of those serious results was the frequent trial of a black defendant by an all-white jury in military courts and civilian courts. The letter obviously was an attempt to rectify that situation, albeit clumsily.

In this case, the legal community made an effort to find a black officer to serve on the panel, but there was no one available in the command or in any command in close proximity. Therefore, Colonel C.B. Mickelwait, an Army Judge Advocate, wrote a letter on April 10, 1945 telling Major Joseph W. Riley, the Staff Judge Advocate, that as no black officers were available to serve on the court-martial panel that Major Riley had complied with the original theater directive. The review of record of trial by the division Judge Advocate approved of Major Joseph W. Riley's actions, even though he failed to carry out the directive. It is this author's opinion that the two officers (Mickelwait and Riley) did not have the authority not to comply with the theater commander's directive. They should have delayed the trial until the conditions expressed by General Eisenhower could be met.

A second issue is in play. Interestingly enough, the division staff judge advocate review was written twenty-three days after the letter to Major Riley. The review was written by Lieutenant Colonel Joseph W. Riley, the Division Judge Advocate. It is possible that the Major Joseph W. Riley of April 10, 1945, the Staff Judge Advocate, is a different person than Lieutenant Colonel Joseph W. Riley, the Division Judge Advocate who approved Major Riley's action. If they are one and the same, the review by Lieutenant Colonel Riley is inappropriate.

One additional element must also be addressed. In Lieutenant Colonel Riley's review, he explains his view of black witnesses and defendants. In deciding, whether leading questions were appropriate or not, Major Riley had stated:

> "Expedience also requires the propounding a leading question to colored witnesses who generally were evasive and reluctant or too voluble, enthusiastic and unrealistic have difficulty in finding language to express accurately their thoughts and knowledge and who often misconceive the purpose of the question."

Although no serious question exists concerning the defendant's guilt, the above procedural matters clearly are offensive to a current day reviewer. Theater Commander instructions on potential life and death issues are there to be followed. Officers are not entitled to review their previous opinions and decisions if they are subsequently promoted to a reviewing position. Finally, general categorizations about individuals smack of racism. In this case, where the evidence clearly demonstrated the guilt of the defendant, these avoidable errors only muddy the waters.

# View from a Potential Juror

*"It is not the critic who counts; not the man who points out how the strong man stumbles, or where the doer of deeds could have done them better. The credit belongs to the man who is actually in the arena ..."*

In each of these cases, I tried to avoid giving my own opinions on the verdict. This section is a summary of how I would have voted – had I been a colonel on a jury during the war – given the benefit of hindsight and the fact that I had much more time to mull over my opinion than the actual jurors had. This is not an exercise in "second guessing" the jury, but rather information for tomorrow's lawyers, as they try significant cases in the future. In a perfect world, we could locate the actual jurors and interview theme to see why a juror voted the way he did.

I must first explain my "internal compass" concerning reasonable doubt. For me to convict, I need to be between 91% and 95% certain that the accused committed the crime. Clearly, anything greater than 95% also falls in this category of beyond reasonable doubt. Imposing a sentence of death would require an even higher standard and I would have to be convinced that the accused committed the crime with 100% certainty, as after an execution,

it cannot be undone. Officers on General Courts-Martial knew that if they voted to execute, very few cases subsequently would be overturned – that would have been my assumption as a jury member.

One additional point concerns my "internal compass." I listened to soldiers for years and have a good sense when a trooper is telling the truth, shading the truth, or lying. In many of these cases in this study, I believed the accused lied in his statements to investigators or lied on the witness stand. In those cases, I frequently overcame reasonable doubt. Having said that, the same was true concerning prosecution witnesses; if I thought they lied, and I thought their testimony was critical in the case, I got to reasonable doubt quickly.

What follows, then, is just my opinion – not a lawyer, but the type of officer who would have been detailed to serve on these General Court-Martial panels in the European and North African/ Mediterranean Theaters of Operations.

**[1] David Cobb:** Cobb knew the official role of Lieutenant Cobner. I believe that Cobb also lied about Cobner's pistol. Cobb made up this story to introduce an element of self-defense. Verdict – Guilty; Sentence – Death.

**[2] Harold A. Smith:** He admitted killing the victim, and he lied in his statement that Jenkins was drawing his weapon. I do not believe that Smith was only sixteen. Concerning clemency, the officers should have thought about that before they voted. They could have then easily sentenced Smith to life. Verdict – Guilty; Sentence – Death.

**[3] James E. Kendrick:** Verdict – Guilty; Sentence – Death.

**[4, 5, 6 & 7] Willie A. Pittman, Harvey Stroud, Armstead White and David White:** The accused admitted they raped the victim. Common sense tells me that if the accused were tried separately, then they should have separate juries. I think the defense should have challenged that. They had a prompt: Lieutenant Schuveiller stated that he had previous knowledge of the case and he was excused. I would have voted to convict, but would want to actually hear and see the accused testify, before deciding on punishment.

**[8] Charles H. Smith:** The evidence was overwhelming that Smith murdered Tackett. While Smith was extremely intoxicated, his actions showed he knew what he was doing. Corporal Tackett was in the official performance of his duty and did nothing to worsen the situation. Verdict – Guilty; Sentence – Death.

**[9] Lee A. Davis:** The accused admitted firing his weapon and the shots killed someone. The expert witnesses confirmed that as well. Had there been no ensuing rape, I would have voted to convict, but would have had enough doubt that I would not have imposed the death penalty, as he appeared to show remorse. When he then committed the rape, his remorse starts to peel away. Verdict – Guilty; Sentence – Death.

**[10] Edwin P. Jones:** He clearly shot and killed the MP. Verdict – Guilty; Sentence – Death.

**[11] John H. Waters:** There is no doubt that the accused killed the victim. I would clearly vote to convict. I have some doubt as to whether or not the murder was premeditated. I would have to listen to and see all the witnesses before I could make that determination.

**[12] Charles E. Spears:** I would have voted to convict; clearly, Spears shot and killed Quick. I also would have listened very carefully to the witness who described Quick's previous behavior. If I believed that in Spears' mind, Quick was armed and dangerous, I would not have voted to hang him. Then again, there were all those previous Special Courts-Martial; this man was never going to be a good soldier.

**[13] J.C. Leatherberry:** Both defendants lied in portions of their testimony; Fowler told more of the truth, although he may have been far more involved than he let on and may have gotten lucky. The travel timeline proves beyond a reasonable doubt that Leatherberry could not have returned from London on December 8; he had to have returned the previous day; this overrides the alibi witnesses for the defense and destroys his entire testimony. Verdict – Guilty; Sentence – Death.

**[14] Wiley Harris, Jr.:** Harris clearly killed the victim. I have gone back and forth on this case and would have bought the self-defense; the pair set Harris up. I will not lose sleep over a pimp getting killed. With this charge, not guilty. Harris should not have been hanged.

**[15] Alex F. Miranda:** There is no doubt that Alex F. Miranda committed this murder; I would not have bought a defense based on alcohol consumption. A unit First Sergeant is the senior non-commissioned officer in charge of anywhere from 70 to 200 soldiers. A unit lives or dies based on the ability and courage of this person. Verdict – Guilty; Sentence – Death.

**[16] Robert L. Donnelly:** The accused deserted and then killed an MP. These are textbook crimes that in wartime the military justice system was designed to punish with the death penalty. Private Donnelly should have been executed, although a case could be made that it should have been by firing squad. Verdict – Guilty; Sentence – Death.

**[17 & 18] Eliga Brinson and Willie Smith:** Dr. Parks seems like a powerful expert witness, and I would have given a lot of weight to his testimony. I believe the men raped the victim; this was not a consensual meeting. Both Brinson's and Smith's stories about other soldiers wearing parts of their uniforms certainly sounds like a fabrication. Obviously, if it had been in existence, DNA testing would have solved this case quickly. Just looking at the files, I personally would have voted to convict, but would have sentenced them to life, because during the penalty phase a little voice of doubt – based on the inability of the victim to identify the assailants – would have crept into my head.

**[19] Clarence Whitfield:** I am inclined to believe the victim; I do not think that two girls would just decide to have sex with four armed men from an invading army in a dirty farm field. I suspect that the accused and his companions did not fully comprehend that "No meant no." Whitfield knew something was wrong with what happened or he would not have changed his story several times. I am not sure that his statements before being advised of his rights should have been considered. Verdict – Guilty; Sentence – Death.

**[20] Ray Watson:** The accused admitting shooting the victim. The MPs were in the performance of their duty and did not inflame the situation with threatening words. Numerous witnesses saw Watson shoot and kill Brockman. I do not buy Watson's claim that he was so drunk as to not be responsible – he avoided capture for several hours with several MPs right on his tail. Verdict – Guilty; Sentence – Death.

**[21] Madison Thomas:** How was the company line-up conducted in which the accused was identified; how strong was the identification of the accused; what were the rules then in admitting evidence of prior bad behavior? That previous court-martial for threatening a woman is pretty damning information. I would need more information before casting a vote in this case.

**[22 & 23] James B. Sanders and Roy W. Anderson:** We may never truly understand this one. How competent was the interpreter? Why did the jury later request life imprisonment? Just looking at the trial records is insufficient for me to render an opinion.

**[24] Paul W. Kluxdal:** He clearly shot the First Sergeant. His Defense Counsels did not do him any favors; they should have met with him more – if we are to believe his letter. They also should have put him on the stand so everything about his knee could have come out. I would have voted to convict, but am not sure about the penalty.

**[25 & 26] Joseph Watson & Willie Wimberly, Jr.:** I have no reasonable doubt in this case. It was good to see a colonel take charge. Verdict – Guilty; Sentence – Death.

**[27] Richard B. Scott:** It is beyond reasonable doubt that Scott raped the woman. If the husband of the rape victim did encourage the accused to have sex with his wife, I do not believe he would later attend Scott's execution – which he did. The prosecution should have produced the bloody shirt and bayonet and for those reasons, I would have found the defendant, Not Guilty on the two specifications related to assault. As a result, I would have voted for life imprisonment.

**[28] William D. Pennyfeather:** The accused obviously had a difficult life, but he knew what he was doing and there appears to be nothing in the conduct of the case that was untoward. Verdict – Guilty; Sentence – Death.

**[29] Curtis L. Maxey:** I am not sure this guy ever told the truth. Verdict – Guilty; Sentence – Death.

**[30] Theron W. McGann:** Verdict – Guilty; Sentence – Death.

**[31 & 32] Arthur E. Davis and Private Charles H. Jordan:** The defense offered no alternative theory to raise reasonable doubt. Verdict – Guilty; Sentence – Death.

**[33] James E. Hendricks:** Hendricks lied at least four times. His most truthful statement may have been months later to the Chaplain – seconds before he was executed – when he said, "Tell all the boys not to do what I did." I would have voted for the death penalty, unless Lieutenant Colonel Sedillo and Captain Orr could have strongly explained why they requested clemency.

**[34] Benjamin Pygate:** There is reasonable doubt in just reviewing the files. I would have needed to hear the witnesses on the stand to assess the credibility of each. I am not even sure they have the correct murder weapon. Pygate was a bad man; maybe the worst of the 96, based on his civilian criminal record, but just because he had been incarcerated in Sing Sing does not mean he did this crime. He probably did it, but probably is not enough to convict.

**[35 & 36] Oscar N. Newman and Leo Valentine, Sr.:** Verdict – Guilty; Sentence – Death.

**[37] William E. Davis:** He clearly shot and killed the woman, but I do not think he intended to kill her. I would have voted to convict and gone with life in prison.

**[38 & 39] Ernest L. Clark and Augustine M. Guerra:** Verdict – Guilty; Sentence – Death. I wonder why they did not plead guilty and go for life imprisonment?

**[40 & 41] John David Cooper and J.P. Wilson:** I would want to hear the witnesses in person to try to determine their certainty of identification; until then I cannot make a decision. After reading Wilson's interview on January 27, 1945, I would order the case to be re-opened.

**[42] Walter J. Baldwin:** Baldwin undoubtedly killed Adolpha Drouin and wounded his wife. I am not certain that his actions were premeditated. Baldwin's statement to Agent Fisher seems "coached," especially (my underline):

"At this time I could see no one around <u>nor was there anyone so far as I could see barring my chance of escaping or running away</u>."

Privates just do not use these types of words and phrases. I would have voted to convict, but would have voted to sentence him to life.

**[43] Arthur J. Farrell:** Farrell committed the rape and that Teton later lied to try to save his friend. I wish I knew what Cowan and Hayden said about disposing of Teton's bloody field jacket. I might have voted to give both Farrell and Teton the death sentence. Verdict – Guilty; Sentence – Death.

**[44] James W. Twiggs:** There is no doubt that Twiggs shot and killed Adams. Given the events and multiple threats that day, I would have voted for life imprisonment.

**[45 & 46] Mervin Holden and Elwood J. Spencer:** They did it; "no" means "no." Verdict – Guilty; Sentence – Death.

**[47] Eddie Slovik:** No doubt about his guilt. I might have inquired on whether he could have been hanged instead. Verdict – Guilty; Sentence – Death.

**[48 & 49] Waiters Yancy and Robert L. Skinner:** This was a brutal attack. Skinner probably heard through "stockade scuttlebutt" that he could claim the rape was consensual, but the victim bit him and he slapped her, which throws his assertion out. Verdict – Guilty; Sentence – Death.

**[50] William Mack:** The most important testimony is that of the neuro-psychiatrist. If Mack was sane and knew what he was doing, I would vote to convict and sentence him to death. He was either an inveterate liar or he was crazy; I would have wanted to carefully hear on the witness stand what the doctors had to say about his mental condition.

**[51] Otis B. Crews:** Crews clearly shot and killed the MP. I do not believe that the MPs were going to shoot the three men, but I am not sure exactly what was said in the bar that might have escalated the situation. I therefore would have voted for a sentence of life imprisonment.

**[52] William C. Downes:** I cannot make a determination without actually hearing and seeing the demeanor of each witness. This study was unable to determine those special considerations that General Eisenhower invoked, but the fact that both General Clay and General Eisenhower reduced portions of the conviction and sentences show they took their responsibility seriously – no one would have objected if both had confirmed the orders to execute all three defendants.

**[53, 54 & 55] Amos Agee, John C. Smith and Frank Watson:** I believe that all three men raped the victim and that Watson robbed two Frenchmen; I do not believe Watson's assertion that the victims lied. I would have voted to convict. This is another case where I would want to actually hear and see the accused testify before deciding whether to vote for life imprisonment or the death penalty.

**[56 & 57] Cubia Jones and Robert L. Pearson:** Reading the file I am filled with reasonable doubt; it seems like a consensual encounter that may have been rough contact but did not turn into an accusation of rape until the woman needed to conceal the nature of the event. Her answers to the investigator seem impertinent. The statements of Jones and Pearson soon after the incident provide several indications that she consented. I would vote to acquit both.

**[58] Kinney Jones:** It is clear that Jones shot and killed an NCO in the performance of his duty. This type of crime seems to be suited for a sentence of "Death by Musketry." Verdict – Guilty; Sentence – Death.

**[59] John H. Mack:** Verdict – Guilty; Sentence – Death.

**[60] John W. Taylor:** I concur with the Theater Judge Advocate. Taylor clearly murdered the victim, but the fact that the victim had earlier pointed his weapon at Taylor would cause me to give him the lesser penalty of life imprisonment.

**[61] Lee A. Burns:** I think Burns probably committed the crime, but "probably" is not good enough. I would want to hear from Corporal Ballard, before rendering a verdict.

**[62] Abraham Smalls:** Private Smalls clearly shot and killed the victim. While this was no defense in committing the crime, I would have taken into consideration how the victim had picked on Smalls and sentenced Smalls to life imprisonment.

**[63] General L. Grant:** I am leaning toward a conviction, but I would like to see the accused in court, as I could be persuaded to vote for life imprisonment.

**[64] Olin W. Williams:** Williams lied in his statement; he also acted guilty in the lineup. Verdict – Guilty; Sentence – Death.

**[65] Tommie Davison:** I think that Davison was so intoxicated he may not have remembered exactly what he did, but that is no excuse. What did he mean on the scaffold that he had five non-commissioned officers who could show he was not guilty? We need to talk to them.

**[66] William Harrison, Jr.:** Verdict – Guilty; Sentence – Death.

**[67] Benjamin F. Hopper:** Hopper shot and killed the victim; that was never in dispute. I concur with the First Army Staff Judge Advocate and the Commander; I would have voted to convict, but would have voted for a sentence of life imprisonment.

**[68, 69 & 70] John Williams, James L. Jones and Milbert Bailey:** With no complete judicial file to review, it is not possible to render an opinion.

**[71] Shelton McGhee, Sr.:** I concur with the findings of guilty, but agree with the opinions that the sentence should have been reduced to life imprisonment. Corporal McGhee's previous excellent service should have carried some weight.

**[72] George E. Smith, Jr.:** Clearly, Smith committed the murder. I am not sure about his mental state so I might have voted for life imprisonment, but I agree with the English psychiatrist that this guy should never be let out of incarceration.

**[73] George Green, Jr.:** Green clearly murdered Corporal Garrett. However, he was a decent young man and could have been rehabilitated. On the other hand, officers have to protect non-commissioned officers doing their duty. I would have voted to convict and however an unpleasant duty, would have voted for the death penalty. Verdict – Guilty; Sentence – Death.

**[74] Haze Heard:** No opinion can be rendered without a review of the judicial file.

**[75] William J. McCarter:** The accused clearly was guilty of pre-meditated murder and I would have voted to convict. If the company commander submitted a strong statement, requesting leniency, I would have voted for life imprisonment.

**[76] Clete O. Norris:** Because of his statement, it appears that the accused was guilty of killing Captain McDonald. The TJA did not present a motive, so I would have voted to convict and voted for life imprisonment. Had Norris not given a statement, I do not believe the Army would have proven the case. This case is a shame, because Norris seemed to be a good soldier.

**[77] Alvin R. Rollins:** The legal reviews are a bit confusing over the issue of whether or not the accused admitted firing his German pistol on the day the crime was committed. However, everyone else in the jeep can be eliminated as potential shooters and the powder burns on both victims show that the bullets had to have been fired from inside the vehicle. Rollins committed the murders and just kept lying about what happened. Verdict – Guilty; Sentence – Death.

**[78] Matthew Clay, Jr.:** Clay murdered Victor Bellery and seriously wounded his wife. Clay lied to an officer the night of the crime and gave a false name to an investigating agent. Even if we throw out the one confession due to possible duress, there is more than enough evidence of guilt. Verdict – Guilty; Sentence – Death.

**[79] Werner E. Schmiedel:** Verdict – Guilty; Sentence – Death.

**[80] Aniceto Martinez:** The accused committed the crime. Despite the fact that the victim's statement, "Let's get it over so you can go back home," is somewhat ambiguous, Martinez roughed her up and gave her a black eye, while he raped her. Verdict – Guilty; Sentence – Death.

**[81] Victor Ortiz:** The accused shot and killed the victim. It was not self-defense. I would have voted to convict and then voted for the death penalty, but I would have pushed for a firing squad. Verdict – Guilty; Sentence – Death.

**[82] Willie Johnson:** The accused committed the crime. Even if his confession is thrown out, he said enough to other soldiers, combined with physical evidence in the truck, to convict him. I believe he also played "dumb" with the three medical doctors. If he was smart enough to know how to drive a truck, he was smart enough to know that driving over someone with that truck would kill her. Verdict – Guilty; Sentence – Death.

**[83 & 84] Fred A. McMurray and Louis Till:** It was a good thing that Private James Thomas, Jr. decided to testify against his fellow accused. He may well have been involved more than he let on. McMurray was liar and Till was a brutal ringleader. Verdict – Guilty; Sentence – Death.

**[85 & 86] Henry W. Nelson and John T. Jones:** I would like to know what made the two jurors initially vote to acquit. I would want to actually hear and see the witnesses before voting. If I did decide to vote guilty, I do not think I would have voted for the death penalty.

**[87] Charles H. Jefferies:** The soldier should have been medically discharged years before, due to complications from his fractured skull. Verdict – Guilty; Sentence – Life.

**[88] Tom Gordon:** There is no doubt that Gordon committed the crime. The witnesses seem split as to how drunk he was on the night in question. I believe I would have voted to convict and follow the Trial Judge Advocate, sentencing Gordon to life.

**[89] Robert Wray:** I do not buy the self-defense theory; he also changed his story. The language got in the gutter quickly in the café; the white soldiers may have used racial epithets; I would vote for life imprisonment. Bar-fights are tough to figure out.

**[90] Henry C. Philpot:** Philpot killed Lieutenant Platt. Verdict – Guilty; Sentence – Death.

**[91] Charles M. Robinson:** I believe that Private Robinson shot and killed the victim. However, I do not think that the division should have gone ahead with the trial and not complied with General Eisenhower's directive; they could have waited until they found a black officer.

**[92] Blake W. Mariano:** I believe that Mariano shot and killed the victim; I am not sure about the two rapes. I would have voted for conviction and using the War Department rationale concerning a "creditable combat record" would have voted for life.

**[93 & 94] Woodrow Parker and Sydney Bennerman:** With no complete judicial file, it is not possible to evaluate the case. This case had a set of heinous circumstances, especially for Bennerman, who had previous problems with non-commissioned officers.

**[95] Mansfield Spinks:** Spinks committed the crimes. However, if his mother was telling the truth in her letter, Spinks never should have been drafted in the first place. I would have voted to convict, but would have voted for life imprisonment.

**[96] Charlie Ervin:** Verdict – Guilty; Sentence – Life. I would have used the Army directive concerning combat actions and as Ervin received a Purple Heart, I would have cut him a tiny bit of slack. Without the combat award, he hangs.

In summary,
I would have voted in the following manner:

| | |
|---|---|
| **Guilty Verdict** <br> Death Sentence | 37 Defendants |
| **Guilty Verdict** <br> Life Imprisonment Sentence | 27 Defendants |
| **Guilty Verdict** <br> Uncertain on Sentence <br> Need More Information <br> (See the defendant) | 10 Defendants |
| **Uncertain Verdict** <br> Need More Information <br> (See and hear witnesses <br> and defendant at trial) | 11 Defendants |
| **Not Guilty** | 4 Defendants |
| **No Verdict Possible** <br> (no judicial file to review) | 6 Defendants |
| **Trial Should Not <br> Have Been Held** <br> (no black juror) | 1 Defendant |

# Conclusions and Future Fields of Study

*"Records of trial of more than 12,000 soldiers by general courts-martial in the European Theater of Operations were received by the Branch Office of the Judge Advocate General before 8 May 1945; other tens of thousands were tried by inferior courts-martial. The causes for this problem population are complex."*[1]

Numerous observations can be made from these 96 cases. Equally important are some recommendations for further examination of issues that were beyond the resources of this study to pursue, but that might lead to some significant findings.

## The Accused

All 96 soldiers were male. Concerning race, seventy-five soldiers were black (78.1%); fifteen soldiers were white (15.6%); four were Hispanic (4.1%) – with three being of Mexican descent, and one of Puerto Rican descent; and two were American Indian (2%), as defined then. One of these last two soldiers was Navajo. Personnel files showed ninety-two exact birthplaces. Georgia was home for eleven of the condemned. North Carolina and Mississippi had eight. South Carolina and Alabama had seven.

The judicial and personnel files for the 96 confirm the birthdates for eighty-eight of those executed. Actual birth years ranged from 1905 to 1924. William J. McCarter was the "old man" at 38½, when he was executed; Arthur J. Farrell and John Waters were 38. Paul Kluxdal was 37. On the other end was Leo Valentine, Sr., who was 19 when executed, as was Robert L. Donnelly. Alvin R. Rollins, Harold A. Smith, Mansfield Spinks, Robert L. Skinner, Alex Miranda, George Green, Jr., Elwood Spencer and Lee A. Davis were 20. For the most part, Eisenhower's advisors had been proven mostly correct when they said:

> "The entire command is composed of young men and every case coming to your attention will be that of a young man."

Sixty-one (63.54%) of those executed had information in the judicial file showing that they had been convicted by a previous court-martial. The infractions ran from absent without leave, which ranked first among previous offenses, to disobeying an officer. Two of the men were convicted by a previous GCM. Six of the men (6.25%) previously had been convicted of a felony in civilian life – a situation that would have seemed intolerable, if the Army had been aware of these convictions.

Every one of the soldiers was a junior enlisted man. The highest ranking was Clete Norris, a Sergeant (1%.) Four men held the rank of corporal (4.1%.) Five men (5.2%) held the rank of Technician Fifth Grade (T/5.) While that rank was officially not a corporal, the individual was paid as a corporal and most units treated them as though they were corporals. Officially, however, a T/5 did not have the authority to give commands or issue orders. Thirteen soldiers (13.5%) held the rank of Private First Class, and seventy-three soldiers were Privates (76%.)

## The Victims

The case of Eddie Slovik, for desertion, had no individual victim. Ninety-five cases had at least one victim of rape, murder or both. Seventy-one victims were civilians; thirty murder victims and thirty-six rape victims; in five cases, the accused raped and murdered the woman. Twenty-six military personnel were murder victims. Seventy of the civilian victims were white; the other was African; none of the civilian victims was an American. Nine of the accused, whose civilian victims were white, were also white. Two of the accused, whose civilian victims were white, were Hispanic. One of the accused, whose civilian victims were white, was a Navajo Native American. Fifty-eight of the accused, whose civilian victims were white, were black. A white soldier murdered the African civilian victim.

Concerning military victims, all were male. In four cases, commissioned officers were the victims. One of the officers was Puerto Rican; a Puerto Rican soldier killed him. Three of the officers murdered were white. A Native American killed one; black soldiers killed two in separate incidents. Twenty-two enlisted men were victims; eleven were black. For these eleven, their killers were black. The other eleven enlisted murder victims were white: five killed by whites; five killed by blacks; one by a Mexican-American.

## The Units

Twenty of the 96 men (20.8%) were assigned to the general category of combat arms units. These types of units do most of the actual fighting and killing of the enemy, although on many battlefields, every soldier in every type of unit is at risk. Another six soldiers (6.2%) could be termed as being assigned to combat support units. Combat support refers to units that provide operational and specialized support to combat forces, such as combat engineers, although in many instances combat engineers fought in direct combat roles. The other seventy men (72.9%) served in combat service support units, providing supply, maintenance, transportation, health care and other services required by combat units.

Company C of the 249th Quartermaster Battalion had four men sentenced to death and executed (for one incident in Sicily), the highest of any battalion-size or lower unit. The 644th Quartermaster Troop Transport Company had three soldiers executed for one incident in France. The 434th Port Company of the 501st Port Battalion also had three soldiers executed for one incident. The 366th Infantry Regiment of the Ninety-Second Infantry Division was home to four soldiers, who were later executed, while the division's 371st Infantry Regiment had three. This division convicted and executed eleven soldiers, far outdistancing any other division; the One Hundredth Infantry Division, with two condemned, was the only other division to have more than one soldier executed.

## The Convening/Approving Authorities

In many cases, convening/approving authorities were base section commanders, in whose areas various combat service support units operated. The leading convening/approving authorities in terms of death penalty executions were:

| | | |
|---|---|---|
| Major General Edward Almond | Ninety-Second Infantry Division (MTO) | 11 executions |
| Brigadier General Ewart Plank | Advance Section of the Communications Zone (ETO) | 10 executions |
| Brigadier General Henry Aurand | Normandy Base Section (ETO) | 9 executions |
| Lieutenant General George Patton | Third Army (ETO) | 7 executions |
| Lieutenant General Omar Bradley | II Corps/First Army (NA & ETO) | 5 executions |
| Brigadier General Francis Oxx | Peninsular Base Section (MTO) | 5 executions |
| Brigadier Charles Thrasher | Southern Base Section/ Oise Intermediate Section (ETO) | 5 execution |

## The Confirming Authorities

Only five senior officers ever sat in the position of confirming authority for the North African/ Mediterranean and the European Theaters of Operation regarding cases, ending with executions. They were General Dwight Eisenhower – seventy-one cases (73.9%); General Joseph McNarney – sixteen cases (16.6%); Lieutenant General Jacob Devers – seven cases (7.2%); Lieutenant General Frank Andrews – one case (1%); and General Omar Bradley – one case (1%.)

However, numbers tell only part of the story. It appears that the confirmation authorities took this responsibility seriously. Having said that, there was

a war on and other decisions made the confirmation of a death sentence seem small in comparison. For example, on June 9, 1944 reports of losses from the June 6, 1944 invasion of Normandy were streaming into the ETO Headquarters of the ETO. On invasion day, 156,000 Allied troops clawed their way ashore in Normandy – and Dwight Eisenhower was responsible for every single one of them. Some 2,499 American soldiers died the first day, with thousands more wounded. After an initial delay, the Germans raced their vaunted *panzer* divisions to the battle to drive the Allies into the sea. Eisenhower won the battle for reinforcements; by June 11, 1944, some 326,547 Allied troops were ashore. Three soldiers, who would not be crossing the beach, were Henry C. Philpot, Willie Smith and Eliga Brinson. On June 7th and 9th, General Eisenhower reviewed their convictions and confirmed the sentences.

On December 16, 1944, General Eisenhower signed the confirmation order for James W. Twiggs. The same day, the German Sixth SS *Panzer* Army, the Fifth *Panzer* Army and the Seventh Army – several hundred thousand men – with hundreds of dreaded *Panther* and *Tiger* tanks – smashed through American lines in the Ardennes sector of Belgium. During the entire four-week struggle, American forces suffered some 19,246 killed in action, 62,489 wounded in action and 26,612 captured or missing; many of the casualties came on that first day – December 16. Eisenhower certainly had to take some time contemplating Twiggs, but he had the hurricane of the German *Wehrmacht* to consider as well.

## The Juries

This study was able to identify **409** personnel as jury members in these cases. Every juror was male and a commissioned officer from the grade of second lieutenant to colonel. While a few of these officers received promotions later to the general officer grades, there was no evidence that service on these juries affected their chances for promotion. A distribution by grade follows:

| COMPANY-GRADE OFFICERS | |
|---|---|
| Second Lieutenant | 13 (3.17%) |
| First Lieutenant | 36 (8.80%) |
| Captain | 105 (25.67%) |
| FIELD-GRADE OFFICERS | |
| Major | 127 (31.05%) |
| Lieutenant Colonel | 80 (19.55%) |
| Colonel | 48 (11.73%) |

It is difficult to generalize about seniority in military juries, except to say that the more senior an officer was, in general, the more experience he had dealing with soldiers. Every officer had another primary job, whether that was as a staff officer at a headquarters or as a commanding officer. Second and first lieutenants often were platoon leaders,

responsible for the lives of thirty soldiers. Captains or first lieutenants commanded companies of between seventy and two-hundred men. In the field-grade positions, lieutenant colonels (majors in their absence) often commanded battalions that ranged of four-hundred to eight-hundred soldiers. Colonels often commanded regiments, whose authorized strength was over two-thousand. While jury duty provided the officers with an opportunity for a hot meal and a shower to the rear of the front line, most officers were anxious to return to their regular responsibilities. There were no minimum requirements for each branch to be represented; commands selected from assigned strength, so an area that had a lot of quartermaster units could be expected to have a fair amount of quartermaster-officers on General Courts-Martial. For identified jurors, the four leading branches represented were Corps of Engineers – sixty-six, Infantry – sixty-one, Quartermaster – fifty-four, and Field Artillery – twenty-five. Sixteen Judge Advocates sat as voting members on juries, often as Law Members. Determining the source of commission for jury members was beyond the scope of this study, although we do know that twenty-two officers (5.37%) on these juries graduated from the United States Military Academy at West Point.

Several officers sat on more than one GCM that resulted in an execution. Sitting on multiple panels that resulted in the deaths of five soldiers were four officers (0.97%): Colonel James Weeks, Lieutenant Colonel James C. Horne, Captain Wendell L. Price and Captain James L. Glymph. Eighteen officers (4.40%) sat on panels that resulted in the executions of four men, and twenty-four officers (6.26%) sat on juries that resulted in executions of three soldiers.

A full analysis of the race for each juror is an important area for future research. It is also not known how strenuously each unit attempted to follow theater guidance to ensure that at least one black officer was on the jury if the accused was black and if the crime was violent, which by definition – with the exception of desertion – these cases were. This study found that **thirteen** of the GCMs had at least one black officer on the jury, but this examination is only preliminary.

## The Executioners

Firing squads ("shot to death by musketry") executed seven of the condemned men; the study identified the commanding officer for **five** of the firing squads – a rough equivalent to an executioner, although the commanding officer did not personally fire his own weapon. First Lieutenant Clyde R. Thorn supervised two executions by firing squad in Italy. Major William Fellman II commanded the firing squad of Eddie Slovik; Captain Philip J. Flynn led the firing squad of Benjamin Pygate. Lieutenant Colonel James C. Cullens presided over the firing squad that executed Alex Miranda.

Eighty-nine men died of hanging by the neck until dead. The executioner in these cases is considered as the person, who directly causes the trap door to open. British official executioner, Thomas Pierrepoint conducted **seventeen** hangings; he had various assistants. English hangmen pushed a lever that released the trap doors. Major Mortimer H. Christian, Commandant, Seine DTC, served as the executioner in **eight** executions (8.98% of the hangings.) Lieutenant Colonel Henry L. Peck, Commandant, Loire DTC, was the executioner for **two** (2.24% of the hangings.) Both men cut a taut rope that put the release of the trap door into motion.

## The "Hidden Hangman"

In the fall of 1944, reports of executions in France stopped naming the actual executioner, which until that point had been Lieutenant Colonel Peck or Major Christian and began referring to "the executioner." Personnel and finance clerks provided the clues concerning their identities. While official reports of execution omitted the name of the hangman, personnel and finance orders could not. These clerks generated rosters, showing name, rank and service number, which allowed transportation, messing and quarters to be provided. In each case, the mission of the group of soldiers was "to carry out the instructions of the Commanding General." Orders from the Headquarters of the Brittany Base Section, dated December 22, 1944, directed that Master Sergeant John C. Woods and Technician Third Grade Thomas F. Robinson go to "necessary places on temporary duty." Those orders took him to the execution of William E. Davis. On January 2, 1945, the Loire DTC published orders requesting that travel documents be issued to two officers, four non-commissioned officers and one junior enlisted man. Three of the non-commissioned officers were Sergeant Cavicchioli, Sergeant Dyro and Sergeant Girvalo – all three had been at numerous executions, serving as immediate guards of the condemned. The fourth non-commissioned officer was Master Sergeant John C. Woods, 37540591; the orders also requested a truck to haul the gallows. A second set of orders directed that Woods go to Beaufay, France on January 16, 1945; Walter Baldwin was executed in Beaufay the next day. Another set of orders, dated January 26, 1945, directed Woods and others to go

to Namur, Belgium and to Lérouville, France after that. The Army hanged Mervin Holden and Elwood J. Spencer at Namur on January 30, 1945 and J.P. Wilson at Lérouville on February 2, 1945.

Orders, dated February 25, 1945, directed that Woods go to Étienville, France two days before the execution of William C. Downes at that village. Another set of orders, dated April 16, 1945, showed this NCO needed orders to attend what was obviously another execution – most likely that of Milbert Bailey, James L. Jones and John Williams who would be hanged at La Pernelle in Normandy on April 19, 1945. Orders, dated May 17, 1945, sent him to Mesnil-Clinchamps for Haze Heard's hanging. These various orders are corroborated by the daily morning reports of the 2913th DTC, showing Master Sergeant Woods on temporary duty to these locations during the period of execution. He attended at least sixteen hangings away from the Loire DTC and was present at Le Mans on the days when twelve additional executions occurred. Policy letters also support the involvement of Woods. On March 5, 1945, the ETO directed that GCM jurisdictions that had a soldier confirmed to be executed, contact the Commanding Officer, Loire DTC and this officer would "furnish an experienced hangman with one assistant, and a recorder for the execution." Woods was the only experienced hangman at the Loire DTC.[2]

An examination of his personnel file reveals that Master Sergeant Woods was assigned to the 2913th DTC. The Commandant of the 2913th, Lieutenant Colonel Henry Peck, oversaw thirty executions (in which he was not the executioner.) It seems likely that Master Sergeant Woods participated in many of these events – certainly at least thirty-four – and travelled to the Seine DTC, where he was an assistant for three other hangings.

In early 1945, two additional names surfaced as attending several executions. They were Technician Fifth Grade George H. Garnand (38395128) and Technician Fifth Grade Norman A. McCllen (36781644.) They were never named as executioners and never served as escorts for the condemned in their final march to the gallows. However, they may have played some role, possibly as drivers of the heavy transporter on which was the portable scaffold.

## "Botched" Executions

The Army thrives on practice and rehearsals, believing that mistakes made in practice can be rectified before the unit or individual has to do the mission in combat. Practicing for an execution was difficult, as the emotions involved could not be adequately replicated. Although every one of the 96 executions ended in death, it appears that **fifteen** (15.62%) could be described as "botched" (or flawed) executions. Two were firing squads – Private Alex F. Miranda and Private Eddie Slovik. For Miranda, officials did not install a bullet-absorbing backstop; as a result, dangerous ricochets flew through the air during the firing squad's volley. In Slovik's firing squad, the marksmanship of the unit did not immediately kill the condemned.

The other **thirteen** executions that did not go according to plan were hangings: Walter J. Baldwin, Lee A. Davis, Tommie Davison, Benjamin F. Hopper, Paul M. Kluxdal, William Mack, Clete Norris, James B. Sanders, John C. Smith, James W. Twiggs, J.P. Wilson, Willie Wimberly, Jr. and Waiters Yancy. In one case (Davis), the hangman was Englishman Thomas Pierrepoint. In **nine** cases (Baldwin, Hopper, Davison, Mack, Norris, Smith, Twiggs, Wilson and Yancy), Master Sergeant Woods was the primary hangman. For one case (Wimberly), Lieutenant Colonel Mortimer H. Christian was the primary hangman; and in two cases (Sanders and Kluxdal) Christian served as the hangman, with Woods serving as the assistant, who would have prepared the equipment and adjusted the rope. In all known instances, the condemned man did not have his spinal cord fatally severed at the end of the drop, but took up to twenty minutes to die.

## "The Dirty Dozen"

The fiction movie *The Dirty Dozen* was an account of a U.S. Army major – played by Lee Marvin – who is to train a dozen Army General Prisoners, convicted of murder and sentenced to death, for a mission to kill German officers in France. On the suicide mission, most of the participants died by the movie's end. The film was based on E.M. Nathanson's fiction book, *The Dirty Dozen*, which was influenced by a small group of real-life airborne pathfinder troopers, known as "The Filthy Thirteen," in the One-Hundred and First Airborne Division. The paratroopers were often in trouble, but none had faced a General Court-Martial.

This study has found that before the Normandy invasion, Major General Clarence Huebner, the Commanding General of the First Infantry Division, suggested that selected General Prisoners fight in special "Engineer (Battlefield) Demolition Removal Units." Their mission would be to deploy in advance of regular combat troops to clear the battlefield of mines and other explosives left by the enemy – in lieu of employing Engineer troops in this dangerous work. The Army would suspend each man's sentence, which would give the men an opportunity

of "redeeming and purging" themselves of blemishes by previous misconduct. Several senior officers thought the suggestion excellent; one officer noted that only volunteer GPs should fight in such units, otherwise "we can expect a great many AWOLs." The plan is believed to have made it to the Deputy Theater Commander for consideration, where wiser heads prevailed.[3]

## Contributing Factors

The General Board, United States Forces, European Theater, Judge Advocate Section, in its analysis, "The Military Offender in the Theater of Operations," stated, "Intoxication was the largest contributing factor to crime in the European Theater of Operations." [4] For at least **seventy** of those convicted and executed (72.91%), alcohol consumption was a contributing factor in the crime. Some of the soldiers were actually searching for alcohol, when they got into trouble. Part of the problem was too much consumption, but unfamiliarity with foreign types of alcohol (e.g. grappa, calvados and schnapps) also contributed to the problem. While the Army of World War II was not the "drinking man's army" that the post-Civil War frontier army was, some commanders seem to have tolerated drinking off duty and sometimes even turned a blind eye toward drinking on duty. Thus, many defendants attempted to use alcohol consumption (e.g. intoxication) as a defense against the charges against them. Finally, there was a plethora of captured enemy firearms; it often seemed that every soldier had a German P-38 or Luger P-08 pistol and at least a handful of ammunition. Unfortunately, that was often enough ammo to commit a serious crime, especially if the soldier mixed carrying firearms with binge drinking.

This leads us to the topic of inadequate supervision. In this study's opinion, one of the reasons that so many offenders came from combat support units was a lack of supervision. At the front, infantry and armor soldiers were under constant supervision by tough, no-nonsense NCOs. A soldier simply could not decide to leave his foxhole in the middle of the Hürtgen Forest to find some alcohol and female companionship – he would probably get lost and step on a mine in just a few minutes. Logistical soldiers received independent missions – such as driving a truck long distances, often without NCO supervision. In fact, sometimes the driver was the only soldier in the vehicle. In several cases in this study, NCOs in these non-combat units could have done a much better job overseeing the activities of junior personnel, but failed to do so.

## Administrative Issues

The Army examined the entire judicial procedure in Europe after the war. On June 17, 1945, General Dwight Eisenhower signed General Order 128, ordering a factual analysis of the strategy, tactics and administration employed by U.S. forces in the ETO. To do this, the headquarters established an analytical group known as the General Board, which temporarily assigned subject matter experts to tackle the various reports. A Judge Advocate Section completed three reports that addressed issues germane to this study: "The Judge Advocate Section in Theater of Operations," Study 82; "Military Justice Administration in Theater of Operations," Study 83; and "The Military Offender in the Theater of Operations," Study 84.

These studies mentioned found significant shortfalls in the generalized administration of justice. First, they noted that there were not nearly enough Judge Advocate officers in the European Theater. On "VE Day," 485 Judge Advocate officers were in the ETO.[5] There simply were not enough JAG officers to go around. There was a great need for trained officers with trial experience to prosecute and defend courts-martial cases, as well as to review the records for legal sufficiency. Not only were Judge Advocates required to bring to technical judicial skill to prevent errors in trial procedure, but also experience and sound judgment to ensure that justice was actually done. As a GCM could impose serious punishment, it was important that both the prosecution and the defense be men, "conscious of their responsibility and qualified by trial experience and training in military law to discharge it." In other words, skilled lawyers were needed as Defense Counsels, Trial Judge Advocates and Law Members. As the report stated:[6]

> "Although Article of War 8 requires the use of a Judge Advocate officer as Law Member on a General Court-Martial, if he is available, in many instances they were not available."

Some officers, lawyers in civilian life, who served in other branches (i.e. Field Artillery, Infantry, or Coast Artillery), occasionally served in legal positions at courts-martial, but this was an inadequate solution. As the report stated:[7]

> "Further, it was too optimistic to expect any officer who assisted with the principal General Court-Martial functions, in addition to his other duties, to handle military justice problems with the skill judgment and thoroughness that was desired."

The report stated that as a rule, Staff Judge Advocates had direct access to commanding generals. SJAs also had an opportunity to present their views either in writing or orally. Many commanding generals dealt directly with their Judge Advocates in person, allowing them access at any time a matter was considered sufficiently important to be brought to the commander's attention. Others directed that the Judge Advocate take military justice matters up with the chief of staff. A few commanders required the submission of military justice matters through the Assistant Chief of Staff, Personnel (G-1.) General Eisenhower permitted his Judge Advocate direct access on all military justice matters.[8]

Finally, the report mentioned that there was an over-emphasis on speed in courts-martial. While it was recognized that military trials should be expeditiously processed, particularly in combat units, where the death of witnesses and the movement of units could make the trial difficult or impossible, it is also desirable that careful pre-trial investigations occur, and that every accused have an opportunity to prepare his defense. As the report stated, "No right of the accused, or any valuable evidence of the prosecution, should be sacrificed for speed."[9]

Ensuring that trained, experienced lawyers served as Defense Counsels was one key change. Another was that the rights of an individual defendant were not subjugated to the Army's need for speed in processing courts-martial in combat zones. Both were just two of the improvements in the implementation of the Uniform Code of Military Justice in 1950.

## Factors of Race

Some existing studies have concluded that that black soldiers were routinely executed, while white soldiers were not. Most start with the percentage of black troops in Europe. According to an article in *Stars & Stripes*, dated June 14, 1945, early in the war Congress set a standard that 10.4% of all soldiers serving overseas would be "Negro." The War Department concurred, but used this figure as an aggregate; in Europe, the department determined that 8.4% of all troops would be black. On May 15, 1945, the count of all troops in Europe was determined to be 3,082,142 of which 259,173 were "colored."[10] Therefore, from a purely mathematical formula, 8.4% of those soldiers executed would be expected to be black. Such was not the case; of the 96 condemned, 78.1% were black. The simplest assumption would be that black soldiers were singled out for execution.

Army policy during the war does not support this assertion. As early as December 7, 1943, General Dwight Eisenhower, the European Theater Commander, directed Brigadier General Edward C. Betts:

"That henceforward, where practicable and available, one or more negro officers be detailed upon all General Courts-Martial before whom are to be tried negro members of this command for serious crimes of violence or disorders such as murder, mutiny, riot, rape and other disorders involving inter-racial relations or interracial sensibilities."

General Betts then directed Colonel W.S. Sully, Chief of the Military Justice Section, of the ETO, to telephone each major subordinate staff judge advocate and inform them of the policy. Betts added that Colonel Sully was to explain that Eisenhower had decided to communicate in this manner "for reasons sufficient," rather than by written communication. Sully accomplished this task and informed General Betts the following day that he had informed the major command judge advocates and that they would pass this information to all subordinate staff judge advocates. He also stated that he had advised the judge advocates that although no positive directive existed concerning Special Courts-Martial, "it would be desirable to apply the same principal when appointing members of such courts."[11]

The actual implementation of the policy immediately ran into problems. In Britain on December 14, 1943, a GCM found two soldiers guilty of rape. The panel had two black officers on it; the court excused one officer – race unknown – at the beginning of trial for "having conscientious scruples against the death sentence." The panel voted to convict, but could then not agree on a sentence; at the discussion in court, it became known that one of the black officers was unwilling to vote for the death sentence "on grounds of conscientious scruples." As a result, both defendants received life imprisonment. Colonel Sully sent a memorandum to General Betts on December 16, 1943, which stated in part,[12]

"If colored members of courts are unwilling to vote the extreme penalty in a case such as this which was extremely aggravated and accompanied by much brutality, it would seem we might recommend reconsideration of TC's [Theater Commander's] policy."

There is no record General Eisenhower ever received this memo. Brigadier General E.C. McNeil jumped in, however, on December 28, 1943 and stated that he would develop questions to be asked members of the court before being sworn in to determine if they had any religious or moral scruples against the death penalty.[13] General Eisenhower, probably not satisfied that his guidance was being obeyed, in March directed that the Deputy Theater Commander, Major General John C.H. Lee, publish a written order; the communication, initially classified as SECRET, and promulgated on March 6, 1944, read:[14]

SUBJECT: Courts-Martial
1. Although in this theater the ratio of negro officers to white officers is not large, it is especially desired that wherever practicable, one or more negro officers be detailed as members of all courts-martial before which are to be tried negro personnel for the more serious crimes, including crimes of violence or disorder and those involving inter-racial sensibilities.
2. Those instructions have been furnished in writing to all commanders exercising General Court-Martial jurisdiction, and will not be reproduced or distributed by them. Such publication as is necessary to carry out this directive into effect will be done orally.

By direction of the Theater Commander

Senior commanders saw other problems. On April 5, 1944, Major General Everett S. Hughes wrote a memo to General Eisenhower, after talking with Lieutenant General George Patton and Major General Wade Haislip. Both generals found fault, not with the policy, but in the manner that it was promulgated, stating that issuing the order in secrecy and then telling subordinates that they could only distribute instructions orally put full responsibility on subordinates. As Major General Haislip opined, "the Theater should take full responsibility and in no way 'pass the buck' to subordinates." General Eisenhower saw this memo and wrote on the bottom, "Why secret?"[15] That question festered. On December 6, 1944, Brigadier General Betts sent a memorandum to the ETO G-1 (Personnel.) Betts' legal opinion was that since the letter of March 6, 1944, additional units had deployed the Theater and,[16]

"Very probably the Theater Commander's policy respecting the detail of Negro officers as members of CM [Courts-Martial] has not come to the attention of the commanders thereof. Republication of this letter – unclassified is believed to be in keeping with the Theater Commander's desire – and in fact there is reason to believe he thinks it has already been so republished in accordance with his purpose made known in April 1944."

At about the same time, on November 16, 1944 a memo discussed the possibility, "For the appointment of associate Negro defense counsel, where practicable, in cases of Negro soldiers involved in major offenses."[17] The idea finally died, with the rationale given by Brigadier General Betts:[18]

"Defense counsel should be selected for their ability to protect and defend the interests of accused soldiers, whether they be white or colored and if competent Negro officers are available their detail is proper. Justice should take no account of race. If injustice is being done because of race it must be corrected – but this proposal is not suited to that need."

This study concludes that there was much confusion over General Eisenhower's policy and that promulgating it as a secret document, and suggesting further oral – not written – distribution was an error that made it very likely that not all subordinate commands would follow, or even be aware of, the commander's intent. However, General Eisenhower was nothing if not clever. In addition to holding the final approval before any death sentence could be carried into execution as the confirmation authority, the Theater Commander instituted one additional safeguard in March 1944. Eisenhower directed that the ETO Assistant JAG (initially Colonel Guy M. Kinman) forward to Eisenhower's attention instances where, in Colonel Kinman's opinion, the verdict of a court appeared to be unwarranted by the evidence adduced at the time of trial. While that opinion could cut both ways – courts-martial that acquitted defendants, when the evidence was overwhelming of their guilt – Eisenhower could also use Kinman's expert eye to determine if black defendants were being convicted with less evidence than would result in a white defendant's conviction.[19] It was clear that General Eisenhower understood the potential ramifications of death penalty convictions and took multiple steps to ensure these General Courts-Martial were fair to every defendant, regardless of color.

The individual trial records of those executed also do not support the assertion of widespread racism. What jumped off the pages of the musty files was that each trial was uniquely different from every other one. For the most part, Trial Judge Advocates and Defense Counsels had different levels of experience and different manners of performance at the trial. Some officers seemed to be content letting the facts drive the trial, while others jumped in with both feet to attempt to have the trial bend to their will. Some defendants testified at trial; others did not. Many defendants made incriminating statements before trial; others kept silent. In one case, General Eisenhower commuted the death sentences for two black soldiers, but confirmed the sentence for the third black defendant in the same trial. In another case, two black soldiers and one white one raped a French woman – one black trooper and the white trooper were executed, while the second black trooper was not.

To conclude that black soldiers were routinely executed, while whites were not, one would have to evaluate every trial that <u>could</u> have led to an execution and then form a theory based on the aggregate observations. To this study's knowledge, that has never been attempted.

The words found in the thousands of pages of trial records speak for themselves; some, perhaps many, officers looked at black soldiers and white soldiers differently; officer views were also shaped by the race of the officer. For many blacks and many whites, members of another race were almost foreign, which bred mistrust or gross generalizations. Language used by many in those days seems shocking by today's standards, although the Army tried to prohibit the most egregious conduct. On February 14, 1942, then Adjutant General, Major General E.S. Adams published the following memorandum to all senior commanders:[20]

"Superiors are forbidden to injure those under their authority by tyrannical or capricious conduct or by abusive language. While maintaining discipline and the thorough and prompt performance of military duty, all officers, in dealing with enlisted men, will bear in mind the absolute necessity of so treating them as to preserve their self-respect. A grave duty rests on all officers and particularly upon organization commanders in this respect. In this connection, the use of epithet deemed insulting to a racial group should be carefully avoided. Similarly, commanders should avoid all practices tending to give the colored soldier cause to feel that the Army makes any differentiation between him and any other soldier."

When officers forgot Major General Adams' wise counsel, tense situations could escalate to violence. However, the demonstrated ability of soldiers influenced officers far more than did skin color. This was not necessarily an altruistic view; high-performing soldiers created outstanding units and outstanding units got their officers promotions, decorations and accolades. When the first all-black armored battalion, the 761st Tank Battalion, arrived at the all-white Twenty-Sixth Infantry Division in November 1944, the division commander, Major General Willard S. Paul, stood atop a halftrack and addressed the massed soldiers of the new battalion:[21]

"I am delighted that you're here. I've got a little work for you to do. You are the first colored tank battalion in this Third Army, and I can tell you I'm proud as hell to have you supporting my division."

Major General Paul knew a good unit when he saw it. Officers tended to promote and present decorations to "good" soldiers, overlook "average" soldiers and get rid of "poor" soldiers, whether that meant reassigning them to other units or putting them in the stockade so they would not adversely influence the majority of soldiers, who were trying their best and obeying orders. In the extreme examples, almost by definition, any soldier who appeared before a GCM was a "poor" soldier, unless his chain of command could show, and testify, otherwise.

**At the end of the day, the primary reasons why these particular 96 men were tried, found guilty, and sentenced to death were because these men committed very serious crimes and because in the penalty phase of trial the jury saw them as "poor" soldiers, not because they were Black, Hispanic, American Indian or White.**

This study could find no example of a soldier committing a capital offense and the Army judicial system "pinning the rap" on another soldier. There is not a scintilla of evidence where the chain of command, after a serious crime, ordered: "Go arrest a black guy, not a white one." While the author, in many cases, may have voted differently on punishment – and even on guilt in a handful of cases – the proper unbiased logic behind most of the verdicts can be seen.

## Areas for Future Study

Future studies can provide greater granularity to the vexing questions of the past. A prospective study could examine all the cases of American soldiers charged with rape and/or murder in North Africa and Europe. Then the study could examine that portion of the cases in which the accused was acquitted, and examine each acquittal by race to see what can be concluded. Another endeavor could examine the cases in North Africa and Europe that are part of the 1,136 accused who were found guilty of rape and/or murder, but were sentenced to life imprisonment and determine the factors that went into this decision. As mentioned at the beginning of this study, this work is primarily historical in nature. The author consulted the legal reviews of the trial extensively, only reading actual trial records in the initial research period – and then looking for case facts, not legal errors. Teams of lawyers could easily dissect every page of those trial records in future research to discover legal peculiarities and possibly legal points that the multiple Army legal reviews missed after trial.

While the study could uncover no incidents of command influence before or during a trial, in one case a commander did write a letter to a jury after they delivered a sentence of life imprisonment instead of the death penalty; he did so not based on the race or rank of the convicted, but on the heinousness of the crime. Letters of admonishment to juries by approving authorities were permitted in the World War II era. Today, unlawful command influence occurs when senior personnel, wittingly or unwittingly, act to influence court members, witnesses, or others participating in military justice cases. Separate research needs to be done concerning how command influence was defined and understood in World War II and any provable role it may have had in judicial matters.

## Resulting Changes

The Army, based in part on its own observations from the General Boards, instituted numerous changes and improvements to its judicial system. More "defense-friendly" improvements, such as enlisted personnel as part of every jury for an enlisted defendant, have been implemented. Today, it can be argued that military juries are generally more educated than civilian juries are, as every commissioned officer, and a great many non-commissioned officers, have college degrees; all are employed and all understand soldiers and those factors that can influence soldier behavior.

In 1948, Congress enacted significant reforms in the Articles of War, including creation of a Judicial Council of three general officers to consider cases involving sentences of death and life imprisonment. Congress also placed the Departments of the Army, Navy, and Air Force under the newly created Department of Defense. The first Secretary of Defense promptly created a committee, under the chairmanship of Professor Edmund Morgan, to study the potential for unifying and revising the services' different military justice systems under a single code. The Morgan Committee recommended:

- A unified system applicable to the Army, Navy, Air Force, Marine Corps, and Coast Guard
- Qualified attorneys serve as presiding officers and counsel
- Measures to enhance the rights of service-members in the context of the disciplinary needs of the Armed Forces
- The creation of an independent, three-judge civilian appellate court, which became known as the Court of Military Appeals (in 1968, this forum became the United States Court of Military Appeals.)

Today, the President of the United States is the final confirming authority concerning military executions, not a military Theater Commander. Additionally, the Army is an all-volunteer force that maintains high standards of entrance. Today the Army does not look to the penal system for recruits, or ignore criminal or psychiatric reports; most of the 96 soldiers in this book would not be able to get within shouting distance of a recruiting officer in the military of today. Mix that with General Orders in today's combat theaters of operation that prohibit taking firearms as war trophies and severely curb alcohol consumption and contributing factors to the commission of serious crimes are significantly curtailed.

• • •

However, back in World War II, in the North African/Mediterranean and European Theaters of Operations life was tough – especially if you had done something really, really stupid. Brigadier General James E. Morrisette's conclusion in 1944 may have been true that:

"Innocent, I would prefer trial by a court-martial of the United States Army than by any other tribunal in the world. Guilty, such a court is the last I would choose."

However, for these 96 soldiers, charged with capital crimes, they had no choice of tribunal. These soldiers would find that a U.S. Army General Court-Martial was a formidable, efficient and unforgiving juggernaut bent on crushing the life out of them, if it thought they were guilty, which was compounded by the fact that World War II had reduced the value of a single human life to insignificance.

# Postscript

After the war, the Allies tried twenty-five leaders of the Third *Reich*. The proceedings ended with verdicts of death for twelve defendants. Martin Bormann, tried *in abstentia*, and was unavailable to meet the hangman. Another defendant, Hermann Göring, cheated the verdict by taking poison, hours before he was to be hanged.

The hangman for the Nürnberg Trial of the Major War Criminals was none other than U.S. Army Master Sergeant John C. Woods. True to form, several of the Nazi condemned did not die quickly that night of October 16, 1946. Equally, true to form, Woods disagreed with his critics. "Never saw a hanging go off any better," he said cheerfully afterwards to a correspondent from *Time*: "10 men in 106 minutes, that's fast work." Woods thus became a notable figure and later requested a transfer out of Germany, due to his fear of retribution by former Nazis for his 106 minutes at Nürnberg. For many reasons, the Army shipped Woods out of Germany, but the former hangman still felt that danger lurked right behind him. The Army subsequently assigned him to the remote Pacific atoll of Eniwetok in the Marshall Islands.

One of the Army facilities at Eniwetok – which would become famous as a testing ground for nuclear weapons – was a rock quarry, the stone used to improve the landing strips on the atoll. On the night of July 21, 1950, two lights went out at the quarry. Master Sergeant John Woods took over, as brash as ever. A young soldier describes what happened next:

"My name is Richard G. Griffin, RA 17260969, Private, Company A, 79th Engineer Construction Battalion. I work in the quarry at Eniwetok. Just before we quit hauling rock on the night of 21 July 1950, two lights went out.

I told Sergeant Woods about it and he said that we would have to fix them because the drillers were going to work. He sent me after two light bulbs because he thought the other two were burned out. We put the two new bulbs in but they still didn't work. We started to check the line running to the switch box and I saw where it was broken and told Sergeant Woods. He told me to turn the switch off. I did, and then went to the building next to the one the switch is located in to get some friction tape and a pair of pliers. When I came out of the building, Sergeant Woods hollered to turn the switch off. I told him I had already done it but he said some current was coming through so he came up and turned it off again. We went back down to splice the wire.

He was telling me about some man that got killed by working with electricity in water. About that time, I felt a shock and threw my wire down. Sergeant Woods screamed and fell backwards into the water. I yelled to Corporal Blanchard to call the ambulance. He took off and I called Corporal Mahone to hold the switch down. Mahone and someone else then pulled Sergeant Woods out of the water. I don't know who the other man was. In just a few minutes, the ambulance came; the Medics gave Sergeant Woods artificial respiration. That is all I know."

Master Sergeant John C. Woods would never respond to the first aid. It was a pedestrian end for a man who had been thrust onto the world stage and had been crafty enough to take full advantage of the opportunity. It was not the death of a grand historical figure, but at least "Top" Woods died faster than many of the men he executerd.[1]

# Epilogue

*"A dead man, being taken down from execution, is a uniquely broken body whether he is a criminal or Christ ..."*

There are two Frances: one is the "City of Light" and its sophisticated suburbs; the other is the "Impressionist" countryside, with its myriad of small villages. In September, this second France is a feast for the senses. In Champagne country, vineyards are ripe with succulent grapes, ready to be delivered to the alchemists of sugar, who will turn them into the world's drink of success. With the crops harvested, it is evident that the fields are rolling, occasionally dissected by thick wood lines. Larger stands of woods have their own names such as the Forêt De Nesles. Fère-en-Tardenois is even more picturesque than I had imagined; it is a warm home for our fallen soldiers from The Great War. It is nice for travelers as well. Ivy covers many of the French homes, giving them the appearance of an earlier, simpler time. One does not merely stay at a hotel or a Bed & Breakfast in Fère-en-Tardenois; one is pampered there.

One and a half miles away – across harvested fields – the grass in a cemetery is even greener than official photographs portray it. The rows of white crosses are at such an angle from the sun that the shadows, cast by each cross, fall to the side, adding to the theme of bright light and brighter deeds. Quite moving are those crosses for the missing in action, which read:

HERE RESTS IN HONORED GLORY
AN AMERICAN SOLDIER
KNOWN BUT TO GOD

On special occasions, small American and French flags stand immediately in front of each cross, reminding onlookers of the shared American and French sacrifices of that war. Along the side of the cemetery – called *Cimetiere Américain Oise-Aisne* by the locals – runs a smooth macadam road, the *Rue du Mémorial Day*, understandable even to an old infantryman, who cannot speak a single sentence of French.

There is much more to the cemetery than meets the eye. Four pairs of brothers are buried side by side; three additional pairs of brothers rest in the cemetery, apart from one another. Nine interred soldiers have brothers buried at other American military cemeteries in France. Seven female Army nurses rest here. The famous poet, Joyce Kilmer – author of "Trees" – is in Plot B, Row 9. He was the victim of an enemy sniper in 1918, while serving as the acting adjutant to Medal of Honor recipient Major William "Wild Bill" Donovan – who later helped found the Office of Strategic Services, forerunner of the Central Intelligence Agency, a clandestine organization shielded from the public eye. What is also shielded from the public eye is Plot E, the Fifth Field, not marked on any map or direction signs. Even the faithful Global Positioning System fails to record its existence.

A reflecting pool causes visitors to redirect their thoughts inward. That became obvious as we entered Plot E, which only can occur legally through the back door of the superintendent's office. Out that door, one descends six wooden steps and walks about eighty feet, before encountering tall pine trees and laurel bushes. Then you are there; like a silent, concealed leopard, it springs on you before you notice its presence behind the foliage.

The field appears to be a rough rectangle, perhaps one-hundred by fifty feet, but it looks much smaller. Perhaps a golf green at first look, but a closer examination reveals scattered patches of clover. Caretakers groom the hedges and cut the grass. The emerald clearing slopes downward, away from the superintendent's building. One gardener told a previous visitor that the plot was called "a house of shame."[1] A single, small, white granite cross stands at the head of the field. There are no words on it. Several feet away begin four rows of small, flat, stone markers sunk into the ground. Each flat marker reveals only the grave number, invisible until you are almost on top of it – like a landmine. The numerals are produced by pouring dark molten lead into the inscribed digits. White marble and black numbers make a stark contrast.

There are no names, no dates of birth and no dates of death – simply a number on each. Row 1 contains grave numbers 1-24. Row 2 begins with 25 and ends with 48. And so forth. Ninety of the 96 soldiers remain in the plot. Four were never buried there in the first place; their remains went home shortly after the war. Grave 27 once held Alex Miranda and Grave 65 was the resting place for

Eddie Slovik. Officials exhumed both and sent their remains home – the plots remained empty, although the markers remain to maintain the field's symmetry. Four of the graves contain the remains of soldiers, convicted of a capital crime and sentenced to life imprisonment, who had died before they could be sent to prison.[2] Black rest next to white. They are not organized as to date or location of death.[3] No one has any choice position based on rank. In fact, there are no choice positions, although the field – as is the entire cemetery – is as immaculate as is the famous Arlington National Cemetery back home. Now the internal reflection sets in. These executed men lay in anonymity, while many of the officers – tasked with operating the legal system – rest in America's most hallowed ground at Arlington. There was never a grand design to distinguish between the two groups – some things just happen.

Albert Pierrepoint, the executioner for several of these American soldiers, later explained that the duties of a hangman did not end when he pulled the lever to release the trap door. His responsibilities continued after death, by removing the rope and ensuring that he either left the shirt on as a shroud – if the body was headed for a coffin – or tied the shirt around the man's waist if the body was headed for a medical examination. Later, Albert began to reflect on this:

> "A dead man, being taken down from execution, is a uniquely broken body whether he is a criminal or Christ, and I received this flesh, leaning helplessly into my arms, with the linen around the loins, gently with the reverence I thought due to the shell of any man who has sinned and suffered."

Thus begins our quandary. We have solved our mystery. Now all that remains is to determine what we should do with our find, for this is now history. That may be the most difficult task of all. Should we leave the history in unnamed graves and obscure archival files or should we "mark the graves" in an identifiable fashion and fully make the legal and personnel files, of those executed, more accessible to the public? On the one hand, should the punishment of any individual stop at the moment of death, or can the nature of the crime be so repugnant that we stamp out all traces of the perpetrator's very existence after his death? Do we have the right and responsibility to ensure that history completely forgets the very presence of a man by making access

to his life story and his crimes exceedingly difficult and by expunging his name from even his marker of death, or are we being dishonest to history by doing so? It has been done before. Totalitarian regimes have attempted this, altering photographic images and official documents, burying the deceased in unmarked graves and even killing-off entire families.

On the other hand, the families of these men have already abandoned them, either intentionally or unintentionally, as some children know nothing of their father's fate. The cemetery has no records of any requests from families to visit the plot nor have they requested that flowers be placed on the graves, since the plot was established in 1949. There have been only a handful of visitors since 2004, when the ABMC informally changed the policy to agree that the plot exists, an admission that had never been openly made, only whispered.

While expunging these men from history was never the intent of the Army, their burial has contributed to a foggy gap in our past, haziest at the cemetery itself. If the past does not belong to us, but to those who made it, should we tinker with it at all, or should we declare that due punishment ends at death and that a marker with each man's name replace the Orwellian stone at each resting place? This is not giving back their honor; they forfeited that when they committed their crimes. It simply would be giving them back their identity. There is a difference.

The Army initially interred each of the executed men at traditional – if temporary – American military cemeteries. Each had a wooden cross to mark the site and on each cross was an identification tag, with the individual's full name on it. Thus, at some time during the interment process, the Army ensured that each set of remains had a name – an identity.

Moreover, how should we handle the few men, who may not have committed these crimes? While there may be none in this category, would it not be better to err on the side of caution and place a traditional marker at the grave of each, should even one young man be truly innocent? On the other hand, the existing system has produced no unwanted attention or exhibitions. There have been no complaints by the French in the area. There have been no demonstrations at Oise-Aisne – the cemetery has remained at rest. Why place all that in jeopardy with more publicity? It is a question that I have been asked and that I have asked of myself.

In the novel, *The Man Without a Country*, the main character, Lieutenant Philip Nolan, during his trial for treason, stated that he never again wanted to hear the name of his country. A court-martial subsequently convicted him and sentenced him to spend the rest of his days at sea, without so much as a word of news about the United States. His punishment would last fifty-five years, confined to various Navy ships off the coast. The crews complied with the directive and Nolan never again heard the words: "The United States of America." Later, as he lay dying, he scribbled a final wish:[4]

"Bury me in the sea; it has been my home, and I love it. But will not someone set up a stone for my memory at Fort Adams or at Orleans, that my disgrace may not be more than I ought to bear?"

For the 96, not having proper grave markers may be a disgrace that is more than they ought to bear. Unlike Lieutenant Nolan, they never cursed their native land. Consider the last words of one of them. As he stood on the gallows in the final minute of his existence, he spoke to his executioners – his fellow soldiers – who would soon take his life, saying,[5]

"I am awful sorry for everything I did ... God bless all you boys. God bless the Army."

**The End**

# APPENDICES

# Officer Branch/ Grade Abbreviations

| | | | | |
|---|---|---|---|---|
| AC | Air Corps | | 2 LT | Second Lieutenant |
| AG | Adjutant General | | 1 LT | First Lieutenant |
| AUS | Army of the US (Specialists) | | CPT | Captain |
| CA | Civil Affairs | | MAJ | Major |
| CAC | Coast Artillery Corps | | LTC | Lieutenant Colonel |
| CAV | Cavalry | | COL | Colonel |
| CC | Chemical Corps | | BG | Brigadier General |
| CE | Corps of Engineers | | MG | Major General |
| DC | Dental Corps | | LTG | Lieutenant General |
| FA | Field Artillery | | GEN | General (4-star) |
| FI | Finance Corps | | | |
| GS | General Staff | | DSC | Distinguished Service Cross |
| IG | Inspector General | | DSM | Distinguished Service Medal |
| IN | Infantry | | SS | Silver Star |
| JAG | Judge Advocate General | | LM | Legion of Merit |
| MC | Medical Corps | | DFC | Distinguished Flying Cross |
| MP | Military Police | | BSM | Bronze Star Medal |
| OD | Ordnance | | PH | Purple Heart |
| QM | Quartermaster | | | |
| SC | Signal Corps | | | |
| TC | Transportation Corps | | | |
| VC | Veterinary Corps | | | |

# Dramatis Personae

**Edward M. Almond (*DSM, SS, PH*):** MG and Commanding General of the Ninety-Second Infantry Division in Italy from October 1942 to August 1945, during which time he approved **eleven** death sentences, ending in execution. He was born in Luray, VA on December 12, 1892 and graduated from the Virginia Military Institute in 1915. He became the Chief of Staff for GEN MacArthur in Japan and commanded the Tenth Corps at the invasion at Inchon during the Korean War. Promoted to lieutenant general, he became the Commandant of the Army War College in 1951. Almond retired in 1953. He died on June 11, 1979; he is buried at Arlington National Cemetery in Section 2, Site 4937-A.

**Frank Maxwell Andrews (*DSM, DFC*):** LTG and Commanding General of the ETO from February 1943 through May 3, 1943, during which time he confirmed **one** death sentence that ended in execution. Born February 3, 1884 in Nashville, TN, he graduated from West Point in 1906. An Air Corps officer, he served as the first chief of General Headquarters Air Force, U.S. Army Assistant Chief of Staff G-3, Commander of the Panama Canal Air Force and Commander of U.S. Forces in the Middle East. He was killed in an aircraft accident on May 3, 1943 in Iceland. He is buried at Arlington National Cemetery in Section 3; Andrews Air Force Base is named in his honor.

**Henry S. Aurand (*DSM, BSM*):** BG and Commanding General of the Normandy Base Section from November 1944 to April 1945, during which time he approved **nine** death sentences, which were later executed. Born in Tamaqua, PA on April 21, 1894, he graduated from West Point in 1915. He later transferred to the Pacific and became the Commanding General, United States SOS, in the China Theater. He retired in 1952 and died on June 18, 1980. He is buried at Arlington National Cemetery in Section 11, Site 813-2.

**Raymond O. Barton (*DSM, SS, BSM*):** MG and Commander Fourth Infantry Division. While in command of this organization, he approved **one** death sentence that was carried out. Barton was born on August 22, 1889 in Granada, CO. He graduated West Point in 1912, commissioned in the Infantry. In World War I, he commanded an infantry battalion.

He commanded the Fourth Infantry Division for over two years in World War II. Raymond Barton died in Augusta, GA on February 27, 1963. He is buried at the Westover Memorial Park Cemetery in Augusta.

**Edward C. Betts (*LM, BSM*):** BG and JAG for the ETO. Born on June 9, 1890 in AL, he received his law degree from the University of Alabama in 1911. In World War I, he served in the IN; he transferred to the JAG Division in 1929. Betts died on May 6, 1946 in Germany; he is buried in the American Military Cemetery in Hamm, Luxembourg.

**Russell E. Boyle:** Sergeant and MP guard at the Loire DTC, during which time he escorted **twenty-four** condemned men to the gallows. He enlisted in Chicago; the Army discharged Boyle at Camp Grant, IL on November 21, 1945.

**Omar N. Bradley (*DSM, SS, LM, BSM*):** GEN and Commanding General of the Twelfth Army Group. Bradley was born on February 12, 1893 in Clark, MO. He graduated from West Point in 1915. He also commanded the Second Corps and First Army. He confirmed **five** death sentences that were carried out. Bradley later headed the Veterans Administration for two years – improving its health care system and helping veterans obtain educational benefits under the "GI. Bill." Bradley later served as the Chairman of the Joint Chiefs of Staff. Omar Bradley died on April 8, 1981 in New York City; he is buried at Arlington National Cemetery, in Section 30, Lot 428-1.

**Ernest M. Brannon:** COL and JAG for the First Army from 1943 to 1945. In this capacity he legally reviewed **three** death sentences, recommending death in two cases and life imprisonment in the other; all ended in execution. Born in FL on December 21, 1895, he graduated from West Point in 1919. He later served as the Army's Assistant JAG and the JAG from 1950 to 1954, retiring as a MG. Brannon died in Silver Spring, MD on June 8, 1982. He is buried at Arlington National Cemetery in Section 11, Site 612-1.

**Kenneth L. Breitenstein:** Sergeant and Military Police guard at **ten** hangings in the 2913th DTC. Born in Reading, PA on August 19, 1922, he finished three years of high school before becoming a metalworker. He was inducted at Allentown, PA on January 2, 1943. He stood 6'1" tall and weighed 175 pounds. In 1945, he attended officer candidate school and served in the Reserves until 1953. He died on May 10, 2009 at Coudersport, PA.

**Jack D. Briscoe:** Sergeant in the 2913th DTC who served as a military police escort guard for the condemned man in at least **four** executions. Born in Sheridan, TX on July 4, 1919, he stood 6' tall and weighed 163 pounds. He was single and had worked as a roustabout on an oil field before enlisted at Camp Bowie, TX on November 4, 1941. His military occupational specialty was listed as a 677 – Disciplinarian. He separated from the Army on September 22, 1945 at Fort Sam Houston, TX. He was awarded the European-African-Middle Eastern Campaign Medal, the Good Conduct Medal and the American Defense Service Medal. He later worked for the Mobil Oil Company, married and had two daughters. He died on July 18, 1985 at Weimar, TX; his remains rest at the Chesterville County Cemetery.

**Withers A. Burress (*DSM, BSM*):** MG and Commander of the One-Hundredth Infantry Division. He approved **two** death sentences that ended in execution. Born on November 24, 1894 in Richmond, VA, he graduated from the Virginia Military Institute in 1914. In World War I, he saw combat in France. He assumed command of the division in November 1942, commanding it for the duration. He died at Arlington, VA on June 13, 1977. He is buried in Arlington National Cemetery in Section 30.

**Eugene M. Caffey (*DSC, SS, LM, BSM, PH*):** COL and temporary commander of the Normandy Base Section. He approved at least **two** death sentences that were later carried out. Caffey was born in GA on December 21, 1895 and graduated from West Point in 1918. A CE officer, who was also a JAG, he was in temporary command of the Normandy Base Section in 1944, while serving as the commander of the 1st Engineer Special Brigade. Caffey also commanded the Beach District. Caffey later served as the JAG of the Army; he retired as a MG in 1956. Eugene Caffey died on May 30, 1961 at Las Cruces, NM. He is buried at the Masonic Cemetery in that city.

**Charles E. Cheever (*LM, BSM*):** COL and Staff JAG for the Third Army. He provided the legal review for **seven** death sentences that were later carried into execution. Born in MA on January 5, 1898, he received his law degree at New York University. He transferred from the Adjutant General branch to the

JAG in 1932. He retired from the Army in 1947 and became the President of USAA Financial Services in San Antonio. He died on January 6, 1985 and is buried at the Fort Sam Houston National Cemetery in Plot 5, in Grave 153-B.

**Mortimer H. Christian:** MAJ and Commandant, Seine DTC, during which time he presided over at least **eleven** executions and actually served as the executioner in **eight** executions. Born on September 28, 1896, he graduated from Virginia Military Institute, serving in the 17th Cavalry in World War I, later entering the MPs. He died on November 1, 1955. He is buried at Arlington National Cemetery in Section 1, Site 931-B.

**Lucius D. Clay (*DSM, BSM*):** MG and Commander of the Normandy Base Section until November 1944, approval authority for **four** GCM cases ending in execution. Born in Marietta, GA on April 23, 1897, he graduated from West Point in 1918. He became the Military Governor of the U.S. Zone of Occupation from 1947 to 1949. He retired with the grade of GEN in 1949. Lucius D. Clay died at Chatham, MA on April 16, 1978. He is buried at the United States Military Academy Post Cemetery in Section 18, Row G, in Grave 79.

**Leroy P. Collins:** BG and Commander Northern Ireland Base Section and Commander of the Loire Section in the Communications Zone. He approved **one** death sentence that was carried out. Born in NY on March 4, 1883, he graduated from Union College in 1905 and received a commission in the FA. He was the Distinguished Graduate in 1924 at the Command and General Staff College and graduated from the Naval War College.

**Frank P. Corbin, Jr.:** COL and Staff Judge Advocate for the Twentieth Corps. Born in Morgantown, WV on April 12, 1907, he graduated from West Point in 1931, receiving a commission in the CAC, and graduated from the Columbia Law School in 1942. After the war, he served as the chief prosecutor at the war crimes trials at Dachau, Germany; he transferred to the Air Force in 1947 and rose to brigadier general. He died on March 1, 1994; he is buried at the Fort Sam Houston National Cemetery in Section B, Site 160-C.

**Norman D. Cota (*DSC, SS, LM, BSM, PH*):** MG and Commanding Officer of the Twenty-Eighth Infantry Division in 1944-1945, during which time he appointed the GCM to try Private Eddie Slovik, approved the sentence and attended the execution. Born in Chelsea, MA on May 30, 1893, he graduated from West Point in 1917. In 1946, he was retired for disability; he died in Wichita, KS on October 4, 1971. Norman D. Cota is buried at the United States Military Academy Post Cemetery in Section X, Site 287.

**Myron C. Cramer (*DSM*):** MG and U.S. Army's JAG in Washington, DC from December 1, 1941 to November 20, 1945, the senior legal officer in the Army. Born on November 6, 1881 in Portland, CT, he graduated from Wesleyan University in 1904 and Harvard Law School in 1907. After the war, he helped try Japanese war criminals and retired in 1949. Myron C. Cramer died on March 25, 1966. He is buried at Arlington National Cemetery in Section 2, Lot 1220.

**James C. Cullens, Jr.:** LTC and Commandant of DTC Number 1/2912th DTC at Shepton Mallet Prison, during which time he presided over **eight** executions; Cullens assumed command of the facility on June 14, 1943 as a MAJ. He commanded the unit until October 1, 1944, when he transferred to the 751st MP Battalion. Cullens was born in Orleans Parish, LA on November 9, 1895. He graduated from West Point in 1918 with a commission in the IN, but resigned the following year. He was recalled to service in 1942 and served until 1947. He died at Ille-et-Vilaine, Dinard, France on December 11, 1961.

**Jacob Devers (*DSM, BSM*):** GEN and Commanding General of the ETO, 1943-1944, and Commanding General of the MTO, during which time he confirmed **seven** death sentences. Devers was born in York, Pennsylvania on September 8, 1887 and died October 15, 1979 in Washington, DC. He graduated from West Point in 1909. He also commanded the Sixth Army Group and Twelfth Army Group in France. He is buried at Arlington National Cemetery, Section 1 at Site 149-F.

**Joseph V. DePaul Dillon (*LM, BSM*):** BG and Provost Marshal of the NATO, during which time he presided over **four** executions. Born in NY on January 4, 1899, he graduated from West Point in 1920. Dillon retired in 1953 as a MG. He died in Washington, DC on July 25, 1971; he is buried in Section 35 in Site 2247 at Arlington National Cemetery.

**Dwight D. Eisenhower (*DSM, LM*):** GEN and Commanding General of the ETO, from 1942 to February 1943 and from December 1943 to 1945, and Commanding General of the MTO from February 1943 to December 1943, during time in both positions, he confirmed **seventy-one** death sentences that were later carried out. He was born October 14, 1890 in Dennison, TX, graduating from West Point in 1915. In the 1930s, he served as the chief aide to Douglas MacArthur. Eisenhower became the 34th President of the United States in 1953. He died on March 28, 1969 in Washington, DC. His remains rest at the Eisenhower Presidential Library in Abilene, Kansas.

**William Fellman II:** MAJ and Director of Execution for Private Eddie Slovik. Born on March 22, 1911, he lived in Philadelphia. Fellman served in the Twenty-Eighth Infantry Division in World War II; he was later promoted to LTC. Fellman died on April 10, 1973; he is buried at Arlington National Cemetery in Section 43, Site 1996-1.

**Philip J. Flynn:** MAJ and Commanding Officer of the United Kingdom Base Guardhouse. In this position, Flynn presided over **two** executions, serving as the commander of the firing squad in the execution of Benjamin Pygate. He was an MP.

**Robert T. Frederick (*DSC-2, SS, LM-2, BSM-2, PH-8*):** MG and Commander of the Forty-Fifth Infantry Division. As commander of this organization, he approved **one** death sentence that was later carried out. Born in San Francisco, CA on March 14, 1907, he graduated from West Point in 1928, receiving a commission in the CAC. In World War II, he commanded the 1st Special Service Force (Devil's Brigade), the 1st Airborne Task Force and from December 1944 to September 1945 the Forty-Fifth Infantry Division. He retired in 1952. MG Frederick died in Stanford, CA on November 29, 1970. He is buried at the San Francisco National Cemetery in Section OS, Row 66A and Site 11.

**Leonard T. Gerow (*DSM, SS, LM*):** MG and Commander Fifth Corps. As commander of this organization, he approved **one** death sentence that was later carried out. Born on July 13, 1888 in Petersburg, VA, he graduated from the Virginia Military Institute, receiving a commission in the IN in 1911. In World War II, he commanded the Twenty-Ninth Infantry Division and then became the commander of the corps. The first corps commander ashore at D-Day, he took command of the Fifteenth Army in January 1945; Gerow was later promoted to LTG. He retired in 1950, but received an appointment to GEN four years later by a special act of Congress. He died in Petersburg, VA on October 12, 1972. He is buried at Arlington National Cemetery at Section 4 Site 5634 EN.

**T.W. Gillard:** LTC and Commandant of DTC Number 1 at Shepton Mallet Prison, during which time he presided over **one** execution. He turned over command of the center to LTC James C. Cullens on June 14, 1943.

**Alfonso Girvalo:** Sergeant and Military Police guard at the Loire DTC, during which time he escorted **twenty-eight** condemned men to the gallows. Nicknamed "Big Al," he was born in 1918 in Ossining, NY; he attended high school for four years prior to his induction on April 16, 1942 at Fort Jay at Governors Island, NY. One prisoner recalled that Girvalo stood about 6'1" tall and weighed 200 pounds. He was a reasonable man, but was very strong and once lifted a 5'11", 175-pound prisoner off the ground with one arm. "Big Al" also always seemed to be too big for his uniform. After the war, he returned to the Ossining. He died there in 1986.

**Roy W. Grower (*LM*):** BG and Commander, Brittany Base Section. He approved at least **three** death sentences that were later carried out, while in this command. He earlier commanded the 351st Engineer General Support Regiment and the Eastern Base Section in England. Grower was born in NY on January 27, 1890. He died on January 31, 1957; he is buried at the Fort Sam Houston National Cemetery, Plot AI, Row O, in Grave 304.

**Damon M. Gunn (*LM, BSM, PH*):** COL and JAG for the Second Corps from November 9, 1942 to August 22, 1943, during which time reviewed the Willie A. Pittman, Harvey Stroud, Armstead White and David White cases. Born in Buckingham, IA on May 27, 1899, he graduated from West Point in 1923 and received his law degree from Yale in 1937. Damon Gunn died on November 5, 1983 in Washington, DC. He is buried at Arlington National Cemetery.

**Wade H. Haislip (*DSM, BSM*):** MG and Commander Fifteenth Corps. In command of this organization, he approved **one** death sentence that was later carried out. Born in Woodstock, VA on July 9, 1889, he graduated from West Point in 1912 in the IN. He served in World War I and then attended several higher U.S. and French Army schools. During World War II, he commanded the Eighty-Fifth Infantry Division, Fifteenth Corps and Seventh Army. He finished his career as the Vice Chief of Staff of the Army; as a four-star general, he retired in 1951. He was later Governor of the Soldiers Home. Wade Haislip died after suffering a stroke at Walter Reed Army Medical Center on December 23, 1971. He is buried at Arlington National Cemetery, Section 7, in Grave 8200.

**Lawrence H. Hedrick:** BG and head of the Branch Office of The JAG with the ETO (BOTJAG) from July 18, 1942 to June 22, 1943. He was born in Warren County, IN on November 22, 1880, but moved to South Dakota. He received his law degree in 1905 from the University of Missouri. He was promoted to COL on November 18, 1939. He died on March 17, 1958. Lawrence Hedrick is buried at Arlington National Cemetery in Section 30.

**Burton S. Hill:** COL and member of Board of Review Number 2, Branch Office of the JAG, with the ETO. He retired from the Army in 1950 and returned to WY, where he became the head of the Bar.

**Courtney H. Hodges (*DSC, DSM, SS, BSM*):** LTG and Commander of the First Army. He approved **two** death sentences that ended in execution while in command of this organization. Born in Perry, GA on January 5, 1887, he entered West Point, but was found deficient in mathematics and forced to leave after his plebe year. He joined the Army as an enlisted man, receiving a commission three years later. During World War I, he earned a DSC. Hodges assumed command of the First Army in August 1944 and commanded this organization until his retirement (GEN) in March 1949. Courtney Hodges died in San Antonio, TX on January 16, 1966. He is buried at Arlington National Cemetery in Section 2, Site 890 AR.

**Samuel T. Holmgren (*LM*):** COL and member of Board of Review, Branch Office of the JAG, North African/Mediterranean Theater of Operations (April 12, 1943 to November 23, 1944.) Born in Mason, MN, he graduated from the George Washington University Law School; before the war, he served as the Assistant United States District Attorney in Concord, NH.

**Hubert D. Hoover (*LM*):** BG and Assistant JAG for the NATO; later Army Assistant JAG in Washington, DC. Born in Bedford, IA in 1887, he graduated from the University of California Law School with a commission in the IN in 1917. He served as the Assistant JAG in charge of the Branch Office of The JAG with the MTO from July 20, 1943 to June 16, 1945.

He served as the Assistant JAG for the Army, retiring in 1948; he died at Walter Reed Hospital on April 9, 1971; he is buried at Arlington National Cemetery.

**John W. Huyssoon:** COL and JAG for the PBS. Born in NJ on December 16, 1899, he graduated from West Point in 1925. Initially a CAC officer, he transferred to the JAG on December 3, 1940. Huyssoon retired on June 30, 1955; he died at Travis Air Force Base, CA on April 2, 1962. He is buried at Arlington National Cemetery in Section 2, Site 3551A.

**O.Z. Ide:** Member of Board of Review, Branch Office of the JAG, NATO. He was born in Ypsilanti, MI on May 26, 1891. He graduated from the Yale Law School in 1915 and served in World War I. He ran for Congress in Michigan in 1938, but lost. After the war, he was a Recorder's Judge in Detroit, MI.

**Arthur Stuart Imell:** MAJ and Commander of the 2615th MP DTC in North Africa, during which time he presided over at least **one** execution and served as the hangman for **two**. Born on July 31, 1889, he served in World War I in the IN and retired as a LTC. He died on February 9, 1956; he is buried at Fort Sam Houston National Cemetery in Section AI, Site 268.

**Mortimer R. Irion (*BSM*):** LTC and member of Board of Review, Branch Office of the JAG, NATO. Born July 26, 1904, he was a graduate of the University of Texas. He died in Dallas, TX on August 30, 1996.

**Fenton Stratton Jacobs (*DSM*):** BG and Commander of the Channel Base Section of the Communications' Zone, ETO. A CAV officer, he approved **one** death sentence that was later carried out. He was born in Gordonsville, VA on April 17, 1892 and served in World War I. He retired in 1952 and died on June 20, 1966.

**William H. Jones, Jr. (*LM, BSM*):** COL and Provost Marshal for the Mediterranean Base Section, NATO. An Infantry officer, he supervised **one** execution. Born in KY on March 4, 1890, he graduated from West Point in 1913. He retired from the Army in 1949 and died on July 1, 1968.

**Anthony Julian:** MAJ and member of Board of Review Number 2, Branch Office of the JAG, ETO. Born on March 25, 1902, he graduated from Harvard Law School in 1929 and was a member of the Massachusetts State Legislature. After the war, he served as U.S. attorney for the District of

Massachusetts and later as a federal judge on the United States District Court for the District of Massachusetts. Judge Julian died in Boston, MA on January 18, 1984.

**Harry Kirk:** British assistant hangman, he served as an assistant to Albert Pierrepoint. He may have participated in a few executions of U.S. soldiers in Britain. In 1950, served as the principal hangman for a woman, but the hanging was botched and it was his last appearance. Kirk was born in Huntington, England in 1893 and died in 1967. He reportedly told another assistant hangman, Syd Dernley, the following story:

"'We hanged twenty-two Yanks in one morning,' he told us. 'They'd got people all over the place who had been sentenced to death in this country and in Europe. They brought them all to Shepton Mallet in Somerset, where they had a big military prison and they brought us in. We did the lot in one morning. It was a production line. Shout the name out … bring the man in … read the crime and sentence … drop … down into the pit, check from the doctor … get them off the rope … re-set the trap and adjust the rope … next one … We had two bloody great American military policemen on the job just in case, but there wasn't anything serious. They had to carry one or two in because they were almost fainting and couldn't walk but they all stood on their own on the drop.' You obviously didn't leave them on the rope for an hour like we do. 'No,' laughed Kirky, 'three or four minutes maybe, no more. They wanted them all out of the way that morning and we did them all in the morning.' Twenty-two, I breathed, I don't suppose you could even remember all their names. 'No I couldn't,' he replied, 'but I can tell you what I can remember: they paid us for each man. Cash on the nail – in dollars!'"

**Herbert A. Kleinbeck:** Technician Fifth Grade and assistant hangman to Master Sergeant John C. Woods. Born on August 9, 1920 in Chicago, IL, he was single, had one year at the University of Illinois and was trained as an apprentice tool and die maker. Kleinbeck, who listed his residence as Elmhurst, IL, was inducted in Chicago on August 14, 1942. He stood 5'10" tall and weighed 164 pounds. He attended military police school and was trained as a clerk, light truck driver and motor dispatcher and arrived in Europe on June 2, 1943. He was discharged from the Army at Fort Sheridan, IL on December 24, 1945. He was awarded the European-African-Middle Eastern Campaign Medal, the World War

II Victory Medal and the Good Conduct Medal. Herbert Kleinbeck died on February 21, 2000 in East La Mirada, CA.

**Edward J. Kotrich (*LM, BSM*):** LTC and JAG for the United Kingdom Base Section. He was born in MN on April 20, 1907.

**Herman F. Kramer (*DSM, BSM*):** MG and Commander Sixty-Sixth Infantry Division from April 1943 to August 18, 1945. He approved **one** death sentence that ended in execution. He was born in NE on November 27, 1892 and served in several infantry regiments in World War I. He died on October 20, 1964; Kramer is buried in Section 34 at Arlington National Cemetery.

**Frank N. Landi:** Sergeant and Military Police guard at the Loire DTC, during which time he escorted **seven** condemned men to the gallows. Nicknamed "Bow Legs" at the DTC, he was likely born on November 3, 1904 in PA. Landi had attended grammar school and had worked in a machine shop prior to enlisting in Los Angeles on April 17, 1942. One prisoner recalled that Landi stood about 5'5" tall and in addition to his very bowed legs had what appeared to be a broken nose, indicative that he may have been a boxer. He was discharged at Indian Gap Military Reservation in PA on November 6, 1945 and returned to Los Angeles. It appears that Frank Landi died in Sacramento, CA on May 1, 1981.

**Thomas B. Larkin (*DSM, SS, LM*):** MG and Deputy Chief of Staff in the Headquarters of the ETO. By virtue of his position, he was authorized by command of GEN Eisenhower to publish final details concerning when and where condemned prisoners would be executed in the ETO. He was born in Louisburg, WI on December 15, 1890. Larkin graduated from Gonzaga University and then entered West Point, graduating in 1915; he was commissioned in the CE. During World War I, he won the Silver Star. During World War II, he served as Commanding General, SOS, Mediterranean Base Sector and Commanding General of Services and Supply NATO. He then became the Commander of the Communications Zone MTO and the Commander of the Southern Line of Communications in the ETO. In January 1946, he became the Quartermaster General of the Army. LTG Larkin died on October 17, 1969; he is buried at Arlington National Cemetery in Section 3, Site 4270-HL.

**Herbert R. Laslett:** LTC and Commandant of the 2912th DTC at Shepton Mallet Prison, England, beginning on October 1, 1944, during which time he presided over **six** executions. Born on August 23, 1891, he died on May 31, 1954. He is buried at the Willamette National Cemetery at Happy Valley, OR in Section G, Site 1409.

**Howard Laux:** First Sergeant and commander of the firing squad for **two** executions. Born in 1915 in California, he had graduated from high school and had been a doorman before becoming an MP.

**Edmond H. Leavey (*LM*):** COL and Commander Mediterranean Base Section in the NATO. He approved **one** death sentence that was later carried out. Born in TX on July 21, 1894, he graduated from West Point in August 1917 with a commission in the CE. He was the chief of staff and commander of the base section in 1942-1943. He later served in the Pacific, retiring in 1949 as a MG. He died in Honolulu, HI on February 11, 1980. He is buried at the National Memorial Cemetery of the Pacific in Honolulu in Section E, Site 46-A.

**John C.H. Lee (*DSM, SS, BSM*):** LTG and Commander of Services of Supply, ETO from May 1942 to 1945. He approved **three** death sentences that were later executed. He was also the Deputy Theater Commander for Supply and Administration, and in January 1944 became the Deputy Commander of U.S. Forces in the ETO – second in command to General Eisenhower. Born in Junction City, KS on August 1, 1887, Lee graduated from West Point in 1909. At the beginning of World War II, he was the Commander of the Second Infantry Division. He was promoted to LTG in February 1944. Lee was considered a "hard-charger," often called – behind his back, of course – "Jesus Christ Himself" and "John Court House," plays on his two middle initials. John C.H. Lee died on August 30, 1958 in York, PA; he is buried at Arlington National Cemetery, Section 2, in Site 3674.

**Lyman Louis Lemnitzer (*DSM, LM*):** MG and Chief of Staff in the Headquarters of the MTO. By virtue of his position, he was authorized by command of GEN Joseph McNarney to publish final details concerning when and where condemned prisoners would be executed in the MTO. Born on August 29, 1899 in Honesdale, PA, he graduated from West Point in 1920 with a commission in the CAC. He was promoted to BG in June 1942 and helped plan the invasion of North Africa, Sicily and Italy. He commanded the Eleventh Airborne Division and the Seventh Infantry Division during the Korean War. He later was the Chief of Staff of the Army and the Chairman of the Joint Chiefs of Staff. Lemnitzer went on to serve as the Supreme Allied Commander of NATO before retiring in 1969. He died on November 12, 1988; Lemnitzer is buried at Arlington National Cemetery in Section 30.

**Royal B. Lord (*DSM, BSM*):** BG (February 1944), later MG (November 1944), and Deputy Chief of Staff in the Headquarters of the ETO. By virtue of his position, he was authorized by command of General Eisenhower to publish final details concerning when and where condemned prisoners would be executed in the ETO. Born on September 19, 1899 in MA, he graduated West Point in 1923. He retired from the service in April 1946 and died at Rancho Santa Fe, CA on October 21, 1963.

**Vincent J. Martino:** Tech Sergeant and MP escort guard at **six** executions. Born in New York City on April 17, 1924, he had served as a stock clerk. Martino stood 5'6" tall and weighed 195 pounds. He arrived overseas on February 13, 1944 to an assignment with the 2913th DTC. He was awarded the European-African-Middle Eastern Campaign Medal, the Good Conduct Medal and the World War II Victory Medal. His file listed him with a military occupational specialty of 564 – Hangman. He died on October 14, 2003 in Naples, FL. Martino is buried at the Florida National Cemetery at Bushnell, FL in Plot 1100 of Section 329.

**Joseph T. McNarney (*DSM, LM*):** GEN and Commanding General of U.S. Army Forces, Mediterranean Theater, during which time he confirmed **sixteen** death sentences that were later executed in Italy. Born at Emporium, PA in 1893, he graduated from West Point in 1915 – a classmate of Dwight Eisenhower and Omar Bradley. McNarney was commissioned an IN officer; he soon became a flier. He became the Deputy Chief of Staff of the Army in March 1942. In October 1944, he was assigned as the Deputy Supreme Commander in the MTO and Commanding General of U.S. Army Forces, Mediterranean Theater. He was promoted to GEN in March 1945. In September 1945, McNarney assumed duties as the Acting Supreme Allied Commander of the Mediterranean Theater. He became the Commanding General of U.S. Forces in the European Theater and Commander in Chief, U.S. Forces of Occupation in Germany in November 1945. He died on February 1, 1972 in LaJolla, CA. He is buried at the Forest Lawn Memorial Park in Glendale, CA.

**Edwin C. McNeil (*DSM, LM, BSM*):** BG, Army Deputy JAG in Washington, DC from 1937 to 1943, and the head of the Branch Office of The JAG with the ETO (BOTJAG) from June 22, 1943 through the end of the war. As such, he was involved in almost every case in some manner. Born in Alexandria, MN on November 13, 1882, he graduated from West Point in 1907 and the Columbia Law School in 1916. He won an Army Distinguished Service Medal for actions in World War I, in which he handled clemency issues for GEN John Pershing. He later taught law at West Point. McNeil died in Washington, DC on October 1, 1965.

**Earl Mendenhall:** Sergeant and Military Police guard, assigned to the Loire DTC, present at **six** hangings. Standing 6' tall and weighing 180 pounds, with gray eyes and blond hair, the former bridge carpenter was easily distinguishable from the other guards that escorted prisoners to the gallows. Born in Bowie, TX on December 8, 1923, he was inducted on November 24, 1941. Discharged from the Army in August 1945, in 1963 he moved to Grand Blanc, MI and worked for 35 years in the Chevy V-8 Engine Plant. He died on April 9, 2011; he is buried in the Evergreen Cemetery at Grand Blanc.

**Claude Bayles Mickelwait (*DSM, LM, BSM*):** COL and Acting JAG for the NATO. He served later as JAG for the Twelfth Army Group. Mickelwait was born in Glenwood, IA on July 29, 1894. He received his law degree from the University of California in 1935. Commissioned in the IN, he transferred to the JAG in 1936. After the war, he served as the Staff Judge Advocate for the European Command and the Assistant JAG for the Army. He retired as a MG and died at age 85 on June 14, 1981. He is buried at Arlington National Cemetery.

**Troy H. Middleton (*DSM, SS, LM*):** MG and Commander of the Eighth Corps. He approved **one** death sentence that was later carried out. Born on October 12, 1889 in Copiah County, MS, he enlisted in the Army in 1910. By the end of World War I, he reached the grade of COL. He initially retired from the service in 1937, but was recalled in 1942 and commanded the Forty-Fifth Infantry Division until March 1944, when he assumed command of the corps. He retired again from the Army in 1950 as a LTG and became president of Louisiana State University. He died in Baton Rouge, LA on October 9, 1976. He is buried at Baton Rouge National Cemetery.

**Frank W. Milburn (*DSM, LM, BSM*):** MG and Commanding General of the Twenty-First Corps. He approved **two** death sentences that were later carried out. Born in Jasper, IN on January 11, 1892, Frank Milburn graduated from West Point in 1914 with a commission in the IN. He commanded the corps from December 1943 through the end of the war. Before he retired in April 1952, he had commanded five army corps and served as the acting commander of the Eighth Army in Korea. Milburn died in Missoula, MT on October 25, 1962. He is buried at the Fort Missoula Post Cemetery.

**Herbert Morris:** British civilian assistant executioner. Born on February 18, 1888 in London, he helped execute 19 condemned prisoners during the period 1939 to 1945. **Four** were American soldiers.

**Richard A. Mosley:** Sergeant and Military Police guard at the Loire DTC, during which time he escorted **seven** condemned men to the gallows. The son of Irish immigrants, Mosley was born in Pineville, KY on February 22, 1904. He joined the Navy in World War I, but received a discharge for being underage. He spent five years at the University of Illinois, studying electrical and mechanical engineering. He subsequently was the foreman for an automobile service center. Although he was partially blind in one eye, he entered the Army at Los Angeles on August 1, 1942 and became a powerhouse engineer. After arriving in Great Britain on June 1, 1943, he was transferred to new duties as a military specialty 635 – disciplinarian. He stood 6'5" tall and weighed 203 pounds. On March 1, 1945, he became a first sergeant in the 1008th Engineer Services Battalion. Mosley was discharged at Fort MacArthur, CA on August 31, 1945. He was awarded the Good Conduct Medal, the World War II Victory Medal and the European-African-Middle Eastern Campaign Medal with a Bronze Service Star for Northern France. Mosley lived in Hanford, CA until his death on January 5, 1953. He is buried at Grangeville Cemetery in Armona, CA.

**W.G. Neiswender:** MAJ and Commander of the PBS Garrison Stockade Number 1 in Italy, during which time he presided over at least **eight** executions.

**Francis H. Oxx (*DSM, LM*):** BG and Commanding General, PBS in Italy. He approved at least **five** death sentences that were later carried out. Born on September 9, 1898 in RI, he graduated from West Point in 1920 with a commission in the CE. He retired from the Army in 1952 because of disability. Francis

H. Oxx died on February 15, 1956 of a heart attack in Frederick, MD. He is buried at the Arlington National Cemetery in Section 30, Site 914 RH.

**Alexander M. Patch (*DSM*):** LTG and Commander Seventh Army. He approved **three** death sentences that were later executed. Born November 23, 1889 at Fort Huachuca, AZ, he graduated from West Point in 1913 with a commission in the IN. In World War II, he first commanded the Americal Division and the Fourteenth Corps at Guadalcanal in the Pacific. He was then selected by GEN Marshall for command of the Seventh Army. In August 1945, he returned to the U.S. to take command of the Fourth Army; he was soon struck by pneumonia. He died at Brooke General Hospital at Fort Sam Houston, TX on November 21, 1945. He is buried at the United States Military Academy Post Cemetery in Section 1, Site 33.

**George S. Patton, Jr. (*DSC-2, DSM-3, SS-2, LM, BSM, PH*):** LTG and Commander Third Army. Patton approved **seven** death sentences that were later carried out. Born in San Gabriel, CA on November 11, 1885, he took five years to graduate from West Point, graduating in 1909. In 1916-1917, he participated in the "Pancho Villa Expedition" along the border with Mexico. He assumed command of the Second Corps on March 6, 1943; he held this position until late 1943, when he was relieved of command for slapping a soldier. He received command of the Third Army after the invasion of Normandy and led this unit the rest of the war. On December 9, 1945, Patton was seriously injured in a highway accident, leaving him paralyzed from the neck down. He died on December 21, 1945 of a pulmonary embolism. He is buried at the American Military Cemetery in Hamm, Luxembourg.

**Henry L. Peck:** LTC and Commanding Officer, Loire DTC, during which time he presided over at least **thirty-two** executions and served as the executioner for at least **two** hangings. Henry Peck was born on August 26, 1910 in New York City. He graduated from the City College of New York in 1931 with a degree in history; he later received a Master's Degree from Columbia University. He relinquished command of the 2913th DTC (Loire DTC) to COL Morris T. Warner on June 26, 1945 and departed the unit on October 11, 1945. Peck was promoted to COL in March 1946. He later worked for the Veteran's Administration and retired as a colonel on August 26, 1970. Henry Peck died on December 5, 1996.

**Walter R. Peck (*SS, LM, DFC*):** BG and Commander of the 96th Combat Bombardment Wing (Heavy.) He approved **one** death sentence that was later carried out. Walter R. Peck was born in Lima, OH on January 15, 1896. He attended West Point for six months, but left and one year later became a Philippine Scout with the grade of 2LT. In May 1944, Peck assumed command of the 96th Combat Bomber Wing. He died on December 24, 1965; he is buried at Fort Rosecrans National Cemetery in San Diego in Plot A-E, Grave 1614.

**Arthur W. Pence (*DSM*):** BG and Commander PBS in the NATO and the Eastern Base Section of the NATO. He approved **two** death sentences that were later carried out. He was born on July 18, 1898 in VA and graduated from West Point in November 1918. He died on November 8, 1954 at Fort Belvoir, VA while in command of the Corps of Engineers Center. He is buried at Arlington National Cemetery in Section 2, Grave 3425-1.

**George D. Pence (*DSM, LM*):** MG and Chief of Staff in the Headquarters of the MTO. By virtue of his position, he was authorized by command of GEN McNarney to publish final details concerning when and where condemned prisoners would be executed in the MTO. Born in AL on July 13, 1902, he graduated from West Point in 1924 with a commission in the FA. He was retired for disability in 1947 and died in Clearwater, FL on February 24, 1977. He is buried at Arlington National Cemetery, Section 2, in Site 3427-1.

**Albert Pierrepoint:** British civilian executioner. Albert Pierrepoint served as the assistant executioner for his uncle, Thomas Pierrepoint, in **seven** executions of American soldiers. The Pierrepoints were a Yorkshire family who provided three of Britain's Chief Executioners (sometimes called "scaffolders") in the first half of the Twentieth century. Henry Pierrepoint (March 1878 – December 14, 1922) took up the craft first, hanging 105 men from 1901 to 1910. According to reputable sources, Henry could execute a man in the time it took the prison clock to strike eight – leading him from his cell to the adjacent death chamber on the first stroke, and having him suspended, dead on the rope, by the eighth and final stroke. Henry persuaded his older brother Thomas W. (see below), to take up the calling. Albert Pierrepoint, born March 30, 1905, Henry's son and Thomas's nephew, outdid his father and uncle combined, and executed 434 people (including sixteen women) between 1932

and 1956. Albert resigned over a disagreement about fees in 1956, when not paid the full fee of 15£ for an execution. In his later memoirs, on the final page, Albert Pierrepoint concluded, "The trouble with the death sentence has always been that nobody wanted it for everybody, but everybody differed about who should get off." Pierrepoint was also the proprietor for two pubs, "Help the Poor Struggler" and the "Rose and Crown." Albert died on July 10, 1992 in a nursing home in Southport, Lancashire.

**Thomas W. Pierrepoint:** British civilian executioner. Born in 1870, Thomas served as a hangman from 1909 to 1946; he is credited with having carried out 294 hangings. Thomas W. Pierrepoint served as the chief executioner of **seventeen** American soldiers – sixteen in Great Britain and one in France. Thomas W. Pierrepoint died on February 10, 1954 in Bradford, England. Later, Albert Pierrepoint recalled that his uncle Thomas on one occasion counseled him on how to conduct an execution stating, "If you can't do it without whisky, don't do it at all."

**Ewart G. Plank (*LM, BSM*):** BG and Commander, Advance Section, Communications Zone and responsible for general support troops in the initial stages of the Normandy invasion. He served as the commander of the Eastern Base Section for the ETO in 1942 and 1943, before being elevated to Commander, Advance Section, Communications Zone; he held this position in 1944-45. He approved **ten** death sentences that were later carried out. Plank then was promoted to MG and named the Commanding General for the Base Section, Philippine Islands. Born in MO on November 4, 1897, graduated from West Point in 1920 and was commissioned in the CE. Ewart Plank retired in 1949 and died on September 2, 1982 at San Francisco, CA. He is buried at the Riverside National Cemetery, Riverside, CA, in Plot 2, Grave 1916.

**Adam Richmond:** BG and Army JAG for the NATO and later the MTO. Born in IA on September 24, 1889, he graduated from the University of Wisconsin in 1912 and received his law degree at the same institution in 1914. In World War I, he served in the IN. Richmond died on December 1, 1959. He is buried at Arlington National Cemetery in Section 34, Site 73-A.

**Alexander Riley:** British civilian executioner. Born July 1, 1908, he assisted in the execution of seven condemned prisoners during the period 1940 to 1946. Of these, **three** were American soldiers. He lived in Manchester, England.

**B. Franklin Riter (*LM*):** COL and member of the Board of Review, Branch Office of the JAG with the ETO. Born in Logan, UT on September 27, 1886, he graduated from Columbia Law School in 1910. Riter had a reserve commission in the JAG from 1923 to 1941, when he was called to active duty. When the JAG section of the ETO deployed to Paris, France, Riter became coordinator for the five boards of review. He left the Army in 1947 as a BG and returned to Salt Lake City. He died on May 23, 1966. He is buried at Mt. Olivet Cemetery in Salt Lake City.

**Thomas F. Robinson:** Technician 3rd Class and assistant to Master Sergeant John C. Woods. He accompanied Woods on at least **eleven** missions to execution sites. Robinson was born in NY in 1920; he was married and had two years of high school. At the time of his enlistment, he lived in Westchester, New York. A baker by trade, he enlisted in 1942 in Bayonne, NJ; prior to working with Woods, Robinson was assigned to the 554th Quartermaster Depot. Robinson was discharged November 9, 1945 in New York City.

**Ellwood W. Sargent (*BSM*):** COL and member of Board of Review, Branch Office of the JAG, ETO and the Mediterranean Theatre of Operations. At the end of the war, he went to the Far East. He was born in 1904 in Pittstown, MA. A graduate of the Harvard Law School in 1930, he entered the Army in 1940. He died in Arlington, VA in 1972 of cancer.

**Cicero C. Sessions:** MAJ and member of Board of Review, Branch Office of the JAG with the NATO. Sessions was born on October 5, 1908. He graduated from the Tulane Law School in 1932. In later years, he lived in Bay Saint Louis, MS. He died on March 22, 1992 and rests in the Gardens of Memory Memorial Park, Bay Saint Louis.

**Gordon Simpson:** LTC and member of Board of Review, Branch Office of the JAG with the NATO. Born in Gilmer, TX on October 30, 1894, he was an Associate Justice on the Texas Supreme Court from January 1945 to September 1945 and a Justice of the Texas Supreme Court from September 1945 to March 1949. During this time, he was a member of a special commission that reviewed the records of the Malmedy Massacre Trial held in 1946 at Dachau, Germany. He died in Dallas, TX on February 13, 1987 of a heart attack.

**William H. Simpson (*DSM, SS*):** LTG and Commander Ninth Army. He approved **three** death sentences that were later carried out. Born on May 18, 1888 in Weatherford, TX, he graduated from West Point in 1909 with a commission in the IN. He served in the Philippines and on the Mexican Punitive Expedition before serving in World War I. He commanded several divisions in World War II, before assuming command of the army. He retired in 1946, but received a promotion eight years later to GEN. Simpson died in San Antonio, TX on August 15, 1980. He is buried at Arlington National Cemetery in Section 30.

**Benjamin R. Sleeper (*BSM*):** MAJ and member of the Board of Review, Branch Office of the JAG with the ETO. Sleeper served in the IN in World War I. He earned a bachelor of laws degree from the University of Texas in 1919. He later taught at Baylor University Law School. He died on November 5, 1972 at Waco, TX. He is buried at the Oakwood Cemetery there.

**Walter Bedell Smith (*DSM, BSM*):** LTG and Chief of Staff in the Headquarters of the ETO. By virtue of his position, he was authorized by command of GEN Eisenhower to publish final details concerning when and where condemned prisoners would be executed in the ETO. Born on October 5, 1895 in Indianapolis, IN, he served as an enlisted man before World War I. He received a commission as a 2LT in the IN. He was wounded in France. He became Eisenhower's Chief of Staff in September 1942. After the war, he served as the Ambassador to the Soviet Union, Director of Central Intelligence and Under Secretary of State. He died of a heart attack on August 9, 1961 in Washington, DC. He is buried at Arlington National Cemetery in Section 7, Grave 8197, close to GEN Marshall (Grave 8198.)

**Henry L. Sommer:** LTC and division judge advocate for the Twenty-Eighth Infantry Division. He reviewed the trial records in the Eddie Slovik case. He was born in Hollidaysburg, PA and graduated from Dickinson College in Carlisle, PA.

**John L. Steele:** LTC and Commandant, MTO DTC. The center was organized in 1943 at Casablanca; it moved to Pisa, Italy on December 24, 1944. Steele was from St. Johnsbury, VT.

**Benjamin B. Talley (*DSC, DSM, LM, BSM*):** COL and Commander Normandy Base Section, during which he approved at **one** death sentence. Born in Greer County, OK on July 29, 1903, he graduated from the Georgia School of Technology in 1925. A CE officer, he was in charge of all Army construction projects in Alaska early in the war. He was promoted to BG. Talley retired in 1956 and died on November 27, 1998 in Homer, AK. He is buried in Section 1 of Arlington National Cemetery.

**Clyde R. Thorn (*BSM*):** 1LT, IN, and Acting Commander of the PBS Garrison Stockade Number 1. In this capacity, he supervised **two** executions by firing squad in Italy and witnessed **two** hangings. He was born on May 13, 1910 at Harrisburg, AR. Enlisting in the Army on April 13, 1942, he later received a commission as a 2LT, after graduating from Officer Candidate School at Fort Benning, GA. He then went to North Africa and later saw combat in the Fifteenth Infantry Regiment of the Third Infantry Division, where he won a Combat Infantryman's Badge in the Naples-Foggia Campaign; overall, he would receive four campaign stars and the Bronze Star. He was later promoted to Captain. Clyde Thorn died in Batesville, AR on March 6, 1992. He is buried there at the Oaklawn Cemetery.

**Charles O. Thrasher (*DSM, LM, BSM*):** BG and Commander of the Southern Base Section in England and later the Oise Intermediate Section of the Communications' Zone. He approved **five** death sentences – that were later carried out – while in command of this organization. Charles O. Thrasher was born on December 9, 1886 in Paxton, IL. He served in the QM in France in World War I. He also received the Chevalier De l' Ordre National De La Legion D'Honneur and the Commander of the Order of the British Empire (CBE) during World War II. He retired in 1946 and died on September 2, 1960.

**William T. Thurman (*BSM*):** LTC and Ninety-Second Infantry Division Judge Advocate from March 1945 through September 1945. He was born in 1909 in Atlanta, GA, graduating from the University of Georgia. In 1947, he transferred to the new United States Air Force. He retired in 1969 as a MG and died on August 24, 1984.

**James A. Ulio (*DSM*):** MG and Adjutant General of the Army. Born June 29, 1882 in Walla Walla, WA, he served as an enlisted man and then a junior officer in the Philippines before World War I. In his World War II position, he was in charge of communications concerning casualties to the next of kin. He served as The Adjutant General from March 1, 1942 to January 31, 1946. He died on July 30, 1958; he is buried at Arlington National Cemetery.

**John C. Urbaitis:** MAJ and medical officer. During the war, he helped serve as an examining medical officer at **ten** executions, more than any other doctor did. His duties included pronouncing the executed man dead. Urbaitis was born on September 5, 1906 and died on April 23, 1984. He is buried at the Forest Lawn Cemetery in McKean County, PA.

**Charles M. Van Benschoten (*LM*):** COL and member of Board of Review Number 2, Branch Office of the JAG with the ETO. Born on January 13, 1886, Charles M. Van Benschoten died on October 13, 1962 in Perry, MI. He is buried at Rose Lawn Cemetery in that city.

**Harry B. Vaughan (*LM, PH*):** BG and Commander of the United Kingdom Base Section. He approved **one** death sentence that resulted in an execution. Born in Norfolk, VA on July 24, 1888, he graduated from Virginia Polytechnic Institute. He was commissioned a 1LT; he died on March 16, 1964. He is buried at Arlington National Cemetery in Section 34 in Site 149-A.

**Stephen Wade:** British civilian executioner. During his career, he hanged 29 people as the principal executioner and assisted in 19 other executions through 1955. Of these latter, several were American soldiers. He was born on December 14, 1887; his regular job was that of a motor dealer in Doncaster, England. Wade died of stomach cancer on December 22, 1956 in Doncaster, South Yorkshire, England.

**Walton H. Walker (*DSC-2, DSM-2, SS-3, LM, DFC-2, BSM*):** MG and Commander of the Twentieth Corps. He approved **one** death sentence that was later carried out. Born on December 3, 1889 in Belton, TX, he graduated from West Point in 1912. Walker helped patrol the Mexican border in 1916 and served in World War I. In World War II, he commanded the Third Armored Division and the corps. He was promoted to LTG in May 1945. Walker assumed command of the Eighth Army in Japan in 1948 and commanded this unit until he was killed in a vehicle accident north of Seoul, Korea on December 23, 1950. His final grade was GEN; he is buried at Arlington National Cemetery in Section 34, Site 86-A.

**Bert E. Ward:** First Sergeant and commander of the firing squad for **one** execution. Born in MI in 1909, he enlisted in the Army on April 10, 1939 in Cordele, GA. Prior to his enlistment, Ward, who was a candy-maker, lived in Genesee County, MI. When he was discharged at Indian Town Gap Military Reservation on August 15, 1945, he went to Eaton Rapids, MI.

**Thomas J. Ward, Sr. (*BSM, PH-4*):** Sergeant, IN, and Supply Sergeant of the Loire Disciplinary Training Center. In this capacity, he witnessed several executions by hanging. He was born on June 9, at Harrisburg, PA. Enlisting in the Army on September 2, 1943, he was assigned to Company I, 23rd Infantry Regiment in the Second Infantry Division and fought in France, Belgium and the Siegfried Line. He was wounded in action four times, before being assigned to the Loire DTC in February 1945. At Le Mans, he was the closest friend of John Woods. He remained at the DTC until November 1945, when he returned to the States. During the war, he also received the following awards: Combat Infantryman's Badge, the European-African-Middle Eastern Campaign Medal (with four campaign stars), the Good Conduct Medal, the Occupation (Germany) Medal and the World War II Victory Medal. In civilian life, he worked as a construction foreman at Miller and Norford Inc., and the New Cumberland Army Depot, before retiring. He is still alive and a true gentleman of the old school.

**Glenn A. Waser:** CPT, MP and Commander of the PBS Garrison Stockade Number 1, during which, he supervised **five** executions. Born in OH on July 17, 1909, he attended the University of Illinois. He entered the service on July 7, 1942 and retired as a COL. He died on January 11, 1984; his remains are at the Fort Sheridan Cemetery, Highwood, IL in Section 13.

**Arthur R. Wilson (*DSM, BSM*):** BG and Commander Mediterranean Base Section and the PBS. He approved **two** death sentences that were later executed, while in command of this organization. Arthur Wilson was born on July 18, 1894 in CA and served as an enlisted man in 1916 on border duty with Mexico. He was later commissioned in the FA, after graduating from the University of California in 1919. Wilson died on August 11, 1956.

**Edward F. Witsell (*DSM*):** MG and Adjutant General of the Army. In his position in World War II, he was in charge of communications concerning casualties to the next of kin. Born March 29, 1891 in SC, he graduated from The Citadel in 1911 and served in World War I in the IN. He transferred to the Chemical Warfare branch in 1924 and to the AG ten years later. After serving as Acting Adjutant

General, he served as The Adjutant General from February 1, 1946 to June 30, 1951. He died on November 27, 1969; Witsell is buried at Arlington National Cemetery at Section 46 in Site 526-7.

**Claudius O. Wolfe (*LM*):** COL and the Judge Advocate at the Headquarters of the Mediterranean Base Section and the PBS. He was born in TX on May 23, 1901. After the war, he defended German Major General Anton Dostler in a war crimes trial. He died on October 31, 1983 in San Patricio County, TX.

**Myron R. Wood (*LM, BSM*):** BG and Commander Ninth Air Force Service Command. While in command of this organization, he approved **two** death sentences that were carried out. He was born on December 12, 1892 in CO and died on October 29, 1946 of a heart attack. He is buried in Arlington National Cemetery in Section 6, Site 8559-A.

**William G. Wood:** CPT and Commander PBS Disciplinary Training Stockade. While in command of this organization, Wood was the presiding officer for **one** execution.

**John C. Woods:** Master Sergeant and hangman assigned to the Loire DTC; in his capacity, he hanged at least **thirty-four** soldiers – and possibly two more – and was the assistant hangman for **five** others in the European Theater of Operation. Woods was born in Wichita, KS on June 5, 1911. He completed freshman year of high school, but then dropped out. He later enlisted in the Navy in 1929, but deserted. Authorities apprehended him, convicted him by a General Court-Martial and dismissed him for being mentally unstable and unsuitable for military service. He received a dishonorable discharge from the Civilian Conservation Corps after six months in 1933, when he went AWOL and refused to work. Prior to his induction in the Army on August 30, 1943, he lived in Eureka, Kansas; he was married with no children. At his induction, he was listed as having blue eyes, brown hair with a ruddy complexion and stood 5'4½" tall and weighed 130 pounds. He reported to Fort Leavenworth, KS to begin training on September 19, 1943; he was assigned to Company B of the 37th Engineer Combat Battalion in the Fifth Engineer Special Brigade on March 30, 1944. Woods may have participated in the landings on Omaha Beach on June 6, 1944 with his unit, but never discussed his past at the Loire DTC. He was attached to the 2913th DTC in October 1944; orders in December 1944 show him assigned to the

Provost Marshal Section in the Headquarters of the Brittany Base Section. Woods was formally assigned to the 2913th DTC on February 12, 1945; on May 7, 1945, he was assigned to the Headquarters of the Normandy Base Section, but was attached back to the 2913th for duty. On September 3, 1945, Woods was released from attachment and assigned to the Headquarters CHANOR Base Section. Sergeant Thomas Ward recalled that at Le Mans, "Johnnie" Woods never talked about his past and when the two non-commissioned officers went to town for a few beers, Woods reminded his friend that they should not discuss any of the executions in public. According to Ward, Woods never got into trouble at Le Mans and had a room of his own in the same barracks as the other NCOs. Woods stayed to himself in this room much of the time. Many of the junior enlisted men looked up to the hangman as having to do a difficult job. Woods gained international fame in October 1946, as the official hangman for the International Military Tribunal at Nürnberg. There, he executed ten senior German military and civilian officials previously convicted of egregious crimes against humanity, crimes against peace and war crimes. By this time, Woods had gained a reputation as a hard drinker. During his career as a hangman, he reportedly executed 347 men, but he likely hanged sixty to seventy men. Woods was accidentally electrocuted on July 21, 1950 on Eniwetok Atoll. He is buried in the city cemetery in Toronto, KS, a small town sixty miles east of Wichita. He received the European-African-Middle Eastern Campaign Medal (with one campaign star), the Good Conduct Medal, the Occupation (Germany) Medal, the World War II Victory Medal and a Distinguished Unit Badge.

**William Henry Sterling Wright (*DSM, LM*):** COL and Provost Marshal of the First Army; he presided over **one** execution in this capacity. He was born in MN on October 29, 1907. He graduated from West Point in 1930; he was a CAV officer. He later commanded the Second Armored Division and retired as a LTG. He died on January 14, 2009 in Irvington, VA. He is buried at the Grace Episcopal Churchyard in Kilmarnock, VA.

# Endnotes

## Prologue

1   The North African Theater of Operations was designated the Mediterranean Theater of Operations on November 1, 1944 and retained this new designation through the end of the war in Europe.

2   Established by an act of Congress in 1923, the ABMC had as its goal the commemoration of the service, achievements and sacrifice of the U.S. Armed Forces wherever they had served overseas since 1917 and at locations within the U.S., when directed by public law. The Commission's first Chairman was John J. Pershing.

3   In 1917, a military cemetery was added to Brookwood; this contained 468 deceased American soldiers.

**Sources, Prologue:** Stephen E. Ambrose, *Citizen Soldiers: The U.S. Army from the Normandy Beaches to the Bulge to the Surrender of Germany*, New York: Touchstone, 1997, 342; "The US Prison at Shepton Mallet," *After the Battle Magazine*, Number 59, London: Battle of Britain Prints International, 1988, 51; "The Execution of Eddie Slovik," *After the Battle Magazine*, Number 32, London: Battle of Britain Prints International, 1981, 41-42; John J. Eddleston, *The Encyclopaedia of Executions*, London: John Blake Publishing, 2004, 683-684; Syd Dernley and David Neumann, *The Hangman's Tale: Memories of a Public Executioner*, London: Pan Press, 1990, 133; Robert J. Lilly, "Dirty Details: Executing U.S. Soldiers During World War II," *Crime & Delinquency*, Volume 42, Number 4, October 1996, Thousand, Oaks, CA: Sage Publications, 509-510; Discussion with David Atkinson, Acting Superintendent, Oise-Aisne American Military Cemetery, Seringes-et-Nesles, France, September 12, 2011.

## Dedication

1   To qualify for inclusion in this study, the individual had to have served in World War II in the North African/Mediterranean or European Theaters. Additionally, the soldier had to have committed the capital offense on or before May 8, 1945 – "VE Day" (Victory in Europe), although the actual date of execution could have been after this date. This work does not include the case of Private Karl Gustav "Ricky" Hulten of the 101st Airborne Division because he was tried by a British civilian court, convicted and hanged – all within the British judicial system.

2   At the U.S. Army Clerk of Court, the judicial files could be found for 88 of the 96 men. However, several of these eight had significant partial judicial files included in their personnel files at the National Records Administration (National Personnel Records Center) at St. Louis, Missouri.

## Introduction

1   The Army Air Corps did not become a separate service until July 26, 1947 with the implementation of the National Security Act of 1947, making it the U.S. Air Force.

2   "Doughboy Does the Dying," *Stars & Stripes*, London Edition, Vol. 5, No. 191, June 16, 1945.

3   William Bradford Huie, *The Execution of Private Slovik*, Yardley, PA: Westholme Publishing, 2004, 11.

4   The General Board, United States Forces, European Theater, Judge Advocate Section, "Military Justice Administration in Theater of Operations," Study 83, 7.

5   Colonel John P. Dinsmore, the Special Assistant to the Chief Legislative and Liaison Division in the U.S. Army in Washington, DC, Memorandum to the Under-Secretary of War, "Comparison of Executions during World War I and World War II," 22 April 1946.

6   Colonel Hubert D. Hoover, Assistant JAG, Memorandum to the Secretary of War, "Courts-Martial executed death sentences December 1941 through March 1946."

7   Major General Thomas M. Green, the U.S. Army JAG, Memorandum to the Under-Secretary of War, "Final disposition of rape and/or murder charges tried by General Courts-Martial, December 1941 to April 1946, and analysis of evidence establishing identity of accused in such cases as resulted in the death of the accused."

8   Ibid.

9   "U.S. Army Tries 3,185 in 2 Year Stay in Britain," *Chicago Tribune*, January 21, 1945, 1.

## The U.S. Army Judicial System in World War II

1   Brigadier General James E. Morrisette, "Military Law and Administration of Military Justice," address delivered before the State Bar Association of Wisconsin, Milwaukee, Wisconsin, 23 June 1944, reprinted in *The Judge Advocate Journal*, Volume I, Number 2, 15 September 1944, 7.

2   "The U.S. Prison at Shepton Mallet," *After the Battle Magazine*, Number 59, London: Battle of Britain Prints International, 1988, 29.

3  "One Out of 185 U.S. Soldiers in Army Custody," *Chicago Tribune*, February 11, 1945, 19.

4  Charles Whiting, *American Deserter: General Eisenhower and the Execution of Eddie Slovik*, York, England: Eskdale Publishing, 2005, 123.

5  The General Board, Study 83, 8.

6  Ibid.

7  Ibid., 7.

8  JAG of the Army, *A Manual for Courts-Martial, U.S. Army*, (Effective April 1, 1928; Corrected to April 20, 1943), 10, 11.

9  Ibid., 237.

10  Ibid., 55.

11  Ibid., 10, 142, 145, 147, 148, 150, 151, 152, 156, 157, 160, 161, 162, 163, 164, 165. No soldiers were executed after being convicted of the following articles that carried a possible death sentence:

*Article 59 – Advising, Persuading or Assisting Desertion*: helping someone else desert.

*Article 66 – Attempting to Create, Beginning, Joining, Causing or Exciting a Mutiny or Sedition*: mutiny was a collective insubordination against military authority; sedition was the raising of "commotion or disturbance" against the State (civil authority.) 22 soldiers were convicted of these crimes in the ETO during the war and 15 received the death penalty, although it was never carried out.

*Article 67 – Failure to Suppress Mutiny or Sedition/Failure to Give Information of Mutiny or Sedition*: not taking action against a mutiny or sedition.

*Article 75 – Misbehavior Before the Enemy/ Running Away Before the Enemy*: any conduct before the enemy that is "not conformable to the standard of behavior before the enemy set by the history of our arms"; any act of treason, cowardice, insubordination and similar conduct in the presence of the enemy. In the ETO, 494 soldiers were tried by GCMs and 29 were sentenced to death for this crime.

*Article 76 – Subordinates Compelling Commander to Surrender*: anyone who attempted to compel or compel their commander to surrender to the enemy.

*Article 77 – Improper Use of Countersign*: anyone who misused the challenge and password system of security.

*Article 78 – Forcing a Safeguard*: overwhelming a guard force protecting a facility.

*Article 81 – Relieving, Corresponding With, or Aiding the Enemy*: helping the enemy with supplies, information, or have correspondence with the enemy.

*Article 82 – Being a Spy*: clandestinely obtaining information with the intention of communicating it to the enemy.

*Article 86 – Being Found Drunk on Post/Being Found Sleeping on Post/Leaving Post Before Being Relieved*: improper conduct while on guard or sentinel duty. One soldier, who was executed in North Africa or Europe was convicted of this article of war.

12  The General Board, Study 83, 10.

13  Ibid., 16.

14  JAG of the Army, *A Manual for Courts-Martial, U.S. Army*, 24, 220.

15  Ibid, 204, 205.

16  The General Board, United States Forces, European Theater, Judge Advocate Section, "The Judge Advocate Section in Theater of Operations," Study 82, 6.

17  JAG of the Army, *A Manual for Courts-Martial, U.S. Army*, 2, 3.

18  Ibid., 6, 229.

19  Ibid., 30.

20  Ibid., 32.

21  Ibid.

22  Ibid., 33, 34.

23  Ibid., 35.

24  Ibid., 28, 39.

25  JAG of the Army, *A Manual for Courts-Martial, U.S. Army*, 39, 40, 205; and The General Board, Study 82, 18.

26  JAG of the Army, *A Manual for Courts-Martial, U.S. Army*, 44, 45, 46.

27  Ibid., 61, 62.

28  Ibid., 62, 63.

29  Ibid., 64, 65.

30  William Bradford Huie, *The Execution of Private Slovik*, 168.

31  JAG of the Army, *A Manual for Courts-Martial, U.S. Army*, 65, 212.

32  Letter to Commanding General Eight Air Force, "SUBJECT: Trial by GCM of George E. Cole," 13 August 1942, Records Group 0498, HQ, ETO, U.S. Army (World War II), Entry #UD1028, Judge Advocate Section, *General Correspondence, Decimal File, 1942-1945, 250.451 Court-Martial Changes August 1945-December 1945 THRU GCM Reviews by Staff Judge Advocates of Subordinate Commands*, Box 4726.

33 Proposed Letter to Commanding General 3rd Bombardment Division, from JAG Office, ETO, 14 November 1944, Records Group 0498, HQ, ETO, U.S. Army (World War II), Entry # UD1028, Box 4726.

34 JAG of the Army, *A Manual for Courts-Martial, U.S. Army*, 73, 74, 75, 76.

35 William Bradford Huie, *The Execution of Private Slovik*, 237.

36 JAG of the Army, *A Manual for Courts-Martial, U.S. Army*, 76, 79, 213.

37 William Bradford Huie, *The Execution of Private Slovik*, 182.

38 JAG of the Army, *A Manual for Courts-Martial, U.S. Army*, 78, 214.

39 Ibid., 92, 93, 212.

40 William Bradford Huie, *The Execution of Private Slovik*, 242. The Army's policy was to inform insurance companies that a client's death was not within the terms of the policy for compensation.

## 1 – David Cobb

1 On the prosecution: 2LT Daniel J. Pinsky (IN) and 2LT James W. Reid (CE.) Two officers served on Cobb's defense team: CPT Richard L. Tracy (CE) and 1LT Ewald M. Kniestedt (CE.) The jury included LTC Joel W. Clayton (CAV), MAJ Lawrence M. Gredinger (IN) – who was also a Law Member, MAJ Roy D. McCarty (CE), MAJ Joseph A. Christ (CE), CPT John Selsemeyer (CE), 1LT Aldine J. Coffman (CE), 1LT John E. Bartmess (CE) and 1LT Clyde W. Spears (CE.) Clayton went to West Point, but did not graduate; he died on March 11, 1977 in Atlanta, GA. McCarty was born in Oklahoma on June 15, 1912. He graduated from West Point in 1936 and retired in 1966.

2 **Charge: Violation of the 92nd Article of War.**
*Specification:* In that Private David Cobb, Company C, 827th Engineer Battalion (Aviation) did at Company C, 827th Engineer Battalion (Aviation) Guardhouse, Ordnance Depot, Desborough, Northamptonshire, England, on 27 December 1942, with malice aforethought, willfully, deliberately, feloniously, unlawfully, and with premeditation kill one, 2nd Lt. Robert J. Cobner, a human being by shooting him with a rifle.

3 Albert Pierrepoint, *Executioner: Pierrepoint*, London: Hodder and Stoughton, 1974, 67, 68, 70, 91, 92, 140, 178 and 182.

4 **Sources, David Cobb:** *from U.S. Army Clerk of Court* – GCM [Private David Cobb], "Organization of the Court," 6 January 1943; "Record of Trial GCM Private David Cobb," Cambridge, Cambridgeshire, England, January 6, 1943; Branch Office of The JAG with the ETO, APO 871, "Board of Review, U.S. v. Private David Cobb (34165248), Company C, 827th Engineer Battalion (Aviation)," 19 February 1943; HQ, ETO, "Sentence confirmation [Private David Cobb]" 1 March 1943; CPT Richard L. Tracy, "Letter of Clemency [Private David Cobb," HQ, 816th Engineer Battalion, 12 January 1943; Brigadier General L. H. Hedrick, "AG 201 Cobb, David, to Commanding General ETOUSA," 4 March 1943; HQ, SOS, "Suggested Procedure Attending Execution of Private David Cobb," 5 March 1943; HQ, SOS, "Proceedings of Execution of Private David Cobb, 34165248, Company C, 827th Engineer Battalion (Aviation)," 13 March 1943; Lieutenant Colonel John B. Hazard, "Autopsy Protocol, U-43-1 [David Cobb],"12 March 1943; HQ DTC #1, "Certificate of Death," 12 March 1943; Community Social Club #47, "Letter to President of the United States [David Cobb]," January 6, 1943; *from NARA (NPRC)* – various personal data forms; HQ, DTC #1, Statement Concerning Reading Execution Order to Private David Cobb," 4 March 1943; Letter from Lieutenant General F. M. Andrews to the Mother of Private David Cobb, 6 March 1943; DTC No. 1, Autopsy Protocol, U-43-1 (David Cobb), 8:30 a.m., 12 March 1943; "SOLDIER IN BRITAIN TO HANG FOR KILLING; Negro Sentenced By Court-Martial For Shooting Officer," *The Philadelphia Inquirer*, January 6, 1943; *from other sources* – "Soldier Sentenced to Die," *New York Times*, January 7, 1943; "U.S. SOLDIER IS HANGED; Private Executed in England for Killing U.S. Officer," *New York Times*, April 21, 1943, 8; "The US Prison at Shepton Mallet," *After the Battle Magazine*, Number 59, London: Battle of Britain Prints International, 1988, 31-32; J. Robert Lilly, "US Military Executions," *After the Battle Magazine*, Number 90, London: Battle of Britain Prints International, 1995; Albert Pierrepoint, *Executioner: Pierrepoint*, 67; John J. Eddleston, *The Encyclopaedia of Executions*, 643; Robert J. Lilly, "Dirty Details: Executing U.S. Soldiers During World War II," 510; Albert Pierrepoint Execution Ledger Entry, courtesy Paul Fraser Collectables; Bristol, England; Adrian Roose, Director.

## 2 – Harold A. Smith

[1] Serving as Trial Judge Advocate was MAJ Artie C. Meedham (QM); CPT Alan P. Hayman (QM) served as Assistant Trial Judge Advocate. MAJ Harold B. Riley (IN) served as Smith's Defense Counsel; 2LT William Frankfurter (QM) sat as Assistant Defense Counsel. The jury included LTC Robert H. Peters (IN), MAJ Edgar A. Kahn (MC) who was the Law Member, CPT Trevor V. Ealey (QM), CPT Joseph B. Farrior (MC), CPT Elmore A. Haney (QM), 1LT Melvin I. Holstein (QM), 2LT Kermit J. McCaslin (MC) and 2LT Kenneth R. Moberg (MC.) None was a West Point officer.

[2] **Charge I: Violation of the 92nd Article of War.** *Specification:* In that Private Harold Adolphus Smith, HQ and HQ Company, First Tank Destroyer Group, did, at Chiseldon Camp. "E" Company, 116th Infantry, near Swindon, Wilts, England, on or about January 9, 1943, with malice aforethought, willfully, deliberately, feloniously, unlawfully and with premeditation kill one Private Harry M. Jenkins, Company "E", 116th Infantry, a human being by shooting him with a pistol.

**Charge II: Violation of the 69th Article of War.** *Specification:* In that Private Harold Adolphus Smith, HQ and HQ Company, First Tank Destroyer Group, having been placed in confinement in the stockade at Chiseldon Camp, Wilts, England, did, at Chiseldon Camp, Wilts, England, on or about December 31, 1942, escape from said confinement before he was set at liberty by proper authority.

[3] "Bob's your uncle" is English slang for "and that's it" or "there you have it."

[4] **Sources, Harold A. Smith:** *from U.S. Army Clerk of Court* – Thomas B. Henley, "Descriptive List of Deserter or Escaped Military Prisoner [Harold A. Smith] from the Army of the United States," January 5, 1943; Soldier's Qualification Card [Harold Alvin Smith]; AGO Form 65-4, "Identification Card [Harold A. Smith]"; "Statement of PVT Harold Adolphus Smith, taken at 33 Davis Street, London at 9:30 am on January 11, 1943"; "Statement of PVT Leroy K. Reed, taken on January 11, 1943"; Branch Office of The JAG with the ETO, "Board of Review, United States v. Private Harold Adolphus Smith (14045090), alias Harold A. Smith, alias Harry Adolphus Smith, HQ and HQ Company, First Tank Destroyer Group"; "Plea for Clemency in the case of PVT Harold A. Smith, 14045090, tried by a GCM appointed by paragraph 16, SO: 41., HQ. Southern Base Section, SOS, ETOUSA, dated 10 February 1943," 22 March 1943; HQ, DTC #1, SBS, SOS, ETOUSA, "Statement of Conduct of General Prisoner Harold

A. Smith," 5 April 1943; HQ, ETO, "Confirmation of Sentence [Private Harold A. Smith]," May 20, 1943; Brigadier General L.H. Hedrick, "Holding of Board of Review [Private Harold Adolphus Smith], to Commanding General ETOUSA," 11 June 1943; DTC #1, "Proceedings of execution of Private Harold A. Smith, 14045090, HQ and HQ Company, First Tank Destroyer Group," 25 June 1943; *from NARA (NPRC)* – various personal data forms; HQ, ETO, "GCM Order No. 9 [Private Harold A. Smith]," 16 June 1943; HQ, Southern Base Section, SOS, "Memorandum for Executive Officer, Southern Base Section concerning Execution of Private Smith, 22 June 1943; *from other sources* – "The US Prison at Shepton Mallet," *After the Battle Magazine*, Number 59, London: Battle of Britain Prints International, 1988; Albert Pierrepoint, *Executioner: Pierrepoint*, 128; Email from Professor J. Robert Lilly concerning burial location, February 7, 2011; Albert Pierrepoint, Albert Pierrepoint Execution Ledger Entry.

## 3 – James E. Kendrick

[1] Trial Judge Advocate was CPT Donald K. Kelley (IN), with 1LT George H. McPherson (AUS) serving as Assistant Trial Judge Advocate. MAJ John Doran (IN) served as Kendrick's Defense Counsel; 1LT Joseph E. King (QM) sat as Assistant Defense Counsel. The jury included COL Harry A. Flint (CAV), LTC Wendell Blanchard (CAV) who was the Law Member, LTC William M. Stokes, Jr. (CAV), LTC Harry L. Hillyard (IN), LTC Charles C. Peterson (QM), LTC Henry W. Hurley (CE) and LTC Carroll H. Prouty (CAV.) LTC Ralph J. Butchers (GS) is listed as present, but may have then been challenged off the jury as his name is stricken from the record of trial. "Paddy" Flint was a legend throughout the Army. Born in VT, he graduated from West Point in 1912 and supposedly drank whiskey and played poker with George Patton on a regular basis. He assumed command of the 39th Infantry Regiment in Sicily in 1943, gave it the motto "Anything, Anywhere, Anytime – Bar Nothing" and turned it into a first-class fighting unit. Flint was shot by a German sniper in Normandy on July 23, 1944 and died the following day. In total, he won two Distinguished Service Crosses, three Silver Stars and two Purple Hearts. He is buried in Arlington National Cemetery in Section 2, Site 310. Blanchard was born on September 19, 1902 in Massachusetts. He graduated from West Point in 1924. In 1944 and 1945, he served as the Commander, Combat Command R, in the 4th Armored Division. He

died in Washington, DC on September 8, 1977. Hillyard was born March 15, 1911 in NE. He graduated from West Point in 1934. Hillyard retired as a MG; he died on October 9, 1991 in Indialantic, FL.

[2] **Charge: Violation of the 92nd Article of War.**
*Specification 1*: In that Private James E. Kendrick, HQ Battery, 14th Armored Field Artillery Battalion, did, near DeBrousseville, Algeria, on or about May 28, 1943, with malice aforethought, willfully, deliberately, feloniously, unlawfully and with premeditation kill one *********, a human being, by suffocating her with his hands or by other means forcefully employed.

*Specification 2*: In that Private James E. Kendrick, HQ Battery, 14th Armored Field Artillery Battalion, did, near DeBrousseville, Algeria, on or about May 28, 1943, forcibly and feloniously, against her will, have carnal knowledge of *********, a human being of about ten years of age.

[3] **Sources, James E. Kendrick:** *from U.S. Army Clerk of Court* – "Statement of Accused [Private James E. Kendrick] Made to CPT William C. Smith (Provost Marshal) on June 2, 1943, After Viewing Dead Body of Carmen Nunez"; Branch Office of the JAG with the NATO, "Board of Review, U.S. v. James E. Kendrick (14026995), HQ Battery, 14th Armored Field Artillery Battalion, 28 June 1943; HQ, 2nd Armored Division, "Approval of Sentence [Private James E. Kendrick]," June 19, 1943; HQ, Ist Armored Corps, "Approval of Sentence [Private James E. Kendrick]," June 20, 1943; HQ, NATO, U.S. Army, "Confirmation of Sentence [Private James E. Kendrick]," June 29, 1943; *from NARA (NPRC)* – various personal data forms; Inventory of Effects (Kendrick, James E.), 18 July 1943; Service Record, James E. Kendrick, October 29, 1949 – July 17, 1943.

**4, 5, 5, 7 – Willie A. Pittman, Harvey Stroud, Armstead White & David White**

[1] MAJ John Wray (OD) served as Trial Judge Advocate. He was assisted by 2LT William H. Crago. MAJ Herbert L. Peavy (FA) sat as White's Defense Counsel. The accused requested that 1LT Joseph F. Kirst, Company C, 249th Quartermaster Battalion, be assigned as the Assistant Defense Counsel, which happened without objection. Serving on the jury was COL Andrew T. McNamara (QM) as the board president, COL Robert H. Krueger (CAC) the Law Member, LTC Russell F. Akers, Jr. (IN), LTC William H. Amspacker (MC), LTC James Holsinger (FA), LTC Russell W. Jenna (IN), MAJ Armistead R. Harper (CAV), CPT James V.

Loftus (QM) and 2LT Daniel M. Schuveiller (IN.) However, Schuveiller stated that he had previous knowledge of the case; he was excused from the court. McNamara was born in RI on May 14, 1905 and graduated from West Point in 1928. He retired in 1964 as a LTG. Krueger was born in MN on November 2, 1899 and graduated from West Point in 1923. He died in VA on August 3, 1974. Akers was born in VA on December 17, 1911. He graduated from West Point in 1933. During the Korean War, he served as the Commander of the 15th Infantry Regiment. He retired as a COL and died in Front Royal, VA on February 6, 1976. Jenna, a West Point graduate of 1934, was born in MA on August 30, 1911. During the war, he served as the Commander, 41st Armored Infantry Regiment. He retired as a COL and died on October 7, 1969 in Tallahassee, FL.

[2] **Charge: Violation of the 92nd Article of War.**
*Specification*: In that Private David White, Company C, 249th Quartermaster Battalion, did, at Marretta, near Gela, Sicily, on or about July 17, 1943, forcibly and feloniously against her will, have carnal knowledge of *********.

[3] **Sources, David White:** *from U.S. Army Clerk of Court* – David White, "Statement of David White," Company C, 249th QM Bn., 1345, 18 July; HQ, II Corps, "Approval of Sentence [Private David White]," July 27, 1943; HQ, NATO, U.S. Army, "Confirmation of Sentence [Private David White]," 4 August 1943; HQ, NATO, Office of the Theater Judge Advocate, "Review of Theater Judge Advocate on Record of Trial by GCM, U.S. v. Private David White (34400884), Company C, 249th Quartermaster Battalion," 2 August 1943; Branch Office of the JAG with the NATO, "Board of Review, U.S. v. Private David White (34400884), Company C, 249th Quartermaster Battalion," 9 August 1943; NATO, "Message No. W-9823," 12 September 1943.

**Sources, Harvey Stroud:** *from U.S. Army Clerk of Court* – Harvey Stroud, "Statement of Harvey Stroud," Company C, 249th QM Bn., 1315, 18 July; HQ, II Corps, "Approval of Sentence [Private Harvey Stroud]," July 27, 1943; "Review of II Corps Judge Advocate on Record of Trial by GCM, U.S. v. Private Harvey Stroud (33215131), Company C, 249th Quartermaster Battalion," 2 August 1943; HQ, NATO, Office of the Theater Judge Advocate, "Review of Theater Judge Advocate on Record of Trial by GCM, U.S. v. Private Harvey Stroud (33215131), Company C, 249th Quartermaster Battalion," 2 August 1943; HQ, NATO, U.S. Army, "Confirmation of Sentence [Private Harvey

Stroud]," 4 August 1943; Branch Office of the JAG with the NATO, "Board of Review, U.S. v. Private Harvey Stroud (33215131), Company C, 249th Quartermaster Battalion," 9 August 1943; NATO, "Message No. W-9823," 12 September 1943; *from NARA (NPRC)* – various personal data forms; HQ, NATO, APO 534, "GCM Order Number 22 [Harvey Stroud]," 9 August 1943; *from American Military Cemetery Oise-Aisne* – "Report of Burial, Stroud, Harvey, 33215131," 30 August 1943; "Report of Burial, Stroud, Harvey, 33215131," 7 July 1947; Office of the Quartermaster General of the Army, Form 638, Intra-office, Reference Stroud, Harvey, 33215131," 22 September 1948; Quartermaster Corps Form 1194, Disinterment Directive # 5265 03026, Stroud, Harvey, 33215131," 7 October 1948; ABMC Synopsis Document Correction of Grave Numbers, Stroud, Harvey, 19 November 1952.

**Sources, Armstead White:** *from U.S. Army Clerk of Court* – Armistead White, "Statement of Armistead White," Company C, 249th QM Bn., 1020, 18 July; "Record of Court-Martial [Private Armstead White]," APO 302, 21 July 1943; HQ, II Corps, "Approval of Sentence [Private Armistead White]," July 27, 1943; HQ, NATO, Office of the Theater Judge Advocate, "Review of Theater Judge Advocate on Record of Trial by GCM, U.S. v. Private Armstead White (34401104), Company C, 249th Quartermaster Battalion," 2 August 1943; HQ, NATO, U.S. Army, "Confirmation of Sentence [Private Armistead White]," 4 August 1943; "Board of Review, U.S. v. Private Armstead White (34401104), Company C, 249th Quartermaster Battalion," 7 August 1943; NATO, "Message No. W-9823," 12 September 1943; *from NARA (NPRC)* – various personal data forms.

**Sources, Willie A. Pittman:** *from U.S. Army Clerk of Court* – Willie Aron Pittman, "Statement of Willie Aron Pittman," Company C, 249th QM Bn., 1245, 18 July; "Record of Court-Martial [Private Willie A. Pittman]," APO 302, 21 July 1943; HQ, II Corps, "Approval of Sentence [Private Willie A. Pittman]," July 27, 1943; HQ, NATO, Office of the Theater Judge Advocate, "Review of Theater Judge Advocate on Record of Trial by GCM, U.S. v. Private Willie A. Pittman (34400976), Company C, 249th Quartermaster Battalion," 2 August 1943; Branch Office of the JAG with the NATO, "Board of Review, U.S. v. Private Willie A. Pittman (34400976), Company C, 249th Quartermaster Battalion," 9 August 1943; HQ, NATO, U.S. Army, "Confirmation of Sentence [Private Willie A. Pittman]," 4 August 1943;

NATO, "Message No. W-9823," 12 September 1943; *from NARA (NPRC)* – various personal data forms; HQ, NATO, APO 534, "GCM Order Number 24 [Willie A. Pittman]," 9 August 1943; HQ, NATO, APO 534, "Execution of Sentence of GCM in the Case of Private Willie A. Pittman, 34400976, Company C, 249th Quartermaster Battalion," 24 August 1943; "Hanging Witness List [Willie A. Pittman]," 30 August 1943; HQ, NATO, Office of the Provost Marshal General, "Report of Execution in the Case of Willie A. Pittman, 34400976," 7 September 1943.

## 8 – Charles H. Smith

[1] COL John H. Manning (IN) served as Defense Counsel; CPT Joseph W. Whelan (JAG) assisted him. Trial Judge Advocate was MAJ William J. Flynn (JAG); he had no Assistant Trial Judge Advocate. On the jury were COL Robert H. Bond (IN) as President and Law Member, COL John W. Keveney (IN), COL Charles W. Rooth (IN), COL Hugh J. Fitzgerald (GS), COL Paul M. Ellman (CE), LTC Harry F. Jager (QM), LTC Forrest W. Andrews (OD), MAJ Thomas B. Randall (QM), CPT Howard C. L. Terzin (TC) and CPT Harry G. Hedges (CE.) None of the court members was a West Pointer.

[2] **Charge: Violation of the 92nd Article of War.**
*Specification*: In that Private Charles H. Smith, 540th Engineer Regiment (C), did, at Oran, Algeria, on or about 7 May 1943, with malice aforethought, willfully, deliberately, feloniously, unlawfully and with premeditation kill one Corporal William L. Tackett, a human being by cutting him with a knife.

[3] **Sources, Charles H. Smith:** *from U.S. Army Clerk of Court* – CID Case #271, "Fatal Assault on Military Policeman Corporal William L. Tackett, 6982857, 281st Military Police Company," 10 May 1943; "Record of Court-Martial [Private Charles H. Smith]," 21 May 1943; HQ, NATO, U.S. Army, "Confirmation of Sentence [Private Charles H. Smith]," 21 July 1943; Branch Office of the JAG with the NATO, "Board of Review, U.S. v. Charles H. Smith (36337437), 540th Engineer Regiment (C)," 2 August 1943; *from NARA (NPRC)* – various personal data forms; HQ, Mediterranean Base Section, "Review of the Staff Judge Advocate U.S. v. Private Charles H. Smith, 36337437, 540th Engineer Regiment," 14 June 1943; HQ, NATO, APO 534, "GCM Order Number 27 (Private Charles H. Smith)," 3 September 1943; HQ, 2615 MP DTC, APO 600, Disposition Form concerning

identity of prisoner in the death cell, 5 September 1943; HQ, 2615 MP Disciplinary Training Center, APO 600, Witnesses for the hanging of Charles H. Smith, 6 September 6, 1943.

## 9 – Lee A. Davis

[1] **Charge: Violation of the 92nd Article of War.**
*Specification 1*: In that Private Lee A. Davis, Company C, 248th Quartermaster Battalion (Service), at or about London Hill, Marlborough, Wilts, England, on or about 28 September 1943, with malice aforethought, willfully, deliberately, feloniously, unlawfully, and with premeditation kill one, Cynthia June Lay, a human being, by shooting her with a rifle.

*Specification 2*: In that Private Lee A. Davis, Company C, 248th Quartermaster Battalion (Service), at or about London Hill, Marlborough, Wilts, England, on or about 28 September 1943, forcibly and feloniously, against her will, have carnal knowledge of *********, a female person.

[2] **Sources, Lee A. Davis:** *from U.S. Army Clerk of Court* – "Statement of Lee Andrew Davis"; "Confirmation of Sentence [Private Lee A. Davis]," 13 November 1943; HQ, ETO, "GCM Orders No. 27," 4 December 1943; "Proceedings of Execution in the Case of Private Lee A. Davis (18023362)," 14 December 1943; *from NARA (NPRC)* – various personal data forms; Service Record, Davis, Lee A. (18023362), March 25, 1941 to December 14, 1943; War Department, The Adjutant General's Office, Washington, "Report of Death Davis, Lee A., 18023363, Private," 23 December 1943; *from other sources* – "Girl Shot After Visit to a Cinema," *Evening Standard*, October 6, 1943; "U.S. Soldier Sentenced to Death," *The Times of London*, October 27, 1943; "SOLDIER DIES FOR MURDER; American Private Hanged at the U.S. Army Center in Britain," *New York Times*, December 15, 1943, 3; "The U.S. Prison at Shepton Mallet"; Albert Pierrepoint, *Executioner: Pierrepoint*, 95; John J. Eddleston, *The Encyclopaedia of Executions*, 656.

## 10 – Edwin P. Jones

[1] COL John H. Manning (IN) served as Defense Counsel; 2LT Maurice Levenbron assisted him. Trial Judge Advocate was MAJ William J. Flynn (JAG); 2LT Thomas K. Roche assisted him. On the jury were COL Robert H. Bond (IN) as President and Law Member, COL Van V. Shufelt (CAV), COL John F. Ehlert (IN), COL Ira W. Black (IN), COL Robert G. St. James (IN) and LTC Harry F. Jager (QM.) None of the court members was a West Point officer.

[2] **Charge I: Violation of the 92nd Article of War.**
*Specification*: In that Private Edwin P. Jones, Battery A, 27th Armored Field Artillery Battalion, did, at Assi Ben Okba, Algeria, on or about 28 August 1943, with malice aforethought, willfully, deliberately, feloniously, unlawfully, and with premeditation kill one Private Alfred E. Raby, a human being, by shooting him with a pistol.

**Charge II: Violation of the 92nd Article of War.**
*Specification*: In that Private Edwin P. Jones, Battery A, 27th Armored Field Artillery Battalion, did, at Assi Ben Okba, Algeria, on or about 28 August 1943, with intent to commit a felony, viz., murder, commit an assault upon Private Norman E. Hippert, by willfully and feloniously shooting him in the chest with a pistol.

[3] **Sources, Edwin P. Jones:** *from U.S. Army Clerk of Court* – "Record of Court-Martial [Private Edwin P. Jones]," 21 September 1943; HQ of the Mediterranean Base Section, "Review of the Staff Judge Advocate, United States vs. Private Edwin P. Jones (15045804), 27th Armored Field Artillery Battalion," 27 October 1943; HQ, NATO, U.S. Army, "Confirmation of Sentence [Private Edwin P. Jones]," 6 December 1943; Branch Office of the JAG with the NATO, "Board of Review, U.S. v. Privates Edwin P. Jones (15045804) and Fred T. Bailey (33090327), both 27th Armored Field Artillery Battalion," 23 December 1943; *from NARA (NPRC)* – various personal data forms; HQ, NATO, "GCM Orders Number 56," 23 December 1943; HQ, Mediterranean Base Section, Office of the Provost Marshal, "Report of Death," 5 January 1944; Letter from Attorney Lewis D. Jones, New Castle, Kentucky, to the Office of the Adjutant General, January 6, 1944; War Department, The Adjutant General's Office, "Letter to [Next of Kin of Private Edwin P. Jones,]" 11 January 1944; *from other sources* – Email from Professor J. Robert Lilly concerning burial location, February 7, 2011; "W.C. Jones Killed; Brother Wounded," *Henry County Local*, August 8, 1941; "Kistner Freed At Examining Trial," *Henry County Local*, August 15, 1941; Interview with Historian for Henry County, Kentucky, February 24, 2011; Interview with family member of Edwin P. Jones, February 25, 2011.

## 11 – John H. Waters

[1] MAJ David M. Hall (JAG) served as Trial Judge Advocate; CPT Howard I. Michaels (IN) served as his assistant. MAJ Richard H. Carnahan (DC) was Defense Counsel, with 1LT David J. Harman (JAG) as his assistant. On the jury were: COL Michael H. Zwicker (QM), MAJ Doyle Joslin (MC), MAJ

John W. Grant (SC), MAJ Harvey R. Fraser (CE) also the Law Member, MAJ Paul J. Desilets (TC), MAJ Andrew J. McKeon (MP), MAJ William E. Hartmann (CE), CPT Louis C. Courtemanche (CE), CPT James R. Sweeney (QM) and 1LT Richard W. Bartsch (CE.) McKeon may have been challenged off the jury. Fraser was born in IL on August 11, 1916, graduating from West Point in 1939. He became a full professor of mechanics at West Point; he retired as a BG in 1965.

[2] **Charge I: Violation of the 92nd Article of War.** *Specification*: In that Private John H. Waters, Engineer Model Makers Detachment, EBS, SOS, ETOUSA, did, at Henley-on-Thames, Oxfordshire, England, on or about 14 July 1943, with malice aforethought, willfully, deliberately, feloniously, unlawfully, and with premeditation kill one Doris May Staples, a human being, by shooting her with a pistol.

**Charge II: Violation of the 86th Article of War** *Specification*: In that Private John H. Waters, Engineer Model Makers Detachment, EBS, SOS, ETOUSA, being on guard and posted as a sentinel at headquarters Engineer Model Makers Detachment, Henley-on-Thames, Oxfordshire, England, on or about 14 July 1943, did leave his post before he was regularly relieved.

**Charge III: Violation of the 96th Article of War.** *Specification*: In that Private John H. Waters, Engineer Model Makers Detachment, EBS, SOS, ETOUSA, did, at Henley-on-Thames, Oxfordshire, England, on or about 14 July 1943, willfully maim himself in the head by shooting himself with a pistol, thereby unfitting himself for the full performance of military service.

[3] **Sources, John H. Waters:** *from U.S. Army Clerk of Court* – Investigation Division Office of the Provost Marshal General, ETO, U.S. Army, "Statement of John Henry Waters," 19 July 1943; 36th Station Hospital, APO 649, US Army, "Clinical Abstract, John H. Waters," 27 October 1943; Engineer Model Makers Detachment, "Letter for Leniency, Private John Waters," 18 December 1943; HQ, ETO, U.S. Army, "Confirmation of Sentence [Private John H. Waters]," 24 December 1943; Branch Office of The JAG with the ETO, "Board of Review, U.S. v. Private John H. Waters (32337934), Engineer Model Makers Detachment," January 31, 1944; HQ, ETO, U.S. Army, "Letter to General McNeil concerning Private John H. Waters," 4 February 1944; Disciplinary Training Center 2912, "Proceedings of execution of Private John H. Waters, 32337934, Engineer Model Makers Detachment," 10 February 1944; *from*

*NARA (NPRC)* – various personal data forms; HQ, ETO, "GCM Order No. 5 [Private John H. Waters]," 4 February 1944; *from other sources* – "U.S. Soldier Sentenced to Death," *The Times of London*, December 1, 1943; "SOLDIER TO BE HANGED; American Sentenced for Murder of Girl in England," *New York Times*, December 1, 1943, 9; "The US Prison at Shepton Mallet"; John J. Eddleston, *The Encyclopaedia of Executions*, 662.

**12 – Charles E. Spears**

[1] **Charge: Violation of the 92nd Article of War.** *Specification*: In that Private Charles E. Spears, Company D, Three Hundred Eighty-seventh Engineer Battalion (Separate), did at Naples, Italy on or about 17 December 1943, with malice aforethought, willfully, deliberately, feloniously, unlawfully, and with premeditation kill one Private David Quick, Company A, Three Hundred Eighty-seventh Engineer Battalion (Separate), a human being, by shooting him with a pistol.

[2] **Sources, Charles E. Spears:** *from U.S. Army Clerk of Court* – HQ, NATO, U.S. Army, "Confirmation of Sentence [Private Charles E. Spears]," 18 March 1944; HQ, PBS, Office of the Staff Judge Advocate, "Letter to Colonel Hubert D. Hoover concerning cases of Private Charles E. Spears, Private Sidney C. Cimental and Private Robert L. Donnelly," 31 March 1944; Branch Office of the JAG with the NATO, "Board of Review, U.S. v. Private Charles E. Spears (32337619), Company D, 387th Engineer Battalion (Separate)," 1 April 1944; *from NARA-NPRC* – various personal data forms; "Proceedings in the Trial of Spears, Charles E. PVT, Company D, 387th Engineer Battalion (Separate), August 7, 1942, Fort George C. Meade, MD; War Department, Office of the Adjutant General, "Non-Battle Report of Death, Spears, Charles E., 32337619," 29 April 1944; *from other sources* – Discussion with Nathalie Le Barbier, Oise-Aisne American Military Cemetery, September 11, 2011.

**13 – J.C. Leatherberry**

[1] For the defense were 1LT Charles E. Crane (CE) and 2LT Herman F. Katz (CE.) The Trial Judge Advocate was CPT Daniel J. Pinsky (JAG) and assistant 2LT Leland B. Howard (CE.) The jury was comprised of: LTC Clyde C. Zeigler (CE), LTC Walter H. Esdorn (CE), MAJ Gerald W. Farrell (DC), MAJ James A. Hargett (CE), MAJ Arthur A. Krudener (CE), CPT William Corbett (CE), CPT James G. Levering, Jr. (IN), CPT Lawrence R. Grangaard (DC), 2LT Henry Winn, Jr. (CE) and

2LT Joseph W. Turner (CE.) Esdorn was born in New York on August 16, 1905, graduating second in his class at West Point in 1931. He retired disabled in 1945 and died in Boca Raton, FL on October 6, 1986.

[2] **Charge I: Violation of the 92nd Article of War.**
*Specification*: In that Private J. C. Leatherberry, Company A, 356th Engineer General Service Regiment, did at or near Birch, Essex, England, on the main Colchester Maldon Road, on or about 7 December 1943, with malice aforethought, willfully, deliberately, feloniously, unlawfully, and with premeditation kill one Harry Claude Hailstone, of 127 Maldon Road, Colchester, a human being by strangling the said Harry Claude Hailstone.

**Charge II: Violation of the 92nd Article of War.**
*Specification*: In that Private J. C. Leatherberry, Company A, 356th Engineer General Service Regiment, did at or near Birch, Essex, England, on the main Colchester Maldon Road, on or about 7 December 1943, by force and violence and by putting him in fear, feloniously take, steal and carry away from the person of one Harry Claude Hailstone, of 127 Maldon Road, Colchester, one cigarette lighter and a Billfold, value of about £2 (American currency equivalent $8.06), the value of the property of Harry Claude Hailstone.

[3] **Sources, J.C. Leatherberry:** *from U.S. Army Clerk of Court* – Investigation Division, Office of the Provost Marshal General, ETO, "Statement of George E. Fowler," 13 December 1943; GCM [Private J.C. Leatherberry], "Organization of the Court," 19 January 1944; Office of the Judge Advocate, HQ, Eastern Base Section, Supply of Services, ETO, "Review of Record of Trial [Private J. C. Leatherberry]," 6 February 1944; HQ, ETO, "Review by Staff Judge Advocate, U.S. v. Private J. C. Leatherberry (34472451), Company A, 356th Engineer General Service Regiment," 4 March 1944; HQ, ETO, "GCM Order No. 26 [Private J. C. Leatherberry]," 1 May 1944; MAJ James C. Cullens, Commandant of the 2912th DTC, "Request for Commutation of Death Sentence [Private J. C. Leatherberry]," 6 May 1944; HQ, 2912th DTC, "Proceedings of execution of Private J. C. Leatherberry, 34472451, Company a, 356th Engineer General Service Regiment," 16 May 1944; Branch Office of the JAG with the ETO, APO 871, "Death Sentence Records," 29 June 1944; *from NARA (NPRC)* – various personal data forms; "Report of Burial, Leatherberry, J.C., 34472451," 16 May 1944; *from NARA, College Park, Maryland* – War Department Message

to ETO concerning Federal District Court ruling on death penalty, 18 June 1944, Records Group 0498, HQ, ETO, U.S. Army (World War II), Entry # UD1028, Judge Advocate Section, *General Correspondence, Decimal File, 1942-1945, 250.4 Court-Martial Miscellaneous, September 1942-August 1944 THRU 250.4 Jurisdiction Policy, May 1945,* Box 4723; *from other sources* – "1.30 a.m. Court Finds Soldier Guilty of Murder," *Daily Express*, January 20, 1944; "U.S. Soldier Guilty of Murder," *The Times of London*, January 25, 1944; "U.S. SOLDIER IS CONVICTED; Leatherberry Is Sentenced in Britain to Die for Murder," *New York Times*, January 25, 1944, 3; "The US Prison at Shepton Mallet"; Albert Pierrepoint, *Executioner: Pierrepoint*, 95.

## 14 – Wiley Harris, Jr.

[1] **Charge: Violation of the 92nd Article of War.**
*Specification*: In that Private Wiley Harris Jr., 626th Ordnance Company, did, on or about 6 March 1944, with malice aforethought, willfully, deliberately, feloniously, unlawfully, and with premeditation kill one Harry Coogan, a human being, by stabbing him in the chest, head and abdomen with a sharp instrument.

[2] **Sources, Wiley Harris, Jr.:** *from U.S. Army Clerk of Court* – "Statement of Accused [Private Wiley Harris Jr.]," 9 March 1944; HQ, ETO, "GCM Order No. 32 [Private Wiley Harris, Jr.]," 19 May 1944; HQ, 2912th DTC, "Proceedings of execution of Private Wiley Harris, Jr., 6924547, 626th Ordnance Ammunition Company, 26 May 1944; HQ, XV Corps, U.S. Army, "Letter of Condolence to Michael Coogan," 31 May 1944; Branch Office of the JAG with the ETO, APO 871, "Death Sentence Records," 29 June 1944; *from NARA (NPRC)* – various personal record forms; Final Financial Statement of Wiley Harris, Private, 2912th DTC; Telegram from Cecil M. Lowe, Member of Parliament, to President Roosevelt, 26 May 1944; Service Record, Wiley Harris, May 21, 1937 to May 26, 1944; *from other sources* – "U.S. Soldier Doomed as Slayer," *New York Times*, May 25, 1944, 4; "U.S. Soldier Hanged as Slayer," *New York Times*, May 27, 1944, 7; "The US Prison at Shepton Mallet"; Albert Pierrepoint, *Executioner: Pierrepoint*, 95.

## 15 – Alex F. Miranda

[1] Trial Judge Advocate was CPT Harold Hillman (FA); assisted by 2LT Richard Ballman. Defense Counsel was 1LT Paul V. Jones (MC); assistant was 2LT Henry B. Yeagley. The jury included:

MAJ Norborne P. Gatling, Jr. (IN), MAJ Linden K. Cannon (FA), MAJ Kenneth M. Alford (MC), CPT Henry C. Borger (FA), CPT George S. Laird, Jr. (MC), 1LT Joseph B. Killgore (FA), 1LT William E. Sheppard, 2LT John H. Irving (CAV) and 2LT William S.C. Bradford (FA.) None was a West Point officer. Bradford was born in PA in 1916. He had served in the PA National Guard. He resided in Philadelphia and had three years of college.

2 **Charge: Violation of the 92nd Article of War.**
*Specification*: In that Private Alex F. Miranda, Battery C, 42$^{nd}$ Field Artillery Battalion, did at Broomhill Camp, Devonshire, England, on or about 5 March 1944, with malice aforethought, willfully, deliberately, feloniously, unlawfully, and with premeditation kill one, First Sergeant Thomas Evison, Battery C, 42nd Field Artillery Battalion, a human being by shooting him with a carbine.

3 **Sources, Alex F. Miranda:** *from U.S. Army Clerk of Court* – GCM [Private Alex F. Miranda], "Organization of the Court," 19 January 1944; HQ, ETO, "GCM Order No. 32 [Private Alex F. Miranda]," 23 May 1944; HQ, 2912th DTC, "Proceedings of execution of Private Alex F. Miranda, 39297382, 42nd Field Artillery Battalion," 30 May 1944; Colonel Hubert D. Hoover, Assistant JAG, Memorandum to the Secretary of War, "Courts-Martial executed death sentences December 1941 through March 1946;" *from NARA (NPRC)* – various personal record forms; HQ, ETO, "Review by Staff Judge Advocate, U.S. v. Private Alex F. Miranda, 39297382, Battery C, 42nd Field Artillery Battalion," 15 April 1944; HQ, 2912th DTC, "Detail for the Firing Squad," 29 May 1944; Federal Bureau of Investigation, Record of Contributor of Fingerprints, Miranda, Alex, October 26, 1944; *from other sources* – "U.S. Soldier Shot for Murder," *The Times of London*, June 1, 1944; "The US Prison at Shepton Mallet"; "From the Editor," *After the Battle Magazine*, Number 66, London: Battle of Britain Prints International, 1989, 41; Jim Carlton, "Army Will Review Soldier's WWII Execution," *Los Angeles Times*, March 29, 1988; "From the Editor," *After the Battle Magazine*, Number 72, London: Battle of Britain Prints International, 1991, 44.

## 16 – Robert L. Donnelly

1 **Charge I: Violation of the 58th Article of War.**
*Specification*: In that Private Robert L. Donnelley, Battery B, 36th Field Artillery, did at Venafro, Italy, on or about 1900 hours, 16 December 1943, desert the service of the United States and did remain absent in desertion until he was apprehended at Naples, Italy, on or about 27 January 1944.
**Charge: Violation of the 92nd Article of War.**
*Specification*: In that Private Robert L. Donnelley, Battery B, 36th Field Artillery, did at Naples, Italy, on or about 20 January 1944, with malice aforethought, willfully, deliberately, feloniously, unlawfully, and with premeditation kill one, Tec 5th Grade John P. Brown, Jr., 57th Military Police Company, a human being by shooting him with a pistol.

2 **Sources, Robert L. Donnelly:** *from U.S. Army Clerk of Court* – HQ, Peninsular Base, Office of the Provost Marshal, "Statement of Private Robert L. Donnelly, 13131982," 27 January 1944; HQ, NATO, "Review of Theater Judge Advocate on Record of Trial, U.S. v. Private Robert L. Donnelly, 13131982, Battery B, Thirty Sixth Field Artillery," 18 April 1944; HQ, NATO, U.S. Army, "Confirmation of Sentence [Private Robert L. Donnelly]," 30 April 1944; *from NARA (NPRC)* – various personal data forms; HQ, Disciplinary Training Stockade, PBS, APO 782, "Report of Death [Robert L. Donnelly], 31 May 1944; HQ, Disciplinary Training Stockade, APO 782, "Death Certificate [Private Robert L. Donnelly, 13131982]," 31 May 1944; HQ, PBS, APO 782, "Execution of sentence by GCM in the case of Private Robert L. Connelly, 13131982, Battery "B," 36th Field Artillery," 1 June 1944.

## 17, 18 – Eliga Brinson and Willie Smith

1 Prosecution: CPT David J. Harman (JAG) and 2LT Frank B. Jones (FA.) Three officers served on Brinson and Smith's defense team, including CPT Joseph G. Roye (SC) and CPT Frederick P. Simmons (OD.) The jury included: COL Jefferson H. Fulton (IN), LTC Wayne A. Hayes (DC), LTC Lyman I. Collins (AC), LTC John C. Doyle (TC), MAJ Richard Weidig (QM), MAJ Willard T. Day (CE), MAJ George J. Kane (AG), CPT John R. Coleman (CE), 1LT David B. Vail (SC) and 1LT Robert N. Cann (QM.) None of the court members was a West Point officer.

2 **Charge: Violation of the 92nd Article of War.**
*Specification*: In that Private Willie Smith, 4090th Quartermaster Service Company, and Private Eliga Brinson, 4090th Quartermaster Service company, acting jointly, and in pursuance of a common intent, did, at Bishops Cleeve, Gloucestershire, England, on or about 5 March 1944, forcibly and feloniously, against her will, have carnal knowledge of *********, Bishops Cleeve, Gloucestershire, England.

[3] **Sources, Eliga Brinson:** *from U.S. Army Clerk of Court* – GCM [Privates Eliga Brinson and Willie Smith], "Organization of the Court," 28 April 1944; Branch Office of The JAG with the ETO APO 871, "Board of Review, U.S. v. Privates Eliga Brinson (34052175) and Willie Smith (34565556), both of 4090th Quartermaster Service Company," 13 July 1944; HQ, ETO, "Sentence confirmation [Private Eliga Brinson]" 9 June 1944; Senator Claude Pepper, "Letter to Major General Myron C. Cramer, The JAG [concerning Private Eliga Brinson]," June 6, 1944; Brigadier General E.C. McNeil, "Letter to Commanding General, ETOUSA, APO 887, US Army [ref. Privates Eliga Brinson and Willie Smith]," July 13, 1944; *from NARA (NPRC)* – HQ, U.S. General Depot G-25, Special Court-Martial Order Number 1 [Corporal Eliga Brinson]," January 3, 1944; HQ, U.S. General Depot G-25, Special Court-Martial Order Number 79 [Private Eliga Brinson]," April 3, 1944; HQ, ETO, "GCM Order Number 62 [Eliga Brinson and Willie Smith]," August 4, 1944; various personnel forms; *from other sources* – "Army Sentences 2 to Hanging," *New York Times*, April 30, 1944, 2; "U.S. Soldiers Sentenced to Death," *The Times of London*, May 1, 1944; "Two U.S. Soldiers Hanged," *The Times of London*, August 12, 1944; "The U.S. Prison at Shepton Mallet"; Albert Pierrepoint, *Executioner: Pierrepoint*, 110.

**Sources, Willie Smith:** *from U.S. Army Clerk of Court* – GCM [Privates Eliga Brinson and Willie Smith], "Organization of the Court," 28 April 1944; Branch Office of The JAG with the ETO APO 871, "Board of Review, U.S. v. Privates Eliga Brinson (34052175) and Willie Smith (34565556), both of 4090th Quartermaster Service Company," 13 July 1944; HQ, ETO, "Sentence confirmation [Private Willie Smith]" 9 June 1944; Brigadier General E. C. McNeil, "Letter to Commanding General, ETOUSA, APO 887, US Army [ref. Privates Eliga Brinson and Willie Smith]," July 13, 1944; *from NARA (NPRC)* – HQ, ETO, "GCM Order Number 62 [Eliga Brinson and Willie Smith]," August 4, 1944; various personnel forms; *from other sources* – "Army Sentences 2 to Hanging," *New York Times*, April 30, 1944, 2; "U.S. Soldiers Sentenced to Death," *The Times of London*, May 1, 1944; "Two U.S. Soldiers Hanged," *The Times of London*, August 12, 1944; "The U.S. Prison at Shepton Mallet"; Albert Pierrepoint, *Executioner: Pierrepoint*, 110.

## 19 – Clarence Whitfield

[1] For the defense were MAJ Claude J. Perry (GS) and CPT Angelo A. Laudani (QM.) Trial Judge Advocate was LTC William A. Lord, Jr.; his assistant was CPT Thomas M. Conway (IN.) On the jury was COL James L. Snyder (MC), LTC Neil L. Crone (MC), LTC Malcolm W. Courser (QM), LTC Thomas T. Taylor (IN), LTC James S. Thurmond (MP) who was also the Law Member, CPT Simon C. Curtis (QM), CPT Byron G. Felkner (CE) and CPT Frank E. Napper (OD.) It appears that Taylor was challenged off the panel by the defense. Laudani was born on October 20, 1917 in MA. He graduated from West Point in 1941, retired from the Army in 1962 as a LTC and then was a mathematics teacher for fourteen years. He died on November 8, 2001. Lord was born in NJ on February 15, 1904. He graduated West Point in 1925 and was commissioned in the IN, but resigned his commission in 1926. He was recalled to active duty in 1940 and was in the Civil Affairs Section of First Army from 1943 to 1945. He left the service as a COL and died in Livingston, NJ on July 14, 1979.

[2] **Charge: Violation of the 92nd Article of War.** *Specification*: In that Clarence Whitfield, Two-hundred Fortieth Port Company, did, at Vierville Sur Mer, France, on or about 1830, 14 June 1944, forcibly and feloniously against her will, have carnal knowledge of *********.

[3] **Sources, Clarence Whitfield:** *from the U.S. Army Clerk of Court* – GCM [Private Clarence Whitfield], "Organization of the Court," 20 June 1944; "Evidence of Previous Convictions in the case of Private Clarence Whitfield;" HQ, First U.S. Army, "Review of the Staff Judge Advocate [Private Clarence Whitfield]," 22 June 1944; HQ, ETO, "Sentence confirmation [Private Clarence Whitfield]" 17 July 1944; HQ, ETO, U.S. Army, Judge Advocate Section, "Execution of death sentence imposed by GCM, Hq FUSA, upon Pvt Clarence (NMI) Whitfield, 34672443, 240th Port Co, 494th Port Bn, TC," 18 July 1944; HQ, First U.S. Army, "Execution of death sentence imposed by GCM, Hq FUSA, upon Pvt Clarence (NMI) Whitfield, 34672443, 240th Port Co, 494th Port Bn, TC," 26 July 1944; Branch Office of The JAG with the ETO, APO 871, "Board of Review, U.S. v. Private Clarence Whitfield (34672443), 240th Port Company, 494th Port Battalion, Transportation Corps," 27 July 1944; HQ, ETO, "GCM Order No. 66 [Private Clarence Whitfield]," 12 August 1944; HQ, First U.S. Army, "Proceedings in the Execution of Private Clarence

(NMI) Whitfield, 34672443," 14 August 1944; *from NARA, College Park, Maryland* – HQ, 12th Army Group, Memorandum, "Courts-Martial Death Sentence," Records Group 338, Records of U.S. Army Operations, Tactical and Support Organizations (World War II and Thereafter), War Department, VIII Corps, *Decimal Subject Files, 1940-1945, Entry UD 42882, Adjutant General Section 250.4 to Adjutant General Section 250.4*, Box 9; *from NARA (NPRC)* – various personnel forms; Service Record, Clarence Whitfield, April 23, 1943 – August 14, 1944; HQ, ETO, APO 887, "Trial of Enlisted Man by GCM," 12 August 1944; "Certificate [Concerning the Reading of GCMO Number 66 to Clarence Whitfield,] 13 August 1944; *from other sources* – Albert Pierrepoint, *Executioner: Pierrepoint*, 95; "Normandy Executions," *After the Battle*, Number 85, London: Battle of Britain Prints International, 1994, 29; Interview with Etienne Viard, Mayor, Canisy, France, September 15, 2011.

## 20 – Ray Watson
[1] **Charge I: Violation of the 92nd Article of War.**
*Specification*: In that Private Ray Watson, Company B, Three Eighty-Sixth Engineer Battalion (Separate) did, at Secondigliano, Italy on or about 15 April 1944, with malice aforethought, willfully, deliberately, feloniously, unlawfully and with premeditation, kill one Private John W. Brockman, One Hundred and Twelfth Military Police, Prisoner of War Detachment, a human being, by shooting him with a pistol.
**Charge II: Violation of the 93rd Article of War.**
*Specification*: In that Private Ray Watson, Company B, Three Eighty-Sixth Engineer Battalion (Separate) did, at Secondigliano, Italy on or about 15 April 1944 with intent to do bodily harm, commit an assault upon Private First Class Philip E. Tobeas, One Hundred and Twelfth Military Police, Prisoner of War Detachment, by willfully and feloniously shooting the said Private First Class Tobeas in the leg with a pistol.
[2] **Sources, Ray Watson:** Branch Office of The JAG with the NATO, APO 534, "Board of Review, U.S. v. Private Ray Watson (33139251), Company B, 386th Engineer Battalion (Separate), 21 August 1944; HQ, NATO, "Sentence confirmation [Private Ray Watson]" 17 July 1944.

## 21 – Madison Thomas
[1] For the defense were: CPT Robert S. Talbert (QM), who was assisted by 1LT Salvatore J. Chianta. The Trial Judge Advocate was 2LT Stuart N. Arkin (JAG); his assistant was 2LT George S. Rassmussen (QM.) On the jury were: LTC H. Beecher Dierdorff (DC), who was also the Law Member, MAJ George B. Gantt (FI), MAJ Robert B. Montgomery (MC), CPT Leonard D. Wright (MC), CPT Albert E. Matson (QM), CPT George B. Taplin (MC) and 2LT John S. Wittman (MC.) None of the court members was a West Point officer.
[2] **Charge: Violation of the 92nd Article of War.**
*Specification*: In that Private Madison Thomas, 964th Quartermaster Service Company, did, at Gunnislake, Cornwall, England, on or about 26 July 1944, forcibly and feloniously, against her will, have carnal knowledge of *********, Gunnislake, Cornwall, England.
[3] **Sources, Madison Thomas:** *from U.S. Army Clerk of Court* – Criminal Investigation Division, Services of Supplies, U.S. Army, ETO, "Statement of Private Madison Thomas," 2 August 1944; HQ, ETO, "GCM Order Number 85 [Private Madison Thomas]," 5 October 1944; HQ, 2912th DTC, APO 508, "Proceedings of execution of Private Madison Thomas, 38265363," 12 October 1944; *from NARA (NPRC)* – Letter from Brigadier General Robert H. Dunlop, Acting Adjutant General to Senator John Overton, October 27, 1944; various personnel forms; *from other sources* – "The US Prison at Shepton Mallet", 43; Albert Pierrepoint, *Executioner: Pierrepoint*, 95; Albert Pierrepoint Execution Ledger Entry.

## 22, 23 – James B. Sanders & Roy W. Anderson
[1] **Charge I: Violation of the 96th Article of War.**
*Specification*: In that Technician Fifth Grade James B. Sanders, Private Roy W. Anderson and Private Florine Wilson, all of Company B, 29th Signal Construction Battalion, acting jointly and in pursuance of a common intent to aid each other in the perpetration of a felony, viz: rape, did, at Neuville-au-Plain, Village Le Port, Manche, France, on or about 20 June 1944, wrongfully and unlawfully, each in turn, threaten and hold at the point of a gun Alphonse Lehot.
**Charge II: Violation of the 92nd Article of War.**
*Specification 1*: In that Technician Fifth Grade James B. Sanders, Company B, 29th Signal

Construction Battalion, did, at Neuville-au-Plain, Village Le Port, Manche, France, on or about 20 June 1944, forcibly and feloniously, against her will, have carnal knowledge of *********** [Rape Victim 1].

*Specification 2*: In that Technician Fifth Grade James B. Sanders, Company B, 29th Signal Construction Battalion, did, at Neuville-au-Plain, Village Le Port, Manche, France, on or about 20 June 1944, forcibly and feloniously, against her will, have carnal knowledge of *********** [Rape Victim 2].

**Charge II: Violation of the 92nd Article of War.**
*Specification 1*: In that Private Roy W. Anderson, Company B, 29th Signal Construction Battalion, did, at Neuville-au-Plain, Village Le Port, Manche, France, on or about 20 June 1944, forcibly and feloniously, against her will, have carnal knowledge of *********** [Rape Victim 1].

*Specification 2*: In that Private Roy W. Anderson, Company B, 29th Signal Construction Battalion, did, at Neuville-au-Plain, Village Le Port, Manche, France, on or about 20 June 1944, forcibly and feloniously, against her will, have carnal knowledge of *********** [Rape Victim 2].

[2] The panel was composed of: COL Ross B. Warren (FA), COL Marshall Stubbs (CC), COL James B. Mason (MC), LTC Thomas B. Bagley (JAG), who was also the Law Member, LTC Daniel J. Murphy (OD), MAJ William B. Clagett (SC), MAJ Marcy Chanin (CE), CPT Joseph M. McNulty (QM), CPT Theodore E. Corpow (MC), 2LT Frank J. Lavender (QM) and 2LT Richard W. Spikes, Jr. (QM.) MAJ Frank McNamee, Jr. (JAG) served as the Trial Judge Advocate; he was assisted by 2LT William R. Vance (JAG.) MAJ Alfred M. Osgood (FA) was the Defense Counsel and was assisted by CPT Carl W. Miller (IN.) Stubbs was born in NE on June 13, 1906. He graduated from West Point in 1929 and was commissioned in the IN; he later branch-transferred to the CC. In 1944, he served in the Chemical Warfare Section of the Advance Section, Communications Zone and later became the G-4 of the organization. He retired in 1963 as a MG; Stubbs died on November 20, 1990 at Raleigh, NC. Murphy was born on July 16, 1912 in NY. He graduated from West Point in 1935 as a FA officer. He commanded the 78th Ordnance Battalion in 1943 and was the Deputy Ordnance Officer for the Advance Section, Communications Zone. He retired in 1956 as a COL and died on August 5, 2005.

[3] **Sources, Army Hangman Problem:** *from NARA, College Park, Maryland* – War Department, The Adjutant General's Office, Pamphlet "Execution of Death Sentences," 31 March 1943; War Department, The Adjutant General's Office, "SUBJECT: Execution of Death Sentences," 8 July 1943; HQ, Normandy Base Section, Communications Zone, ETO, Memorandum, "SUBJECT: Report of Personnel Experienced as Hangmen," 10 September 1944; "Employment of French National as Hangman," 14 September 1944; "Experienced Hangman," 15 September 1944; Message, Survey concerning Qualified Hangman, from Major General John C.H. Lee to all Base Sections, 16 September 1944; HQ, Communications Zone, ETO, Memorandum "SUBJECT: Construction of Portable Gallows," 21 September 1944; Message from Loire Section to European Theater of Operation ref identification of a potential hangman, 27 September 1944; Message from Normandy Base Section to European Theater of Operation ref Private John C. Woods and Private First Class Thomas S. Robinson, 2 October 1944; Note from the ETO thru the Provost Marshal to the Judge Advocate concerning the use of enlisted hangmen, 12 October 1944, all in , Records Group 0498, HQ, ETO, U.S. Army (World War II), Entry # UD1028, Judge Advocate Section, *General Correspondence, Decimal File, 1942-1945, 250.451 Court-Martial Changes August 1945-December 1945 THRU GCM Reviews by Staff Judge Advocates of Subordinate Commands,* Box 4726; HQ, ETO, "Standing Operating Procedure, No. 54, Execution of Death Sentences Imposed by Courts-Martial," 14 December 1944, Records Group 338, Records of U.S. Army Operations, Tactical and Support Organizations (World War II and Thereafter), War Department, VIII Corps, *Decimal Subject Files, 1940-1945, Entry UD 42882, Adjutant General Section 247 to Adjutant General Section 250 (Discipline, January 1944-May 1945),* Box 7; *from NARA (NPRC)* – Army Personnel File of John C. Woods; HQ, ETO, Office of the Theater Provost Marshal, APO 887, Memorandum to General Lord concerning Hangmen, 28 September 1944.

[4] **Sources, James B. Sanders:** *from U.S. Army Clerk of Court* – HQ, ETO, GCM Order Number 91 [Technician Fifth Grade James B. Sanders], 21 October 1944; HQ, Seine DTC, APO 887, "Report of Proceedings in the Death Chamber [General Prisoner James B. Sanders]," 26 October 1944; Letter from the GCM Board "Recommendation as to Clemency [James B. Sanders], no date; HQ, ETO,

Review of Staff Judge Advocate, *U.S. v. Technician Fifth Grade James B. Sanders*, 34124233, Company B, 29th Signal Construction Battalion and Private Roy W. Anderson, 35407199, Company B, 29th Signal Construction Battalion; Court Roster, Ste. Mere-Eglise, France, 17 July 1944; *from NARA (NPRC)* – Cover Sheet, Military Personnel Records Jacket, James B. Sanders, 34124233; HQ, ETO, GCM Order Number 91 [Technician Fifth Grade James B. Sanders], 21 October 1944; HQ, Seine Section, Communications Zone, ETO, "Execution of General Prisoner James B. Sanders," 23 October 1944; HQ, Seine Section, DTC, APO 887, Special Order Number 1, 24 October 1944; HQ, Seine Section, DTC, APO 887, Special Order Number 2, 25 October 1944; Officer of the Surgeon, Seine Section, DTC, Physical and Mental Condition Certification for General Prisoner James B. Sanders, 25 October 1944; Service Record, James B. Sanders, May 27, 1942 – October 25, 1944; various personnel forms; *from other sources* – "Two Soldiers Hanged for Rape," *New York Times*, October 31, 1944, 4.

**Sources, Roy W. Anderson:** *from U.S. Army Clerk of Court* – HQ, ETO, GCM Order Number 91 [Private Roy W. Anderson], 21 October 1944; HQ, Seine DTC, APO 887, "Report of Proceedings in the Death Chamber [General Prisoner Roy W. Anderson]," 26 October 1944; Letter from the GCM Board "Recommendation as to Clemency [Roy W. Anderson], no date; HQ, ETO, Review of Staff Judge Advocate, U.S. v. Technician Fifth Grade James B. Sanders, 34124233, Company B, 29th Signal Construction Battalion and Private Roy W. Anderson, 35407199, Company B, 29th Signal Construction Battalion; Court Roster, Ste. Mere-Eglise, France, 17 July 1944; *from NARA (NPRC)* – "Report of Physical Examination and Induction, Anderson, Roy William"; HQ, ETO, GCM Order Number 92 [Private Roy W. Anderson], 21 October 1944; various personnel forms.

**Sources, John C. Woods:** *from NARA (NPRC)* – U.S. Navy Personnel File, Board of Medical Survey, "Report of Medical Survey, Woods, John Clarence," 23 April 1930.

## 24 – Paul W. Kluxdal

[1] **Charge: Violation of the 92nd Article of War.**
*Specification*: In that Private First Class Paul M. Kluxdal, HQ Battery, 200th Field Artillery Battalion, did, in the vicinity of Vire, France, on or about 12 August 1944, with malice aforethought, willfully, deliberately, feloniously, unlawfully, and with premeditation kill one First Sergeant Loyce M. Robertson, HQ Battery, 200th Field Artillery Battalion, a human being, by shooting him with a carbine.

[2] Hearing the case were: COL Louis A. Hawkins (FI), LTC John W. McCaslin (IG), MAJ Robert L. Slingluff, Jr. (FA), MAJ Carroll J. Williams (OD), MAJ Spencer D. Smith (FI), CPT Abraham I. Doktorsky (MC) and CPT Stephen W. Guzy (MP.) CPT Lynn G. Grimson (IN) and 2LT John R. Graney (FA) served as Defense Counsels; both men were lawyers in civilian life. Serving as Trial Judge Advocates were CPT Valentine L. Fine (JAG) and 1LT Elroy B. Suneson (AG.) None of the officers graduated from West Point.

[3] **Sources, Paul M. Kluxdal:** *from U.S. Army Clerk of Court* – HQ, V Corps, Rear Echelon Command Post, Moussy le Vieux, France, List of Court Members, Page 3 of Record of Trial G.C.M., 4 September 1944; HQ V Corps, APO 305, Letter to the Commanding General, HQ, V Corps, concerning requested clemency for Private First Class Kluxdal, 8 September 1944; Branch Office of The JAG with the ETO, APO 871, "Board of Review Number 1, U.S. v. Private First Class Paul M. Kluxdal (36395076), HQ Battery, 200th Field Artillery Battalion," 12 October 1944; HQ, V Corps, Office of the Commanding General, APO 305, "Sentence Approved [Private 1st Class Paul W. Kluxdal]," September 17, 1944; HQ, ETO, "Confirmation of Sentence, Private First Class Paul M. Kluxdal," 30 September 1944; HQ, ETO, GCM Order Number 94 [Private First Class Paul M. Kluxdal], 26 October 1944; Letter to the Office of the Clerk of the Court, U.S. Army Judiciary by Emmett N. Bailey, Jr., February 23, 1998; *from NARA (NPRC)* – HQ, Seine Section, Communications Zone, ETO, "Execution of General Prisoner Paul M. Kluxdal," 27 October 1944; Office of the Surgeon, Seine DTC, APO 667, Certificate of Physical and Mental Examination for Paul M. Kluxdal, 31 October 1944; Service Record, Paul M. Kluxdal, March 17, 1942 – October 31, 1044; HQ, Seine DTC, APO 887, "Report of Proceedings in the Death Chamber," 1 November 1944; various personnel forms; *from other sources* – "Chicago Soldier Hanged for Killing Sergeant in France," *Chicago Tribune*, November 3, 1944, 10; "PFC Hanged in France for Murder of Topkick," *Stars & Stripes*, London Edition, Vol. 5, No. 2, November 3, 1944, 1; "Soldier Hanged for Murder," *New York Times*, November 5, 1944, 5.

## 25, 26 – Joseph Watson & Willie Wimberly, Jr.

[1] COL Thomas H. Nixon was born in PA. He graduated from West Point in June 1918 and became an Engineer officer. During the war, he was awarded two Legions of Merit, two Bronze Stars and a Distinguished Service Medal. He retired with disability in 1954 and died in York, PA on May 21, 1985.

[2] **Charge I: Violation of the 92nd Article of War.**
*Specification*: In that Private Joseph Watson and Technician Fifth Grade Willie Wimberly, Jr., both of the 257th Signal Construction Company, acting jointly and in pursuance of a common intent, did, at or near Le Pas En Ferre, France, on or about 8 August 1944, forcibly and feloniously, against her will, have carnal knowledge of ************, a female.

**Charge II: Violation of the 93rd Article of War.**
*Specification 1*: In that Private Joseph Watson and Technician Fifth Grade Willie Wimberly, Jr., both of the 257th Signal Construction Company, acting jointly and in pursuance of a common intent, did, at or near Le Pas En Ferre, France, on or about 8 August 1944, with intent to do him bodily harm, commit an assault upon Pierre Gourdin, a human being, by shooting him in the leg with a dangerous weapon, to wit, a submachine gun.

*Specification 2*: In that Private Joseph Watson and Technician Fifth Grade Willie Wimberly, Jr., both of the 257th Signal Construction Company, acting jointly and in pursuance of a common intent, did, at or near Le Pas En Ferre, France, on or about 8 August 1944, with intent to do him bodily harm, commit an assault upon *************, a human being, by shooting her in the leg with a dangerous weapon, to wit, a submachine gun.

*Specification 3*: In that Private Joseph Watson and Technician Fifth Grade Willie Wimberly, Jr., both of the 257th Signal Construction Company, acting jointly and in pursuance of a common intent, did, at or near Le Pas En Ferre, France, on or about 8 August 1944 in the night time, feloniously and burglariously break and enter the dwelling house of Pierre Gourdin and ************* with intent to commit a felony, viz., rape therein.

[3] It would be a senior jury that would decide the case: COL Nicholas W. Campanole (GS), COL Clell B. Perkins (VC), COL Robert E. Cummings (AG), COL Clarence C. Park (IG), COL James J. Weeks (DC), COL Fenton M. Wood (QM) and MAJ Andre B. Moore (JAG), who was also the Law Member on the court. The Defense Counsels were LTC John K. Patterson (CA) and CPT Everett E. Smith (JAG.) The Trial Judge Advocates

included MAJ Merrit Y. Hughes (AUS) and CPT Edwin L. Mayall (JAG.) Mayall spoke French due to the nature of the trial and the fact that the two victims were not believed to speak any English. Campanole was the Third Army G-5, and monitored the effects of military operations on civilian personnel. None of the officers graduated from West Point.

[4] **Sources, Willie Wimberly, Jr.:** *from U.S. Army Clerk of Court* – HQ, Third U.S. Army, APO 403, Special Orders Number 170, Detail for Court-Martial, 12 August 1944; Branch Office of The JAG with the ETO, APO 871, "Board of Review No. 1, U.S. v. Private Joseph Watson (396101250 and Technician Fifth Grade Willie Wimberly, Jr. (36392154), both of 257th Signal Construction Company," 11 October 1944; HQ, Seine DTC, APO 887, "Report of Proceedings in the Death Chamber [Willie Wimberly]," 10 November 1944; HQ, Third U.S. Army, Office of the Commanding General, Letter of Condolence, 17 November 1944; *from NARA (NPRC)* – various personal data forms; HQ, Seine DTC, APO 687, "Special Order Number 5," 8 November 1944.

**Sources, Joseph Watson:** *from U.S. Army Clerk of Court* – HQ, Third U.S. Army, APO 403, Special Orders Number 170, Detail for Court-Martial, 12 August 1944; Branch Office of The JAG with the ETO, APO 871, "Board of Review No. 1, U.S. v. Private Joseph Watson (396101250 and Technician Fifth Grade Willie Wimberly, Jr. (36392154), both of 257th Signal Construction Company," 11 October 1944; HQ, Seine DTC, APO 887, "Report of Proceedings in the Death Chamber [Joseph Watson]," 10 November 1944; HQ, Third U.S. Army, Office of the Commanding General, Letter of Condolence, 17 November 1944; *from NARA (NPRC)* – various personal data forms.

## 27 – Richard B. Scott

[1] None of the officers graduated from West Point.

[2] **Charge I: Violation of the 92nd Article of War.**
*Specification*: In that Technician Fifth Grade Richard B. Scott, 229th Quartermaster Salvage Collecting Company, did, at Octeville, near Cherbourg, France, on or about 20 July 1944, forcibly and feloniously, against her will, have carnal knowledge of ************.

**Charge II: Violation of the 93rd Article of War.**
*Specification 1*: In that Technician Fifth Grade Richard B. Scott, 229th Quartermaster Salvage Collecting Company, did, at Octeville, near Cherbourg, France, on or about 20 July 1944, with intent to do him bodily harm, commit an assault

upon Mr. Joseph Chatel by cutting him on the left side of his body just above the belt line with a dangerous weapon, to wit, a bayonet.

*Specification 2*: In that Technician Fifth Grade Richard B. Scott, 229th Quartermaster Salvage Collecting Company, did, at Octeville, near Cherbourg, France, on or about 20 July 1944, with intent to do him bodily harm, commit an assault upon Mr. Marcel Dupont, by willfully and feloniously threatening him with a dangerous weapon to wit, a bayonet.

[3] **Sources, Richard B. Scott: *from U.S. Army Clerk of Court*** – HQ, Normandy Base Section, Communications Zone, ETO, APO 562, Special Orders Number 11 [Detail for the Court, GCM], 21 August 1944; HQ, Normandy Base Section, Communications Zone, ETO, APO 562, Record of Trial GCM, "Arraignment and Charges," 7 September 1944; HQ, Normandy Base Section, Communications Zone, ETO, APO 562, "Review by Staff Judge Advocate, U.S. v. Technician Fifth Grade, Richard B. Scott, 38040012, 229th QM Salvage Collecting Company," 20 September 1944; HQ, ETO, "Confirmation Order [Technician Fifth Grade Richard B. Scott, 38040012, 229th Quartermaster Salvage Collecting Company," 20 October 1944; 298th General Hospital, Communications Zone, ETO, APO 562, "Proceedings of a board of officers convened pursuant to Para 4, SO 195, 27 October 1944 to determine the mental status of Technician Fifth Grade Richard B. Scott, 38040012, 229th QM Salvage Collecting Company," 27 October 1944; Branch Office of The JAG with the ETO, APO 871, "Board of Review No. 1, U.S. v. Technician Fifth Grade, Richard B. Scott, 38040012, 229th QM Salvage Collecting Company," 4 November 1944; Office of the Surgeon, Fort Du Roule, Cherbourg, France, "Death Certificate [General Prisoner Richard B. Scott, 38040012, 229th QM Salvage Coll. Co.]", 18 November 1944; HQ, Guard House Overhead Detachment Number 5, U.S. Army, APO 562, "Report of Proceedings at the Execution of General Prisoner, Richard B. Scott, 38040012 (formerly Technician 5th Grade, 229th Quartermaster Salvage Collecting Company), 18 November 1944; *from NARA (NPRC)* – various personal data forms; Service Record, Richard B. Scott, March 7, 1941 – November 18, 1944; *from other sources* – "Two U.S. Soldiers Are Hanged," *New York Times*, November 20, 1944.

## 28 – William D. Pennyfeather

[1] LTC Paul H. Googe (TC), LTC William C. Hollis (TC), MAJ George W. Seckinger (IN), MAJ Raymond J. Lamar (CE), MAJ Eugene T. Shields (QM) and Law Member, CPT Dean A. Van Deventer (QM) and CPT Henry D. Bonneau (SC.) Serving as the Trial Judge Advocate was 1LT Vincent P. Clarke (TC), who was assisted by 2LT Joseph A. Bruggeman (QM.) For the defense was CPT Jean E. Pierson (TC), 1LT Joseph L. Weiser (CE) and 1LT Meade C. Harris, Jr. (CE.) Court-martial members were usually assigned to serve for a limited period of time – often a week or two – and would sit in judgment of all cases brought to them during that period. Harris was born in IL in 1917. He was a college graduate and was inducted in Chicago on June 8, 1942.

[2] **Charge: Violation of the 92nd Article of War.**

*Specification*: In that Private William D. Pennyfeather, 3868th Quartermaster Truck Company (TC), did, at Cherbourg, France, on or about 1 August 1944, forcibly and feloniously, against her will, have carnal knowledge of ************.

[3] **Sources, William D. Pennyfeather: *from U.S. Army Clerk of Court*** – Criminal Investigation Division, SOS, U.S. Army, ETO, "Statement of Pvt. William D. Pennyfeather (Col) Date: 2 August 1944;" HQ, Normandy Base Section, Communications Zone, ETO, APO 562, Special Orders Number 11 [Detail for the Court, GCM], 21 August 1944; HQ, Normandy Base Section, Communications Zone, ETO, APO 562, Record of Trial GCM, "Arraignment and Charges," 2 September 1944; HQ, Normandy Base Section, Communications Zone, ETO, APO 562, "Review by Staff Judge Advocate, U.S. v. Private William D. Pennyfeather, 32801627, 3868th Quartermaster Truck Company," 14 September 1944; HQ, ETO, "Confirmation Order [Private William D. Pennyfeather, 32801627, 3868th Quartermaster Truck Company]" 4 October 1944; Branch Office of The JAG with the ETO, APO 871, "Board of Review No. 1, U.S. v. Private William D. Pennyfeather, 32801627, 3868th Quartermaster Truck Company," 4 November 1944; HQ, Guard House Overhead Detachment Number 5, U.S. Army, APO 562, "Report of Proceedings at the Execution of General Prisoner, William D. Pennyfeather, 32801627, (formerly Private, 3868th Quartermaster Truck Company), 18 November 1944"; *from NARA (NPRC)* – various personal data forms; State of New York,

Executive Department, Division of Parole, "Letter Concerning Parole of William D. Pennyfeather," January 26, 1943; *from other sources* – "Two U.S. Soldiers Are Hanged," *New York Times*, November 20, 1944.

## 29 – Curtis L. Maxey
[1] Sitting on the panel were LTC Charles A. Luckie (JAG) – who was also the Law Member, LTC James B. Chubbuck (CE), LTC Paul S. Lawrence (QM), MAJ August Koukol, Jr., MAJ Clyde P. Younger (QM), MAJ William Rybak (CE), MAJ Joseph Lombard, (CE), CPT Charles A. Lonn (CE) and CPT Saul Fraint, (CE.) Trial Judge Advocate was MAJ Gilbert C. St. Clair (IN), who was assisted by CPT John E. Stadig (CE.) CPT Paul Therretta (CE) served as Defense Counsel; he was assisted by 1LT Carl A. Gelb (QM.) Chubbuck was born in NY on December 15, 1915, graduating from West Point in 1938. During the war, he rose to command the 36th Engineer Regiment. In Korea, he commanded the 1169th Engineer Combat Group. He retired in 1960; he died on April 19, 1974.

[2] **Charge: Violation of the 92nd Article of War.** *Specification*: In that Private Curtis L. Maxey, 3277th Quartermaster Service Company, did, at Saint Tropez, France, on or about 15 August 1944, forcibly and feloniously, against her will, have carnal knowledge of ************.

[3] **Sources, Curtis L. Maxey: *from U.S. Clerk of Court* – "Report of Interrogation of Private L. E. Hollingsworth, 34429655, by 1st LT Lewis Bernstein, CID, 504th MP Battalion," 21 August 1944; "Report of Interrogation of Private Curtis L. Maxie, 34554198, by 1st LT Lewis Bernstein, CID, 504th MP Battalion," 21 August 1944; HQ, Seventh Army, Office of the Surgeon, APO 758, "Psychiatric Examination of Prisoners," 22 August 1944; HQ, NATO, "Confirmation Order [Private Curtis L. Maxey, 34554198, and Private L. B. Hollingsworth, 34429655, both of 3277th Quartermaster Service Company]," 17 October 1944; Branch Office of The JAG with the NATO, APO 534, "Review by the Board of Review, U.S. v. Privates Curtis L. Maxey (34554198) and L. B. Hollingsworth (34429655) both of 3277th Quartermaster Service Company," 31 October 1944; *from NARA (NPRC)* – HQ, NATO, APO 534, "GCM Order Number 79 [Curtis L. Maxey]," 28 October 1944; various personnel forms.**

## 30 – Theron W. McGann
[1] The General Board, United States Forces, European Theater, Judge Advocate Section, "The Military Offender in the Theater of Operations," Study 84, 5. The report cited Eugene S. Sernans, Executive Secretary of the General Howard Association, quoted in *Stars and Stripes* on October 10, 1945.

[2] William Bradford Huie, *The Execution of Private Slovik*, 10.

[3] **Charge: Violation of the 92nd Article of War.** *Specification*: In that Private Theron W. McGann, Company A, 32nd Signal Construction Battalion, did, at Quibou, Manche, France, on or about 5 August 1944, forcibly and feloniously, against her will, have carnal knowledge of ************.

[4] Sitting on the panel were COL Hurley E. Fuller (IN), MAJ Carmon C. Harris (JAG), Law Member, MAJ Clayton S. Davis (QM), CPT Owen M. Lynch (OD), CPT Boyd V. Hill (CE) and CPT Wayne S. Aho (CAC.) MAJ Julian E. Weisler (JAG) stood as the Trial Judge Advocate; he was assisted by CPT Ralph A. Newman (Sp Res.) CPT Copentius B. Maynard (JAG) served as the Defense Counsel. None of the officers graduated from West Point.

[5] **Sources, Theron W. McGann: *from U.S. Army Clerk of Court* – "A Chronology of the Case of: McGann, Theron W., 39332102, Private, Company A, 32nd Signal Battalion;" "Report of Agent John B. Goodall, CIC Detachment, HQ, 1st U.S. Army," 6 August 1944; HQ, 1st U.S. Army, APO 230, Investigation Division, Office of the Provost Marshal, "Statement of Private Theron W. McGann," 8 August 1944; HQ, 32nd Signal Construction Battalion, "Personal History of Accused," 14 August 1944; HQ, First U.S. Army, "Organization of the Court, Trial of Private Theron W. McGann," 28 August 1944; HQ, First U.S. Army, APO 230, "Review of the Staff Judge Advocate of the Record of Trial by GCM of McGann, Theron W., 39332102, Private, Company A, 32nd Signal Battalion," 21 September 1944; HQ, ETO, "Review by Staff Judge Advocate, U.S. v. Private Theron W. McGann, 39332102, Company A, 32nd Signal Construction Battalion," 26 October 1944; HQ, ETO, "Confirmation Order [Private Theron W. McGann, 39332102, Company A, 32nd Signal Construction Battalion]," 27 October 1944; Branch Office of The JAG with the ETO, APO 887, "Board of Review Number 1, U.S. v. Private Theron W. McGann (39332102), Company A, 32nd Signal Construction Battalion," 7 November 1944; HQ, ETO, "GCM Orders Number 104, [Private Theron W. McGann]," 15 November 1944; HQ, Normandy Base Section, Communications**

Zone, ETO, APO 562, "Execution of General Prisoner Theron W. McGann," 17 November 1944; "Report of Proceedings at the Execution of General Prisoner Theron W. McGann, 39332102," 20 November 1944; "Hand Receipt for Remains of General Prisoner Theron W. McGann," 20 November 1944; "HQ, First U.S. Army, Letter to Chief of Gendarmerie, Quibou, Manche, France," 8 December 1944; "Death Book" Ledger; *from NARA (NPRC)* – various personal data forms; Inventory of Effects of McGann, Theron J., 20 November 1944; "Report of Burial, McGann, Theron W.," 21 November 1944; *from other sources* – J. Robert Lilly, "Military Executions," in Clifton D. Bryant, *Handbook of Death and Dying*, Thousand, Oaks, CA: Sage Publications, 2003, 379, 380; Email from Professor J. Robert Lilly concerning burial location, February 7, 2011.

## 31 – Arthur E. Davis

[1] William Bradford Huie, *The Execution of Private Slovik*, 15.

[2] Sitting on the jury were COL Clell B. Perkins (VC), COL Robert E. Cummings (AG), COL Clarence C. Park (IG), COL James J. Weeks (DC), LTC Kenneth E. Van Buskirk (FA) and MAJ Andre B. Moore (JAG), who served as the Law Member. All officers were assigned to the Third Army headquarters. MAJ Merrit Y. Hughes (AUS) served as the Trial Judge Advocate; he was assisted by CPT Edwin L. Mayall (JAG.) LTC John K. Patterson (CAC) sat as the Defense Counsel for the two accused. He was assisted by CPT Everett E. Smith (JAG.) The defendants requested that 1LT Delbert V. Whitenack (MP) be assigned to their defense team. Their request was granted. None of the officers was a West Pointer.

[3] **Charge I: Violation of the 92nd Article of War.**
*Specification*: In that Private Arthur E. Davis, 3326th Quartermaster Company, and Private Charles H. Jordan, 3327th Quartermaster Truck Company, did, at or near La Rouennerie En Montour, Ile et Vilaine, France, on or about 10 August 1944, acting jointly and in pursuance of a common intent, forcibly and felonious, against her will, have carnal knowledge of **************, a French woman.

**Charge II: Violation of the 93rd Article of War.**
*Specification*: In that Private Arthur E. Davis, 3326th Quartermaster Company, and Private Charles H. Jordan, 3327th Quartermaster Truck Company, acting jointly and in pursuance of a common intent, did, at or near La Rouennerie En Montour, Ile et Vilaine, France, on or about 10

August 1944, with intent to commit a felony, viz. murder, commit an assault upon Amand Honore and Joseph Taburel by willfully and feloniously firing at the said Amand Honore and Joseph Taburel with a dangerous weapon, to wit, a rifle.

**Charge III: Violation of the 96th Article of War.**
*Specification*: In that Private Arthur E. Davis, 3326th Quartermaster Company, and Private Charles H. Jordan, 3327th Quartermaster Truck Company, acting jointly and in pursuance of a common intent, did, at or near La Rouennerie En Montour, Ile et Vilaine, France, on or about 10 August 1944, commit an assault upon Amand Honore by wrongfully placing the muzzle of a rifle to the forehead of the said Amand Honore and firing shots over his head.

[4] **Sources, Arthur E. Davis:** *from U.S. Army Clerk of Court* – Record of Trial, General Court-Martial, Third U.S. Army, Davis, Arthur E. and Jordan, Charles H., 16 August 1944; HQ, Third U.S. Army, Office of the Judge Advocate, "Review of the Staff Judge Advocate, U.S. v. Private Arthur E. Davis, 36788637, 3326th Quartermaster Truck Company and Private Charles H. Jordan, 14066430, 3327th Quartermaster Truck Company," 28 August 1944; "GCM Check List, Davis, Arthur E., PVT," "Organization of the Court," Poilley, France," 16 August 1944; HQ, Third U.S. Army, Office of the Judge Advocate, "Review of the Staff Judge Advocate, U.S. v. Private Arthur E. Davis, 36788637, 3326th Quartermaster Truck Company and Private Charles H. Jordan, 14066430, 3327th Quartermaster Truck Company," 28 August 1944; HQ, Third U.S. Army, "Approval of Sentence [Private Arthur E. Davis]," 30 August 1944; HQ, ETO, "Review by Staff Judge Advocate, U.S. v. Private Arthur E. Davis, 36788637, 3326th Quartermaster Truck Company and Private Charles H. Jordan, 14066430, 3327th Quartermaster Truck Company," 23 September 1944; HQ, ETO, "Confirmation Order [Private Arthur E. Davis, 36788637, 3326th Quartermaster Truck Company and Private Charles H. Jordan, 14066430, 3327th Quartermaster Truck Company]," 23 September 1944; Branch Office of The JAG with the ETO, APO 887, "Board of Review No. 2, U.S. v. Private Arthur E. Davis, 36788637, 3326th Quartermaster Truck Company and Private Charles H. Jordan, 14066430, 3327th Quartermaster Truck Company," 2 November 1944; HQ, ETO, "GCM Orders Number 105 [Private Arthur E. Davis and Private Charles H. Jordan]," 15 November 1944; *from NARA (NPRC)* – various personnel forms; Service Record, Arthur E. Davis, November 8, 1943 – November 22, 1944.

## 32 – Charles H. Jordan

[1] **Sources, Charles H. Jordan:** *from U.S. Army Clerk of Court* – Record of Trial, General Court-Martial, Third U.S. Army, Davis, Arthur E. and Jordan, Charles H., 16 August 1944; "Organization of the Court," Poilley, France," 16 August 1944; HQ, Third U.S. Army, Office of the Judge Advocate, "Review of the Staff Judge Advocate, U.S. v. Private Arthur E. Davis, 36788637, 3326th Quartermaster Truck Company and Private Charles H. Jordan, 14066430, 3327th Quartermaster Truck Company," 28 August 1944; "Evidence of Previous Convictions in the Case of Jordan, Charles H., 14066430, Private, 3327th Quartermaster Truck Company," 16 August 1944; "GCM Check List, Jordan, Charles E., PVT," HQ, Third U.S. Army, "Approval of Sentence [Private Charles H. Jordan]," 30 August 1944; HQ, ETO, "Review by Staff Judge Advocate, U.S. v. Private Arthur E. Davis, 36788637, 3326th Quartermaster Truck Company and Private Charles H. Jordan, 14066430, 3327th Quartermaster Truck Company," 23 September 1944; HQ, ETO, "Confirmation Order [Private Arthur E. Davis, 36788637, 3326th Quartermaster Truck Company and Private Charles H. Jordan, 14066430, 3327th Quartermaster Truck Company]," 23 September 1944; Branch Office of The JAG with the ETO, APO 887, "Board of Review No. 2, U.S. v. Private Arthur E. Davis, 36788637, 3326th Quartermaster Truck Company and Private Charles H. Jordan, 14066430, 3327th Quartermaster Truck Company," 2 November 1944; HQ, ETO, "GCM Orders Number 105 [Private Arthur E. Davis and Private Charles H. Jordan]," 15 November 1944; *from NARA (NPRC)* – various personnel forms; HQ, Third Army, "Circular 55," 14 September 1944; War Department, The Adjutant General's Office, "Non-Battle Casualty Report, Jordan, Charlie M., 14066430," 12 March 1945.

## 33 – James E. Hendricks

[1] **Charge I: Violation of the 92nd Article of War.**
*Specification:* In that Private First Class, James E. Hendricks, 3326th Quartermaster Truck Company, 80th Quartermaster Battalion (Mobile), did, at Plumaudan, Cotes du Nord, France, on or about 21 August 1944, with malice aforethought, willfully, deliberately, feloniously, unlawfully, and with premeditation kill one Victor Bignon, a human being by shooting him with a rifle.
**Charge II: Violation of the 93rd Article of War.**
*Specification 1:* In that Private First Class, James E. Hendricks, 3326th Quartermaster Truck Company, 80th Quartermaster Battalion (Mobile), did, at Plumaudan, Cotes du Nord, France, on or about 21 August 1944, unlawfully enter the dwelling of Victor Bignon, with intent to commit a criminal offense, to wit, rape therein.
*Specification 2:* In that Private First Class, James E. Hendricks, 3326th Quartermaster Truck Company, 80th Quartermaster Battalion (Mobile), did, at Plumaudan, Cotes du Nord, France, on or about 21 August 1944, with intent to commit a felony, viz; rape, commit an assault upon Noemie Bignon, by willfully and feloniously grasping her and pointing a rifle at her and attempting to have sexual intercourse with her.

[2] Sitting on the panel were the following officers: COL Claud T. Gunn (FI), LTC Juan A.A. Sedillo (JAG) who served as Law Member, LTC Kenneth Clark (AG), MAJ Clayton T. Hathaway (FI), CPT John J. Silbernagel (AG), CPT Frederick L. Orr (FI), 1LT Gerald W. Stone (QM) and 1LT Paul E. Stewart (AG.) 2LT Joseph D. Greene (AG) served as the Trial Judge Advocate; he was assisted by 2LT James P. Reed. 2LT Ralph M. Fogarty (IN) sat as Defense Counsel; 2LT Robert F. Seager (OD) was his assistant. None of the officers graduated from West Point. Gunn hailed from Georgia; in World War I, he had been a coast artillery officer assigned to Fort Strong, MA; he died on August 29, 1991. Sedillo, an actor and lawyer, was born on February 14, 1894 in Socorro, New Mexico; he died on November 3, 1982 in NM. Silbernagel was from Madison, WI. He commanded the 13th Machine Records Unit attached to the VIII Corps. Ralph Fogarty died in 2003 in IL.

[3] **Sources, James E. Hendricks:** *from U.S. Army Clerk of Court* – "Court-Martial Charges, Time Data Sheet in the Case of Hendricks, James E., PFC, 33453189, 3326th Quartermaster Truck Company;" "Statement of James E. Hendricks, ASN 33453189, 3326th Quartermaster Truck Company;" HQ, VIII Corps, APO 308, "Recommendation for Clemency, James E. Hendricks," 14 September 1944; HQ, VIII Corps, APO 308, "Review of Staff Judge Advocate, U.S. v. Private First Class James E. Hendricks, 33453189, 3326th Quartermaster Truck Company," 18 September 1944; HQ, VIII Corps, APO 308, "Commendation, 1LT Donald F. Tucker, o-1574355, QMC, 3326th Quartermaster Truck Company, APO 308," September 1944; HQ, ETO, "Review by Staff Judge Advocate, U.S. v. Private First Class James E. Hendricks, 33453189, 3326th Quartermaster Truck Company," October 1944; HQ, ETO, "Confirmation Order in the Case of

Private First Class James E. Hendricks, 33453189, 3326th Quartermaster Truck Company," 27 October 1944; HQ, ETO, "GCM Orders Number 109 [Private First Class James E. Hendricks]," 19 November 1944; HQ, Brittany Base Section, Communications Zone, ETO, APO 517, "Orders [for Movement to Plumaudan, France], 21 November 1944; "Report of Proceedings at the Execution of General Prisoner James E. Hendricks, 33453189," 24 November 1944; "Receipt of Remains of General Prisoner James H. Hendricks," 24 November 1945; *from NARA (NPRC)* – various personal data forms; Service Record, James E. Hendricks, February 1, 1943 to November 24, 1944; *from other sources* – Alice Kaplan, *The Interpreter*, NY: Free Press, 2005, 28-33, 81.

[4] Alice Kaplan, *The Interpreter*, 83-84.

### 34 – Benjamin Pygate

[1] The following officers sat in judgment: LTC Norman W. Whited (CAC), CPT Everett H. Wing (OD); CPT William A. Parks (OD) Law Member, CPT James S. Raper (MC), CPT Victor N. Green (CE) and 1LT Pieter J. Van der Lijn (OD.) 2LT Myron J. Borawiak (OD) served as the Trial Judge Advocate; he was assisted by 2LT Robert F. Hunt (OD.) 2LT Richard W. Dudley (OD) served as Defense Counsel. None graduated from West Point.

[2] **Charge: Violation of the 92nd Article of War.** *Specification*: In that Private Benjamin Pygate, 960th Quartermaster Service Company, did, at Drill Hall Camp, Westbury, Wiltshire, England, on or about 17 June 1944, with malice aforethought, willfully, deliberately, feloniously, unlawfully, and with premeditation kill one Private First Class James E. Alexander, a human being by stabbing him in the throat with a knife.

[3] **Sources, Benjamin Pygate:** *from U.S. Army Clerk of Court* – "Organization of the Court, GCM of Private Benjamin (NMI) Pygate," 15 July 1944; HQ, Southern Base Section, Communications Zone, ETO, APO 519, "Office of the Staff Judge Advocate, Review of Record of Trial by GCM, United States vs. Benjamin Pygate, 33741021, Private, 960th Quartermaster Service Company, General Depot G-47," 5 August 1944; HQ, ETO, "Confirmation Order in the Case of Private Benjamin Pygate, 33741021, 960th Quartermaster Service Company, General Depot G-47," 31 August 1944; Branch Office of The JAG with the ETO, APO 887, "Board of Review No. 1, U.S. v. Benjamin Pygate, 33741021, Private,

960th Quartermaster Service Company, General Depot G-47," 5 August 1944; Letters from Private Benjamin Pygate to Family Members, October 22, 1944; HQ, 2912th DTC, APO 508, "Appointment of Detail for the Execution of Private Benjamin (NMI) Pygate, 33741021," 24 November 1944; HQ, 2912th DTC, APO 508, "Proceeding of Execution of Private Benjamin (NMI) Pygate, 33741021," 28 November 1944; *from NARA (NPRC)* – various personal data forms; "Report of Physical Examination and Induction [Benjamin Pygate]"; HQ, 96th General Hospital, APO 121, Sanity Hearing for Pygate, Benjamin, Private, 33741021, 26 September 1944; Service Record, Benjamin Pygate, May 5, 1943 – November 28, 1944; Federal Bureau of Investigation, "Record of Fingerprints, Benjamin Pygate, FBI Record Number 331317," February 6, 1945; *from other sources* – "The US Prison at Shepton Mallet."

### 35, 36 – Oscar N. Newman & Leo Valentine, Sr.

[1] **Charge: Violation of the 92nd Article of War.** *Specification*: In that Sergeant Johnnie E. Hudson, 396th Quartermaster Truck Company, did, at or near Beaunay, France, on or about 18 September 1944, forcibly and feloniously, against her will, have carnal knowledge of *************.

**Charge: Violation of the 92nd Article of War.** *Specification*: In that Technician Fifth Grade Leo Valentine, Sr., 396th Quartermaster Truck Company, did, at or near Beaunay, France, on or about 18 September 1944, forcibly and feloniously, against her will, have carnal knowledge of *************.

**Charge: Violation of the 92nd Article of War.** *Specification*: In that Technician Fifth Grade Oscar N. Newman, HQ and HQ Company, 712th Railway Operating Battalion, did, at or near Beaunay, France, on or about 18 September 1944, forcibly and feloniously, against her will, have carnal knowledge of *************.

[2] The following sat on the court COL Russell R. Klanderman (OD), LTC William E. Ryan (CE), LTC John C. Williams (IN), MAJ Louis M. Haas (FA), MAJ Thomas C. Adams (FA), MAJ Walter L. Winegar (CE), MAJ Sewall D. Andrews (QM), MAJ Nicholas S. Strider (FI), CPT William G. Walley, Jr. (JAG) and Law Member, CPT Lawrence C. McNeil (MP.) 1LT William H. Vance (JAG) served as the Trial Judge Advocate; he was assisted by 2LT Harley H. Stipp (JAG.) CPT Fred J. Stegmaier (CC) sat as one of two assistant Defense Counsels; the other was 2LT William J. Durisek. Klanderman was born in MI on June

28, 1910; he graduated from West Point in 1933. He retired from the Army as a COL in 1962 and died at Scott Air Force Base in IL on December 31, 1964. Winegar was born in UT on July 11, 1914; he graduated from West Point in 1939. He won a Bronze Star as an engineer group commander. He retired in 1969.

3  **Sources, Oscar N. Newman:** *from U.S. Army Clerk of Court* – HQ, 712th Railway Operation Battalion, APO 350, Office of the Chaplain, Request for Clemency for Oscar N. Newton, 8 November 1944; Branch Office of The JAG with the ETO, APO 887, "Board of Review No. 1, U.S. v. Sergeant Johnnie E. Hudson (34741799), and Technician Fifth Grade Leo Valentine, Sr. (32954278), both of 396th Quartermaster Truck Company, and Technician Fifth Grade Oscar N. Newman (35226382), HQ and HQ Company, 712th Railway Operation Battalion," 18 November 1944; HQ, ETO, GCM Order Number 115 (Technician Fifth Grade Oscar N. Newman), 25 November 1944; HQ, Oise Section, Communications Zone, APO 513, "Report of Proceedings at the Execution of General Prisoner Oscar N. Newman, 35226382 (formerly Technician Fifth Grade, HQ and HQ Company, 712th Railway Operating Battalion," 29 November 1944; HQ, 2913th Detention Training Center, APO 573, "Receipt for Remains of General Prisoner Oscar N. Newman," 29 November 1944; War Department, The Adjutant General's Office, Washington, DC, Battle Casualty Report, Newman, Oscar N., 35226382, 27 Feb 45; *from NARA (NPRC)* – Service Record for Oscar N. Newman from August 13, 1943 to November 29, 1944, "Report of Physical Examination and Induction, Oscar Neill Newman," September 13, 1943; various personnel forms; *from other sources* – Interview with Michel Jacquesson, Beaunay, France, September 10, 2011.

**Sources, Leo Valentine:** *from U.S. Army Clerk of Court* – HQ, Third U.S. Army, Office of the Commanding General, APO 403, "Court-Martial Charges," 22 September 1944; Branch Office of The JAG with the ETO, APO 887, "Board of Review No. 1, U.S. v. Sergeant Johnnie E. Hudson (34741799), and Technician Fifth Grade Leo Valentine, Sr. (32954278), both of 396th Quartermaster Truck Company, and Technician Fifth Grade Oscar N. Newman (35226382), HQ and HQ Company, 712th Railway Operation Battalion," 18 November 1944; HQ, ETO, GCM Order Number 114 (Technician Fifth Grade Leo Valentine, Sr.), 25 November 1944; HQ, Oise Section, Communications Zone, APO 513,

"Report of Proceedings at the Execution of General Prisoner Leo Valentine, Sr., 32954278 (formerly Technician Fifth Grade, 396th Quartermaster Truck Company," 29 November 1944; HQ, 2913th Detention Training Center, APO 573, "Receipt for Remains of General Prisoner Leo Valentine, Sr.," 29 November 1944; HQ, 712th Railway Operating Battalion, APO 350, "Letter to Mayor Jules Babiot, Fromontiers, Marne, France," 7 December 1944; *from other sources* – Interview with Michel Jacquesson, Beaunay, France, September 10, 2011.

## 37 – William E. Davis

1  Colonel John M. Collins, "World War II NCOs," *Army Magazine*, Arlington, VA: Association of the U.S. Army, February 2005.

2  "GIs Today Are Smarter Than '17 Soldier Dads," *Stars & Stripes*, London Edition, Vol. 4, No. 307, October 27, 1944, 4.

3  Also in attendance were: COL Ray C. Fountain, Provost Marshall of Brittany Base Section of the Communications Zone; and officials LTC Frederick Whittaker, LTC Francis S. Gabel, 1LT James E. Watson, 1LT Onan W. Trowbridge and 1LT Paul G. Lincavage. Thorrolf P. "Ralph" Dyro was born on March 21, 1921 at Port Arthur, TX; he stood 5'10" tall and weighed 187 pounds. He was white, finished three years of high school and was married. He enlisted on March 18, 1939 at Fort McDowell, CA and arrived in Europe on January 14, 1943. He was qualified expert with the M-1 rifle. Dyro was discharged from the Army on July 7, 1945 at Fort Dix, NJ. He moved to Ormand Beach, FL in 1993 and died on August 10, 1999 after retiring from a furniture moving company.

4  **Charge I: Violation of the 92nd Article of War.**
*Specification*: In that Private First Class William E. Davis and Private First Class J.C. Potts, both of 3121st Quartermaster Service Company, 563rd Quartermaster Battalion, acting jointly, and in pursuance of a common intent, did, at Guiclan, Finistere, France, on or about 22 August 1944, with malice aforethought, willfully, deliberately, feloniously, unlawfully, and with premeditation, kill one Germaine Pouliquen, a human being, by shooting her with a rifle.

**Charge II: Violation of the 93rd Article of War.**
*Specification*: In that Private First Class William E. Davis and Private First Class J.C. Potts, both of 3121st Quartermaster Service Company, 563rd Quartermaster Battalion, acting jointly, and in pursuance of a common intent, did, at Guiclan, Finistere, France, on or about 22 August 1944, with intent to commit a felony, viz, rape,

commit an assault upon Germaine Pouliquen, by willfully, forcibly, and feloniously holding her and attempting to have carnal knowledge.

[5] **Sources, William E. Davis:** *from U.S. Army Clerk of Court* – "Statement of PFC William E. Davis, ASN 33541888, 3121 QM Serv. Co., APO 403," 28 August 1944; HQ, Ninth U.S. Army, Office of the Surgeon, APO 339, Neuropsychiatric Examination of Private William E. D. Davis, ASN 33541888, 30 September 1944; HQ, Ninth U.S. Army, Office of the Army Judge Advocate, "Review of the Army Judge Advocate, in the Case of Potts, J.C. and Davis, William E.," 6 October 1944; HQ, ETO, "Confirmation of Sentence of Private First Class William E. Davis, 33541888, 3121st Quartermaster Services Company, " 27 October 1944; Branch Office of The JAG with the ETO, APO 887, "Board of Review No. 1, U.S. v. Privates First Class William E. Davis (33541888) and J.C. Potts (34759592), both of 3121st Quartermaster Service Company," 29 November 1944; HQ, Loire DTC, APO 517, "Report of Proceedings at the Execution of General Prisoner William E. Davis, formerly Private First Class, 3121st Quartermaster Service Company," 28 December 1944; *from NARA (NPRC)* – various personnel forms; Service Record for William E. Davis, October 7, 1943 – December 27, 1944; HQ, Brittany Base Section, Communications Zone, ETO, APO 517, Orders to Officers and Enlisted Concerned, 22 December 1944; HQ, ETO, APO 887, "Execution of Death Sentence (Davis, William E.)," 22 December 1944; HQ, ETO, GCM Order Number 146 (Private First Class William E. Davis), 21 December 1944; Certificate (Physical and Mental Condition of William E. Davis), 26 December 1944; Receipt for Remains of General William E. Davis, 27 December 1944; HQ, Loire DTC, Special Orders Number 154, 23 December 1944; HQ, Loire DTC, "Report of Execution," 29 December 1944; *from other sources* – Alice Kaplan, *The Interpreter*, 174.

## 38, 39 – Ernest L. Clark & Augustine M. Guerra

[1] **Charge: Violation of the 92nd Article of War.**

*Specification 1:* In that Private Augustine M. Guerra, 306th Fighter Control Squadron, IX Air Defense Command, did, in conjunction with Corporal Ernest Lee Clark, at Ashford, Kent, England, on or about 22 August 1944, with malice aforethought, willfully, deliberately, feloniously, unlawfully, and with premeditation, kill one Betty Dorian Pearl Green, a human being, by choking and strangling the said Betty Dorian Pearl Green.

*Specification 2:* In that Private Augustine M. Guerra,
306th Fighter Control Squadron, IX Air Defense Command, acting jointly and in pursuance of a common intent with Corporal Ernest Lee Clark, did, at Ashford, Kent, England, on or about 22 August 1944, forcibly and feloniously, against her will, have carnal knowledge of Betty Dorian Pearl Green, a female child below the age of sixteen years, the said Private Augustine M. Guerra penetrating the sexual organs of the said Betty Dorian Pearl Green with his penis, being aided and abetted therein by the said Corporal Ernest Lee Clark who held and subdued the said Betty Dorian Pearl Green during such action.

*Specification 3:* In that Private Augustine M. Guerra, 306th Fighter Control Squadron, IX Air Defense Command, acting jointly and in pursuance of a common intent with Corporal Ernest Lee Clark, did, at Ashford, Kent, England, on or about 22 August 1944, forcibly and feloniously, against her will, have carnal knowledge of Betty Dorian Pearl Green, a female child below the age of sixteen years, the said Private Augustine M. Guerra penetrating the sexual organs of the said Betty Dorian Pearl Green with his penis, being aided and abetted therein by the said Corporal Ernest Lee Clark who held and subdued the said Betty Dorian Pearl Green during such action.

[2] The panel included the following officers: COL Neal J. O'Brien (AG), COL Aaron L. Johnson (AC), COL Reginald B. Sentenne (CC), LTC Kermit R. Kann (QM), MAJ Raymond A. Nelson (IN), MAJ Sidney D. Nielson (AC), MAJ Starbuck Smith, Jr. (AC) and MAJ Harold J. Geradot (QM.) CPT Hiram P. Todd, Jr. (AC) sat as the Trial Judge Advocate; CPT Joseph P. Correia (MP) was the Defense Counsel. None of the officers was from West Point.

[3] **Charge: Violation of the 92nd Article of War.**

*Specification 1:* In that Corporal Ernest Lee Clark, 306th Fighter Control Squadron, IX Air Defense Command, did, in conjunction with Private Augustine M. Guerra, at Ashford, Kent, England, on or about 22 August 1944, with malice aforethought, willfully, deliberately, feloniously, unlawfully, and with premeditation, kill one Betty Dorian Pearl Green, a human being, by choking and strangling the said Betty Dorian Pearl Green.

*Specification 2:* In that Corporal Ernest Lee Clark, 306th Fighter Control Squadron, IX Air Defense Command, did, in conjunction with Private Augustine M. Guerra, at Ashford, Kent, England, on or about 22 August 1944, forcibly and feloniously, against her will, have carnal knowledge of Betty Dorian Pearl Green, a female child below the age of sixteen years, the said Corporal Ernest Lee Clark penetrating the sexual organs of the said Betty Dorian Pearl Green with his penis, being aided and abetted therein by the said Private Augustine M. Guerra who held and subdued the said Betty Dorian Pearl Green during such action.

*Specification 3*: In that Corporal Ernest Lee Clark, 306th Fighter Control Squadron, IX Air Defense Command, did, in conjunction with Private Augustine M. Guerra, at Ashford, Kent, England, on or about 22 August 1944, forcibly and feloniously, against her will, have carnal knowledge of Betty Dorian Pearl Green, a female child below the age of sixteen years, the said Private Augustine M. Guerra penetrating the sexual organs of the said Betty Dorian Pearl Green with his penis, being aided and abetted therein by the said Corporal Ernest Lee Clark during such action.

[4] **Sources, Ernest Lee Clark:** *from U.S. Army Clerk of Court* – "Statement Made Voluntarily by a Witness, William Ernest Green, 180 Newtown, Ashford," 23 August 1944; Investigation Division, Office of the Provost Marshal General, ETO, Statement of Corporal Ernest Lee Cark, dated 25 August 1944; HQ, IX Air Force Service Command, Office of the Staff Judge Advocate, "Review of the Staff Judge Advocate, United States vs. Corporal Ernest Lee Clark, 33212946, 306th Fighter Control Squadron, IX Air Defense Command," 22 October 1944; Branch Office of The JAG with the ETO, APO 887, "Board of Review No. 2, U.S. v. Corporal Ernest Lee Clark (33212946), 306th Fighter Control Squadron, IX Air Defense Command," 14 December 1944; HQ, ETO, GCM Order Number 152 (Corporal Ernest Lee Clark), 30 December 1945; HQ, 2912th DTC, APO 508, Proceedings of Execution of Corporal Ernest L. Clark, 33212946, and Private Augustine M. Guerra, 38458032, formerly members of the 306th Fighter Control Squadron, IX Air Defense Command, 8 January 1945; *from NARA (NPRC)* – "Service Record, Clark, Ernest Lee, 33212946, from September 17, 1942 to January 8, 1945; Federal Bureau of Investigation Fingerprint Record, Clark, Ernest Lee," 16 February 1945; various personnel records; *from other sources* – "SOLDIER DOOMED TO HANG; American Convicted of Murder of English Girl, 15," *New York Times*, October 10, 1944, 4; "The US Prison at Shepton Mallet"; Albert Pierrepoint Execution Ledger Entry.

**Sources, Augustine M. Guerra:** *from U.S. Army Clerk of Court* – HQ, ETO, GCM Order Number 151 (Private Augustine M. Guerra), 30 December 1945; HQ, 2912th DTC, APO 508, Proceedings of Execution of Corporal Ernest L. Clark, 33212946, and Private Augustine M. Guerra, 38458032, formerly members of the 306th Fighter Control Squadron, IX Air Defense Command, 8 January 1945; *from NARA (NPRC)* – "Service Record, Guerra, Augustine M., 38458032, from April 15, 1943 to January 8, 1945; Federal Bureau of Investigation Fingerprint Record, Guerra, Augustine M.," 16 February 1945; various personnel forms; *from other sources* – "SOLDIER DOOMED TO HANG; American Convicted of Murder of English Girl, 15," *New York Times*, October 10, 1944, 4; "The US Prison at Shepton Mallet"; Albert Pierrepoint Execution Ledger Entry.

**40, 41 – John David Cooper & J.P. Wilson**

[1] "Normandy Executions," *After the Battle*, 29; and War Department, Pamphlet Number 27-4, *Procedure for Military Executions.*

[2] **Charge I: Violation of the 92nd Article of War.**
*Specification 1*: In that Private J.P. Wilson and Private First Class John David Cooper, both of the 3966th Quartermaster Truck Company, acting jointly and in pursuance of a common intent, did, at Lérouville, Meuse, France, on or about 19 September 1944, forcibly and feloniously, against her will, have carnal knowledge of ∗∗∗∗∗∗∗∗∗∗∗∗ [Rape Victim 1.]

*Specification 2*: In that Private J.P. Wilson and Private First Class John David Cooper, both of the 3966th Quartermaster Truck Company, acting jointly and in pursuance of a common intent, did, at Lérouville, Meuse, France, on or about 19 September 1944, forcibly and feloniously, against her will, have carnal knowledge of ∗∗∗∗∗∗∗∗∗∗∗∗ [Rape Victim 2.]

*Specification 3*: In that Private J.P. Wilson and Private First Class John David Cooper, both of the 3966th Quartermaster Truck Company, acting jointly and in pursuance of a common intent, did, at Ferme de Marville, par Chonville, Meuse, France, on or about 21 September 1944, forcibly and feloniously, against her will, have carnal knowledge of ∗∗∗∗∗∗∗∗∗∗∗∗ [Rape Victim 3.]

*Specification 4*: In that Private J.P. Wilson and Private First Class John David Cooper, both of the 3966th Quartermaster Truck Company, acting jointly and in pursuance of a common intent, did, at Ferme de Marville, par Chonville, Meuse, France, on or about 21 September 1944, forcibly and feloniously, against her will, have carnal knowledge of *********** [Rape Victim 4.]

**Charge II: Violation of the 93rd Article of War.**

*Specification 1*: In that Private J.P. Wilson and Private First Class John David Cooper, both of the 3966th Quartermaster Truck Company, acting jointly and in pursuance of a common intent, did, at Lérouville, Meuse, France, on or about 19 September 1944, unlawfully enter the dwelling house of Gustave Pivel with intent to commit a criminal offense, to-wit, a wrongful search and trespass, therein.

*Specification 2*: In that Private J.P. Wilson and Private First Class John David Cooper, both of the 3966th Quartermaster Truck Company, acting jointly and in pursuance of a common intent, did, at Ferme de Marville, par Chonville, Meuse, France, on or about 21 September 1944, unlawfully enter the dwelling house occupied by Mme. Lucienne Barry and others, the ownership of which is unknown, with intent to commit a criminal offense, to-wit, a wrongful search and trespass, therein.

**Charge III: Violation of the 96th Article of War.**

*Specification 1*: In that Private J.P. Wilson and Private First Class John David Cooper, both of the 3966th Quartermaster Truck Company, acting jointly and in pursuance of a common intent, did, at Lérouville, Meuse, France, on or about 19 September 1944, commit an assault upon Gustave Pivel by threatening him with a bayonet and by tying his hands and feet.

*Specification 2*: In that Private J.P. Wilson and Private First Class John David Cooper, both of the 3966th Quartermaster Truck Company, acting jointly and in pursuance of a common intent, did, at Lérouville, Meuse, France, on or about 19 September 1944, commit an assault upon Mme. Gustave Pivel, by threatening her with a bayonet.

*Specification 3*: In that Private J.P. Wilson and Private First Class John David Cooper, both of the 3966th Quartermaster Truck Company, acting jointly and in pursuance of a common intent, did, at Ferme de Marville, par Chonville, Meuse, France, on or about 21 September 1944, wrongfully imprison by locking them in a cellar M. Paul Weber, M. Edouard Weber and other male occupants of a dwelling house occupied by Mme. Lucienne Barry and others, the ownership of which is unknown.

*Specification 4*: In that Private J.P. Wilson and Private First Class John David Cooper, both of the 3966th Quartermaster Truck Company, acting jointly and in pursuance of a common intent, did, at Lérouville, Meuse, France, on or about 19 September 1944, forcibly enter and wrongfully search the dwelling house occupied by Mme. Henriette Boidin, M. Sylvain Boidin and others, the ownership of which is unknown.

*Specification 5*: In that Private J.P. Wilson and Private First Class John David Cooper, both of the 3966th Quartermaster Truck Company, acting jointly and in pursuance of a common intent, did, at Lérouville, Meuse, France, on or about 19 September 1944, wrongfully enter and trespass in the dwelling on M. Jean Frey.

³ **Sources, J.P. Wilson:** *from U.S. Army Clerk of Court* – HQ, Third U.S. Army, APO 403, "Approval of Sentence, Private J.P. Wilson, 32484756, 3966th Quartermaster Truck Company," 15 November 1944; HQ, ETO, "Confirmation of Sentence, Private J.P. Wilson, 32484756, 3966th Quartermaster Truck Company," 14 December 1944; Branch Office of The JAG with the ETO, APO 887, "Board of Review No. 2, U.S. v. Private First Class John David Cooper (34562464) and Private J. P. Wilson (32484756), both of 3966th Quartermaster Truck Company," 28 December 1944; "Interview of Prisoner J. P. Wilson by Colonel Warren Hayford III," 27 January 1945; HQ Loire DTC, APO 517, "Report of Proceedings at the Execution of General Prisoner J. P. Wilson, formerly Private, 3966th Quartermaster Truck Company," 6 February 1945; War Department, The Adjutant General's Office, Washington, DC, "Non-Battle Casualty Report, J. P. Wilson, 32484756," 1 March 1945; *from NARA (NPRC)* – HQ, Third U.S. Army, Office of the Judge Advocate, "Review of U.S. v. Private First Class John David Cooper, 3456464, 3966th Quartermaster Truck Company and Private J. P. Wilson, 32484756, 3966th Quartermaster Truck Company," 9 November 1944; HQ, ETO, "GCM Order Number 30 [Wilson, J. P.]" 26 January 1945; Letter from Adjutant General's Office to Henry Wilson, May 18, 1948; Letter from Henry Wilson to War Department, October 26, 1948; various personnel forms; Morning Report, 2913th DTC, January 27, 1945.

**Sources, John David Cooper:** *from U.S. Army Clerk of Court* – HQ, Third U.S. Army, APO 403, "Approval of Sentence, Private First Class John David Cooper, 34562464, 3966th Quartermaster Truck Company," 15 November 1944; HQ, ETO, "Confirmation of Sentence, Private First Class John

David Cooper, 34562464, 3966th Quartermaster Truck Company," 14 December 1944; Branch Office of The JAG with the ETO, APO 887, "Board of Review No. 2, U.S. v. Private First Class John David Cooper (34562464) and Private J. P. Wilson (32484756), both of 3966th Quartermaster Truck Company," 28 December 1944; HQ Loire DTC, APO 517, "Report of Proceedings at the Execution of General Prisoner John D. Cooper, formerly Private First Class, 3966th Quartermaster Truck Company," 12 January 1945; *from NARA (NPRC)* – Morning Report, 2913th DTC, January 7, 1945; HQ, Loire DTC, APO 517, "Request for Orders," 2 January 1945; HQ, Seine Section, Com Z, ETO, APO 887, "Release from Confinement," 8 January 1945; various personnel forms; *from other sources* – "Two U.S. Soldiers Hanged," *Stars & Stripes*, London Edition, Vol. 5, No. 6, January 19, 1945, 1.

## 42 – Walter J. Baldwin

[1] Cunningham was born in IL, graduating from West Point in 1916. He retired in 1946 and died on March 5, 1949 at St. Petersburg, FL.

[2] **Charge I: Violation of the 61st Article of War.**
*Specification*: In that Private Walter J. Baldwin, 574th Ordnance Company, did, without proper leave, absent himself from his organization at or near Beaufay, France, from about 18 August 1944 to about 23 August 1944.
**Charge II: Violation of the 92nd Article of War.**
*Specification*: In that Private Walter J. Baldwin, 574th Ordnance Company, did, at or near Beaufay, France, on or about 23 August 1944, with malice aforethought, willfully, deliberately, feloniously, unlawfully, and with premeditation kill one Adolpha Drouin, a human being, by shooting him with a carbine.
**Charge III: Violation of the 93rd Article of War.**
*Specification*: In that Private Walter J. Baldwin, 574th Ordnance Company, did, at or near Beaufay, France, on or about 23 August 1944, with intent to commit a felony, viz., murder, commit an assault upon Madame Louise Drouin by willfully and feloniously shooting her with a carbine.

[3] **Sources, Walter J. Baldwin:** *from U.S. Army Clerk of Court* – HQ, Loire DTC, APO 517, "Report of Proceedings at the Execution of General Prisoner Walter J. Baldwin, formerly Private, 574th Ordnance Ammunition Company," 17 January 1945; HQ, Loire Section, Communications' Zone, ETO, "Report on Charges preliminary to trial [Private Walter J. Baldwin]," 12 September 1944; 19th General Hospital Office of Chief of

Neuropsychiatric Section, "Board Proceedings [Private Walter J. Baldwin]," 8 September 1944; Criminal Investigation Division, SOS, U.S. Army, ETO, "Statement of Agent John G. Poust, 14th Military Police CIS," 28 August 1944; Criminal Investigation Division, SOS, U.S. Army, ETO, "Statement of Pvt. Walter J. Baldwin (Col)," 26 August 1944; "Record of Trial GCM Private Walter J. Baldwin," Palais de Justice, Le Mans, France, October 6, 1944; Staff Judge Advocate, Loire Section, Communications' Zone, ETO, "Review of the Staff Judge Advocate, Trial by GCM [Private Walter J. Baldwin]," 4 November 1944; *from NARA (NPRC)* – various personnel forms; "Consultation Request and Report, Baldwin, Walter J., Private, "C" 206th," October 29, 1942; HQ, ETO, "GCM Orders Number 10," 10 January 1945; HQ, ETO, APO 887, "Execution of Death Sentence," 10 January 1945; HQ, Brittany Base Section, APO 517, "Orders," 10 January 1945; Checklist, General Prisoner Walter J. Baldwin concerning execution; Letter of Condolence from CPT Frank N. Ford to the Mother of Private Baldwin, 27 March 1945; *from other sources* – "Two U.S. Soldiers Hanged," *Stars & Stripes*, London Edition, Vol. 5, No. 6, January 19, 1945, 1.

## 43 – Arthur J. Farrell

[1] Present were LTC James S. Keller (QM), LTC Volney E. Bradley (QM), MAJ William C. Hopkins (TC), MAJ Arnold N. Davis (JAG) – who would serve as the Law Member, MAJ Logan B. Hendrixson (MC), MAJ Henry Fisher, Jr. (CE), MAJ Walter W. Peacock (OD) and MAJ Allen C. Graham (QM.) CPT George W. Thompson (QM) was assigned as the Trial Judge Advocate; he would be assisted by 1LT Paul A. Robblee (CA) and 2LT Frederick T. Donald (CE.) CPT Arthur T. Harris, Jr. (CE) was the Defense Counsel. Assisting him were 1LT Lindley J. Hanson (MC) and 2LT Ralph J. White (MC.)

[2] **Charge: Violation of the 92nd Article of War.**
*Specification*: In that Corporal Wilford Teton, Troop C, 17th Cavalry Reconnaissance Squadron, did, at Au Fayel, Brittany, France, on or about 24 September 1944, forcibly and feloniously, against her will, have carnal knowledge of ************.
**Charge: Violation of the 92nd Article of War.**
*Specification*: In that Private Arthur J. Farrell, Troop C, 17th Cavalry Reconnaissance Squadron, did, at Au Fayel, Brittany, France, on or about 24 September 1944, forcibly and feloniously, against her will, have carnal knowledge of ************.

[3] **Sources, Arthur J, Farrell:** *from U.S. Army Clerk of Court* – Record of Trial, Teton, Wilford and Farrell, Arthur J., both of Troop C, 17th Cavalry Reconnaissance Squadron, Rennes, Brittany, France, 16 and 23 October 1944; HQ, ETO, "Confirmation of Sentence, Private Arthur J. Farrell, 32559163, Troop C, 17th Cavalry Reconnaissance Squadron," 19 November 1944; Branch Office of The JAG with the ETO, APO 887, "Board of Review No. 1, U.S. v. Corporal Wilford Teton (39315061), and Private Arthur J. Farrell (32559163), both of Troop C, 17th Cavalry Reconnaissance Squadron," 29 November 1944; HQ, Brittany Base Section, Communications Zone, ETO, APO 517, "Report of Investigation of the Facts Surrounding the Statement of Private Wilford (NMI) Teton, 39315061," 21 December 1944; HQ, ETO, GCM Orders Number 11, 10 January 1945; HQ, Brittany Base Section, Memo to Branch Office of The JAG with the ETO from Lieutenant Colonel R.A. McWilliams, Assistant Adjutant General of the Brittany Base Section, 11 January 1945; Letter from Arthur Farrell to his Mother dated January 18, 1945; Certificate on the Physical and Mental Condition of General Prisoner Arthur J. Farrell, January 18, 1945; HQ, Loire DTC, APO 517, "Report of the Proceedings at the Execution of General Prisoner Arthur J. Farrell, formerly Private, Troop C, 17th Cavalry Reconnaissance Squadron," 20 January 1945; Letter from Senator Francis J. Myers to Major General Myron C. Cramer concerning Private Arthur J. Farrell, September 5, 1945; *from NARA (NPRC)* – Morning Report, 2913th DTC, January 17, 1945; various personnel forms.

## 44 – James W. Twiggs

[1] On the court were LTC Irwin M. Rice (CE) – who was also the Law Member, MAJ Richard L. Powell (CE), CPT James J. Powell, Jr. (TC), CPT James A. Bartlett (CE), 1LT Vinson K. Robinson (CE), 1LT William S. Mayeaux (QM) and 2LT James M. Kidd (CE.) The assigned Trial Judge Advocate was absent at the beginning of the trial, which made 1LT John B. Stone (MC) lead the prosecution. CPT Erling J. Hangerud (MC) was the Defense Counsel; he was assisted by 1LT Maurice F. Quinn (MP.) None of the court members graduated from West Point.

[2] **Charge: Violation of the 92nd Article of War.**
*Specification*: In that Private James W. Twiggs, Company F, 1323rd Engineer General Service Regiment, did, at Bellefontaine, ¼ MI N, T 7085, French Lambert, Zone 1, France, on or about 20 September 1944, with malice aforethought, willfully, deliberately, feloniously, unlawfully, and with premeditation, kill William D. Adams, a human being, by shooting him with a rifle.

[3] The Loire DTC was closed in early 1946. Source for much of the information on the DTC was from Dr. Stephen Weiss, incarcerated at the Loire DTC for several months, but overall had a distinguished record of service.

[4] **Sources, James W. Twiggs:** *U.S. Army Clerk of Court* – Statement, Private James W. Twiggs, 38265086, Company F, 1323rd Engineer General Support Regiment, 21 September 1944; Organization of the Court, 25 October 1944; HQ, Normandy Base Section, Communications Zone, "Review by the Staff Judge Advocate, U.S. v. Private James W. Twiggs, 38265086, Company F, 1323rd Engineer General Services Regiment," 18 November 1944; HQ, ETO, "Confirmation Order for Private James W. Twiggs, 38265086, Company F, 1323rd Engineer General Service Regiment," 16 December 1944; HQ, ETO, GCM Order Number 16, 13 January 1945; Letter, James Twiggs to Commanding General Supreme HQ Allied Expeditionary Forces, ETO, Plea for Clemency, 12 January 1945; HQ, Loire DTC, "Report of Proceedings at the Execution of General Prisoner James W. Twiggs, 38265086, formerly Private, Company F, 1323rd Engineer General Service Regiment," 22 January 1945; *from NARA (NPRC)* – various personnel forms; Company C, 389th Military Police Battalion, APO 517, "Supplemental Guard," 18 January 1945; "Execution Check List"; HQ, Brittany Base Section, Communications Zone, ETO, APO 517, "Subject: Orders," 14 January 1945; "Certificate of Physical and Mental Condition [General Prisoner James W. Twiggs]," 21 January 1945; "Certificate of Death [General Prisoner James W. Twiggs], 22 January 1945; "Receipt of Remains [General Prisoner James W. Twiggs]," 22 January 1945; *various other sources* – "Army & Navy: The Black Hole of Le Mans," *Time Magazine*, February 4, 1946; Discussions with Thomas Ward, former supply sergeant of the Loire Disciplinary Training Center, beginning April 2013.

## 45, 46 – Mervin Holden & Elwood J. Spencer

[1] COL James M. Epperly (DC), LTC Ernest R. Baltzell (JAG) – who was also the Law Member, MAJ Charles H. Stephens (AC), MAJ John C. Ward (AG), MAJ Albert L. Hatch (IN), CPT Oscar L. Scarborough (FA), CPT Friend L. Kilburn (VC), CPT James R. Burdick (AG) and 1LT Joseph

C. Hurley (AG.) 1LT James B. Craighill served as the Trial Judge Advocate; he was assisted by 2LT Robert B. McBride III (IN.) CPT Robert L. Ingalls (OD) was the Defense Counsel, with CPT John T. Middlebrooks (IN) as his assistant. None of the court officers was a West Point graduate.

[2] **Charge I: Violation of the 92nd Article of War.**
*Specification*: In that Private Elwood J. Spencer, 646th Quartermaster Truck Company, did, at Namur, Belgium, on or about 24 October 1944, forcibly and feloniously, against her will, have carnal knowledge of \*\*\*\*\*\*\*\*\*\*\*\*.

**Charge II: Violation of the 96th Article of War.**
*Specification 1*: In that Private Elwood J. Spencer, 646th Quartermaster Truck Company, did, at Namur, Belgium, on or about 24 October 1944, commit the crime of sodomy by feloniously and against the order of nature having carnal connection per os [oral sex] with \*\*\*\*\*\*\*\*\*\*\*\*.
*Specification 2*: In that Private Elwood J. Spencer, 646th Quartermaster Truck Company, did, at Namur, Belgium, on or about 24 October 1944, wrongfully commit an assault upon Emile Deremince by threatening to do him bodily harm with a dangerous weapon, to wit, a knife.

**Charge I: Violation of the 92nd Article of War.**
*Specification*: In that Private Mervin Holden, 646th Quartermaster Truck Company, did, at Namur, Belgium, on or about 24 October 1944, forcibly and feloniously, against her will, have carnal knowledge of \*\*\*\*\*\*\*\*\*\*\*\*.

**Charge II: Violation of the 96th Article of War.**
*Specification*: In that Private Mervin Holden, 646th Quartermaster Truck Company, did, at Namur, Belgium, on or about 24 October 1944, wrongfully commit an assault upon Emile Deremince by threatening to do him bodily harm with a dangerous weapon, to wit, a knife.

[3] **Sources, Elwood J. Spencer:** *from U.S. Army Clerk of Court* – Criminal Investigation Division, SOS, ETO, Statement of Private Elwood J. Spencer, 26 October 1944; HQ, Ninth U.S. Army, Office of the Surgeon, APO 339, Neuropsychiatric Examination of Private Elwood Spencer, 33739343, 5 November 1944; HQ, Ninth U.S. Army, Office of the Judge Advocate, APO 339, Review of the Army Judge Advocate in the Case of Private Mervin Holden, 38226564, and Private Elwood J. Spencer, 33739343, both of the 646th Quartermaster Truck Company, 24 November 1944; Branch Office of The JAG with the ETO, APO 887, "Board of Review No. 1, U.S. v. Privates Mervin Holden (38226564), and Elwood J.

Spencer (33739343), both of 646th Quartermaster Truck Company," 11 January 1945; HQ, ETO, GCM Orders Number 21, 20 January 1945; HQ, Loire DTC, APO 517, "Report of Proceedings at the Execution of General Prisoner Elwood J. Spencer, formerly Private, 646th Quartermaster Truck Company," 6 February 1945; *from NARA (NPRC)* – set of orders from personnel file of J. P. Wilson, HQ, Loire DTC, APO 517, "Orders," 26 January 1945; Morning Report, 2913th DTC, January 27, 1945; various personnel forms.

**Sources, Mervin Holden:** *from U.S. Army Clerk of Court* – Criminal Investigation Division, SOS, ETO, Statement of Private Mervin Holden, 26 October 1944; HQ, Ninth U.S. Army, Office of the Surgeon, APO 339, Neuropsychiatric Examination of Private Mervin Holden, 38226564, 5 November 1944; HQ, Ninth U.S. Army, Office of the Judge Advocate, APO 339, Review of the Army Judge Advocate in the Case of Private Mervin Holden, 38226564, and Private Elwood J. Spencer, 33739343, both of the 646th Quartermaster Truck Company, 24 November 1944; Branch Office of The JAG with the ETO, APO 887, "Board of Review No. 1, U.S. v. Privates Mervin Holden (38226564), and Elwood J. Spencer (33739343), both of 646th Quartermaster Truck Company," 11 January 1945; HQ, ETO, GCM Orders Number 20, 20 January 1945; HQ, Loire DTC, APO 517, "Report of Proceedings at the Execution of General Prisoner Mervin Holden, formerly Private, 646th Quartermaster Truck Company," 6 February 1945; *from NARA (NPRC)* – set of orders from personnel file of J. P. Wilson, HQ, Loire DTC, APO 517, "Orders," 26 January 1945; Morning Report, 2913th DTC, January 27, 1945.

### 47 – Eddie Slovik

[1] William Bradford Huie, *The Execution of Private Slovik*, 111.

[2] There were no West Point graduates among the court. Williams of Harrisburg, PA, was the division finance officer. Altman was fatally wounded a month later in the "Battle of the Bulge" and died in a German prisoner of war camp; he was awarded the Silver Star, Bronze Star and the Purple Heart. Green was from Antonito, CO. Kimmelman was a dentist; he won the Silver Star during the "Battle of the Bulge."

[3] Edward G. Miller, *A Dark and Bloody Ground: The Hürtgen Forest and the Roer River Dams, 1944-1945*, College Station, TX: Texas A&M University Press, 1995, 45-90.

[4] **Sources, Eddie Slovik:** *from U.S. Army Clerk of Court* – Record of Trial by GCM of Eddie D. Slovik, 3689415, Private, Company G, 109th Infantry, Rötgen, Germany 11 November 1944; HQ, 28th Infantry Division, Staff Judge Advocate, APO 28, Review of the Staff Judge Advocate in the Case of Slovik, Eddie D., 36896415, Private, Company G, 109th Infantry, 26 November 1944; Letter from Private Eddie Slovik to the Theater Judge Advocate, European Theater of Operation, 9 December 1944; Branch Office of The JAG with the ETO, APO 887, "Board of Review No. 1, U.S. v. Private Eddie D. Slovik (36896415), Company G, 109th Infantry," 6 January 1945; HQ, ETO, GCM Orders Number 27, 23 January 1945; HQ, 28th Infantry Division, Designation of 109th Infantry Area, 31 January 1945; HQ, 28th Infantry Division, Office of the JAG, APO 28, "Report of Execution by Shooting," 31 January 1945; *from NARA, College Park, Maryland* – Memorandum "SUBJECT: Commutation of Unexecuted Death Sentences for Military Offenses After Cessation of Hostilities," from Eisenhower to Colonel H. W. Hollers, Chief, Military Justice Division, Judge Advocate Section," 30 January 1945; *from other sources* – "The Execution of Eddie Slovik," *After the Battle Magazine*, Number 32, London: Battle of Britain Prints International, 1981, 28-41; Benedict B. Kimmelman, "The Example of Private Slovik," *American Heritage*, The Magazine of History, Volume 38, Number 6, September/October 1987, NY: Forbes, 97-104; William Bradford Huie, *The Execution of Private Slovik*, 20, 21, 27, 98, 121, 129, 152, 153, 156, 157, 164, 168, 169, 174, 178, 179, 181, 185, 209, 211, 212, 232, 233; Charles Whiting, *American Deserter: General Eisenhower and the Execution of Eddie Slovik*, 12, 13, 191.

## 48, 49 – Waiters Yancy & Robert L. Skinner

[1] William Bradford Huie, *The Execution of Private Slovik*, 59.

[2] On the court were COL Burwell B. Wilkes (TC), MAJ Fred A. Palumbo (TC), MAJ Linn K. Twinem (JAG) who was also the Law Member, CPT John F. Kottnauer (QM), CPT Louis M. Prager (TC), CPT William P. Elliott (CE), 1LT Thomas M. Taft (TC) and 2LT Joseph O. Curtis (CE.) 2LT Joseph A. Bruggeman (QM) served as the Trial Judge Advocate. CPT Lemuel Y. Morehead (TC) was the Defense Counsel; he was assisted by 2LT Otway B. Noble (QM.) None of the officers was from West Point.

[3] **Charge I: Violation of the 92nd Article of War**
*Specification 1:* In that Private Waiters Yancy, 1511th Engineer Water Supply Company, did at Hameau-Pigeon, France, on or about 1 August 1944, forcibly and feloniously, against her will, have carnal knowledge of **************.
*Specification 2:* In that Private Waiters Yancy, 1511th Engineer Water Supply Company, did at Hameau-Pigeon, France, on or about 1 August 1944, with malice aforethought, willfully, deliberately, feloniously unlawfully and with premeditation kill one Auguste Lebarillier, a human being, by shooting him with a rifle.
**Charge II: Violation of the 93rd Article of War**
*Specification 1:* In that Private Waiters Yancy, 1511th Engineer Water Supply Company, did at Hameau-Pigeon, France, on or about 1 August 1944, with intent to do him bodily harm, commit an assault upon Auguste Mace, by shooting him with a dangerous weapon, to-wit: a rifle.
*Specification 2:* In that Private Waiters Yancy, 1511th Engineer Water Supply Company, did at Hameau-Pigeon, France, on or about 1 August 1944, with intent to do him bodily harm, commit an assault upon Xaver M. Hébert, by shooting him with a dangerous weapon, to-wit: a rifle.
*Specification 3:* In that Private Waiters Yancy, 1511th Engineer Water Supply Company, did at Hameau-Pigeon, France, on or about 1 August 1944, with intent to bodily harm, commit an assault upon Renee Jeanne Clementine Hébert, by hitting her on the head and face with his fists and helmet.

[4] None of the officers was from West Point.

[5] Bradham was born in FL on October 30, 1908. He later was promoted to MAJ. After his military service, he went on to be a distinguished civic leader in Jacksonville, FL. He died in Jacksonville on May 1, 1989.

[6] **Charge: Violation of the 92nd Article of War**
*Specification:* In that Private Robert L. Skinner, 1511th Engineer Water Supply Company, did at Hameau-Pigeon, France, on or about 1 August 1944, forcibly and feloniously, against her will, have carnal knowledge of **************.

[7] **Sources, Waiters Yancy:** *from U.S. Army Clerk of Court* – Statement made by Waiters Yancy, 37499079, 1511th Engineer Water Supply Company, APO 403, 11:30 a.m., 4 August 1944; HQ, XII Corps, Office of the Provost Marshal, APO 312, "Report on Investigation of Shooting and Alleged Rape in Hameau-Pigeon on 1 August 1944," 9 August 1944; Statement made by Waiters Yancy, 37499079, 1511th Engineer Water Supply

Company, APO 403, 23 August 1944; 298th General Hospital, "Report of Proceedings of Board of Officers to examine Private Waiters Yancy," 3 October 1944; Organization of the Court (GCM of Private Waiters Yancy), 7 November 1944; HQ, Normandy Base Section, Communications Zone, ETO, APO 562, "Letter of Regret," 25 November 1944; HQ, Normandy Base Section, Communications Zone, ETO, APO 562, Review by the Staff Judge Advocate, U.S. v. Private Waiters Yancy, 37499079, 1511th Engineer Water Supply Company, APO 403, 25 November 1944; HQ, ETO, Review by the Staff Judge Advocate, U.S. v. Private Waiters Yancy, 37499079, 1511th Engineer Water Supply Company, APO 403, 22 December 1944; HQ, ETO, "Confirmation of Sentence, Private Waiters Yancy, 37499079, 1511th Engineer Water Supply Company, 23 December 1944"; HQ, ETO, GCM Order Number 33 (Private Waiters Yancy), 3 February 1945; Hand Receipt for the Remains of General Prisoner Waiters Yancy, 37499079, 10 February 1945; HQ, Loire DTC, APO 517, "Report of Proceedings at the Execution of General Prisoner Waiters Yancy, formerly Private, 1511th Engineer Water Supply," 11 February 1945; War Department, The Adjutant General's Office, Washington, DC, "Non-Battle Casualty Report, Yancy Waiters, 37499079," 24 February 1945; *from NARA (NPRC)* – various personnel forms; Branch Office of The JAG with the ETO, APO 887, "Board of Review No. 1, U.S. v. Private Waiters Yancy (37499079), 1511th Engineer Water Supply Company," 16 January 1945; *from other sources* – "Normandy Executions," 31-32; Philippe Esvelin, *Forgotten Wings*, Bayeux, France: Heimdal, 2006, 41-42.

**Sources, Robert L. Skinner:** *from U.S. Army Clerk of Court* – Statement made by Robert L. Skinner, 35802328, 1511th Engineer Water Supply Company, APO 403, 5 August 1944; HQ, XII Corps, Office of the Provost Marshal, APO 312, "Report on Investigation of Shooting and Alleged Rape in Hameau-Pigeon on 1 August 1944," 9 August 1944; 298th General Hospital, "Report of Proceedings of Board of Officers to examine Private Waiters Yancy," 3 October 1944; Organization of the Court (GCM of Private Robert L. Skinner), 8 November 1944; HQ, Normandy Base Section, Communications Zone, ETO, APO 562, Review by the Staff Judge Advocate, U.S. v. Private Robert L. Yancy, 35802328, 1511th Engineer Water Supply Company, APO 403, 21 November 1944; HQ, ETO, "Confirmation of Sentence, Private Robert L. Skinner, 35802328,

1511th Engineer Water Supply Company, 14 December 1944"; HQ, ETO, Review by the Staff Judge Advocate, U.S. v. Private Robert L. Skinner, 35802328, 1511th Engineer Water Supply Company, APO 403, 29 December 1944; Letter to Supreme Allied Commander from Private Robert L. Skinner, 16 January 1945; Interview of Private Robert L. Skinner by Colonel Warren Hayford III, 25 January 1945; Certificate of Physical and Mental Condition of Robert L. Skinner by CPT Louis J. Baronberg, 9 February 1945; Hand Receipt for the Remains of General Prisoner Robert L. Skinner, 35802328, 10 February 1945; HQ, Loire DTC, APO 517, "Report of Proceedings at the Execution of General Prisoner Robert L. Skinner, formerly Private, 1511th Engineer Water Supply," 11 February 1945; War Department, The Adjutant General's Office, Washington, DC, "Non-Battle Casualty Report, Robert L. Skinner, 35802328," 24 February 1945; *from NARA (NPRC)* – HQ, Loire DTC, APO 517, "Orders," 8 February 1945; various personnel forms; Service Record, Skinner, Robert L., 35802328, May 21, 1943 to February 10, 1945; *from other sources* – "Normandy Executions," 31-32; Philippe Esvelin, *Forgotten Wings*, 41-42.

## 50 – William Mack

[1] **Charge I: Violation of the 92nd Article of War.**
*Specification:* In that Private William Mack, Battery A, 578th Field Artillery Battalion, did, at Pentreff, Le Drennec, Finistere, France, on or about 20 August 1944, with malice aforethought, willfully, deliberately, feloniously, unlawfully, and with premeditation kill one Eugene Tournellec, a human being, by shooting him with a carbine.

**Charge II: Violation of the 93rd Article of War.**
*Specification:* In that Private William Mack, Battery A, 578th Field Artillery Battalion, did, at Pentreff, Le Drennec, Finistere, France, on or about 20 August 1944, with intent to commit a felony, viz, rape, commit an assault on Catherine Tournellec, by willfully and feloniously grasping her, forcibly tearing her clothing from her body, and exposing his private parts to her.

[2] The panel included LTC Francis Sullivan (JAG) who was also the Law Member, LTC Horace D. Brown (CE), MAJ Lewis A. Convis (IN), MAJ William N. Gerety (OD), MAJ Francis P. O'Neil (TC), CPT Robert A. Smoak (CAC), CPT William T. Doughtry, Jr. (TC), CPT Henry A. Campbell (IN) and CPT David Leskowitz (MC.) CPT James L. Hornbostel (JAG) served as the Trial Judge Advocate; he was assisted by 2LT Sidney Hertz (QM.)

[3] **Sources, William Mack:** *from U.S. Army Clerk of Court* – Investigation Division, Provost Marshal General's Detachment (Prov), SOS, ETO, Statement of William (NMI) Mack (Col), 8 September 1944; Statement by Private William Mack, 32620461, Battery A, 578th Field Artillery Battalion, taken by Colonel R. E. Bower, Inspector General, VIII Corps, 23 September 1944; Statement by Private William Mack, 32620461, Battery A, 578th Field Artillery Battalion, taken by Colonel R. E. Bower, Inspector General, VIII Corps, 25 September 1944; Statement of Investigating Officer Made at Rennes, Brittany, France in the Case of the Accused, Mack, William, 32620461, Private, Battery A, 578th Field Artillery Battalion, APO 339, 2 October 1944; Organization of the Court (GCM of Private William Mack), 23 November 1944; HQ, Brittany Base Section, Communications Zone, ETO, APO 517, Review of the Staff Judge Advocate, 5 December 1944; Branch Office of The JAG with the ETO, APO 887, "Board of Review No. 1, U.S. v. Private William Mack (32620461), Battery A, 578th Field Artillery Battalion," 30 January 1945; HQ, ETO, GCM Order Number 40 (Private William Mack), 9 February 1945; Certificate of Physical and Mental Condition of General Prisoner William Mack, 32620461, 14 February 1945; Hand Receipt for Remains of General Prisoner William Mack, 32629461, 15 February 1945; HQ, Loire DTC, APO 562, "Report of Proceedings at the Execution of General Prisoner William Mack, formerly Private, 578th Artillery Battalion," 17 February 1945; War Department, The Adjutant General's Office, Washington, DC, "Non-Battle Casualty Report, William Mack, 32620461, 5 March 1945"; *from NARA-NPRC* – Morning Report, 2913th DTC, February 12, 1945; various personal data forms; *from other sources* – "U.S. Army Hangs Yank for Murder Near Brest," *Chicago Tribune*, February 17, 1945, 4.

**Sources, John C. Woods:** *from NARA (NPRC)* – U.S. Navy Personnel File, Letter from USNAVPERS to The Adjutant General of the Army on John C. Woods.

## 51 – Otis B. Crews

[1] Milton K. Ziegler was born in Ste. Genevieve, MO on September 27, 1921. He finished grammar school, was single and was a cement and concrete worker, before his induction on May 7, 1942. He was discharged as a corporal from Jefferson Barracks, MO on September 24, 1945 and later lived in Ste. Genevieve, where he married and had several children.

[2] The members were COL Charles R. Johnson, Jr. (CAV) who was also the Law Member, COL Lester A. Hancock (IN), COL Elijah G. Arnold (TC), COL Leigh Bell (IN), COL Antulio Segarra (IN) and LTC George A. Ramsey (MC.) CPT Stanley Timmins, Sr. (JAG) served as the Trial Judge Advocate; he was assisted by CPT Daniel K. Greenfield (IN.) CPT Wendell C. Hamacher (CAV) sat as the Defense Counsel. His assistant was absent on official business as were two additional assistant Trial Judge Advocates. Johnson was born in Washington, DC on April 3, 1894. He graduated from West Point in April 1917 with a commission in the CAV. Johnson later served as a cavalry instructor at West Point and the Cavalry School. In 1932, he was part of the United States Olympic team. From 1940 to 1942, Johnson commanded the 106th Cavalry Regiment, before serving as a military attaché to Morocco and Algeria. In 1943, COL Johnson was the commander of the 15th Infantry Regiment. He retired as a COL in 1947 and died in San Antonio, TX on May 10, 1981. Segarra was born in Cayey, PR on January 20, 1906. He graduated from West Point in 1927. From 1929 to 1931, he served as the aide to the military governor of Puerto Rico, Theodore Roosevelt, Jr. In 1942, he assumed command of the 296th Puerto Rican (National Guard) Infantry Regiment; he commanded the 65th Infantry Regiment from November 25, 1943 to June 21, 1944 in Italy and Corsica. He retired from the Army in 1957 and died in San Juan, PR on September 13, 1999.

[3] **Charge: Violation of the 92nd Article of War**
*Specification:* In that Private Otis B. Crews, 3423rd Quartermaster Truck Company, did, at or near No. 53 Via San Donato, Orto D'Atella, Italy, on or about 16 January 1944, with malice aforethought, willfully, deliberately, feloniously, unlawfully, and with premeditation, kill one Private Wilbur Bryant, (NMI) a human being, by shooting him with a US Army Pistol, Cal. 45.

[4] **Sources, Otis B. Crews:** *from U.S. Army Clerk of Court* – HQ, PBS, Office of the Provost Marshal, APO 782, Statement of M/Sgt. John A. Ganobcik, 35027362, 334th QM Company, in the Case of the Shooting of Pvt. Bryant, 18 January 1944; HQ, PBS, Office of the Provost Marshal, APO 782, Statement of M/Sgt. James E. Collier, 20426137, 334th QM Company, in the Case of the Shooting of Pvt. Bryant, 18 January 1944; 262nd Station Hospital, APO 782, Report of Autopsy, Private Wilbur Bryant, 2651st MP Company, 19 January 1944; HQ, PBS, Office of the Provost Marshal,

APO 782, Statement of Pvt. Richard W. Coleman, 14044521, 3423rd QM Truck Company, in the Case of the Fatal Shooting of an American Military Policeman, 2 August 1944; HQ, PBS, Office of the Provost Marshal, APO 782, Statement of Pvt. David Morris, 34156395, 304th QM, in the Case of MP Bryant, 4 August 1944; Office of the Provost Marshal, Criminal Investigation Division, APO 782, "Private Otis B. Crews, Homicide, Naples, Italy," 4 August 1944; HQ, PBS, Office of the Staff Judge Advocate, APO 782, Advice of the Staff Judge Advocate in the case of Private Otis B. Crews, 25 August 1944; Organization of the Court (GCM of Private Otis B. Crews), 26 September 1944; Branch Office of The JAG with the MTO, APO 512, "Board of Review, U.S. v. Private Otis B. Crews (14057830), 3423rd Quartermaster Truck Company," 13 February 1945; HQ, MTO, APO 512, GCM Order Number 28 (Private Otis B. Crews), 13 February 1945; *from NARA (NPRC)* – HQ, Disciplinary Training Stockade, Southern District, PBS, APO 782, "Report of Death [General Prisoner Otis B. Crews, 14057830]," 21 February 1945; HQ, Disciplinary Training Stockade, Southern District, PBS, APO 782, "Death Certificate [General Prisoner Otis B. Crews, 14057830], 21 February 1945; HQ, PBS Stockade Number 1, APO 782, Summary of Execution of Otis Crews, 8 March 1945; HQ, PBS Stockade Number 1, APO 782, Letter of Condolence to the Mother of Otis Crews, 12 April 1945; various personnel forms.

## 52 – William C. Downes

[1] **Charge I: Violation of the 92nd Article of War.**
*Specification 1:* In that Private James R. Parrott, 597th Ordnance Ammunition Company, and Private Grant U. Smith, 597th Ordnance Ammunition Company, and Private William C. Downes, 597th Ordnance Ammunition Company, acting jointly and in pursuance of a common intent, did, at Étienville, France, on or about 2400 hours, 12 July 1944, forcibly and feloniously, against her will have carnal knowledge of ************ [Rape Victim 1.]
*Specification 2:* In that Private James R. Parrott, 597th Ordnance Ammunition Company, and Private Grant U. Smith, 597th Ordnance Ammunition Company, and Private William C. Downes, 597th Ordnance Ammunition Company, acting jointly and in pursuance of a common intent, did, at Étienville, France, on or about 2400 hours, 12 July 1944, forcibly and feloniously, against her will have carnal knowledge of ************ [Rape Victim 2.]
*Specification 3:* In that Private James R. Parrott, 597th Ordnance Ammunition Company, and Private Grant U. Smith, 597th Ordnance Ammunition Company, and Private William C. Downes, 597th Ordnance Ammunition Company, acting jointly and in pursuance of a common intent, did, at Étienville, France, on or about 2400 hours, 26 July 1944, forcibly and feloniously, against her will have carnal knowledge of ************ [Rape Victim 3.]

**Charge II: Violation of the 93rd Article of War.**
*Specification 1:* In that Private James R. Parrott, 597th Ordnance Ammunition Company, and Private Grant U. Smith, 597th Ordnance Ammunition Company, and Private William C. Downes, 597th Ordnance Ammunition Company, acting jointly and in pursuance of a common intent, did, at Étienville, France, on or about 2400 hours, 12 July 1944, wrongfully and unlawfully enter the dwelling of ************, with intent to commit a criminal offense, to wit: rape, therein.
*Specification 2:* In that Private James R. Parrott, 597th Ordnance Ammunition Company, and Private Grant U. Smith, 597th Ordnance Ammunition Company, and Private William C. Downes, 597th Ordnance Ammunition Company, acting jointly and in pursuance of a common intent, did, at Étienville, France, 26 July 1944, in the night-time feloniously and burglariously break and enter the dwelling house of Monsieur Just Hebeurt, Étienville, France with intent to commit a felony, to wit: rape, therein.

[2] **Sources, William C. Downes:** *from U.S. Clerk of Court* – Branch Office of The JAG with the ETO, APO 887, "Board of Review No. 1, U.S. v. Privates James R. Parrott (32483580), Grant U. Smith (35688909) and William C. Downes (33519814), all of 597th Ordnance Ammunition Company," 9 February 1945; HQ, Loire DTC, APO 562, "Report of Proceedings at the Execution of General Prisoner William C. Downes, formerly Private, 597th Ordnance Ammunition Company," 1 March 1945; HQ, Normandy Base Section, Communications Zone, ETO, APO 562, Letter to the Mayor of Étienville, France, 10 March 1945; War Department, The Adjutant General's Office, Washington, DC, "Non-Battle Casualty Report, William C. Downes, 33519814," 15 March 1945; *from NARA (NPRC)* – HQ, ETO, APO 562, "GCM Order Number 50 [William C. Clifton]," 23 February 1945; HQ, Loire DTC, APO 562,

"Orders," 25 February 1945; "Report of Burial, Downes, William C., 33519814," 28 February 1945, various personnel forms; Morning Report, 2913th DTC, February 26, 1945; *from other sources* –Interview with Georges René, Mayor, Étienville, France, September 15, 2011.

## 53, 54, 55 – Amos Agee, John C. Smith & Frank Watson

[1] None of the court members was a West Point officer. Griggs was born in Mansfield, GA on February 19, 1916. After attending high school in Akron, OH, he went to Alabama State University. After the war, Griggs graduated from Tennessee State University and moved to Detroit, MI, where he worked at the Wayne County Youth Home for over 30 years, finishing as its director. He died in Detroit on September 13, 1997.

[2] **Charge: Violation of the 93rd Article of War.**
*Specification*: In that Private Amos Agee, 644th Quartermaster Troop Transport company, did, at Le Noyer, Commune de Bure, Orne, France, on or about 2 September 1944, forcibly and feloniously, against her will, have carnal knowledge of Madame ******************.

**Charge: Violation of the 93rd Article of War.**
*Specification*: In that Private John C. Smith, 644th Quartermaster Troop Transport company, did, at Le Noyer, Commune de Bure, Orne, France, on or about 2 September 1944, forcibly and feloniously, against her will, have carnal knowledge of Madame ******************.

**Charge: Violation of the 93rd Article of War.**
*Specification*: In that Private Frank Watson, 644th Quartermaster Troop Transport company, did, at Le Noyer, Commune de Bure, Orne, France, on or about 2 September 1944, forcibly and feloniously, against her will, have carnal knowledge of Madame ******************.

[3] The War Department notified Smith's mother of his death on March 15, 1945; she immediately replied stating that she had ten children of which three were serving overseas. She wrote the Veterans Administration in 1951 for more information and desired that his name be cleared so she could receive his insurance.

[4] The War Department notified Watson's father of his death on March 15, 1945.

[5] **Sources, Amos Agee: *from U.S. Army Clerk of Court*** – HQ, ETO, "Sentence confirmation [Private Amos Agee]" 14 January 1945; Branch Office of The JAG with the ETO APO 887, "Board of Review No. 2, U.S. v. Privates Amos Agee (34163762), Frank Watson (34793522)

and John C. Smith (33214953), all of 644th Quartermaster Troop Transport Company," 14 February 1945; GCM [Privates Amos Agee, Frank Watson and John C. Smith], "Organization of the Court," 18 October 1944; HQ, Loire DTC, APO 562, "Report of Proceedings at the Execution of General Prisoner Amos Agee, formerly Private, 644th Quartermaster Troop Transport Company," 5 March 1945; *from NARA (NPRC)* – various personal data forms; Physical and Mental Examination Certification of General Prisoner Amos Agee, 2 March 1945; HQ, 644th Quartermaster Truck Company, APO 758, "M.D. Form #78," 1 August 1945; Service Record, Amos Agee, November 19, 1941 to March 5, 1945; Letter from Chaplain Kilian R. Bowler to Agee Family, 8 August 1945.

**Sources, John C. Smith: *from U.S. Army Clerk of Court*** – HQ, ETO, "Sentence confirmation [Private John C. Smith]" 14 January 1945; Branch Office of The JAG with the ETO APO 887, "Board of Review No. 2, U.S. v. Privates Amos Agee (34163762), Frank Watson (34793522) and John C. Smith (33214953), all of 644th Quartermaster Troop Transport Company," 14 February 1945; GCM [Privates Amos Agee, Frank Watson and John C. Smith], "Organization of the Court," 18 October 1944; HQ, Loire DTC, APO 562, "Report of Proceedings at the Execution of General Prisoner John C. Smith, formerly Private, 644th Quartermaster Troop Transport Company," 5 March 1945; War Department, The Adjutant General's Office, "Non-Battle Casualty Report, PVT. John C. Smith," Washington, DC; *from NARA (NPRC)* – various personal data forms; HQ, ETO, "GCM Order Number 52 (Private John C. Smith)," 26 February 1945; HQ, 644th Quartermaster Truck Company, APO 758, "M.D. Form #78," 1 August 1945.

**Sources, Frank Watson: *from U.S. Army Clerk of Court*** – HQ, ETO, "Sentence confirmation [Private Frank Watson]" 14 January 1945; Branch Office of The JAG with the ETO APO 887, "Interview of PVT Frank Watson by COL Warren Hayford III (FA)," 25 January 1945; "Board of Review No. 2, U.S. v. Privates Amos Agee (34163762), Frank Watson (34793522) and John C. Smith (33214953), all of 644th Quartermaster Troop Transport Company," 14 February 1945; GCM [Privates Amos Agee, Frank Watson and John C. Smith], "Organization of the Court," 18 October 1944; HQ, Loire DTC, APO 562, "Report of Proceedings at the Execution of General Prisoner Frank Watson, formerly Private,

644th Quartermaster Troop Transport Company," 5 March 1945; War Department, The Adjutant General's Office, "Non-Battle Casualty Report, PVT. Frank Watson, Jr.," Washington, DC; *from NARA (NPRC)* – various personal data forms.

**56, 57 – Cubia Jones & Robert L. Pearson**
[1] None of the court members was a West Point officer.

[2] **Charge: Violation of the 92nd Article of War.**
*Specification:* in that Private Cubia Jones and Corporal Robert L. Pearson, both of Company A, 1698th Engineer Combat Battalion, acting jointly and in pursuance of a common intent, did, at Chard, Somerset, England, on or about 3 December 1944, forcibly and feloniously, against her will, have carnal knowledge of ***********.

[3] **Sources, Cubia Jones: *from U.S. Army Clerk of Court*** – Criminal Investigation Division, SOS, ETO, Statement of Private Cubia Jones, 4 December 1944; HQ, 2912th DTC, APO 508, "Report of Psychiatric Examination of General Prisoner Cubia Jones, 34563790," 11 December 1944; Proceedings of a GCM, Chard, Somerset, England, Pursuant to SO 290 Hq XXI Corps; HQ, ETO, "Confirmation of Sentence, Corporal Robert L. Pearson (38326741), Company A, 1698th Engineer Combat Battalion and Private Cubia Jones (34563790), Company A, 1698th Engineer Combat Battalion, 12 February 1945; Branch Office of The JAG with the ETO APO 887, "Board of Review No. 1, U.S. v. Corporal Robert L. Pearson (38326741) and Private Cubia Jones (34563790), both of Company A, 1698th Engineer Combat Battalion; 5 March 1945; HQ, 2912th DTC, APO 508, "Proceeding of Execution of Corporal Robert L. Pearson, 38326741, and Private Cubia Jones, 34563790, formerly Members of Company A, 1698th Engineer Combat Battalion," 17 March 1945; *from NARA (NPRC)* – various personal data forms; Service Record, Cubia Jones, December 29, 1943 to March 17, 1945; Letter from Chaplain Berkestresser to the Wife of Cubia Jones, 20 March 1945; *from other sources* – "The US Prison at Shepton Mallet."
**Sources, Robert L. Pearson: *from U.S. Army Clerk of Court*** – Criminal Investigation Division, SOS, ETO, Statement of Corporal Robert L. Pearson, 4 December 1944; HQ, 2912th DTC, APO 508, "Report of Psychiatric Examination of General Prisoner Robert L. Pearson, 38326741," 11 December 1944; Proceedings of a GCM, Chard, Somerset, England, Pursuant to SO 290 Hq XXI Corps; HQ, ETO, "Confirmation of Sentence,

Corporal Robert L. Pearson (38326741), Company A, 1698th Engineer Combat Battalion and Private Cubia Jones (34563790), Company A, 1698th Engineer Combat Battalion, 12 February 1945; Branch Office of The JAG with the ETO APO 887, "Board of Review No. 1, U.S. v. Corporal Robert L. Pearson (38326741) and Private Cubia Jones (34563790), both of Company A, 1698th Engineer Combat Battalion; 5 March 1945; HQ, 2912th DTC, APO 508, "Proceeding of Execution of Corporal Robert L. Pearson, 38326741, and Private Cubia Jones, 34563790, formerly Members of Company A, 1698th Engineer Combat Battalion," 17 March 1945; War Department, The Adjutant General's Office, "Non-Battle Casualty Report, Robert L. Pearson," 26 March 1945; *from NARA (NPRC)* – various personal data forms; *from other sources* – "The US Prison at Shepton Mallet."

**58 – John W. Taylor**
[1] Notestein was born on July 19, 1893 in Poland, OH and died in CA in November 1963.
[2] The jury included: LTC Courtenay C. Crozier (IG), LTC Louis G. Osborne (AG), who was also the Law Member, LTC Eldon L. Bolton (MC), MAJ Frederick R. Krug (DC), CPT James L. Glymph (IN) and CPT Wendell L. Price (DC.) LTC Gaston M. Wood (IN) served as the Trial Judge Advocate; he was assisted by CPT John L. Duggan (FI.) CPT Francis L. Robinson (MC) held the position of Defense Counsel; his assistant was 2LT William T. Josey (IN.) Crozier attended West Point but did not graduate. He died on March 1, 1971.
[3] **Charge: Violation of the 92nd Article of War.**
*Specification:* In that Private John W. Taylor, Company D, 371st Infantry, did at Pietrasanta, Italy, on or about 23 January 1945 with malice aforethought, willfully, deliberately, feloniously, unlawfully, and with premeditation kill one Private First Class Earl Johnson, a human being by shooting him with a rifle.
[4] **Sources, John W. Taylor: *from U.S. Army Clerk of Court*** – HQ, 92nd Infantry Division, Office of the Staff Judge Advocate, Memorandum to Accompany the Record of Trial in the Case of Private John W. Taylor, 37485128, Company D, 371st Infantry Regiment; Statement by Private John W. Taylor, 37485128, Company D, 371st Infantry, Taken by CPT Fred A. Brewer, Investigating Officer, 24 January 1945; Organization of the Court, Court-Martial of Private John W. Taylor, 30 January 1945; HQ, MTO, Office of the Theater Judge Advocate, APO 512, Review of Theater Judge Advocate on Record of Trial by GCM U.S.

v. Private John W. Taylor, 37485128, Company D, 371st Infantry, 24 February 1945; HQ, MTO, APO 512, "Confirmation of Sentence for Private John W. Taylor, 37485128, Company D, 371st Infantry Regiment," 26 February 1945; Branch Office of the JAG with the MTO, APO 512, "Board of Review in the Case of U.S. v. Private John W. Taylor, (37485128), Company D, 371st Infantry," 8 March 1945; War Department, The Adjutant General's Office, "Non-Battle Casualty Report for John W. Taylor," 3 April 1945; *from NARA (NPRC)* – various personal data forms; HQ, PBS, APO 782, "Execution of Sentence by GCMO in the Case of General Prisoner John W. Taylor," 28 March 1945; HQ, PBS Garrison Stockade Number 1, APO 782, "Special Orders Number 42," 19 March 1945 (from personnel file of John H. Mack); HQ, PBS Garrison Stockade Number 1, APO 782, "Death Certificate [General Prisoner John W. Taylor, 37485128, PBS Garrison Stockade Number 1]," 20 March 1945.

## 59 – Kinney Jones

[1] Sitting in judgment were the following officers: LTC Henry C. Britt (IN), who was also the Law Member, LTC John J. Phelan (IN), MAJ Samuel A. Montgomery (MC), MAJ John W. Halterman, Jr. (IN), MAJ John A. Campbell (CE) and CPT James P. Carter (IN.) MAJ Harry B. Lane (FA) served as the Trial Judge Advocate; he was assisted by MAJ Alvin D. Wilder, Jr. (CE.) CPT Chester C. Heizer (IN) was assigned as the Defense Counsel. Phelan was born in NY on July 15, 1914. He graduated from West Point in 1936 and commissioned in the IN. He won three Silver Stars and three Purple Hearts. Enemy fire killed Phelan in Italy on April 15, 1945, while he was a battalion commander in the 473rd Infantry Regiment. He is buried at the United States Military Academy Post Cemetery in Section VII, Site 101. Lane was born in NE on December 15, 1916. He graduated from West Point in 1940 with a commission in the FA. He served as the commanding officer of the 598th Field Artillery Battalion in the Ninety-Second Infantry Division. He served in Vietnam at the end of his career before retiring in 1970 as a COL. He last resided at Sanibel, FL. Wilder was born on May 11, 1918 in CA. He graduated from West Point in 1942 with a commission in the CE. In 1944-45, he served as the commanding officer for the engineer battalion in the Ninety-Second Infantry Division. He retired in 1972 as a COL and died in Berkeley, CA on February 4, 1993.

[2] **Charge: Violation of the 92nd Article of War.**
*Specification:* In that Private First Class Kinney Jones, Cannon Company, 371st Infantry, did, north of Pietrasanta, Italy, on or about 2 January 1945, with malice a forethought, willfully, deliberately, feloniously, unlawfully and with premeditation kill one Corporal Milton M. Winstead, Cannon Company, 371st Infantry, a human being by shooting him with a U.S. Carbine, caliber .30 M1.

[3] **Sources, Kinney Jones:** *from U.S. Army Clerk of Court* – Sworn Statement of 1LT Leonard S. Morgan, 371st Infantry, 7 January 1945; Sworn Statement of Technician Grade Five Benjamin H. Belcher, Cannon Company, 371st Infantry, 7 January 1945; Sworn Statement by Private First Class Kinney Jones, Cannon Company, 371st Infantry, 9 January 1945; HQ, 92nd Infantry Division, Office of the Staff Judge Advocate, Memorandum to Accompany the Record of Trial in the Case of Private First Class Kinney Jones, Cannon Company, 371st Infantry Regiment, 92nd Infantry Division; Record of Trial Private First Class Kinney Jones, Cannon Company, 371st Infantry Regiment, 92nd Infantry Division, 17 January 1945; HQ, 92nd Infantry Division, Office of the Staff Judge Advocate, Review of the Staff Judge Advocate, U.S. v. Private First Class Kinney Jones, Cannon Company, 371st Infantry Regiment, 92nd Infantry Division, 18 January 1945; HQ, MTO, APO 512, Office of the Theater Judge Advocate, Review of Theater Judge Advocate on Record of Trial by GCM, U.S. v. Private First Class Kinney Jones, Cannon Company, 371st Infantry Regiment, 92nd Infantry Division, 12 February 1945; HQ, MTO, APO 512, "Confirmation of Sentence for Private First Class Kinney Jones, Cannon Company, 371st Infantry Regiment, 92nd Infantry Division," 19 February 1945; Branch Office of the JAG with the MTO, APO 512, "Board of Review in the Case of U.S. v. Private First Class Kinney Jones, Cannon Company, 371st Infantry Regiment, 92nd Infantry Division," 3 March 1945; War Department, The Adjutant General's Office, "Non-Battle Casualty Report for Kinney Jones," 3 April 1945; *from NARA (NPRC)* – various personnel forms; HQ, MTO, APO 512, "GCM Orders Number 36 (Private First Class Kinney Jones, 34120505)," 3 March 1945; HQ, PBS Garrison Stockade Number 1, APO 782, "Execution of Death Sentence," 20 March 1945; HQ, PBS Garrison Stockade Number 1, APO 782, "Special Orders Number 42," 19 March 1945 (from personnel file of John H. Mack); HQ, PBS Garrison Stockade Number 1, APO 782, "Death Certificate

(Private First Class Kinney Jones, 34120505)," 20 March 20, 1945; HQ, PBS, APO 782, "Execution of Sentence by GCMO in the Case of General Prisoner Kinney Jones," 29 March 1945; HQ, PBS Garrison Stockade Number 1, APO 782, Letter to Mrs. Ida Bonnans, 19 April 1945.

## 60 – John H. Mack

[1] The jury included LTC Louis G. Osborne (AG), who was also the Law Member, LTC Thomas S. Gasiorowski (FI), MAJ William M. Campbell (MP), CPT Raymond B. Ochsner (AG), CPT James L. Glymph (IN) and CPT Wendell L. Price (DC.) LTC Gaston M. Wood (IN) served as the Trial Judge Advocate; he was assisted by CPT John L. Duggan (FI.) CPT Francis L. Robinson (MC) held the position of Defense Counsel; his assistant was 2LT William T. Josey (IN.) None of the officers attended West Point.

[2] **Charge: Violation of the 92nd Article of War.**
*Specification 1:* In that Private John H. Mack, Battery C, 599th Field Artillery Battalion, did, at Pietrasanta, Italy, on or about 31 December 1944, with malice aforethought, willfully, deliberately, feloniously, unlawfully, and with pre-meditation kill one Lombardi, Ettore, a human being by shooting him with a carbine.
*Specification 2:* In that Private John H. Mack, Battery C, 599th Field Artillery Battalion, did, at Pietrasanta, Italy, on or about 31 December 1944, with malice aforethought, willfully, deliberately, feloniously, unlawfully, and with pre-meditation kill one Lombardi, Galleni Palmira, a human being by shooting her with a carbine.
*Specification 3:* In that Private John H. Mack, Battery C, 599th Field Artillery Battalion, did, at Pietrasanta, Italy, on or about 31 December 1944, with malice aforethought, willfully, deliberately, feloniously, unlawfully, and with pre-meditation kill one Lombardi, Carmela, a human being by shooting her with a carbine.

[3] **Sources, John H. Mack:** *from U.S. Army Clerk of Court* – Charge Sheet, John H. Mack, Private, Battery C, 599th Field Artillery Battalion, 4 January 1945; HQ, 92nd Infantry Division, Office of the Staff Judge Advocate, Memorandum to Accompany the Record of Trial in the Case of Private John H. Mack, Battery C, 599th Field Artillery Battalion; HQ, 92nd Infantry Division, Office of the Provost Marshal, APO 92, Testimony of Private John H. Mack, 34042053, Battery C, 599th Field Artillery Battalion, 31 December 1944; Oral Statement of Accused, John H. Mack, 2 January 1945; "Organization of the Court, GCM of Private John H. Mack, 18 January

1945"; HQ, 92nd Infantry Division, Office of the Staff Judge Advocate, Review of the Staff Judge Advocate, U.S. v. Private John Mack, 34042053, Battery C, 599th Field Artillery Battalion, 21 January 1945; HQ, MTO, APO 512, Office of the Theater Judge Advocate, Review of Theater Judge Advocate on Record of Trial by GCM, U.S. v. Private John Mack, 34042053, Battery C, 599th Field Artillery Battalion, 14 February 1945; HQ, MTO, APO 512, "Confirmation of Sentence for Private John H. Mack, 34042053, Battery C, 599th Field Artillery Battalion," 19 February 1945; Branch Office of the JAG with the MTO, APO 512, "Board of Review in the Case of U.S. v. Private John H. Mack, (34042053), Battery C, 599th Field Artillery Battalion," 6 March 1945; HQ, MTO, APO 512, GCM Order Number 37, 6 March 1945; War Department, The Adjutant General's Office, "Non-Battle Casualty Report for John H. Mack," 3 April 1945; *from NARA (NPRC)* – various personnel forms; HQ, Southern District PBS, "Routing Slip, Subject: Executions, 20 March 1945; HQ, PBS, APO 782, "Execution of Death Sentence by GCMO in the Case of General Prisoner John H. Mack," 29 March 1945; HQ, PBS Garrison Stockade Number 1, APO 782, "Special Orders Number 42," 19 March 1945; HQ, PBS Garrison Stockade Number 1, APO 782, "Death Certificate, General Prisoner John H. Mack, 34042053," 20 March 1945.

## 61 – Lee A. Burns

[1] **Charge: Violation of the 92nd Article of War.**
*Specification:* in that Private Lee A. Burns, 792nd Ordnance (LM) Company, did on or about 2300 [11:00 p.m.], at the home of Fedora Sabatini Coste Festone Maggiano Street Pro di Lucca Italy, forcibly and feloniously, against her will, have carnal knowledge of ***********.

[2] Britt was born on January 19, 1910 in Georgia. He graduated from West Point in 1932. In 1944-45, he served as a battalion commander in the 365th Infantry Regiment and won two Bronze Stars. In the Korean War, he served as the commanding officer of the 24th Infantry Regiment, winning two Silver Stars. He retired with disability as a COL in 1962; Britt died in Bradenton, FL on July 12, 1977.

[3] **Sources, Private Lee A. Burns:** *from U.S. Army Clerk of Court* – HQ, 92nd Infantry Division, Office of the Staff Judge Advocate, Memorandum to Accompany the Record of Trial in the Case of Private Lee A. Burns, 38520648, 792nd Ordnance (LM) Company; HQ, 92nd Infantry Division, Office of the Provost Marshal, APO 92, Testimony of Sabatini Fedora, Resident at Coste Festone

Maggiano, Pro di Lucca, 4 December 1944; Statement, Private Lee A. Burns, 24 December 1944; Statement, Private Aldene Worthey, 26 December 1944; Organization of the Court, Court-Martial of Private Lee A. Burns, 19 January 1945; HQ, MTO, Office of the Theater Judge Advocate, APO 512, Review of Theater Judge Advocate on Record of Trial by GCM U.S. v. Private Lee A. Burns, 38520648, 792nd Ordnance (LM) Company, 12 February 1945; HQ, MTO, APO 512, "Confirmation of Sentence for Private Lee A. Burns, 38520648, 792nd Ordnance (LM) Company, "19 February 1945; Branch Office of the JAG with the MTO, APO 512, "Board of Review in the Case of U.S. v. Private Lee A. Burns, 38520648, 792nd Ordnance (LM) Company," 17 March 1945; War Department, The Adjutant General's Office, "Non-Battle Casualty Report for Lee A. Burns," 12 April 1945; *from NARA (NPRC)* – various personnel forms; HQ, PBS Garrison Stockade Number 1, APO 782, "Execution of Death Sentence," 27 March 1945.

## 62 – Abraham Smalls

[1] None of the officers graduated from West Point.

[2] **Charge: Violation of the 92nd Article of War.**
*Specification:* In that Private Abraham Smalls, Company L, 370th Infantry, did at Viareggio, Italy, on or about 4 February 1945 with malice aforethought, willfully, deliberately, feloniously, unlawfully, and with premeditation kill one Private First Class George W. Jones, a human being by shooting him with a rifle.

[3] **Sources, Abraham Smalls:** *from U.S. Army Clerk of Court* – HQ, 92nd Infantry Division, Office of the Staff Judge Advocate, Memorandum to Accompany the Record of Trial in the Case of Private Abraham Smalls, 34512812, Company L, 370th Infantry Regiment; Organization of the Court, Court-Martial of Private Abraham Smalls, 17 February 1945; Branch Office of the JAG with the MTO, APO 512, "Board of Review in the Case of U.S. v. Private Abraham Smalls, (34512812), Company L, 370th Infantry," 19 March 1945; War Department, The Adjutant General's Office, "Non-Battle Casualty Report for Private Abraham Smalls," 12 April 1945; *from NARA (NPRC)* – Information from Hospital Admission Cards; various personnel forms; Service Record, Smalls, Abraham, 34512812, November 7, 1942 to March 27, 1945; HQ, PBS Garrison Stockade Number 1, APO 782, "Execution of Death Sentence [General Prisoner Abraham Smalls]," 27 March 1945.

## 63 – General L. Grant

[1] Jamison, a black officer, retired from the U.S. Army as a LTC. During the Korean War, he served as a company commander in the 24th Infantry Regiment. He died in 1986 in Cuyahoga, OH.

[2] None of the officers graduated from West Point.

[3] **Charge I: Violation of the 61st Article of War.**
*Specification:* In that, Private First Class General L. Grant, Company D, 366th Infantry, did without proper leave, absent himself from his organization and station at Viareggio, Italy, from 1800 hours 8 January 1945 to about 2100 hours 8 January 1945.
**Charge II: Violation of the 92nd Article of War.**
*Specification:* In that Private First Class General L. Grant, Company D, 366th Infantry, did at Viareggio, Italy, on or about 8 January 1945 with malice aforethought, willfully, deliberately, feloniously, unlawfully, and with premeditation kill one Carlo Franceschi, a human being by shooting him with a rifle.

[4] **Sources, General L. Grant:** *from U.S. Army Clerk of Court* – HQ, 92nd Infantry Division, Office of the Staff Judge Advocate, Memorandum to Accompany the Record of Trial in the Case of Private General L. Grant, 34557976, Company D, 366th Infantry Regiment; Record of Trials by Courts-Martial; HQ, 92nd Infantry Division, Office of the Provost Marshal, APO 92, Testimony of Private General Lee Grant, 34557976, Company D, 366th Infantry, 9 January 1945; Organization of the Court, Court-Martial of Private First Class General L. Grant, 8 February 1945; HQ, MTO, Office of the Theater Judge Advocate, APO 512, Review of Theater Judge Advocate on Record of Trial by GCM U.S. v. Private First Class General L. Grant, 34557976, Company D, 366th Infantry, 28 February 1945; HQ, MTO, APO 512, "Confirmation of Sentence for Private First Class General L. Grant, 34557976, Company D, 366th Infantry, 28 February 1945; Branch Office of the JAG with the MTO, APO 512, "Board of Review in the Case of U.S. v. Private First Class General L. Grant, 34557976, Company D, 366th Infantry," 10 March 1945; War Department, The Adjutant General's Office, "Non-Battle Casualty Report for General L. Grant," 16 April 1945; *from NARA (NPRC)* – various personal data forms; Memo from ABMC to Memorial Division, Correction of Grave Numbers, Oise-Aisne Cemetery, Fère-en-Tardenois, 19 November 1952.

### 64 – Olin W. Williams

[1] On the panel were LTC George R. Anderson (QM), MAJ Samuel H. Berry (JAG), who was also the Law Member, MAJ George M. Seckinger (TC), CPT Phillip H. Carlin (OD), 1LT Jason R. Gray (TC), 1LT Lafayette Parker (QM), 1LT Lloyd R. Hagen (AG) and 1LT Francis Harkins (FI.) CPT Robert G. Hisey (IN) sat as the Trial Judge Advocate. CPT Carl W. Miller (IN) served as the Defense Counsel. He was assisted by 2LT Michael P. Murphy (TC.) None of the officers graduated from West Point.

[2] **Charge: Violation of the 92nd Article of War.**
*Specification 1*: In that, Private Olin W. Williams, 4194th Quartermaster Service Company, did, at Le Chene Daniel, A Cherence Le Heron, France, on or about 0250 hours, 24 September 1944, with malice aforethought, willfully, deliberately, feloniously, unlawfully, and with premeditation, kill one Albert Lebocey, a human being, by shooting him with a carbine rifle.
*Specification 2*: In that Private Olin W. Williams, 4194th Quartermaster Service Company, did, at Le Chene Daniel, A Cherence Le Heron, France, on or about 0250 hours, 24 September 1944, forcibly and feloniously, against her will, have carnal knowledge of ***********.

[3] **Sources, Olin W. Williams:** *from U.S. Army Clerk of Court* – "Serious Complaint Report, Mr. Lebocey, Albert, Case No. 793B1," 24 September 1944; Sworn Statement, 1LT Gus N. Bacalis, 589th Ordnance Ammunition Company, 26 September; Sworn Statement, Private Odell Austin, 38302522, 589th Ordnance Ammunition Company, 1 October 1944; Sworn Statement, Private Chester Coet, 32805481, 589th Ordnance Ammunition Company, 1 October 1944; Sworn Statement, Private Olin W. Williams, 34649494, 4194th Quartermaster Service Company, 4 October 1944; HQ, ETO, "Confirmation Order for Private Olin W. Williams, 4194th Quartermaster Service Company," 4 March 1945; Branch Office of The JAG with the ETO APO 887, "Board of Review No. 1, U.S. v. Private Olin W. Williams, 34649494, 4194th Quartermaster Service Company," 14 March 1945; HQ, ETO, GCM Order Number 85, 24 March 1945; HQ, Loire DTC, APO 562, "Report of Proceedings at the Execution of General Prisoner Olin W. Williams, formerly Private, 4194th Quartermaster Service Company," 31 March 1945; Certificate of Death, Olin W. Williams, 4194th Quartermaster Service Company, 29 March 1945; HQ, Normandy Base Section, Communications Zone, ETO, APO 562, Letter of Regret, 9 April 1945; War Department,

The Adjutant General's Office, "Non-Battle Casualty Report for Private Olin W. Williams," 10 April 1945; *from NARA-NPRC* – various personnel forms; HQ, Loire DTC, APO 562, "Special Orders Number 56," 24 March 1945; HQ, Normandy Base Section, APO 562, "Execution of General Prisoners Tommie Davison and Olin W. Williams," 25 March 1945; HQ, Beach District Guardhouse, Normandy Base Section, APO 562, "Certificate [Reading the Execution Order to the Condemned]," 28 March 1945; "Certificate [Concerning Physical and Mental Health of the Condemned]," 28 March 1945; HQ, Beach District, Normandy Base Section, APO 562, "Rosters of Personnel for Execution," 28 March 1945; HQ, 3059 QM Graves Registration Company, APO 562, "Travel Orders," 29 March 1945.

### 65 – Tommie Davison

[1] None of the officers graduated from West Point.
[2] **Charge I: Violation of the 92nd Article of War.**
*Specification*: In that Private Tommie (NMI) Davison, 427th Quartermaster Troop Transport Company did, at Prise Guinment, France, on or about 23 August 1944 forcibly and feloniously, against her will, have carnal knowledge of ***********.

**Charge II: Violation of the 93rd Article of War.**
*Specification*: In that Private Tommie (NMI) Davison, 427th Quartermaster Troop Transport Company did, at Prise Guinment, France, on or about 23 August 1944 with intent to do him bodily harm commit an assault upon M. Henri Duqueroux, by shooting at him with a dangerous weapon to wit, a pistol.

**Charge III: Violation of the 65th Article of War.**
*Specification*: In that Private Tommie (NMI) Davison, 427th Quartermaster Troop Transport Company did, at Prise Guinment, France, attempt to assault a warrant officer, CWO Earl E. Lane, Jr., with a pistol while said warrant officer was in the execution of his office.

[3] **Sources, Tommie Davison:** *from U.S. Army Clerk of Court* – Criminal Investigation Division, First U.S. Army, APO 230, "Statement of Private Odell Kirby, 34561870, 429th Quartermaster Troop Transport Company, 26 August 1944"; Organization of the Court, Court-Martial of Private Tommie Davison, 9 December 1944; HQ, Normandy Base Section, Communications Zone, ETO, APO 562, "Review by the Staff Judge Advocate, U.S. v. Private Tommie Davison, 34485174, 427th Quartermaster Troop Transport Company," 25 January 1945; Branch Office of The JAG with the ETO APO 887, "Board of Review

No. 1, U.S. v. Tommie Davison, 34485174, 427th Quartermaster Troop Transport Company," 14 March 1945; HQ, Loire DTC, APO 562, "Report of Proceedings at the Execution of General Prisoner Tommie Davison, formerly Private, 427th Quartermaster Troop Transport Company," 31 March 1945; War Department, The Adjutant General's Office, "Non-Battle Casualty Report for Private Tommie Davison," 9 April 1945.

### 66 – William Harrison, Jr.

[1] Sitting on the panel were: COL Tom W. Scott (AC), MAJ Ira D. Cope (AC), MAJ Bates L. Scoggins (AC), MAJ James H. Maloney (AC), MAJ James Eshelby (AC), MAJ Eugene E. McEwan (AC), CPT Luther C. Morrill (AC), CPT Frank E. Moss (JAG and Law Member), CPT Leonard J. Rosen (QM), CPT Ross E. Clark (AC) and CPT Timothy W. Goodrich (AC.) 1LT Morris C. McGee (AC) served as the Trial Judge Advocate. 1LT Randolph J. Soker assisted him. MAJ Clarence R. Liggit (AC) served as the Defense Counsel. 1LT Theodor Kadin (AC) was his assistant. None of the officers was a West Point graduate.

[2] **Sources, William Harrison, Jr.:** *from U.S. Army Clerk of Court –* Death Book" Ledger located at the U.S. Army Clerk of the Court in Ballston, Virginia; "Final dispositions of rape and/or murder charges tried by General Courts-Martial, December 1941 to April 1946, and analysis of evidence establishing identity of accused in such cases as resulted in death of the accused," Memorandum for the Under Secretary of War, Room 3E-714, The Pentagon, Washington, 25, DC from Major General Thomas M. Green, Major General, The JAG, undated; *from NARA-NPRC –* various personnel forms; various medical evaluation forms; cover sheet to personnel file; HQ, Army Air Force Station 238, APO 639, "Special Court-Martial Orders Number 30," 26 June 1944; HQ, Army Air Force Station 238, APO 639, "Special Court-Martial Orders Number 45," 23 September 1944; "Neuropsychiatric Examination of Enlisted Man," 29 September 1944; HQ, Base Air Depot Area, Air Service Command, United States Strategic Air Forces in Europe, "Special Orders Number 294," 24 October 1944; "Record of Trial of Harrison, William Jr., 15089828, Private, HQ & HQ Squadron, 2nd Combat Crew Replacement Center Group, AAF Station 238, APO 639," 6, 7, 17 and 18 November 1944; Letter from Dr. Douglas Lothian, Down Mental Hospital, to the mother of William Harrison, 9 December 1944; Branch Office of The JAG with the ETO, APO 887, "Board

of Review Number 1, U.S. v. Private William Harrison, Jr., 15089828, HQ and HQ Squadron, 2nd Combat Crew Replacement Center," 19 January 1945; Note to Colonel Kunkel from J.B.S., dated 25 January 1945; War Department, Office of the Chief of Staff, "Pleas for Executive Clemency in the GCM Case of Private William Harrison, Jr., ASN 15089828," 26 March 1945; HQ, ETO, "GCM Orders Number 88," 30 March 1945; Office of the Chaplain, U. K. Base Guardhouse, APO 508, "Letter of Condolence from Chaplain John E. Berkstresser," 8 April 1945; War Department, The Adjutant General's Office, "Non-Battle Casualty Report, Harrison, William Jr., Private, ASN 15089828," 16 April 1945; *from other sources –* "Soldier's Execution Delayed," *New York Times*, December 3, 1944; "The US Prison at Shepton Mallet"; John J. Eddleston, *The Encyclopaedia of Executions*, 687.

### 67 – Benjamin F. Hopper

[1] Sitting on the panel were COL Frederic P. Van Duzee (QM), MAJ Alvis P. Jackson (CAC), MAJ Lee H. Burnham (CAC), MAJ Merle A. Cook (CE), MAJ Joseph J. Walsh (SP), who was the Law Member, MAJ Richard F. Armitage (OD), CPT Charles E. Knox (FA), CPT Vernon Jones (CAC) and CPT J.W. Barnes (CE.) 2LT Clay V. Spear served as the Trial Judge Advocate and CPT Wayne S. Aho (CAC) served as the Defense Counsel. None of the officers graduated from West Point.

[2] **Charge: Violation of the 92nd Article of War.**
*Specification:* In that, Private Benjamin F. Hopper, Thirty-One Hundred Seventieth Quartermaster Service Company, did, at Welkenraedt, Belgium on or about 28 October 1944, with malice aforethought, willfully, deliberately, feloniously, unlawfully, and with premeditation kill one Private Randolph Jackson, Jr., a human being, by shooting him with a carbine.

[3] **Sources, Benjamin F. Hopper:** *from U.S. Army Clerk of Court –* HQ, First U.S. Army, Office of the Surgeon, Neuropsychiatric Section, APO 230, "Psychiatric Report in Disciplinary Cases, Hopper, Benjamin, 32720571," November 23, 1944; HQ, First U.S. Army, Organization of the Court, GCM of Private Benjamin F. Hopper, 23 November, 1944; HQ, First U.S. Army, APO 230, Review of the Staff Judge Advocate, Case of Private Benjamin F. Hopper, 32720571, 3170th Quartermaster Service Company, 12 December 1944; Interview of Prisoner Benjamin Hopper by Colonel Warren Hayford III, 25 January 1945; ETO,

APO 887, "Review by Staff Judge Advocate, U.S. v. Private Benjamin F. Hopper, 32720571, 3170th Quartermaster Service Company," February 1945; HQ, ETO, "Confirmation Order in the Case of Private Benjamin F. Hopper, 32720571, 3170th Quartermaster Service Company," 12 February 1945; Branch Office of the JAG with the ETO, APO 887, "Board of Review No. 2, U.S. v. Private Benjamin F. Hopper, 32720571, 3170th Quartermaster Service Company," 4 April 1945; HQ, European Theater of Command, GCM Orders Number 107, 7 April 1945; Certificate of Examination for Cause of Death for Benjamin F. Hopper, 32702571, formerly of 3170th Quartermaster Service Company, 11 April 1945; HQ, Loire DTC, APO 562, "Report of Proceedings at the Execution of General Prisoner Benjamin F. Hopper, Formerly Private, 3170th Quartermaster Service Company," 12 April 1945; War Department, The Adjutant General's Office, "Non-Battle Casualty Report, Private Benjamin F. Hopper," 18 April 1945; Letter to the Office of the Clerk of the Court, U.S. Army Judiciary by Emmett N. Bailey, Jr., February 23, 1998; *from NARA-NPRC* – various personnel forms; various medical evaluation forms; "Certificate [of Medical Condition]," 10 April 1945; Delta DTC, Office of the Chaplain, APO 772, Letter of Condolence, 4 July 1945; *from other sources* – Discussions with Thomas Ward, former supply sergeant of the Loire Disciplinary Training Center, beginning April 2013.

## 68, 69, 70 – John Williams, James L. Jones & Milbert Bailey

[1] **Charge: Violation of the 92nd Article of War.**
*Specification 1:* In that, Private John Williams, Private Milbert Bailey, and Private James L. Jones, all of 434th Port Company, 501st Port Battalion, acting jointly and in pursuance of a common intent, did, at La Pernelle, Hameau, Scipion, Normandy, France, on or about 11 October 1944, with malice aforethought, willfully, deliberately, feloniously, unlawfully, and with premeditation kill one ************, a human being, by stabbing him with a knife.
*Specification 2:* In that, Private John Williams, Private Milbert Bailey, and Private James L. Jones, all of 434th Port Company, 501st Port Battalion, acting jointly and in pursuance of a common intent, did, at La Pernelle, Hameau, Scipion, Normandy, France, on or about 11 October 1944, forcibly and feloniously against her will, have carnal knowledge of ************.

[2] **Sources, John Williams:** *from U.S. Army Clerk of Court* – "Death Book" Ledger; "Final dispositions of rape and/or murder charges tried by General Courts-Martial, December 1941 to April 1946, and analysis of evidence establishing identity of accused in such cases as resulted in death of the accused," Memorandum for the Under Secretary of War, Room 3E-714, The Pentagon, Washington, 25, DC from Major General Thomas M. Green, Major General, The JAG, undated; *from NARA (NPRC)* – various personal data forms; Service Record John Williams, February 6, 1943 – April 19, 1945; Letter from the wife of John Williams to President Franklin D. Roosevelt, March 1945; HQ, Normandy Base Section, Communications Zone, ETO, APO 562, "Execution of General Prisoners Milbert Bailey, James L. Jones and John Williams," 14 April 1945; HQ, ETO, "GCM Order Number 116 [Bailey, Jones & Williams]," 15 April 1945; HQ, Loire DTC, APO 562, "Orders [Temporary Duty for Personnel La Pernelle, Hameau, Manche, France]," 16 April 1945; HQ, Loire DTC, APO 562, "Rosters of Personnel for Execution," 16 April 1945; HQ, Loire DTC, APO 562, "Official Observers," 16 April 1945; HQ, Loire DTC, APO 562, "Orders [Temporary Duty for Personnel La Pernelle, Hameau, Manche, France]," 16 April 1945; HQ, Beach District Guardhouse, Normandy Base Section, APO 562, Certificate concerning reading of GCM Orders to the Condemned, 18 April 1945; HQ, Loire DTC, APO 562, "Report of Proceedings at the Execution of General Prisoner John Williams, formerly Private, 434th Port Company, 501st Port Battalion," 21 April 1945; Certificate of Physical and Mental Condition [General Prisoner John Williams], 18 April 1945; Certificate of Death John Williams, 32794118, 19 April 1945; Receipt for Remains for John Williams, 32794118, 19 April 1945; War Department, The Adjutant General's Office, "Report of Death [Williams, John]," 3 May 1945; HQ, 434th Port Company, U.S. Ordnance Depot 0-656, Channel Base Section, Communications Zone, ETO, APO 228, Letter of Condolence to Wife of John Williams, 3 May 1945; Letter from The Adjutant General Major General J. A. Ulio to the Wife of John Williams, 27 April 1945; War Department, The Adjutant General's Office, "Report of Non-Battle Casualty [Williams, John, 32794118]," 27 April 1945; Letter from The Adjutant General Major General J. A. Ulio to the wife of John Williams, 9 May 1945; *from other sources* – Discussion with Daniel Bellamy, Mayor, Le Pernelle, France, September 16, 2011.

**Sources, James L. Jones:** *from U.S. Army Clerk of Court* – "Death Book" Ledger; "Final dispositions of rape and/or murder charges tried by General Courts-Martial, December 1941 to April 1946, and analysis of evidence establishing identity of accused in such cases as resulted in death of the accused," Memorandum for the Under Secretary of War," Room 3E-714, The Pentagon, Washington, 25, DC from Major General Thomas M. Green, Major General, The JAG, undated; *from NARA (NPRC)* – various personal data forms; HQ, ETO, "GCM Order Number 116 [Bailey, Jones & Williams]," 15 April 1945; HQ, Loire DTC, APO 562, "Orders [Temporary Duty for Personnel La Pernelle, Hameau, Manche, France]," 16 April 1945; "Certificate [of Physical and Mental Condition of James L. Jones], 18 April 1945; HQ, Loire DTC, APO 562, "Report of Proceedings at the Execution of General Prisoner James L. Jones, formerly Private, 434th Port Company, 501st Port Battalion," 21 April 1945; War Department, The Adjutant General's Office, "Report of Non-Battle Casualty [Jones, James L., 34221343]," 27 April 1945; War Department, The Adjutant General's Office, "Report of Death [Jones, James L.]," 10 May 1945; *from other sources* – Discussion with Daniel Bellamy, Mayor, Le Pernelle, France, September 16, 2011.

**Sources, Milbert Bailey:** *from U.S. Army Clerk of Court* – "Death Book" Ledger; "Final dispositions of rape and/or murder charges tried by General Courts-Martial, December 1941 to April 1946, and analysis of evidence establishing identity of accused in such cases as resulted in death of the accused," Memorandum for the Under Secretary of War, Room 3E-714, The Pentagon, Washington, 25, DC from Major General Thomas M. Green, Major General, The JAG, undated; *from NARA (NPRC)* – various personal data forms; HQ, Beach District Guardhouse, Normandy Base Section, APO 562, "Execution of General Prisoners Milbert Bailey, James L. Jones and John Williams," 14 April 1945; HQ, Beach District Guardhouse, Normandy Base Section, APO 562, Office of the Provost Marshal, "Rosters of Personnel for Execution," 16 April 1945; HQ, Loire DTC, APO 562, "Orders," 16 April 1945; HQ, Beach District Guardhouse, Normandy Base Section, APO 562, "Certificate [concerning reading the execution order,] 18 April 1945; HQ, Loire DTC, APO 562, "Report of Proceedings at the Execution of General Prisoner Milbert Bailey, formerly Private, 434th Port Company, 501st Port Battalion," 21 April 1943; *from other sources* – Discussion with Daniel Bellamy, Mayor, Le Pernelle, France, September 16, 2011.

**Sources, John C. Woods:** *from NARA (NPRC)* – U.S. Navy Personnel File, Letter from Major General J.A. Ulio, The Adjutant General, to The Chief of Naval Personnel concerning John C. Woods, 22 April 1945; Letter from USNAVPERS to The Adjutant General of the Army on John C. Woods; Navy Service Record, John Clarence Woods, (341-73-98.)

## 71 – Shelton McGhee, Sr.

[1] On the panel were COL Roger W. Whitman (QM), who was the Law Member, LTC Charles H. Dobbs (IN), LTC Leo S. Strawn (MC), MAJ John M. Sanders (OD), CPT Lloyd J. Roberts (AG), and CPT Gerald D. Bertram (QM.) 2LT Mervin R. Samuel (QM) was to have served as the Assistant Trial Judge Advocate, but due to the absence of another officer, Samuel became the Trial Judge Advocate. 1LT John W. Wynne (CAC) served as Defense Counsel due to another officer's absence. Dobbs graduated from West Point in 1922. He was born in NC on July 10, 1899. He resigned his commission in 1925, but came back in the service in World War II. He died at Midland, TX on February 18, 1985. None of the other officers graduated from West Point.

[2] **Charge I: Violation of the 92nd Article of War.**
*Specification:* In that Corporal Shelton McGhee, Sr., 3823rd Quartermaster Truck Company, 133rd Quartermaster Battalion (Mobile), did at Livorno, Italy, on or about 15 December 1944, with malice aforethought, willfully, deliberately, feloniously, unlawfully, and with premeditation kill one Technician 5th Grade George W. Brown, 3823rd Quartermaster Truck Company, 133rd Quartermaster Battalion (Mobile), a human being by shooting him with a pistol.

**Charge II: Violation of the 64th Article of War.**
*Specification:* In that Corporal Shelton McGhee, Sr., 3823rd Quartermaster Truck Company, 133rd Quartermaster Battalion (Mobile), did at Livorno, Italy, on or about 15 December 1944,, draw a weapon, to wit a pistol against 1LT James A. Green, 3823rd Quartermaster Truck Company, 133rd Quartermaster Battalion (Mobile), his superior officer, who was then in the execution of his office.

[3] **Sources, Shelton McGhee, Sr.:** *from U.S. Army Clerk of Court* – HQ, PBS, Office of the Provost Marshal, Criminal Investigations Division, Accused Background Information, 19 December 1944; Court-Martial Form #2 – Evidence of Previous Convictions, McGhee, Shelton Sr., Corporal, 34529025, 23 December 1944; 114th

Station Hospital, Neuropsychiatric Service, "Psychiatric Report in Disciplinary Case, McGhee, Shelton Sr., Corporal, 34529025," 24 January 1945; HQ, PBS, Organization of the Court, GCM of Corporal Shelton McGhee, Sr., 3 February 1945; HQ, PBS, "Review of the Staff Judge Advocate, U.S. v. Corporal Shelton McGhee, Sr., 34529025, 3823rd Quartermaster Truck Company, 133rd Quartermaster Battalion (Mobile)," 26 March 1945; HQ, PBS, "Court-martial, Corporal Shelton McGhee," 30 March 1945; HQ, MTO, Office of the Theater Judge Advocate, "Review of Theater Judge Advocate, U.S. v. Corporal Shelton McGhee, Sr., 34529025, 3823rd Quartermaster Truck Company, 133rd Quartermaster Battalion (Mobile)," 14 April 1945; HQ, MTO, "Confirmation Order in the Case of McGhee, Shelton Sr., Corporal, 34529025" 14 April 1945; Branch Office of the JAG with the MTO, "Board of Review, U.S. v. Corporal Shelton McGhee, Sr., 34529025, 3823rd Quartermaster Truck Company, 133rd Quartermaster Battalion (Mobile)," 21 April 1945; HQ, Mediterranean Theater of Command, GCM Orders Number 67, 21 April 1945; *from NARA (NPRC)* – various personal record forms; Laboratory Service, 64th General Hospital, APO 428, "Autopsy Report, Brown, George W.," 16 December 1944.

## 72 – George E. Smith, Jr.

[1] Wojtacha was tried for being an accessory to murder, but was not sentenced to death.

[2] Sitting in judgment were COL Olin F. McIlnay (MC), LTC James R. Clarke (SC), LTC John R. Philpott (AC), MAJ Robert R. Dickey (JAG) the Law Member, MAJ Robert M. Stonesifer (AC), MAJ Dana E. Smith (AC), MAJ Ralph E. Riegelman (MC), MAJ Clark E. Holland (AC), MAJ Richard D. Conrad (AC), MAJ Joseph L. Mann (MC) and CPT George R. Kaiser, Jr. (AC) MAJ Charles F. Brockus (JAG) served as the Trial Judge Advocate; he was assisted by CPT Rolando J. Matteucci (AC.) MAJ Peter A. Deisch (AC) sat as the Defense Counsel. He was assisted by 1LT Max M. Sokarl. None of the officers was a West Pointer. Sokarl was from CT.

[3] **Charge: Violation of the 92nd Article of War.**
*Specification:* In that Private George E. Smith, Jr., 784th Bombardment Squadron, 466th Bombardment Group (H), did at Honingham, Norfolk, England, on or about 3 December 1944, with malice aforethought, willfully, deliberately, feloniously, unlawfully, and with premeditation kill one Eric Teichman, a human being by shooting him with a rifle.

[4] **Sources, George E. Smith:** *from U.S. Army Clerk of Court* – 231st Station Hospital, Office of the Chief of Medical Service, "Psychiatric Report on Enlisted Man (Prisoner) [George W. Smith, Jr.]," 9 December 1944; "Statement of Findings, Psychiatric Examination of George E. Smith, Jr. by Dr. John Vincent Morris," 4 January 1945; "Record of Trial, GCM, Private George E. Smith, Jr., 33288266;" "Records of [Previous] Trials by Courts-Martial, [Private George E. Smith, Jr.]; 755th Bombardment Squadron, 458th Bombardment Group (H), "Request for Clemency, Private George E. Smith, Jr.," 13 February 1945; HQ, ETO, "Confirmation of Sentence [Private George W. Smith, Jr., 33288266]," 3 April 1945; Branch Office of The JAG with the ETO, APO 887, "Board of Review Number 1, U.S. v. Private George E. Smith, Jr. (33288266), 784th Bombardment Squadron, 466th Bombardment Group (H)," 26 April 1945; HQ, Guardhouse Overhead Detachment Number 6833, APO 508, "Proceeding of Execution of Private George E. Smith," 8 May 1945; HQ, 2nd Air Division, APO 558, "Letter of Regret to Lady Teichman, Honingham Hall, Honingham, England," 22 May 1945; *from NARA (NPRC)* – various personal data forms; Service Record, Smith, George E., Jr., 33288266, March 15, 1943 to May 8, 1945; Commonwealth of Pennsylvania, Pennsylvania Board of Parole, Harrisburg, "George E. Smith, Parole No. 6856-A," August 24, 1949; Adjutant Generals Division, Information Concerning George E. Smith, Jr., 10 October 1949; *from other sources* – "Hunt for Briton's Slayer Turns to Yank Airdrome," *Chicago Tribune*, December 6, 1944, 1; "Inspect U.S. Carbines in Death of Briton," *Stars & Stripes*, London Edition, Vol. 5, No. 31, December 7, 1944, 8; "2 Indicted in Teichman Death," *New York Times*, December 8, 1944; "Two U.S. Soldiers Held in Diplomat's Killing," *Stars & Stripes*, London Edition, Vol. 5, No. 32, December 8, 1944, 8; "2 GIs Charged in Death of Briton," *Stars & Stripes*, London Edition, Vol. 5, No. 33, December 9, 1944, 4; "TEICHMAN SHOOTING CITED; Statement by Pvt. Smith Read at Court-Martial in England," *New York Times*, January 10, 1945, 6; "SOLDIER PLEADS INSANITY; Slayer of British Diplomat Called Homicidal Degenerate," *New York Times*, January 11, 1945, 4; "Pleads Insanity for GI Killer," *Stars & Stripes*, London Edition, Vol. 5, No. 59, January 11, 1945, 4; "U.S. Troops' Mental Age Put at 13 to 14 In Defense of Private Who Shot Diplomat," *New York Times*, January 12, 1945; "Calls GI Killer Mentally Only 9," *Stars & Stripes*,

London Edition, Vol. 5, No. 60, January 12, 1945, 4; "ARMY COURT CONVICTS SLAYER OF TEICHMAN," *New York Times*, January 13, 1945, 16; "U.S. PRIVATE IS HANGED; Pays Penalty for Having Shot Briton Who Challenged Him," *New York Times*, May 11, 1945, 4; "The US Prison at Shepton Mallet," 47-48; John J. Eddleston, *The Encyclopaedia of Executions*, 686.

## 73 – George Green, Jr.

[1] On the court were: COL James J. Weeks (DC), LTC Karl W. Curtis (IG), LTC Robert E. Joseph (JAG), MAJ Frank Kemmerer (QM) and CPT Everett E. Smith, (JAG) Law Member. 1LT Fred W. Hofstetter (IN) sat as the Trial Judge Advocate. CPT Victor L. Thom (CAV) served as Defense Counsel; he was assisted by CPT Frederic C. Blake (OD.) None of the officers was a West Point graduate.

[2] **Charge: Violation of the 92nd Article of War.**
*Specification*: In that Private George Green, Jr., 998th Quartermaster Salvage Collecting Company, did, at Champigneulles, France, on or about 18 November 1944, with malice aforethought, willfully, deliberately, feloniously, unlawfully, and with premeditation kill one Corporal Tommie Lee Garrett, a human being, by shooting him with a carbine.

[3] **Sources, George Green, Jr.: *from U.S. Army Clerk of Court*** – 998th Quartermaster Salvage Company, "Evidence of Previous Convictions, Private George Green, Jr.," 18 November 1944; "Record of Trial, George Green, Jr., 38476751, Private, 998th Quartermaster Salvage Collecting Company;" HQ, Third U.S. Army, APO 403, "Approval of Sentence for Private George Green, Jr., 38476751, 998th Quartermaster Salvage Collecting Company;" 9 January 1945; "Letter from Private George Green, Jr. to General Dwight D. Eisenhower," January 23, 1945; "Sworn Statement by J.A. Ford Concerning George Green, Jr.," 14 February 1945; HQ, ETO, "Review by Staff Judge Advocate, U.S. v. Private George Green, Jr., 38476751, 998th Quartermaster Salvage Collecting Company," 25 February 1945; HQ, ETO, "Confirmation of Sentence, Private George Green, Jr. 38476751," 25 February 1945; HQ, ETO, "GCM Order Number 129, Private George Green, Jr., 38476751, 998th Quartermaster Salvage Collecting Company;" 1 May 1945; HQ, Loire DTC, APO 562, "Report of Proceedings at the Execution of General Prisoner George Green, Jr., formerly Private 998th Quartermaster Salvage Collecting Company," 15 May 1945; War Department, The Adjutant General's Office, "Non-

Battle Casualty Report, Private George Green, Jr., 38476751," 26 May 1945; *from NARA (NPRC)* – various personal data forms; War Department, The Adjutant General's Office, "Report of Death, Green, George Jr., 38476751," 1 June 1945; *from other sources* – Discussions with Thomas Ward, former supply sergeant of the Loire Disciplinary Training Center, beginning April 2013.

## 74 – Haze Heard

[1] **Sources, Haze Heard: *from U.S. Army Clerk of Court*** – "Death Book" Ledger; "Final dispositions of rape and/or murder charges tried by General Courts-Martial, December 1941 to April 1946, and analysis of evidence establishing identity of accused in such cases as resulted in death of the accused," Memorandum for the Under Secretary of War, Room 3E-714, The Pentagon, Washington, 25, DC from MAJ General Thomas M. Green, MAJ General, The JAG, undated; *from NARA (NPRC)* – HQ, ETO, "GCM Order Number 137 [Haze Heard]," 11 May 1945; HQ, Normandy Base Section, APO 562, "Execution of General Prisoner Haze Heard," May 15, 1945; Loire DTC, APO 562, "Orders," May 17, 1945; HQ, Loire DTC, APO 562, "Report of Execution, Haze Heard, 34562354," 23 May 1945; War Department, The Adjutant General's Office, "Report of Death, Heard, Haze, 34562354," 1 June 1945; various personnel forms; *from other sources* – Discussion with Anita Queruel, Secretary to the Mayor, Guy Lebrec, Deputy Mayor, and with the grandson of Madame Berthe Robert, Mesnil-Clinchamps, France, September 15, 2011.

## 75 – William J. McCarter

[1] The following in attendance LTC Lester C. Ayers (IN), MAJ Melvin A. Hoherz (AG), CPT Melwood W. Van Scoyoc (FA), CPT Kenneth W. Sinish (MC), CPT Melvan M. Jacobs (FI) and 1LT Stephan G. Clark, Jr. MAJ Andre B. Moore (JAG) served as the Trial Judge Advocate while MAJ Thomas L. Kirkpatrick (IG) served as Defense Counsel. None of the officers was West Pointers.

[2] **Charge: Violation of the 92nd Article of War.**
*Specification*: In that Private First Class William J. McCarter, 465th Quartermaster Laundry Company, did, at Thionville, France, on or about 1 February 1945, with malice aforethought, willfully, deliberately, feloniously, unlawfully, and with premeditation kill one Private Charles P. Williams, a human being, by shooting him with a carbine.

[3] **Sources, William J. McCarter:** *from U.S. Army Clerk of Court* – HQ, 32nd Evacuation Hospital, "Clinical Diagnosis of Charles P. Williams, Private," 1 February 1945; HQ, 32nd Evacuation Hospital, "Annex Number 1 to Report of Investigation Conducted Pursuant to Par 1, Special Order Number 13," 1 February 1945; "A Sworn Statement of William McCarter, 465th Quartermaster Laundry," 4 February 1945; "Record of Trial by GCM in the Case of Private First Class William J. McCarter, 34675988, 465th Quartermaster Laundry Co. Tried at HQ, XX Corps on 16 February 1945"; HQ, XX Corps, APO 340, "Review of the Staff Judge Advocate, Private First Class William J. McCarter, 34675988," 27 February 1945; "A Chronology of the Case of: PFC William J. McCarter, 24675988 [SP], 465th Quartermaster Laundry Company," 3 March 1945; HQ, ETO, "Confirmation Order in the Case of McCarter, William J., Private First Class, 34675988" 29 March 1945; Branch Office of The JAG with the ETO, APO 887, "Board of Review Number 2, U.S. v. Private First Class William J. McCarter, 34675988, 465th Quartermaster Laundry Company," 3 May 1945; HQ, ETO, "GCM Orders Number 138," 12 May 1945; Letter to General Dwight D. Eisenhower from Mrs. Alice M. Eccles, May 28, 1945; War Department, The Adjutant General's Office, "Non-Battle Casualty Report, Private First Class William J. McCarter," 7 June 1945; *from NARA (NPRC)* – Record of Trial by Court-Martial, McCarter, William J., Private First Class, 465th Quartermaster Laundry Company, 16 February 1945; various personnel forms; *from other sources* – Discussions with Thomas Ward, former supply sergeant of the Loire Disciplinary Training Center, beginning April 2013.

## 76 – Clete O. Norris

[1] On the court were MAJ Robert F. Durbin (IN), MAJ Quincy V. Tuma (FA), MAJ William H, Harrison, Jr. (IN and Law Member), CPT Robert T. Baldwin (CAC), CPT George F. Roberts (IN), CPT Edward J. Hirz (IN), CPT Jacob J. Urman (FA), 2LT Frank R. La Budde (IN), and 2LT Joseph N. McCord (IN.) 1LT John F. Finch (AUS) served as the Trial Judge Advocate; he was assisted by 1LT Julian J. Case (FA.) 1LT Chester H. Stewart (IN) served as the Defense Counsel; 1LT Thomas Clancey (FA) assisted him. Hirz graduated from West Point in 1926. He was born in OH on June 25, 1901. He served in the 10th Infantry Regiment and the 65th Infantry Regiment in Puerto Rico, before resigning from the Army in 1929. Recalled to duty, he was later assigned to the 85th Ordnance Battalion. He died at Mourmelon, France on May 8, 1946. Tuma was born in TX in 1914. He graduated from college and went into the Texas National Guard as an enlisted man. He died in Harris, TX in 1979.

[2] **Sources, Clete O. Norris:** *from U.S. Army Clerk of Court* – "Death Book" Ledger; "Final dispositions of rape and/or murder charges tried by General Courts-Martial, December 1941 to April 1946, and analysis of evidence establishing identity of accused in such cases as resulted in death of the accused," Memorandum for the Under Secretary of War, Room 3E-714, The Pentagon, Washington, 25, DC from Major General Thomas M. Green, Major General, The JAG, undated; *from NARA (NPRC)* – Service Record, Norris Clete O., 25 September 1941 – 31 May 1945; "Report of Induction, Norris, Clete O.," 25 September 1941; HQ, Southern California Sector, Western Defense Command, Pasadena, California, "Special Court-Martial Order Number 19," 30 June 1943; HQ, ETO, "Review by the Staff Judge Advocate, U.S. v. Sergeant Clete O. Norris, 37082314, 3384th Quartermaster Truck Company," 2 May 1945; Branch Office of The JAG with the ETO, APO 887, "Board of Review No. 2, U.S. v. Sergeant Clete O. Norris, 37082314, 3384th Quartermaster Truck Company," 18 May 1945; HQ, Southern District, Normandy Base Section, APO 562, "Letter Order Number 5-106," 19 May 1945; HQ, ETO, APO 887, "Execution of Death Sentence (Norris, Clete O.)," 25 May 1945; HQ, ETO, GCM Orders Number 174, 26 May 1945; Certificate [of health concerning Clete O. Norris], signed by Major Ernest A. Weizer, 30 May 1945; Certificate [concerning cause of death of Clete O. Norris], 31 May 1945; Receipt for Remains [for General Prisoner Clete O. Norris], 31 May 1945; Commanding Officer, Loire DTC, APO 562, "Message to Commanding General, ETO, APO 887 (Execution of General Prisoner Clete O. Norris)," 31 May 1945; HQ, ETO, "GCM Orders Number 174," 26 May 1945; HQ, Loire DTC, APO 562, "Report of Execution, Clete O. Norris," 31 May 1945; *from other sources* – Discussions with Thomas Ward, former supply sergeant of the Loire Disciplinary Training Center, beginning April 2013.

## 77 – Alvin R. Rollins

[1] On the panel were LTC Albert L. Sayre (SC), MAJ William R. Weightman (MP) the Law Member, MAJ Lockwood Thompson (AC), MAJ Ralph L. Hunter (TC), CPT Anthony C. Prestifilippo (IN), CPT Norman F. Swanson (FI), CPT Leonard Lustig (CE), CPT Robert H. Wormhoudt (CAS)

and CPT Lincoln H. Brown, Jr. (QM.) MAJ Clem H. Block (JAG) served as Trial Judge Advocate; he was assisted by 1LT David P. Tarbell (IN.) CPT William E. Davis (SC) sat as the sole Defense Counsel after the primary counsel, CPT William Peeteas excused by verbal order of the Oise Section commander, BG Charles O. Thrasher. None of the officers graduated from West Point. Wormhoudt was born on December 12, 1910. He died on August 27, 1991. He is buried at the Riverside National Cemetery, Riverside, CA in Plot 42, Grave 1183.

[2] **Charge: Violation of the 92nd Article of War.**
*Specification 1*: In that Private First Class Alvin R. Rollins, 306th Quartermaster Railhead Company, did, at Troyes, France, on or about 23 February 1945, with malice aforethought, willfully, deliberately, feloniously, unlawfully, and with premeditation kill one Private First Class John H. Hoogewind, a human being, by shooting him with a pistol.

*Specification 2*: In that Private First Class Alvin R. Rollins, 306th Quartermaster Railhead Company, did, at Troyes, France, on or about 23 February 1945, with malice aforethought, willfully, deliberately, feloniously, unlawfully, and with premeditation kill one Sergeant Royce A. Judd, Jr., a human being, by shooting him with a pistol.

[3] **Sources, Alvin R. Rollins:** *from U.S. Army Clerk of Court* – "Organization of the Court [Private First Class Alvin R. Rollins]," 13 March 1945; HQ, Oise Section, Communications Zone, ETO, Office of the Staff Judge Advocate, "Review of Record of Trial by GCM, United States vs. Alvin R. Rollins, 34716953, Private First Class, 306th Quartermaster Railhead Company," 27 March 1945; HQ, Oise Section, Communications Zone, ETO, "Approval of Sentence, Private First Class Alvin R. Rollins," 28 March 1945; HQ, ETO, Office of the Staff Judge Advocate, "Review of Record of Trial by GCM, United States vs. Alvin R. Rollins, 34716953, Private First Class, 306th Quartermaster Railhead Company," 25 April; HQ, ETO, "Confirmation Order in the Case of Private First Class Alvin R. Rollins, 34716953, 306th Quartermaster Railhead Company," 29 April 1945; Branch Office of The JAG with the ETO, APO 887, "Board of Review Number 1, United States vs. Private First Class Alvin R. Rollins (34716953), 306th Quartermaster Railhead Company," 18 May 1945; "Certificate of Death for Alvin R. Rollins," 31 May 1945; "Receipt for the Remains of General Prisoner Alvin R. Rollins), 31 May 1945; HQ, Loire DTC, APO

562, "Report of Proceedings at the Execution of General Prisoner Alvin R. Rollins, formerly Private First Class, 306th Quartermaster Railhead Company," 1 June 1945; War Department, The Adjutant General's Office, "Non-Battle Casualty Report Rollins, Alvin R., 34716953," 7 June 1945; *from NARA (NPRC)* – HQ, 306th Quartermaster Railhead Company, "Letter of Condolence," 21 July 1945; "Report of Burial [Rollins, Alvin R.]"; various personnel records; *from other sources* – Discussions with Thomas Ward, former supply sergeant of the Loire Disciplinary Training Center, beginning April 2013.

## 78 – Matthew Clay, Jr.

[1] None of the court members was a West Point officer.

[2] **Charge I: Violation of the 92nd Article of War.**
*Specification*: In that Private First Class Matthew Clay Jr., 3236th Quartermaster Service Company, did, at Fontenay-Sur-Mer, Manche, France, on or about 9 October 1944, with malice aforethought, willfully, deliberately, feloniously, unlawfully, and with premeditation kill one Victor Bellery, a human being, by stabbing him with a bayonet.

**Charge II: Violation of the 93rd Article of War.**
*Specification*: In that Private First Class Matthew Clay Jr., 3236th Quartermaster Service Company, did, at Fontenay-Sur-Mer, Manche, France, on or about 9 October 1944, with intent to do her bodily harm, commit an assault on Madame Augustine Bellery, by cutting her on the body with a dangerous instrument, to wit, a bayonet.

[3] **Sources, Matthew Clay, Jr.:** *from U.S. Army Clerk of Court* – HQ, ETO, "Sentence confirmation [Private First Class Matthew Clay Jr.,]" 29 March 1945; Matthew Clay, "Letter to General Dwight D. Eisenhower," April 7, 1945; Branch Office of The JAG with the ETO APO 887, "Board of Review No. 2, U.S. v. Private First Class Matthew Clay, Jr. (38490561), 3236th Quartermaster Service Company," 18 May 1945; GCM [Private First Class Matthew Clay, Jr.], "Organization of the Court," 20 January 1945; HQ, Loire DTC, APO 562, "Report of Proceedings at the Execution of General Prisoner Matthew Clay, Jr., formerly Private First Class, 3236th Quartermaster Service Company," 5 June 1945; War Department, The Adjutant General, "Non-Battle Casualty Report, Clay, Matthew Jr., 38490561," 12 June 1945; Letter to the Office of the Clerk of the Court, U.S. Army Judiciary by Emmett N. Bailey, Jr., February 23, 1998.

## 79 – Werner E. Schmiedel

[1] **Charge I: Violation of the 92nd Article of War.**

*Specification*: In that General Prisoner Werner E. Schmiedel, formerly Private, 403 Replacement Company, 18th Replacement Battalion, 2nd Replacement Depot, and Private James W. Adams, Company M, 157th Infantry, 45th Division, acting jointly and in pursuance of a common intent, did, at Rome, Italy, on or about 10 October 1944, with malice aforethought, willfully, deliberately, feloniously, unlawfully, and with premeditation kill one Eolo Ferretti, a human being, by shooting him with a pistol.

**Charge II: Violation of the 93rd Article of War.**

*Specification 1*: In that General Prisoner Werner E. Schmiedel, formerly Private, 403 Replacement Company, 18th Replacement Battalion, 2nd Replacement Depot, and Private James W. Adams, Company M, 157th Infantry, 45th Division, acting jointly and in pursuance of a common intent, did, at Rome, Italy, on or about 10 October 1944, by force and violence and by putting them in fear, feloniously take, steal and carry away from the persons of Eolo Ferretti, Camillo Bochinni, Antonio Ferretti and Alfredo Venanzoni, money and personal papers of some value, the property of the said Eolo Ferretti, Camillo Bochinni, Antonio Ferretti and Alfredo Venanzoni.

*Specification 2*: In that General Prisoner Werner E. Schmiedel, formerly Private, 403 Replacement Company, 18th Replacement Battalion, 2nd Replacement Depot, and Private James W. Adams, Company M, 157th Infantry, 45th Division, acting jointly and in pursuance of a common intent, did, at or near Capua, Italy, on or about 17 September 1944, by force and violence and by putting him in fear, feloniously take, steal and carry away from the person and presence of Sergeant Stefan Pawluk, an automobile, one wallet, 18,000 lire, one Egyptian pound sterling, one wrist watch, two rings, three gold chains, four gold coins, one cigarette case, one cigarette holder, and one pistol, of a total value in excess of fifty dollars, property of the said Stephan Pawluk.

**Additional Charge:**
**Violation of the 93rd Article of War.**

*Specification 1:* In that General Prisoner Werner E. Schmiedel, formerly Private, 403 Replacement Company, 18th Replacement Battalion, 2nd Replacement Depot, and Private James W. Adams, Company M, 157th Infantry, 45th Division, acting jointly and in pursuance of a common intent, did, at or near Sparanise, Italy, on or about 7 September 1944, by force and violence and by putting him in fear, feloniously take, steal and carry away from the person of Salvatore Starace, 125,000 lire, the property of the said Salvatore Starace.

*Specification 2*: The prosecution elected not to prosecute this specification.

*Specification 3*: In that General Prisoner Werner E. Schmiedel, formerly Private, 403 Replacement Company, 18th Replacement Battalion, 2nd Replacement Depot, and Private James W. Adams, Company M, 157th Infantry, 45th Division, acting jointly and in pursuance of a common intent, did, at or near Formia, Italy, on or about 17 September 1944, by force and violence and by putting him in fear, feloniously take, steal and carry away from the person of Private First Class Willie L. Traughber, a military police brassard and a pistol, of some value, property of the said Private First Class Willie L. Traughber.

*Specification 4*: In that General Prisoner Werner E. Schmiedel, formerly Private, 403 Replacement Company, 18th Replacement Battalion, 2nd Replacement Depot, and Private James W. Adams, Company M, 157th Infantry, 45th Division, acting jointly and in pursuance of a common intent, did, at or near Formia, Italy, on or about 17 September 1944, by force and violence and by putting him in fear, feloniously take, steal and carry away from the person of Sergeant Donald Tinkham, a military police brassard and a pistol, of some value, property of the said Sergeant Donald Tinkham.

**Additional Charge II:**
**Violation of the 61st Article of War.**

*Specification*: In that General Prisoner Werner E. Schmiedel, formerly Private, 403 Replacement Company, 18th Replacement Battalion, 2nd Replacement Depot, did without proper leave, absent himself from his station at or near Aversa, Italy, from on or about 2 September 1944 to about 3 November 1944.

[2] Albert was from Santa Fe, NM; Corso was from California, PA. Medding was from Memphis, TN.

[3] **Sources, Werner E. Schmiedel:** *from U.S. Army Clerk of Court* – Branch Office of The JAG with the MTO, APO 512, "Board of Review, U.S. v. General Prisoner Werner E. Schmiedel, formerly Private, 7041115, 403rd Replacement Company, 18th Replacement Battalion, 2nd Replacement Depot, and Private James W. Adams, 6956616, Company M, 157th Infantry Regiment, 45th Division," 26 May 1945; The War Department, The JAG's Office, "Non-Battle Casualty Report for Schmiedel, Werner E., 7041115," 25 June 1945; *from NARA (NPRC)* – various personnel forms; HQ, PBS, APO 782, "GCM Orders Number 594,"

15 November 1944; HQ, PBS, APO 782, "GCM Orders Number 82," 28 May 1945; *from other sources* – "Army & Navy: Mobster Abroad," *Time Magazine*, November 20, 1944; "2 U.S. SOLDIERS GO ON TRIAL IN ROME," *New York Times*, March 27, 1945, 7; "TWO GIs IN ROME SENTENCED TO HANG; Court-Martial Finds Lane Gang Leader and Aide Guilty of Murdering Civilian," *New York Times*, March 28, 1945, 8; "2 Yanks Sentenced to Hang for Killing in Holdup in Italy," *Chicago Tribune*, March 28, 1945, 14; "U.S. DESERTER HANGED; Convicted of Having Murdered Italian During Hold-Up," *New York Times*, June 12, 1945.

## 80 – Aniceto Martinez

[1] **Charge: Violation of the 92nd Article of War.**
*Specification:* In that Private First Class Aniceto Martinez, HQ Detachment, Prisoner of War Inclosure Number 2, did, at Rugeley, Staffordshire, England, on or about 6 August 1944 forcibly and feloniously, against her will, have carnal knowledge of ***********.

[2] **Sources, Aniceto Martinez:** *from U.S. Army Clerk of Court* – HQ, United Kingdom Base, Communications Zone, ETO, APO 413, "Review of Staff Judge Advocate, GCM of Aniceto Martinez, 38168482, Private, Guardhouse Number Three, Sudbury, Derbyshire, England," 2 March 1945; Branch Office of The JAG with the ETO APO 887, "Board of Review No. 3, U.S. v. Private Aniceto Martinez (38168482), HQ' Detachment, Prisoner of War Inclosure Number 2," 29 May 1945; United Kingdom Base DTC, APO 508, "Proceeding of execution of Private Aniceto Martinez, 38168482, U.K. Base DTC," 15 June 1945; The War Department, The JAG's Office, "Non-Battle Casualty Report for Martinez, Aniceto, PFC, 38168482," 28 June 1945; *from NARA (NPRC)* – "Service Record, Aniceto Martinez, 38168482, October 19, 1942 to June 15, 1945"; HQ United Kingdom Base DTC, APO 508, "Letter of Condolence from Chaplain (CPT) George E. Montie," 16 June 1945; various personnel data forms; *from other sources* – "The US Prison at Shepton Mallet," 44; John J. Eddleston, *The Encyclopaedia of Executions*, 689; Discussion with Nathalie Le Barbier, Oise-Aisne American Military Cemetery, September 11, 2011; Albert Pierrepoint Execution Ledger Entry.

## 81 – Victor Ortiz

[1] **Charge: Violation of the 92nd Article of War.**
*Specification*: In that Private Victor (NMI) Ortiz, 3269th Quartermaster Service Company, did, at Marquette, France, on or about 28 January 1945, with malice aforethought, willfully, deliberately, feloniously, unlawfully, and with premeditation kill one Captain Ignacio Bonit, 3269th Quartermaster Service Company, a human being, by shooting him with a carbine, M1, .30 caliber.

[2] The court included COL Harry B. Parris (IN), LTC Walter F. Plank (CC), LTC Gordon A. Miller (SC), MAJ Joseph M. Commander, Jr. (AC), MAJ John F. Tarrant (AC and Law Member) and 1LT Stanford A. Wright (QM.) CPT Carl L. Stevens (QM) served as the Trial Judge Advocate; he was assisted by CPT Hugh M. Rose (AUS.) CPT Paul B. Madden (AUS) was assigned as the Defense Counsel, with 1LT David L. Price (SC) serving as the Assistant Defense Counsel.

[3] **Sources, Victor Ortiz:** *from U.S. Army Clerk of Court* – Office of the Surgeon, 558th Quartermaster Group Infirmary, APO 228, Description of Wounds to Captain Ignacio Bonit, 29 January 1945; HQ, 3269th Quartermaster Service Company, "Summary of Expected Testimony," 30 January 1945; HQ, Channel Base Section, Communications' Zone, ETO, APO 228, "Review of the Staff Judge Advocate, Ortiz, Victor, 30405077," 22 March 1945; HQ, Channel Base Section, Communications' Zone, ETO, APO 228, "Approval of Sentence for Private Victor Ortiz, 30405077," 25 March 1945; HQ, ETO, "Confirmation Order in the Case of Private Victor Ortiz, 30405077, 3269th Quartermaster Service Company," 6 May 1945; Branch Office of The JAG with the ETO, APO 887, "Board of Review, U.S. v. Private Victor Ortiz, 30405077, 3269th Quartermaster Service Company," 8 June 1945; HQ, ETO, "GCM Orders Number 213," 16 June 1945; HQ, Loire DTC, APO 562, Certificate Stating that GCM Order Number 213 Was Read In Its Entirety to Private Victor Ortiz," 20 June 1945; HQ, Loire DTC, APO 562, "Report of Proceedings at the Execution of General Prisoner Victor Ortiz, formerly Private, 3269th Quartermaster Service Company," 23 June 1945; War Department, The Adjutant General's Office, "Non-Battle Casualty Report, Private Victor Ortiz," 26 June 1945; HQ, Army Service Forces, Office of The JAG, Letter to Mrs. Victor Ortiz, Bella Vista, Hato Rey, Puerto Rico, 6 March 1946; Letter to Adjutant General's Office from Ms. Aurelia Reyes, May 17, 1955; Letter to Adjutant General's Office from Mr. Frank

Torres, Attorney at Law and Counselor for Mrs. Aurelia Reyes Ortiz, December 29, 1960; *from NARA (NPRC)* – Letter from Chaplain Kilian R. Bowler to Ms. Aurelia Reyes, August 3, 1945; various personnel forms; *from other sources* – Discussions with Thomas Ward, former supply sergeant of the Loire Disciplinary Training Center, beginning April 2013.

## 82 – Willie Johnson

[1] **Charge: Violation of the 92nd Article of War.**
*Specification*: In that Private Willie Johnson, 3984th Quartermaster Truck Company, did, on or about 24 August 1944, at or near Equilly, Normandy, France, with malice aforethought, willfully, deliberately, feloniously, unlawfully, and with premeditation kill one Madame Julien Fontaine, a human being, by driving over her body with a gasoline tank truck.

[2] None of the officers was a West Pointer.

[3] **Sources, Willie Johnson:** *from U.S. Army Clerk of Court* – "Chronology of the Case of Johnson, Willie, Private, 38270465, 3984th Quartermaster Truck Company;" "Record of Trials by Courts-Martial, Private Willie Johnson, 38270465, 3984th Quartermaster Truck Company," 21 November 1944; HQ, 165th General Hospital, APO 562, "Insanity Board Proceedings for Johnson, Willie, Private, 38270465, 3984th Quartermaster Truck Company," 23 January 1945; "Organization of the Court, GCM, Private Willie Johnson, 38270465, 3984th Quartermaster Truck Company," 27 January 1945; HQ, Normandy Base Section, Communications Zone, ETO, APO 562, "Review by Staff Judge Advocate, U.S. v. Private Willie Johnson, 38270465, 3984th Quartermaster Truck Company," 17 February 1945; HQ, ETO, "Confirmation Order in the Case of Private Willie Johnson, 38270465, 3984th Quartermaster Truck Company," 29 March 1945; Letter from Brigadier General E. C. Betts, Theater Judge Advocate, to Mrs. Kittie Johnson, 30 May 1945; Branch Office of The JAG with the ETO, APO 887, "Board of Review Number 3, U.S. v. Private Willie Johnson 38270465, 3984th Quartermaster Truck Company," 11 June 1945; HQ, ETO, "GCM Orders Number 218, " 21 June 1945; Letter from Brigadier General E. C. Betts, Theater Judge Advocate, to Private Willie Johnson, 38270465, Loire DTC, 23 June 1945; HQ, Loire DTC, APO 562, "Report of Proceedings at the Execution of General Prisoner Willie Johnson, formerly Private, 3984th Quartermaster Truck Company," 26 June 1945; "Receipt for Remains of Willie Johnson, 38270465,

3984th Quartermaster Truck Company," 26 June 1945; Certificate of Death for Willie Johnson, 38270465, 3984th Quartermaster Truck Company, 26 June 1945; HQ, CHANOR Base Section, APO 562, "Letter of Regret to the Mayor of Equilly, France," 9 July 1945; War Department, The Adjutant General's Office, "Non-Battle Casualty Report, Johnson, Willie, Private, 38270465," 9 July 1945; War Department, The Adjutant General's Office, "Report of Death, Johnson, Willie, Private, 38270465," 10 July 1945; Letter from Colonel Albert W. Johnson, Acting Chief, Military Justice Division, to Mrs. Kittie Johnson, 12 December 1945; *from NARA (NPRC)* – HQ, Loire DTC, APO 562, "Special Order Number 130," 22 June 1945; Office of the Chaplain, 46th Quartermaster Group (TC), APO 758, "Letter of Condolence," 7 August 1945; various personnel forms.

## 83, 84 – Fred A. McMurray & Louis Till

[1] Dobbs graduated last in his class at West Point in 1922. He was born in NC on July 10, 1899. He died on February 18, 1985 at Midland, TX.

[2] **Charge I: Violation of the 92nd Article of War.**
*Specification 1*: In that Private Fred A. McMurray, One Hundred Seventy-Seventh Port Company, Three Hundred Seventy-Ninth Port Battalion, Transportation Corps, did, at Civitavecchia, Italy, on or about 27 June 1944, with malice aforethought, willfully, deliberately, feloniously, unlawfully, and with premeditation kill one Anna Zanchi, a human being, by shooting her with a pistol.
*Specification 2*: In that Private Fred A. McMurray, One Hundred Seventy-Seventh Port Company, Three Hundred Seventy-Ninth Port Battalion, Transportation Corps, did, at Civitavecchia, Italy, on or about 27 June 1944, forcibly and feloniously, against her will, have carnal knowledge of *********** [Rape Victim 1.]
*Specification 3*: In that Private Fred A. McMurray, One Hundred Seventy-Seventh Port Company, Three Hundred Seventy-Ninth Port Battalion, Transportation Corps, did, at Civitavecchia, Italy, on or about 27 June 1944, forcibly and feloniously, against her will, have carnal knowledge of *********** [Rape Victim 2.]
**Charge II: Violation of the 93rd Article of War.** (The accused was not arraigned on this charge.)
**Charge I: Violation of the 92nd Article of War.**
*Specification 1*: In that Private Louis Till, One Hundred Seventy-Seventh Port Company, Three Hundred Seventy-Ninth Port Battalion, Transportation Corps, did, at Civitavecchia, Italy,

on or about 27 June 1944, with malice aforethought, willfully, deliberately, feloniously, unlawfully, and with premeditation kill one Anna Zanchi, a human being, by shooting her with a pistol.

*Specification 2*: In that Private Louis Till, One Hundred Seventy-Seventh Port Company, Three Hundred Seventy-Ninth Port Battalion, Transportation Corps, did, at Civitavecchia, Italy, on or about 27 June 1944, forcibly and feloniously, against her will, have carnal knowledge of *********** [Rape Victim 1.]

*Specification 3*: In that Private Louis Till, One Hundred Seventy-Seventh Port Company, Three Hundred Seventy-Ninth Port Battalion, Transportation Corps, did, at Civitavecchia, Italy, on or about 27 June 1944, forcibly and feloniously, against her will, have carnal knowledge of *********** [Rape Victim 2.]

**Charge II: Violation of the 93rd Article of War.** (The accused was not arraigned on this charge.

3 **Sources, Fred A. McMurray:** *from U.S. Army Clerk of Court* – Statement by John Masi to Agent L. H. Rousseau, 30 June 1944; Sworn Statement by Private James Thomas, Jr. to 1LT Lewis Bernstein, Summary Court Officer, 8 July 1944; Statement by Private Fred A. McMurray to 1LT Ralph A. Hamilton, Jr., 19 July 1944; HQ, PBS, Office of the Provost Marshal, APO 782, "Statement of James E. Carter, Mo MM 1/c, 7212980, U.S. Navy Salvage Fleet," 30 July 1944; Certificate Concerning the Service Record of Private Fred A. McMurray, 38184335, 8 September 1944; Statement by John Masi to Agent L. H. Rousseau, 27 October 1944; Sworn Statement by Emma Zanchi to Captain James D. Barnes, Investigating Officer, 27 October 1944; Sworn Statement by Benni Lucretzia to Captain James D. Barnes, Investigating Officer, 28 October 1944; Sworn Statement by Frieda Mari to Captain James D. Barnes, Investigating Officer, 28 October 1944; HQ, PBS, Office of the Staff Judge Advocate, APO 782, "Memorandum to Accompany the Record of Trial in the Case of Private Fred A. McMurray, 38184335, and Private Louis Till, 36392273, both of 177th Port Company, 379th Port Battalion, TC; Memorandum from Captain Eugene J. Ralston, Subject: Clemency in U.S. v. James Thomas Jr., 9 February 1945; Organization of the Court, GCM of Private Fred A. McMurray, 38184335, and Private Louis Till, 36392273, both of 177th Port Company, 379th Port Battalion," 17 February, 1945; HQ, PBS, Office of the Staff Judge Advocate, APO 782, "Review of the Staff Judge Advocate in the Common Trial of Private Fred A. McMurray, 38184335, 177th Port Company, 379th Port Battalion, Transportation Corps and Private Louis Till, 36392273, 177th Port Company, 379th Port Battalion, Transportation Corps," 18 April 1945; HQ, MTO, "Confirmation Order in the Case of Private Fred A. McMurray, 38184335, and Private Louis Till, 36392273, both of 177th Port Company, 379th Port Battalion, Transportation Corps," 17 May 1945; Branch Office of The JAG with the MTO, "Board of Review, U.S. v. Privates Fred A. McMurray (38184335) and Louis Till (36392273), both of 177th Port Company, 379th Port Battalion, Transportation Corps," 13 June 1945; CG US Army Forces MTO, Caserta, Italy, Message to War Department on Private Fred A. McMurray, 10 July 1945; War Department, The Adjutant General's Office, "Non-Battle Casualty Report, McMurray, Fred A., Private, 38184335," 13 July 1945; *from NARA (NPRC)* – various personal data forms; HQ, PBS Garrison Stockade Number 1, APO 782, "Execution Order (Fred A. McMurray, 38184336)," 1 July 1945; HQ, PBS, APO 782, "Execution of Sentence by GCMO in the case of PVT Fred A. McMurray," 7 July 1945.

**Sources, Louis Till:** *from U.S. Army Clerk of Court* – Statement by John Masi to Agent L. H. Rousseau, 30 June 1944; Sworn Statement by Private James Thomas, Jr. to 1LT Lewis Bernstein, Summary Court Officer, 8 July 1944; Statement by Private Fred A. McMurray to 1LT Ralph A. Hamilton, Jr., 19 July 1944; HQ, PBS, Office of the Provost Marshal, APO 782, "Statement of James E. Carter, Mo MM 1/c, 7212980, U.S. Navy Salvage Fleet," 30 July 1944; Certificate Concerning the Service Record of Private Louis Till, 36392273, 8 September 1944; Statement by John Masi to Agent L. H. Rousseau, 27 October 1944; Sworn Statement by Emma Zanchi to Captain James D. Barnes, Investigating Officer, 27 October 1944; Sworn Statement by Benni Lucretzia to Captain James D. Barnes, Investigating Officer, 28 October 1944; Sworn Statement by Frieda Mari to Captain James D. Barnes, Investigating Officer, 28 October 1944; HQ, PBS, Office of the Staff Judge Advocate, APO 782, "Memorandum to Accompany the Record of Trial in the Case of Private Fred A. McMurray, 38184335, and Private Louis Till (36392273), both of 177th Port Company, 379th Port Battalion, TC"; Memorandum from Captain Eugene J. Ralston, Subject: Clemency in U.S. v. James Thomas Jr., 9 February 1945; Organization of the Court, GCM of Private Fred A. McMurray, 38184335, and Private Louis Till, 36392273, both of 177th Port Company, 379th Port Battalion, 17 February, 1945; HQ, PBS, Office of the Staff Judge

Advocate, APO 782, "Review of the Staff Judge Advocate in the Common Trial of Private Fred A. McMurray, 38184335, 177th Port Company, 379th Port Battalion, Transportation Corps and Private Louis Till, 36392273, 177th Port Company, 379th Port Battalion, Transportation Corps," 18 April 1945; HQ, MTO, "Confirmation Order in the Case of Private Fred A. McMurray, 38184335, and Private Louis Till, 36392273, both of 177th Port Company, 379th Port Battalion, Transportation Corps," 17 May 1945; Branch Office of The JAG with the MTO, "Board of Review, U.S. v. Privates Fred A. McMurray (38184335) and Louis Till (36392273), both of 177th Port Company, 379th Port Battalion, Transportation Corps," 13 June 1945; CG US Army Forces MTO, Caserta, Italy, Message to War Department on Private Louis Till, 11 July 1945; War Department, The Adjutant General's Office, "Non-Battle Casualty Report, Till, Louis, Private, 36392273," 13 July 1945; *from NARA (NPRC)* – various personal data forms.

[4] Christopher Paul Moore, *Fighting for America: Black Soldiers – The Unsung Heroes of World War II*, NY: Random House Publishing, 2005, 219.

[5] Ezra Pound, *The Pisan Cantos*, edited by Richard Sieburth, NY: New Directions, 2003, 8.

## 85, 86 – John T. Jones & Henry Nelson

[1] None of the officers graduated from West Point.

[2] **Charge I: Violation of the 92nd Article of War.**
*Specification:* In that Private John T. Jones, Battery B, 599th Field Artillery Battalion, and Private Henry W. Nelson, Company A, 371st Infantry Regiment, acting jointly, and in pursuance of a common intent, did, at Massa Maciniai, Italy, on or about 29 January 1945, forcibly and feloniously, against her will, have carnal knowledge of \*\*\*\*\*\*\*\*\*\*\*.

**Charge 2: Violation of the 93rd Article of War**
*Specification 1:* In that Private John T. Jones, Battery B, 599th Field Artillery Battalion, and Private Henry W. Nelson, Company A, 371st Infantry Regiment, acting jointly, and in pursuance of a common intent, did, at Massa Maciniai, Italy, on or about 29 January 1945, by force and violence and by putting him in fear, feloniously take, steal and carry away from the presence of Luigi Decanini, a watch, two rings, two bicycles, the property of Luigi Decanini, value about $70.00.
*Specification 2:* In that Private John T. Jones, Battery B, 599th Field Artillery Battalion, and Private Henry W. Nelson, Company A, 371st Infantry Regiment, acting jointly, and in pursuance of a common intent, did, at Massa Maciniai, Italy, on

or about 29 January 1945, with intent to do him bodily harm, commit an assault upon Attilio Rovai by shooting him in the eye with a dangerous weapon, to wit, a carbine.

[3] **Sources, Henry W. Nelson: *from U.S. Army Clerk of Court* –** Statement of Private Henry W. Nelson, 35726029, undated; Evidence of Previous Convictions in the Case of Nelson, Henry W., 35726029, Private, Company A, 371st Infantry, 27 February 1945; Organization of the Court in the Joint Trial of Private Henry W. Nelson and Private John T. Jones, 17 March 1945; HQ, 92nd Infantry Division, Office of the Division Judge Advocate, APO 92, "Review of the Staff Judge Advocate in Joint Trial Case of Private Henry W. Nelson, 35726029, Company A, 371st Infantry Regiment and Private John T. Jones, 38315973, Battery B, 599th Field Artillery Battalion," 29 March 1945; HQ, MTO, Office of the Theater Judge Advocate, APO 512, "Review of the Theater Judge Advocate on Record of Trial by GCM of U.S. v. Private Henry W. Nelson, 35726029, Company A, 371st Infantry Regiment and Private John T. Jones, 38315973, Battery B, 599th Field Artillery Battalion," 13 April 1945; HQ, MTO, "Confirmation Order in the Case of Private Henry W. Nelson, 35726029, Company A, 371st Infantry Regiment and Private John T. Jones, 38315973, Battery B, 599th Field Artillery Battalion," 21 April 1945; Branch Office of The JAG with the MTO, APO 512, "Board of Review U.S. v. Private Henry W. Nelson, 35726029, Company A, 371st Infantry Regiment and Private John T. Jones, 38315973, Battery B, 599th Field Artillery Battalion," 11 May 1945; War Department, The Adjutant General's Office, "Non-Battle Casualty Report, Nelson, Henry W., 35726029," 15 July 1945; *from NARA (NPRC)* – various personal data forms; Service Record, Henry W. Nelson, February 26, 1943 – July 5, 1945; HQ, PBS Garrison Stockade Number 1, APO 782, "Execution of Death Sentence," 5 July 1945.

**Sources, John T. Jones: *from U.S. Army Clerk of Court* –** Statement of Private John T. Jones, 38315973, undated; Organization of the Court in the Joint Trial of Private Henry W. Nelson and Private John T. Jones, 17 March 1945; HQ, 92nd Infantry Division, Office of the Division Judge Advocate, APO 92, "Review of the Staff Judge Advocate in Joint Trial Case of Private Henry W. Nelson, 35726029, Company A, 371st Infantry Regiment and Private John T. Jones, 38315973, Battery B, 599th Field Artillery Battalion," 29 March 1945; HQ, MTO, Office of the Theater Judge Advocate, APO 512, "Review of the Theater

Judge Advocate on Record of Trial by GCM of U.S. v. Private Henry W. Nelson, 35726029, Company A, 371st Infantry Regiment and Private John T. Jones, 38315973, Battery B, 599th Field Artillery Battalion," 13 April 1945; HQ, MTO, "Confirmation Order in the Case of Private Henry W. Nelson, 35726029, Company A, 371st Infantry Regiment and Private John T. Jones, 38315973, Battery B, 599th Field Artillery Battalion," 21 April 1945; Branch Office of The JAG with the MTO, APO 512, "Board of Review U.S. v. Private Henry W. Nelson, 35726029, Company A, 371st Infantry Regiment and Private John T. Jones, 38315973, Battery B, 599th Field Artillery Battalion," 11 May 1945; War Department, The Adjutant General's Office, "Non-Battle Casualty Report, Jones, John T., 38315973," 23 July 1945; *from NARA (NPRC)* – various personal data forms; Service Record, John T. Jones, November 3, 1943 – July 5, 1945; "Burial Report, John T. Jones," 5 July 1945; HQ, PBS Garrison Stockade Number 1, APO 782, "Report of Death, Jones, John T.," 5 July 1945; HQ, PBS Garrison Stockade Number 1, APO 782, "Death Certificate, Jones, John T.," 5 July 1945; HQ, PBS Garrison Stockade Number 1, APO 782, "Execution of Death Sentence," 5 July 1945.

### 87 – Charles H. Jeffries

[1] Crockett was born in the Philippine Islands on August 9, 1914. He graduated from West Point in 1936. In World War II, he served as the Operations Officer for the 92nd Infantry Division, Division Artillery. He retired disabled in 1946 and died in Palo Alto, CA on February 19, 1981. Born in RI, Brownlee was the first black commissioned FA officer in World War II; he was assigned to the 600th Field Artillery Battalion in the 92nd Infantry Division. After the war, he graduated from Northwestern University in 1947. He later worked for the *Chicago Daily News* and later won an Emmy while working for *WLS* radio. Brownlee died on November 21, 2005 in Evanston, IL. Richardson was born in MN in 1915. Previously a member of the Minnesota National Guard, he lived in Chicago when he was inducted on January 6, 1941.

[2] **Charge I: Violation of the 92nd Article of War.**
*Specification:* In that Private Charles H. Jeffries, Company F, 366th Infantry, did, at Barga, Italy, on or about 22 December 1944, with malice aforethought, willfully, deliberately, feloniously, unlawfully and with premeditation, kill one Alfredo Bechelli, a human being by shooting him with a rifle.

**Charge II: Violation of the 93rd Article of War.**
*Specification 1:* In that Private Charles H. Jeffries, Company F, 366th Infantry, did, at Barga, Italy, on or about 22 December 1944, with intent to do him bodily harm, commit an assault on Private First Class James Livingston, Company F, 366th Infantry, by shooting him in the leg, with a dangerous weapon, to wit, one (1) rifle.

*Specification 2:* In that Private Charles H. Jeffries, Company F, 366th Infantry, did, at Barga, Italy, on or about 22 December 1944, with intent to do him bodily harm, commit an assault on Private First Class John B. Walker, Company F, 366th Infantry, by shooting him in the shoulder, with a dangerous weapon, to wit, one (1) rifle.

*Specification 3:* In that Private Charles H. Jeffries, Company F, 366th Infantry, did, at Barga, Italy, on or about 22 December 1944, with intent to do him bodily harm, commit an assault on Private First Class Mansee Bonnett, Company F, 366th Infantry, by shooting him with a dangerous weapon, to wit, one (1) rifle.

*Specification 4:* In that Private Charles H. Jeffries, Company F, 366th Infantry, did, at Barga, Italy, on or about 22 December 1944, with intent to do her bodily harm, commit an assault on Silvana Bechelli by shooting her with a dangerous weapon, to wit, one (1) rifle.

*Specification 5:* In that Private Charles H. Jeffries, Company F, 366th Infantry, did, at Barga, Italy, on or about 22 December 1944, with intent to do her bodily harm, commit an assault on Giaconda Bonini by shooting her with a dangerous weapon, to wit, one (1) rifle.

*Specification 6:* In that Private Charles H. Jeffries, Company F, 366th Infantry, did, at Barga, Italy, on or about 22 December 1944, with intent to do her bodily harm, commit an assault on Alda Bonini by shooting her in the leg with a dangerous weapon, to wit, one (1) rifle.

[3] **Sources, Charles H. Jeffries: *from U.S. Army Clerk of Court* –** "Organization of the Court in the Case of Private Charles H. Jeffries, 33181343," 28 February 1945; HQ, MTO, Office of the Theater Judge Advocate, APO 512, "Review of the Theater Judge Advocate U.S. v. Private Charles H. Jeffries, 33181343, Company F, 366th Infantry Regiment," 8 April 1945; HQ, MTO, APO 512, "Confirmation of Sentence, Private Charles H. Jeffries, 33181343, Company F, 366th Infantry Regiment," 21 April 1945; Branch Office of The JAG with the MTO, APO 512, "Board of Review, U.S. v. Private Charles H. Jeffries (33181343), Company F, 366th Infantry Regiment," 2 May 1945; War Department,

The Adjutant General's Office, "Non-Battle Casualty Report, Jeffries, Charles H., 33181343," 16 July 1945; *from NARA (NPRC)* – various personal data forms; "Report of Proceedings of a Board of Officers, 366th Infantry, Fort Devens, Massachusetts," February 17, 1943; HQ, MTO, APO 512, "GCM Orders Number 94," 22 June 1945; HQ, PBS Garrison Stockade Number 1, APO 782, "Execution Order (Charles H. Jeffries, 33181343)," 5 July 1945; War Department, The Adjutant General's Office, Letter to Next of Kin for Private Charles H. Jeffries, 18 August 1945.

## 88 – Tom Gordon

[1] On the court were LTC Daniel S. Stevenson (VC), LTC Joseph W. Clough (IN), LTC Albert C. Kraft (CE), MAJ Charley S. Hedrick (OD), MAJ Robert A. Bieber (CAV), MAJ Frank T. Heinemann (QM), CPT Lawrence L. Hill (AG) and CPT Theodore Loveless (TC.) 1LT John E. Walsh (JAG) served as the Trial Judge Advocate and 1LT Ben Baime (CAC) sat as Defense Counsel. None of the officers graduated from West Point.

[2] **Charge I: Violation of the 92nd Article of War.** *Specification*: In that Private Tom Gordon, 3251st Quartermaster Service Company, did, at Marseille, France, on or about 12 November 1944, with malice aforethought willfully, deliberately, feloniously, unlawfully, and with premeditation kill one Laurence Broussard, 3251st Quartermaster Service Company, a human being by shooting him with a rifle.

**Charge II: Violation of the 93rd Article of War.** *Specification*: In that Private Tom Gordon, 3251st Quartermaster Service Company, did, at Marseille, France, on or about 12 November 1944, with intent to commit a felony, viz murder commit an assault upon Corporal Willie J. Best, 3251st Quartermaster Service Company, by willfully and feloniously shooting the said Corporal Willie J. Best 3251st Quartermaster Service Company in the leg with a rifle.

**Charge III: Violation of the 61st Article of War.** *Specification*: In that Private Tom Gordon, 3251st Quartermaster Service Company, did, without proper leave absent himself from his camp at Marseille, France from about 12 November 1944 to about 13 November 1944.

[3] **Sources, Tom E. Gordon:** *from U.S. Army Clerk of Court* – 80th Station Hospital, APO 772, "Certificate Concerning Death of Corporal Lawrence Broussard, 37053033," 27 November 1944; Evidence of Previous Convictions in the Case of Gordon, Tom, Private 34091950, 3251st

Quartermaster Service Company, 30 December 1944; HQ, Seventh Army, Office of the Trial Judge Advocate, APO 758, "Recommendation for Clemency in the Case of Private Tom Gordon," 22 February 1945; HQ, Seventh Army, Office of the Staff Judge Advocate, "Review of the Staff Judge Advocate in the Case of Gordon, Tom, 34091950, Private, 3251st Quartermaster Service Company," 30 March 1945; Letter from Private Tom Gordon to General Dwight Eisenhower, Pardon Request from Private Gordon, 25 April 1945; HQ, ETO, "Confirmation Order in the Case of Private Tom Gordon, 34091950, 3251st Quartermaster Service Company," 6 May 1945; Branch Office of The JAG with the ETO, APO 887, "Board of Review Number 1, U.S. v. Private Tom Gordon (34091950), 3251st Quartermaster Service Company," 20 June 1945; Telegram from HQ, Communications Zone, ETO to the War Department, Date of Execution for Private Tom Gordon, 2 July 1945; Certificate, Cause of Death for Tom Gordon, 34091950, 10 July 1945; Receipt for Remains of Tom Gordon, 34091950, 10 July 1945; HQ, Loire DTC, "Report of Proceedings at the Execution of General Prisoner Tom Gordon, 34091950, formerly Private, 3251st Quartermaster Service Company," 12 July 1945; War Department, The Adjutant General's Office, "Non-Battle Casualty Report, Gordon, Tom, 34091950," 20 July 1945; *from NARA (NPRC)* – various personal data forms; "Report of Burial, Gordon, Tom," 10 July 1945.

## 89 – Robert Wray

[1] **Charge: Violation of the 92nd Article of War.** *Specification*: In that Private Robert (NMI) Wray, 3299th Quartermaster Service Company, did, at Golbey, France, on or about 17 December 1944, with malice aforethought willfully, deliberately, feloniously, unlawfully, and with premeditation kill one Private Billy B. Betts, a human being by shooting him with a rifle.

[2] **Sources, Robert Wray:** *from U.S. Army Clerk of Court* – HQ, 68th Military Police Company, APO 667, "Statement by Charles Herbert Carey, 12096222, Private First Class," 18 December 1944; Company D, 65th Infantry, APO 758, "Statement by Ismael Torres, 10402697, Sergeant," 19 December 1944; Company D, 65th Infantry, APO 758, "Additional Statement by Ismael Torres, 10402697, Sergeant," 19 December 1944; 2nd Field Hospital, APO 371, "Certificate Concerning Death of Private Billy Betts, 39573932," 22 December 1944; Continental Advance Section, Criminal Investigation Division, Office of

the Provost Marshal, APO 667, "Report on Murder Case Private Robert Wray, 34461589," 21 January 1945; HQ, 3299th Quartermaster Service Company, APO 758, "Statement by John J. Harkins, Captain, Quartermaster on Private Robert Wray, 34461589," 28 January 1945; Evidence of Previous Convictions in the Case of Wray, Robert, 34461589, undated; 682nd Medical Clearing, NP Hospital Number 2, APO 758, "Psychiatric Report in Disciplinary Cases, Private Robert Wray, 34461589," 22 March 1945; HQ, Seventh Army, Staff Judge Advocate, APO 758, "Review of the Staff Judge Advocate of the Record of Trial for Wray, Robert (NMI), 34461589, Private, 3299th Quartermaster Service Company," 6 May 1945; HQ, ETO, "Review by the Staff Judge Advocate, U.S. v. Private Robert Wray, 34461589, 3299th Quartermaster Service Company," 19 June 1945; HQ, ETO, "Confirmation Order in the Case of Private Robert Wray, 34461589, 3299th Quartermaster Service Company," 26 June 1945; Branch Office of The JAG with the ETO, APO 887, "Board of Review U.S. v. Private Robert Wray (34461589), 3299th Quartermaster Service Company," 3 August 1945; Certificate, Cause of Death for Robert Wray, 34461589, 20 August 1945; "Receipt for Remains of Robert Wray, 34461589," 20 August 1945; HQ, Loire DTC, APO 562, "Report of Proceedings at the Execution of Robert Wray, formerly Private, 3299th Quartermaster Service Company," 22 August 1945; War Department, The Adjutant General's Office, "Non-Battle Casualty Report, Wray, Robert, 34461589," 6 September 1945; Letter from Mrs. Maggie M. Wray to Major General Edward F. Witsell, War Department, The Adjutant General's Office, Reference Wray, Robert, 34461589, September 11, 1945; *from NARA (NPRC)* – various personal data forms.

### 90 – Henry C. Philpot

[1] On the panel were COL James J. Shea (IN), MAJ Kenneth J. Schwoerke (CAC), MAJ Rollins S. Emmerich (IN), MAJ William H. Harrison (IN) who was the Law Member, CPT Jacob J. Urman (FA), CPT George M. Oliver (AG) and 1LT Frank P. Laney (IN.) 1LT John F. Finch (AUS) sat as the Trial Judge Advocate and assisted by 2LT Benjamin D. Tissue (IN.) 1LT Chester H. Stewart (IN) served as the Defense Counsel. None of the officers graduated from West Point.

[2] **Charge: Violation of the 92nd Article of War.** *Specification*: In that Private Henry C. Philpot, attached-unassigned 234th Replacement Company, 90th Replacement Battalion, did, at or

near Bad Neuenahr, Germany, on or about 30 March 1945, with malice aforethought willfully, deliberately, feloniously, unlawfully, and with premeditation kill one 2LT John B. Platt, a human being, by shooting him with a rifle.

[3] **Sources, Henry Philpot:** *from U.S. Army Clerk of Court* – Evidence of Previous Convictions in the Case of Philpot, Henry C., 39080069, Private, 31 March 1945; Organization of the Court in the GCM of Henry C. Philpot, 23 April 1945; "A Chronology of the Case of: Private Henry C. Philpot, 39080069, attached unassigned 234th Replacement Company, 90th Replacement Battalion," undated; HQ, ETO, "Confirmation Order in the Case of Private Henry C. Philpot, 39080069, 234th Replacement Company, 90th Replacement Battalion," 7 June 1945; War Department, Branch Office of The JAG with the ETO, APO 887, "Cover Memorandum Forwarding Board of Review Number 1 Findings in the Case of Private Henry C. Philpot (39080069)," 26 June 1945; War Department, Branch Office of The JAG with the ETO, APO 887, "Board of Review Number 1 Findings in the Case of Private Henry C. Philpot (39080069)," 26 June 1945; War Department, Branch Office of The JAG with the ETO, APO 887, "Clemency Memorandum, Philpot," 26 June 1945; HQ, 235th General Hospital, APO 746, "Report of Proceedings of Board of Officers in the Case of Private Henry C. Philpot, 39080069, attached unassigned 234th Replacement Company, 90th Replacement Battalion," 28 July 1945; HQ, U.S. Forces, European Theater, "GCM Orders Number 365," 30 August 1945; HQ, Loire DTC, APO 562, "Report of Proceedings at the Execution of Henry C. Philpot, formerly Private, 234th Replacement Company, 90th Replacement Battalion," 13 September 1945; Certificate, Cause of Death for Henry C. Philpot, 39080069, 10 September 1945; Receipt for Remains of Henry C. Philpot, 39080069, 10 September 1945; War Department, The Adjutant General's Office, "Non-Battle Casualty Report, Philpot, Henry C., 39080069," 25 September 1945; *from NARA (NPRC)* – various personal data forms; Letter from Chaplain Charles O. Dutton to the Family of Henry Philpot, dated 12 September 1945.

### 91 – Charles M. Robinson

[1] On the panel were COL Fredrik L. Knudsen, Jr. (IN), LTC Henry C. Springer (AG), LTC Erwin O. Gibson (IN), LTC Wilmer C. Landry (QM), MAJ John R. Philbrick (FA), MAJ William Scholz, Jr. (IN), MAJ Charles C. Smith (AG), MAJ Frederick

W. Gilbert (FA) who was the Law Member, CPT Leon S. Thomas (FI) and 1LT Willard K. West (IN.) 1LT Malcolm E. Stewart (JAG) served as the Trial Judge Advocate; he was assisted by 1LT Charles E. Lapp, Jr. (IN.) CPT Harry R.P. Niehoff (FA) sat as Defense Counsel with CPT Charles H. Gresham (CC) as his assistant. Landry was born on March 9, 1913 in LA. He graduated from West Point in 1936 with a commission in the Infantry before transferring to become a Quartermaster. He was the Quartermaster for the Sixty-Sixth Infantry Division. He retired in 1966 as a COL and died on June 13, 1987 in Berkeley, CA.

[2] **Charge: Violation of the 92nd Article of War.**
*Specification:* In that Private Charles M. Robinson, 667th Quartermaster Truck Company did, at Messac, France, on or about 1 April 1945, with malice aforethought, willfully, deliberately, feloniously, unlawfully, and with premeditation kill one Yvonne Le Ny, a human being, by shooting her with a pistol, caliber 45.

[3] **Sources, Charles M. Robinson:** *from U.S. Army Clerk of Court* – HQ, 66th Infantry Division, APO 454, "Supplement Number 1, Form Book, Memorandum, Administration of Justice, Personal Data Concerning Accused, Robinson, Charles M. 38164425, Private, 667th Quartermaster Truck Company," undated; Prosecution Exhibit 1, Identity Booklet for Medical Examinations Mademoiselle Le Ny; HQ, 12th Army Group, Office of the Staff Judge Advocate, APO 655, Letter to Major Joseph W. Riley, Staff Judge Advocate, 66th Infantry Division, Concerning Negro Officers on the Court, 10 April 1945; HQ, 66th Infantry Division, Office of the Surgeon, APO 454, "Neuropsychiatric Examination of Private Charles M. Robinson, 38164425, 667th Quartermaster Truck Company," 12 April 1945; HQ, 66th Infantry Division, Office of the Division Judge Advocate, APO 454, "Review of Record of Trial by Division Judge Advocate, U.S. v. Private Charles M. Robinson, 38164425, 667th Quartermaster Truck Company," 3 May 1945; HQ, ETO, "Confirmation Order in the Case of Private Charles M. Robinson, 38164425, 667th Quartermaster Truck Company," 26 June 1945; Branch Office of The JAG with the European Theater, APO 887, "Board of Review Number 2, U.S. v. Private Charles M. Robinson, 38164425, 667th Quartermaster Truck Company," 1 September 1945; HQ, U.S. Forces, European Theater, "GCM Orders Number 416," 17 September 1945; Receipt for Remains of Charles M. Robinson, 38164425, 28 September 1945; HQ, Loire DTC, APO 562, "Report of Proceedings at the Execution of Charles M. Robinson, formerly Private, 667th Quartermaster Truck Company," 30 September 1945; War Department, The Adjutant General's Office, "Non-Battle Casualty Report, Robinson, Charles M., 38164425," 9 October 1945; Note from Member of Congress, Albert Thomas from Texas, to Major General Witsell, November 30, 1945; *from NARA (NPRC)* – various personal data forms.

### 92 – Blake W. Mariano

[1] **Charge: Violation of the 92nd Article of War.**
*Specification 1:* In that Private First Class Blake W. Mariano, Company C, 191st Tank Battalion, did, at or near Lauf, Germany, on or about 16 April 1945, forcibly and feloniously, against her will, have carnal knowledge of ************ [Rape Victim 1].
*Specification 2:* In that Private First Class Blake W. Mariano, Company C, 191st Tank Battalion, did, at or near Lauf, Germany, on or about 16 April 1945, forcibly and feloniously, against her will, have carnal knowledge of ************ [Rape Victim 2].
*Specification 3:* In that Private First Class Blake W. Mariano, Company C, 191st Tank Battalion, did, at or near Lauf, Germany, on or about 16 April 1945, with malice aforethought, willfully, deliberately, feloniously and unlawfully, and with premeditation kill one, Martha Gary, a human being, by shooting her with a sub-machinegun.

[2] **Sources, Blake W. Mariano:** *from U.S. Army Clerk of Court* – "Affidavit, Private First Class Blake W. Mariano, 38011593," 1 May 1945; HQ, Forty-Fifth Infantry Division, APO 45, "Proceedings of a Board of Officers Which Convened at Munich, Germany, for Private First Class Blake W. Mariano, 38011593, Company C, 191st Tank Battalion," 10 May 1945; HQ, United States Forces, European Theater, "Confirmation Order in the Case of Private First Class Blake W. Mariano, 38011593, Company C, 191st Tank Battalion," 4 August 1945; Branch Office of The JAG with the European Theater, APO 887, "Board of Review Number 3 U.S. v. Private First Class Blake W. Mariano (38011593), Company C, 191st Tank Battalion," 6 September 1945; Branch Office of The JAG with the European Theater, APO 887, "First Enclosure to Board of Review Number 3 U.S. v. Private First Class Blake W. Mariano (38011593), Company C, 191st Tank Battalion," 7 September 1945; HQ, Loire DTC, APO 562, "Report of Proceedings at the Execution of Blake W. Mariano, 38011593, formerly Private First

Class, Company C, 191st Tank Battalion," 10 October 1945; War Department, The Adjutant General's Office, "Report of Death, Mariano, Blake W. 38011593," 25 October 1945; *from NARA (NPRC)* – various personal data forms; Letter from Mrs. H. P. Powers, Gallup, New Mexico to the Office of the Adjutant General, War Department, July 28, 1945; HQ, United States Forces, European Theater, "Designation of Officer Courier," 8 October 1945; Extract [Receipt for Remains,] 10 October 1945.

## 93, 94 – Woodrow Parker & Sydney Bennerman

[1] **Charge: Violation of the 92nd Article of War.**
*Specification 1:* In that Private Woodrow Parker, and Private Sidney Bennerman, Jr., both of the 163rd Chemical Smoke Generator Company, acting jointly, and in pursuance of a common intent, did, at Heilbronn, Germany, on or about 15 April 1945, with malice aforethought, willfully, deliberately, feloniously and unlawfully, and with premeditation kill one, **********, a human being, by striking her on the head and face with rifles.
*Specification 2:* In that Private Woodrow Parker, and Private Sidney Bennerman, Jr., both of the 163rd Chemical Smoke Generator Company, acting jointly, and in pursuance of a common intent, did, at Heilbronn, Germany, on or about 15 April 1945, with malice aforethought, willfully, deliberately, feloniously and unlawfully, and with premeditation kill one, **********, a human being, by striking him on the head and face with rifles.
*Specification 3:* (Not Applicable to accused)
*Specification 4:* In that Private Sidney Bennerman, Jr., 163rd Chemical Smoke Generator Company did, at Heilbronn, Germany, on or about 15 April 1945, forcibly and feloniously, against her will, have carnal knowledge of ************ [Rape Victim.]

[2] **Source, Woodrow Parker:** *from U.S. Army Clerk of Court* – "Death Book" Ledger; "Final dispositions of rape and/or murder charges tried by General Courts-Martial, December 1941 to April 1946, and analysis of evidence establishing identity of accused in such cases as resulted in death of the accused," Memorandum for the Under Secretary of War, Room 3E-714, The Pentagon, Washington, 25, DC from Major General Thomas M. Green, Major General, The JAG, undated; *from other sources* – "Normandy Executions," *After the Battle Magazine*, Number 85, London: Battle of Britain Prints International, 1994, 29.
**Source, Sidney Bennerman:** *from U.S. Army Clerk of Court* – "Death Book" Ledger; "Final dispositions of rape and/or murder charges tried

by General Courts-Martial, December 1941 to April 1946, and analysis of evidence establishing identity of accused in such cases as resulted in death of the accused," Memorandum for the Under Secretary of War, Room 3E-714, The Pentagon, Washington, 25, DC from Major General Thomas M. Green, Major General, The JAG, undated; *from NARA (NPRC)* – various personal data forms; HQ, Metropolitan Area, APO 782, "Special Court-Martial Order Number 43," 11 March 1944; HQ, 163rd Chemical SG Company, "Battle Participation Award," 17 November 1944; HQ, U.S. Forces, European Theater, "GCM Order Number 479, "Private Sydney Bennerman, Jr., 34174757," 10 October 1945; War Department, The Adjutant General's Office, "Report of Death, Bennerman, Sidney, 34174757," 31 October 1945; *from other sources* – "Normandy Executions," 29.

## 95 – Mansfield Spinks

[1] **Charge: Violation of the 92nd Article of War.**
*Specification 1:* In that Private Mansfield Spinks, Company I, 366th Infantry, did, at Forte Dei Marmi, Italy, on or about 16 January 1945, with malice aforethought, willfully, deliberately, feloniously, unlawfully, and with premeditation kill one Arnolfo Carresi, a human being by shooting him with a rifle.
*Specification 2:* In that Private Mansfield Spinks, Company I, 366th Infantry, did, at Forte Dei Marmi, Italy, on or about 16 January 1945, forcibly and feloniously, against her will, have carnal knowledge of ************.

[2] **Sources, Mansfield Spinks:** *from U.S. Army Clerk of Court* – HQ, 92nd Infantry Division, Office of the Provost Marshal, APO 92, Testimony of Private Mansfield Spinks, 36793241, Company I, 366th Infantry, 21 January 1945; HQ, 92nd Infantry Division, Office of the Provost Marshal, APO 92, Testimony of ********* [Rape Victim], 21 January 1945; HQ, Allied Force, Caserta, Italy, Message to War Department Concerning Death Sentence for Mansfield Spinks, Private, 36793241, 2 May 1945; HQ, Allied Force, Caserta, Italy, Message to War Department Concerning Approval of Death Sentence for Mansfield Spinks, Private, 36793241, 24 May 1945; HQ, MTO, "Confirmation Order in the Case of Private Mansfield Spinks, 36793241, Company I, 366th Infantry," 20 June 1945; HQ, Allied Force, Caserta, Italy, Message to War Department Concerning Confirmation of Death Sentence for Mansfield Spinks, Private, 36793241, 21 June 1945; Branch Office of The JAG with the MTO, APO 512, "Board of Review U.S. v.

Private Mansfield Spinks (36793241) Company I, 366th Infantry," 18 July 1945; War Department, The Adjutant General's Office, "Non-Battle Casualty Report, Spinks, Mansfield, 36793241," 7 November 1945; War Department, The Adjutant General's Office, "Report of Death, Spinks, Mansfield, 36793241," 8 November 1945; Letter from Mother of Mansfield Spinks to The Adjutant General's Office, November 23, 1945; Letter from Mother of Mansfield Spinks to The President of the United States, November 27, 1945; Letter from Colonel Albert W. Johnson to Mrs. Mabel Spinks, December 19, 1945; *from NARA (NPRC)* – HQ, MTO, APO 512, "Trial by GCM (Spinks, Mansfield)," 3 August 1945; HQ, MTO, APO 512, "GCM Orders Number 122," 4 October 1945; HQ, PBS Garrison Stockade Number 1, APO 782, "Special Orders Number 116," 18 October 1945; HQ , PBS Garrison Stockade Number 1, APO 782, "Execution Order (Mansfield (NMI) Spinks, 36793241)," 18 October 1945; HQ , PBS Garrison Stockade Number 1, APO 782, "Execution of Death Sentence," 19 October 1945; HQ , PBS Garrison Stockade Number 1, APO 782, "Death Certificate," 19 October 1945; Letter from Mother of Mansfield Spinks to the Veterans Administration, August 20, 1946; Letter from Mother of Mansfield Spinks to the Director of Insurance, Veterans Administration, October 25, 1946; various personal data forms.

## 96 – Charlie Ervin

[1] Vails was born in AL in 1916, lived in Tuscaloosa and entered the Army at Fort Bragg, NC on May 1, 1942. He served as a MAJ in the Korean War with the 3rd Battalion of the 9th Infantry Regiment. He was wounded in action in November 1950 and taken prisoner; he died of his wounds several weeks later; his family received his Silver Star. Worthen was born in Pensacola, FL on May 12, 1914. He resided in Jamaica, NY, before being inducted on March 20, 1941. He would command Company B of the 365th Infantry Regiment during the war and later command Company H and Company K of the 25th Infantry Regiment. He was awarded a Silver Star and a Purple Heart for shrapnel wounds. None of the officers graduated from West Point.

[2] **Charge I: Violation of the 92nd Article of War.**
*Specification:* In that Private Charlie Ervin, Jr., Company E, 226th Engineer General Service Regiment (formerly Company I, 366th Infantry), and Private Elmer Sussex, Company F, 371st Infantry, acting jointly and in pursuance of a common intent, did, near Pietrasanta, Italy, on or about 31 July 1945, with malice aforethought, willfully, deliberately, feloniously, unlawfully, and with premeditation kill one Pietro Testini by shooting him with a carbine.

**Charge II: Violation of the 93rd Article of War.**
*Specification 1:* In that Private Charlie Ervin, Jr., Company E, 226th Engineer General Service Regiment (formerly Company I, 366th Infantry), and Private Elmer Sussex, Company F, 371st Infantry, acting jointly and in pursuance of a common intent, did, near Pietrasanta, Italy, on or about 31 July 1945, with intent to do him bodily harm, commit an assault upon Giorgio Gamberini, by cutting him on the hand with a dangerous weapon to wit, a knife.

*Specification 2:* In that Private Charlie Ervin, Jr., Company E, 226th Engineer General Service Regiment (formerly Company I, 366th Infantry), and Private Elmer Sussex, Company F, 371st Infantry, acting jointly and in pursuance of a common intent, did, near Pietrasanta, Italy, on or about 31 July 1945, with intent to do him bodily harm, commit an assault upon Giorgio Gamberini, by shooting him in the leg with a dangerous weapon to wit, a carbine.

[3] **Sources, Charlie Ervin, Jr.:** *from U.S. Army Clerk of Court* – HQ, 92nd Infantry Division, Office of the Provost Marshall, APO 92, "Statement of Charlie Ervin, Jr., Private, 34042926, Company I, 366th Infantry Regiment," 4 August 1945; "Organization of the Court, Case of Elmer Sussex (38354458), Company F, 371st Infantry Regiment, and Charlie Ervin, Jr. (34042926), Company I, 366th Infantry Regiment," 22 August 1945; Branch Office of The JAG with the MTO, APO 512, "Board of Review U.S. v. Elmer Sussex (38354458), Company F, 371st Infantry Regiment, and Charlie Ervin, Jr. (34042926), Company I, 366th Infantry Regiment," 22 September 1945; *from NARA (NPRC)* – various personal data forms; HQ, Fifth Army, APO 464, "Soldier wanted for murder and rape," 19 May 1945.

### View from a Potential Defense Counsel or Trial Judge Advocate

[1] **Sources for View from a Potential Defense Counsel or Trial Judge Advocate:** Major General Myron C. Cramer, "Equalization of Court-Martial Sentences," from an address delivered at The JAG's Conference, Ann Arbor, Michigan, 22 May 1945, reprinted in *The Judge Advocate Journal*, Volume II, Number 2, Summer 1945, 7.

**Conclusions and Future Fields of Study**

1  The General Board, Study 84, 4.

2  HQ, ETO, Memorandum, "SUBJECT: Procedure for Execution of Death Sentences on the Continent," 5 March 1945, Records Group 0498, HQ, ETO, U.S. Army (World War II), Entry # UD1028, Box 4726.

3  JAG Section, ETO, Memorandum for G-1, "SUBJECT: Training and Organization of Our General Prisoners as Engineer (Battlefield) Demolition Removal Units," 7 April 1944, Records Group 0498, HQ, ETO, U.S. Army (World War II), Entry # UD1028, Judge Advocate Section, *General Correspondence, Decimal File, 1942-1945, 250.4 Court-Martial Before Trial THRU 250.4 Court-Martial Appointments – General, July-October 1945,* Box 4722.

4  The General Board, Study 84, 11.

5  The General Board, Study 82, 6.

6  Ibid., 16, 18.

7  Ibid., 19.

8  Ibid.

9  Ibid., 39.

10  "Reich Force 10 Pct. Negro," *Stars & Stripes,* London Edition, Vol. 4, No. 189, June 14, 1945.

11  HQ, ETO, Judge Advocate Section, Memorandum for Colonel W. S. Sully, Chief, Military Justice Section, from Brigadier General Edward C. Betts, "Personnel of GCM for Trial of Certain Cases," 7 December, 1943; HQ, ETO, Judge Advocate Section, Memorandum for Brigadier General Edward C. Betts from Colonel W. S. Sully, Chief, Military Justice Section, Compliance with Oral Directions, 8 December 1943, all in Records Group 0498, HQ, ETO, U.S. Army (World War II), Entry # UD1028, Box 4722.

12  "Memorandum for General Betts," from Colonel Scully, 16 December 1943, Records Group 0498, HQ, ETO, U.S. Army (World War II), Entry # UD1028, Judge Advocate Section, *General Correspondence, Decimal File, 1942-1945, 250 Discipline – Individual Cases, January 1944-June 1945 THRU 250.1 Fraternization,* Box 4719.

13  War Department, Branch Office of The JAG for the ETO, Letter to Brigadier General Betts concerning conscientious opposition to the death penalty, 28 December 1943, Records Group 0498, HQ, ETO, U.S. Army (World War II), Entry # UD1028, Judge Advocate Section, *General Correspondence, Decimal File, 1942-1945, 250.4 Court-Martial Miscellaneous, September 1942-August 1944 THRU 250.4 Jurisdiction Policy, May 1945,* Box 4723.

14  HQ, ETO, APO 887, Memorandum, "SUBJECT: Courts-Martial," 6 March 1944, Records Group 0498, HQ, ETO, U.S. Army (World War II), Entry # UD1028, Judge Advocate Section, *General Correspondence, Decimal File, 1942-1945, 250.4 Court-Martial Before Trial THRU 250.4 Court-Martial Appointments – General, July-October 1945,* Box 4722.

15  HQ, ETO, "Memorandum for General Eisenhower," from Major General E. S. Hughes, 5 April 1944, Records Group 0498, HQ, ETO, U.S. Army (World War II), Entry # UD1028, Box 4722.

16  Memorandum, "SUBJECT: Negro Troops and Military Justice," 6 December 1944, Records Group 0498, HQ, ETO, U.S. Army (World War II), Entry # UD1028, Box 4722.

17  Memorandum, "SUBJECT: Study of Major Crimes Involving Negro Soldiers," 16 November 1944, Records Group 0498, HQ, ETO, U.S. Army (World War II), Entry # UD1028, Judge Advocate Section, *General Correspondence, Decimal File, 1942-1945, 250 Discipline – Individual Cases, January 1944-June 1945 THRU 250.1 Fraternization,* Box 4719.

18  Ibid.

19  HQ, ETO, Memorandum thru Commanding General Third U.S. Army to Commanding General 8th Infantry General, reference AG 201 Robinson, Ralph R., 31 March 1944, Records Group 0498, HQ, ETO, U.S. Army (World War II), Entry # UD1028, Judge Advocate Section, *General Correspondence, Decimal File, 1942-1945, 250.451 Court-Martial Changes August 1945-December 1945 THRU GCM Reviews by Staff Judge Advocates of Subordinate Commands,* Box 4726.

20  War Department, The Adjutant General's Office, Memorandum, "SUBJECT: Treatment of Negro Soldiers," 14 February 1942, Records Group 338, Records of U.S. Army Operations, Tactical and Support Organizations (World War II and Thereafter), War Department, VIII Corps, *Decimal Subject Files, 1940-1945, Entry UD 42882, Adjutant General Section 250.4 to Adjutant General Section 293,* Box 10.

21  "Negro Tankers Join Third Army," *Stars & Stripes,* London Edition, Vol. 5, No. 4, November 6, 1944, 5.

**Postscript**

[1]  **NARA** *(NPRC)* – Army Personnel File John C. Woods; Eniwetok, Marshall Islands, Testimony of Richard G. Griffin, RA 17260969, Private, 22 July 1950.

**Epilogue**

[1]  Alice Kaplan, *The Interpreter*, 172-173.

[2]  #11 – Joseph Mahoney; #32 – Ellsworth Williams; #83 – Willie Hall; and #96 – William Lucas.

[3]  The only linkage seems in the plots of Parker and Bennerman; both were executed (for the same crime) on October 15, 1945 and are buried next to each other in Row 3 in Grave 56 and Grave 57.

[4]  Edward Everett Hale, *The Man Without a Country*, NY: Little, Brown, 1898.

[5]  **Sources, Epilogue:** Discussion with Nathalie Le Barbier, Oise-Aisne American Military Cemetery, September 11, 2011; Discussion with David Atkinson, Oise-Aisne American Military Cemetery, September 12, 2011.

# Bibliography

**Primary Sources**
*The General Board, United States Forces, European Theater*
Judge Advocate Section, "The Judge Advocate Section in Theater of Operations," Study 82.
Judge Advocate Section, "Military Justice Administration in Theater of Operations," Study 83.
Judge Advocate Section, "The Military Offender in the Theater of Operations," Study 84.

*United States Army Clerk of Court Office, Ballston, Virginia*
Court-Martial (CM) cases for the 96 were originally viewed at this location. They were later transferred to NARA St. Louis and are shown below at the NPRC.

Office of the Clerk of Court, U.S. Army, Letter from the Deputy Clerk to Mr. Solomon Bogard on compilation of Army personnel executions in World War II, dated November 14, 1985.

"Final dispositions of rape and/or murder charges tried by General Courts-Martial, December 1941 to April 1946, and analysis of evidence establishing identity of accused in such cases as resulted in death of the accused," Memorandum for the Under Secretary of War, Room 3E-714, The Pentagon, Washington, 25, DC from Major General Thomas M. Green, Major General, The Judge Advocate General, undated.

*National Archives and Records Administration, National Personnel Records Center (NPRC), St. Louis, Missouri*

| | | | |
|---|---|---|---|
| CM Case # 287315/Personnel File | Agee, Amos | 34163762 | PVT |
| CM Case # 285969/Personnel File | Anderson, Roy W. | 35497199 | PVT |
| Personnel File | Asbell, Milton | O-472209 | CPT |
| Personnel File | Bailey, Milbert | 34151488 | PVT |
| CM Case # 287413/Personnel File | Baldwin, Walter J. | 34020111 | PVT |
| Personnel File | Bennerman, Sydney | 34174757 | PVT |
| Personnel File | Boyle, Russell E. | 36721587 | SGT |
| CM Case # 262475/Personnel File | Brinson, Eliga | 34052175 | PVT |
| Personnel File | Breitenstein, Kenneth L. | 33486597 | SGT |
| Personnel File | Briscoe, Jack D. | 38051551 | SGT |
| CM Case # 265788/Personnel File | Burns, Lee A. | 38520648 | PVT |
| CM Case # 286482/Personnel File | Clark, Ernest Lee | 33212946 | CPL |
| CM Case # 286393 | Clay, Matthew Jr. | 38490561 | PFC |
| CM Case # 258068/Personnel File | Cobb, David | 165248 | PVT |
| CM Case # 287064 | Cooper, John David | 34562464 | PFC |
| CM Case # 286303/Personnel File | Crews, Otis B. | 14057830 | PVT |
| CM Case # 286559/Personnel File | Davis, Arthur E. | 36788637 | PVT |
| CM Case # 258072/Personnel File | Davis, Lee A. | 18023362 | PVT |
| CM Case # 283439/Personnel File | Davis, William E. | 33541888 | PFC |
| CM Case # 287135/Personnel File | Davison, Tommie | 34485174 | PVT |
| CM Case # 262462/Personnel File | Donnelly, Robert L. | 13132982 | PVT |
| CM Case # 285325/Personnel File | Downes, William C. | 33519814 | PVT |
| Personnel File | Dyro, Thorroff P. | 6577908 | SGT |
| CM Case # 295534 | Ervin, Charlie Jr. | 34042926 | PVT |
| CM Case # 286064 | Farrell, Arthur J. | 32559163 | PVT |
| Personnel File | Girvalo, Alfonso | 32316672 | SGT |
| CM Case # 286910/Personnel File | Gordon, Tom E. | 34091950 | PVT |
| CM Case # 287617 | Grant, General L. | 34557976 | PFC |
| CM Case # 287605/Personnel File | Green, George Jr. | 38476751 | PFC |
| Personnel File | Griggs, Yancey F. | O-1045442 | CPT |
| CM Case # 286911/Personnel File | Guerra, Augustine M. | 38458023 | PVT |

| | | | |
|---|---|---|---|
| CM Case # 302743/Personnel File | Harris, Wiley Jr. | 6924547 | PVT |
| CM Case # 276262/Personnel File | Harrison, William Jr. | 15089828 | PVT |
| Personnel File | Heard, Haze | 34562354 | PFC |
| CM Case # 288129/Personnel File | Hendricks, James E. | 33453189 | PFC |
| CM Case # 287773 | Holden, Mervin | 38226564 | PVT |
| CM Case # 288114/Personnel File | Hopper, Benjamin F. | 32720571 | PVT |
| CM Case # 289052/Personnel File | Jefferies, Charles H. | 33181343 | PVT |
| CM Case # 288384/Personnel File | Johnson, Willie | 38270465 | PVT |
| CM Case # 289141/Personnel File | Jones, Cubia | 34563790 | PVT |
| CM Case # 267488/Personnel File | Jones, Edwin P. | 15045804 | PVT |
| Personnel File | Jones, James L. | 34221343 | PVT |
| CM Case # 289035/Personnel File | Jones, John T. | 38315973 | PVT |
| CM Case # 289127/Personnel File | Jones, Kinney | 34120505 | PFC |
| CM Case # 286559/Personnel File | Jordan, Charles H. | 14066430 | PVT |
| CM Case # 270659/Personnel File | Kendrick, James E. | 14026995 | PVT |
| Personnel File | Kleinbeck, Herbert A. | 16100440 | T5 |
| CM Case # 288505/Personnel File | Kluxdal, Paul M. | 36395076 | PFC |
| Personnel File | Landi, Frank N. | 39237105 | SGT |
| CM Case # 306769/Personnel File | Leatherberry, J.C. | 34472451 | PVT |
| CM Case # 288670/Personnel File | Mack, John H. | 34042053 | PVT |
| CM Case # 288771/Personnel File | Mack, William | 32620461 | PVT |
| CM Case # 296582/Personnel File | Mariano, Blake W. | 38011593 | PFC |
| CM Case # 306312/Personnel File | Martinez, Aniceto | 38168482 | PFC |
| Personnel File | Martino, Vincent J. | 32819220 | T/5 |
| CM Case # 269746/Personnel File | Maxey, Curtis L. | 34544198 | PVT |
| CM Case # 288535/Personnel File | McCarter, William J. | 34675977 | PFC |
| CM Case # 289263/Medical File | McGann, Theron W. | 39332102 | PVT |
| CM Case # 289257/Personnel File | McGhee, Shelton Sr. | 34529025 | CPL |
| CM Case # 288642/Personnel File | McMurray, Fred A. | 38184335 | PVT |
| Personnel File | Mendenhall, Earl | 20817862 | SGT |
| CM Case # 301544/Personnel File | Miranda, Alex F. | 39297382 | PVT |
| Personnel File | Mosley, Richard A. | 39529780 | SGT |
| CM Case # 289035/Personnel File | Nelson, Henry W. | 35726029 | PVT |
| CM Case # 287783/Personnel File | Newman, Oscar N. | 35226382 | T/5 |
| CM Case # 289745/Personnel File | Norris, Clete O. | 37082314 | SGT |
| CM Case # 289785/Personnel File | Ortiz, Victor | 30405077 | PVT |
| CM Case # 289141/Personnel File | Pearson, Robert L. | 38326741 | CPL |
| Personnel File | Peck, Henry L. | O-289263 | LTC |
| CM Case # 290137/Personnel File | Pennyfeather, William D. | 32801627 | PVT |
| CM Case # 298666/Personnel File | Philpot, Henry C. | 39080069 | PVT |
| CM Case # 311696/Personnel File | Pittman, Willie Aron | 34400976 | PVT |
| CM Case # 289917/Personnel File | Pygate, Benjamin | 33741021 | PVT |
| CM Case # 303097/Personnel File | Robinson, Charles M. | 38164425 | PVT |
| Personnel File | Robinson, Thomas F. | 32555124 | T/3 |

| | | | |
|---|---|---|---|
| CM Case # 300615/Personnel File | Rollins, Alvin R. | 34716953 | PFC |
| CM Case # 285969/Personnel File | Sanders, James B. | 34124233 | T/5 |
| CM Case # 284636/Personnel File | Schmiedel, Werner | 7041115 | PVT |
| CM Case # 291138/Personnel File | Scott, Richard B. | 38040012 | T/5 |
| CM Case # 289454/Personnel File | Skinner, Robert L. | 35802328 | PVT |
| CM Case # 290498 | Slovik, Eddie | 36896415 | PVT |
| CM Case # 291404/Personnel File | Smalls, Abraham | 34512812 | PVT |
| CM Case # 267198/Personnel File | Smith, Charles H. | 36337437 | PVT |
| CM Case # 289955/Personnel File | Smith, George E. Jr. | 33288266 | PVT |
| CM Case # 258070/Personnel File | Smith, Harold A. | 14045090 | CPL |
| CM Case # 287315/Personnel File | Smith, John C. | 33214953 | PVT |
| CM Case # 262475 | Smith, Willie | 34565556 | PVT |
| CM Case # 267110/Personnel File | Spears, Charles E. | 32337619 | PVT |
| CM Case # 287773/Personnel File | Spencer, Elwood J. | 33739343 | PVT |
| CM Case # 295486/Personnel File | Spinks, Mansfield | 36793241 | PVT |
| CM Case # 311647/Personnel File | Stroud, Harvey L. | 33215131 | PVT |
| CM Case # 290761/Personnel File | Taylor, John W. | 37485128 | PVT |
| CM Case # 290546/Personnel File | Thomas, Madison | 38265363 | PVT |
| Personnel File | Thorn, Clyde R. | O-1305859 | 1LT |
| CM Case # 288642/Personnel File | Till, Louis | 36392273 | PVT |
| CM Case # 291296/Personnel File | Twiggs, James W. | 38265086 | PVT |
| CM Case # 287783 | Valentine, Leo Sr. | 32954278 | T/5 |
| Personnel File | Ward, Bert E. | 6828589 | 1SG |
| CM Case # 258069/Personnel File | Waters, John H. | 32337934 | PVT |
| CM Case # 287315/Personnel File | Watson, Frank | 34793522 | PVT |
| CM Case # 290540/Personnel File | Watson, Joseph | 39610125 | PVT |
| CM Case # 264698/Personnel File | Watson, Ray | 33139251 | PVT |
| CM Case # 311662/Personnel File | White, Armstead | 34401104 | PVT |
| CM Case # 311653/Personnel File | White, David | 34400884 | PVT |
| CM Case # 293083/Personnel File | Whitfield, Clarence | 34672443 | PVT |
| CM Case # 303439 | Williams, Ellsworth | 34200976 | PVT |
| Personnel File | Williams, John | 32794118 | PVT |
| CM Case # 291944/Personnel File | Williams, Olin W. | 34649494 | PVT |
| CM Case # 287064/Personnel File | Wilson, J. P. | 32484756 | PVT |
| CM Case # 290540/Personnel File | Wimberly, Willie Jr. | 36392154 | T/5 |
| Personnel File | Woods, John C. | 37540591 | MSG |
| Navy Personnel File | Woods, John C. | 3417398 | AS |
| Personnel File | Worthen, Clyde A. | O-1294762 | CPT |
| CM Case # 296038/Personnel File | Wray, Robert | 34461589 | PVT |
| CM Case # 293448 | Yancy, Waiters | 37499079 | PVT |
| Personnel File | Ziegler, Milton K. | 17046765 | CPL |

## Office of the Adjutant General Morning Reports, 2912th Disciplinary Training Center

July 1944 – Item Number 23252; Box Number 676; Reel Number 12.112

August 1944 – Item Number 15308; Box Number 522; Reel Number 17.166

September 1944 – Item Number 27205; Box Number 773; Reel Number 6.225

October 1944 – Item Number 16658; Box Number 578; Reel Number 17.214

November 1944 – Item Number 14382; Box Number 493; Reel Number 8.207

December 1944 – Item Number 15590; Box Number 525; Reel Number 4.365

March 1945 – Item Number 24573; Box Number 708; Reel Number 9.463

April 1945 – Item Number 13062; Box Number 468; Reel Number 5.421

May 1945 – Item Number 16374; Box Number 578; Reel Number 18.525

## Office of the Adjutant General Morning Reports, 2913th Disciplinary Training Center

July 1944 – Item Number 23252; Box Number 676; Reel Number 12.112

August 1944 – Item Number 15308; Box Number 522; Reel Number 17.166

September 1944 – Item Number 27205; Box Number 773; Reel Number 6.225

October 1944 – Item Number 16658; Box Number 578; Reel Number 17.214

January 1945 – Item Number 10145; Box Number 398; Reel Number 16.328

February 1945 – Item Number 22613; Box Number 608; Reel Number 13.162

March 1945 – Item Number 24573; Box Number 708; Reel Number 9.463

April 1945 – Item Number 13062; Box Number 468; Reel Number 5.421

May 1945 – Item Number 16374; Box Number 578; Reel Number 18.525

June 1945 – Item Number 14366; Box Number 528; Reel Number 14.408

July 1945 – Item Number 22816; Box Number 716; Reel Number 10.451

August 1945 – Item Number 21218; Box Number 678; Reel Number 2.697

September 1945 – Item Number 10648; Box Number 415; Reel Number 18.703

October 1945 – Item Number 20809; Box Number 724; Reel Number 15.488

## National Archives and Records Administration, College Park, Maryland

Records Group 338, Records of U.S. Army Operations, Tactical and Support Organizations (World War II and Thereafter), War Department, VIII Corps, *Decimal Subject Files, 1940-1945,* Entry UD 42882, *Adjutant General Section 247 to Adjutant General Section 250 (Discipline, January 1944-May 1945),* Box 7.

Records Group 338, Records of U. S. Army Operations, Tactical and Support Organizations (World War II and Thereafter), War Department, VIII Corps, *Decimal Subject Files, 1940-1945,* Entry UD 42882, *Adjutant General Section 250.4 to Adjutant General Section 250.4,* Box 9.

Records Group 338, Records of U.S. Army Operations, Tactical and Support Organizations (World War II and Thereafter), War Department, VIII Corps, *Decimal Subject Files, 1940-1945,* Entry UD 42882, *Adjutant General Section 250.4 to Adjutant General Section 293,* Box 10.

Records Group 0498, Headquarters, European Theater of Operations, U.S. Army (World War II), Entry # UD1028, Judge Advocate Section, *General Correspondence, Decimal File, 1942-1945, 250 Discipline – Individual Cases, January 1944-June 1945 THRU 250.1 Fraternization,* Box 4719.

Records Group 0498, Headquarters, European Theater of Operations, U.S. Army (World War II), Entry # UD1028, Judge Advocate Section, *General Correspondence, Decimal File, 1942-1945, 250.4 Court-Martial Before Trial THRU 250.4 Court-Martial Appointments – General, July-October 1945,* Box 4722.

Records Group 0498, Headquarters, European Theater of Operations, U.S. Army (World War II), Entry # UD1028, Judge Advocate Section, *General Correspondence, Decimal File, 1942-1945, 250.4 Court-Martial Miscellaneous, September 1942-August 1944 THRU 250.4 Jurisdiction Policy, May 1945,* Box 4723.

Records Group 0498, Headquarters, European Theater of Operations, U.S. Army (World War II), Entry # UD1028, Judge Advocate Section, *General Correspondence, Decimal File, 1942-1945, 250.451 Court-Martial Changes August 1945-December 1945 THRU General Court-Martial Reviews by Staff Judge Advocates of Subordinate Commands,* Box 4726.

## American Military Cemetery Oise-Aisne

"Report of Burial, Stroud, Harvey, 33215131," 30 August 1943.

"Report of Burial, Stroud, Harvey, 33215131," 7 July 1947.

Office of the Quartermaster General of the Army, Form 638, Intra-office, Reference Stroud, Harvey, 33215131," 22 September 1948.

Quartermaster Corps Form 1194, Disinterment Directive # 5265 03026, Stroud, Harvey, 33215131," 7 October 1948.

ABMC Synopsis Document Correction of Grave Numbers, Stroud, Harvey, 19 November 1952.

## Paul Fraser Collectables; Bristol, England; Adrian Roose, Director

Albert Pierrepoint Execution Ledger

## Secondary Sources

Ambrose, Stephen E. *Citizen Soldiers: The U.S. Army from the Normandy Beaches to the Bulge to the Surrender of Germany,* NY: Touchstone, 1997.

"Army Court Convicts Slayer of Teichman," *New York Times,* January 13, 1945.

"Army Sentences 2 to Hanging," *New York Times,* April 30, 1944.

"Army & Navy: Mobster Abroad," *Time Magazine,* November 20, 1944.

"Army & Navy: The Black Hole of Le Mans," *Time Magazine,* February 4, 1946.

"Army & Navy: Murder at Honingham Hall," *Time Magazine,* December 18, 1944.

"Calls GI Killer Mentally Only 9," *Stars & Stripes,* London Edition, Vol. 5, No. 60, January 12, 1945.

Carlton, Jim. "Army Will Review Soldier's WWII Execution," *Los Angeles Times,* March 29, 1988.

"Chicago Soldier Hanged for Killing Sergeant in France," *Chicago Tribune,* November 3, 1944.

Collins, Colonel John M. "World War II NCOs," *Army Magazine,* Arlington, VA: Association of the United States Army, February 2005.

Cramer, Major General Myron C. "Equalization of Court-Martial Sentences," from an address delivered at TJAG Conference, Ann Arbor, Michigan, 22 May 1945, reprinted in *The Judge Advocate Journal*, Volume II, Number 2, Summer 1945.

"Death Penalty Upheld in Cleft-Chin Case," *Stars & Stripes*, London Edition, Vol. 5, No. 94, February 21, 1945.

Dernley, Syd & Neumann, David. *The Hangman's Tale: Memories of a Public Executioner*, London: Pan Press, 1990.

Disney, Francis J. *Shepton Mallet Prison*, Shepton Mallet, England: Whitstone Press, 1992.

"Doughboy Does the Dying," *Stars & Stripes*, London Edition, Vol. 5, No. 191, June 16, 1945.

Eddleston, John J. *The Encyclopaedia of Executions*, London: John Blake Publishing, 2004.

Esvelin, Philippe. *Forgotten Wings*, Bayeux, France: Heimdal, 2006.

"The Execution of Eddie Slovik," *After the Battle Magazine*, Number 32, London: Battle of Britain Prints International, 1981.

"From the Editor," *After the Battle Magazine*, Number 66, London: Battle of Britain Prints International, 1989.

"From the Editor," *After the Battle Magazine*, Number 72, London: Battle of Britain Prints International, 1991.

"GI Deserter Shot," *Stars & Stripes* (London Edition), Vol. 5, No. 82, February 7, 1945.

"GI, Girl to Die in 'Cleft' Case," *Stars & Stripes*, London Edition, Vol. 5, No. 70, January 24, 1945.

"Girl Shot After Visit to a Cinema," *Evening Standard*, October 6, 1943.

"GIs Today Are Smarter Than '17 Soldier Dads," *Stars & Stripes*, London Edition, Vol. 4, No. 307, October 27, 1944.

Hale, Edward Everett. *The Man Without a Country*, NY: Little, Brown, 1898.

"Hangman's End, *Time Magazine*, August 7, 1950.

Huie, William Bradford. *The Execution of Private Slovik*, Yardley, PA: Westholme Publishing, 2004.

"Hunt for Briton's Slayer Turns to Yank Airdrome," *Chicago Tribune*, December 6, 1944.

"Inspect U.S. Carbines in Death of Briton," *Stars & Stripes*, London Edition, Vol. 5, No. 31, December 7, 1944.

Kaplan, Alice. *The Interpreter*, NY: Free Press, 2005.

Kimmelman, Benedict B. "The Example of Private Slovik," *American Heritage*, The Magazine of History, Volume 38, Number 6, September/October 1987, NY: Forbes.

"Kistner Freed At Examining Trial," *Henry County Local*, August 15, 1941.

Ligné, André. "La region mancelle à l'heure américaine," *Maine Découvertes*, No. 60, avril-mai 2009.

Lilly, J. Robert. "Dirty Details: Executing U.S. Soldiers During World War II," *Crime & Delinquency*, Volume 42, Number 4, October 1996, Thousand, Oaks, CA: Sage Publications.

Lilly, J. Robert. "Military Executions," in Clifton D. Bryant, *Handbook of Death and Dying*, Thousand, Oaks, CA: Sage Publications, 2003.

Lilly, J. Robert. "US Military Executions," *After the Battle Magazine*, Number 90, London: Battle of Britain Prints International, 1995.

"Lore of the Corps – Shot by Firing Squad: The Trial and Execution of Pvt. Eddie Slovik, *The Army Lawyer*, Department of the Army Pamphlet 27-50-444, May 2010.

Miller, Edward G. *A Dark and Bloody Ground: The Hürtgen Forest and the Roer River Dams, 1944-1945*, College Station, TX: Texas A&M University Press, 1995.

Moore, Christopher Paul. *Fighting for America: Black Soldiers – The Unsung Heroes of World War II*, NY: Random House Publishing, 2005.

Morrisette, Brigadier General James E. "Military Law and Administration of Military Justice," from an address delivered before the State Bar Association of Wisconsin, Milwaukee, Wisconsin, 23 June 1944, reprinted in *The Judge Advocate Journal*, Volume I, Number 2, 15 September 1944.

Motley, Mary Penick. *The Invisible Soldier: The Experience of the Black Soldier, World War II*, Detroit, MI: Wayne State University Press, 1975.

Moyer, Steve. "Found in Translation," *Humanities Magazine*, Volume 29, Number 4, July/August 2008.

"Negro Tankers Join Third Army," *Stars & Stripes*, London Edition, Vol. 5, No. 4, November 6, 1944.

"Normandy Executions," *After the Battle Magazine*, Number 85, London: Battle of Britain Prints International, 1994.

Obermayer, Herman J. *Soldiering for Freedom: A GI's Account of World War II*, College Station, Texas: Texas A&M University Press, 2005.

*Official Army Register, 1956, Volume 1*, Washington, DC: U.S. Government Printing Office, 1956.

"One Out of 185 U.S. Soldiers in Army Custody," *Chicago Tribune*, February 11, 1945.

"1.30 a.m. Court Finds Soldier Guilty of Murder," *Daily Express*, January 20, 1944.

"Paris Black Market Robs U.S. Army," *Life Magazine*, Volume 18, Number 13, March 26, 1945.

Peters, James Edward. "Arlington National Cemetery," *After the Battle Magazine*, Number 131, London: Battle of Britain Prints International, 2006.

"PFC Hanged in France for Murder of Topkick," *Stars & Stripes*, London Edition, Vol. 5, No. 2, November 3, 1944.

Pierrepoint, Albert. *Executioner: Pierrepoint*, London: Hodder and Stoughton, 1974.

"Pleads Insanity for GI Killer," *Stars & Stripes*, London Edition, Vol. 5, No. 59, January 11, 1945.

Pound, Ezra. *The Pisan Cantos*, edited by Richard Sieburth, New York: New Directions, 2003.

Ramsey, Winston, Editor. *Scenes of Murder Then and Now*, Essex, England: Battle of Britain International Ltd, 2011.

"Reich Force 10 Pct. Negro," *Stars & Stripes*, London Edition, Vol. 4, No. 189, June 14, 1945.

"Sergeant Who Hanged Nazis Is Slain – 'In Army,'" *Chicago Daily Tribune*, July 25, 1950.

"SOLDIER DIES FOR MURDER; American Private Hanged at the U.S. Army Center in Britain," *New York Times*, December 15, 1943.

"SOLDIER DOOMED TO HANG; American Convicted of Murder of English Girl, 15," *New York Times*, October 10, 1944.

"Soldier Hanged for Murder," *New York Times*, November 5, 1944.

"SOLDIER IN BRITAIN TO HANG FOR KILLING; Negro Sentenced By Court-Martial For Shooting Officer," *The Philadelphia Inquirer*, January 6, 1943.

"SOLDIER IS HANGED AS LONDON SLAYER; Woman Foe of Death Penalty Protests at Prison Gate as Paratrooper Dies Attack on Prison Blocked Family in Boston Grieves," *New York Times*, March 9, 1945.

"Soldier Pleads Insanity; Slayer of British Diplomat Called Homicidal Degenerate," *New York Times*, January 11, 1945.

"Soldier Sentenced to Die," *New York Times*, January 7, 1943.

"SOLDIER TO BE HANGED; American Sentenced for Murder of Girl in England," *New York Times*, December 1, 1943.

"Soldier's Execution Delayed," *New York Times*, December 3, 1944.

Stanton, Shelby L. *World War II Order of Battle*, NY: Galahad Books, 1991.

Stonehouse, Cheryl. "Dark Side of the Good-Time G.I.s," *Daily Express*, April 26, 2006.

"TEICHMAN SHOOTING CITED; Statement by Pvt. Smith Read at Court-Martial in England," *New York Times*, January 10, 1945.

"The US Prison at Shepton Mallet," *After the Battle Magazine*, Number 59, London: Battle of Britain Prints International, 1988.

"3 Germans Hanged for Slaying Airman," *New York Times*, June 30, 1945.

"2 GIs Charged in Death of Briton," *Stars & Stripes*, London Edition, Vol. 5, No. 33, December 9, 1944.

"TWO GIs IN ROME SENTENCED TO HANG; Court-Martial Finds Lane Gang Leader and Aide Guilty of Murdering Civilian," *New York Times*, March 28, 1945.

"2 Indicted in Teichman Death," *New York Times*, December 8, 1944.

"Two Soldiers Hanged for Rape," *New York Times*, October 31, 1944.

"Two U.S. Soldiers Are Hanged," *New York Times*, November 20, 1944.

"2 U.S. SOLDIERS GO ON TRIAL IN ROME," *New York Times*, March 27, 1945.

"Two U.S. Soldiers Hanged," *Stars & Stripes*, London Edition, Vol. 5, No. 6, January 19, 1945.

"Two U.S. Soldiers Hanged," *The Times of London*, August 12, 1944.

"Two U.S. Soldiers Held in Diplomat's Killing," *Stars & Stripes*, London Edition, Vol. 5, No. 32, December 8, 1944.

"2 Yanks Sentenced to Hang for Killing in Holdup in Italy," *Chicago Tribune*, March 28, 1945.

"U.S. Army Hangs Yank for Murder Near Brest," *Chicago Tribune*, February 17, 1945.

"U.S. Army Tries 3,185 in 2 Year Stay in Britain," *Chicago Tribune*, January 21, 1945.

"U.S. DESERTER HANGED; Convicted of Having Murdered Italian During Hold-Up," *New York Times*, June 12, 1945.

"U.S. Private Is Hanged; Pays Penalty for Having Shot Briton Who Challenged Him," *New York Times*, May 11, 1945.

"U.S. Soldier Doomed as Slayer," *New York Times*, May 25, 1944.

"U.S. Soldier Guilty of Murder," *The Times of London*, January 25, 1944.

"U.S. Soldier Hanged as Slayer," *New York Times*, May 27, 1944.

"U.S. Soldier in Britain to Hang," *New York Times*, February 6, 1944.

"U.S. SOLDIER IS CONVICTED; Leatherberry Is Sentenced in Britain to Die for Murder," *New York Times*, January 25, 1944.

"U.S. SOLDIER IS HANGED; Private Executed in England for Killing U.S. Officer," *New York Times*, April 21, 1943.

"U.S. Soldier Sentenced to Death," *The Times of London*, October 27, 1943.

"U.S. Soldier Sentenced to Death," *The Times of London*, December 1, 1943.

"U.S. Soldiers Sentenced to Death," *The Times of London*, May 1, 1944.

"U.S. Soldier Shot for Murder," *The Times of London*, June 1, 1944.

"U.S. Troops' Mental Age Put at 13 to 14 In Defense of Private Who Shot Diplomat," *New York Times*, January 12, 1945.

War Department, Field Manual 10-10, *Quartermaster Service in Theater of Operations*, Washington, DC: War Department, 2 March 1942.

War Department, Pamphlet Number 27-4, *Procedure for Military Executions*, Washington, DC: War Department, 12 June 1942.

"W. C. Jones Killed; Brother Wounded," *Henry County Local*, August 8, 1941.

Weber, Thomas. *Hitler's First War: Adolf Hitler, the Men of the List Regiment, and the First World War*, Oxford, England: Oxford University Press, 2010.

Weiss, Stephen J. *Second Chance*, Shire Hill, England: Military History Publishing, 2011.

Whiting, Charles. *American Deserter: General Eisenhower and the Execution of Eddie Slovik*, York, England: Eskdale Publishing, 2005.

### Media

DVD Documentary – *The Untold Story of Louis Emmett Louis Till*, ThinkFilm, 2005.

### *Discussions, Interviews and Correspondence*

Email from Professor J. Robert Lilly concerning burial locations, February 7, 2011.

Interview with the Historian for Henry County, Kentucky, February 24, 2011.

Interview with family member of Edwin P. Jones, February 25, 2011.

Discussions and emails with Colonel (Retired) Fred Borch III, Judge Advocate General Regimental Historian & Archivist, beginning August 2011.

Discussions and emails with Herman J. Obermayer, editor, publisher and author, who was assigned to legal section in the ETO, beginning September 2011.

Interview with Michel & Aurelien Jacquesson, Beaunay, France, September 10, 2011.

Discussion with Nathalie Le Barbier, Cemetery Associate, Oise-Aisne American Military Cemetery, Seringes-et-Nesles, France, September 10 & 11, 2011.

Discussion with David Atkinson, Acting Superintendent, and Nathalie Le Barbier, Oise-Aisne American Military Cemetery, Seringes-et-Nesles, France, September 12, 2011.

Discussion with Louis Massard, Plumaudan, France, September 13, 2011.

Discussion with Anita Queruel, Secretary to the Mayor, and Guy Lebrec, Deputy Mayor, Mesnil-Clinchamps, France, September 15, 2011.

Discussion with grandson of Madame Robert, Mesnil-Clinchamps, France, September 15, 2011.

Interview with Etienne Viard, Mayor, Canisy, France, September 15, 2011.

Interview with Georges René, Mayor, Étienville, France, September 15, 2011.

Discussion with Daniel Bellamy, Mayor, Le Pernelle, France, September 16, 2011.

E-mail interviews with Dr. Stephen Weiss, London, beginning November 2011.

Discussions with family member of Shelton McGhee, Sr., beginning July 2012.

Discussions with Thomas Ward, former supply sergeant of the Loire Disciplinary Training Center, beginning April 2013.

# Personnel Index

**David Cobb #1, General Court-Martial**
(Picture used with permission of the
*Northamptonshire Telegraph*, Kettering, UK)

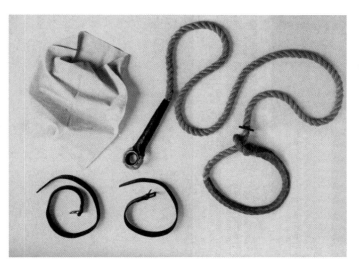

**British Hanging Equipment**
(publisher of *The Hangman's Tale: Memories of a
Public Executioner*, used the photograph in the book,
but was unable to locate the family of the author
who died in 1994)

**Firing Squad for Mansfield Spinks #95
and Charlie Ervin Jr. #96**
(image may not be reproduced in any material
form without written permission of the author.)

**First Lieutenant Clyde R. Thorn**
(private photo, courtesy of family)

**John C. Woods checking rope November 1945**
(courtesy *Associated Press*)

**John C. Woods celebrating October 1946** (courtesy *Associated Press*)

**John C. Woods on troop ship 1946**
(courtesy *Associated Press*)

**John C. Woods with wife 1946**
(courtesy *Associated Press*)

**Lieutenant Colonel Henry Peck**
(courtesy Herman Obermayer)

**Master Sergeant John C Woods**
(courtesy National Archives)

**Mortimer A. Christian, Seine DTC**
(courtesy VMI yearbook)

| Town | Executioner | Date | Name | AGE. | HEIGHT. | WEIGHT | DROP | Town | Executioner |
|---|---|---|---|---|---|---|---|---|---|
| ERMAN. SPY. | A. P | JULY 7 1942 | EUGENE TIMMERMAN. | 38 | 5·4½ | 120 | 8-7 | BELGIUM SPY WANDSWORTH | A·P· H·KIRK S.WADE A·P |
| ENTONVILLE | H·KIRK | JULY.21 1942. | ARTHUR ANDERSON. | 52 | 5·10½ | 154 | 7-3 | WANDSWORTH | H. MORRIS T.W.P H·KIRK |
| DUBLIN OUNTJOY. | T. W. P A. P | SEP. 2. 1942. | THOMAS. JOSEPH. WILLIAMS | 19 | 5·6 | 127½ | 8·9. | BELFAST. | A·P |
| DUBLIN OUNTJOY. - | T. W. P A. P. | SEP. 10 1942 | SAMUEL. SIDNEY DASHWOOD | 22 | 5·5 | 162 | 6-11 | PENTONVILLE | H. MORRIS S. WADE |
| ANDSWORTH | T. W. P S.CROSS | SEP. 10 1942 | GEORGE WILLIAM SILVEROSO. | 23 | 5·11 | 169 | 6-9 | PENTONVILLE | H·KIRK A·P |
| ANDSWORTH | H. KIRK A. P | OCT. 6 1942. | PATRICK. WILLIAM KINGSTONE | 38 | 5·3½ | 122 | 8-7 | WANDSWORTH | H. MORRIS T.W.P. |
| PENTONVILLE | S. WADE A. D | OCT. 28. 1942. | WILLIAM. AMBROSE COLLINS | 21 | 5·9½ | 140 | 7-11 | DURHAM. | A. P. |
| VANDSWORTH ERMAN. SPY | H. ALLEN A. P. | NOV. 3 1942 | DUNCAN. ALEXANDRA SCOTT. FORD. | 21 | 5·5½ | 130 | 8·5 | WANDSWORTH DUTCH. SPY | H. KIRK A. P |
| VANDSWORTH MOUNTJOY | S.WADE T. W. P | DEC. 31 1942 | JOHANNES. MARINUS DRONKERS. | 46 | 6·0½ | 182. | 6·3. | WANDSWORTH BELGIUM SPY | S. WADE A·P |
| DUBLIN | T. W. P A. P | JAN. 26 1943 | JOHANNER WINTER | 39 | 5·0 | 145 | 7-8. | WANDSWORTH JEW | H. CRITCHELL A. P. |
| LEICESTER | A. P. | JAN. 27 1943 | HARRY DOBKIN | 49 | 5·4 | 202½ | 5-9. | WANDSWORTH U.S.A. NEGRO | H. MORRIS T.W.P. |
| VANDSWORTH | H. MORRIS T. W. P | MARCH. 12 1943 | DAVID COBB | 21 | 5·10 | 158 | 7·2 | SHEPTON. MALLET | A·D· A· P |
| OXFORD | A. P. H·P | MARCH. 31 1943. | DUDLEY GEORGE RAYNOR. | 26 | 5·7½ | 150 | 7-4 | WANDSWORTH FRENCH. INDIAN | S. WADE A·P |
| WANDSWORTH BRITISH. SUB | H. KIRK A. P | APRIL. 29 1943 | AUGUST. SANGRET. | 28. | 5·5½ | 146 | 7·6 | WANDSWORTH BURMESE | H.CRITCHEL |
| WANDSWORTH | H.CRITCHEL | ⑤ 1943 | | | | | | | |

**Pierrepoint Execution Ledger 1** (courtesy Paul Fraser Collectibles)

**Thomas (seated) and Albert Pierrepoint**
(courtesy Paul Fraser Collectibles)

**George E. Smith #72, in newspaper**
(photo from Army JAG file)

**Aniceto Martinez #80** (photo from Army JAG file)

**Augustine Guerra #39** (photo from Army JAG file)

**Charlie Ervin Jr. #96, Being tied to the post for the firing squad**
(image may not be reproduced in any material form without written permission of the author.)

**Charles Robinson #91**
(photo from Army JAG file)

**Edwin P. Jones #10** (courtesy Jones family member)

**Fred A McMurray #83, Being led to the gallows**

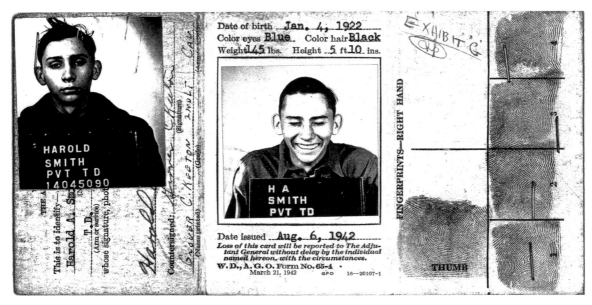

**Harold A. Smith #2, Identification card** (photo from Army JAG file)

**J.C. Leatherberry #13** (photo from Army JAG file)

**Louis Till #84, Being led to the gallows**
(image may not be reproduced in any material form without written permission of the author.)

**Louis Till #84, Standing on the scaffold**
(image may not be reproduced in any material form without written permission of the author.)

Pvt. Robert Lee Scofield, son of Lucille Scofield, Murphysboro, died in France, Feb. 10, 1945.

**Robert Skinner #49**
(courtesy Jackson County Historical Society)

**William Harrison #66** (photo from Army JAG file)

**Madison Thomas #21** (photo from Army JAG file)

**Paris Disciplinary Training Center** (photo from Army JAG file)

**Shepton Mallet Prison** (original photographer unknown)

**Mervin Holden #45 and Elwood Johnnie Spencer #46, Entrance to Fort d'Orange execution site**
(author photo from 2011)

**Mervin Holden #45 and Elwood Johnnie Spencer #46, Execution site, Fort d'Orange**
(author photo from 2011)

**Charles M. Robinson #91, Murder victim**
(photo from Army JAG file)

**Ernest L. Clark #38 and Augustine M. Guerra #39, Murder victim** (photo from Army JAG file)

**George Smith #72, Murder victim Sir Eric Teichmann**
(photo from Army JAG file)

**James E. Kendrick #3, Murder victim** (photo from Army JAG file)

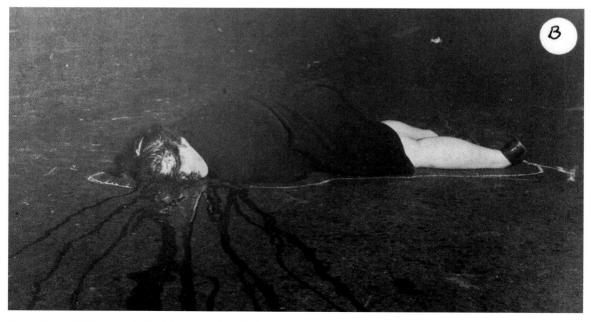

**Lee A. Davis #9, Murder victim** (photo from Army JAG file)

**The Fifth Field from Superintendent's office**
(author photo from 2011)

**The Fifth Field, the single, unmarked cross**
(author photo from 2011)

**The Fifth Field, Row 1 is closest to the cross** (author photo from 2011)